Eddie Kelly

THE DEFINITIVE LISTING OF IRELAND'S
TOP TEN HITS 1954 – 1979

ISBN: 978-1-907179-33-4

A CIP catalogue for this book is available from the National Library.

Published by Original Writing Ltd., Dublin, 2009

Printed in Great Britain by the MPG Books Group, Bodmin and Kings Lynn.

Contents

Picture sleeves and photographs selected from the personal collections of Eddie Kelly and John Murphy.

Introduction

Listings of the best selling records, have been compiled in the USA since 1942, and since 1952 in the UK. In Ireland however, it was a much different story.

During the fifties, with a population of less than three million, the ownership on this island of gramophones, radiograms and record players, was still considered a luxury item and the resulting sales of records was relatively small.

Despite this, interest in the popular music of the day was steadily increasing, thanks to the hit recordings being featured on Radio Luxembourg, AFN, the BBC Light programme and the Irish national station, Radio Eireann.

The first published listing of best selling records in Ireland was in late 1954 when the Evening Herald, one of two national evening newspapers of the day, included the 'top three best sellers in Dublin' in their September 14 issue. This continued on a fortnightly basis for several months.

On January 4, 1955, a new type of listing was introduced, and the top three recording and distribution companies in the Republic, Decca, EMI and Philips, provided the titles of their two best selling records, every two weeks.

This continued in the Evening Herald until on February 14, 1956, when a new record company, Nixa, was added to the list, bringing the total number of discs featured to eight.

As with any self-compiled submission, it was generally accepted that one hundred per cent accuracy might not have been the order of the *day,* however even a casual glance at the song title index, confirms that the selection did give a good indication of the most popular recordings.

On February 12, 1959, the Evening Herald introduced the 'Herald Top Ten', based on returns from record stores. Unlike the old best sellers listing, the 'Herald Top Ten' showed the nation's favourite discs in numerical order. Published weekly, Ireland at last had a chart of its own.

The Evening Herald was the main player in compiling a recognised weekly listing of best selling records in Ireland, until October 1, 1962, when Radio Eireann, commenced broadcasting 'Ireland's Top Ten'. This continued until December 1966, when the station decided to axe the programme.

The resulting void was filled by Spotlight Magazine, who published a weekly chart of the top thirty best selling records. This was subsequently reduced to a top twenty by late 1968. With the sudden demise of Spotlight Magazine in December 1975, music lovers had to wait until February of the following year for Starlight Magazine to appear on the news stands.

Throughout the seventies, there were many problems and disagreements over the compilation of the weekly charts, and for a period, a public opinion poll was the preferred method. Starlight Magazine avoided this compilation method, except for a brief period from August 12, 1976 to November 18, 1976, when they bowed to pressure from the record industry. Fortunately I did manage to obtain 'sales' charts for this period.

In June 1978, the Mechanical Copyright Protection Society (Ireland) (MCPS) started to compile and publish their official weekly Top Thirty, and this became the accepted industry standard.

In this book, the definitive Irish chart book of the period, we provide for the first time, the history of the weekly chart of Ireland's ten best selling records from February 12, 1959 to December 31, 1979.

They're all here - the hit records, the artists, complete with full details of their chart performance. Also included are their date of entry, their highest position achieved, and the number of weeks spent in the charts.

We don't say how and why records were hits, but we do tell you the ones that were. We hope this book will bring back many treasured memories, and no doubt, it will also serve to settle that all important argument as to who had that hit and when!

Happy reading.

Author's Note

Ever since I was a little boy, growing up in the small Co. Tipperary village of Cullen, I've had a love affair with hit records and record charts.

I have fond memories of pleading with my late mother, to allow me to stay up late on a Sunday night to listen to the wireless, as it strained the last flicker of energy in its valves to pick up the Top Twenty as broadcast from Radio Luxembourg.

In later years, the BBC Light Programme fuelled my passion for the chart toppers, with their 'Pick of the Pops' show, hosted by David Jacobs.

In the fifties and sixties, Britain was well served on the music front, with several music publications, such as the New Musical Express, Melody Maker, Disc and Record Mirror, all publishing a weekly chart of the best selling records. Ireland had to wait until 1967 for the publication of its first weekly music magazine, however in the meantime, the national newspaper the Evening Herald, compiled their own weekly top ten list of best selling records.

I continued to enter each published chart of Ireland's best selling records in my notebooks, throughout the fifties, sixties and seventies. The idea of this book, dealing exclusively with the Irish charts, was first suggested to me many years ago, by my good friend and fellow chart enthusiast, the late John Dwyer.

Having considered many formats, and burning the midnight oil over drafts and redrafts, I finally settled on the format used in this book. I have listed every record which made the best sellers list from September 14, 1954 to September 17, 1958 and the Top Ten, from February 14, 1959 to December 31, 1979.

In addition, I have included biographical information on each artist and full details of the relevant record labels and catalogue numbers. While every effort has been made to verify the accuracy of the content, it is possible that some errors may come to light after publication. Any additions or amendments are welcome and will be included in future editions.

Eddie Kelly
September 2009

Part One

Alphabetically by Artist

The information given in this part of the book is as follows:

Date disc first came on chart

Highest position reached on chart

Number of weeks on chart, individually by single and in total by artist

Title, label and catalogue number

• Number One Single

◆ Instrumental

Date	Pos	Wks	ARTIST / Record Title *Label & Number*

ABBA ***112 Weeks***

Swedish group formed in 1970. Personnel: Anna-Frid (Frida) Lyngstad-Ruess (born November 15, 1945 in Bjorkasen, Norway), Agnetha Ase Faltskog (born April 5, 1950 in Jonkoping, Sweden), Benny Andersson (born Goran Bror Benny Andersson on December 16, 1946 in Stockholm, Sweden), Bjorn Ulvaeus (born on April 25, 1945 in Gothenburg, Sweden). Represented Sweden in the 1974 Eurovision Song Contest with their own song, *Waterloo*, Group name made up with their initials. Bjorn and Agnetha married in 1971 and divorced in 1979. Benny and Frida married in 1978 and divorced in 1979. Group split in 1984 with Anna and Frida going on to pursue solo careers. Benny and Bjorn teamed up with Tim Rice to compose the stage musical, *Chess*.

Date	Pos	Wks	ARTIST / Record Title *Label & Number*
25 Apr 74	1(2)	7	• 1. WATERLOO *Epic EPC 2240*
16 Oct 75	4	5	2. SOS *Epic EPC 3576*
22 Jan 76	1(3)	9	• 3. MAMA MIA *Epic Sep C 3790*
15 Apr 76	1(7)	10	• 4. FERNANDO *Epic EPC 4036*
02 Sep 76	1(6)	11	• 5. DANCING QUEEN *Epic EPC 4499*
25 Nov 76	2	11	6. MONEY MONEY MONEY *Epic EPC 4713*
24 Mar 77	1(5)	8	• 7. KNOWING YOU KNOWING ME *Epic EPC 4955*
03 Nov 77	2	7	8. THE NAME OF THE GAME *Epic EPC 5750*
19 Jan 78	1(1)	8	• 9. TAKE A CHANCE ON ME *Epic Sep C 5950*
14 Sep 78	1(1)	3	• 10. SUMMER NIGHT CITY *Epic Sep C 6579*
01 Feb 79	1(3)	6	• 11. CHIQUITITA *Epic EPC 7030*
03 May 79	3	8	12. DOES YOUR MOTHER KNOW *Epic EPC 7316*
19 Jul 79	3	6	13. ANGELEYES / VOULEZ VOUS *Epic EPC 7499*
01 Nov 79	1(2)	5	• 14. GIMME GIMME GIMME (A MAN AFTER MIDNIGHT) *Epic EPC 7914*
14 Dec 79	2	8	15. I HAVE A DREAM *Epic Sep C 8088*

Date	Pos	Wks	ARTIST / Record Title *Label & Number*

Morris ALBERT — *3 Weeks*

Born Mauricio Alberto Kaisermann on September 7, 1951 in Sao Paulo, Brazil. *Feelings* was first issued on record, in Brazil in 1973. In 1985, a Federal District Court in Manhattan, New York, found that more than eighty per cent of *Feelings* had been plagiarized from *Pour Toi*, a 1956 composition by French composer, Louis Gaste. A settlement of $500,000 was awarded to Gaste.

Date	Pos	Wks	ARTIST / Record Title *Label & Number*
30 Oct 75	5	3	1. FEELINGS *Decca F 13591*

Denis ALLEN — *14 Weeks*

Singer/songwriter. Born on October 15, 1942 in Limerick, Ireland. Had an appreciation of music from an early age. Played the tin whistle in the school band while attending John Street National School. On leaving secondary school worked in an architect's office training as a draftsman. Joined a local group, The Casuals. First job as a professional musician with Brendan Frawley at the Royal George Hotel. Joined the Berwyn Showband. Left to join a newly formed group, Bojangle. In 1973, Tommy Drennan invited him to join Top League. In September 1975, formed a new band, Ding A Ling, with Shaun O'Dowd. Performed his own composition, *Da Dum Da Dum I Love You So*, in the 1977 National Song Contest. In 1979, was approached by Shay Kinsella and John Loftus, to write a song to promote a Limerick Lady Festiva l that they were starting. Wrote the song, *Limerick You're A Lady*, at three o'clock in the morning after getting home from a gig. Recorded it in Dublin and took the demo tape around all the main record companies, but no one interested. Decided to put it out on his own Middle 8 label, and as a result of radio plays and demand for it from public, Release Records took it on. The song is now regarded as Limerick city's unofficial anthem. In October 1979, decided to leave Ding A Ling and form his own band.

Date	Pos	Wks	ARTIST / Record Title *Label & Number*
17 Mar 77	7	4	1. DA DUM DA DUM I LOVE YOU SO *Skylark BK 005*
09 Aug 79	2	10	2. LIMERICK YOU'RE A LADY *Release RL 973*

Date	Pos	Wks	ARTIST / Record Title *Label & Number*

The ALLISONS — *8 weeks*

Male vocal duo. John Allison (born Brian Henry John Alford on December 31, 1939 in London) and Bob Allison (born Bernard Colin Day on February 2, 1942 in Trowbridge, Wiltshire). First met when they were members of the same choir at St. Dionis, Parsons Green, London. Discovered by impresario Tito Burns, who saw them as Britain's answer to the Everly Brothers. Represented the UK in the 1961 Eurovision Song Contest with John's composition, *Are You Sure*, finishing in second position. The duo broke up in 1963.

Date	Pos	Wks	ARTIST / Record Title *Label & Number*
30 Mar 61	2	8	1. ARE YOU SURE *Fontana EH 294*

Herb ALPERT and the TIJUANA BRASS — *3 Weeks*

Band leader/trumpeter/vocalist born on March 31, 1935 in Los Angeles, California, USA. Played trumpet since age of eight. Played at weddings and parties in the Los Angeles area. Co-wrote the song, *Wonderful World*, with Sam Cooke. In 1962, founded A & M Records with Jerry Moss. Formed the Tijuana Brass in 1962. It was made up of session musicians until 1965, when a touring band was formed. Burt Bacharach played piano and did arrangement on *This Guy's In Love With You.*

Date	Pos	Wks	ARTIST / Record Title *Label & Number*
12 Sep 68	8	3	1. THIS GUY'S IN LOVE WITH YOU *Pye AMS 727*

AMEN CORNER — *13 Weeks*

Group formed in Cardiff, Wales in 1966. Personnel: Andy Fairweather-Low (lead vocals, guitar), Neil Jones (lead guitar), Clive Taylor (bass), Blue Weaver (organ), Dennis Byron (drums), Alan Jones (baritone sax) and Mike Smith (tenor sax). Played farewell concert on October 4, 1969 at the Boston Gliderdrome.

continues over

Date	Pos	Wks	ARTIST / Record Title *Label & Number*
			Alan and Mike joined Judas Jump while the remnants of Amen Corner emerged in the early 70's as Fair Weather. Andy Fairweather-Low enjoyed a successful solo career in the 1970's.
08 Feb 68	5	5	1. BEND ME SHAPE ME *Deram DM(I) 172*
26 Sep 68	9	2	2. HIGH IN THE SKY *Deram DM(I) 197*
13 Mar 69	4	2	3. (IF PARADISE IS) HALF AS NICE *Immediate IM 073*
17 Jul 69	7	4	4. HELLO SUSIE *Immediate IM 081*
			See also Fair Weather; Andy Fairweather-Low

The AMES BROTHERS — *3 Weeks*

Family vocal group formed in Boston, Massachusetts, USA in 1947. Personnel: Gene, Joe, Vic and Ed Uricks. Disc debut: *Bye Bye Blackbird* on which they were billed as Russ Morgan and his orchestra with Vocal Chorus by the Ames Brothers. In early 1953 the brothers left Coral to sign with RCA Victor. In 1958, were named Billboard magazines's Male Vocal Group of the Year. The group disbanded in 1965. Ed Ames went on to achieve success as a solo artist. Vic Ames died in a road accident on January 23, 1978.

Date	Pos	Wks	ARTIST / Record Title *Label & Number*
15 Feb 55	-	2	1. THE NAUGHTY LADY OF SHADY LANE *HMV IP 958*
12 Feb 59	9	1	2. PUSSY CAT *RCA ERC 1091*

ALTHIA and DONNA — *3 Weeks*

Jamaican female vocal duo. Personnel: Althia Forest and Donna Reid.

Date	Pos	Wks	ARTIST / Record Title *Label & Number*
02 Feb 78	2	3	1. UP TOWN TOP RANKING *Lightning LIG 506*

AMERICA — *4 Weeks*

Formed in London in 1970. The sons of American servicemen stationed in England, they first met while attending Central High School in Watford. Personnel: Dan Peek (born Florida), Gerry Beckley (born Texas) and Dewey Bunnell (born Yorkshire).

continues over

Date	Pos	Wks	ARTIST / Record Title *Label & Number*

Signed to Warner Brothers Records by talent scout Ian Samwell (former guitarist with Cliff Richard and The Drifters and composer of *Move It*). Disc debut: *I Need You* (1971). Relocated to the USA in 1972. Dan Peek left the group in 1977. *Horse With No Name* was originally titled, *Desert Song.*

27 Jan 72	4	4	1. A HORSE WITH NO NAME *Warner Bros. K 16128*

Leroy ANDERSON and his 'Pops' Concert Orchestra — *1 Weeks*

Born on June 29, 1908 in Cambridge, Massachusetts, USA. In 1919, began piano and music studies at the New England Conservatory of Music. Studied musical harmony at Harvard where he earned an MA with a major in music in 1930. Played trombone in the Harvard University Band. Began arranging for Arthur Fiedler's Boston Pops Orchestra in 1936. Musical compositions include *Blue Tango*, *Buglers Holiday*, *The Typewriter*, *Sleigh Ride* and *Forgotten Dreams*. In 1958, he scored a Broadway musical. Died on May 18, 1975. Elected posthumously to the Songwriters Hall of Fame in 1988.

27 Aug 57	-	1	1. FORGOTTEN DREAMS • *Brunswick 05485*

Lynn ANDERSON — *9 Weeks*

Born on September 26, 1947 in Grand Forks, North Dakota, USA. Raised in California. The daughter of country songwriters Casey and Liz Anderson. She started performing at the age of six. Won major awards as a horse rider at shows all over California. Won the California Horse Show Queen title in 1966. Won CMA female vocalist award in 1971. *Rose Garden* was composed by Joe South

18 Mar 71	1(2)	9	• 1. ROSE GARDEN *CBS 5360*

Date	Pos	Wks	ARTIST / Record Title *Label & Number*

Chris ANDREWS **8 Weeks**

Born Christopher Frederick Andrews on October 15, 1942 in Romford, Essex, England. In the early sixties formed his own group Chris Ravell and the Ravers. Composed hit songs for Adam Faith and Sandie Shaw including *The First Time*, *Someone's Taken Maria Away*, *Girl Don't Come* and *Long Live Love*. *To Whom It Concerns* was used as the theme tune for the Irish television chat show, *The Late Late Show*, for almost thirty years.

Date	Pos	Wks	ARTIST / Record Title *Label & Number*
01 Nov 65	1(2)	6	• 1. YESTERDAY MAN *Decca F 12236*
10 Jan 66	9	2	2. TO WHOM IT CONCERNS *Decca F 22285*

Eamonn ANDREWS **2 Weeks**

Born on December 19, 1922 in Dublin, Ireland. Worked on Irish state radio (Radio Eireann) as a presenter and boxing commentator before moving to England to work for the BBC. Voted Television Personality of the Year on four different occasions. Hosted *What's My Line* BBC 1951-63, ITV 1984-87, *Crackerjack* 1955-64 and *This Is Your Life* 1955-88. Moved to ITV in 1964. Hosted the Eamonn Andrews Show on ITV 1964-69. When the Irish national Television service was launched in 1961 he was appointed Chairman of its state run governing body, the RTE Authority. Owner and founder of the Eamonn Andrews Recording Studios in Dublin, where many of the chart hits by Irish artists were recorded. Died on November 5, 1987.

Date	Pos	Wks	ARTIST / Record Title *Label & Number*
03 Jan 56	-	2	1. SHIFTING WHISPERING SANDS *Parlophone DIP 204*

Julie ANDREWS **1 Weeks**

Born Julia Elizabeth Wells on October 1, 1935 in Walton on Thames, Surrey, England. In 1945, made her first public singing appearance in her parents vaudeville act. Made her Broadway debut in 1954 in *The Boyfriend*. Shot to world fame in 1956 when she played role of Eliza Doolittle in the stage musical *My Fair Lady*.

continues over

Date	Pos	Wks	ARTIST / Record Title *Label & Number*

She stayed in the production for two years. Made her film debut in *Mary Poppins* (1964) for which she won Academy Award for Best Actress. Other film credits include *Sound Of Music* (1965), *Torn Curtain* (1966) and *Thoroughly Modern Millie* (1967). Wrote two children's books in the 1970's. In 1997 had surgery to remove non-cancerous nodules on her vocal chords but the operation backfired and robbed Julie of her singing voice. Julie is the voice of Queen Lillian in the animated film, *Shrek 2*.

Date	Pos	Wks	ARTIST / Record Title *Label & Number*
17 Sep 58	-	1	1. I COULD HAVE DANCED ALL NIGHT *Philips EPB 846*

The ANIMALS — *13 Weeks*

Originally formed in Newcastle, England in 1960 as the Alan Price Combo, the group changed its name to the Animals when Eric Burdon joined in 1962. Personnel: Eric Burdon (born May 11, 1941 in Newcastle, lead vocals), Alan Price (organ, vocals), Chas Chandler (bass), Hilton Valentine (lead guitar), and John Steel (drums). Alan Price left in May 1965 to pursue a solo career. Replaced by Dave Rowberry. Barry Jenkins replaced John Steel in 1966. Group split in September 1966. Eric Burdon kept the name until December 1968. Reformed in 1977 and 1983. Chas Chandler died on July 17, 1996.

Date	Pos	Wks	ARTIST / Record Title *Label & Number*
27 Jul 64	10	2	1. THE HOUSE OF THE RISING SUN *Columbia DB(I) 7301*
15 Mar 65	7	1	2. DON'T LET ME BE MISUNDERSTOOD *Columbia DB(I) 7445*
03 May 65	6	2	3. BRING IT ON HOME TO ME *Columbia DB(I) 7539*
02 Aug 65	5	5	4. WE'VE GOTTA GET OUT OF THIS PLACE *Columbia DB(I) 7639*
29 Nov 65	9	1	5. IT'S MY LIFE *Columbia DB(I) 7741*
13 Jun 66	7	2	6. DON'T BRING ME DOWN *Decca F 12407*

Paul ANKA — *18 Weeks*

Singer/songwriter. Born on July 30, 1941 in Ottawa, Canada. Had his first international hit at age of sixteen with his own song, *Diana*.

continues over

Date	Pos	Wks	ARTIST / Record Title *Label & Number*

Penned the song as a tribute to his baby sitter, Diana Ayoub. In 1975, Paul recorded a sequel, *Remember Diana*. A songwriter of distinction he composed, *It Doesn't Matter Anymore,* for Buddy Holly and wrote English lyrics to a French song, *My Way*, for Frank Sinatra. Film appearances include *Girls Town* (1959) and *The Longest Day* (1962). Released the critically acclaimed album, *Rock Swings*, in 2005. Inducted into the Canadian Songwriters Hall of fame in March 2008. Odia Coates who is featured on *You're Having My Baby,* was born on July 6 1942 in Mississippi, USA. Died of breast cancer on May 19, 1991.

24 Sep 57	-	4	1. DIANA *Columbia IDB 719*
21 Jan 58	-	1	2. I LOVE YOU BABY *Columbia DB(I) 4022*
18 Feb 58	-	1	3. YOU ARE MY DESTINY *Columbia DB(I) 4063*
03 Sep 59	4	7	4. LONELY BOY *Columbia DB(I) 4324*
17 Dec 59	6	1	5. PUT YOUR HEAD ON MY SHOULDER *Columbia DB(I) 4355*
16 Aug 62	9	1	6. A STEEL GUITAR AND A GLASS OF WINE *RCA ERC 1292*
31 Oct 74	4	3	7. (YOU'RE) HAVING MY BABY *United Artists UP 35713*

You're Having My Baby credit *Paul Anka featuring Odia Coates*

Billie ANTHONY *3 Weeks*

Born Philomena McGeachie Levy on October 11, 1932 in Glasgow, Scotland. Began her professional career as a dancer in the chorus line. In 1953 on the suggestion of Tony Brent she decided to try to make a living as a singer. In October of 1953, under the name Billie Anthony, she recorded her first single for Columbia, *I'd Rather Take My Time*. Retired from world of showbiz in 1968 to concentrate on motherhood. Died on January 5, 1991 following a series of strokes, aged 58.

09 Nov 54	2	1	1. THIS OLE HOUSE *Columbia IDB 527*
30 Oct 56	-	1	2. LAY DOWN YOUR ARMS *Columbia IDB 667*
12 Feb 57	-	1	3. I DREAMED *Columbia IDB 694*

Date	Pos	Wks	ARTIST / Record Title *Label & Number*

The ARCHIES *15 Weeks*

The Archies were animated cartoon characters who topped the ratings all over the USA with their Saturday morning television series on the CBS network. The single, *Sugar Sugar*, and subsequent recordings featured studio singers and session musicians. Ron Dante (born August 22, 1945 in Staten Island, New York) was featured as lead vocalist on all Archies recordings. He went on to produce a series of multi-platinum albums for Barry Manilow.

Date	Pos	Wks	ARTIST / Record Title *Label & Number*
30 Oct 69	1(6)	15	• 1. SUGAR SUGAR *RCA Victor RCA 1872*

See also The Cufflinks

Louis ARMSTRONG and his All Stars *19 Weeks*

Born on July 4, 1901 in New Orleans, USA. At the age of eleven, following an incident in which Louis fired a gun in a public place, he was arrested and sent to the Waif's Home in New Orleans. The Home's bandmaster offered him a place in the institution's band, where he learned to play drums, trombone and cornet. Following his release he was hired by Kid Ory's Band. Formed his own band, the Hot Five, in 1925. Numerous film appearances including *Pennies From Heaven* (1936), *High Society* (1956) and *Hello Dolly* (1969). Influenced legions of singers and trumpet players worldwide. Died in his sleep on July 6, 1971 in New York.

Date	Pos	Wks	ARTIST / Record Title *Label & Number*
14 Mar 56	-	5	1. THEME FROM THE THREEPENNY OPERA *Philips PB 574*
22 Jun 64	5	6	2. HELLO DOLLY *London HLR 9878*
02 May 68	2	8	3. WHAT A WONDERFUL WORLD *HMV POP(I) 1615*

ARRIVAL *2 Weeks*

Formed in Liverpool, England in 1969. Personnel: Dyan Birch (vocals), Frank Collins (vocals), Carol Carter (vocals), Paddy McHugh (vocals), Don Hume, (bass), Lloyd Courtney (drums) and Tony O'Malley (piano).

continues over

Date	Pos	Wks	ARTIST / Record Title *Label & Number*
			Disc debut: "Friends" (1969). Broke up in 1973 when Birch, Collins, McHugh and O'Malley left to form Kokomo. Dyan Birch lead vocals on *Friends*.
05 Feb 70	8	2	1. FRIENDS *Decca F 12986*

ASHTON, GARDNER and DYKE — *3 Weeks*

Formed in London, England in 1968. Personnel: Tony Ashton (born March 1, 1946 in Blackburn) keyboards/vocals. Kim Gardner (born January 27, 1948 in London) bass, Roy Dyke (born February 13, 1945 in Liverpool), drums and Mick Liber (guitar). Disbanded in 1972. Tony Ashton died from cancer on May 28, 2001. Kim Gardner died on October 24, 2001.

Date	Pos	Wks	ARTIST / Record Title *Label & Number*
25 Feb 71	6	3	1. RESURRECTION SHUFFLE *Capitol CL(I) 15665*

ATOMIC ROOSTER — *2 Weeks*

Formed in London in 1969. Made debut at Lyceum, London on August 29, 1969. Personnel: Vincent Crane (organ), Nick Graham (bass, vocals) and Carl Palmer (drums). Carl Palmer came up with the group name. Palmer left in May 1970 to form Emerson, Lake and Palmer (ELP). Replaced by Paul Hammond. In April 1970 Nick Graham quit. John Cann (vocals, guitar) joined. Paul French joined in May 1971. Numerous personnel changes over the lifespan of the group. Disbanded in February 1975. Vincent Crane committed suicide by overdosing on sleeping pills on February 14, 1989. Paul Hammond died 1992.

Date	Pos	Wks	ARTIST / Record Title *Label & Number*
19 Aug 71	9	2	1. DEVILS ANSWER *B&C CB 157*

Winifred ATWELL — *6 Weeks*

Born Una Winifred Atwell on April 27, 1914 in Tuna Puna, Port of Spain, Trinidad. Began playing piano at an early age. At the age of 5 played Chopin concerts in public. Relocated to New York in 1945 where she spent six months before moving to London where she studied at The Royal Academy of Music.

continues over

Date	Pos	Wks	ARTIST / Record Title *Label & Number*

Signed to Decca Records in 1951. Moved to Philips in 1953, returning to Decca in 1955. Winnie achieved her success playing her 'other' piano, which reputedly cost her £2.50 and which she later insured for £10,000. Film appearances include *It's A Grand Life* (1953) and *It's Great To Be Young* (1956). Moved to Australia in the 1972. Retired from music business in 1978. Died on February 28, 1983.

Date	Pos	Wks	ARTIST / Record Title *Label & Number*
01 Mar 55	-	1	1. LET'S HAVE ANOTHER PARTY • *Philips PB 268*
27 Mar 56	-	3	2. POOR PEOPLE OF PARIS (POOR JOHN) • *Decca F 10681*
13 Nov 56	-	2	3. MAKE IT A PARTY • *Decca F 10796*

Various hits listed above were medleys: **Let's Have Another Party**: Somebody Stole My Gal / I Wonder Where My Baby Is Tonight / When The Red Red Robin / Bye Bye Blackbird / Sheik Of Araby. **Make It A Party**: Who Were You With Last Night / Hello Hello Who's Your Lady Friend / Yes Sir That's My Baby / Don't Dilly Dally On The Way / Beer Barrel Polka.

Frankie AVALON — *7 Weeks*

Born Francis Thomas Avallone, on September 18, 1939 in Philadelphia, USA. Learned to play trumpet at an early age. Made his recording debut, as a trumpeter, in 1954 with the release of *Trumpet Sorrento*, on the RCA offshoot X Records. Joined the band Rocco and the Saints (in which future star Bobby Rydell played drums). In early 1957, signed with Chancellor Records and later that year had his first vocal single, *Cupid*, issued. His career as an actor blossomed in the Sixties with appearances in films such as *Guns Of The Timberland* (1960) *The Alamo* (1960) *Drums Of Africa* (1963) and *Beach Party* (1963). Returned to the singles chart in 1976 with a disco version of *Venus*.

Date	Pos	Wks	ARTIST / Record Title *Label & Number*
07 May 59	5	4	1. VENUS *HMV POP(I) 605*
21 Jan 60	2	3	2. WHY *HMV POP(I) 688*

Date	Pos	Wks	ARTIST / Record Title *Label & Number*

AVERAGE WHITE BAND — *1 Weeks*

Scottish band formed in London, England in 1971. Personnel: Alan Gorrie (born on July 19, 1946 in Glasgow, Scotland) (lead vocals, bass), Onnie McIntyre (guitar), Hamish Stuart (guitar/bass/vocals), Robbie McIntosh (drums), Malcolm 'Molly' Duncan (saxophone) and Roger Ball (keyboards, saxophone). Film actor, Stanley Baker, was persuaded to finance the making of their first album. McIntosh died from drug poisoning on September 23, 1974. Replaced by Steve Ferrone. *Pick Up The Pieces* on their 1974 album, *AWB*.

Date	Pos	Wks	ARTIST / Record Title *Label & Number*
20 Mar 75	10	1	1. PICK UP THE PIECES *Atlantic K 10489*

The AVONS — *7 Weeks*

Vocal trio. Personnel: Valerie Avon (born in London), Elaine Murtagh (born in Cork, Ireland) and Ray Adams (born in Jersey). Sisters-in-law Valerie and Elaine originally performed as the Avon Sisters. Discovered singing at the 1958 BBC Radio Exhibition. Released a single, *Jerri-Lee*, in 1959. Added Ray Adams (who was vocalist with the Nat Gonella Band) to the lineup and changed name to the Avons. Signed to EMI. Penned *Dance On*, a hit for The Shadows and Kathy Kirby and *In Summer*, a hit for Billy Fury.

Date	Pos	Wks	ARTIST / Record Title *Label & Number*
17 Dec 59	2	7	1. SEVEN LITTLE GIRLS SITTING IN THE BACK SEAT *Columbia DB(I) 4363*

Charles AZNAVOUR — *5 Weeks*

Born Shahnour Varenagh Aznavourian on May 22, 1924 in Paris, France. Attended acting school as a child and made his first professional stage appearance at the age of nine. In 1941, met songwriter and composer Pierre Roche, and they teamed up as a double act, performing their own songs. Split in 1952. Began having success with his own songs through recordings by Juliette Greco and Edith Piaf. By 1956 had established himself as one of the top names of French chanson.

continues over

Date	Pos	Wks	ARTIST / Record Title *Label & Number*
			A talented songwriter, his songs have been recorded by many international stars including Bing Crosby, Sammy Davis Jr. and Ray Charles. *She* was used as the theme to the TV series, *Seven Faces Of Woman.*
11 Jul 74	1(1)	5	• 1. SHE *Barclay BAR 26*

Date	Pos	Wks	ARTIST / Record Title *Label & Number*

B

BACCARA *15 Weeks*

Spanish female duo formed in 1977 as Spanish Flamenco. Spotted by RCA executive Leon Dean. Renamed Baccara. Personnel: Maria Mendiolo and Mayte Mateus. Represented Luxembourg in the 1978 Eurovision Song Contest with *Parlez vous Francais*. The duo split in 1983, with both ladies forming their own versions of Baccara.

20 Oct 77	1(1)	8	• 1. YES SIR I CAN BOOGIE *RCA PB 5526*
26 Jan 78	4	7	2. SORRY I'M A LADY *RCA PB 5555*

Burt BACHARACH his Orchestra and Chorus *4 Weeks*

Born on May 12, 1928 in Kansas City, Missouri, USA. In 1932, family moved to New York. At the age of twelve, started to learn cello, drums and piano. Studied music theory and composition at the Mannes School of Music in New York. In 1952, became Vic Damone's piano accompanist. In 1957, collaborated for the first time with lyricist, Hal David. Enjoyed success with songs such as *The Story Of My Life* and *Magic Moments*. For the period 1958-61 toured Europe and America as musical director for Marlene Dietrich. Married Angie Dickinson in 1966, were divorced in 1980.

14 Jun 65	7	4	1. TRAINS AND BOATS AND PLANES *London HLR 9968*

The BACHELORS *44 Weeks*

Vocal trio from Dublin, Ireland. Personnel: Con Cluskey, (born November 18, 1941, lead vocals, guitar); Dec Cluskey (vocals, guitar) and John Stokes (vocals, double bass). Started out in late 1950's as an instrumental (harmonica's) group called The Harmonichords. In 1962, spotted by Dick Rowe who signed the trio to Decca.

continues over

Date	Pos	Wks	ARTIST / Record Title *Label & Number*
			Changed their name to the Bachelors. Appeared in the 1965 film, *I've Gotta Horse*. Peter Phibbs replaced John Stokes in 1984. Following the departure of Peter Phibbs, in 1993, Con and Dec continued as a duo.
01 Apr 63	8	3	1. CHARMAINE *Decca F 11559*
30 Dec 63	9	1	2. LONG TIME AGO *Decca F 11772*
17 Feb 64	2	8	3. DIANE *Decca F 11799*
30 Mar 64	2	10	4. I BELIEVE *Decca F 11857*
15 Jun 64	6	7	5. RAMONA *Decca F 11910*
31 Aug 64	1(1)	10	• 6. I WOULDN'T TRADE YOU FOR THE WORLD *Decca F 1194*
11 Jan 65	8	3	7. NO ARMS CAN EVER HOLD YOU *Decca F 12034*
18 Apr 66	9	2	8. THE SOUND OF SILENCE *Decca F 12351*
			BACHMAN-TURNER OVERDRIVE 6 Weeks
			Rock group formed in Vancouver, Canada in 1972 by brothers Randy (vocals, guitar), Tim (guitar) and Robin Bachman (drums) with C. Fred Turner (vocals, bass). Randy left in 1977 to pursue a solo career.
12 Dec 74	4	6	1. YOU AIN'T SEEN NOTHING YET *Mercury 6167 025*
			BADFINGER 7 Weeks
			Formed in Swansea, Wales in 1964 as the Iveys. Changed name to Badfinger in November 1969. Neil Aspinall of Apple Records came up with the Badfinger name. Personnel: Pete Ham (vocals, guitar, keyboards), Tom Evans (guitar), Joey Molland (bass) and Mike Gibbins (drums). Split in April 1975. Reformed in 1978 and continued until 1983. Paul McCartney wrote their debut hit, *Come And Get It*. Ham and Evans composed *Without You*, a million seller for both Nilsson (1972) and Mariah Carey (1994). Pete Ham and Tom Evans both committed suicide (by hanging), Ham on April 24, 1975 and Evans on November 19, 1983. Mike Gibbins died in his sleep on October 4, 2005.
12 Feb 70	5	4	1. COME AND GET IT *Apple APPLE 20*
11 Feb 71	7	3	2. NO MATTER WHAT *Apple APPLE 31*

Date	Pos	Wks	ARTIST / Record Title *Label & Number*
			Joan BAEZ ***2 Weeks***
			Born on January 9, 1941 in Staten Island, New York City, USA. Bought her first guitar in 1956. First gained recognition at the 1958 Newport Folk Festival. Signed to Vanguard Records. Disc debut: *Joan Baez* LP (1960). During the 60's began to champion the work of Bob Dylan.
18 Nov 71	8	2	1. THE NIGHT THEY DROVE OLD DIXIE DOWN *Vanguard VS 35138*
			Long John BALDRY ***8 Weeks***
			Born John William Baldry on January 12, 1941 in East Haddon, Derbyshire, England. Started his career playing folk and jazz in the 1950's. During the early 60's he was vocalist with a number of blues groups, including Blues Incorporated, Cyril Davies All Stars, the Hoochie Coochie Men (with a young Rod Stewart as second vocalist), Steampacket and Bluesology (whose lineup included pianist, Reg Dwight, later to achieve fame as Elton John). Emigrated to Canada in the early 1980's. Was the voice for Robotnik on the popular Sonic the Hedgehog computer game. Died from complications following a chest infection, on July 21, 2005.
30 Nov 67	2	8	1. LET THE HEARTACHES BEGIN *Pye 7N 17385*
			Kenny BALL and his JAZZMEN ***16 Weeks***
			Bandleader/trumpeter/vocalist. Born on May 22, 1930 in Ilford, Essex, England. Played with several local bands before beginning his professional musical career in 1953, with Sid Phillips. Moved to Eric Delaney Band in 1956. Formed the Jazzmen in October 1958. Lonnie Donegan helped the band secure a recording contract with Pye. Disc debut: *Teddy Bears Picnic* (1960).
21 Dec 61	3	5	1. MIDNIGHT IN MOSCOW • *Pye Jazz 7NJ 2049*
15 Mar 62	3	4	• 2. MARCH OF THE SIAMESE CHILDREN • *Pye Jazz 7NJ 2051*
31 May 62	7	4	3. THE GREEN LEAVES OF SUMMER • *Pye Jazz 7NJ 2054*
08 Oct 62	10	1	4. SO DO I *Pye Jazz 7NJ 2056*

continues over

Date	Pos	Wks	ARTIST / Record Title *Label & Number*
29 Oct 62	10	1	5. THE PAY OFF • *Pye Jazz 7NJ 2061*
02 Sep 63	8	1	6. ACAPULCO 1922 • *Pye Jazz 7NJ 2067*

BANDWAGON - See Johnny Johnson and the Bandwagon

CHRIS BARBER JAZZBAND ***18 Weeks***

Born Donald Christopher Barber on April 17, 1930 in Welwyn Garden City, Hertfordshire, England. As a child played the violin. Purchased his first trombone from a member of Humphrey Lyttelton's Band. Formed his first band in 1948, turned professional in 1952. Took over Ken Colyer's Jazzmen in 1954, renaming it the Chris Barber Jazzband. Disc debut: *New Orleans Joys* LP (1954). Personnel: Chris Barber (trombone), Monty Sunshine (clarinet), Pat Halcox (trumpet), Dickie Bishop (banjo, guitar), Dick Smith (bass), Ron Bowden (drums) and Ottillie Patterson (vocals). Chris married Ottillie in 1959 (they divorced in 1983). Monty Sunshine is the featured instrumentalist (clarinet) on *Petite Fleur.*

Date	Pos	Wks	ARTIST / Record Title *Label & Number*
12 Mar 59	1(5)	18	• 1. PETITE FLEUR • *Pye Nixa NJ 2026*

See also Monty Sunshine Quartet

BARBRA and NEIL ***3 Weeks***

Female/male vocal duo. Barbra Streisand born on April 24, 1942 in Brooklyn, New York City, USA. Neil Diamond born on January 24, 1941 in Brooklyn, New York City, USA.

Date	Pos	Wks	ARTIST / Record Title *Label & Number*
31 Dec 78	4	3	1. YOU DON'T BRING ME FLOWERS *CBS 6803*

BARLEYCORN ***46 Weeks***

Formed in Belfast, N. Ireland in June 1971. Personnel: Paddy McGuigan (vocals, harmonica), Liam Tiernan (banjo), Brian McCormack (bass, vocals on hit) and John Delaney (banjo).

continues over

Date	Pos	Wks	ARTIST / Record Title *Label & Number*

Recorded *The Men Behind The Wire* in November 1971, but had difficulty (due to lyrical content) in getting a record company to release it. The song composed by Pat McGuigan was written about Long Kesh internment camp outside Lisburn. On December 14, 1971 Pat McGuigan was lifted by the British army and interned on the prison ship Maidstone in Belfast Lough. Released in February 1972 and returned to the group. Liam Tiernan left group in 1981 to pursue a solo career. Brian McCormack left group in 1982. Replaced by Derek McCormack. Over the years the group had many personel changes in its lineup. Group disbanded in 1995. John Delaney the only ever present member. Derek McCormack died on January 30, 2005.

Date	Pos	Wks	Record
06 Jan 72	1(5)	35	• 1. THE MEN BEHIND THE WIRE *CRC CRC 71*
01 Feb 73	4	8	2. SING IRISHMEN SING *Solo SOLO 110*
07 Mar 74	4	3	3. BRING THEM HOME *Dolphin DOS 116*

J J BARRIE — *3 Weeks*

Born Barrie Authors on July 7, 1933 in Ottawa, Canada. Began his showbiz career as one half of a comedy duo, Authors and Swinson. Moved into management and agency work. Has written several screen plays. *No Charge* is a cover of a Tammy Wynnette composition. Vicky Brown is backing vocalist on *No Charge.*

Date	Pos	Wks	Record
10 Jun 76	5	3	1. NO CHARGE *Power Exchange PX 209*

The BARRON KNIGHTS with Duke D'Mond — *8 Weeks*

Comedy/vocal group formed in Leighton Buzzard, Bedfordshire, England in 1960. Originally known as the Knights Of The Round Table. First professional gig in October 1960.

continues over

Date	Pos	Wks	ARTIST / Record Title *Label & Number*
			Personnel: Duke D'Mond (born Richard Palmer on February 23, 1943 in Dunstable, Bedfordshire, lead vocals), Barron Anthony (born Tony Osmond, bass, vocals), Butch Baker (guitar, vocals), Dave Ballinger (drums) and Pete Langford (lead guitar). Duke D'Mond died on April 9, 2009.
03 Aug 64	2	6	1. **CALL UP THE GROUPS** *Columbia DB(I) 7317*
03 May 65	7	2	2. **POP GO THE WORKERS** *Columbia DB(I) 7525*
			The John BARRY SEVEN **4 Weeks**
			Born John Barry Prendergast on November 3, 1933 in York, England. Formed the John Barry Seven in 1957. Personnel: John Barry (trumpet), Vic Flick (lead guitar), Les Reed (piano), Mike Peters (bass), Denis King (saxophone), Jimmy Snead (saxophone) and Dougie Wright (drums). Resident on BBC TV pop programme *Drumbeat* (1959). Barry composed the music score for a dozen James Bond films. Won Oscar for Best Song and Best Score for 1966 film "Born Free". Awarded OBE in 1999.
27 Oct 60	8	4	1. **WALK DON'T RUN** • *Columbia DB(I) 4505*
			Len BARRY **2 Weeks**
			Born Leonard Borisoff on June 12, 1942 in Philadelphia, USA. In 1959, joined The Dovells as lead singer. The group placed several records in the US charts. In late 1963, left the group to pursue a solo career. Debut solo disc: *Don't Come Back* (1964).
29 Nov 65	8	2	1. **1-2-3** *Brunswick 05942*
			Shirley BASSEY **21 Weeks**
			Born Shirley Veronica Bassey on January 8, 1937 in Tiger Bay, Cardiff, Wales. Discovered in 1955 by comedian Al Read while appearing in a touring revue, *Memories Of Al Jolson*. A season at the prestigious Café de Paris in London was followed in 1956 by a residency in Las Vegas. Disc debut: *Burn My Candle* (1956).

continues over

Date	Pos	Wks	ARTIST / Record Title *Label & Number*
			In 1964 sang the theme song in the James Bond film, *Goldfinger.* Made a Dame of the British Empire in 1999.
27 Feb 57	-	5	1. BANANA BOAT SONG *Philips EPB 668*
19 Feb 59	5	4	2. AS I LOVE YOU *Philips EPB 845*
05 Mar 59	6	1	3. KISS ME HONEY HONEY KISS ME *Philips EPB 860*
25 May 61	5	2	4. YOU'LL NEVER KNOW *Columbia DB(I) 4643*
24 Aug 61	3	8	5. REACH FOR THE STARS *Columbia DB(I) 4685*
18 Nov 63	10	1	6. I (WHO HAVE NOTHING) *Columbia DB(I) 7113*

Mike BATT — *1 Weeks*

Born on February 6, 1950 in London, England. Began his career in popular music at the age of eighteen. Talented songwriter/producer he wrote, produced and provided vocals for the The Wombles recordings. Also produced or composed hit recordings for Steeleye Span, Elkie Brooks, Cliff Richard, David Essex and Katie Melua. Made his debut as a conductor at London's Barbican with the London Symphony Orchestra in 1984. He also composed the score for the 1978 film, *Watership Down*, including the hit song, *Bright Eyes*.

Date	Pos	Wks	ARTIST / Record Title *Label & Number*
02 Oct 75	4	1	1. SUMMERTIME CITY *Epic EPC 3460*

See also The Wombles

BAY CITY ROLLERS — *44 Weeks*

Formed in Edinburgh, Scotland in 1967, as The Saxons. Discovered by Tom Paton, who became their manager. He chose their name, by sticking a pin in a map of the USA. Personnel: Leslie McKeown (born on November 12, 1955 in Edinburgh, Scotland, lead vocals), Eric Faulkner (guitar), Stuart 'Woody' Wood (guitar), Alan Longmuir (bass) and Derek Longmuir (drums). Disc debut: *Keep On Dancing* (1971). Alan Longmuir left in August 1976, replaced by Ian Mitchell. He left in January 1977, replaced by Pat McGlynn, who departed after six months, in July 1977.

continues over

Date	Pos	Wks	ARTIST / Record Title *Label & Number*
			The group continued as a four piece. Les McKeown departed in late 1978. Band split in 1979. Reformed in 1998 for a Japanese TV show.
22 Aug 74	5	4	1. SUMMERLOVE SENSATION *Bell BELL 1369*
31 Oct 74	5	6	2. ALL OF ME LOVES ALL OF YOU *Bell BELL 1382*
13 Mar 75	1(4)	11	• 3. BYE BYE BABY *Bell BELL 1409*
17 Jul 75	1(2)	7	• 4. GIVE A LITTLE LOVE *Bell BELL 1425*
20 Nov 75	4	4	5. MONEY HONEY *Bell BELL 1461*
22 Apr 76	3	5	6. LOVE ME LIKE I LOVE YOU *Bell BELL 1477*
07 Oct 76	4	3	7. I ONLY WANNA TO BE WITH YOU *Bell BELL 1493*
16 Jun 77	6	4	8. IT'S A GAME *Arista ARST 108*

Gilbert BECAUD — *1 Weeks*

Born Francois Gilbert Silly on October 24, 1927 in Toulon, France. Learned to play the piano at a young age. Studied at the Conservatoire de Nice. In 1942 joined the French Resistance. In 1953 while touring as a pianist met Edith Piaf at whose suggestion he began singing. A gifted songwriter, he composed the original French versions of *The Day The Rain Came Down*, *Let It Be* and *What Now My Love*. Died from lung cancer on December 18, 2001.

Date	Pos	Wks	ARTIST / Record Title *Label & Number*
01 May 75	9	1	1. A LITTLE LOVE AND UNDERSTANDING *Decca FR 13537*

The BEACH BOYS — *52 Weeks*

The most successful American group of the sixties. Formed in Hawthorne, California in 1961 as The Pendeltones. The change of name to Beach Boys came in October 1961. Was a family affair with Wilson brothers, Brian, Denis, and Carl, and their cousin Mike Love. A close friend Al Jardine made up the group. When Brian Wilson stopped touring with the group in 1964, Bruce Johnston was brought in. Group were inducted into the Rock and Roll Hall of Fame in 1988.

continues over

Date	Pos	Wks	ARTIST / Record Title *Label & Number*
			Denis Wilson died of drowning on December 28, 1983. Carl Wilson died from cancer on February 6, 1998.
14 Mar 66	7	4	1. BARBARA ANN *Capitol CL(I) 15432*
02 May 66	2	9	2. SLOOP JOHN B *Capitol CL(I) 15441*
29 Aug 66	6	4	3. GOD ONLY KNOWS *Capitol CL(I) 15459*
14 Nov 66	3	7	4. GOOD VIBRATIONS *Capitol CL(I) 15475*
25 May 67	4	8	5. THEN I KISSED HER *Capitol CL(I) 15502*
05 Sep 68	5	7	6. DO IT AGAIN *Capitol CL(I) 15554*
24 Jul 69	10	1	7. BREAK AWAY *Capitol CL(I) 15598*
11 Jun 70	3	10	8. COTTONFIELDS *Capitol CL 15640*
02 Aug 79	8	2	9. LADY LYNDA *Caribou CRB 7427*

The BEATLES ***174 Weeks***

Formed in Liverpool in late 1950's. Were known as The Quarrymen, Johnny and the Moondogs and the Silver Beatles before finally settling on The Beatles. Original personnel: John Lennon (guitar), George Harrison (lead guitar), Paul McCartney (guitar), Stu Sutcliffe (bass) and Pete Best (drums). Sutcliffe left in April 1961 (he died on April 10, 1962 of a brain hemorrhage) and Paul moved to bass. Pete Best was replaced by Ringo Starr in August 1962. Group were managed by Brian Epstein and produced by George Martin. Beatles starred in films *A Hard Day's Night* (1964). *Help!* (1965) and *Magical Mystery Tour* (1967) and did the voices on the animated cartoon film, *Yellow Submarine* (1968). Formed own record label, Apple, in 1968. The Beatles were all born in Liverpool: John Lennon (October 9, 1940, he was shot dead on December 8, 1980 in New York City), Paul McCartney (June 19, 1942), George Harrison (February 25, 1943) and Ringo Starr (born Richard Starkey on July 7, 1940). Group disbanded in late 1970 with individual members moving on to successful solo careers. Inducted into the Rock 'n' Roll Hall of Fame in 1988.

continues over

Date	Pos	Wks	ARTIST / Record Title *Label & Number*
			In 1995 Paul, George and Ringo got together in the studio to play on a track, *Free As A Bird* (a John Lennon Demo from 1977). Released as a Beatles single it took the Fab Four back into the upper echelons of the charts world wide. John Lennon was shot to death on December 8, 1980 in New York City. George Harrison died from cancer November 29, 2001.
25 Mar 63	10	2	1. PLEASE PLEASE ME *Parlophone R(I) 4983*
06 May 63	1(1)	12	• 2. FROM ME TO YOU *Parlophone R(I) 5015*
09 Sep 63	2	19	3. SHE LOVES YOU *Parlophone R(I) 5055*
16 Dec 63	2	9	4. I WANT TO HOLD YOUR HAND *Parlophone R(I) 5084*
30 Mar 64	1(3)	8	• 5. CAN'T BUY ME LOVE *Parlophone R(I) 5114*
20 Jul y 64	1(3)	9	• 6. A HARD DAY'S NIGHT *Parlophone R(I) 5160*
07 Dec 64	1(5)	8	• 7. I FEEL FINE *Parlophone R(I) 5200*
26 Apr 65	1(4)	6	• 8. TICKET TO RIDE *Parlophone R(I) 5265*
02 Aug 65	1(5)	9	• 9. HELP! *Parlophone R(I) 5305*
13 Dec 65	1(5)	7	• 10. DAY TRIPPER / WE CAN WORK IT OUT *Parlophone R(I) 5389*
20 Jun 66	1(4)	6	• 11. PAPERBACK WRITER *Parlophone R(I) 5452*
15 Aug 66	1(2)	8	• 12. YELLOW SUBMARINE / ELEANOR RIGBY *Parlophone R(I) 5493*
02 Mar 67	2	6	13. PENNY LANE *Parlophone R(I) 5570*
20 Jul 67	1(2)	8	• 14. ALL YOU NEED IS LOVE *Parlophone R(I) 5620*
14 Dec 67	2	7	15. HELLO GOODBYE *Parlophone R(I) 5655*
28 Mar 68	3	6	16. LADY MADONNA *Parlophone R(I) 5675*
12 Sep 68	1(3)	10	• 17. HEY JUDE *Parlophone DP(I) 570*
01 May 69	1(6)	10	• 18. GET BACK *Apple R 5777*
19 Jun 69	1(4)	8	• 19. THE BALLAD OF JOHN AND YOKO *Apple R(I) 5786*
20 Nov 69	3	7	20. SOMETHING *Apple R(I) 5814*
12 Mar 70	3	6	21. LET IT BE *Apple R(I) 5833*
22 Apr 76	5	3	22. YESTERDAY *Apple R 6013*

Get Back credit *The Beatles with Billy Preston*

See also George Harrison; John Lennon; Paul McCartney; Ringo Starr

The BEE GEES — *76 Weeks*

The Gibb brothers, Barry and twins Robin and Maurice were born in Douglas, Isle of Man. Family moved to Manchester in 1950's. Emigrated to Australia in 1958. Performed there as the Gibbs and later as the B. G's. Had several hit recordings in Australia. Disc debut: *Three Kisses Of Love* (1960). Returned to England in early 1967 and signed a management contract with Robert Stigwood. Personnel: Barry Gibb (guitar/vocals), Robin Gibb (keyboards/vocals), Maurice Gibb (bass, guitar, keyboards, vocals), Vince Melouney (lead guitar) and Colin Peterson (drums). Vince Melouney left in late 1968. Robin Gibb left in March 1969 to pursue a solo career. Colin Peterson was dimissed in August 1969. Barry and Maurice continued as the Bee Gees recording an album "Cucumber". Robin rejoined Barry and Maurice in 1971. Composed the music for the film, *Saturday Night Fever.* Maurice Gibb died on January 12, 2003.

Date	Pos	Wks	ARTIST / Record Title *Label & Number*
19 Oct 67	2	8	1. MASSACHUSETTS *Polydor 56192*
05 Sep 68	1(1)	6	• 2. I'VE GOTTA GET A MESSAGE TO YOU *Polydor 56273*
27 Mar 69	4	3	3. FIRST OF MAY *Polydor 56304*
04 Sep 69	1(2)	11	• 4. DON'T FORGET TO REMEMBER *Polydor 56343*
28 Sep 72	7	1	5. RUN TO ME *Polydor 2058 255*
07 Aug 75	5	5	6. JIVE TALKIN' *Polydor 2090 160*
09 Sep 76	4	3	7. YOU SHOULD BE DANCING *Polydor 2090 195*
08 Dec 77	2	7	8. HOW DEEP IS YOUR LOVE *Polydor 2090 259*
02 Mar 78	4	7	9. STAYIN' ALIVE *Polydor 2090 267*
20 Apr 78	1(3)	7	• 10. NIGHT FEVER *RSO 002*
30 Nov 78	2	8	11. TOO MUCH HEAVEN *RSO 25*
15 Feb 79	1(2)	7	• 12. TRAGEDY *RSO 27*
19 Apr 79	6	3	13. LOVE YOU INSIDE OUT *RSO 31*

See also Robin Gibb

Date	Pos	Wks	ARTIST / Record Title *Label & Number*
			Philomena BEGLEY ***26 Weeks***
			Born on October 20, 1939 in Pomeroy, Co. Tyrone, N. Ireland. While working in Fishers Hat Factory in Cookstown, Co. Tyrone she made a few guest appearances with the Old Cross Ceili Band. Joined the band full time in mid 1966. Disc debut: *My Little Son* (1968). In late 1970, the Old Cross Bandshow changed their name to Country Flavour, and embarked on a country and Irish musical direction. In 1974, Philomena decided to leave the Old Cross and on March 17, 1974 made her debut with her own band, The Ramblin' Men at the Four Seasons, Monaghan. Recorded an album of duets with Ray Lynam in 1976. Won the European Gold star Award in Holland in 1983.
30 Sep 71	7	1	1. HERE TODAY GONE TOMORROW *Release RL 588*
12 Oct 72	9	1	2. RAMBLIN' MAN *Release RL 640*
25 Oct 73	7	3	3. LIGHT IN THE WINDOW *Release RL 690*
05 Dec 74	5	2	4. WAIT A LITTLE LONGER PLEASE JESUS *Top Spin TSS 51*
21 Aug 75	5	8	5. BLANKET ON THE GROUND *Top Spin TSS 57*
24 Jun 76	3	7	6. ONCE AROUND THE DANCE FLOOR *Top Spin TSS 60*
14 Jul 77	5	4	7. FOR THE FIRST TIME IN A LONG TIME *Top Spin TSS 74*
			See also Ray Lynam and Philomena Begley
			Dominic BEHAN ***3 Weeks***
			Born on October 22, 1929 in Dublin. Brother of playwright Brendan Behan. Wrote several plays including *Posterity Be Damned* in which he sang *The Patriot Game* during its run at the Gaiety Theatre, Dublin in February 1960. Composed many successful songs including *The Sea Around Us*, *Avondale*, *The Patriot Game* and *Arkle*, a song about the great steeplechaser. His first novel, *The Public World of Parable Jones*, was published just before his death. Died of cancer on August 3, 1989 in Glasgow.
04 May 64	8	3	1. LIVERPOOL LOU *Piccadilly 7N 35172*

Date	Pos	Wks	ARTIST / Record Title *Label & Number*

Harry BELAFONTE *8 Weeks*

Born Harold George Belafonte on March 1, 1927 in Harlem, New York, USA. As a young boy moved with his family to Jamaica. On his return to New York he attended the George Washington High School. An interest in the theatre led to his becoming a member of the American Negro Theatre. Disc debut: *Lean On Me* (1949). Film appearances include *Carmen Jones* (1954), Won Broadway's 1954 Tony Award as Best Supporting or Featured Actor (Musical) for *John Murray Anderson's Almanac*. Signed to RCA Victor Records in 1955. His 1955 album, *Calypso*, became the first album in the world to sell over a million copies. In 1987, replaced Danny Kaye as UNICEF's Goodwill Ambassador. In 2006 was presented with the inaugural Amilcar Cabral International Freedom Award for his life contribution to all humanity.

Date	Pos	Wks	ARTIST / Record Title *Label & Number*
12 Mar 57	-	3	1. BANANA BOAT SONG (DAY-O) *HMV IP 1225*
23 Apr 57	-	1	2. JAMAICA FAREWELL *HMV IP 1225*
21 May 57	-	1	3. MAMA LOOK A BOO BOO *HMV IP 1241*
30 Jul 57	-	3	4. ISLAND IN THE SUN *RCA ERC 1007*

Freddie BELL and the BELL BOYS *4 Weeks*

Born Freddie Bello on September 29, 1931 in South Philadelphia, USA. Learned to play bass, trombone and drums. Member of the Ernie Ventura Band. Formed Bell Boys in 1951. Personnel: Freddie Bell (lead vocals), Frankie Brent (bass), Russ Conti (piano), Chick Keeney (drums), Jerry Mayo (trumpet) and Jack Kane (tenor saxophone). Disc debut: "Hound Dog" (1955). Signed to Mercury Records in 1956. Film appearances include *Rock Around The Clock* (1956) and *Don't Knock The Rock* (1956). Toured Britain in 1957 as support to Tommy Steele. Died of lung cancer on February 10, 2008.

Date	Pos	Wks	ARTIST / Record Title *Label & Number*
30 Oct 56	-	3	1. GIDDY UP A DING DONG *Mercury MT 122*
04 Jun 57	-	1	2. ROMPIN' AND STOMPIN' *Mercury MT 141*

Date	Pos	Wks	ARTIST / Record Title *Label & Number*
			The BELLAMY BROTHERS ***10 Weeks***
			Brothers, Howard (born on February 2, 1946 in Darby, Florida) and David Bellamy (born on September 16, 1950 in Darby, Florida, USA). Learned how to play a number of instruments during their childhood. Played first official gig, in 1968, with their father at the Rattlesnake Roundup, in San Antonio, Florida. Moved to Atlanta in 1968, where they formed Jericho. In 1973, Jim Stafford recorded David's song, *Spiders And Snakes*. The success of the record gave the brothers enough money to move to LA, where they began to concentrate on a full time musical career. In 1975, they signed to Curb Records and issued their first single, *Nothin' Heavy*.
27 May 76	3	7	1. **LET YOUR LOVE FLOW** *Warner Bros K 16690*
30 Sep 79	8	3	2. **IF I SAID YOU HAD A BEAUTIFUL BODY (Would You Hold It Against Me)** *Warner Bros K 17405*
			Tony BENNETT ***11 Weeks***
			Born Anthony Dominick Benedetto on August 3, 1926 in Long Island, New York, USA. Studied music and painting at the New York High School of Industrial Arts. Drafted into the U. S. Army in 1944. While on a concert tour with Bob Hope it was suggested by Hope that a change of name to Tony Bennett would be beneficial. Disc debut: *Fascinating Rhythm* (1947). Signed to Columbia in 1950. Inducted into the Big Band and Jazz Hall of Fame in 1997. Received a Lifetime Achievement Award from ASCAP in 2002.
12 Apr 55	-	8	1. **STRANGER IN PARADISE** *Philips PB 420*
27 Aug 57	-	3	2. **IN THE MIDDLE OF AN ISLAND** *Philips EPB 724*

Date	Pos	Wks	ARTIST / Record Title *Label & Number*

Chuck BERRY — *18 Weeks*

Singer/guitarist/songwriter. Born Charles Edward Berry on October 16, 1926 in San Jose, California, USA. Grew up in St. Louis. Blues legend Muddy Waters introduced him to Leonard Chess founder of Chess Records. The 'Poet Laureate' of Rock 'n' Roll made his disc debut in 1955 with *Maybelline*. Appeared in several films including *Rock Rock Rock* and *Hail Hail Rock 'n' Roll*, a film documentary/concert tribute to Chuck. Acclaimed as one of the most influential artists to emerge from the rock 'n' roll era. Inducted into the Rock and Roll Hall of Fame in 1986. *My Ding A Ling* was recorded live at the Lancaster Arts Festival in England in 1972.

Date	Pos	Wks	ARTIST / Record Title *Label & Number*
11 Nov 63	3	5	1. **MEMPHIS TENNESSEE** *Pye Int. 7N 25218*
15 Jun 64	7	5	2. **NO PARTICULAR PLACE TO GO** *Pye Int. 7N 25242*
30 Nov 72	1(2)	8	• 3. **MY DING A LING** *Chess 6145 019*

Dave BERRY — *12 Weeks*

Born David Holgate Grundy on February 6, 1941 in Woodhouse, Sheffield, England. Formed the Cruisers in 1962. Spotted by Decca A & R man Mike Smith while performing at a dance hall in Doncaster in 1963. Changed his surname in tribute to his musical hero Chuck Berry.

Date	Pos	Wks	ARTIST / Record Title *Label & Number*
28 Oct 63	9	1	1. **MEMPHIS TENNESSEE** *Decca F 11734*
14 Sep 64	7	2	2. **THE CRYING GAME** *Decca F 11937*
03 May 65	9	2	3. **LITTLE THINGS** *Decca F 12103*
08 Aug 66	6	7	4. **MAMA** *Decca F 12435*

Memphis Tennessee credit *Dave Berry and The Cruisers*

Mike BERRY with the OUTLAWS — *2 Weeks*

Born Michael Bourne on September 24, 1942 in Northampton, England. Legendary independent producer Joe Meek renamed him Mike Berry and produced his early recordings. Turned to acting when the hits dried up and enjoyed success in two top television series' *Worzel Gummidge* (Mr Peters) and *Are You Being Served* (Mr Spooner) (1981-85).

continues over

Date	Pos	Wks	ARTIST / Record Title *Label & Number*
			The Outlaws lineup included Ritchie Blackmore and Chas Hodges. In 2005 he fulfilled one of his lifelong ambitions when he recorded the album, *About Time Too*, with The Crickets.
23 Mar 61	6	2	1. WILL YOU LOVE ME TOMORROW *Decca F 11314*
			The BEVERLEY SISTERS ***11 Weeks***
			London born family vocal trio. Joy (born May 5, 1929) and twins Teddie and Babs (born May 5, 1932). Parents were a variety act known as Coram and Mills. During WW11 were evacuated to the British Midlands. Discovered by Jock Ware who was auditioning children for an advertising campaign to promote bedtime drink, Ovaltine. Impressed by their vocal harmony he put them in touch with Cecil Madden of the BBC. The end result was six radio shows featuring the sisters on the BBC. In December 1944, The Beverley Sisters began their professional career. Own television show, *Those Beverley Sisters*, on BBC for seven years. Signed by Norman Newell to a recording contract with EMI. Disc debut: *Ferry Boat Inn* (1951). Joy married England football captain, Billy Wright in 1958. He died of cancer in 1992. Signature tune: *Sisters*. Awarded the MBE for their services to music in January 2006.
02 Oct 56	-	2	1. BORN TO BE WITH YOU *Decca F 10770*
12 Mar 59	6	5	2. LITTLE DRUMMER BOY *Decca F 11107*
24 Dec 59	7	4	3. LITTLE DONKEY *Decca F 11172*
			BIG BEN ACCORDION BAND ***1 Weeks***
			Studio group of British session musicians assembled for recording purposes by orchestra leader/producer, Norrie Paramor.
13 Nov 56	-	1	1. ROCK 'N' ROLL *Columbia IDB 672*
			Medley: Rock Around The Clock/See You Later Alligator/Saints Rock n Roll/Blue Suede Shoes/ Rock Island Line/Why Do Fools Fall In Love

Date	Pos	Wks	ARTIST / Record Title *Label & Number*

BIG BEN BANJO BAND — *2 Weeks*

Formed in London, England in 1955 by Norrie Paramor as a recording entity, utilizing the top British session musicians. The popularity of the group led to the situation that live performances had to be organised. The group appeared at the 1958 Royal Variety Performance. Resident on the BBC radio programme, *Everybody Step Together.* Also had their own series on Radio Luxembourg.

Date	Pos	Wks	ARTIST / Record Title *Label & Number*
04 Jan 55	-	2	1. LET'S GET TOGETHER No. 1 *Columbia IDB 540*

Tracks on **Let's Get Together No. 1**: I'm Just Wild About Harry/April Showers/Rock A Bye Your Baby/Swanee/Darktown Strutters Ball/For Me And My Gal/Oh You Beautiful Doll/Yes Sir That's My Baby.

BIG TOM and the MAINLINERS — *60 Weeks*

Irish showband. Big Tom was born Thomas McBride on September 18, 1938 in Drumnakill, Oram, County Monaghan, Ireland. Emigrated to England in late 1950's. Returned home in 1960. Big break arrived in 1966, when the Mainliners were invited to appear on Telifis Eireann's music programme, *The Showband Show.* Tom performed the song, *Gentle Mother*, on the show and was an immediate hit. The Mainliners from Castleblaney, County Monaghan were formed in 1964. Personnel: Big Tom (lead vocals, guitar), Henry McMahon (leader, tenor sax), Seamus McMahon (lead guitar), Ginger Morgan (bass), Ronnie Duffy (drums), John Beattie (organ), and Cyril McKevitt (trombone). Tom and the Mainliners parted company in May 1975. Tom teamed up with The Everglades who underwent a name change to The Travellers. Re-united with original members of Mainliners in 1989.

Date	Pos	Wks	ARTIST / Record Title *Label & Number*
09 Feb 67	7	5	1. GENTLE MOTHER *Emerald MD 1060*
09 Nov 67	4	8	2. AN OLD LOG CABIN FOR SALE *Emerald MD 1084*
20 Aug 70	3	10	3. SUNSET YEARS OF LIFE *Emerald MD 1147*

continues over

Date	Pos	Wks	ARTIST / Record Title *Label & Number*
24 Feb 72	1(2)	10	• 4. BROKEN MARRIAGE VOWS *Denver DMC 1007*
11 Jan 73	1(2)	13	• 5. I LOVE YOU STILL *Denver DMC 1010*
30 May 74	1(I)	14	• 6. OLD LOVE LETTERS *Denver DMC 1012*

Mr. Acker BILK and his PARAMOUNT JAZZ BAND — *19 Weeks*

Clarinetist Bernard Stanley Bilk was born on January 28, 1929 in Pensfort, Somerset, England. Originally started playing the clarinet when he was serving with the Royal Engineers in the Canal Zone in Egypt, where he borrowed and practiced on a clarinet while in the Glasshouse for sleeping on guard duty. On his demob formed his first band in Bristol, then moved to London as a clarinet player with Ken Colyers Band. Returned to Bristol where he formed the Bristol Paramount Jazz Band in 1958. *Stranger On The Shore* started out life under the title, *Jenny*, Acker's daughters name. It was used as the theme music for the 1961 BBC television series, *Stranger On The Shore*, and under its new title topped the Irish, British and American singles chart. In 2001 he was awarded an MBE for his services to the music industry.

Date	Pos	Wks	ARTIST / Record Title *Label & Number*
10 Mar 60	3	5	1. SUMMER SET • *Columbia DB(I) 4382*
09 Feb 61	7	3	2. BUONA SERA *Columbia DB(I) 4544*
05 Oct 61	9	3	3. THAT'S MY HOME *Columbia DB(I) 4673*
04 Jan 62	1(2)	7	• 4. STRANGER ON THE SHORE • *Columbia DB(I) 4750*
30 Sep 76	9	1	5. ARIA • *Pye 7N 45607*

Stranger On The Shore credit Mr Acker Bilk with the Leon Young String Chorale

Aria credit Acker Bilk, his Clarinet and Strings

BIMBO JET — *3 Weeks*

French studio group. *El Bimbo* was composed by Claude Morgan who played it to producer Laurent Rossi, who immediately saw the commercial possibilities and arranged to record the number with studio musicians.

Date	Pos	Wks	ARTIST / Record Title *Label & Number*
28 Aug 75	4	3	1. EL BIMBO *Columbia OC 006*

Date	Pos	Wks	ARTIST / Record Title *Label & Number*

Jane BIRKIN and Serge GAINSBOURG **3 Weeks**

Female/male vocal duo. Jane Birkin born on December 12, 1947 in London, England. Serge Gainsbourg born on April 2, 1928 in Paris, France. One of the most controversial records of the sixties, it was banned by the BBC and RTE. Gainsbourg originally intended to record *Je T'aime* with Brigette Bardot, but she turned it down. Serge Gainsbourg died of a heart attack on March 2, 1991.

Date	Pos	Wks	ARTIST / Record Title *Label & Number*
09 Oct 69	2	3	1. JE T'AIME...MOI NON PLUS *Major Minor MM 645*

Cilla BLACK ***29 Weeks***

Born Priscilla Maria Veronica White on May 27, 1943 in Liverpool, England. Signed by Brian Epstein in September 1963. He gave her a new name, arranged a recording contract with EMI, and for her debut single obtained a Lennon and McCartney song, *Love of the Loved*. Went on to host some of television's top programmes including *Blind Date* and *Surprise Surprise*. Awarded an OBE in 1996. Her husband (and manager), Bobby Willis, died of cancer on October 23, 1999. Her autobiography, *What's It All About*, published in 2004.

Date	Pos	Wks	ARTIST / Record Title *Label & Number*
02 Mar 64	1(1)	7	• 1. ANYONE WHO HAD A HEART *Parlophone R(I) 5101*
25 May 64	2	8	2. YOU'RE MY WORLD *Parlophone R(I) 5133*
14 Feb 66	10	1	3. LOVE'S JUST A BROKEN HEART *Parlophone R(I) 5395*
20 Mar 69	5	4	4. SURROUND YOURSELF WITH SORROW *Parlophone R(I) 5759*
21 Aug 69	5	4	5. CONVERSATIONS *Parlophone R(I) 5785*
16 Dec 71	3	5	6. SOMETHING TELLS ME (SOMETHING'S GONNA HAPPEN TONIGHT) *Parlophone R(I) 5924*

Gerry BLACK and the SEASONS ***4 Weeks***

Born Gerald Black on November 29, 1944 in Bessbrook, Co. Armagh, N. Ireland. A member of several bands including the Hilton and Finnavons. Disc debut: *An Exiles Dream* (1969). Teamed up with the Seasons in 1971.

continues over

Date	Pos	Wks	ARTIST / Record Title *Label & Number*
			Personnel: Gerry Black (lead vocals/trumpet), Peadar McGeough (bass), Thomas Kiernan (lead guitar), Brendan Murray (drums), Gabriel McQuillan (guitar), Freddy Ryan (trombone) and John McIntyre (tenor sax). Gerry Black left the Seasons in April 1974. Joined Big Valley in October 1974. Left in August 1975 and returned to the Seasons. In May 1976, Gerry Black and Gay McQuillan joined the Roly Daniels Band. Gerry Black operates the Piano Studio in Castleblaney, Co. Monaghan. Brendan Murray died on August 23, 2002.
24 May 73	7	4	1. MEET ME TONIGHT IN LAREDO *Denver DMC 1011*
			Jeanne BLACK ***8 Weeks***
			Born Gloria Jeanne Black on October 25, 1937 in Pomona, California, USA. Began her singing career as vocalist with Cliffie Stone's band in 1956. Also recorded with her sister as Jeanne and Janie. *He'll Have To Stay* was an answer song to the Jim Reeves hit, *He'll Have To Go.*
16 Jun 60	4	8	1. HE'LL HAVE TO STAY *Capitol CL(I) 15131*
			BLACKTHORN ***2 Weeks***
			Ballad group formed in Belfast, N. Ireland in 1970 by Pat Brady and Brian Aldwinkle who were students at Queens University. Disc debut: *London's Derry.* Personnel (1979): Sean Fitzpatrick (bass), John McCormac (vocals/bodhran), Gordon Manley (banjo), Desi McHenry (vocals/guitar) and Stephen Mulhern (fiddle). Numerous personnel changes over the years. Gordon Manley left in 2003.
21 Dec 79	8	2	1. A CHILDREN'S WINTER / FAREWELL TO NANCY *RCI 844*
			The BLARNEY FOLK ***2 Weeks***
			Ballad group formed in Dublin, Ireland in 1966. Personnel: Mick O'Brien (vocals, double bass), Eugene Byrne (vocals, guitar, banjo) and Brendan O'Brien (vocals, guitar, harmonica).
26 Sep 66	7	2	1. THE MERRY PLOUGHBOY *Major MJS 101*

Date	Pos	Wks	ARTIST / Record Title *Label & Number*

BLONDIE — *25 Weeks*

Formed in New York City, USA in 1974. Personnel: Debbie Harry (born July 1, 1945 in Miami, Florida, lead vocals), Chris Stein (guitar), Jimmy Destri (keyboards) and Clem Burke (drums). Group disbanded in 1982 with Debbie Harry pursuing a solo career. Reformed in 1998. *Denis* was a remake of Randy and The Rainbows 1963 USA top ten hit, *Denise*.

Date	Pos	Wks	Title
23 Mar 78	3	6	1. DENIS *Chrysalis CHS 2204*
01 Feb 79	2	8	2. HEART OF GLASS *Chrysalis CHS 2275*
17 May 79	1(4)	8	• 3. SUNDAY GIRL *Chrysalis CHS 2320*
04 Oct 79	3	3	4. DREAMING *Chrysalis CHS 2350*

Barry BLUE — *4 Weeks*

Born Barry Ian Green on December 4, 1950 in London, England. Struck up a songwriting partnership with Lynsey De Paul and composed several hits including *Sugar Me* and *Dancing On A Saturday Night*. Wrote hits *I Eat Cannibals*, for Toto Coelo (1982) and *Escaping*, for Dina Carroll (1996).

Date	Pos	Wks	Title
06 Sep 73	4	4	1. DANCIN' (ON A SATURDAY NIGHT) *Bell BELL 1295*

BLUE MINK — *10 Weeks*

Formed in London, England in 1969. Personnel: Roger Cook (born on August 19, 1940 in Bristol, vocals), Madeline Bell (born on July 23, 1942 in N ewark, New Jersey, vocals), Roger Coulam (keyboards), Herbie Flowers (bass), Alan Parker (guitar), and Barry Morgan (drums). Disc debut: *Melting Pot* (1969). Disbanded in 1974.

Date	Pos	Wks	Title
30 Apr 70	10	1	1. GOOD MORNING FREEDOM *Philips EBF 1838*
17 Jun 71	3	9	2. BANNER MAN *Columbia RZ(I) 3034*

Colin BLUNSTONE — *1 Weeks*

Born on June 24, 1945 in Hatfield, Hertfordshire, England. Lead singer with the Zombies until their disbandment in 1967. Signed to Deram Records in 1969 and recorded under the pseudonym, Neil MacArthur.

continues over

Date	Pos	Wks	ARTIST / Record Title *Label & Number*
			Enjoyed hit status under that name in Britain with a remake of *She's Not There.*
16 Mar 72	10	1	1. SAY YOU DON'T MIND *Epic EPC 7765*
			BONEY M ***55 Weeks***
			Vocal group created by German record producer, Frank Farian, in 1976. Personnel : Liz Mitchell (lead vocal), Marcia Barrett, Bobby Farrell and Maizi Williams. Marcia Barrett was lead singer on *Belfast.* Group split in 1986. A musical, *Daddy Cool*, based on the hits of Boney M, was staged in 2006.
12 May 77	4	6	1. SUNNY *Atlantic* K *10892*
11 Aug 77	4	4	2. MA BAKER *Atlantic K 10965*
17 Nov 77	1(1)	7	• 3. BELFAST *Atlantic K 11020*
11 May 78	1(4)	19	• 4. RIVERS OF BABYLON / BROWN GIRL IN THE RING *Atlantic K 11120*
28 Sep 78	3	8	5. RASPUTIN *Atlantic K11192*
23 Nov 78	1(7)	8	• 6. MARY'S BOY CHILD - OH MY LORD *Atlantic K 11221*
03 May 79	5	3	7. HOORAY HOORAY, IT'S A HOLI-HOLIDAY *Atlantic K 11279*
			The BOOMTOWN RATS ***33 Weeks***
			Formed in Dun Laoghaire, Co. Dublin, Ireland in 1975. Bands first gig was on October 31, 1975, under the name, Nightlife Thugs, at the Bolton Street Technical College. Legend has it, that halfway through the gig they changed the name to the Boomtown Rats. In 1976, relocated to London in search of a record deal. Signed to a new record company, Ensign. Personnel: Bob Geldof (born on October 5, 1954 in Dublin, vocals), Johnnie Fingers (keyboards), Pete Briquette (bass), Garry Roberts (guitar), Gerry Cott (guitar) and Simon Crowe (drums). In 1978, became the first Irish band to achieve a UK Number One hit single, when *Rat Trap*, climbed to the top. Gerry Cott left group in April 1981. Rats disbanded in 1986 when Bob Geldof decided to pursue a solo career.

continues over

Date	Pos	Wks	ARTIST / Record Title *Label & Number*
			Bob Geldof and Johnnie Fingers were inspired to write the song, *I Don't Like Mondays,* by an incident at Cleveland Elementary School in San Diego, California. On Monday, January 29, 1979, sixteen year old, Brenda Spencer, shot dead the school principal Burton Wragg and head custodian Mike Sucher and wounded eight pupils and a police officer. When asked why she carried out the shooting, she replied "I don't like Mondays. This livens up the day". The quote inspired Geldof and Fingers to write the song. Bob Geldof went on to enjoy success as a solo artist. His biggest achievements being the launch of the charity, Band Aid in 1984 and Live 8 in 2005. Received an Honorary Knighthood from the Queen of England, in 2006.
15 Sep 77	2	8	1. LOOKING AFTER No. *1 Mulligan LUNS 011*
18 May 78	10	1	2. SHE'S SO MODERN *Mulligan LUNS 715*
06 Jul 78	5	4	3. LIKE CLOCKWORK *Mulligan LUNS 716*
26 Oct 78	2	9	4. RAT TRAP *Mulligan LUNS 717*
02 Aug 79	1(4)	7	• 5. I DON'T LIKE MONDAYS *Mulligan LUNS 727*
22 Nov 79	3	4	6. DIAMOND SMILES *Mulligan LUNS 733*

Pat BOONE — ***61 Weeks***

Born Charles Eugene Boone on June 1, 1934 in Jacksonville, Florida, USA. Signed to Republic Records in 1954. Disc debut: *Until You Tell Me So*. Film appearances include *Bernadine* (1957), *April Love* (1957), *State Fair* (1962) *Journey To The Centre Of The Earth* and *The Main Attraction* (1962). In 1963, came to Ireland to shoot the film, *Never Put It In Writing*, in which he starred with Milo O'Shea and Fidelma Murphy. In 1997, aged 62, Pat was back in the spotlight with *In A Metal Mood (No More Mr Nice Guy),* an album of heavy metal standards. Made first concert tour of Ireland in July 2005. Issued an album of Irish songs titled, *Dreams Of Ireland*, to coincide with the tour.

Date	Pos	Wks	ARTIST / Record Title *Label & Number*
03 Jun 56	-	3	1. I'LL BE HOME *London HLD 8253*
27 Feb 57	-	3	2. DON'T FORBID ME *London HLD 8370*

continues over

Date	Pos	Wks	ARTIST / Record Title *Label & Number*
16 Jul 57	-	5	3. LOVE LETTERS IN THE SAND *London HLD 8445*
08 Oct 57	-	1	4. THERE'S A GOLDMINE IN THE SKY *London HLD 8479*
23 Oct 57	-	3	5. REMEMBER YOU'RE MINE *London HLD 8479*
04 Feb 58	-	2	6. APRIL LOVE *London HLD 8512*
01 Apr 58	-	6	7. A WONDERFUL TIME UP THERE *London HL 8574*
23 Jul 58	-	1	8. SUGAR MOON *London HL 8640*
17 Sep 58	-	1	9. IF DREAMS CAME TRUE *London HLD 8675*
12 Feb 59	3	6	10. I'LL REMEMBER TONIGHT *London HLD 8775*
16 Apr 59	6	7	11. WITH THE WIND AND RAIN IN YOUR HAIR *London HLD 8824*
11 Jun 59	9	3	12. FOR A PENNY *London HLD 8855*
27 Jul 61	2	4	13. MOODY RIVER *London HLD 9350*
21 Dec 61	2	8	14. JOHNNY WILL *London HLD 9461*
26 Jul 62	4	8	15. SPEEDY GONZALES *London HLD 9573*

The female vocalist on Speedy Gonzales is Jackie Ward. The voice of Speedy is Mel Blanc.

Ken BOOTHE — *7 Weeks*

Born on March 22, 1948 in Denham Town, Kingston, Jamaica. When he was only eight years old he won his first singing contest. Musical career began in the early 1960's. Began his recording career in 1963 with Winston Stranger' Cole in the duo, *Stranger and Ken*. Inducted into the Caribbean Hall of Fame in 2004. *Everything I Own* was composed by David Gates.

Date	Pos	Wks	ARTIST / Record Title *Label & Number*
31 Oct 74	1(3)	7	• 1. EVERYTHING I OWN *TroJan TR 7920*

BOSTON — *2 Weeks*

Formed in Boston, USA in 1975. Personnel: Brad Delp (born on June 12, 1951 in Boston, vocals, keyboards), Tom Scholz (guitar), Barry Goudreau (guitar), Fran Sheehan (bass) and John 'Sib' Hashian (drums). The bands debut album, *Boston*, released in 1976, was at the time the best selling debut album in U.S. history, with sales of over seventeen million copies. Brad Delph died of carbon monoxide poisoning on March 9, 2007.

Date	Pos	Wks	ARTIST / Record Title *Label & Number*
16 Nov 78	8	2	1. DON'T LOOK BACK *Epic Sep C 6653*

Date	Pos	Wks	ARTIST / Record Title *Label & Number*

Eve BOSWELL *3 Weeks*

Born Eva Keleti on May 11, 1924 in Budapest, Hungary. Educated in Lausanne, Switzerland where she studied classical piano at Lausanne Academy. Her parents were involved in showbusiness and Eve joined them in the family act, the Three Hugos. Moved to South Africa in 1939 and secured a position as vocalist with the Roy Martin Band. Dick jockey, Ala Dell, who was then a local record producer, made some private recordings with Eve and took them to London. Orchestra leader, Geraldo, heard the demos and offered Eve a job as vocalist. On June 1, 1949, she made her debut with Geraldo and his Orchestra at the Blackpool Winter Gardens. In January 1952 she left Geraldo to pursue a solo career. Was the singing voice of Vera Ellen, in the 1951 film, *Happy Go Lucky*. Died of a heart attack on August 13, 1998 in Durban, South Africa.

Date	Pos	Wks	ARTIST / Record Title *Label & Number*
14 Feb 56	-	3	1. PICKIN' A-CHICKEN *Parlophone DIP 215*

David BOWIE *35 Weeks*

Born David Robert Jones on January 8, 1947 in Brixton, London, England. Disc debut: *Liza Jane*,as Davy Jones with the King Bees (1964). Changed name to David Bowie. Signed to Deram in 1966. His second single for the label *The Laughing Gnome*, didn't chart until 1973. Turned down by Apple, Bowie released *Space Oddity* on Philips before signing for RCA in 1971. Moved to EMI in 1983. Film appearances include *The Man Who Fell To Earth* (1976) and *Elephant Man* (1980). Inducted into the Rock and Roll Hall of Fame in 1996.

Date	Pos	Wks	ARTIST / Record Title *Label & Number*
18 Jan 73	3	3	1. THE JEAN GENIE *RCA 2302*
12 Jul 73	4	7	2. LIFE ON MARS *RCA 2316*
18 Oct 73	5	4	3. THE LAUGHING GNOME *Deram DM 123*
25 Oct 73	2	6	4. SORROW RCA *RCA 2424*
28 Feb 74	2	4	5. REBEL REBEL *RCA LPBO 5009*
17 Oct 74	4	2	6. KNOCK ON WOOD *RCA 2466*

continues over

Date	Pos	Wks	ARTIST / Record Title *Label & Number*
30 Oct 75	3	6	7. SPACE ODDITY *RCA 2593*
08 Jan 76	9	2	8. GOLDEN YEARS *RCA 2640*
24 Nov 77	8	1	9. HEROES *RCA PB 1121*

Denis BOWLER and the SUN VALLEY BOYS — *6 Weeks*

Born in Glenbeigh, Co. Kerry. Former male nurse. Sun Valley Boys formed in Dublin in April 1970. Personnel: Denis Bowler (vocals), Joe Monks (lead guitar), Danny Heery (organ), John Quarsey (drums), Eamonn Donnelly (bass), Paddy Burns (trumpet) and Jas Fagan (trombone). Disc debut: *Dingle Bay* (1970). Band broke up in 1973. *The Ireland Of Tomorrow,* composed by the band's lead guitarist, Joe Monks.

Date	Pos	Wks	ARTIST / Record Title *Label & Number*
22 Jun 72	6	6	1. THE IRELAND OF TOMORROW *Release RL 633*

BRENDAN BOWYER — *96 Weeks*

Born on October 12, 1938 in Waterford, Ireland. Moved to Limerick at the age of two, where his father, Stanley, became organist and choirmaster in the Redemptorist Church. Family relocated to Waterford in 1946. Attended Waterpark College, Waterford and during his student days won a College inter-provincal rugby cap. On leaving college became a junior clerk with a local firm. A work colleague, Tom Dunphy, invited him to join the Harry Boland Band as trombonist. In September 1957, the band was relaunched as the Royal Showband. Ireland's first home based pop idol hit the number one spot in Ireland's Top Ten with his debut single, *Kiss Me Quick*. Achieved one of his life time ambitions, on March 26, 1966, when he met his idol, Elvis Presley, on the film set of *Spinout*, in Los Angeles, USA. In August 1971, decided to leave the Royal Showband, to form his own band, the Big 8. Relocated to Las Vegas in the early 1970's. In 2001, his recording career was given a new lease of life with the success of the album, *Follow On*.

continues over

Date	Pos	Wks	ARTIST / Record Title *Label & Number*
12 Aug 63	1(7)	14	• 1. KISS ME QUICK *HMV IP 1293*
09 Dec 63	1(1)	9	• 2. NO MORE *HMV POP(I) 1238*
15 Jun 64	1(2)	11	• 3. BLESS YOU (for being an angel) *HMV IP 1295*
21 Dec 64	1(7)	14	• 4. I RAN ALL THE WAY HOME / HUCKLEBUCK *HMV POP(I) 1377*
09 Aug 65	1(1)	11	• 5. DON'T LOSE YOUR HUCKLEBUCK SHOES *HMV IP 1301*
18 Oct 65	2	6	6. THE WONDER OF YOU *HMV POP(I) 1481*
18 Apr 66	6	5	7. THE FLY *HMV POP(I) 1521*
19 Sep 66	4	5	8. I CAN'T GET YOU OUT OF MY HEART *HMV IP 1304*
21 Dec 67	7	3	9. THE HOLY CITY *King KG 1066*
29 Aug 68	9	2	10. LADY WILLPOWER / WOMAN WOMAN *King KG 1078*
19 Dec 68	9	2	11. THE SAME OLD SONG *Dolphin DOS 19*
11 Nov 71	6	3	12. YOU GAVE ME A MOUNTAIN *Play PLAY 8*
01 Apr 76	7	5	13. HUCKLEBUCK (re-issue) *EMI IEMI 5038*
06 Oct 77	4	6	14. THANK YOU ELVIS *Hawk HASP 411*

See also Tom Dunphy and the Royal Showband
See also Charlie Matthews and the Royal Showband

The BRANAGAN BROTHERS — *1 Weeks*

Family duo formed in Dublin, Ireland. Personnel: Donal (born 1950 in Dublin, guitar) and Declan Branagan (born 1956 in Dublin, bass). Made their musical debut (with their sister Geraldine) as The Branagans in 1973. Performed the song, *Fado Fado*, in the 1973 National Song Contest. As a trio signed to Release Records in November 1974. Disc debut *Singer Of Songs*. Geraldine left group in 1975 to pursue a solo career. Brothers continued as a duo. In April 1977, augmented lineup with Alan Shiels (piano) and Alan Barton (drums). Geraldine rejoined the brothers in 1979 when under the name the GB Band they concentrated on the ballroom circuit. Declan Brannagan gave up music business in the early 1980's. Donal is still doing some solo work.

Date	Pos	Wks	ARTIST / Record Title *Label & Number*
09 Jun 77	10	1	1. GLITTER AND GLEAM *CBS 5192*

Date	Pos	Wks	ARTIST / Record Title *Label & Number*

Rossano BRAZZI ***1 Weeks***

Singer, stage and film actor. Born on September 18, 1916 in Bologna, Italy. As a young man very interested in sport including boxing and football. At college he played as goalkeeper with the City of Florence soccer team. Film appearances include *Little Women* (1949), *Three Coins In A Fountain* (1954), *South Pacific* (1958) and *The Italian Job* (1969). Died on December 24, 1994.

Date	Pos	Wks	ARTIST / Record Title *Label & Number*
10 Apr 56	-	1	1. SUMMERTIME IN VENICE *HMV IP 1094*

BREAD ***1 Weeks***

Formed in Los Angeles, California, USA in 1969. Personnel: David Gates (born on December 11, 1940 in Tulsa, Oklahoma, vocals, guitar, keyboards), James Griffin (guitar), Robb Royer (guitar) and Jim Gordon (drums). Mike Botts replaced Robb Royer in 1970 with Larry Knetchel replacing Jim Gordon the following year. James Griffin died on January 11, 2005. Mike Botts died on December 9, 2005. Larry Knetchel died on August 20, 2009.

Date	Pos	Wks	ARTIST / Record Title *Label & Number*
01 Oct 70	10	1	1. MAKE IT WITH YOU *Elektra 2101 010*

Rose BRENNAN ***2 Weeks***

Born on January 1, 1931 in Dublin, Ireland. In 1942 won a talent contest which made her decide on a professional singing career. Broadcast on Radio Eireann and sang with the bands of Roy Fox (at the Theatre Royal) and Billy Watson (at Clerys). In May 1951 joined the Joe Loss Orchestra. Left in November 1966 and retired from music business. Disc debut: *Goodbye Sweetheart*, in 1952 with Joe Loss Orchestra. In 1955 was voted the NME Top Dance Band Female Singer.

Date	Pos	Wks	ARTIST / Record Title *Label & Number*
18 Jan 55	-	2	1. THE SPINNING WHEEL *HMV IP 944*

Date	Pos	Wks	ARTIST / Record Title *Label & Number*

Tony BRENT — *2 Weeks*

Born Reginald Bretagne on August 13 1926 in Bombay, India. Relocated to England in 1947. Success in a talent contest, in 1949, led to work as vocalist with Ambrose and his Orchestra. Signed with Columbia Records in 1952. Disc debut: *Dancing On The Grapes* (1952). Died of a heart attack on June 19, 1993.

Date	Pos	Wks	ARTIST / Record Title *Label & Number*
10 Sep 57	-	1	1. DARK MOON *Columbia IDB 715*
15 May 58	-	1	2. THE CLOUDS WILL SOON ROLL BY *Columbia DB(I) 4066*

BRIAN and MICHAEL — *8 Weeks*

British vocal duo formed in 1975. Personnel: Michael Coleman (vocals/bass) and Brian Burke (vocals/guitar). The song is a tribute to the painter L S Lowry. Michael had the idea for the song during the early 1970's and after Lowry's death he finished it. Following the recording, Brian Burke decided to leave and Michael brought in Kevin Parrott, who had worked with Michael in the group, the Big Sound. St. Winifred's School Choir provided the backing vocals on the record. The Tinwhistle Brass Band are also featured on the record.

Date	Pos	Wks	ARTIST / Record Title *Label & Number*
30 Mar 78	1(3)	8	• 1. MATCHSTALK MEN AND MATCHSTALK CATS AND DOGS *Pye 7N 46035*

BRIGHOUSE and RASTRICK BRASS BAND — *4 Weeks*

Formed in 1881, when the people of the West Yorkshire villages of Brighouse and Rastrick made the decision to establish a brass band. One of the most successful British brass bands their list of achievements and honours is second to none. Have won over 400 prizes since 1910, including the British Open Championship, National Brass Band Championship of Great Britain, World Championship, All England Masters Brass Band Championship, Champion Band of Europe and All England Masters Championship.

continues over

Date	Pos	Wks	ARTIST / Record Title *Label & Number*
			Featured in the 2000 film, *Brassed Off.* In 1977, earned Silver and Gold discs for sales of over a million copies of *The Floral Dance.*
05 Jan 78	2	4	1. THE FLORAL DANCE *Transatlantic BIG 548*
			***Sarah BRIGHTMAN and HOT GOSSIP* 6 Weeks**
			Born on August 14, 1960 in Berkhampstead, England. Began dancing at the age of three. Trained in classical ballet at Elmhurst, studied jazz and acting at Arts Educational. In 1976, aged sixteen, joined the BBC television Top of the Pops dance group Pan's People. A year later she teamed up their raunchier ITV counterpart Hot Gossip. Appeared in the stage musicals *Phantom Of The Opera*, *Cats, Requiem* and *Aspects Of Love.* Married composer Andrew Lloyd Webber in 1984, separated in 1990 and divorced in 1991. Moved to Germany in the early 1990's. Made her film debut in the 2008 film, *Repo! The Genetic Opera.*
14 Dec 78	5	6	1. I LOST MY HEART TO A STARSHIP TROOPER *Ariola AHA 527*
			***The BROADSIDERS* 1 Weeks**
			Ballad group formed in Dublin, Ireland in 1966. Personnel: Deirdre Downes (lead vocals, mandolin), Johnny Way (vocals, banjo), Paddy O'Sullivan (guitar) and Noel Fitzmaurice (vocals guitar).Johnny McEvoy produced *Shores Of Amerikay.*
12 Oct 67	7	1	1. THE SHORES OF AMERIKAY *Pye 7N 17382*
			***Elkie BROOKS* 5 Weeks**
			Born Elaine Bookbinder on February 25, 1945 in Manchester, England. After a period in the early 60's touring with Eric Delaney and Humphrey Lyttleton, she signed to Decca as a solo artist. Disc debut: *Something's Got A Hold Of Me* (1964). In 1970, joined rock group Dada. The following year she formed the group, Vinegar Joe, with Robert Palmer and Pete Gage.

continues over

Date	Pos	Wks	ARTIST / Record Title *Label & Number*
			Departed in 1974 to pursue a solo career. *Pearl's A Singer,* was produced by Mike Leiber and Jerry Stoller.
30 Jun 77	9	1	1. PEARL'S A SINGER *A&M AMS 7275*
13 Oct 77	7	2	2. SUNSHINE AFTER THE RAIN *A&M AMS 7306*
30 Mar 78	8	2	3. LILAC WINE *A&M AMS 7333*
			BROTHERHOOD OF MAN ***31 Weeks***
			Formed by record producer/songwriter Tony Hiller in London, England in late 1969. Disc debut: *United We Stand* (1970). Several personnel changes in the early years. In 1972, Martin Lee, Lee Sheridan and Nicky Stevens joined the group. Sandra Stevens joined in 1973. This lineup continues to the present day. In 1976 represented the UK in the Eurovision Song Contest, winning with *Save Your Kisses For Me.*
25 Mar 76	1(1)	11	• 1. SAVE YOUR KISSES FOR ME *Pye 7N 45569*
14 Apr 77	6	3	2. OH BOY (The Mood I'm In) *Pye 7N 45656*
04 Aug 77	1(1)	6	• 3. ANGELO *Pye 7N 45699*
02 Feb 78	1(1)	7	• 4. FIGARO *Pye 7N 46037*
08 Jun 78	6	4	5. BEAUTIFUL LOVER *Pye 7N 46071*
			The BROTHERS ***4 Weeks***
			Family group of five brothers based in London, who originally hailed from Mauritius. Personnel: Clarel (lead vocals), Lindsay (guitar), Gervais (keyboards), Daniel (bass) and Clarey Bayou (drums). Sprang to fame in 1976 by winning top TV talent show, *Opportunity Knocks.*
03 Mar 77	4	4	1. SING ME *BUS 1054*
			The Crazy World of Arthur BROWN ***2 Weeks***
			Formed in 1967. Personnel: Arthur Brown (born Arthur Wilton on June 24, 1944 in Whitby, Yorkshire, England, vocals), Vincent Crane, keyboards and Drachen Theaker, drums. Theaker replaced by Carl Palmer. Broke up in late 1968. Vincent Crane committed suicide on February 14, 1999.
29 Aug 68	8	2	1. FIRE *Track 604022*

Date	Pos	Wks	ARTIST / Record Title *Label & Number*

Billy BROWN — *8 Weeks*

Born William John Brown on October 11, 1943 in Larne, Co. Antrim, N. Ireland. Made his first public performance at the age of eight, as a member of a vocal trio. Began playing music in school at the age of thirteen. After leaving school attended Belfast College of Art. A member of the Billy McFarland Band, he left along with fellow members, Torry McGahey and Maurice Henry in July 1962, to form the Freshmen. In February 1971, left the Freshmen and formed the short lived Billy Brown Band. In October 1971 broke up the Billy Brown Band and teamed up with ex Real McCoy vocalist, Mike O'Brien to form the Brown and O'Brien Band. Returned to the ranks of the Freshmen in November 1972. In late 1976, while passing through Longford, he met Suzanne Murphy, ex We 4 member and at that time a member of the Irish Opera Company. Being a friend of Billy, she presented him with a couple of tickets for the opera, La Cemerentola. Billy went along to the opera, and liking all he saw and heard, felt he had to commemorate the occasion by writing a song about it. The song turned out to be *Cinderella*. Died on June 6, 1999.

Date	Pos	Wks	ARTIST / Record Title *Label & Number*
14 Mar 74	5	1	1. THE LEAVING OF LIVERPOOL *Dolphin DOS 113*
31 Mar 77	3	7	2. CINDERELLA *CBS 5079*

See also Derek Dean; The Freshmen

Joe BROWN and the BRUVVERS — *20 Weeks*

Born Joseph Roger Brown on May 13, 1941 in Swarby, Lincolnshire, England. Signed by producer Jack Good as a guitarist for studio band on pop TV programme, *Boy Meets Girl* (1959-60). Signed to Decca as a singer in 1959. Worked as guitarist with top rock 'n' roll performers including Eddie Cochran and Gene Vincent. Starred in film, *What A Crazy World* (1964) and London West End musical, *Charlie Girl* (1965-68).

continues over

Date	Pos	Wks	ARTIST / Record Title *Label & Number*
			The Bruvvers: Pete Oakman (bass), Tony Oakman (guitar), John Beveridge (guitar) and Tommy Brown (drums) replaced by Howie Gee who in turn was replaced by Bobby Graham.
21 Jun 62	2	8	1. A PICTURE OF YOU *Piccadilly 7N 35047*
14 Jan 63	8	2	2. IT ONLY TOOK A MINUTE *Piccadilly 7N 35082*
25 Feb 63	2	10	3. THAT'S WHAT LOVE WILL DO *Piccadilly 7N 35106*

The BROWNS — *9 Weeks*

Family vocal trio formed in 1955. Personnel: Jim Ed Brown, and his sisters, Maxine and Bonnie. In 1952, Jim and his sister Maxine formed a vocal duo, performing on local radio shows. Signed to Fabor Records. The duo enjoyed chart success with *Looking Back To See.* In 1955, younger sister, Bonnie joined and they became The Browns. Following appearances on Shreveport's 'Louisiana Hayride' were signed by RCA in 1956. Group disbanded in 1967, with Maxine and Bonnie leaving to concentrate on their families. Jim Ed embarked on a solo career, that he had launched in 1965, while the group were still together. In 1975, began a six season run as co-host of syndicated television series, *Nashville On The Road.* In 1976, teamed up with singer Helen Cornelius, the duo enjoyed a long run of chart success in the country music field.

Date	Pos	Wks	ARTIST / Record Title *Label & Number*
17 Sep 59	2	9	1. THE THREE BELLS *RCA ERC 1140*

BUBBLEROCK — *2 Weeks*

Singer/songwriter/producer, Jonathan King (born Kenneth George King on December 6, 1944 in London, England) under one of his many pseudonyms.

Date	Pos	Wks	ARTIST / Record Title *Label & Number*
07 Feb 74	9	2	1. (I Can't Get No) SATISFACTION *UK 53*

The BUGGLES — *5 Weeks*

Formed in London, England in 1979. Personnel: Trevor Horn (vocals, bass) and Geoff Downes (keyboards). Disc debut: *Age Of Plastic* LP (1979).

continues over

Date	Pos	Wks	ARTIST / Record Title *Label & Number*
			Geoff Downes joined Yes in 1980. Trevor Horn formed ZTT Records and produced hits for Frankie Goes To Hollywood and ABC. *Video Killed The Radio Star,* has the historic honour of being the first video shown on MTV (August 1, 1981).
18 Oct 79	1(2)	5	• 1. VIDEO KILLED THE RADIO STAR *Island WIP 6524*
			B. BUMBLE and the STINGERS ***8 Weeks***
			A group of Los Angeles, California session men – Lincoln Mayorga (piano), Rene Hall (guitar), Earl Palmer (drums), Plas Johnson (tenor sax), and Al Hassan (bass). Following the success of "Nut Rocker", pianist RC Gamble toured as B Bumble. *Nut Rocker* was adapted from Tchaikovsky's, *The Nutcracker.*
17 May 62	2	8	1. NUT ROCKER • *Top Rank JAR 611*
			Johnny BURNETTE ***14 weeks***
			Born Johnny Joseph Burnette on March 25, 1934 in Memphis, Tennessee, USA. Formed the Rock 'n' Roll Trio with his brother Dorsey and Paul Burlison in 1953. Signed to Coral Records in 1956. Trio folded in 1957. Wrote several hit songs for Ricky Nelson including *Believe What You Say* and *Just A Little Too Much.* Died in a boating accident on Clear Lake, California on August 14, 1964. His son, Rocky Burnette, enjoyed chart success in 1979.
17 Nov 60	3	9	1. DREAMIN' *London HLG 9172*
09 Feb 61	4	5	2. YOU'RE SIXTEEN *London HLG 9254*
			Terry BURTON ***1 Weeks***
			Female vocalist. Born 1934 in Stratford, England. Father was a trumpeter with Joe Loss Orchestra. At age of fifteen, employed as vocalist with the Percy Pease Orchestra. In the mid 1950's sang with the Malcolm Mitchell Orchestra. Pianist Bill McGuffie introduced her to Johnny Franz of Philips Records. A successful test resulted in a recording contract.
01 Jan 57	-	1	1. A LETTER TO A SOLDIER *Philips PB 653*

Date	Pos	Wks	ARTIST / Record Title *Label & Number*

Lou BUSCH and his Orchestra and Chorus — *4 Weeks*

Born Louis Ferdinand Bush on July 18, 1910 in Louisville, Kentucky, USA. Led his own band at age of twelve. Left home at age sixteen to work as a professional musician. In 1945, A&R with Capitol Records. Played piano on Jo Stafford's recording of *Ragtime Cowboy Joe*. In 1950 made honky tonk piano recordings under the name Joe 'Fingers' Carr. Married to singer Margaret Whiting. In late 50's, left Capitol for Warner Brothers, where he produced several albums with comedian, Allan Sherman, including the hit single, *Hello Muddah*. Died in a car accident on September 19, 1979.

Date	Pos	Wks	ARTIST / Record Title *Label & Number*
14 Feb 56	-	4	1. ZAMBESI • *Capitol CL 14504*

Kate BUSH — 9 Weeks

Born Catherine Bush on July 30, 1958 in Bexleyheath, Kent, England. From a musical family, began playing piano at the age of eleven. By her mid teens had composed over 200 songs. Discovered by Dave Gilmour of Pink Floyd who helped her obtain a recording contract with EMI Records. Signed with EMI whilst still attending school. Her debut disc, *Wuthering Heights*, was inspired by Emily Bronte's novel of the same name. In 1987 received a BRIT Award for Best British Female Solo Artist. In 2002, won an Ivor Novello Award for Outstanding Contribution to British Music.

Date	Pos	Wks	ARTIST / Record Title *Label & Number*
16 Mar 78	1(3)	6	• 1. WUTHERING HEIGHTS *EMI 2719*
29 Jun 78	3	2	2. THE MAN WITH THE CHILD IN HIS EYES *EMI 2806*
23 Nov 78	10	1	3. HAMMER HORROR *EMI 2887*

Date	Pos	Wks	ARTIST / Record Title *Label & Number*

Max BYGRAVES — *8 Weeks*

Born Walter William Bygraves on October 16, 1922 in Rotherhithe, London, England. Adopted the name Max in tribute to his hero, comedian Max Miller. Made his debut as a performer at RAF concerts during World War II. In 1951, signed by BBC radio to co-star with ventriloquist Peter Brough and his dummy Archie Andrews. It turned Max into a household name. Film appearances include *Cry From The Streets* (1958) and *Spare The Rod* (1961). Catch phrase: *I wanna tell you a story*. Hosted the popular television game show, *Family Fortunes* 1983-1985.

Date	Pos	Wks	ARTIST / Record Title *Label & Number*
12 Oct 54	3	1	1. GILLY GILLY OSSENFEFFER KATZENELLEN BOGEN BY THE SEA *HMV IP 915*
24 Dec 59	5	2	2. JINGLE BELL ROCK *Decca F 11176*
14 Apr 60	3	5	3. FINGS AIN'T WOT THEY USED T'BE *Decca F 11214*

The BYRDS — *9 Weeks*

Formed in Los Angeles, California, USA in 1964. First recorded as The Beefeaters in 1964. Personnel: Roger McGuinn (born July 13, 1942 in Chicago, lead vocals, guitar), Chris Hillman (bass), David Crosby (guitar), Gene Clark (percussion), and Michael Clarke (drums). David Crosby left in 1967 to form Crosby, Stills & Nash. Gram Parsons was a member for a period in 1968 before leaving to form the Flying Burrito Brothers. Original members reunited in 1973 and 1979. Gram Parsons died of a heroin overdose on September 19, 1973. Gene Clark died of natural causes on May 24, 1991. Michael Clarke died from liver failure on December 19, 1993. Inducted into the Rock and Roll Hall of Fame in 1991.

Date	Pos	Wks	ARTIST / Record Title *Label & Number*
12 Jul 65	1(1)	7	• 1. MR. TAMBOURINE MAN *CBS 201765*
30 Aug 65	8	2	2. ALL I REALLY WANT TO DO *CBS 201796*

Date	Pos	Wks	ARTIST / Record Title *Label & Number*

C

Patricia CAHILL ***4 Weeks***

Born in 1944 in Drimnagh, Dublin. Ireland. By the age of twelve was singing solo at school concerts. Won medals at the Father Matthew Feis and at the Feis Ceol. Commenced her professional career with the Jack Cruise Company. In the early 1960's appeared in many successful stage productions at the Theatre Royal and Olympia Theatre. Disc debut: *Ireland's Patricia Cahill Sings For You* L.P. (1962). *One And One Are Two* won the 'Straight Songs Section' at the 1967 Castlebar International Song Contest. In 1970, was signed to the Deram Record Company in England. Now lives and works in Spain.

Date	Pos	Wks	ARTIST / Record Title *Label & Number*
11 Jan 68	6	4	1. ONE AND ONE ARE TWO *Rex R 11031*

Eddie CALVERT ***3 Weeks***

Born Albert Edward Calvert on March 15, 1922 in Preston, Lancashire, England. Eddie's father taught him to play the trumpet and by age eleven he was a member of the Preston Town Silver Band. Formed his own band in late 1940's. Moved to South Africa in 1968. Died on August 8, 1978.

Date	Pos	Wks	ARTIST / Record Title *Label & Number*
21 Jun 55	-	2	1. CHERRY PINK AND APPLE BLOSSOM WHITE • *Columbia IDB 556*
17 Jan 56	-	1	2. LOVE IS A MANY SPLENDORED THING • *Columbia IDB 593*

Glen CAMPBELL ***41 Weeks***

Multi instrumentalist/vocalist. Born on April 22, 1936 in Billstown, Arkansas USA. Disc debut: *Turn Around Look At Me* (1961). A much sought after session musician in the early 1960's, his talents as a guitarist can be heard on records by Frank Sinatra, Dean Martin and Elvis Presley.

continues over

Date	Pos	Wks	ARTIST / Record Title *Label & Number*

Worked on stage and in the recording studios with the Champs, Beach Boys and the Crickets. Hosted his own show on American television from 1966-1972. Appeared in several films including *True Grit* (1969). In 1967, won a Grammy in both the country and pop categories for *Gentle On My Mind* (Country) and *By The Time I Get To Phoenix* (Pop).

Date	Pos	Wks	ARTIST / Record Title *Label & Number*
12 Jun 69	9	2	1. GALVESTON *Ember EMBS 263*
04 Jun 70	2	9	2. HONEY COME BACK *Capitol CL 15638*
31 Dec 70	3	8	3. IT'S ONLY MAKE BELIEVE *Capitol 15663*
02 Oct 75	1(6)	12	• 4. RHINESTONE COWBOY *Capitol CL(I) 15824*
12 Feb 76	5	3	5. COUNTRY BOY (You Got Your Feet In LA) *Capitol CL(I) 15845*
28 Apr 77	2	7	6. SOUTHERN NIGHTS *Capitol CL 15907*

See also Bobbie Gentry and Glen Campbell

CANNED HEAT — *1 Weeks*

Formed in Los Angeles, USA in 1966. Personnel: Bob 'The Bear' Hite (vocals /harmonica), Al 'Blind Owl' Wilson (guitar/vocals), Henry Vestine (guitar) Larry Taylor (bass) and Fito De La Parra (drums). Group took their name from a 1928 recording by Tommy Johnson. Al Wilson committed suicide on September 3, 1970. Bob Hite died of a heart attack on April 5, 1981. Henry Vestine died on October 20, 1997

Date	Pos	Wks	ARTIST / Record Title *Label & Number*
12 Mar 70	6	1	1. LET'S WORK TOGETHER *Liberty LBF 15302*

Freddy CANNON — *9 Weeks*

Born Frederick Picariello on December 4, 1939 in Lynn, Massachusetts, USA. In 1957 formed his own group Freddy Karmon and The Hurricanes. Made his vocal debut on a 1958 single, *Cha Cha Doo*, by the Spindrifts. His nickname *Boom Boom*, came from the big bass drum sound on his records.

Date	Pos	Wks	ARTIST / Record Title *Label & Number*
04 Feb 60	3	9	1. WAY DOWN YONDER IN NEW ORLEANS *Top Rank JAR 247*

Date	Pos	Wks	ARTIST / Record Title *Label & Number*
			Jim CAPALDI ***3 Weeks***
			Born on August 2, 1944 in Evesham, Worcestershire, England. Began his career in music in the early 1960's as a member of The Hellions. Went on to become a founding member (drums) of Traffic. Composed (with Stevie Winwood) many of the groups classic songs including *Paper Sun*, *No Face, No Name, No Number* and *Here We Go Round The Mulberry Bush*. He made his first solo recordings in 1972. Died from stomach cancer on January 28, 2005.
11 Dec 75	8	3	1. LOVE HURTS *Island WIP 6246*
			The CARAVELLES ***2 Weeks***
			Female vocal duo formed in London, England in 1963. Personnel: Lois Wilkinson (born on April 3, 1944 in Sleaford, Lincolnshire) and Andrea Simpson (born on September 9, 1946 in Finchley, London). The girls both worked at the same office in London and started singing together at parties. Named themselves after the French airliner. Lois Wilkinson left in 1966 to pursue a solo career under the name, Lois Lane. Replaced by Lynne Hamilton.
09 Sep 63	8	2	1.YOU DON'T HAVE TO BE A BABY TO CRY *Decca F 11697*
			The CARPENTERS ***23 Weeks***
			Brother and sister duo born in New Haven, Connecticut, USA. Richard (born on October 15, 1946) and Karen Carpenter (born on March 2, 1950). In the mid 1960's formed the Richard Carpenter Trio (Richard, keyboards, Karen, drums and Wes Jacobs, bass). In 1966 the trio disbanded with Richard, Karen and John Bettis forming Spectrum, a vocal harmony sextet. Following their failure to attract a recording contract they disbanded in 1968.

continues over

Date	Pos	Wks	ARTIST / Record Title *Label & Number*

In 1969, Richard and Karen, recorded a demo, which found its way to Herb Alpert, who suitably impressed, signed the duo, to A&M Records, in April 1969. Disc debut: *Offering* (1969). Karen Carpenter died on February 4, 1983.

15 Oct 70	6	3	1. (THEY LONG TO BE) CLOSE TO YOU *Pye AMS 800*
30 Aug 73	8	2	2. YESTERDAY ONCE MORE *A&M AMS 7023*
15 Nov 73	3	4	3. TOP OF THE WORLD *A&M AMS 7086*
13 Feb 75	2	5	4. PLEASE MR. POSTMAN *A&M 7141*
22 May 75	5	4	5. ONLY YESTERDAY *A&M AMS 7159*
03 Nov 77	1(2)	5	• 6. CALLING OCCUPANTS OF INTERPLANATERARY CRAFT (The Recognised Anthem of World Contact Day) *A&M AMS 7318*

Cathy CARR — *1 Weeks*

Born Angelina Helen Catherine Cordovano on June 28, 1936 in the Bronx, New York, USA. Died in November, 1988.

03 Jul 56	-	1	1. IVORY TOWER *London HLH 8274*

Raffaella CARRA — *1 Weeks*

Actress/vocalist/television hostess. Born Raffaella Pelloni on June 18, 1943 in Bologna, Italy. Appeared in several films including *Von Ryans Express* (1965).

18 May 78	9	1	1. DO IT, DO IT AGAIN *Epic EPC 6094*

Doc CARROLL and the ROYAL BLUES — *10 Weeks*

Irish showband. Doc Carroll was born Martin O'Carroll on November 19, 1940 in Tourmakeady, County Mayo, Ireland. A founder member of the Royal Blues. Hit the number one spot with his debut single, *Old Man Trouble*. Left the Blues in March 1972 to form his own band, The Nightrunners. The Royal Blues from Claremorris, Co. Mayo were formed in 1962.

continues over

Date	Pos	Wks	ARTIST / Record Title *Label & Number*

Personnel: Doc Carroll (vocals, lead guitar), Shay O'Hara (vocals), Brian Carr (bass), Don Flanagan (drums), Brendan Arnold (rhythm guitar), Bobby Smith (trumpet), Frank Gill (tenor sax) and Vincent Gill (trombone). Disbanded in 1972. Doc Carroll died on May 1, 2005.

24 Jan 66	1(2)	7	• 1. OLD MAN TROUBLE *Parlophone DIP 508*
10 Oct 66	8	3	2. FAR AWAY FROM YOU *Pye 7N 17166*

See also Shay O'Hara and The Royal Blues

Ronnie CARROLL — *7 Weeks*

Born Ronald Cleghorn on August 18, 1934 in Belfast, Co. Antrim, N. Ireland. First public appearance: Belfast Opera House. Signed to Philips Records by A&R manager Johnny Franz who had seen him perform at the Metropolitan on Edgeware Road, London. Met singer and actress Millicent Martin on a television show, they were married in 1959. They separated in 1965. Represented the UK in two Eurovision Song Contests, in 1962 with *Ring A Ding Girl* and in 1963 with *Say Wonderful Things*. He finished in fourth position on both occasions.. In 1997, stood for Parliament on a, Home Rule for Hampstead, ticket at the British General Election.

27 Sep 62	7	3	1. ROSES ARE RED *Philips 326532 EBF*
08 Apr 63	6	4	2. SAY WONDERFUL THINGS *Philips 326574 EBF*

Mindy CARSON — *1 Weeks*

Born on July 16, 1927 in New York City, USA. Big break occurred when she got to sing with the Harry Cool Orchestra. Signed with RCA in 1951. Moved to CBS in 1952. In late 1950's was encouraged by songwriter Richard Rodgers to enter the world of the stage musical. Appeared in several Broadway productions including *South Pacific* and *The Body Beautiful*. Retired from showbusiness in 1967.

28 Feb 56	-	1	1. MEMORIES ARE MADE OF THIS *Philips PB 548*

Date	Pos	Wks	ARTIST / Record Title *Label & Number*

Clarence CARTER — *2 Weeks*

Born on January 14, 11936 in Montgomery, Alabama, USA. Blind since age of one. Attended Alabama State College in Montgomery, graduated in 1960 with a B. S. Degree in Music. In 1964 teamed up with a school pal, Calvin Scott. Signed to Duke Records and had a record, *You Stole My Heart*, released under the name, Clarence and Calvin. Split with Calvin in 1966, and signed as a solo artist with Fame Records. First disc on Fame, *Tell Daddy All About It.* Discovered singer, Candi Staton, who he later married.

Date	Pos	Wks	ARTIST / Record Title *Label & Number*
19 Nov 70	4	2	1. PATCHES *Atlantic 2091030*

The CASCADES — *7 Weeks*

Male vocal group formed in 1960 in San Diego, California, USA. as The Silver Strands. Changed name to Thunder Notes before a final name change in 1962 to Cascades. Personnel: John Gummoe (born August 2, 1938 in Cleveland, Ohio, lead vocals), Eddie Snyder (guitar), David Stevens (bass), David Wilson (vocals, drums) and David Szabo (vocals, keyboards). Disc debut: *There's A Reason* (1962). Disbanded in 1975. David Wilson died of cancer in 2004.

Date	Pos	Wks	ARTIST / Record Title *Label & Number*
08 Apr 63	1(1)	7	• 1. RHYTHM OF THE RAIN *Warner Bros. EWB 88*

Johnny CASH — *18 Weeks*

Born J R Cash on February 26, 1932 in Kingsland, Arkansas, USA. Began playing guitar and writing songs as a young boy. While attending high school he sang on a local radio station. Enlisted in US Air Force in 1950. On his discharge in August 1954, he married Vivian Liberto. Divorced in 1966. Moved to Memphis in 1954 where he met up with guitarist Luther Perkins and bassist Marshall Grant, who operated under the name, The Tennesse Two. Auditioned for Sam Phillips at Sun records. Disc debut: *Hey Porter* (1955). Left Sun in 1958, to sign with Columbia Records.

continues over

Date	Pos	Wks	ARTIST / Record Title *Label & Number*

In the mid 1960's struck up a friendship with Bob Dylan, and sang a duet with him on Dylan's album, *Nashville Skyline* (1963). Began performing concerts at various prisons and these performances resulted in a pair of successful live albums, *Johnny Cash At Folsom Prison* (1968) and *Johnny Cash At San Quentin* (1969). Married June Carter in 1968. Hosted the Johnny Cash Show on ABC-TV during the period 1969-71. Visited Ireland on several occasions. On his first visit in 1959, he composed the classic song, *Forty Shades Of Green*. His autobiography, *Man In Black*, published in 1975, and *Cash: The Autobiography*, published in 1997. Signed with Mercury Records in 1987, left in 1991. Inducted into the Nashville Songwriters Hall of Fame in 1977. Inducted into the Country Music Hall of Fame in 1980. Inducted into the Rock and Roll Hall of Fame in 1992. Made his final public appearance on July 5, 2003. June Carter Cash died on May 15, 2003. His first wife, Vivian Liberto, died on May 24, 2005. *Walk The Line* a bio-pic starring Joaquin Phoenix as Johnny Cash was released in 2005. Johnny Cash died on September 12, 2003.

Date	Pos	Wks	ARTIST / Record Title *Label & Number*
25 Sep 69	3	7	1. A BOY NAMED SUE *CBS 4460*
18 May 72	1(4)	11	• 2. A THING CALLED LOVE *CBS 7797*

David CASSIDY — *13 Weeks*

Born on April 12, 1950 in New York, USA. Son of actor Jack Cassidy. In 1970 achieved the role of Keith Partridge in the TV series, *The Partridge Family*. Signed to Bell Records. 'The Family' achieved chart success both home and abroad. When the Partridge Family series finished in 1974, he took time off before returning to work in TV drama. Appeared in the 1993 Broadway production of *Blood Brothers*, with Petula Clark. His autobiography, *Could It Be Forever*, published in 2007.

Date	Pos	Wks	ARTIST / Record Title *Label & Number*
11 May 72	3	6	1. COULD IT BE FOREVER *Bell BELL 1224*
05 Oct 72	1(1)	4	• 2. HOW CAN I BE SURE *Bell BELL 1258*

continues over

Date	Pos	Wks	ARTIST / Record Title *Label & Number*
19 Apr 73	9	1	3. I'M A CLOWN *Bell MABEL 4*
01 Nov 73	3	2	4. DAYDREAMER / THE PUPPY SONG *Bell* BELL *1334*
			See also The Partridge Family

The CASUALS ***9 Weeks***

Formed in Lincoln, England in 1961. Personnel: John Tebb (vocals/organ), Howard Newcombe (guitar), Alan Taylor (bass) and Robert O'Brien (drums). Disc debut: *If You Walk Out* (1965). In 1968, the group was victorious for three consecutive weeks on the top TV talent show, Opportunity Knocks. Group split in 1975. *Jesamine* co-written by 1950's pop idol, Marty Wilde, was originally recorded by the Bystanders, under the title, *When Jezamine Goes.*

19 Sep 68	3	9	1. JESAMINE *Decca F 22784*

The CHAIRMEN OF THE BOARD ***4 Weeks***

Formed in Detroit, Michigan, USA in 1968. Personnel: General Norman Johnson, Danny Woods, Eddie Curtis and Harrison Kennedy. Disc debut: 1969. Johnson was lead vocals with The Showmen on hit record, *It Will Stand,* and composed, *Patches*, for Clarence Carter. Johnson left the group in 1974 to pursue a solo career, he returned to group in 1978.

17 Sep 70	5	4	1. GIVE ME JUST A LITTLE MORE TIME *Columbia INV 501*

Bruce CHANNEL ***10 Weeks***

Born on November 28, 1940 in Jacksonville, Texas, USA. In 1978 moved to Nashville and began writing hit songs for artists including T. G. Shepherd, John Conlee and Anne Murray. The harmonica player on *Hey Baby* is Delbert McClinton. The harmonica intro on the record is said to have influenced the Beatles, particularly with their debut recording, *Love Me Do.*

12 Apr 62	3	10	1. HEY BABY *Mercury AMT (I) 1171*

Date	Pos	Wks	ARTIST / Record Title *Label & Number*

Ray CHARLES — *29 Weeks*

Born Ray Charles Robinson on September 23, 1930 in Albany, Georgia, USA. Blind from the age seven due to glaucoma. Moved to Seattle in 1948. Made his first recording, *I Love You, I Love You*, backed by *Confession Blues*, as a member of the Maxin Trio. It was released in 1949 on Downbeat records. Signed to Atlantic Records in 1952. Switched to ABC-Paramount in 1960. Starred in film, *Ballad In Blue*, which was shot in Dublin, Ireland in 1964. Inducted into the Rock and Roll Hall of Fame in 1986. Died on June 10, 2004. A biopic, *Ray*, starring Jamie Foxx, as Ray Charles, was released in 2005.

Date	Pos	Wks	ARTIST / Record Title *Label & Number*
05 Jul 62	1(2)	9	• 1. I CAN'T STOP LOVING YOU *HMV POP(I) 1034*
20 Sep 62	2	9	2. YOU DON'T KNOW ME *HMV POP(I) 1064*
24 Jun 63	2	11	3. TAKE THESE CHAINS FROM MY HEART *HMV POP(I) 1161*

Tina CHARLES — *11 Weeks*

Born Tina Hoskins on March 10, 1954 in London, England. Disc debut: *In The Middle Of The Day* (1969). Backing vocalist on Cockney Rebel's, *Come Up And See Me Make Me Smile*. Working as a session singer when invited to sing lead vocals on the hit single, *I'm On Fire*, by 5,000 Volts.

Date	Pos	Wks	ARTIST / Record Title *Label & Number*
11 Mar 76	2	8	1. I LOVE TO LOVE *CBS 3937*
14 Oct 76	4	3	2. DANCE LITTLE LADY DANCE *CBS 4480*

Chubby CHECKER — *24 Weeks*

Born Ernest Evans on October 3, 1941 in Spring Gulley, South Carolina, USA. Grew up in South Philadelphia. Formed a street harmony group when he was eleven years old. Attended South Philadelphia High School with Fabian Forte. Because of his heavy build he got his nickname, Chubby, while working after school at the local Produce Market. Signed to Parkway Records in 1959. Disc debut: *The Class*. Started a world wide craze with his recording of *The Twist*.

continues over

Date	Pos	Wks	ARTIST / Record Title *Label & Number*
			Barbara Clark, wife of Dick Clark, host of top TV show American Bandstand, named him Chubby Checker.
25 Jan 62	2	14	1. LET'S TWIST AGAIN *Columbia DB(I) 4691*
03 Dec 62	4	10	2. LIMBO ROCK *Cameo Parkway P 849*

CHELSEA F.C. — *1 Weeks*

Professional football club formed in London, England in 1905. Home ground Stamford Bridge. *Blue Is The Colour* was issued to coincide with Chelsea's appearance versus Stoke City in the 1972 English League Cup Final. Stoke defeated Chelsea 2-1. The song was performed by the team squad: Tommy Baldwin, Peter Bonetti, Charlie Cooke, John Dempsey, Ron Harris, Marvin Hinton, John Hollins, Peter Houseman, Alan Hudson, Steve Kember, Eddie McCreadie, Paddy Mulligan, Peter Osgood and David Webb. The song was composed by Daniel Boone and Rod McQueen.

Date	Pos	Wks	ARTIST / Record Title *Label & Number*
23 Mar 72	8	1	1. BLUE IS THE COLOUR *Penny Farthing PEN 782*

CHER — *8 Weeks*

Born Cherilyn La Piere on May 20, 1946 in El Centro, California, USA. Met Sonny Bono in 1962 at a Ronettes recording session. Had her first solo recording, *Ringo I Love You*, released in 1964, under the name Bonnie Jo Mason. Early recordings with Sonny Bono released under the name, Caesar and Cleo. The duo recorded as Sonny & Cher from 1964 to 1973. Married Sonny in 1965, divorced in 1974. Won Academy Award as Best Actress for her performance in the 1987 film, *Moonstruck*.

Date	Pos	Wks	ARTIST / Record Title *Label & Number*
02 May 66	3	5	1. BANG BANG (My Baby Shot Me Down) *Liberty LIB(I) 66160*
09 Dec 71	3	3	2. GYPSYS TRAMPS AND THIEVES *MCA MU 1142*

See also Sonny and Cher

Don CHERRY — *4 Weeks*

Born on January 11, 1924 in Wichita Falls, Texas, USA. After military service in the 1940's he began to sing in nightclub's in the Dallas area and hosted his own radio show. He also began to play in regional golf tournaments.

continues over

Date	Pos	Wks	ARTIST / Record Title *Label & Number*

Made his disc debut in 1950 when he recorded tracks with bandleader Tommy Dorsey. Signed to Columbia in 1955. In 1962, he decided to take golf seriously and turned professional and became a touring member of the PGA. A talented golfer he played in the Masters 9 times, US Open 8 times and Walker Cup 3 times.

14 Feb 56	-	4	1. BAND OF GOLD *Philips PB 549*

CHIC — *2 Weeks*

Disco group formed in New York City in 1977. Personnel: Bernard Evans (bass), Nile Rodgers (guitar), Tony Thompson (drums), Luci Martin (vocals) and Alfa Anderson (vocals). Disbanded in 1983. Bernard Evans died on April 18, 1996. Tony Thompson died of cancer on November 12, 2003.

18 May 78	6	2	1. EVERYBODY DANCE *Atlantic K 11038*

CHICAGO — *10 Weeks*

Formed in Chicago, Illinois, USA in 1967 as the Big Thing. Moved to Los Angeles in 1968 where they signed to Columbia Records as the Chicago Transit Authority. Personnel: Terry Kath (vocals, guitar), Peter Cetera (vocals, bass), Robert Lamm (vocals, piano), Danny Seraphine (drums), James Pankow (trombone), Lee Loughnane (trumpet) and Walt Parazaider (saxophone). Disc debut: *Chicago Transit Authority* L.P. (1969). A name change to Chicago, happened in January 1970, as a result of threatened legal action by the real Chicago Transit Authority. Terry Kath died on January 23, 1978. Peter Cetera left band in 1985.

04 Nov 76	1(6)	10	• 1. IF YOU LEAVE ME NOW *CBS 4603*

CHICKORY TIP — *4 Weeks*

Formed in Maidstone, Kent, England in 1961 as The Sonics. Changed name in 1967. Personnel: Peter Hewson (lead vocals), Rick Foster (guitar), Barry Magyer (bass) and Brian Shearer (drums).

continues over

Date	Pos	Wks	ARTIST / Record Title *Label & Number*
			Disc debut: *Monday After Sunday* (1970). Chris Thomas, a recording engineer at AIR London Studios, played the moog synthesiser on *Son Of My Father.*
24 Feb 72	3	4	1. SON OF MY FATHER *CBS 7237*

CHILD — *2 Weeks*

Formed in London, England in 1978. Personnel: Graham Billbrough (vocal/guitar), Mike McKenzie (bass), Keith Attack (guitar) and Tim Attack (drums).

Date	Pos	Wks	ARTIST / Record Title *Label & Number*
10 Aug 78	7	2	1. IT'S ONLY MAKE BELIEVE *Ariola AHA 522*

CHI-LITES — *1 Weeks*

Formed in Chicago, USA in 1963 as the Hi-Lites. To avoid competition with a an already established act of the same name, decided on a name change. Personnel: Eugene Record (lead vocals), Robert 'Squirel' Lester, Marshall Thompson and Creadel 'Red' Jones. Record left in 1976 to pursue a solo career, rejoined in 1979. Eugene Record died from cancer on July 22, 2005.

Date	Pos	Wks	ARTIST / Record Title *Label & Number*
23 May 74	10	1	1. HOMELY GIRL *Brunswick BR 9*

CHIPS — *9 Weeks*

Formed in Belfast, N. Ireland in 1970 from elements of two bands, The Group and Heart N' Soul. Disc debut: *Sock It To 'Em Sister Nell* (1971). Personnel: Linda Martin (vocals), Irene McIlroy (vocals), Paul Lyttle (lead guitar), Adrian Mullen (keyboards), Shaun Magee (bass) and Brian Donaghy (drums). Linda Martin and Paul Lyttle left Chips in January1972 and formed Lyttle People. Returned to Chips lineup in 1974. Chips supported the Bay City Rollers on their 1976 UK tour. Performed *Goodbye Goodbye* in 1977 National Song Contest. Adrian Mullen composed Ireland's 1974 Eurovision entry, *Cross Your Heart.* Group disbanded in 1986. Linda Martin represented Ireland in two Eurovision Song Contests.

continues over

Date	Pos	Wks	ARTIST / Record Title *Label & Number*
			In 1984, she performed *Terminal Three*, finishing in second position. In 1992, she won the Eurovision with the song, *Why Me?*.
05 Jun 75	6	4	1. LOVE MATTERS *TON TO 701*
28 Apr 77	2	5	2. GOODBYE GOODBYE *Rex R 11116*
			The CHORDETTES ***2 Weeks***
			Formed in Sheboygan, Wisconsin, USA in 1948. Won an audition for Arthur Godfrey's Talent Scouts daily TV show in 1949, leading to a four year stint on the show. Personnel: Jinny Osborn, Janet Ertel, Carol Bushman and Lynn Evans. Signed to Cadence Records in 1953.. Disbanded in 1961. Inducted into Vocal Group Hall of Fame in 2001. Janet Ertel died on November 22, 1988.
18 Sep 56	-	1	1. BORN TO BE WITH YOU *London HL 8302*
15 May 58	-	1	2. LOLLIPOP *London HLA 8584*
			CHRISTIE ***15 Weeks***
			Formed in London, England in 1970. Personnel: Jeff Christie (born July 12, 1946 in Leeds, vocals, guitar), Vic Elmes (bass, vocals) and Mike Blakely (drums). In early 1970, Jeff Christie sent a demo tape of his songs to Tremeloes guitarist Alan Blakely. A recording session was arranged in London with The Tremeloes providing backing for Jeff's vocals. None of the tracks were issued. Jeff formed a group, Christie, and signed to CBS. *Yellow River* featured Jeff Christie and Vic Elmes on vocals, dubbed over the Tremeloes backing track cut at Christie's first sessions. *Yellow River* won the Ivor Novello Award for Best Song of 1970. Group split in 1975.
28 May 70	1(2)	9	• 1. YELLOW RIVER *CBS 4922*
26 Nov 70	4	6	2. SAN BERNADINO *CBS 5169*
			Lou CHRISTIE ***5 Weeks***
			Born Lugee Alfredo Sacco on February 19, 1943 in Glenwillard, Pensylvania, USA. Member of vocal group the Classics in 1960.

continues over

Date	Pos	Wks	ARTIST / Record Title *Label & Number*

Recorded as Lugel and the Lions in 1961. Moved to New York in 1963, where he began a musical association with classically trained musician, Twyla Herbert, who started to write songs with Lou. Debut solo single: *The Gypsy Cried* (1963).

Date	Pos	Wks	ARTIST / Record Title *Label & Number*
30 Oct 69	4	5	1. I'M GONNA MAKE YOU MINE *Buddah 201057*

Tony CHRISTIE — *18 Weeks*

Born Anthony Fitzgerald on April 25, 1943 in Conisborough, South Yorkshire, England. Embarked on a musical career by fronting various bands on the club circuit. Spotted singing with The Trackers, at a club in Wales. Disc debut: *Life's Too Good To Waste* (1966). Signed to MCA in 1969. In 1976, was signed by Andrew Lloyd Webber and Tim Rice to sing the part of Migaldi in the original concept album of *Evita*.

Date	Pos	Wks	ARTIST / Record Title *Label & Number*
17 Jun 71	2	8	1. I DID WHAT I DID FOR MARIA *MCA MK 5064*
16 Dec 71	3	7	2. (Is This The Way To) AMARILLO *MCA MKS(I) 5073*
11 May 72	8	3	3. DON'T GO DOWN TO RENO *MCA MKS 5089*

Gigliola CINQUETTI — *10 Weeks*

Born on December 20, 1947 in Verona, Italy. Won the 1964 Eurovision Song Contest for Italy with *Non Ho L'eta Per Amarti*. Won San Remo Song Festival in 1966. Finished second in the 1974 Eurovison Song Contest, performing, *Si*. English title, *Go (Before You Break My Heart)*.

Date	Pos	Wks	ARTIST / Record Title *Label & Number*
18 May 64	4	7	1. NON HO L'ETA PER AMARTI *Decca F 21882*
30 May 74	6	3	2. GO (Before You Break My Heart) *CBS 2294*

CITY BOY — *2 Weeks*

Formed in Birmingham, England in 1973. Personnel: Lol Mason (vocals), Steve Broughton, Mike 'Max' Slamer (guitar), Chris Dunn (bass), Max Thomas (keyboards) and Roger Kent (drums). Disc debut: *Hap-Ki-Do* (1976). Disbanded in 1982.

Date	Pos	Wks	ARTIST / Record Title *Label & Number*
27 Jul 78	6	2	1. 5-7-0-5 *Vertigo 6059 207*

Date	Pos	Wks	ARTIST / Record Title *Label & Number*

The Dave CLARK FIVE ***25 Weeks***

Formed in London, England in 1960. Personnel: Dave Clark (drums), Mike Smith (vocals, keyboards), Lenny Davidson (guitar), Rick Huxley (bass) and Denis Payton (saxophone). Disc debut: *That's What I Said* (1962). Discovered by an EMI A&R man during their residency at the Tottenham Royal Ballroom in London. Group starred in the 1965 film, *Catch Us If You Can*. Disbanded in May 1970. Dave Clark wrote the musical, *Time*, which was staged at London's Dominion Theatre in April 1986, with Cliff Richard in the lead role. Mike Smith suffered serious head and back injuries in a fall from an eight foot high fence at his home in Spain in October 2003, which left him paralysed from the waist down. Denis Peyton died on December 17, 2006. Mike Smith died of pneumonia on February 28, 2008.

Date	Pos	Wks	ARTIST / Record Title *Label & Number*
06 Jan 64	1(2)	8	• 1. GLAD ALL OVER *Columbia DB(I) 7154*
02 Mar 64	1(1)	8	• 2. BITS AND PIECES *Columbia DB(I) 7210*
04 Jan 68	6	3	3. EVERYBODY KNOWS *Columbia DB (I) 8286*
17 Oct 68	5	5	4. THE RED BALLOON *Columbia DB(I) 8465*
29 Jan 70	10	1	5. GOOD OLD ROCK 'N' ROLL *Columbia DB(I) 8638*

Petula CLARK ***42 Weeks***

Born Petula Sally Olwen Clark on November 15, 1932 in West Ewell, Surrey, England. A child star, she had her own radio series, *Pet's Parlour*, at the age of ten. Made her first film appearance in the 1943 film, *Medal For The General*. Disc debut: *Put Your Shoes On Lucy* (1949). Appeared in over twenty films including starring roles in *Finian's Rainbow* (1968) and *Goodbye Mr Chips* (1969). Has also enjoyed success in several stage musicals including *The* Sound *Of Music*, *Blood Brothers* and *Sunset Boulevard*.

Date	Pos	Wks	ARTIST / Record Title *Label & Number*
28 Feb 56	-	5	1. MEMORIES ARE MADE OF THIS *Nixa N 15040*
10 Sep 57	-	3	2. WITH ALL MY HEART *Nixa N 15096*
21 Jan 58	-	3	3. ALONE *Nixa N 15112*

continues over

Date	Pos	Wks	ARTIST / Record Title *Label & Number*
18 Mar 58	-	3	4. BABY LOVER *Nixa N 15126*
02 Feb 61	2	7	• 5. SAILOR *Pye 7N 15324*
31 Aug 61	2	5	6. ROMEO *Pye 7N 15361*
07 Jan 65	2	5	7. DOWNTOWN *Pye 7N 15722*
03 Mar 66	6	3	8. MY LOVE *Pye 7N 17038*
23 Feb 67	1(3)	8	• 9. THIS IS MY SONG *Pye 7N 17258*

Rosemary CLOONEY ***19 Weeks***

Born on May 23, 1928 in Maysville, Kentucky, USA. Rosemary and her sister, Betty, were schoolgirls when they started singing on WLW Radio in Cincinnati, as the Clooney Sisters. Came to the attention of band leader, Tony Pastor, who signed the sisters as vocalists with his band. The sisters toured for three years, 1946-49, with the Tony Pastor Orchestra. Rosemary went solo in 1949, following her signing with Columbia Records. Made her first official solo recording, *Bargain Day*, in 1949. Film appearances include : *The Stars Are Singing* (1953), *Red Garters* (1954), *White Christmas* (1954) and *Radioland Murders* (1994). Her career declined in the 1960's when she experienced serious psychiatric problems. Her autobiography, *Girl Singer*, was published in 1999. Returned to the music scene in the late 1970's and continued to perform until her illness in 2001. Honoured with a Lifetime Achievement Grammy Award in February 2002. Died of lung cancer on June 29, 2002.

Date	Pos	Wks	ARTIST / Record Title *Label & Number*
12 Oct 54	2	2	1. THIS OLE HOUSE *Philips PB 336*
18 Jan 55	-	6	2. MAMBO ITALIANO *Philips PB 382*
24 May 55	-	1	3. WHERE WILL THE DIMPLE BE *Philips PB 428*
27 Sep 55	-	5	4. HEY THERE *Philips PB 494*
09 Dec 55	-	2	5. CHRISTMAS *Philips PB 530*
08 May 56	-	1	6. KEY TO MY HEART *Philips PB 582*
15 May 58	-	2	7. I COULD HAVE DANCED ALL NIGHT *Philips EPB 800*

Date	Pos	Wks	ARTIST / Record Title *Label & Number*

CLOUT — *7 Weeks*

Formed in Johannesburg, South Africa in 1977. Personnel: Lee Tomlinson (vocals), Cindi Alter (vocals,guitar), Jenni Garson (vocals,guitar), Ingrid Herbst (vocals, drums), Sandy Robbie (guitar) and Bones Brettell (keyboards).

Date	Pos	Wks	ARTIST / Record Title *Label & Number*
13 Jul 78	1(1)	7	• 1. SUBSTITUTE *EMI EMI 2788*

The COASTERS — *5 Weeks*

Formed in Los Angeles, USA in 1955 when Carl Gardner and Bobby Nunn left the Robins vocal group to team up with songwriters/record producers, Jerry Leiber and Mike Stoller, at Atlantic Records. Disc debut: *Down In Mexico* (1956). Personnel (1959): Carl Gardner (tenor), Billy Guy (baritone), Cornell Gunter (tenor) and Will 'Dub' Jones(bass). Many changes in personnel over the years. Inducted into the Rock and Roll Hall of Fame in 1987. Inducted into Vocal Group Hall of Fame in 1999. Cornell Gunter died on February 26, 1990. Will Dub Jones died on January 16, 2000. Billy Guy died on November 5, 2002. Carl Gardner and Billy Guy are lead vocals on *Charlie Brown*.

Date	Pos	Wks	ARTIST / Record Title *Label & Number*
16 Apr 59	6	5	1. CHARLIE BROWN *London* HLE *8819*

Eddie COCHRAN — *13 Weeks*

Born Edward Ray Cochrane on October 3, 1938 in Oklahoma City, USA. Toured the UK with Gene Vincent in 1960. Died on April 17, 1960 in a car accident in Chippenham, Wiltshire, England. Appeared in films *The Girl Can't Help It* (1956) and *Untamed Youth* (1957). Inducted into Rock and Rock Hall of Fame in 1987.

Date	Pos	Wks	ARTIST / Record Title *Label & Number*
16 Jun 60	1(5)	13	• 1. THREE STEPS TO HEAVEN *London HLG 9115*

Joe COCKER — *4 Weeks*

Born John Robert Cocker on May 20, 1944 in Sheffield England. Started his career with a local group the Cavaliers.

continues over

Date	Pos	Wks	ARTIST / Record Title *Label & Number*

Worked for a period as Vance Arnold and the Avengers. Disc debut: *I'll Cry Instead* (1964). Formed the Grease Band in 1965. *With A Little Help From My Friends* was a cover of a track from the Beatles album, *Sgt. Pepper's Lonely Hearts Club Band*. Performed with the Grease Band at Woodstock Festival in 1969.

07 Nov 68	2	4	1. WITH A LITTLE HELP FROM MY FRIENDS *Regal Zonophone RZ(I) 3013*

Alma COGAN — *3 Weeks*

Born Alma Angela Cohen on May 19, 1932 in Golders Green, London, England. From a young age had a burning desire to succeed as a vocalist. In 1947 she unsuccessfully auditioned for the B.B.C. Joined the Denis Hale Band in Brighton and later joined the chorus of *High Button Shoes*, which ran at the London Hippodrome in 1948-49. Disc debut: *To Be Worthy Of You* (1952). In 1956 given her own radio show, *The Song's The Thing*, on the BBC. The following year, *The Alma Cogan Show*, was launched on B.B.C. Television. Died from cancer on October 26, 1966. In 1991, her sister, Sandra Caron wrote the book, *Alma Cogan: A Memoir.*

01 Feb 55	-	1	1. I CAN'T TELL A WALTZ FROM A TANGO *HMV IP 938*
01 Mar 55	-	1	2. PAPER KISSES *HMV IP 961*
01 Apr 58	-	1	3. SUGARTIME *Columbia IDB 540*

Nat King COLE — *16 Weeks*

Pianist/vocalist. Born Nathaniel Adams Coles on March 17, 1917 in Montgomery, Alabama, USA. Joined his brother Eddie's group in 1936. Formed the King Cole Trio in 1939. Signed to Capitol Records in 1943. Embarked on a solo career in 1950. One of the first black jazz artists to have a radio show 1948-49, and the first black entertainer to have a national television show in 1956-57. Appeared in films *St Louis Blues* (1958) and *Cat Ballou* (1965).

continues over

Date	Pos	Wks	ARTIST / Record Title *Label & Number*
			Stopped performing in 1964 due to ill health. Died of lung cancer on February 15, 1965. Father of recording star, Natalie Cole.
26 Oct 54	3	1	1. SMILE *Capitol CL 14149*
18 Jun 57	-	6	2. WHEN I FALL IN LOVE *Capitol CL(I) 14709*
19 Nov 57	-	1	3. STARDUST *Capitol CL(I) 14787*
15 Oct 62	4	8	4. RAMBLIN' ROSE Capitol *CL(I) 15270*

Brian COLL — *17 Weeks*

Born on March 6, 1941 in Drumquin, near Omagh, Co.Tyrone, N.Ireland. Began his music career with the Polka Dots on September 20, 1960. Joined the Plattermen as lead vocalist in 1961. Left in 1962 but returned in 1965. Disc debut: *I'll Take You Home Again Kathleen* (1966). In May 1968, Brian left Plattermen to form his own band, the Buckaroos. In the autumn of 1989, while travelling from Drogheda to Omagh, Brian suffered a severe brain haemorrhage, which resulted in a long stay in hospital and an extended period of time away from the music business.

Date	Pos	Wks	ARTIST / Record Title *Label & Number*
03 Dec 70	7	2	1. GIVE AN IRISH GIRL TO ME *Release RL 548*
30 Sep 71	3	9	2. THESE ARE MY MOUNTAINS *Release RL 594*
09 Mar 72	8	1	3. WHEN MY BLUE MOON TURNS TO GOLD *Release RL 619*
30 May 74	5	5	4. HOMETOWN ON THE FOYLE *Release RL 727*

Dave and Ansil COLLINS — *1 Weeks*

Jamaican male duo formed in 1971. Personnel: Dave Barker (vocals) and Ansil Collins (keyboards). Met in 1971, while working in Jamaica for reggae producer, Lee Perry.

Date	Pos	Wks	ARTIST / Record Title *Label & Number*
06 May 71	10	1	1. DOUBLE BARRELL *Technique TE 901*

The Donie COLLINS SHOWBAND featuring CHRIS — *3 Weeks*

Irish showband. Donie Collins born in Askeaton, Co. Limerick, Ireland. His father wanted him to join the family business (cobbler) but Donie saw his future in the music world and joined the local brass band.

continues over

Date	Pos	Wks	ARTIST / Record Title *Label & Number*

Formed his first band in 1950. In 1964, he formed the Associated Ballrooms chain of dance halls with Con Hynes and Jack O'Rourke. Retired from the performing side of the music business in 1973. Donie Collins died on February 25, 1987. Band personnel: Donie Collins (tenor sax, trumpet), Eddie Sheehan (bass), Liam Foley (lead guitar), Austin Graham (rhythm guitar), Henry Kiely (drums), Pat McDonald (tenor sax), Mick Falahee (tenor sax) and Chris Grace (lead vocals). Grace left band in 1967 to join the Raindrops. Band split in 1973. Mick Falahee died in November 1999.

Date	Pos	Wks	ARTIST / Record Title *Label & Number*
24 Jan 66	6	3	1. YOUNG LOVE *Pye 7N 17004*

Judy COLLINS — *4 Weeks*

Born on May 1, 1939 in Seattle, Washington, USA. Raised in Denver she trained as a classical pianist. Made her public debut at age thirteen, performing Mozart's, *Concerto For Two Pianos*. Inspired by the work of Woody Guthrie and Pete Seeger she turned to folk music in late 1950's. Signed to Elektra Records in 1961. Disc debut: *A Maid Of Constant Sorrow* (1961).

Date	Pos	Wks	ARTIST / Record Title *Label & Number*
12 Jun 75	3	4	1. SEND IN THE CLOWNS *Elektra* K *12177*

COLM and the SUNDOWNERS — *1 Weeks*

Born Colm Gilmore in Portaferry, Co Down, N. Ireland. Disc debut: *Memory Of An Old Christmas Card* (1972). The Sundowners formed in 1968 as a four piece cabaret group. Spotted by promoter Cecil Thompson of C.T. Promotions who suggested enlarging the group and doing the dancehall circuit. Turned pro in December 1971. Personnel: Colm Gilmore (lead vocals), Henry Magee (lead guitar), Dermot Hamilton (rhythm guitar), Francis Hamilton (bass), Paddy Stewart (organ), Patsy Smith (tenor saxophone) and Ivan McKeague (drums). Colm Gilmore died of cancer on August 21, 1997.

Date	Pos	Wks	ARTIST / Record Title *Label & Number*
25 Oct 73	10	1	1. YOU'RE STILL THE ONLY ONE *Release RL 685*

Date	Pos	Wks	ARTIST / Record Title *Label & Number*

The COMMODORES — *14 Weeks*

Formed in Tuskegee, Alabama, USA in 1970. Met as freshmen at Tuskegee Institute in 1967 and decided to form a band for a talent contest. Called themselves, The Mystics, later joined forces with a couple of members of a disbanded campus band called The Jays. A name change was called for and the guys came up with The Commodores. Personnel: Lionel Ritchie (born on June 20, 1949 in Tuskegee, lead vocals, saxophone), William King (trumpet), Thomas McClary (guitar), Milan Williams (keyboards), Ronald LaPread (bass) and Walter 'Clyde' Orange (drums). Signed to Motown Records in 1972. Lionel Ritchie left in 1982 to pursue a solo career.

Date	Pos	Wks	ARTIST / Record Title *Label & Number*
24 Aug 78	1(3)	6	• 1. **THREE TIMES A LADY** *Motown TMG 1113*
11 Oct 79	7	4	2. **SAIL ON** *Motown TMG 1155*
22 Nov 79	3	4	3. **STILL** *Motown TMG 1166*

Perry COMO — *47 Weeks*

Born Pierino Ronald Como on May 18, 1912 in Canonsburg, Pennsylvania, USA. The seventh of thirteen children, he worked after school in a local barbershop. Later, while attending high school he operated his own barber shop. Performed at local functions and gained recognition for his singing ability. In 1933, he successfully auditioned for Freddie Carlone's Band. That same year he married his childhood sweetheart, Roselle Belline. She died in August 1998, two weeks after the couple celebrated their sixty fifth wedding anniversary. In 1936 joined the Ted Weems Orchestra. Made his disc debut with the band in 1938 with *A Gypsy Told Me.* Film appearances include *Something For The Boys* (1944), *Doll Face* (1945) and *If I'm Lucky* (1946). Own TV show from 1948 to 1963. Made first visit to Ireland in 1994 to film a Christmas TV special.

continues over

Date	Pos	Wks	ARTIST / Record Title *Label & Number*
			On May 15, 1999 a life size statue of Perry Como was unveiled in his home town of Canonsburg, as a permanent reminder of the honour he brought to his home town and his contribution to the world of entertainment. Died in his sleep on May 12, 2001.
08 May 56	-	1	1. JUKE BOX BABY *HMV IP 1097*
19 Jun 56	-	2	2. HOT DIGGITY (Dog Ziggity Boom) *HMV IP 1112*
02 Oct 56	-	2	3. GLENDORA *HMV IP 1154*
12 Feb 59	7	2	4. LOVE MAKES THE WORLD GO ROUND / MANDOLINS IN THE MOONLIGHT *RCA ERC 1086*
19 Mar 59	8	2	5. TOMBOY *RCA ERC 1111*
23 Jul 59	7	3	6. I KNOW *RCA ERC 1126*
31 Mar 60	2	9	7. DELAWARE *RCA ERC 1170*
04 Mar 71	6	1	8. IT'S IMPOSSIBLE *RCA 2043*
17 May 73	2	12	9. AND I LOVE YOU SO *RCA 2346*
27 Sep 73	1(2)	11	• 10. FOR THE GOOD TIMES *RCA 2402*
06 Jun 74	6	2	11. I WANT TO GIVE *RCA LPBO 7518*

CONGREGATION — *4 Weeks*

Studio vocal group formed by songwriters Roger Cook and Roger Greenaway to record their song, *Softly Whispering I Love You*. Brian Keith, ex Plastic Penny, is lead vocals on the track.

Date	Pos	Wks	ARTIST / Record Title *Label & Number*
13 Jan 72	7	4	1. SOFTLY WHISPERING I LOVE YOU *Columbia DB(I) 8830*

Billy CONNOLLY — *3 Weeks*

Born on November 24, 1942 in Anderston, Glasgow, Scotland. In the early 1960's began performing solo at the Folk Attic Club in Paisley. Formed a bluegrass group the Skillet Lickers. At the same time was serving an apprenticeship as a welder on the Clyde shipyards. Teamed up with Tam Harvey in 1967 and began gigging as the Humblebums. In 1968 signed to Transatlantic Records. Gerry Rafferty joined up with Billy and Tam in January 1969. Tam left in mid 1969 and Billy and Gerry continued as a duo. Split up in September 1970.

continues over

Date	Pos	Wks	ARTIST / Record Title *Label & Number*
			Billy went on to develop his comic talents and establish himself as one of the leading British comedians. Film appearances include *Mrs Brown* (1997).
20 Nov 75	6	3	1. D.I.V.O.R.C.E. *Polydor 2058 652*
			Russ CONWAY ***47 Weeks***
			Born Trevor Herbert Stanford on September 2, 1925 in Bristol, England. In the early 1940's joined the Royal Navy. Demobbed in 1946, he soon got bored with civilian life and joined the Merchant Navy. During his career at sea, he lost the tip of a finger in an accident with a bread slicer. Left the Merchant Navy in 1955. Spotted playing piano in a London club by choreographer Irving Davies, who hired him as a rehearsal pianist. This led to a meeting with Norman Newell, an A & R man with EMI. Signed to Columbia Records Disc debut: *Roll The Carpet Up* (1957). Died of cancer on November 16, 2000.
12 Mar 59	2	18	1. SIDE SADDLE • *Columbia DB(I) 4256*
04 Jun 59	1(2)	13	•2. ROULETTE • *Columbia DB(I) 4298*
03 Sep 59	1(1)	8	•3. CHINA TEA • *Columbia DB(I) 4337*
19 Nov 59	2	8	4. SNOWCOACH • *Columbia* DB(I) *4368*
			Sam COOKE ***12 Weeks***
			Born on January 22, 1931 in Clarksdale, Mississippi, USA. Son of a Baptist Minister. Lead singer of the Soul Stirrers gospel group 1950-1957. In 1956, released a single, *Lovable*, under the name Dale Cook on Specialty Records. A string of hits on the Keen label led to RCA Records signing Cooke. Shot to death by a female motel manager on December 11, 1964 in Los Angeles. Inducted into the Rock and Roll Hall of Fame in 1986.
27 Oct 60	6	4	1. CHAIN GANG *RCA ERC 1202*
31 Aug 61	9	3	2. CUPID *RCA ERC 1242*
12 Apr 62	6	5	3. TWISTIN' THE NIGHT AWAY *RCA ERC 1277*

Date	Pos	Wks	ARTIST / Record Title *Label & Number*
			Rita COOLIDGE ***7 Weeks***
			Born May 1, 1944 in Lafayette, Nashville, Tennessee, USA. Started out singing with her sisters, Pricilla and Linda, as the Coolidge Sisters. Worked with Joe Cocker, Delaney and Bonnie and Leon Russell as backing vocalist before setting out as a solo artist. Solo disc debut: *Turn Around And Love You* (1969). Signed to A&M Records in 1971. Married to Kris Kristofferson 1973-1980.
01 Sep 77	6	3	1. WE'RE ALL ALONE *A&M AMS 7295*
02 Mar 78	7	4	2. WORDS *A&M 7330*
			Alice COOPER **6 Weeks**
			Rock group formed in Detroit, USA in 1966. Personnel: Alice Cooper (born Vincent Furnier on February 4, 1948 in Detroit, lead vocals), Glen Buxton (guitar), Michael Bruce (guitar), Dennis Dunaway (bass) and Neal Smith (drums). Following the demise of the group Cooper re-emerged as a solo artist in the late 80's. Film appearances include *A Nightmare On Elm Street* (1984) and *Prince Of Darkness* (1987). Glen Buxton died on October 19, 1997.
10 Aug 72	2	4	1. SCHOOL'S OUT *Warner Bros. K 16188*
09 Nov 72	8	2	2. ELECTED *Warner Bros. K 16241*
			Don CORNELL ***2 Weeks***
			Born Luigi Francesco Varlard on April 21, 1919 in The Bronx, New York, USA. Worked as vocalist at New York's Edison Hotel with the Bobby Hayes Orchestra. Made his first recordings under the name, Lou Varlaro. In 1942 he came to the attention of bandleader Sammy Kaye. Kaye renamed the young crooner, Don Cornell. Left Kaye in 1949 to pursue a solo career. Signed to Coral Records in 1952. Was inducted into the Big Band Hall of Fame in February 1993. Died on February 23, 2004.
23 Nov 54	3	2	1. HOLD MY HAND *Vogue Q 2013*

Date	Pos	Wks	ARTIST / Record Title *Label & Number*

Elvis COSTELLO — *4 Weeks*

Born Declan Patrick McManus on August 25, 1954 in Liverpool, England. Son of vocalist/trumpeter, Ross McManus, who was a member of the Joe Loss Orchestra. First performed his own songs in public at a London Folk Club in 1970. In 1972, formed a duo, Rusty, with Allan Mayes. Formed band Flip City in 1974. The band folded at the end of 1975 and he embarked on a solo career as D P Costello (Costello being the maiden name of his paternal great grandmother To make ends meet he also got a job as a computer operator for the Elizabeth Arden factory. Signed to Stiff Records in 1976. It was Jake Riveria of Stiff who decided to give D P the new Christian name, Elvis. Disc debut: *Less Than Zero* (1977). Performed his first live gig as Elvis Costello at London's Nashville on May 27, 1977. Formed The Attractions in July 1977. Personnel: Pete Thomas (drums), Steve Naïve (keyboards) and Bruce Thomas (bass). Elvis split with The Attractions in late 1984. Inducted into the Rock and Roll Hall of Fame in 2003.

Date	Pos	Wks	ARTIST / Record Title *Label & Number*
01 Mar 79	4	4	1. OLIVER'S ARMY *Radar ADA 31*

The COTTON MILL BOYS — *17 Weeks*

Formed in Dublin in 1968 by Gerry Madigan as four piece folk/bluegrass group. Launched as a seven piece showband on the ballroom circuit on June 20, 1969, making their debut at Dublin's Crystal Ballroom. Personnel: Gerry Madigan (vocals, banjo), Mick McManus (fiddle), Mike Scott (vocals), Tony Hughes (vocals, guitar), Tommy Kinsella (bass), Buddy Boland (guitar) and Martin McGregor (drums). Won European Best Country Act Award at the 1972 Wembley International Country Music Festival. Band got a new lease of life in 1976, when they had four successive wins on the top British TV talent show, Opportunity Knocks. Own six week series on RTE television. During their lifetime the band had many personnel changes in their lineup.

continues over

Date	Pos	Wks	ARTIST / Record Title *Label & Number*

Here are some of the major ones. In August 1972, Tommy Kinsella, Buddy Boland and Martin McGregor left to form Buckshot. Vocalist Mike Scott left in March 1974 to front The Hootenannys. Replaced by Des Wilson. Mick McManus departed in 1975, replaced by Charlie Arkins. Des Wilson and Gerry Madigan left in 1978. Vocalist/guitarist Tony Hughes departed in 1982. The group disbanded in 1984. Des Wilson, (lead vocal on *Lucille*), died on December 12, 1990.

Date	Pos	Wks	ARTIST / Record Title *Label & Number*
16 Nov 72	7	3	1. **MEET THE COTTONS** *Hawk HASP 307*
03 May 73	7	2	2. **JUDY** *Hawk HASP 315*
14 Oct 76	9	1	3. **THE WEDDING SONG** *Hawk HASP 393*
25 Nov 76	3	4	4. **RAINING IN MY HEART** *Hawk HASP 396*
26 May 77	2	7	5. **LUCILLE** *Hawk HASP 404*

Tracks on **Meet The Cottons**: Katy Clyne / Try A Little Kindness / Does My Ring Hurt Your Finger / A Maidens Prayer.

Julie COVINGTON — *7 Weeks*

Born on September 11, 1947 in London, England. Trained to be a teacher at Homerton College of Education in Cambridge. Gave up her studies to perform in the Cambridge Footlights Revue. Met Clive James who encouraged her to continue with Footlights in the Edinburgh Festival. Disc debut: *While The Music Lasts* LP (private pressing) (1967). Achieved international recognition when her recording of, *Don't Cry For Me Argentina*, was lifted from original *Evita* album, and released as a single. Won a Britiannia Award (later renamed Brit Award) in 1977 as the Most Outstanding New British Recording Artist (female). Starred with Charlotte Cornwall and Rula Lenska in the 1976 TV series, *Rock Follies*.

Date	Pos	Wks	ARTIST / Record Title *Label & Number*
27 Jan 77	2	7	1. **DON'T CRY FOR ME ARGENTINA** *MCA MCA 260*

Floyd CRAMER — *3 Weeks*

Born on October 27, 1933 in Shreveport, Louisiana, USA. Moved to Nashville in 1955 where he quickly became Nashville's top session piano player.

continues over

Date	Pos	Wks	ARTIST / Record Title *Label & Number*
			Played on countless hit records by artists such as Elvis Presley, Patsy Cline and Roy Orbison. Co-wrote the classic country song, *Last Date*. Died from lung cancer on December 31, 1997.
01 Jun 61	4	3	1. ON THE REBOUND • *RCA ERC 1231*
			Les CRANE ***2 Weeks***
			Born on December 3, 1935 in San Francisco, California, USA. In the mid 1960's hosted a number of late night television talk shows. Won Grammy, for *Desiderata* in 1971, for Best Spoken Word Recording. Appeared in the 1966 film, *An American Dream*. Left the entertainment business in the 1980's to work in the software industry. The poem, *Desiderata*, was written in 1906 by Max Ehrmann. Died of natural causes on July 13, 2008.
30 Mar 72	9	2	1. DESIDERATA *Warner Bros. K 16119*
			CREEDENCE CLEARWATER REVIVAL ***13 Weeks***
			American vocal/instrumental group formed while members still at High School in El Cerrito, California, USA. Made disc debut as the Golliwogs in 1964. Changed name to Creedence Clearwater Reviva l in 1967. Personnel: John Fogarty (lead vocals, guitar), Tom Fogarty (guitar), Stu Cook (bass) and Doug Clifford (drums). Disbanded in 1972. Tom Fogerty died on September 6, 1990. John Fogerty continues to enjoy a successful solo career.
18 Sep 69	1(1)	6	• 1. BAD MOON RISING *Liberty LBF 15230*
14 May 70	8	1	2. TRAVELLIN' BAND *Liberty LBF 15310*
09 Jul 70	3	6	3. UP AROUND THE BEND *Liberty LBF 15354*
			The CREW CUTS ***1 Weeks***
			Vocal group formed in Toronto, Canada in 1952 under the name The Canadaires. Members met while attending St. Michael's Cathedral Choir School in Toronto.

continues over

Date	Pos	Wks	ARTIST / Record Title *Label & Number*

In 1953, made their disc debut, *Chirp, Chirp, Sing A Song Little Sparrow*. In January 1954, the group decided on a name change and The Crew Cuts were born. They signed to Mercury records and released their first single as The Crewcuts, *Crazy Bout Ya Baby*. Personnel: John Perkins (born on August 28, 1931 in Toronto, lead vocal), Rudi Maugeri (baritone), Ray Perkins (bass) and Pat Barrett (tenor). Disbanded following a farewell concert in Pittsburg in June 1964.

Date	Pos	Wks	ARTIST / Record Title *Label & Number*
12 Oct 54	1	1	• 1. SH-BOOM *Mercury MB 3140*

The CRICKETS **1 Weeks**

Rock 'n' roll group from Lubbock, Texas, USA. Formed by Buddy Holly and Jerry Allison in 1957, the lineup also included Joe B Mauldin (bass) and Nikki Sullivan (rhythm guitar). Disc debut: *That'll Be The Day* (1957). Sullivan left in December 1957. Group continued as a trio. Holly left in October 1958 with Allison taking over as leader and keeper of the flame. Buddy Holly died on February 3, 1959 in an air crash. Nikki Sullivan died of a heart attack on April 6, 2004. Personnel (1962): Jerry Allison (drums), Sonny Curtis (vocals, lead guitar), Glen D. Hardin (keyboards) and Jerry Naylor (lead vocals). Numerous personnel changes over the years but Allison, Curtis and Mauldin have remained constant fixtures in the lineup. Made first visit to Ireland in 1990. Still active as recording and touring artists.

Date	Pos	Wks	ARTIST / Record Title *Label & Number*
26 Jul 62	9	1	1. DON'T EVER CHANGE *Liberty LIB(I) 55441*

See also Buddy Holly

Bing CROSBY **6 Weeks**

Born Harry Lillis Crosby on May 3, 1903 in Tacoma, Washington, USA. He started his professional musical career as a member of Paul Whiteman's Orchestra in 1926. Formed Rhythm Boys. In 1926, made his first recording (with Al Rinker), *I've Got The Girl*. Split from Whiteman in 1930.

continues over

Date	Pos	Wks	ARTIST / Record Title *Label & Number*

Launched his solo career in 1931. Made fifty five full length films during his career, starting with, *The Big Broadcast*, in 1932 and ending with a television film, *Dr. Crooks Garden* in 1971. Won Oscar for Best Actor in 1945, for his portrayal of a priest, Father O'Malley, in the 1944 Paramount film, *Going My Way*. Starred, with Bob Hope, in seven 'Road' comedy films. Made his final recording, *Once In A While*, on October 11, 1977. Collapsed and died from a massive heart attack on October 14, 1977, as he was walking to the club house after completing a round of golf on the Le Moraleja golf course near Madrid, Spain. Theme song, *When The Blue Of The Night (Meets The Gold Of The Day.*

Date	Pos	Wks	ARTIST / Record Title *Label & Number*
04 Jan 55	-	1	1. COUNT YOUR BLESSINGS INSTEAD OF SHEEP *Brunswick 05339*
10 May 55	-	2	2. STRANGER IN PARADISE *Brunswick 05410*
04 Jun 57	-	3	3. AROUND THE WORLD *Brunswick 05674*

Bing CROSBY and Grace KELLY ***2 Weeks***

Male / female vocal duo. Grace Patricia Kelly born on November 12, 1929 in Philadelphia, USA. After her graduation from high school in 1947, she relocated to New York. Made her debut on Broadway in 1949. Made her film debut in the 1951 film, *Fourteen Hours*. Other film appearances include *High Noon* (1952), *Mogambo* (1953), *Dial M For Murder* (1954) and *Rear Window* (1954). Won an Academy Award for Best Actress for her role in the 1954 film, *Country Girl*. Her appearance in the 1956 film, *High Society*, was her final acting performance. Met Prince Ranier of Monaco, in May 1955, at the Cannes Film Festival. They married on April 19, 1956 and she received the title Princess Grace. Died on September 14, 1982, from injuries received in a car accident. *True Love* featured in the 1956 film *High Society*.

Date	Pos	Wks	ARTIST / Record Title *Label & Number*
15 Jan 57	-	2	1. TRUE LOVE *Capitol CL(I) 14645*

Date	Pos	Wks	ARTIST / Record Title *Label & Number*

Bing CROSBY and Louis ARMSTRONG ALL STARS 1 Weeks

Bing Crosby born on May 3, 1903 in Tacoma, Washington, USA. Louis Armstrong born on July 4, 1901 in New Orleans, USA. The number, *Now You Has Jazz,* featured in the 1956 film *High Society*, starring Bing Crosby, Frank Sinatra, Grace Kelly and Celeste Holm. Louis Armstrong and his All Stars also appeared in the film. All Stars personnel: Louis Armstrong (trumpet/vocals), Barrett Deems (drums), Edmond Hall (clarinet), Billy Kyle (piano), Arvell Shaw (double bass) and Trummy Young (trombone).

Date	Pos	Wks	ARTIST / Record Title *Label & Number*
27 Nov 56	-	1	1. NOW YOU HAS JAZZ *Capitol CL(I) 14643*

The CRYSTALS 13 weeks

Female vocal group formed in Brooklyn, New York, USA in 1960. Discovered by 'wall of sound' producer Phil Spector. Personnel: Dolores 'Dee Dee' Kenniebrew, Barbara Alston, Mary Thomas, Myrna Girard and Patricia 'Patsy' Wright. Signed to Philles Records. Disc debut: *There's No Other Like My Baby* (1961). Myrna Girard left in 1962, replaced by Dolores 'La La' Brooks, who took over as lead vocals from Barbara Alston. Mary Thomas left in 1963. Patsy Wright left in 1964, replaced by Frances Collins. In late 1964 left Philles to sign with United Artists. Barbara Alston left in late 1964. Group disbanded in 1967. Reunited in 1971 (Dee Dee, Mary and La La). Stayed together until 1973. Dee Dee Kenniebrew continues to keep the group name alive on the touring front. On several of the hits no member of group performed. Darlene Love was lead vocals on *He's A Rebel* and *He's Sure The Boy I Love.* La La Brooks, lead vocals on *Da Doo Ron Ron* and *Then He Kissed Me.* Barbara Alston's biography, *There's No Other*, published in 2007.

Date	Pos	Wks	ARTIST / Record Title *Label & Number*
05 Aug 63	3	6	1. DA DOO RON RON *London HLU 9732*
14 Oct 63	3	7	2. THEN HE KISSED ME *London HLU 9773*

Date	Pos	Wks	ARTIST / Record Title *Label & Number*

Joe CUDDY — *41 Weeks*

Born on March 4, 1942 in Sutton, Dublin, Ireland. Began his singing career as a member of his school choir at St. Fintan's Christian Brothers School in Sutton. Continued singing at the Redemptorist College in Limerick. On leaving college he joined his local church choir. Out of this was born the Michael O'Connell Singers who appeared on radio and TV and various recording sessions. Started on the cabaret scene in Dublin in 1966 while working as a butcher by day. In 1966, decided to pack in his day job and concentrate on a full time career in showbusiness with a cabaret season at the Grand Hotel, Malahide, Dublin. Went professional in 1970. Signed to Rex Records he made his disc debut in 1972 with *Sticks And Stones*. Won the 1973 Castlebar International Song Contest performing, *I'm Gonna Make It*, which was composed by Vince Hill. Won an RMI Award in 1973. In March 1974, won a heat on ITV's *Opportunity Knocks*. Appeared in the 1991 film, *Hear My Song*.

Date	Pos	Wks	ARTIST / Record Title *Label & Number*
13 Dec 73	1(2)	11	•1. I'M GONNA MAKE IT *Rex R 11086*
04 Apr 74	1(5)	18	•2. ANY DREAM WILL DO *Rex R 11090*
18 Mar 76	2	12	3. DON'T LET LIFE GET YOU DOWN *Rex R 11109*

The CUFF LINKS — *4 Weeks*

Studio creation put together by songwriters Paul Vance and Lee Pockriss who hired Ron Dante, the singing voice of the Archies, to record one of their songs *Tracy*. Dante promised that if *Tracy* was successful he would record an album as the Cuff Links. Following the success of *Tracy*, Vance and Pockriss put together a seven piece touring group to go out on the road as the Cuff Links. Personnel: Joe Cord (lead vocals), Pat Rizzo (sax, flute), Rich Dimino (organ), Bob Gill (trumpet), Dave Lavender (guitar), Andrew 'Jr' Denno (bass) and Danny Valentine (drums).

continues over

Date	Pos	Wks	ARTIST / Record Title *Label & Number*
			Ron Dante was also lead vocal on UK hit single *When Julie Comes Around.* Joe Cord was lead vocal on single, *Run Sally Run.*
15 Jan 70	6	4	1. TRACY *MCA MU 1101*
			See also The Archies

Larry CUNNINGHAM *73 Weeks*

Born on February 13, 1938 in Mullinalaghta, Granard, Co. Longford, Ireland. Began musical career with Grafton Showband. In 1960 was approached by members of St. Bridget's Ceili Band to join them as lead singer and baritone saxophone player, in a new showband (the Mighty Avons) they were launching. Disc debut: *Tribute To Jim Reeves* (1964). First Irish showband artist to make British singles chart., when *Tribute To Jim Reeves* made it to number forty in December 1964. Cunningham left Avons in August 1969 to form his own band, the Country Blue Boys. In October 1973, travelled to Nashville to record the album, *Good Old Country Music.* Teamed up with Margo in 1975-76. His biography, *A Showband Legend,* published in 2009.

Date	Pos	Wks	ARTIST / Record Title *Label & Number*
11 Jan 65	9	1	1. TRIBUTE TO JIM REEVES *King KG 1016*
27 May 65	4	9	2. I GUESS I'M CRAZY *King KG 1020*
22 Nov 65	5	6	3. THERE'S THAT SMILE AGAIN *King KG 1030*
03 Jan 66	1(2)	9	• 4. LOVELY LEITRIM *King KG 1030*
09 May 66	2	7	5. AMONG THE WICKLOW HILLS *King KG 1034*
28 Nov 66	2	6	6. SNOWFLAKE *King KG 1046*
09 Mar 67	5	5	7. FOOLS PARADISE *King KG 1053*
24 Aug 67	8	5	8. THREE STEPS TO THE PHONE *King KG 1061*
11 Apr 68	10	1	9. THE EMIGRANT *King KG 1073*
30 Oct 69	10	1	10. BALLAD OF JAMES CONNOLLY/ PRETTY LITTLE GIRL FROM OMAGH *Release RL 524*
29 Jan 70	7	1	11. DON'T LET ME CROSS OVER *Release RL 529*
23 Dec 71	1(1)	7	• 12. SLANEY VALLEY *Release RL 608*
26 Apr 73	5	3	13. GOODBYE COMES HARD TO ME *Release RL 667*

continues over

Date	Pos	Wks	ARTIST / Record Title *Label & Number*
14 Feb 74	3	4	14. THIS TIME OF THE YEAR *Release RL 712*
17 Jul 75	3	7	15. MY KATHLEEN *Release RL 775*
07 Oct 76	9	1	16. ANNAGHDOWN *Release RL 836*

See also Larry and Margo

CUPID'S INSPIRATION *2 Weeks*

Group from Stanford, Lincolnshire, England. Personnel: Terry Rice-Milton (lead vocals), Laughton James (bass), Wyndham George (lead guitar), Roger Gray (drums) and Garfield Tomkin (piano). Terry Rice-Milton left the group in 1970, to pursue a solo career. Replaced by Martin Cure.

Date	Pos	Wks	ARTIST / Record Title *Label & Number*
25 Jul 68	5	2	1. YESTERDAY HAS GONE *CBS 56-3500*

D.J. CURTIN and the KERRY BLUES *12 Weeks*

Born Denis Joseph Curtin on February 22, 1945 in Tralee, Co. Kerry, Ireland. Joined the Derek Joys Showband in 1964, as vocalist/tenor sax player. Formed the Kerry Blues in 1965. Resident group at the Mount Brandon Hotel, Tralee, until 1967 when they turned pro and embarked on showband circuit. Personnel: D.J. (lead vocals), Tommy O'Connor (bass), Alfie Curtin (guitar), Tommy Griffin (drums), Johnny Wall (guitar), Bernie O'Connor (trumpet) and John Curtin (tenor sax). Disc debut: *My Elusive Dreams* (1968). In January 1978, D.J. decided to leave the Kerry Blues and join Brendan Bowyer and the Big 8.

Date	Pos	Wks	ARTIST / Record Title *Label & Number*
11 Oct 73	3	7	1. ALMOST PERSUADED *Release RL 693*
16 May 74	7	4	2. LOSING YOU *THE THE 101*
15 Sep 77	9	1	3. NOREEN BAWN *Release RL 885*

Date	Pos	Wks	ARTIST / Record Title *Label & Number*
			Glen CURTIN ***4 Weeks***
			Born Harry Curtin on April 2, 1943 in Cork, Ireland. Moved to England with his family at the age of thirteen. Formed a group with his sister and brother called The Nomads. In 1972, while on holiday in Cork was asked to front a new band, Xanadu. Disc debut: *Little Children* (1972). Joined the New Blues as lead vocalist in April 1972. Moved to the Nevada showband in July 1974 to replace Red Hurley. In September 1975 formed his own band, Galaxy. The following year he became only Irish artist to win a heat on ITV's *New Faces* talent show. Relocated to the USA in 1980. Died on September 20, 2009.
31 Jan 74	7	3	1. I'D LOVE YOU TO WANT ME *Polydor 2078 041*
08 Sep 77	10	1	2. ME AND THE ELEPHANT *Release RL 881*

Date	Pos	Wks	ARTIST / Record Title *Label & Number*

D

Roger DALTREY ***1 Weeks***

Born on March 1, 1944 in Hammersmith, London, England. Formed a skiffle group called The Detours who evolved into The Who. Lead vocalist with the Who from 1962. Embarked on various solo projects during the 70's. Released his first solo album, *Daltrey,* in 1973. Film appearances include *Tommy* (1975), *Lisztomania* (1975) and *McVicar* (1980). In 2004, was awarded a OBE for services to music and charity. *Giving It All Away* composed by Leo Sayer.

Date	Pos	Wks	ARTIST / Record Title *Label & Number*
31 May 73	10	1	1. GIVING IT ALL AWAY *Track 2094 110*

See also The Who

Vic DAMONE ***11 Weeks***

Born Vito Rocco Farinola on June 12, 1928 in Brooklyn, New York, USA. While working as a part time usher at New York's Paramount Theatre Perry Como heard him singing and encouraged him in his ambitions to be a singer. A winning appearance on Arthur Godfrey's Talent Scouts programme resulted in Vic coming to the attention of Mercury Records founder Berle Adams. Disc debut: *I Have But One Heart* (1947). Adopted his mothers maiden name as his stage name. In late 1955, signed to Columbia Records. Film appearances include *Rich Young And Pretty* (1951), *Hit The Deck* (1955) and *Kismet* (1955).

Date	Pos	Wks	ARTIST / Record Title *Label & Number*
07 Jan 58	-	2	1. AN AFFAIR TO REMEMBER *Philips EPB 745*
15 May 58	-	6	2. ON THE STREET WHERE YOU LIVE *Philips EPB 819*
17 Sep 58	-	1	3. ONLY MAN ON THE ISLAND *Philips EPB 837*
12 Feb 59	7	2	4. GIGI *Philips EPB 889*

Date	Pos	Wks	ARTIST / Record Title *Label & Number*

DANA — *32 Weeks*

Born Rosemary Brown on August 30, 1951 in London, England. Family relocated to Derry, N. Ireland. Made her first public appearance age of six in a local talent contest at St. Columbs Hall in Derry, singing an Irish lullaby she had learned from her grandmother. In 1967, sent a tape of some songs she had written, to Michael Geogheghan, head of Rex Records. Suitably impressed he signed her to a recording contract. Disc debut: *Sixteen* (1968). Represented Ireland in the 1970 Eurovision Song Contest, winning with *All Kinds Of Everything.* Married Damian Scallon on October 5, 1978. Appeared in the 1971 film, *Flight Of The Doves*. Inspired by the visit of Pope John Paul 11 to Ireland in 1979, to write (with her husband) the song, *Totus Tous*. Moved to the USA in 1987. In the 1990's she entered the political arena, running unsuccessfully for the Presidency of Ireland in 1997. Two years later, she successfully contested the Connaught Ulster Constituency in the European elections, being elected an MEP. Her autobiography, *All Kinds Of Everything*, published in 2007. Paul Ryan, of Paul and Barry Ryan pop duo, wrote *Who Put the Lights Out*.

Date	Pos	Wks	ARTIST / Record Title *Label & Number*
26 Mar 70	1(9)	11	• 1. ALL KINDS OF EVERYTHING *Rex R 11054*
04 Mar 71	5	6	2. WHO PUT THE LIGHTS OUT *Rex R 11062*
20 Dec 73	4	6	3. SUNDAY MONDAY TUESDAY *Rex R 11087*
21 Nov 74	7	5	4. PLEASE TELL HIM THAT I SAID HELLO *Polydor GT 6*
01 Jan 76	3	4	5. IT'S GOING TO BE A COLD COLD CHRISTMAS *GTO GT 45*

Mike DANIELS — *1 Weeks*

Trumpeter and band leader. Born on April 13, 1928 in Stanmore, England. Formed his own band in the late 1940's. Now fronts the Delta Jazzmen.

Date	Pos	Wks	ARTIST / Record Title *Label & Number*
09 Apr 59	10	1	1. HIAWATHA • *Parlophone R(I) 4285*

Date	Pos	Wks	ARTIST / Record Title *Label & Number*

Roly DANIELS — *37 Weeks*

Born on May 1, 1942 in Jahalpur, India. Came to England in 1961 and quickly picked up on a recording contract with Parlophone. Disc debut: *Bella Bella Marie* (1961). In 1962, signed by Decca who issued a single, *Yo-Yo Boy*, under the name, Rolly Yo Yo Daniels. A regular on many of the pop package tours of the UK, appearing on same bill as Johnny Burnette, U.S. Bonds, Gene McDaniels, Mark Wynter etc. In late 1964, received an offer to front the Irish based Memphis Showband. On 24 January 1965, made his Irish debut with the band. A move to the Jim Farley Showband followed in October 1965. The Nevada Showband signed him as lead singer in December 1967. A recording contract with CBS followed. In January 1971, formed Green County.

Date	Pos	Wks	ARTIST / Record Title *Label & Number*
18 Jul 66	9	1	1. THROW A LITTLE LOVING *Emerald MD 1051*
07 Aug 69	10	1	2. ANGEL SHE WAS LOVE *CBS 4297*
20 Jan 72	2	8	3. HELLO DARLING *Release RL 609*
14 Dec 72	6	6	4. DON'T FORGET TO SAY I LOVE YOU *Release RL 653*
21 Jun 73	4	11	5. FUNNY FACE *Release RL 680*
21 Mar 74	2	8	6. THE MOST BEAUTIFUL GIRL *Release RL 723*
10 Jun 76	9	1	7. WHERE LOVE BEGINS *Release RL 809*
23 Jun 77	10	1	8. THINKIN' OF A RENDEVOUZ *Kim KM 001*

Johnny DANKWORTH and his Orchestra — *1 Weeks*

Born on September 20, 1927 in London, England. Enrolled at the Royal Academy of Music in London at the age of 17, where he studied the saxophone. Disc debut: *Ladybird* (1948) on Esquire label. In 1950, formed the Johnny Dankworth Seven (with himself on alto sax and clarinet). Formed big band in 1953. From 1949 to 1955 voted Musician of the Year in the Melody Maker Jazz Poll. On July 3, 1959 performed at America's Newport Jazz Festival. Married his band's vocalist, Cleo Laine, in 1958.

continues over

Date	Pos	Wks	ARTIST / Record Title *Label & Number*
			Composed film scores for *Saturday Night and Sunday Morning*, *The Servant* and *Modesty Blaise*. Received a CBE in 2006 for his services to music.
21 Aug 56	-	1	1. EXPERIMENTS WITH MICE • *Parlophone DIP 231*

Bobby DARIN *60 Weeks*

Born Walden Robert Cassotto on May 14, 1936 in the Bronx, New York, USA. Made his first recordings with The Jaybirds in 1956. Signed to Atlantic Records in 1957. In 1960, he married actress Sandra Dee. Film appearances include *State Fair* (1962), *If A Man Answers* (1962) and *Captain Newman MD* (1963), for which he received an Academy Award nomination for Best Supporting Actor. Died of heart failure on December 20, 1973 in Los Angeles, California at the age of 37. *Beyond The Sea* a bio-pic starring Kevin Spacey (as Darin), was released in 2004.

Date	Pos	Wks	ARTIST / Record Title *Label & Number*
09 Jul 59	1(2)	10	• 1. DREAM LOVER *London HLE 8867*
29 Oct 59	1(3)	14	• 2. MACK THE KNIFE *London HLK 8939*
11 Feb 60	5	7	3. LA MER (Beyond The Sea) *London HLE 9034*
06 Apr 61	2	8	4. LAZY RIVER *London HLK 9303*
23 Nov 61	2	9	5. YOU MUST HAVE BEEN A BEAUTIFUL BABY *London HLK 9429*
25 Jan 62	3	4	6. MULTIPLICATION *London HLK 9474*
23 Aug 62	2	7	7. THINGS *London HLK 9575*
01 Jul 63	10	1	8. EIGHTEEN YELLOW ROSES *Capitol CL(I) 15306*

DARTS *19 Weeks*

Doo wop revival group formed in London in 1976. Personnel: Den Hegarty (vocals), Rita Ray (vocals), Griff Fender (vocals), Bob Fish (vocals), George Currie (lead guitar), Hammy Howell (piano), Ian 'Thump' Thompson (bass), Horatio Hornblower (saxophone) and John Drummer (drums). Following an appearance on Charlie Gillet's radio show, *Honky Tonk Demo's*, in October 1976 the band with help from Charlie signed to Magnet in 1977.

continues over

Date	Pos	Wks	ARTIST / Record Title *Label & Number*

Disc debut: *Daddy Cool/The Girl Can't Help It.* Den Hegarty left in late 1978, replaced by Kenny Andrews. Hammy Howell left in 1978. John Dummer, George Currie and Bob Fish left in 1980. In 1983, the group moved into the West End theatre appearing in *Yakety Yak*, a musical based on the songs of Leiber and Stoller. Following the West End run the group embarked on a theatre tour of Britain and Ireland with the musical. Group disbanded in 1985.

Date	Pos	Wks	ARTIST / Record Title *Label & Number*
08 Dec 77	10	4	1. DADDY COOL - THE GIRL CAN'T HELP IT *Magnet MAG 100*
09 Mar 78	7	2	2. COME BACK MY LOVE *Magnet MAG 110*
25 May 78	3	3	3. THE BOY FROM NEW YORK CITY *Magnet MAG 116*
03 Aug 78	2	6	4. IT'S RAINING *Magnet MAG 126*
22 Feb 79	9	2	5. GET IT *Magnet MAG 140*
06 Sep 79	10	2	6. DUKE OF EARL *Magnet MAG 147*

Shaun DAVEY — *1 Weeks*

Composer/musician. Born in 1947in Belfast, N. Ireland. After finishing school moved to Dublin. Graduated from Trinity college in 1971 with an MA in history, a subject he taught in Trinity College and at the College of Art in Dublin. Music credits include TV and film scores for for *Waking Ned*, *Twelfth Night* and *Ballykissangel*. Received an Ivor Novello Novello Award for his score for his score for the BBC mini-series, *The Hanging Gale*. Received international recognition for his work *Brendan Voyage* (1982) and *Granuaile* (1985). *Pride Of The Herd* started out as a piece of music specially written by Shaun Davey for a television and radio advertising campaign by the National Dairy Council of Ireland.

Date	Pos	Wks	ARTIST / Record Title *Label & Number*
07 Dec 78	7	1	1. PRIDE OF THE HERD *CBS CBS 6816*

Anne-Marie DAVID — *5 Weeks*

Born on May 23, 1952 in France. First came to national prominence via her appearance as Mary Magdalene in the 1972 stage production of *Jesus Christ Superstar.*

continues over

Date	Pos	Wks	ARTIST / Record Title *Label & Number*

Represented Luxembourg in the 1973 Eurovision Song Contest and won with song titled *Tu Te Reconnaitras*. The song was re-recorded in English under the title, *Wonderful Dream*. In 1979, she represented France in the Eurovision Song Contest performing *Je Suis l'enfant Soleil*. Retired in 1987.

Date	Pos	Wks	ARTIST / Record Title *Label & Number*
10 May 73	3	5	1. WONDERFUL DREAM *Epic EPC 1446*

Dave DAVIES — *5 Weeks*

Born David Russell Gordon Davies on February 3, 1947 in Muswell Hill, London England. Founder member of The Kinks. Solo debut disc: *Death Of A Clown*. Composed music score for the 1995 film remake of, *Village Of The Damned*. His autobiography, *Kink - An Autobiography*, published in 1996. Suffered a stroke in June 2004.

Date	Pos	Wks	ARTIST / Record Title *Label & Number*
17 Aug 67	6	5	1. DEATH OF A CLOWN *Pye 7N 17356*

The Spencer DAVIS GROUP — *9 Weeks*

Formed in Birmingham, England in April 1963. Personnel: Spencer Davis (vocals, rhythm guitar; Stevie Winwood (born May 12, 1948 in Birmingham, lead vocals, keyboards), Muff Winwood (bass) and Pete York (drums). Stevie Winwood left in 1967 to form Traffic. Muff Winwood lef t the group the same year. Replaced by Eddie Hardin (organ/vocal) and Phil Sawyer (guitar/vocal). Ray Fenwick replaced Sawyer in 1968. Disbanded in 1969.

Date	Pos	Wks	ARTIST / Record Title *Label & Number*
10 Jan 66	3	5	1. KEEP ON RUNNING *Fontana ETF 632*
18 Apr 66	5	2	2. SOMEBODY HELP ME *Fontana ETF 679*
28 Nov 66	7	2	3. GIMME SOME LOVING *Fontana ETF 762*

See also Traffic

DAWN — *28 Weeks*

Vocal trio formed in 1970 in New York City, USA. Personnel: Tony Orlando (born Michael Cassavitis on April 3, 1944 in New York City, lead vocals), Telma Hopkins and Joyce Vincent.

continues over

Date	Pos	Wks	ARTIST / Record Title *Label & Number*
			Orlando enjoyed solo success during the 1960's. Dawn had own television show during the years 1974-76. Disbanded in July 1977. Reformed in 1988.
20 May 71	3	6	1. KNOCK THREE TIMES *Columbia BELL 1146*
26 Aug 71	1(1)	7	•2. WHAT ARE YOU DOING SUNDAY *Columbia BELL 1169*
05 Apr 73	1(6)	12	•3. TIE A YELLOW RIBBON ROUND THE OLE OAK TREE *Bell 1287*
06 Sep 73	8	3	4. SAY, HAS ANYBODY SEEN MY SWEET GYPSY ROSE *Bell 1322*

Johnny DAWSON — *4 Weeks*

Born on August 29, 1953 in Athlone, Co. Westmeath, Ireland. Learned piano at a young age. While still at school formed a group with some friends, called The Pyramids. Also worked at the local Prince of Wales Hotel entertaining American tourists during the summer months dressing up as a leprechaun. After leaving school joined the Ciaran Kelly Ceili Band. In 1969, was invited to join the Brendan Shine Country Band, as drummer/ vocalist. Eurovision winning songwriter, Shay Healy, wrote *I'm Little But There's Lots Of Me To Love.*

Date	Pos	Wks	ARTIST / Record Title *Label & Number*
21 Mar 74	5	4	1. I'M LITTLE BUT THERE'S LOTS OF ME TO LOVE *Play 72*

See also Brendan Shine Superband

Doris DAY — *12 Weeks*

Born Doris Mary Ann Von Kappelhoff on April 3, 1924 in Cincinnati, Ohio, USA. Her dream of becoming a dancer was dashed when she was involved in a car accident. Started taking singing lessons and performing with local bands. Made breakthrough in 1944 when she recorded *Sentimental Journey* with the Les Brown Band. Launched her solo career in 1947. Made her film debut in the 1948 film *Romance On The High Seas*. Other film appearances include *Calamity Jane* (1953), *Pyjama Game* (1957) and *Pillow Talk* (1959). Made her television debut in *The Doris Day Show*, a comedy series that ran from 1968 to 1973.

continues over

Date	Pos	Wks	ARTIST / Record Title *Label & Number*
			On retiring from the world of showbusiness she moved to Carmel, California and decided to dedicate her life to animal welfare, founding the Doris Day Animal Foundation and the Doris Day Animal League. In 1991 she received a Lifetime Achievement Award from the American Comedy Awards. *Whatever Will Be Will Be* was featured in the 1956 film, *The Man Who Knew Too Much.*
04 Jan 55	-	1	1. BLUEBELLS OF BROADWAY *Philips PB 295*
18 Jan 55	-	1	2. IF I GIVE MY HEART TO YOU *Philips PB 325*
19 Jun 56	-	8	3. WHATEVER WILL BE WILL BE (QUE SERA SERA) *Philips PB 586*
16 Apr 58	-	2	4. TEACHER'S PET *Philips EPB 799*

Muriel DAY — *7 Weeks*

Born Muriel Galway on January 11, 1942 in Newtownards, County Down. N. Ireland. Big break happened when Peter Leigh signed her for a series of cabaret dates in England. Performed the song *Twisterella* in the 1963 film *Billy Liar.* Represented Ireland in the 1969 Eurovision Song Contest with *Wages of Love*, finishing in 7th place. Vocalist with Dave Glover Showband 1965-1969.

Date	Pos	Wks	ARTIST / Record Title *Label & Number*
20 Mar 69	1(1)	7	• 1. WAGES OF LOVE *Dolphin DOS 28*

DEAD END KIDS — *7 Weeks*

Formed in Ayrshire, Scotland in 1976. Originally known as Vehicle the new name was suggested by the bass player's mum. Personnel: Robbie Gray (vocals), Alistair Kerr (bass), Colin Ivory (guitar), Davey Johnston (keyboards) and Ricky Squires (drums). Big break arrived when asked to support Bay City Rollers on their 1976 UK tour. The groups debut disc, *Have I The Right*, was a revamp of the Honeycombs 1964 number one hit.

Date	Pos	Wks	ARTIST / Record Title *Label & Number*
12 May 77	1(2)	7	• 1. HAVE I THE RIGHT *CBS SCBS 4972*

Date	Pos	Wks	ARTIST / Record Title *Label & Number*

Chris DE BURGH ***7 Weeks***

Born Christopher John Davison on October 15, 1948 in Buenos Aires, Argentina. Relocated to Ireland with his family in 1960. Began composing songs while studying at Trinity College, Dublin. Moved to London in 1971 and began performing in clubs and doing the rounds of the music companies. Adopted his mothers maiden surname (Maeve Emily de Burgh) as his stage name. Signed to A&M Records in 1974. Disc debut: *Hold On* (1975). His daughter, Rosanna Davidson, won the Miss World title in 2003.

06 Jan 77	3	7	1. A SPACEMAN CAME TRAVELLING *A&M AMS 7267*

DE MARCO SISTERS ***1 Weeks***

Family vocal group formed in Brooklyn, New York, USA. The five DeMarco sisters, Anne, Gina, Gloria, Terri and Arlene, began singing together at a very young age. Spotted by arranger/conductor Gordon Jenkins singing in an elevator. Impressed with their harmony he introduced them to Fred Allen, who signed them up his radio show. The girls spent four years with Allen. Appeared in the 1958 film *Skirts Ahoy*. Split in 1955 to pursue solo careers. Gloria died in 1997. Terri died in 1999. Anne died in 2004.

21 Jun 55	-	1	1. DREAMBOAT *Brunswick 05425*

Lynsey DE PAUL ***1 Weeks***

Born Lynsey Rubin on June 11, 1950 in London, England. Worked as a graphic designer before starting her musical career. Composed hit songs for The Fortunes *Storm In A Teacup*, Dana *Crossword Puzzle* and Barry Blue *Dancing On A Saturday Night*. Won Ivor Novello Award, Best Ballad, for *Won't Somebody Dance With Me*, in 1973. The following year she picked up the Ivor Novello Award for Best Theme, *No Honestly*. In 1977, formed duo with musician/producer/keyboard player, Mike Moran.

continues over

Date	Pos	Wks	ARTIST / Record Title *Label & Number*

They performed and co-wrote the UK's 1977 Eurovision Song Contest entry, Rock Bottom, finishing in second position.

06 Dec 73	9	1	1. WON'T SOMEBODY DANCE WITH ME *Mam MAM 109*

Lynsey DE PAUL and Mike MORAN **2 Weeks**

Female/male vocal duo. Formed in London, England in 1977 to participate in the 1977 Eurovision Song Contest. Performed their own song, *Rock Bottom*, finishing in second position. Lyndsey De Paul born Lynsey Rubin on June 11, 1950 in London, England. Mike Moran began his musical career studying at the Royal College of Music. Has worked with many international stars including Paul McCartney, Cliff Richard, Paul Simon and Kate Bush. Co-wrote *Barcelona* with Freddie Mercury. Has composed music for several films including *Time Bandits* (1981), *Death Wish 3* (1985) and *Whoops Apocalypse* (1986).

19 May 77	7	2	1. ROCK BOTTOM *Polydor 2058 859*

Stephanie DE SYKES **2 Weeks**

Born Stephanie Ryton in 1948. Spotted by Len Beadle who saw her on *Opportunity Knocks* in 1974. In 1974 played the role of Holly Brown in the television soap, *Crossroads*. Appeared in the 1975 film, *Side By Side*. Co-wrote the UK's 1978 Eurovision Song Contest entry, *Bad Old Days*. Performed by Co Co it finished in eleventh position. Also co-wrote the 1980 entry, *Love Enough For Two*. Performed by Prima Donna, it finished in third position.

08 Aug 74	6	2	1. BORN WITH A SMILE ON MY FACE *Pye BRAD 7409*

Derek DEAN and the FRESHMEN **2 Weeks**

Born Derek McMenamin on March 3, 1943 in Ballyshannon, Co. Donegal, Ireland. Moved to Strabane, Co. Tyrone in 1947. Interested in singing from an early age.

continues over

Date	Pos	Wks	ARTIST / Record Title *Label & Number*

Made his public debut at a concert in Strabane, at the age of twelve. Attended St Joseph's Teacher Training College in Belfast. During this time formed a beat group. In 1963, approached by members of the Freshmen, who offered him a position in the band as lead vocalist. Left the band after six months, to return to college to take his teachers diploma. Returned to Freshmen in mid 1964. Disc debut: *I Stand Alone* (1965). Derek's account of his life and times with the band can be found in his book, *The Freshmen Unzipped,* published in 2007.

25 Oct 65	10	2	**1. LA YENKA** *Pye 7N 15964*

See also Billy Brown; The Freshmen

Jimmy DEAN — *5 Weeks*

Born Jimmy Ray Dean on August 10, 1928 in Olton, Texas, USA. Had his first country hit in 1953 with, *Bummin' Around*, on the 4-Star label. Formed own group The Texas Wildcats in the early 1950's. In April 1957 signed to Columbia Records. *Big Bad John* was a number one hit on both the Country and Pop charts in the USA.

16 Nov 61	3	5	**1. BIG BAD JOHN** *Philips EPB 1187*

Alan DEE and the CHESSMEN — *4 Weeks*

Irish showband. Alan Dee born Alan Donaldson in 1944 in Dublin, Ireland. Wrote stage musical *Adam and Eve.* It was staged in the State Theatre, Dublin in 1976, with Colm Wilkinson, in the role of the Devil. Alan Dee left Chessmen in 1966. Replaced by Ricky Valance (of *Tell Laura I Love Her* fame). Chessmen formed in 1963 in Dublin. Had operated as a beat group before joining the showband circuit. Personnel: Alan Dee (vocals, organ), Willie Halpin (lead guitar), Bobby Balla (bass), Terry Brady (drums), Paschal Haverty (tenor sax), John L. Sullivan (baritone sax) and Davey Martin (trumpet). Disbanded in 1971. Paschal Haverty died on March 14, 2008.

01 Aug 66	5	4	**1. MICHAEL MURPHY'S BOY** *Pye 7N 17142*

Date	Pos	Wks	ARTIST / Record Title *Label & Number*

Dave DEE,
DOZY, BEAKY, MICK and TICH *19 Weeks*

Formed in 1961 in Salisbury, England as Dave Dee and The Bostons. A meeting with The Honeycombs management team of Ken Howard and Alan Blaikley resulted in a change of name and a recording contract with Fontana. Personnel: Dave Dee (born David Harman on December 17, 1941 in Salisbury, lead vocals), Dozy (born Trevor Davies, bass), Beaky (born John Dymond, guitar), Mick (born Mick Wilson, drums) and Tich (born Ian Amey, guitar). Dave Dee left in 1969 to pursue a solo career. Dozy, Beaky, Mick and Tich continued until 1972. Reformed in the 1990's. Dave Dee died January 9, 2009.

Date	Pos	Wks	ARTIST / Record Title *Label & Number*
11 Jul 66	10	1	1. HIDEAWAY *Fontana ETF 711*
10 Oct 66	3	4	2. BEND IT! Fontana *ETF 746*
05 Jan 67	4	4	3. SAVE ME *Fontana ETF 775*
06 Jul 67	7	2	4. OKAY! *Fontana ETF 830*
23 Nov 67	7	1	5. ZABADAK *Fontana ETF 873*
07 Mar 68	1(1)	7	• 6. THE LEGEND OF XANADU *Fontana ETF 903*

Tommy DEE *2 Weeks*

Born Thomas Donaldson on July 15, 1936 in Vicker, Virginia, USA. Worked as a deejay at radio station KFXM in San Bernardino, California. Composed *Three Stars* as a tribute to Buddy Holly, Ritchie Valens and The Big Bopper, who died in a plane crash on February 3, 1959. Narration by Tommy Dee with vocals by Carol Kaye and the Teen Aires. In the 1970's became a country music promoter. Died on January 26, 2007.

Date	Pos	Wks	ARTIST / Record Title *Label & Number*
18 Jun 59	5	2	1. THREE STARS *Melodisc 1516*

DEEP PURPLE *8 Weeks*

Formed in London, England in 1968 under the name Roundabout. Changed name to Deep Purple later that year.

continues over

Date	Pos	Wks	ARTIST / Record Title *Label & Number*

Personnel: Ritchie Blackmore (guitar), Jon Lord (keyboards), Roger Glover (bass) and Ian Gillen (vocals). Signed to EMI's Harvest label in May 1968. Gillian and Glover left in 1973, replaced by David Coverdale and Glenn Hughes. Blackmore quit in 1975 to form Rainbow.

Date	Pos	Wks	ARTIST / Record Title *Label & Number*
01 Oct 70	4	8	1. BLACK NIGHT *Harvest HAR 5020*

Rick DEES and his CAST OF IDIOTS 1 Weeks

Born Rigdon Osmond Dees on March 14, 1950 in Jacksonville, Florida, USA. Working as a radio DJ, when he thought up idea for *Disco Duck*. It reached the number one spot in the USA. Inducted into the Radio Hall of Fame in 1999.

Date	Pos	Wks	ARTIST / Record Title *Label & Number*
21 Oct 76	10	1	1. DISCO DUCK *RSO 2090 204*

Desmond DEKKER and the ACES 7 Weeks

Born Desmond Dacres on July 16, 1941 in Kingston, Jamaica. Made disc debut in 1963 with *Honour Your Father And Mother.* Teamed up with his backing group, The Aces, in late 1963, and enjoyed spectacular success in Jamaica. The Aces: Steve Roberts (guitar), Aubrey Mulrain (keyboards), Ian Austin (bass), Gordon Mulrain (drums) and Delroy Williams (backing vocals / MC). Relocated to England in 1969. Died from a heart attack on May 25, 2006

Date	Pos	Wks	ARTIST / Record Title *Label & Number*
08 May 69	7	2	1. ISRAELITES *Pyramid PYR 6058*
08 Oct 70	4	5	2. YOU CAN GET IT IF YOU REALLY WANT IT *TroJan TR 7777*

You Can Get It If You Really Want It credit Desmond Dekker

Eric DELANEY BAND 4 Weeks

Born on May 22, 1924 in London, England. Learned to play drums at a young age. Played to his first live audience at the age of six. From 1947 to 1954 was a member of Geraldo's Orchestra. Formed the Eric Delaney Band in 1954.

Date	Pos	Wks	ARTIST / Record Title *Label & Number*
08 May 56	-	4	1. COCKLES AND MUSSELS • *Nixa N 15046*

Date	Pos	Wks	ARTIST / Record Title *Label & Number*

Terry DENE — *1 Weeks*

Born Terence Williams on December 20, 1938 in London, England. Spotted by producer Jack Good who signed him for a regular slot on the BBC TV hit show *Six-Five Special.* A recording contract with Decca Records quickly followed. Disc debut: *A White Sport Coat* (1957). Starred in the 1958 film, *The Golden Disc.* Married singer Edna Savage on July 8, 1958. In early 1959 received his call-up papers for National Service. Joined the Kings Royal Rifle Corps but within two months was discharged as unfit. By the early sixties his career was over. The eighties saw a revival of interest in Dene, and he built up a reputation as one of Britain's true rock and rollers.

Date	Pos	Wks	ARTIST / Record Title *Label & Number*
29 May 58	-	1	1. STAIRWAY OF LOVE *Decca F 11016*

John DENVER — *9 Weeks*

Born Henry John Deutschendorf on December 31, 1943 in Roswell, New Mexico, USA. Moved to Los Angeles 1963. Lead singer with the Chad Mitchell Trio from 1965 to 1968. His reputation as a songwriter of distinction was recognised when Peter, Paul and Mary took his song, *Leaving On A Jet Plane* to the top of the American charts. Undertook a concert tour of Russia in 1986. In October 1992 toured mainland China. Inducted into the Songwriters Hall of Fame in 1996. Died in a plane crash on October 12, 1997. *Annie's Song* was inspired and composed for Denver's then wife Ann Martell. On November 9, 2005 a new musical, *Almost Heaven: The Songs of John Denver*, got its New York premiere at off-Broadway's Promenade Theatre.

Date	Pos	Wks	ARTIST / Record Title *Label & Number*
19 Sep 74	1(2)	9	• 1. ANNIE'S SONG *RCA APBO 0295*

Karl DENVER — *20 Weeks*

Born Angus Murdo McKenzie on December 16, 1931 in Glasgow, Scotland. Formed the Karl Denver Trio in 1959.

continues over

Date	Pos	Wks	ARTIST / Record Title *Label & Number*
			Personnel: Karl Denver (vocals/guitar), Kevin Neill (guitar) and Gerry Cottrell (bass). Discovered singing in a pub in Manchester by TV and record producer Jack Good, who persuaded Decca to sign him. Appeared in the 1963 film *Just For Fun*. In 1989, invited to sing lead vocals on Happy Mondays recording of *Lazyitis*. Died of brain tumour on December 21, 1998. Gerry Cottrell died on November 24, 2006.
10 Aug 61	5	5	1. MARCHETA *Decca F 11360*
09 Nov 61	4	4	2. MEXICALI ROSE *Decca F 11395*
15 Feb 62	6	4	3. WIMOWEH *Decca F 11420*
26 Apr 62	7	1	4. NEVER GOODBYE *Decca F 11431*
23 Sep 63	3	6	5. STILL *Decca F 11720*

DEREK and the DOMINOS — *1 Weeks*

Formed in London, England in August 1970 when Eric Clapton (guitar/vocals) teamed up with three ex-members of Dealaney and Bonnie's band, Bobby Whitlock (organ/ piano/ vocals), Carl Radle (bass) and Jim Gordon (drums/ piano). Clapton wished to avoid using his own name and billed the band as Derek and the Dominos. Clapton was inspired to write *Layla* by a Persian love story, *The Story of Layla and Majnun*, he had read. Guitarist Duane Allman guested on the recording of *Layla*. Band broke up in 1971. Carl Radle died in 1980.

Date	Pos	Wks	ARTIST / Record Title *Label & Number*
21 Sep 72	10	1	1. LAYLA *Polydor 2058 130*

Neil DIAMOND — *31 Weeks*

Born Neil Leslie Diamond on January 24, 1941 in Brooklyn, New York City, USA. Family moved to Cheyenne, Wyoming in 1945. Moved back to Brooklyn in 1956. In 1962, began working as a songwriter in the Brill Building. One of his first successes, *Ten Lonely Guys*, was recorded by Pat Boone. Disc debut: *What Will I Do* (1962) with Jack Packer as part of a duo, Neil and Jack. Signed to Bang Records in 1966.

continues over

Date	Pos	Wks	ARTIST / Record Title *Label & Number*

Two years later signed recording deal with UNI. Composed music score for 1973 film, *Jonathan Livingston Seagull*. In 1980 starred in a remake of the film, *The Jazz Singer*. Inducted into the Songwriters Hall of Fame in 1984. Made his Irish concert debut in 1984.

Date	Pos	Wks	ARTIST / Record Title *Label & Number*
03 Dec 70	2	12	1. CRACKLIN' ROSE *UNI UNS 529*
18 Mar 71	7	3	2. SWEET CAROLINE *UNI UN 531*
03 Jun 71	1(2)	7	• 3. I AM ... I SAID *UNI UN 532*
23 Dec 76	6	1	4. BEAUTIFUL NOISE *CBS 4601*
12 Jan 78	6	2	5. DESIREE *CBS 5869*
29 Mar 79	4	6	6. FOREVER IN BLUE JEANS *CBS 7047*

See also Barbra and Neil

The DIAMONDS — *2 Weeks*

Vocal group formed in Toronto, Canada in 1953 as the Four Diamonds. Personnel: Dave Somerville (lead vocal), Ted Kowalski (tenor), Phil Levitt (baritone) and Bill Reed (bass). Signed to Coral in 1955. Spotted by Cleveland deejay Bill Randle who got the group a deal with Mercury in 1956. Split in 1961. Bill Reed died on October 22, 2004.

Date	Pos	Wks	ARTIST / Record Title *Label & Number*
30 Jul 57	-	1	1. LITTLE DARLIN' *Mercury MT 148*
05 Mar 58	-	1	2. LAND OF BEAUTY *Mercury MT 195*

DION and the BELMONTS — *12 Weeks*

Formed in New York, USA in 1957. Personnel: Dion (lead vocals), Angelo D'Alea (first tenor), Fred Milano (second tenor) and Carlo Mastrangelo (bass). Disc debut: *We Went Away* (1957). Group took their name from Belmont Avenue in the Bronx. Signed with Laurie Records in 1958. Dion born Dion Di Mucci on July 18, 1939 in the Bronx, New York.. Split from the Belmonts in October 1960. Inducted into the Rock and Roll Hall of Fame in 1989.

Date	Pos	Wks	ARTIST / Record Title *Label & Number*
16 Jul 59	1(2)	12	• 1. A TEENAGER IN LOVE *London HLU 8874*

Date	Pos	Wks	ARTIST / Record Title *Label & Number*
			DIRE STRAITS ***3 Weeks***
			Formed in London, England in June 1977 as the Café Racers. Changed name to Dire Straits for their second gig. Personnel: Mark Knopfler (born August 12, 1949 in Glasgow, Scotland, lead guitar, vocals), David Knopfler (guitar), John Illsley (bass) and Pick Withers (drums). Disc debut: *Sultans Of Swing* (1978). David Knopfler left in July 1980, replaced by Hal Lindes and Alan Clark (keyboards). In September 1983 Terry Williams replaces Pick Withers. Mark Knopfler formed the Notting Hillbillies in 1989.
15 Mar 79	6	3	1. SULTANS OF SWING *Vertigo 6059 206*
			DR FEELGOOD ***1 Weeks***
			Formed in Canvey Island, London in 1971. Personnel: Lee Brilleaux (guitar/vocals), Wilko Johnson (guitar), John B Sparks (bass) and The Big Figure (drums). Took their name from a record by American bluesman, Piano Red. Lee Brilleaux died of throat cancer on April 7, 1994.
22 Feb 79	8	1	1. MILK AND ALCOHOL *United Artists UP 36468*
			DR HOOK ***31 Weeks***
			American group formed in Union City, New Jersey in 1968 as Dr. Hook and the Medicine show. Personnel: Ray Sawyer (guitar/vocals), Dennis Locorriere (guitar/vocals), George Cummings (lead guitar), Billy Francis (keyboards) and Jay David (drums). Shortened name to Dr Hook in 1975 and signed to Capitol Records. Ray Sawyer left in 1982 to pursue a solo career. Disbanded in 1985.
06 Jul 72	1(7)	10	• 1. SYLVIA'S MOTHER *CBS 57929*
05 Aug 76	2	6	2. A LITTLE BIT MORE *Capitol CL 15871*
23 Dec 76	4	2	3. IF NOT YOU *Capitol CL 15885*
11 May 78	5	3	4. MORE LIKE THE MOVIES *Capitol 15967*
25 Oct 79	1(3)	10	• 5. WHEN YOU'RE IN LOVE WITH A BEAUTIFUL WOMAN *Capitol CL 16039*

Sylvia's Mother credit Dr. Hook and the Medicine Show.

Date	Pos	Wks	ARTIST / Record Title *Label & Number*

Ken DODD — *16 Weeks*

Born Kenneth Arthur Dodd on November 8, 1927 in Liverpool, England. Sang in a church choir before developing a comedy act as Professor Yaffle Chuckabutty, Operatic Singer and Sausage Knotter. Became a full time professional comedian in 1954. Made his debut on record as a singer in 1960 with *Love Is Like A Violin* on the Decca label.

Date	Pos	Wks	ARTIST / Record Title *Label & Number*
01 Mar 62	9	1	1. PIANISSIMO *Decca F 114222*
27 Sep 65	1(4)	9	• 2. TEARS *Columbia DB(I) 7659*
20 Dec 65	3	6	3. THE RIVER *Columbia DB(I) 7750*

Joe DOLAN — *126 Weeks*

Born on October 16, 1939 in Mullingar, Co. Westmeath, Ireland. After leaving school, joined the local newspaper, the Westmeath Examiner, as an apprentice compositor. In 1959, with his brother Ben, formed the Drifters Showband. The band received a major boost when Pat Quinn, head of the Quinnsworth Supermarket, employed the band to play relief to the Mighty Rhythm Boys, at the nationwide heats for the 'Miss Quinnsworth' contest. Band turned professional in April 1963. Signed to Pye Records in July 1964. Disc debut: *The Answer To Everything* (1964). In July 1968, faced a major setback when five members of the Drifters handed in their notice. Joe and Ben quickly recruited new members and were back in business. On April 9, 1969, Joe recorded the song that was to change his life. On the suggestion of Geoffrey Everitt, Joe recorded the Hammond and Hazlewood song, *Make Me An Island*, in London. In the mid 1970's, teamed up with Italian songwriter/producer, Roberto Danova and enjoyed international success with many of his recordings. Died on December 26, 2007.

Date	Pos	Wks	ARTIST / Record Title *Label & Number*
14 Sep 64	4	7	1. THE ANSWER TO EVERYTHING *Pye 7N 15681*
08 Feb 65	3	7	2. I LOVE YOU MORE AND MORE EACH DAY *Pye 7N 15760*
26 Jul 65	2	12	3. MY OWN PECULIAR WAY *Pye 7N 15902*

continues over

Date	Pos	Wks	ARTIST / Record Title *Label & Number*
06 Dec 65	2	9	4. ACHING BREAKING HEART *Pye 7N 17003*
30 May 66	10	2	5. TWO OF A KIND E.P. *Pye NEP 24250*
08 Aug 66	1(3)	10	• 6. PRETTY BROWN EYES *Pye 7N 17152*
09 Feb 67	1(1)	8	7. THE HOUSE WITH THE WHITE WASHED GABLE *Pye 7N 17265*
27 Jul 67	3	10	8. TAR AND CEMENT *Pye 7N 17354*
11 Apr 68	8	1	9. LOVE OF THE COMMON PEOPLE *Pye 7N 17484*
22 May 69	2	19	10. MAKE ME AN ISLAND *Pye 7N 17738*
23 Oct 69	1(1)	11	• 11. TERESA *Pye 7N 17833*
12 Feb 70	4	6	12. YOU'RE SUCH A GOOD LOOKING WOMAN *Pye 7N 17891*
13 May 76	1(4)	11	• 13. SISTER MARY *Release RL 811*
18 Aug 77	1(2)	7	• 14. I NEED YOU *Release RL 877*
07 Dec 79	2	6	15. SILENT NIGHT *Release RL 988*

Tracks on **Two Of A Kind EP**: Two Of A Kind / I've Got Five Dollars And It's Saturday Night / I'll Sit On Your Doorstep / Minutes To Midnight / The Jolly Tinker.

Fats DOMINO — *23 Weeks*

Born Antoine Domino Junior on February 26, 1928 in New Orleans, USA. Taught to play piano by local jazz musician Harrison Verrett. Discovered by Imperial Records boss Lew Chudd in 1949. Recorded extensively for Imperial between December 1949 and April 1962. Moved to ABC Paramount in 1962. Film appearances include *The Girl Can't Help It* (1956) and *The Big Beat* (1958). Inducted into the Rock and Roll Hall of Fame in 1986. Also recorded for Mercury, Reprise and Warner Brothers.

Date	Pos	Wks	ARTIST / Record Title *Label & Number*
15 Jan 57	-	1	1. BLUEBERRY HILL *London HLU 8330*
29 Jan 57	-	1	2. HONEY CHILE *London HL 8356*
21 Jan 58	-	1	3. WAIT AND SEE *London HL 8518*
12 Nov 59	6	5	4. I WANT TO WALK YOU HOME *London HLP 8942*
31 Dec 59	2	8	5. BE MY GUEST *London HLP 9005*
07 Apr 60	6	5	6. COUNTRY BOY *London HLP 9073*
05 Apr 62	7	2	7. JAMBALAYA *London HLP 9520*

Date	Pos	Wks	ARTIST / Record Title *Label & Number*
			Lonnie DONEGAN ***73 Weeks***
			Born Anthony James Donegan on April 29, 1931 in Glasgow, Scotland. Family moved to East London while Lonnie was still a child. Bought his first guitar at the age of fourteen. In 1951, following a period of National service in the British Army, he formed the Tony Donegan Jazz Band. In 1952, he adopted the Christian name of his idol, blues singer Lonnie Johnson. Joined the Chris Barber Jazz Band in 1953. The following year, at a Decca recording session recorded, *Rock Island Line*, as a contribution to the band's L.P. In late 1955 *Rock Island Line* began to get radio play from Jack Jackson and Eamonn Andrews and in response to demand, Decca issued it as a single. It provided Lonnie with his first chart hit in Britain and the USA. In 1956, Lonnie departed from the Chris Barber Band, and formed his own Skiffle group and signed to the Pye-Nixa label. *Nobody Loves Like An Irishman* was launched at a reception in Belfast. Died on November 4, 2002.
17 Jul 56	-	2	1. LOST JOHN *Nixa N 15036*
17 Oct 56	-	1	2. DEAD OR ALIVE *Nixa N 15071*
27 Feb 57	-	2	3. DON'T YOU ROCK ME DADDY-O *Nixa N 15080*
07 May 57	-	2	4. CUMBERLAND GAP *Nixa N 15087*
16 Jul 57	-	5	5. PUTTIN' ON THE STYLE *Nixa N 15093*
30 Jul 57	-	2	6. GAMBLIN' MAN *Nixa N 15093*
23 Oct 57	-	5	7. MY DIXIE DARLING *Nixa N 15108*
21 Jan 58	-	3	8. JACK O' DIAMONDS *Nixa N 15116*
01 May 58	-	3	9. NOBODY LOVES LIKE AN IRISH MAN *Nixa N 15129*
11 Jun 58	-	5	10. GRAND COOLIE DAM *Nixa N 15129*
07 Aug 58	-	1	11. SALLY DON'T YOU GRIEVE *Nixa N 15148*
05 Mar 59	5	7	12. DOES YOUR CHEWING GUM LOSE ITS FLAVOUR (ON THE BEDPOST OVERNIGHT) *Pye Nixa 7N 15181*
02 Jul 59	1(2)	10	13. BATTLE OF NEW ORLEANS *Pye Nixa 7N 15206*
29 Oct 59	5	3	14. KEVIN BARRY *Pye Nixa 7N 15219*
07 Apr 60	1(4)	10	• 15. MY OLD MAN'S A DUSTMAN *Pye 7N 15256*
23 Jun 60	8	2	16. I WANNA GO HOME *Pye 7N 15267*
22 Dec 60	10	3	17. LIVELY *Pye 7N 15312*

continues over

Date	Pos	Wks	ARTIST / Record Title *Label & Number*
13 Jul 61	5	1	18. HAVE A DRINK ON ME *Pye 7N 15354*
21 Sep 61	2	3	19. MICHAEL ROW THE BOAT *Pye 7N 15371*
06 Sep 62	8	3	20. PICK A BALE OF COTTON *Pye 7N 15455*

DONOVAN — *20 Weeks*

Born Donovan Philip Leitch on May 10, 1946 in Maryhill, Glasgow, Scotland. In 1956, relocated with his family to Hatfield, England. Began playing guitar at age fourteen. In late 1964, travelled to London and recorded some demos in the hope of getting a record company interested. The demo tape was heard by the producer of TV music programme, Ready Steady Go, who was so impressed that he invited Donovan to appear on the show. This led to a recording contract with Pye Records. In 1966, parted with his management and began a successful association with independent record producer, Mickie Most. Parted with Most in 1969. Appeared in the 1967 film, *Poor Cow*. His autobiography, *The Hurdy Gurdy Man*, published in 2005. Now living in Ireland.

Date	Pos	Wks	ARTIST / Record Title *Label & Number*
12 Apr 65	9	3	1. CATCH THE WIND *Pye 7N 15801*
05 Jul 65	10	1	2. COLOURS *Pye 7N 15866*
05 Jan 67	3	5	3. SUNSHINE SUPERMAN *Pye 7N 17241*
30 Nov 67	9	2	4. THERE IS A MOUNTAIN *Pye 7N 17403*
21 Mar 68	7	3	5. JENNIFER JUNIPER *Pye 7N 17457*
13 Jun 68	5	6	6. HURDY GURDY MAN *Pye 7N 17537*

The DOOLEYS — *12 Weeks*

Family group formed in Ilford, Essex, England in 1967 as The Dooley Family. Relocated to Salford in 1973. Personnel: Jim Dooley (vocals), Anne Dooley (vocals), Kathy Dooley (vocals), Helen Dooley (keyboards), John Dooley (guitar), Frank Dooley (guitar), Bob Walsh (Anne's husband) (bass) and Alan Bogan (drums). Made their recording debut, *Hands Across The Sea*, in 1974. Signed to GTO in 1977. Jim Dooley lead vocals on *A Rose Has To Die*.

continues over

Date	Pos	Wks	ARTIST / Record Title *Label & Number*
			Anne and Kathy lead vocals on *Wanted* and *The Chosen Few*. In early 1982, Anne, Bob and Helen left the group. Vicki Roe replaced Anne on vocals. John, Frank and Alan left in 1985 and later formed a group, the New Dooleys. Jim and Kathy continued the group with the help of a series of new musicians until 1992. Kathy then embarked on a solo career.
12 Oct 78	9	2	1. A ROSE HAS TO DIE *GTO GT 229*
26 Jul 79	3	6	2. WANTED *GTO GT 249*
25 Oct 79	4	4	3. THE CHOSEN FEW *GTO GT 258*
			Val DOONICAN ***47 Weeks***
			Born Michael Valentine Doonican on February 3, 1927 in Waterford, Ireland. Started out in showbusiness in 1946, obtaining a job as a danceband guitarist. In 1953, was invited to join the Four Ramblers and moved to England. Stayed with the group for seven years. Met his wife, Lynnette Rae, when both she and the Four Ramblers supported Anthony Newley on tour. On the advice of Anthony Newley he went solo in 1960. Secured a radio programme on the BBC Light Programme. Comedian, Dickie Henderson recommended Val to impresario, Val Parnell, as a result Val was booked for a spot on the top light entertainment show on British television, *Sunday Night At The London Palladium*. It changed his life! Voted Television Personality of the Year on three occasions. Published his autobiography, *The Special Years* in 1980 and *Walking Tall* (1986).
02 Nov 64	2	14	1. WALK TALL *Decca F 11982*
08 Feb 65	2	6	2. THE SPECIAL YEARS *Decca F 12049*
04 Apr 66	3	9	3. ELUSIVE BUTTERFLY *Decca F 12358*
12 Dec 66	3	7	4. WHAT WOULD I BE *Decca F 12505*
16 Nov 67	2	10	5. IF THE WHOLE WORLD STOPPED LOVING *Pye 7N 17396*
13 Jan 72	5	1	6. MORNING *Philips 6006 177*

Date	Pos	Wks	ARTIST / Record Title *Label & Number*

Carl DOUGLAS — *6 Weeks*

Born in 1942 in Jamaica, West Indies. Raised in California, USA. In 1964 formed the group the Big Stampede. Relocated to England in 1970. *Kung Fu Fighting* was originally intended as the B side of his single, but due to the popularity of the Bruce Lee films, a decision was made to make it the 'A' side.

Date	Pos	Wks	ARTIST / Record Title *Label & Number*
19 Sep 74	1(2)	6	• 1. KUNG FU FIGHTING *Pye 7N 45377*

Craig DOUGLAS — *18 Weeks*

Born Terence Perkins on August 13, 1941 in Newport, Isle of Wight, England. Made his showbusiness debut aged fifteen when he won a local talent contest. His manager Bunny Lewis chose his stage name. Made disc debut on Decca in 1958 with *Sitting In A Tree House*. Moved to Top Rank in 1959, before returning to Decca in 1962. Starred with Helen Shapiro in the 1962 film, *It's Trad Dad*.

Date	Pos	Wks	ARTIST / Record Title *Label & Number*
03 Sep 59	1(2)	10	• 1. ONLY SIXTEEN *Top Rank JAR 159*
10 Mar 60	3	3	2. PRETTY BLUE EYES *Top Rank JAR 268*
19 Nov 62	7	5	3. OH, LONESOME ME *Decca F 11523*

Danny DOYLE — *51 Weeks*

Born in 1944 in Dublin, Ireland. Began singing in his school choir. After leaving school played harmonica in a ceili band. Moving to guitar he entertained at variety shows in the Dublin area. Spent two years in England performing in folk clubs before returning to Dublin. While performing on the folk circuit was spotted and signed to Major label. Disc debut: *Step It Out Mary* (1967). In August 1971, hosted his own TV series, *The Doyle Folk*, on UTV. Represented Ireland at the Malta Song Festival in July 1971. After a successful career as a solo artist on the ballad scene he formed a danceband, Music Box, in April 1972, and concentrated on the ballroom circuit. Disbanded Music Box in May 1974 and formed Country Music Box.

continues over

Date	Pos	Wks	ARTIST / Record Title *Label & Number*
			In February 1976 left the band to resume his career as a solo artist. Emigrated to the USA in 1983.
02 Feb 67	4	4	1. STEP IT OUT MARY *Major MJS 104*
20 Apr 67	9	3	2. THE IRISH SOLDIER LADDIE *Tribune TRS 103*
12 Oct 67	1(7)	15	• 3. WHISKEY ON A SUNDAY *Tribune TRS 107*
17 May 73	1(3)	14	• 4. DAISY A DAY *Release RL 671*
31 Jan 74	2	4	5. THANKS FOR THE MEMORIES *Release RL 709*
07 Oct 76	8	2	6. SOMEWHERE SOMEBODY'S WAITING *Music Box MBS 001*
02 Feb 78	1(2)	9	• 7. THE RARE OLD TIMES *Galaxy E 100*

The DREAM WEAVERS — *7 Weeks*

Formed in Miami, USA in 1953 by college students, Gene Adkinson and Wade Buff (lead vocals). Composed *It's Almost Tomorrow* while attending high school. Wade wrote lyrics and Gene the music. Made a demo of the song and as a result of plays on Miami radio, a number of record companies expressed an interest. Milt Gabler of Decca signed the group. Made their first national TV appearance on January 1, 1956 on the Ed Sullivan Show. Wade Buff left in mid 1956, replaced by Lee Raymond. Group disbanded when Gene was drafted into US Army in 1957.

Date	Pos	Wks	ARTIST / Record Title *Label & Number*
14 Feb 56	-	7	1. IT'S ALMOST TOMORROW *Brunswick 05515*

The DREAMS — *2 Weeks*

Showband formed in Dublin, Ireland in June 1968. Personnel: John Farrell (born on October 30, 1946 in Dublin, lead vocals), Eric Bell (lead guitar), Jim Hudson (bass), Douglas McIlwaine (drums), Shay O'Donoghue (leader, organ), Mark McCormack (trumpet), Joey Geoghan (tenor sax) and Pat McCarthy (trombone). Debut single: *I Will See You There* (1968), composed by members of the Tremeloes. Eric Bell left in late 1969 to join Thin Lizzy. John Farrell left in 1970. After numerous personnel changes the Dreams disbanded in the early 1970's.

Date	Pos	Wks	ARTIST / Record Title *Label & Number*
03 Jul 69	5	2	1. THE CASATSCHOK *Dolphin DOS 40*

Date	Pos	Wks	ARTIST / Record Title *Label & Number*

Tommy DRENNAN *35 Weeks*

Born on October 12, 1941 in Limerick, Ireland. Began his singing career with the Redemptorist church choir in Limerick city. Joined the Freshmen as lead singer in 1963. In January 1964, returned to Limerick to front the Monarchs Showband. In March 1972, decides to leave Monarchs and form a new band, the Top League. Departed from ranks of the Top League in September 1975 to embark on a solo career. The recording of *O Holy Night*, is a combination of the two voices of Tommy Drennan (a) as a twelve year old boy soprano with the choir of Mount St. Alphonsus Church, Limerick, with whom Tommy was a leading soloist. (b) features the voice of Tommy Drennan in the Eamonn Andrews Studios, Dublin in 1971. All made possible by the skill of producer, Bill Sommerville Large.

Date	Pos	Wks	ARTIST / Record Title *Label & Number*
14 Dec 64	4	8	1. BOULAVOGUE *Ember EMBS 201*
17 May 65	9	1	2. MOLLY *Ember EMBS 214*
20 Aug 70	6	6	3. LITTLE BOY LOST *Columbia IDB 751*
22 Jul 71	8	2	4. TAXES BY THE SCORE *Columbia IDB 785*
16 Dec 71	1(2)	3	• 5. O HOLY NIGHT *Columbia IDB 794*
26 Oct 72	3	7	6. THE PROMISE AND THE DREAM *Columbia IDB 818*
29 Mar 73	6	2	7. LEAD US THROUGH *Columbia IDB 826*
18 Oct 73	8	1	8. LOVE AND THE COUNTRY *EMI EMD 4003*
20 Dec 73	2	5	9. BEAUTIFUL PEACE *EMI EMD 4011*

The DRIFTERS *26 Weeks*

Vocal group formed in 1953 in New York, USA. In 1958 the groups manager, George Treadwell, fired all of the Drifters and hired the Five Crowns (who had Ben E King in their lineup) to be the new Drifters. Ben E King, lead vocals on *Save The Last Dance For Me*, left the group in 1960 to pursue a solo career. In 1971, the group decided to relocate to England and approached songwriters Roger Cook and Roger Greenaway to produce and write for the group.

continues over

Date	Pos	Wks	ARTIST / Record Title *Label & Number*
			Personnel: Johnny Moore (born on December 15, 1934 in Selina, Alabama), Bill Fredericks, Butch Leake, Grant Kitchings and Butch Leake. Bill Fredericks left in November 1974, replaced by Clyde Brown. In mid 1975, Grant Kitchings departed, replaced by Billy Lewis. In December 1975, Butch Leake departed, his replacement, Joe Blunt. The Drifters were inducted into the Rock and Roll Hall of Fame in 1988. Johnny Moore died on December 30, 1998. Grant Kitchings died on April 5, 2005.
24 Nov 60	1(2)	14	• 1. SAVE THE LAST DANCE FOR ME *London HLK 9201*
18 Jul 74	2	4	2. KISSING IN THE BACK ROW OF THE MOVIES *Bell* BLL *1358*
07 Nov 74	4	4	3. DOWN ON THE BEACH TONIGHT *Bell 1381*
09 Oct 75	2	4	4. THERE GOES MY FIRST LOVE *Bell 1433*

The DUBLINERS — *33 Weeks*

Formed in 1962 as the Ronnie Drew Group. Changed name on the advice of Luke Kelly. Success at the Edinburgh Festival led to the group signing to Transatlantic Records. Disc debut: *The Dubliners* L.P. (1964). Made international break through in 1967 with *Seven Drunken Nights*. The record was banned from the airwaves by Radio Eireann, Personnel: Ronnie Drew (born September 16, 1934 in Dublin, vocals, guitar), Luke Kelly (born November 17, 1940 in Dublin, vocals, banjo), Ciaran Bourke (tin whistle). John Sheehan (fiddle) and Barney McKenna (banjo). Ronnie Drew left group in July 1974 to pursue a solo career, returned in 1979. Replaced by Jim McCann. Ronnie left in 1996 was replaced by Paddy Reilly. Luke Kelly died on January 30, 1984. Ciaran Bourke died on May 10, 1988. Ronnie Drew died on August 16, 2008.

Date	Pos	Wks	ARTIST / Record Title *Label & Number*
25 Apr 66	6	2	1. NELSON'S FAREWELL *Transatlantic TRA SP 9*
13 Apr 67	1(1)	9	• 2. SEVEN DRUNKEN NIGHTS *Major Minor MM 506*
20 Jul 67	10	2	3. ALL FOR ME GROG *Major Minor MM 521*
21 Sep 67	4	10	4. BLACK VELVET BAND *Major Minor MM 530*

continues over

Date	Pos	Wks	ARTIST / Record Title *Label & Number*
15 Feb 68	10	1	5. DIRTY OLD TOWN *Major Minor MM 552*
03 Jun 71	7	7	6. HAND ME DOWN MY BIBLE *Tribune TRS 152*
28 Oct 71	7	2	7. FREE THE PEOPLE *Plough PLS 003*

Hugo DUNCAN and the TALLMEN 15 Weeks

Born on March 26, 1950 in Strabane, Co Tyrone, N. Ireland. While still at tending school he secured a position as vocalist with local group the Rhythm Aces. In 1970, he was offered a job with leading showband, the Melody Aces. Left after six months to join the Polka Dots replacement for Frankie McBride Came to national prominence in August 1971 when he reached the finals of the RTE Television talent show *Reach For The Stars*, finishing joint third. Disc debut: *Little Sweetheart* (1971). The Tallmen made their debut in April 1971. Personnel: Hugo Duncan (vocals), Pio McCann (bass), Paddy Phillips (organ) Sean Phillips (drums), Damian Given (trumpet) and Adam McPeake (guitar). Left Tallmen in November 1974. In 1992, joined Radio Foyle as a presenter doing holiday relief. In October 1998, moved to BBC Radio Ulster.

Date	Pos	Wks	ARTIST / Record Title *Label & Number*
05 Aug 71	3	10	1. DEAR GOD *Release RL 585*
23 Mar 72	7	1	2. THREE LEAF SHAMROCK *Rex R 11074*
27 Jul 72	10	1	3. EILEEN O'GRADY *Release RL 629*
14 Dec 72	8	2	4. CRY CRY AGAIN *Release RL 649*
29 Nov 73	10	1	5. TWO OF THE USUAL *Release RL 695*

Johnny DUNCAN and the BLUE GRASS BOYS 2 Weeks

Born John Franklin Duncan on September 7, 1932 in Windrock Oliver Springs, Tennesse, USA. Joined the U.S. Army and served in Germany and England. Joined the Chris Barber Jazz Band in 1956. Made his first recordings as a member of the Chris Barber Skiffle Group in September 1956. On leaving Chris Barber signed as a solo artist to Columbia Records. First solo disc: *Kaw-Liga* (1957).

continues over

Date	Pos	Wks	ARTIST / Record Title *Label & Number*

Record producer, Denis Preston, suggested recording *Last Train To San Fernando* and put together the Blue Grass Boys. Personnel Denny Wright (guitar), Jack Fallon (bass), Danny Lavan (fiddle) and Lennie Hastings (drums). Johnny hosted his own BBC radio series, *Tennessee Songbag*. Relocated to Australia in 1972. Died of bowel cancer on July 15, 2000.

Date	Pos	Wks	ARTIST / Record Title *Label & Number*
08 Oct 57	-	2	1. LAST TRAIN TO SAN FERNANDO *Columbia IDB 716*

David DUNDAS — *5 Weeks*

Born on June 2, 1945 in Oxford, England. Pursued an acting career before embarking on a singing career. *Jeans On* originated from a jingle he had composed for a television commercial for Brutus Jeans in the UK. Co-wrote the song with Roger Greenaway. Has composed music for TV.

Date	Pos	Wks	ARTIST / Record Title *Label & Number*
19 Aug 76	3	5	1. JEANS ON *Chrysalis CHS 2094*

Clive DUNN — *5 Weeks*

Born Robert Bertram Dunn on January 9, 1920 in London, England. Was a prisoner of war in Austria for four years during WW11. Became a household name in Britain for his role as Corporal Jones in the hit TV comedy series *Dad's Army*. Film appearances include *What A Whopper* (1961) and *Dad's Army* (1971). Appeared in the popular television series' *Bootsie And Snudge* (1960-63), *Dad's Army* (1968-77) and *Grandad* (1979-84). Awarded an OBE in 1975 for his services to drama.

Date	Pos	Wks	ARTIST / Record Title *Label & Number*
14 Jan 71	6	5	1. GRANDAD *Columbia DB(I) 8726*

Cathal DUNNE — *3 Weeks*

Singer/songwriter/pianist. Born on February 14, 1955 in Cork, Ireland. Nephew of former Taoiseach, Jack Lynch. Music was an essential part of his life when growing up. Started playing piano at age of three. Attended Cork School of Music and while there became musical director of the Montfort Choral Group.

continues over

Date	Pos	Wks	ARTIST / Record Title *Label & Number*
			Graduated from University College Cork in 1974 with a Bachelor of Music Degree. Won the 1974 Castlebar International Song Contest with his own song, *Shalom*. Represented Ireland at the 1976 Yamaha World Song Contest in Japan, with *Lover, Not Just A Wife*. Joined up with, Stateside in May 1978 as lead singer. Represented Ireland in the 1979 Eurovision Song Contest with his own composition, *Happy Man*, finishing in fifth position. Formed his own band, The Formula, in September 1979. Left the band in late 1982. Relocated to the USA in 1983.
08 Mar 79	3	3	1. HAPPY MAN *CBS CBS 7190*
			Sean DUNPHY and the HOEDOWNERS ***71 Weeks***
			Irish showband. Sean Dunphy born on November 30, 1932 in Dublin, Ireland. After leaving school formed a quartet, the Four Lyrics. Moved to London where he became resident singer at the Hibernian Club, Fulham Broadway. Returned to Dublin in 1962 to join the Earl Gill Band. In March 1965, the band received an offer of a residency on the RTE TV music series, *Hoedown*, and decided on a change of name to The Hoedowners. Disc debut: *Oh How I Miss You Tonight* (1965). Represented Ireland in 1967 Eurovision Song Contest, finishing second with, *If I Could Choose*. Sean Dunphy left Hoedowners in June 1973 to pursue a solo career.
07 Mar 66	5	3	1. WONDERFUL WORLD OF MY DREAMS *Pye 7N 17056*
26 Sep 66	2	5	2. SHOWBALL CRAZY *Pye 7N 17182*
06 Apr 67	2	7	3. IF I COULD CHOOSE *Pye 7N 17291*
14 Mar 68	2	9	4. TWO LOVES *Dolphin DOS 1*
19 Dec 68	2	5	5. CHRISTMAS POLKA *Dolphin DOS 18*
23 Jan 69	1(8)	17	• 6. THE LONELY WOODS OF UPTON *Dolphin DOS 22*
31 Jul 69	1(1)	9	• 7. WHEN THE FIELDS ARE WHITE WITH DAISIES *Dolphin* DOS 36
16 Apr 70	5	6	8. THE OLD FENIAN GUN *Dolphin DOS 58*

continues over

Date	Pos	Wks	ARTIST / Record Title *Label & Number*
02 Mar 72	10	1	9. THERE'S AN ISLAND IN THE SUN *Dolphin DOS 93*
11 May 72	2	2	10. MICHAEL COLLINS *Dolphin DOS 96*
22 Nov 73	3	7	11. PAL OF MY CRADLE DAYS *Dolphin DOS 110*

Showball Crazy credit the Hoedowners with commentary by Michael O'Heihi r

Tom DUNPHY and the ROYAL SHOWBAND *11 Weeks*

Tom Dunphy born on February 9, 1936 in Waterford, Ireland. Founder member of the Royal Showband. First Irish showband artist to be featured on record, *Come Down the Mountain Katie Daly,* April 1962. Left the Royal in August 1971 to form The Big 8. Died in a car accident on July 29, 1975, while on his way to a gig in Co. Donegal. Royal Showband formed in Waterford in 1958. Turned professional in April 1959. Personnel: Brendan Bowyer (lead vocals/trombone), Tom Dunphy (vocals/bass), Charlie Matthews (vocals/drums), Jim Conlon (vocals/lead guitar), Michael Coppinger (leader/tenor sax), Eddie Sullivan (trumpet) and Gerry Cullen (keyboards). Following the departure of Brendan Bowyer and Tom Dunphy in July 1971, the band suffered numerous personnel changes until the bands demise in February 1975. In July 1978, a memorial was erected to mark the spot where Tom Dunphy was killed. The memorial is situated on a short bypassed section of the N4, a mile south of Drumsna, Co. Leitrim.

Date	Pos	Wks	ARTIST / Record Title *Label & Number*
03 May 62	8	2	1. COME DOWN THE MOUNTAIN KATIE DALY *HMV POP(I) 1011*
08 Mar 65	1(2)	9	• 2. IF I DIDN'T HAVE A DIME (To Play The Jukebox) *HMV IP 1296*

See also Brendan Bowyer; Charlie Matthews.

Ian DURY and the BLOCKHEADS *3 Weeks*

Born May 12, 1942 in Upminster, Essex, England. Contracted polio at the age of seven, leaving him partially disabled. Worked as an art teacher from 1966-73.

continues over

Date	Pos	Wks	ARTIST / Record Title *Label & Number*

Started his musical career with Kilburn and The High Roads. Disbanded the group in 1977, and from the ashes formed the Blockheads in the same year. Personnel: Ian Dury (vocals), Chaz Jankel (guitar), John Turnball (guitar), Norman Watt-Roy (bass), Mickey Gallagher (keyboards), Gilad Atzman (saxophone) and Dylan Howe (drums). Ian Dury died on March 27, 2000.

Date	Pos	Wks	ARTIST / Record Title *Label & Number*
25 Jan 79	3	3	**1. HIT ME WITH YOUR RHYTHM STICK** *Stiff BUY 38*

Slim DUSTY **11 Weeks**

Born David Gordon Kirkpatrick on June 13, 1927 in Kempsey, New South Wales, Australia. Wrote his first song, *The Way The Cowboy Dies*, at the age of ten. In 1938 began to call himself Slim Dusty. Signed to Columbia Regal Zonophone in 1946. Disc debut: *When The Rain Tumbles Down In July* (1946). Recorded *A Pub With No Beer* in 1957. Awarded an MBE in 1970 for his services to music. His autobiography, *Walk A Country Mile*, published in 1979. Died of cancer on September 19, 2003.

Date	Pos	Wks	ARTIST / Record Title *Label & Number*
12 Feb 59	1(6)	11	• **1. A PUB WITH NO BEER** *Columbia DB(I) 4212*

Bob DYLAN **7 Weeks**

Born Robert Allan Zimmerman on May 24, 1941 in Duluth, Minnesota, USA. While attending high school formed the Shadow Blasters and the Golden Chords, playing a programme of covers of popular songs of the period. In 1959, enrolled at the University of Minnesota. Around this time his love of rock 'n' roll gave way to an interest in American Folk Music. Began to perform at a coffee house and become involved in the local folk music circuit. Adopted the name, Bob Dylan, after he became acquainted with the poetry of Dylan Thomas. In 1961, relocated to New York and played various clubs around Greenwich Village. Came to the attention of John Hammond who signed Dylan to Columbia Records in October 1961.

continues over

Date	Pos	Wks	ARTIST / Record Title *Label & Number*
			Disc debut: *Bob Dylan* L.P. (1962). Provoked an outraged response from the folk music establishment following his performance at the 1965 Newport Folk Festival. In July 1966, suffered injuries in a motorcycle accident that led to his withdrawal from the public eye until his return to Nashville in October 1967 to record what turned out to be the album, *John Wesley Hardin.* Appeared in the 1972 film, *Pat Garrett And Billy the Kid*, also provided songs for the film. Starred in the 1987 film, *Hearts Of Fire.* In the spring of 1988, joined Roy Orbison, Tom Petty, Jeff Lynne and George Harrison, to record an album as, *The Traveling Wilburys.* Recorded a second album in 1990, titled *Traveling Wilburys Volume 3.* Nominated for three Grammy awards for his 2006 album, Modern Times. Won Grammy for Best Contemporary Folk/Americana Album. On May 3, 2006, made his debut as a disc jockey, hosting a weekly radio programme, *Theme Time Radio Hour*, for XM Satellite Radio.
13 Sep 65	9	1	1. LIKE A ROLLING STONE *CBS 201811*
08 Nov 73	9	2	2. KNOCKIN' ON HEAVENS DOOR *CBS 1762*
17 Aug 78	5	4	3. BABY STOP CRYING *CBS 6499*

Date	Pos	Wks	ARTIST / Record Title *Label & Number*

E

The EAGLES — *10 Weeks*

Vocal/instrumental group formed in Los Angeles, USA in 1971. Personnel: Glenn Frey (vocals, guitar), Bernie Leadon (guitar), Randy Meisner (bass) and Don Henley (drums). Don Felder (guitar) was added to lineup in 1975. Leadon left in 1975, replaced by Joe Walsh. Meisner was replaced by Timothy Schmidt in 1977. Disbanded in 1982, with Frey and Henley achieving solo success. Reformed for a farewell tour in 2006.

Date	Pos	Wks	ARTIST / Record Title *Label & Number*
18 Dec 75	5	9	1. LYIN' EYES *Asylum AYM 548*
08 Nov 79	10	1	2. HEARTACHE TONIGHT *Asylum K 12394*

Robert EARL — *7 Weeks*

Born Brian Budge on November 17, 1926 in London, England. Began singing at a young age. During the late 1940's worked as a semi-professional with the Nat Temple and Sidney Lipton Orchestras, as vocalist. Turned professional in 1950. Signed to Philips Record company in 1953. Disc debut: *If You Love Me* (1953). Stayed with the label throughout his recording career.

Date	Pos	Wks	ARTIST / Record Title *Label & Number*
04 Feb 58	-	1	1. MY SPECIAL ANGEL *Philips EPB 767*
16 Apr 58	-	6	2. I MAY NEVER PASS THIS WAY AGAIN *Philips EPB 805*

EARTH WIND and FIRE — *10 Weeks*

Formed in 1969, under the name, the Salty Peppers. Changed name to Earth Wind and Fire in 1970. Personnel: Maurice White (vocals, percussion), Verdine White (vocals, bass), Philip Bailey (vocals), Larry Dunn (keyboards), Al McKay (guitar), Ralph Johnson (drums), Johnny Graham (guitar), Andrew Woolfolk (saxophone), Don Myrick (trumpet), Louis Satterfield (trumpet) and Michael Harris (trumpet). Disc debut: *Earth Wind And Fire* LP (1971).

continues over

Date	Pos	Wks	ARTIST / Record Title *Label & Number*
			Group appeared in 1978 film, *Sgt. Pepper's Lonely Hearts Club Band.*
06 Apr 78	4	4	1. FANTASY *CBS 6056*
25 Jan 79	8	1	2. SEPTEMBER *CBS 6922*
14 Jun 79	5	4	3. BOOGIE WONDERLAND *CBS 7292*
30 Aug 79	8	1	4. AFTER THE LOVE HAS GONE *CBS 7721*

The EASYBEATS — *2 Weeks*

Formed in Sydney, Australia in 1964 as The Starfighters, changed name to Easybeats in 1965. Disc debut: *For My Woman* (1965). Moved to England in 1966. Personnel: Steve Wright (born December 20, 1948 in Leeds, England, vocals), Dick Diamonde (bass), Gordon Fleet (drums), George Young (guitar) and Harry Vanda (lead guitar). Disbanded in 1970. George Young is the older brother of AC/DC's Angus and Malcolm Young.

Date	Pos	Wks	ARTIST / Record Title *Label & Number*
05 Jan 67	7	2	1. FRIDAY ON MY MIN*D United Artists UP 1157*

Billy ECKSTINE — *10 Weeks*

Born William Clarence Eckstein on July 8, 1914 in Pittsburg, Pennsylvania, USA. Began singing at eleven years of age. Sang in night-clubs and with various bands before signing with Earl Hines in 1939. Formed his own band in 1944 and during its three year existence the lineup boasted the talents of Miles Davis, Art Blakey and a young Sarah Vaughan. Signed to the newly formed MGM record label in 1947. Died of a stroke on March 8, 1993.

Date	Pos	Wks	ARTIST / Record Title *Label & Number*
05 Mar 58	-	1	1. IF I CAN HELP SOMEBODY *Mercury MT 191*
19 Feb 59	5	9	2. GIGI *Mercury AMT(I) 1018*

Duane EDDY — *49 Weeks*

Guitarist born on April 26, 1938 in Corring, New York, USA. Moved with his family to Coolidge near Phoenix, Arizona, in 1955. Given his first guitar at age of five. By the age of thirteen was playing guitar in local bands.

continues over

Date	Pos	Wks	ARTIST / Record Title *Label & Number*

Met up with producer/songwriter, Lee Hazlewood, with whom he had a long and successful association. Disc debut: *Soda Fountain Girl* (1956). Signed to Jamie Records, and formed the Rebel Rousers, in 1957. The Rebels: Al Casey (guitar), Corky Casey (rhythm guitar), Buddy Wheeler (bass), Steve Douglas (tenor sax) and Mike Bermani (drums). Moved from Jamie to RCA Records in 1962. Film appearances include *A Thunder Of Drums* (1961), *Wild Westerners* (1962) and *The Savage Seven* (1968). Famous for his 'Twangy' guitar sound. Won Grammy Award in 1986, for Best Rock Instrumental Performance (Orchestra, group or soloist) for his recording of *Peter Gunn* with rock group the Art Of Noise. Inducted into the Rock and Roll Hall of Fame in 1994.

Date	Pos	Wks	ARTIST / Record Title *Label & Number*
31 Dec 59	3	2	1. SOME KIND-A EARTHQUAKE • *London HLW 9007*
26 May 60	3	9	2. SHAZAMI • *London HLW 9104*
25 Aug 60	3	8	3. BECAUSE THEY'RE YOUNG • *London HLW 9162*
26 Jan 61	3	8	4. PEPE • *London HLW 9257*
25 May 61	4	2	5. THEME FROM DIXIE • *London HLW 9324*
30 Aug 62	3	6	6. BALLAD OF PALADIN • *RCA ERC 1300*
03 Dec 62	4	10	7. (Dance With The) GUITAR MAN *RCA ERC 1316*
03 Apr 75	5	4	8. PLAY ME LIKE YOU PLAY YOUR GUITAR *GTO GT 11*

(Dance With The) Guitar Man and Play Me Like You Play Your Guitar credit Duane Eddy and the Rebelettes

EDISON LIGHTHOUSE — *8 Weeks*

British studio group put together by songwriters Tony Macauley and Barry Mason Lead singer, Tony Burrows (born April 14, 1942 in Exeter, England) also featured as a member of The Pipkins, White Plains and First Class. Following the success of, *Love Grows*, members of the group, Greenfield Hammer, adopted the name Edison Lighthouse. Personnel: Ray Dorey (vocals, guitar), Stuart Edwards (lead guitar), David Taylor (bass), and George Wayman (bass).

Date	Pos	Wks	ARTIST / Record Title *Label & Number*
12 Feb 70	1(4)	8	• 1. LOVE GROWS (Where My Rosemary Goes) *Bell BLL 1091*

Date	Pos	Wks	ARTIST / Record Title *Label & Number*

Dave EDMUNDS *10 Weeks*

Guitarist/producer/vocalist. Born on April 15, 1943 in Cardiff, Wales. As a teenager played with several local groups in the Cardiff area. In 1966, joined the Human Beans, who evolved into Love Sculpture the following year. Group broke up in 1969. In 1970, while producing Shakin' Stevens and the Sunsets first album, *A Legend*, he came across the Smiley Lewis recording of *I Hear You Knocking*, and decided to record it. Though credited to Dave Edmunds Rockpile, the recording of, *I Hear You Knocking*, was a solo effort by Dave, apart from bassist John Williams.

Date	Pos	Wks	ARTIST / Record Title *Label & Number*
10 Dec 70	1(1)	9	• 1. I HEAR YOU KNOCKING *Mam MAM 1*
01 Mar 73	6	1	2. BABY I LOVE YOU *Rockfield ROC 1*

ELECTRIC LIGHT ORCHESTRA *17 Weeks*

Formed in Birmingham, England in October 1970 by Roy Wood, Jeff Lynne and Bev Bevan of the Move. Roy Wood left the group in 1972, following the release of the first album, to form his own group, Wizzard. Personnel: Jeff Lynne (vocals/guitar), Bev Bevan (drums), Richard Tandy (keyboards), Kelly Groucutt (bass/vocals), Melvyn Gale (cello), Hugh McDowell (cello) and Mik Kaminski (violin). Group officially disbanded in 1988. Jeff Lynne reformed ELO with new members in 2001. Kelly Groucutt died on February 19, 2009.

Date	Pos	Wks	ARTIST / Record Title *Label & Number*
23 Dec 76	5	4	1. LIVIN' THING *UA UP 36184*
27 Jul 78	9	2	2. WILD WEST HERO *Jet 109*
19 Oct 78	6	3	3. SWEET TALKIN' WOMAN *Jet 121*
07 Jun 79	4	3	4. SHINE A LITTLE LOVE *Jet 144*
16 Aug 79	10	1	5. THE DIARY OF HORACE WIMP *Jet 150*
20 Sep 79	6	4	6. DON'T BRING ME DOWN *Jet 153*

Yvonne ELLIMAN *1 Weeks*

Born Yvonne Marianne Elliman on December 29, 1951 in Honolulu, Hawaii. Relocated to England in 1969.

continues over

Date	Pos	Wks	ARTIST / Record Title *Label & Number*

Spotted by Tim Rice and Andrew Lloyd Webber who offered her the part of Mary Maagdalene in their new rock opera *Jesus Christ Superstar.* She went on to recreate the role in the 1973 film version. Disc debut: *I Don't Know How To Love Him* (1972). Worked as a backing vocalist with Eric Clapton over the course of five albums.

01 Jun 78	9	1	1. IF I CAN'T HAVE YOU *RSO 2090 266*

Pat ELY and the ROCKY TOPS — *12 Weeks*

Born Patrick Healy in Thurles, Co. Tipperary, Ireland. Emmigrated to England in the late 1950's where he sang in the Irish clubs and dance halls around Manchester. Returned to Ireland in the 1960's to join the Savoy Swing Seven. Spotted by Des Kelly who invited him to join the Smokey Mountain Ramblers as lead singer. The SMR launched on the showband circuit in October 1968. Pat left the SMR's in January 1972. Teamed up with ex founder members of the Smokey Mountain Ramblers in March 1972 to form the Rocky Tops. Left Rocky Tops in November 1974 to form his own band, The Storytellers. Retired from the performing side of the music business in the 1980's. The Rocky Tops line-up: Pat Ely (lead vocals), George Kaye (fiddle), Bernie Fallon (drums), Martin Johnson (bass), Dave Kearney (lead guitar), Tommy Higgins (organ) and Tony Cannon (rhythm guitar/tenor sax). Band split in late 1974. Bernie Fallon died on October 23, 2007.

18 Feb 71	8	2	1. JUST BEYOND THE MOON *Ruby RUB 117*
07 Dec 72	9	1	2. ALL I HAVE TO OFFER YOU IS ME *Release RL 650*
23 Aug 73	5	7	3. THE SHORES OF LOUGH BRAN *Release RL 683*
03 Oct 74	9	2	4. ANY TIPPERARY TOWN *Release RL 702*

Just Beyond The Moon credit Pat Ely and Smokey Mountain Ramblers.

Date	Pos	Wks	ARTIST / Record Title *Label & Number*

The EMMET SPICELAND *13 Weeks*

Ballad/folk group formed in Dublin, Ireland in April 1967 from elements of two two groups – the Emmet Folk and the Spiceland Folk. Personnel: Donal Lunny (vocals, mandolin), Mick Byrne (guitar), Brian Byrne (guitar) and Brian Bolger (who left in December 1967). Disc debut: *Mary from Dungloe*. Were the first artists to place a record in the Irish language, *Baidin Fheidhlimi*, on the chart. Performed *Bunclody* at the 1968 All Ireland Senior Hurling Final at Croke Park, Dublin. Donal Lunny left the group in 1969 to be followed in September of the same year by Mick Byrne. Group broke up in 1970. Reformed for a brief period in 1973 with a lineup of Mick Byrne, Honor Heffernan, Dave Murphy and Paul Ashford. Mick Byrne lead vocal on *Bunclody*.

Date	Pos	Wks	ARTIST / Record Title *Label & Number*
15 Feb 68	1(1)	8	1. MARY FROM DUNGLOE *Inset IN 702*
16 May 68	6	3	2. BAIDIN FHEIDHLIMI *Gael-linn CES 002*
17 Oct 68	8	2	3. BUNCLODY *Page One POF 089*

ENGLAND WORLD CUP SQUAD *6 Weeks*

Back Home composed by Phil Coulter and Bill Martin was issued by Pye Records to coincide with England's appearance in the 1970 World Cup Finals in Mexico. England reached the quarter finals where they were defeated by West Germany after extra time on a score of 3-2. *Back Home* performed by the World Cup Squad. Personnel: Gordon Banks, Peter Bonetti, Alex Stepney, Keith Newton, Terry Cooper, Alan Mullery, Brian Labone, Bobby Moore, Tommy Wright, Jackie Charlton, Norman Hunter, Francis Lee, Alan Ball, Martin Peters, Nobby Stiles, Emlyn Hughes, Colin Bell, Bobby Charlton, Geoff Hurst, Peter Osgood, Allan Clarke and Jeff Astle.

Date	Pos	Wks	ARTIST / Record Title *Label & Number*
14 May 70	2	6	1. BACK HOME *Pye 7N 17920*

Date	Pos	Wks	ARTIST / Record Title *Label & Number*

The EQUALS ***10 Weeks***

Group formed in London, England in 1965. Personnel: Derv Gordon (born June 29, 1948 in Jamaica, lead vocals), Eddie Grant (lead guitar), Lincoln Gordon (bass), John Hall (drums) and Pat Lloyd (rhythm guitar). Disc debut: *I Won't Be There* (1966). Eddie Grant left the group in 1972 and went on to enjoy a successful solo career in the 80's as Eddy Grant.

25 Jul 68	2	5	1. BABY COME BACK *President PT 135*
11 Sep 69	3	5	2. VIVA BOBBY JOE *President PT 260*

ERUPTION ***4 Weeks***

Formed in London, England in 1974 by Jamaica natives Precious Wilson (vocals), Greg Perrineau (guitar), Morgan Perrineau (bass), Gerry Williams (keyboards) and Eric Kingsley (drums). Disc debut: *Let Me Take You Back In Time* (1976). Precious Wilson left group in 1979 to pursue a solo career. Group disbanded in 1985.

16 Mar 78	6	4	1. I CAN'T STAND THE RAIN *Atlantic K 11068*

David ESSEX ***19 Weeks***

Born David Albert Cook on July 23, 1947 in Plaistow, London, England. Had a run of unsuccessful singles on Fontana, Pye and Decca before hitting the jackpot on CBS. Disc debut: *Can't Nobody Love You* (1965). Shot to fame following his appearance, in the role of Jesus, in the 1972 London production of *Godspell*. For his performance in *Godspell* won the Variety Club of Great Britain 'Most Promising Newcomer' Award. Film producer, David Puttnam, saw him in *Godspel* and offered him the lead role in the 1973 film *That'll Be The Day*. He also starred in the sequel, *Stardust*. Composed and recorded his debut hit, *Rock On*, while filming *That'll Be The Day*.

Date	Pos	Wks	ARTIST / Record Title *Label & Number*

In 1978, played the role of 'Che' in the stage musical *Evita* at London's Prince Edward Theatre. In 1985, wrote with Richard Crane, the stage musical *Mutiny*, which ran for sixteen months at London's Piccadilly Theatre. David also starred in the production. In 1994, starred in *She Stoops To Conquer* for seven months at the Queens Theatre, London. Awarded an OBE in 1999. His autobiography *A Charmed Life* was published in 2002.

Date	Pos	Wks	ARTIST / Record Title *Label & Number*
07 Nov 74	1(4)	8	• 1. GONNA MAKE YOU A STAR *CBS 2492*
09 Jan 75	3	3	2. STARDUST *CBS SCBS 2828*
25 Sep 75	1(2)	7	• 3. HOLD ME CLOSE *CBS 3572*
31Aug 78	8	1	4. OH WHAT A CIRCUS *Mercury 6007 185*

Don ESTELLE and Windsor DAVIES — *3 Weeks*

Male actors/vocal duo. Don Estelle born born on May 22, 1933 in Manchester, England.. Windsor Davies born on August 28, 1930 in Canning Town, London, England. Moved to Wales in 1940. Worked as a teacher and a miner before becoming an actor in 1961. Both appeared in the top TV comedy *It Ain't Half Hot Mom*. Davies played role of, Sgt Major Williams, while Estelle played, Gunner 'Lofty' Sugden. Don Estelle died on August 2, 2003.

Date	Pos	Wks	ARTIST / Record Title *Label & Number*
19 Jun 75	4	3	1. WHISPERING GRASS *EMI EMI 2290*

Maureen EVANS — *4 Weeks*

Born on March 23, 1940 in Cardiff, Wales. Discovered by comedian Arthur Askey. Disc debut: *Stupid Cupid* (1958). Now runs a drama school, the Maureen Evans Centre Theatre School in Cardiff. *Like I Do* is based on Ponchielli's *Dance Of The Hours* from the opera, *La Gioconda*.

Date	Pos	Wks	ARTIST / Record Title *Label & Number*
28 Jan 63	4	4	1. LIKE I DO *Oriole CB 1760*

Date	Pos	Wks	ARTIST / Record Title *Label & Number*

Paul EVANS ***5 Weeks***

Born on March 5, 1938 in New York City, USA. Came from a musical family. Attended Andrew Jackson High School in Queens. Gave up an engineering scholarship to Columbia University to seek fame and fortune in the music business. Disc debut: *What Do You Know* on the Groove label in 1957. First major success came as a songwriter, when in 1958, the Kalin Twins recorded one of his songs. Tasted chart success as a performer in 1959 when he had a hit with, *Seven Little Girls Sitting In The Back Seat*. His song writing successes include: *When*, (Kalin Twins), *Johnny Will* (Pat Boone), *Roses Are Red* (Bobby Vinton), *I Gotta Know* (Elvis Presley), *Happiness Is* (Ray Conniff) and *Worried Guy* (Johnny Tillotson).

Date	Pos	Wks	ARTIST / Record Title *Label & Number*
18 Jan 79	2	5	1. HELLO THIS IS JOANNIE (The Telephone Answering Machine Song) *Polydor 2066 932*

The EVERLY BROTHERS ***76 Weeks***

Male vocal duo. Brothers, Don (born Isaac Donald Everly on February 1, 1937 in Brownie, Kentucky, USA) and Phil (born Philip Everly on January 19, 1939 in Chicago USA). Disc debut: *The Sun Keeps Shining* on Columbia Records in 1955. Signed to Cadence Records in 1957. In February 1960 the brothers quit Cadence and moved to the newly formed Warner Brothers Records label, signing a ten year contract, reputedly worth in excess of a million dollars. Moved to RCA Records in the early 1970's. The duo split in July 1973 with both brothers pursuing solo careers. Reunited in September 1983. Inducted into the Rock and Roll Hall of Fame in 1986.

Date	Pos	Wks	ARTIST / Record Title *Label & Number*
03 Dec 57	-	1	1. WAKE UP LITTLE SUSIE *London HLA 8498*
23 Jul 58	-	1	2. ALL I HAVE TO DO IS DREAM *London HLA 8618*
12 Mar 59	8	1	3. PROBLEMS *London HLA 8781*
05 Nov 59	6	5	4. ('TIL) I KISSED YOU *London HLA 8934*
12 May 60	1(5)	18	• 5. CATHY'S CLOWN *Warner Bros. EWB 1*

Date	Pos	Wks	ARTIST / Record Title *Label & Number*
25 Aug 60	4	4	6. WHEN WILL I BE LOVED *London HLA 9157*
20 Oct 60	3	6	7. SO SAD (To Watch Good Love Go Bad) *Warner Bros. EWB 19*
02 Mar 61	1(2)	10	• 8. EBONY EYES *Warner Bros. EWB 33*
09 Mar 61	2	8	9. WALK RIGHT BACK *Warner Bros EWB 33*
29 Jun 61	3	8	10. TEMPTATION *Warner Bros. EWB 42*
26 Oct 61	8	1	11. MUSKRAT *Warner Bros. EWB 50*
22 Feb 62	6	4	12. CRYING IN THE RAIN *Warner Bros. EWB 56*
28 Jun 62	4	4	13. HOW CAN I MEET HER *Warner Bros. EWB 67*
21 Jun 65	3	5	14. THE PRICE OF LOVE *Warner Bros. EWB 161*

EXILE — *1 Weeks*

Formed in Lexington, Kentucky, USA in 1963 as The Exiles. Shortenened name to Exile in 1973. Personnel: J.P. Pennington (lead vocals), Jimmy Stokley (vocals), Buzz Cornelison (keyboards), Sonny Lemaire (bass) and Steve Goetzman (drums). J P Pennington left in 1980. Group disbanded in 1993.

Date	Pos	Wks	ARTIST / Record Title *Label & Number*
14 Sep 78	7	1	1. KISS YOU ALL OVER *Rak RAK 279*

Date	Pos	Wks	ARTIST / Record Title *Label & Number*

F

The FACES *4 Weeks*

When Steve Marriott left the Small Faces in 1969 to form Humble Pie, the three remaining members, Ronnie Lane (bass), Ian McLagan (keyboards) and Kenny Jones (drums) recruited Ron Wood (guitar) and Rod Stewart (vocals) to replace him, and changed their name to The Faces. Signed to Warner Brothers Records and enjoyed success as a live and recording act. Rod Stewart left the Faces in December 1975 to pursue a solo career. Ron Wood joined the Rolling Stones in 1976. Ronnie Lane died of multiple sclerosis on June 4, 1997.

01 Mar 73	8	4	1. CINDY INCIDENTALLY *Warner Bros. 16247*

Sean FAGAN
and the PACIFIC SHOWBAND *18 Weeks*

Sean Fagan born on July 11, 1937 in Dublin, Ireland. A member of the Earl Gill Band he joined the Pacific Showband in 1963. Made his recording debut in December 1962, with a pop song in the Irish language, *Neili Mhici Oig*. He now resides in Canada. The Pacific Showband formed in Dublin in 1963 from elements of the Royal Olympics and the Earl Gill Showband. Personnel: Sean Fagan (lead vocals), Sonny Knowles (vocals, tenor sax), Harry Parker (bass), Marty Fanning (drums), Jimmy Dumpleton (lead guitar), Shay Curran (trombone) and Freddie Martin (trumpet). Band moved to Canada in 1970 and changed name to Dublin Corporation.

24 Aug 64	3	9	1. SHE WEARS MY RING *Pye 7N 15675*
30 Nov 64	5	6	2. DISTANT DRUMS *Pye 7N 15728*
02 Jan 69	7	3	3. MY LOVELY ROSE AND YOU *Tribune TRS 124*

Distant Drums credit The Pacific Showband

See also Sonny Knowles and the Pacific Showband; Sonny and Sean

Date	Pos	Wks	ARTIST / Record Title *Label & Number*

FAIR WEATHER — *3 Weeks*

Formed in 1970, by ex members of Amen Corner. Signed to RCA and issued their debut single, *Road To Freedom*, in 1970. Personnel: Andy Fairweather-Low (vocals), Clive Taylor (bass), Neil Jones (guitar), Blue Weaver (organ) and Denis Byron (drums). Disbanded in mid 1971.

Date	Pos	Wks	ARTIST / Record Title *Label & Number*
27 Aug 70	9	3	1. NATURAL SINNER *RCA 1977*

Andy FAIRWEATHER-LOW — *3 Weeks*

Born on August 2, 1950 in Ystrad Mynach, Wales. Founding member of Amen Corner and Fairweather. Following the break up of Fair Weather he retired from the music business. Returned as a solo artist in 1974. Signed to A&M records. When his solo career started to wind down in the 1980's, he began to do a lot of session work as guitarist, bassist and backing vocalist. A member of Eric Clapton's band since the early nineties, touring with Clapton up until 2003. Also worked with George Harrison, Roger Waters and a regular member of Bill Wyman's Rhythm Kings. In 2006, released *Sweet Soulful Music*, his first solo album in twenty six years.

Date	Pos	Wks	ARTIST / Record Title *Label & Number*
22 Jan 76	7	3	1. WIDE EYED AND LEGLESS *A&M AMS 7202*

Adam FAITH — *35 Weeks*

Born Terence Nelhams on June 23, 1940 in Acton, London, England. Recorded for HMV and Top Rank before teaming up with songwriter Johnny Worth and bandleader John Barry at Parlophone. Appeared in several films including *Never Let Go* (1960) *What A Whopper* (1961) and *Mix Me A Person* (1962). Enjoyed success as an actor in several popular TV series', *Budgie* (1970), *Love Hurts* (1992) and *The House That Jack Built* (2002). *The Time Has Come* was featured in the film, *What A Whopper.* Died as result of a heart attack on March 8, 2003.

continues over

Date	Pos	Wks	ARTIST / Record Title *Label & Number*
17 Dec 59	1(1)	7	• 1. WHAT DO YOU WANT? *Parlophone R(I) 4591*
18 Feb 60	3	6	2. POOR ME *Parlophone R(I) 4623*
12 Jan 61	9	1	3. LONELY PUP (In A Christmas Shop) *Parlophone R(I) 4708*
30 Mar 61	9	1	4. WHO AM I? *Parlophone R(I) 4735*
10 Aug 61	2	1	5. DON'T YOU KNOW IT? *Parlophone R(I) 4807*
16 Nov 61	5	8	6. THE TIME HAS COME *Parlophone R(I) 4837*
22 Feb 62	9	3	7. LONESOME *Parlophone R(I) 4864*
17 May 62	4	8	8. AS YOU LIKE IT *Parlophone R(I) 4896*

Marianne FAITHFULL — *24 Weeks*

Born on December 29, 1946 in Hampstead, London, England. Discovered by Rolling Stones manager, Andrew Loog Oldham. Appeared in several films including *I'll Never Forget Whatshisname* (1967) and *Girl On A Motorcycle* (1968). Her autobiography, *Faithfull*, published in 1994.

Date	Pos	Wks	ARTIST / Record Title *Label & Number*
28 Sep 64	9	3	1. AS TEARS GO BY *Decca F 11923*
31 May 65	9	3	2. THIS LITTLE BIRD *Decca F 12162*
04 Mar 76	1(5)	12	• 3. DREAMING MY DREAMS *Nems NES 004*
27 May 76	6	6	4. WRONG ROAD AGAIN *Nems NES 014*

Georgie FAME and the BLUE FLAMES — *9 Weeks*

Born Clive Powell on June 26, 1943 in Leigh, Lancashire, England. Discovered by songwriter Lionel Bart who recommended him to top manager, Larry Parnes. In 1961 joined Billy Fury's backing group the Blue Flames, as piano player. When Blue Flames left Fury in 1962 Fame took over as leader. Had residency at London's West End Jazz Club the Flamingo. In 1964 released the acclaimed album, *Rhythm And Blues At The Flamingo*. Blue Flames broke up in September 1966. Teamed up with Alan Price 1971- 1973.

Date	Pos	Wks	ARTIST / Record Title *Label & Number*
18 Jan 65	3	3	1. YEH YEH *Columbia DB(I) 7428*
25 Jul 66	6	3	2. GET AWAY *Columbia DB(I) 7946*
25 Jan 68	4	3	3. THE BALLAD OF BONNIE AND CLYDE *CBS 3124*

The Ballad Of Bonnie And Clyde credit Georgie Fame

Date	Pos	Wks	ARTIST / Record Title *Label & Number*

The FAMILY DOGG — *3 Weeks*

Male/female vocal group formed in London, England in 1967. Personnel: Steve Rowland (lead vocal), Mike Hazlewood (guitar/vocals, Albert Hammond (guitar/vocals), Doreen de Veuve and Christine Holmes. Disc debut: *Family Dogg* (1967). Hammond and Hazlewood composed hit songs for many international and Irish artists including Joe Dolan, The Dixies, Leo Sayer and The Hollies.

Date	Pos	Wks	ARTIST / Record Title *Label & Number*
17 Jul 69	6	3	1. A WAY OF LIFE *Bell* BLL*(I) 1055*

FAMILY PRIDE — *4 Weeks*

Formed in October 1972, by a group of Irish session singers and musicians who came together to make some recordings. Personnel: Des Smyth, Anne Bushnell, Johnny Christopher, Johnny Curran, Rita Madigan, Gerry Hughes and Pat O'Reilly. *Give Me Your Hand*, is based on the traditional gaelic song, *Tabair Dom Do Lamh*. After cutting two singles and an album the members went their separate ways.

Date	Pos	Wks	ARTIST / Record Title *Label & Number*
16 Nov 72	5	4	1. GIVE ME YOUR HAND *Columbia* IDB *819*

Don FARDON — *6 Weeks*

Born Donald Maughn on August 19, 1943 in Coventry, England. Started his music career in the early sixties as lead singer with a group The Sorrows. Don left group in 1969 and had decided to give up the music business until he was persuaded by record producer, Miki Dallon, to record *Indian Reservation*. Retired from music business in 1975. In 1992, joined BBC Radio as a presenter

Date	Pos	Wks	ARTIST / Record Title *Label & Number*
03 Dec 70	5	6	1. INDIAN RESERVATION *Young Blood YB 1015*

Angela FARRELL — *3 Weeks*

Born in Portadown, Co. Down, N. Ireland. Was working in a chemist shop, when she was chosen by RTE producer, Tom McGrath, to sing *One Day Love* in the 1971 National Song Contest.

continues over

Date	Pos	Wks	ARTIST / Record Title *Label & Number*
			She won and went on to represent Ireland in the Eurovision Song Contest of 1971, finishing in eleventh position.
08 Apr 71	4	2	1. ONE DAY LOVE *Rex R 11063*
10 Feb 72	9	1	2. I AM *Rex R 11071*

FATHER ABRAHAM and the SMURFS *4 Weeks*

Dutch musician, Pierre Kartner, who sings under the alias Father Abraham. Born on April 11, 1935 in Elst, Holland. In 1977 was asked to record a promotional song for an animated cartoon film of The Smurfs. The Smurfs, a fictional group of small sky blue coloured creatures who live in the woods, were created by Belgian cartoonist Peyo in a series of comic strips. In 1981, were launched on television worldwide in the animated television series, *The Smurfs*.

Date	Pos	Wks	ARTIST / Record Title *Label & Number*
22 Jun 78	5	4	1. THE SMURF SONG *Decca F 13759*

Johnny FERGUSON *4 Weeks*

Born on March 22, 1937 in Nashville, Tennessee, USA. Worked as a disc jockey on radio stations in Tennessee and Georgia. Signed a recording contract with MGM in 1959. *Angela Jones* was composed by John D Loudermilk.

Date	Pos	Wks	ARTIST / Record Title *Label & Number*
28 Jul 60	6	4	1. ANGELA JONES *MGM MGM(I) 1059*

FERRANTE and TEICHER *6 Weeks*

Piano duo. Arthur Ferrante (born September 7, 1921 in New York City, USA) and Louis Teicher (born August 24, 1924 in Wilkes Barre, Pennsylvania, USA). After meeting as students and then working as teachers, at Juilliard School in Manhattan, they began to perform together as a duo in 1946. Formed their own record label, Avante Garde, in 1979. Retired from performing in 1989. Teicher died on August 3, 2008. Ferrante died on September 19, 2009.

Date	Pos	Wks	ARTIST / Record Title *Label & Number*
06 Apr 61	3	6	1. EXODUS (Theme from 'Exodus') • *United Artists POP 881*

Date	Pos	Wks	ARTIST / Record Title *Label & Number*

Gracie FIELDS *3 Weeks*

Born Grace Stansfield on January 9, 1898 in Rochdale, Lancashire, England. Changed her name on the advice of a theatrical manager who said her real name was too long. Her mother came up with Gracie Fields. Made disc debut in 1928 with *My Blue Heaven*. Her film career began in 1931 with *Sally In Our Alley*. She went on to make fourteen more including *Sing As We Go* (1934), *Keep Smiling* (1938), *Stage Door Canteen* (1943) and *Madame Pimpernel* (1946). Made her last public appearance on November 13, 1978 in the Royal Variety Show at the London Palladium, when she performed her signature song, *Sally*. Made a Dame in 1979. Died on September 27, 1979.

30 Jul 57	-	2	1. AROUND THE WORLD *Columbia IDB 712*
17 Dec 59	2	1	2. LITTLE DONKEY *Columbia DB(I) 4360*

Eddie FISHER *2 Weeks*

Born Edwin Jack Fisher on August 10, 1928 in Philadelphia, USA. Started singing in synagogues and socials at a young age. In 1945 received an offer to sing with the Buddy Morrow Orchestra. A move to New York in 1947 found him singing in lounges and nightclubs. A tie in with Eddie Cantor saw Fisher sign to Bluebird a subsidiary of RCA. In 1950 moved to parent company RCA and released *Thinking Of You*.For period 1951 to 1953 served in US Army. In September 1954 married actress Debbie Reynolds. Film appearances include *Bundle Of Joy* (1956) and *Butterfield 8* (1960). Left RCA in 1956, returned in 1976. Divorced Debbie Reynolds in 1959 and married Elizabeth Taylor. Divorced from Elizabeth Taylor in 1964. His autobiography, *My Life, My Loves*, was published in 1982.

15 Jan 57	-	2	1. CINDY OH CINDY *HMV IP 1194*

Date	Pos	Wks	ARTIST / Record Title *Label & Number*
			Scott FITZGERALD and Yvonne KEELEY ***2 Weeks***
			Male/female vocal duo. Scott Fitzgerald born William McPhail in Glasgow, Scotland. In 1975 was a member of the Scottish Touring Company in their production of the rock opera, *Hair*. Represented UK in 1988 Eurovision Song contest with *Go*, finishing in second position. Yvonne Keeley born on September 6, 1952 in Holland. *If I Had Words* was adapted from the third movement of Charles Camille Saint-Saens, *Symphony No. 3 (Opus 78).*
23 Feb 78	9	2	1. IF I HAD WORDS *Pepper* UP 36333
			5000 VOLTS ***3 Weeks***
			British studio group formed by session singers, Martin Jay and Tina Charles, in London in 1975. Following the success of *I'm On Fire*, Kevin Wells (drums), Martin Cohen (bass) and Mike Nelson (keyboards) were added to the line-up. Just as the group were about to embark on tour, Tina Charles left the group to pursue a solo career. Vocalist Linda Kelly was drafted in and the group celebrated with another top ten hit, *Doctor Kiss Kiss*. Disbanded in 1977
02 Oct 75	9	2	1. I'M ON FIRE *Philips 6006 464*
19 Aug 76	9	1	2. DOCTOR KISS KISS *Philips 6006 533*
			Roberta FLACK ***1 Weeks***
			Born February 10, 1937 in Black Mountain, Asheville, North Carolina, USA. Earned a music scholarship to Howard University and graduated with a BA in music. Discovered singing and playing jazz in a Washington night club by pianist Des McCann, who introduced her to Atlantic Records. *Killing Me Softly With His Song* is a tribute to singer, Don McLean.
29 Mar 73	10	1	1. KILLING ME SOFTLY WITH HIS SONG *Atlantic K 10282*

Date	Pos	Wks	ARTIST / Record Title *Label & Number*
			Michael FLANDERS ***8 Weeks***
			Born on March 1, 1922 in London, England. A classmate of actor Peter Ustinov and Donald Swann at Westminster School, London. Contracted polio in 1943 and was confined to a wheelchair. In the 1950's formed a very successful musical partnership with Donald Swann. Michael sang and Donald played piano. The duo's most successful revue, *At The Drop Of A Hat*, ran at London's Fortune Theatre from January 24, 1957 to May 2, 1959. Film appearances include *Doctor In Distress* (1963) and *The Raging Moon* (1971). Michael Flanders died on April 14, 1975.
05 Mar 59	2	8	1. LITTLE DRUMMER BOY *Parlophone R(I) 4528*
			FLEETWOOD MAC ***21 Weeks***
			Formed as a Blues band in 1967 in London, England by Mick Fleetwood and John McVie who provided the group with its name. Personnel: Peter Green (vocals, guitar), Jeremy Spencer (vocals, guitar), John McVie (bass), Danny Kirwan (guitar) and Mick Fleetwood (drums). Peter Green left in mid 1970. Jeremy Spencer left in 1971. Replaced by Christine Perfect of Chicken Shack, who later married John McVie. Group relocated to California, USA in 1974, where they added Lindsey Buckingham and Stevie Nicks to the lineup.
16 Jan 69	5	6	1. ALBATROSS • *CBS 57-3145*
22 May 69	5	5	2. MAN OF THE WORLD *Immediate IM 080*
30 Oct 69	5	7	3. OH WELL *Reprise RS 27000*
21 Jun 73	8	3	4. ALBATROSS • (re-issue) *CBS 8306*

Date	Pos	Wks	ARTIST / Record Title *Label & Number*

The FLEETWOODS *7 Weeks*

Female/male vocal trio formed in high school in Olympia, Washington, USA under the name *Two Girls And A Guy*. Personnel: Gretchen Christopher (born February 29, 1940), Barbara Ellis (born February 20, 1940) and Gary Troxel (born November 28, 1939). On signing to Dolphin Records Bob Reisdorf, the owner of Dolphin Records, decided on a change of name to The Fleetwoods. When lead singer Gary Troxel was called up for military service, his place was taken by Vic Dana. Barbara Ellis retired in 1974. Gary Troxel resigned in 1983. Gretchen Christopher (composer of *Come Softly To Me*) is still touring.

Date	Pos	Wks	ARTIST / Record Title *Label & Number*
14 May 59	4	7	1. COME SOFTLY TO ME *London HL 8841*

Berni FLINT *5 Weeks*

Born on May 26, 1952 in Southport, England. On leaving school at fifteen worked as a French polisher and a television aerial rigger. Joined Royal Naval at age eighteen. During his period in the navy learned to play the guitar. On his demob from the navy in 1974 he joined a local beat group before eventually going out as a solo artist, playing the pubs and clubs in the Merseyside area. During a residency at the Sands Club in Liverpool, the manager of the club arranged an audition on the popular television talent show, *Opportunity Knocks*. Berni went on to win for twelve consecutive weeks. In September 1979 hosted Granada TV series, *Pop Gospel*.

Date	Pos	Wks	ARTIST / Record Title *Label & Number*
07 Apr 77	4	5	1. I DON'T WANT TO PUT A HOLD ON YOU *EMI 2599*

The FLOATERS *4 Weeks*

Formed in Detroit, USA in 1976. A popular club act in their home town. Discovered and signed by ABC Records executive, Otis Smith. Personnel: Charles Clark (lead vocals), Larry Cunningham, Paul Mitchell, Ralph Mitchell and Marvin Willis. Disc debut: *I'm So Glad I Took My Time*.

Date	Pos	Wks	ARTIST / Record Title *Label & Number*
29 Sep 77	5	4	1. FLOAT ON *ABC 4187*

Date	Pos	Wks	ARTIST / Record Title *Label & Number*

The FLOWERPOT MEN — *2 Weeks*

Formed in London, England in 1967. Personnel on record: John Carter (lead vocal/acoustic guitar), Ken Lewis (backing vocal/keyboards), Tony Burrows (backing vocals), Rob Shaw (backing vocal/bass), Micky Keen (lead guitar) and Clem Cattini (drums). *Let's Go To San Francisco* was composed and produced by John Carter and Ken Lewis. The tape was turned down by Fontana but Dick Rowe of Decca, liked it and suggested it for their Deram label. With the success of the record a touring Flowerpot Men was needed and Tony Burrows and Neil Landon (from the Ivy League) plus session singers, Robin Shaw and Pete Nelson, went out on the road as the Flowerpot Men.

Date	Pos	Wks	ARTIST / Record Title *Label & Number*
28 Sep 67	8	2	1. LET'S GO TO SAN FRANCISCO *Deram* DM*(I) 142*

See also The Ivy League

The FLYING COLUMN — *1 Weeks*

Ballad group formed in Belfast, N. Ireland in 1969. Personnel: Eamonn Largey (vocals, tin whistle), Kathleen Largey (lead vocals), Tony Lynch (guitar), Paul Anderson (fiddle) and Benny McKeating (banjo). *Four Green Fields* was composed by Tommy Makem. Eamonn Largey died in a car accident in 1973. Kathleen Largey died of cancer in February 1979.

Date	Pos	Wks	ARTIST / Record Title *Label & Number*
06 Apr 72	6	1	1. FOUR GREEN FIELDS *Emerald MDS 1158*

FOCUS — *1 Weeks*

Rock group formed in Amsterdam, Holland in 1969. Personnel: Jan Akkerman (guitar), Thijs Van Leer (flute, keyboards), Cyril Havermans (bass) and Pierre Van der Linden (drums). Disbanded in 1978. Reformed in the late 1990's.

Date	Pos	Wks	ARTIST / Record Title *Label & Number*
22 Feb 73	9	1	1. SYLVIA • *Polydor 2001 422*

Date	Pos	Wks	ARTIST / Record Title *Label & Number*

WAYNE FONTANA and the MINDBENDERS — *2 Weeks*

Formed in Manchester in 1962 by Wayne Fontana (born Glyn Geoffrey Ellis on October 28, 1945 in Manchester, England). Mindbenders personnel: Eric Stewart (lead guitar/vocals), Bob Land (bass) and Ric Rothwell (drums). Signed to Fontana Records by A&R man Jack Baverstock, who auditioned the group at the Oasis Club, Manchester. In October 1965, Wayne Fontana left to pursue a solo career..

Date	Pos	Wks	ARTIST / Record Title *Label & Number*
08 Mar 65	10	1	1. GAME OF LOVE *Fontana ETF 535*
05 Jan 67	10	1	2. PAMELA PAMELA *Fontana ETF 770*

Pamela Pamela credit Wayne Fontana

See also The Mindbenders

FONTANE SISTERS — *3 Weeks*

Family vocal trio from New Milford, New Jersey, USA. Personnel: Marge, Bea and Geri Rosse. Appeared in the 1944 film, *Abbot And Costello In Society*. Signed by RCA in 1949. Enjoyed several major hits with Perry Como. Were working as backing vocalists on Perry Como's TV show when Randy Wood signed them to Dot Records, in 1954.

Date	Pos	Wks	ARTIST / Record Title *Label & Number*
29 Mar 55	-	3	1. HEARTS OF STONE *London HL 8113*

EMILE FORD and the CHECKMATES — *15 Weeks*

Born Michael Emile Ford Miller on October 16, 1937 in Castries, St. Lucia, West Indies. Moved to London, England in 1955 to study engineering. Formed the Checkmates in 1957 and started playing local clubs and ballrooms. Spotted by Les Cox, an A & R talent scout for Pye Records. Checkmates personnel: John Cuffley (drums), Ken Street (guitar), George Ford (bass), Dave Ford (sax), Peter Carter (guitar), Les Hart (sax) and Alan Hawkshaw (piano). Emile parted company with the Checkmates in September 1962. Relocated to Sweden.

continues over

Date	Pos	Wks	ARTIST / Record Title *Label & Number*
10 Dec 59	1(7)	8	• 1. WHAT DO YOU WANT TO MAKE THOSE EYES AT ME FOR? *Pye 7N 15225*
18 Feb 60	4	7	2. ON A SLOW BOAT TO CHINA *Pye 7N 15245*

Tennessee Ernie FORD — *5 Weeks*

Born Ernest Jennings Ford on February 13, 1919 in Bristol, Tennessee, USA. At the age of eighteen was employed by local radio station WOPI as a staff announcer. In 1939, studied at the Cincinnati Conservatory of Music. As a young man worked on radio stations in Atlanta, San Bernadino, Reno and Pasadena. Joined the US Air Force in 1941. His recordings of hymns and scared music achieved gold status with the albums, *Hymns* (1957) and *Sing A Hymn With Me* (1961). Performed, *River Of No Return*, over credits of the 1954 film of same name. Inducted into the Country Music Hall of Fame in 1990. Died of liver complications on October 17, 1991.

Date	Pos	Wks	ARTIST / Record Title *Label & Number*
18 Jan 55	-	4	1. GIVE ME YOUR WORD *Capitol CL 14005*
05 Jul 55	-	1	2. LOSING YOU *Capitol CL 14273*

The FORTUNES — *14 Weeks*

Originally called the Clifftones when they were formed as a vocal harmony trio in Birmingham, England in 1961 by Rod Allen, Glen Dale and Barry Pritchard. In 1963, two new members, David Carr (keyboards) and Andy Brown (drums) joined and were renamed the Fortunes Rhythm Group. Signed to Decca Records. Disc debut: *Summertime Summertime* (1963). Glen Dale left in July 1966 replaced by Shel MacRae. David Carr left in August 1968. Group signed to Capitol in 1971. Barry Pritchard left in 1995 due to ill health. He died on January 11, 1999. In August 2005, Geoff Turton (ex Rockin' Berries lead singer) joined the group for a short period. Rod Allen born (Rodney Bainbridge on March 31, 1944 in Leicester, lead vocals, bass), died of liver cancer on January 10, 2008.

Date	Pos	Wks	ARTIST / Record Title *Label & Number*
02 Aug 65	3	4	1. YOU'VE GOT YOUR TROUBLES *Decca F 12173*

continues over

Date	Pos	Wks	ARTIST / Record Title *Label & Number*
01 Nov 65	5	5	2. HERE IT COMES AGAIN *Decca F 12243*
21 Oct 71	5	4	3. FREEDOM COME FREEDOM GO *Capitol CL(I) 15693*
02 Mar 72	9	1	4. STORM IN A TEA CUP *Capitol CL 15707*

FOSTER and ALLEN — *3 Weeks*

Irish vocal/instrumental duo. Formed in 1975. Personnel: Mick Foster (born on December 6, 1947 in Ballymore Eustace, Co. Kildare. Accordion/vocals) and Tony Allen (born on February 24, 1944 in Mount Temple, Co. Westmeath. Vocals/guitar). Disc debut: *Rambles Of Spring* (1978). Mick Foster won the All Ireland Junior Piano Accordion Championship in 1964 and captured the Senior title in 1968 and 1970. Tony Allen started his musical career playing in various local bands including the Merrylanders, the Finnavons and the Nightrunners. It was while both Tony and Mick were with the Nightrunners that the idea of forming a duo was first mentioned. In late 1975, Mick and Tony teamed up as a duo and Foster and Allen were born.

Date	Pos	Wks	ARTIST / Record Title *Label & Number*
29 Nov 79	8	3	1. A BUNCH OF THYME *CMR CM 003*

The FOUNDATIONS — *21 Weeks*

Formed in January 1967 in London, England. Personnel: Clem Curtis (born November 28, 1940 in Trinidad, lead vocals), Eric Allandale (trombone), Pat Burke (flute), Mike Elliot (tenor sax), Tony Gomez (organ), Tim Harris (drums), Peter Macbeth (bass) and Alan Warner (lead guitar). Clem Curtis left in 1968. Replaced by Colin Young (born September 12, 1944 in Barbados) who is lead vocalist on *Buttercup* and *Bad Old Days*. Group disbanded in 1970.

Date	Pos	Wks	ARTIST / Record Title *Label & Number*
23 Nov 67	3	4	1. BABY NOW THAT I'VE FOUND YOU *Pye 7N 17366*
12 Dec 68	3	13	2. BUILD ME UP BUTTERCUP *Pye 7N 17638*
10 Apr 69	7	4	3. IN THE BAD BAD OLD DAYS *Pye 7N 17702*

The FOUR ACES — *2 Weeks*

Formed in Philadelphia, USA in 1949. Started out as an instrumental combo before concentrating on vocals.

continues over

Date	Pos	Wks	ARTIST / Record Title *Label & Number*
			Personnel: Al Alberts (lead), Dave Mahoney (tenor), Sod Voccaro (baritone) and Lou Silvestri (bass). Disc debut: *It's No Sin* (1951). Al Alberts left in 1958 to pursue a solo career. Al died on November 27, 2009.
01 Mar 55	-	1	1. MELODY OF LOVE *Brunswick 05379*
30 Oct 56	-	1	2. A WOMAN IN LOVE *Brunswick 05589*

The FOUR PENNIES **4 Weeks**

Formed in 1963 in Blackburn, England. Personnel: Lionel Morton (born August 8, 1942 in Blackburn, lead vocals, rhythm guitar), Mike Wilsh (vocals, bass), Fritz Fryer (vocals, lead guitar), and Alan Buck (vocals, drums). *Juliet* originally started out life as the 'B' side to *Tell Me Girl*. Lionel Morton left for a solo career in 1966. He presented children's TV programme, *Play School*, and took the lead in several stage musicals including *Hair*, *Owl And The Pussycat* and *Jesus Christ Superstar*. Fritz Fryer died of cancer on September 2, 2007.

Date	Pos	Wks	ARTIST / Record Title *Label & Number*
18 May 64	3	4	1. JULIET *Philips EBF 1322*

The FOUR SEASONS **14 Weeks**

Vocal group formed in Newark, New Jersey, USA in 1949, as the Variety Trio Were known as The Varitones and also the Four Lovers during the years 1953 to 1962. Renamed The Four Seasons in 1962. Signed to Vee-Jay Records. Disc debut: *Bermuda* (1962). Personnel: Frankie Valli (born Francis C astelluccio on May 3, 1934 in Newark, New Jersey), (lead vocals), Bob Gaudio (piano), Nick Massi (bass) and Tommy De Vito (lead guitar). Nick Massi left in 1965, was replaced by Joe Long. Tommy De Vito left group in April 1970. In 1975 Bob Gaudio left group. In 1975 a new group of Four Seasons was recruited to back Frankie Valli. Disbanded in 1978. Inducted into Rock and Roll Hall of Fame in 1990. Inducted into Vocal Group Hall of Fame in 1999. In 2004, a stage musical based on the groups life was premiered in New York. In 2006, *Jersey Boys*, won four Tony Awards including 'Best Musical'.

Date	Pos	Wks	ARTIST / Record Title *Label & Number*
			Gerry Polci is lead vocal on *December 1963 (Oh What A Night)*. Nick Massi died of cancer on December 24, 2000.
21 Sep 64	4	8	1. RAG DOLL *Philips EBF 1347*
04 Mar 76	3	6	2. DECEMBER 63 (Oh What A Night) *Warner Bros. K 16688*
			See also Frankie Valli

The FOUR TOPS — *10 Weeks*

Formed in Detroit in 1954 as the Four Aims. Changed name to Four Tops in 1956. Disc debut: *Kiss Me Baby* (1956). Signed to Motown in 1964. Personnel: Levi Stubbs, (born June 6, 1936 in Detroit, lead vocals), Renaldo Benson, Lawrence Payton and Abdul Fakir. In 1986, Levi Stubbs provided the voice for the man eating plant in the film, *Little Shop Of Horrors*. Inducted into the Rock and Roll Hall of Fame in 1990. Lawrence Payton died on June 10, 1997. Renaldo 'Obie' Benson died from lung cancer on July 2, 2005. Levi Stubbs died on October 17, 2008.

Date	Pos	Wks	ARTIST / Record Title *Label & Number*
31 Oct 66	4	4	1. REACH OUT I'LL BE THERE *Tamla Motown TMG(I) 579*
25 Jan 68	5	3	2. WALK AWAY RENEE *Tamla Motown TMG(I) 634*
04 Apr 68	6	3	3. IF I WERE A CARPENTER *Tamla Motown TMG(I) 647*

FOX — *5 Weeks*

Formed in London, England in 1970. Personnel: Noosha Fox (born Susie Taylor, vocals), Herbie Armstrong (lead guitar), Kenny Young (rhythm guitar, vocals), Pete Solley (keyboards), Gary Taylor (bass) and Jim Frank (drums). Group broke up in 1976. Noosha Fox pursued a solo career, while Kenny Young and Herbie Armstrong went on to form Yellow Dog.

Date	Pos	Wks	ARTIST / Record Title *Label & Number*
06 Mar 75	3	5	1. ONLY YOU CAN *GTO GT 8*

Mattie FOX — *7 Weeks*

Born on December 9, 1949 in Ballinalee, Co. Longford. Ireland. Vocalist with a local group The Virginians. Invited to join the Country Blue Boys as a replacement for Larry Cunningham (who was retiring).

continues over

Date	Pos	Wks	ARTIST / Record Title *Label & Number*
			Made his debut with the Country Blue Boys on March 17, 1972 at the Fairways Hotel, Dundalk. Left Country Blue Boys in July 1973. Joined up with The Grassroots later that year. In December 1974, teamed up with Margo, to front Country Pride. Formed his own group Misty in May 1976 and embarked on a successful cabaret career. Gave up performing side of business in 1985, to concentrate on management. Looked after the affairs of Christy Moore from 1982 to 2005.
19 Oct 72	5	6	1. DOES MY RING HURT YOUR FINGER *Release RL 646*
29 Aug 74	10	1	2. COTTAGE IN OLD DONEGAL *Release MRL 1008*

Connie FRANCIS — *49 Weeks*

Born Constance Rosa Maria Franconero on December 12, 1938 in Newark, New Jersey, USA. At the age of four her father gave her an accordion. In 1950 she won the Arthur Godfrey Talent Show. He suggested she change her name to something shorter and Connie Francis was born. First recorded for MGM in 1955. Disc debut: *Freddy*. Starred in several films including *Where The Boys Are* (1960), *Follow The Boys* (1963) and *When The Boys Meet The Girls* (1965). Stopped performing after she was raped at a motel on November 8, 1974. Made a comeback in the eighties. Her autobiography, *Who's Sorry Now*, was published in 1984.

Date	Pos	Wks	ARTIST / Record Title *Label & Number*
01 May 58	-	5	1. WHO'S SORRY NOW *MGM MGM(I) 975*
19 Feb 59	6	3	2. MY HAPPINESS *MGM MGM(I) 1001*
23 Jul 59	2	15	3. LIPSTICK ON YOUR COLLAR *MGM MGM(I) 1018*
19 May 60	10	1	4. MAMA *MGM MGM(I) 1076*
14 Jul 60	3	9	5. ROBOT MAN *MGM MGM(I) 1076*
29 Sep 60	9	1	6. EVERYBODY'S SOMEBODY'S FOOL *MGM MGM(I) 1086*
24 Nov 60	5	4	7. MY HEART HAS A MIND OF ITS OWN *MGM (I) 1100*
09 Feb 61	9	4	8. MANY TEARS AGO *MGM* MGM*(I) 1111*
20 Apr 61	8	4	9. WHERE THE BOYS ARE *MGM MGM(I) 1121*
20 Jul 61	10	1	10. BREAKIN' IN A BRAND NEW BROKEN HEART *MGM MGM(I) 1136*
05 Oct 61	5	2	11. TOGETHER *MGM MGM(I) 1138*

Date	Pos	Wks	ARTIST / Record Title *Label & Number*

Stan FREBERG — *2 Weeks*

Pop satirist/comedy writer. Born Stanley Victor Freberg on August 7, 1926 in Los Angeles, California, USA. The only son of a Bapist minister, his first taste of showbusiness came at the age of 11, working as assistant with his uncle Raymond, a magican. After graduating from high school he moved to Hollywood where he quickly found work doing voice-overs for animated cartoon characters for Walt Disney, Warner Bros. and MGM. Also worked as a radio actor appearing on such programmes as *The Jack Benny Show*. Disc debut: *John and Marsha* (1951). Over the following years, Stan trained his sights on many of the hits of the period and turned his parodies of them into classic comedy moments that continue to be aired to this day. His autobiography, *It Only Hurts When I Laugh*, was published in 1989.

Date	Pos	Wks	ARTIST / Record Title *Label & Number*
23 Nov 54	2	1	1. SH-BOOM *Capitol CL 14187*
21 Aug 56	-	1	2. HEARTBREAK HOTEL *Capitol CL 14608*

John FRED and the PLAYBOY BAND — *6 Weeks*

Formed in Baton Rouge, Louisiana, USA in 1956. Personnel: John Fred (born John Gourrier on May 8, 1941 in Baton Rouge, Louisiana. vocals), Tommy Dee (organ), Charlie Spinosa (trumpet), Ronnie Goodson (trumpet), Andrew Bernard (sax), James O'Rourke (guitar), Harold Cowert (bass) and Joe Micelli (drums). John Fred died on April 15, 2005.

Date	Pos	Wks	ARTIST / Record Title *Label & Number*
25 Jan 68	3	6	1. JUDY IN DISGUISE (With Glasses) *Pye 7N 25442*

FREDDIE and the DREAMERS — *1 Weeks*

Formed in Manchester, England in October 1961 when Freddie Garrity took over the Kingfishers and they decided to rename themselves, Freddie and The Dreamers. Personnel: Freddie (born Freddy Garrity on November 14, 1936 in Manchester), Derek Quinn (lead guitar), Roy Crewdson (guitar), Peter Birrell (bass) and Bernie Dwyer (drums). Discovered by John Barry, who was responsible for the group signing to Columbia in March 1963.

continues over

Date	Pos	Wks	ARTIST / Record Title *Label & Number*

Disc debut: *If You Gotta Make A Fool Of Somebody* (1963). Film appearances include *What A Crazy World* (1964), *Just For You* (1964) and *Cuckoo Patrol* (1967). In 1967, the original Dreamers split. From 1971 to 1973 Freddie starred in the UK children's TV show, *Little Big Time*. In July 2002, Freddie suffered a heart attack and had to retire from showbusiness. Bernie Dwyer died on December 4, 2002. Freddie died on May 19, 2006.

16 Dec 63	10	1	1. **YOU WERE MADE FOR ME** *Columbia DB(I) 7147*

FREE — *4 Weeks*

Formed in London, England in 1968. Personnel: Paul Rodgers (vocals), Paul Kossoff (guitar), Andy Fraser (bass) and Simon Kirke (drums). Kossoff and Fraser left in 1972, replaced by Tetsu Yamauchi and John Bundrick. Rodgers and Kirke departed in 1974 to form Bad Company. Kossoff died on March 19, 1976. Paul Rodgers, fronted Queen on their 2005 World tour.

02 Jul 70	5	4	1. **ALL RIGHT NOW** *Island WIP 6082*

The FRESHMEN — *8 Weeks*

Showband formed in Ballymena, County Antrim, Ireland in August 1962 by ex members of the Billy McFarland Band. Made disc debut, *He's The One You Love*, in 1964, under the name, *Six of One*. Supported the Beach Boys on their concert dates in Ireland in May 1967. Signed to CBS in 1970, and released the innovative and highly praised concept album, *Peace on Earth*. Personnel: Derek Dean (lead vocals), Billy Brown (lead vocals, keyboards, tenor sax), Maurice Henry (leader, tenor sax), Torry McGahey (vocals, bass), Davy McKnight (vocals, drums), Damian McIllroy (vocals, lead guitar), and Sean Mahon (vocals, trumpet). Billy Brown left the Freshman in February 1971 to form his own band. Replaced by Ivan Laybourne. Billy returned to the fold in November 1972. Numerous personnel changes throughout seventies. Band broke up in November 1980. Re-formed in 1983 for a brief period. Billy Brown died on June 6, 1999. Sean Mahon died on May 29, 2009.

continues over

Date	Pos	Wks	ARTIST / Record Title *Label & Number*
11 Jan 68	7	5	1. PAPA-OOH-MOW-MOW *Target 7N 17432*
06 Mar 69	9	2	2. JUST TO SEE YOU SMILE *Target 7N 17689*
09 Apr 70	10	1	3. HALFWAY TO WHERE *CBS 4842*

See also Billy Brown; Derek Dean and The Freshmen

Dean FRIEDMAN — *5 Weeks*

Born in 1955 in Paramus, New Jersey, USA. Member of group Marsha and the Self Portraits. Signed to Lifesong in 1976. Disc debut: *Dean Friedman* LP (1977). During the 1980's turned his hand to composing and producing music soundtracks for television and film. Composed the soundtrack music for the hit UK television series *Boon*. Has authored several best selling MIDI synthesizer books for Music Sales Publicity.

Date	Pos	Wks	ARTIST / Record Title *Label & Number*
19 Oct 78	3	5	1. LUCKY STARS *Lifesong LS 402*

FRIJID PINK — *3 Weeks*

Formed by some high school friends in Detroit, USA in 1963, under the name, the Detroit Vibrations. Changed name to Frijid Pink in 1967. Personnel: Kelly Green (vocals), Gary Ray Thompson (guitar), Tom Beaudry (bass), Larry Zelanka (keyboards) and Richard 'Rich' Stevens (drums). Disc debut: 'Tell Me Why'. Disbanded in 1978.

Date	Pos	Wks	ARTIST / Record Title *Label & Number*
21 May 70	7	3	1. THE HOUSE OF THE RISING SUN *Deram* DM *288*

The FUREY BROTHERS and Davy ARTHUR — *33 Weeks*

Folk/ballad group formed in 1974. Personnel: Finbar (vocals, uileann pipes), Paul, George and Eddie Furey (fiddle, guitar) and Davy Arthur. The Fureys were born and raised in Ballyfermott, Dublin, Ireland. Davey Arthur born in Edinburgh, Scotland. Finbar and Eddie started out as a duo in the late 1950's. Performed in folk clubs, colleges and Universities in Britain. Relocated to Scotland in 1966. Paul and George met up with Davey Arthur in Germany in 1970 and formed a group called The Buskers.

continues over

Date	Pos	Wks	ARTIST / Record Title *Label & Number*

Following an appearance at the 1974 Cambridge Folk Festival Finbar, Eddie, Paul, George and Davey decided to amalgamate and form a new group. Davy Arthur left in 1992 to pursue a solo career. Rejoined in 2003. Finbar Furey departed in 1993 to embark on a solo career. Paul Furey died on June 16, 2002.

08 Mar 79	1(1)	28	• 1. GREEN FIELDS OF FRANCE *Banshee SHE 001*
21 Dec 79	5	5	2. LEAVING NANCY *Banshee SHE 002*

Billy FURY — *56 Weeks*

Born Ronald Wycherley on April 17, 1940 in Liverpool, England. In 1958 sent demo of five tracks he had recorded at Percy F Phillips recording studio in Liverpool, to impresario Larry Parnes. Parnes arranged to meet Billy at the Essoldo Theatre in Birkenhead on October 1, 1958 when his current package show with Marty Wilde would play there. Parnes was impressed by Ronnie's talent and looks and after a rehearsal gave him a spot on the second half of the show. He was a smash hit. Parnes signed him on the spot and renamed him Billy Fury. Recorded the classic rock 'n' roll album, *The Sound of Fury* in 1960. Starred in the films, *Play it Cool* (1962) and *I've Gotta Horse* (1965). The sport of kings appealed to Billy and in the 1964 Epsom Derby Billy's horse *Anselmo* finished in fourth place. Dogged by ill health, Billy spent several years out of the business. Made a comeback in July 1981. Died of heart failure on January 29, 1983.

08 Jun 61	5	16	1. HALFWAY TO PARADISE *Decca F 11349*
28 Sep 61	1(1)	6	• 2. JEALOUSY *Decca F 11384*
11 Jan 62	3	10	3. I'D NEVER FIND ANOTHER YOU *Decca F 11409*
21 Jun 62	6	4	4. LAST NIGHT WAS MADE FOR LOVE *Decca F 11458*
25 Mar 63	5	7	5. LIKE I'VE NEVER BEEN GONE *Decca F 11582*
10 Jun 63	4	5	6. WHEN WILL YOU SAY I LOVE YOU *Decca F 11655*
19 Aug 63	4	4	7. IN SUMMER *Decca F 11701*
17 Aug 64	7	4	8. IT'S ONLY MAKE BELIEVE *Decca F 11939*

Date	Pos	Wks	ARTIST / Record Title *Label & Number*

G

Bridie GALLAGHER *3 Weeks*

Born on September 7, 1924 in Ards, Creeslough, Co. Donegal, Ireland. Moved to Belfast while still a teenager to live with her aunt. Began her professional singing career at the age of fourteen performing at local dances and concerts. In the mid 1950's was spotted by Belfast promoter, Mervyn Solomon, who arranged an audition and subsequently a recording contract with Beltona Records. Disc debut: *A Mothers Love's A Blessing* (1956). Holds the attendance record (7,500 set in 1959) for the Royal Albert Hall. Retired from performing in 2000. On July 10, 2000 Donegal Co. Council honoured her at a special ceremony to mark her contribution to music and to her native county.

Date	Pos	Wks	ARTIST / Record Title *Label & Number*
25 Jun 58	-	2	1. THE BOYS FROM THE COUNTY ARMAGH *Beltona BE 2679*
09 Jul 58	-	1	2. THE GIRL FROM DONEGAL L.P. *Beltona LB 17*

Tracks on **The Girl From Donegal L.P.**: The Girl From Donegal / Take This Message To My Mother / At The Close Of An Irish Day / Two Little Orphans / Goodbye Johnny / My Mother's Last Goodbye / The Faithful Sailor Boy / Killarney And You / The Road By The River / Hills Of Donegal / I'll Forgive But I'll Never Forget / The Boys From County Armagh / The Poor Orphan Boy.

GALLAGHER and LYLE *8 Weeks*

Scottish vocal duo. Benny Gallagher born on January 10, 1945 in Largs, Ayrshire. Graham Lyle born on March 11, 1944 in Bellshill, Glasgow. Gallagher and Lyle began their musical careers in the early sixties in Glasgow performing with local groups. In 1968, Paul McCartney signed the duo as staff writers for artists on the Beatles Apple label. In 1969, the duo joined McGuinness Flint, writing two of the band's hits, *When I'm Dead And Gone* and *Malt and Barley Blues*.

continues over

Date	Pos	Wks	ARTIST / Record Title *Label & Number*
			In 1974 made the decision to leave McGuinness Flint and work together as a duo. Disc debut: *Gallagher and Lyle* LP issued on Capitol in 1972. Signed to A&M in 1973. Decided to go their separate ways in 1979. Gallagher to concentrate on production and Lyle to concentrate on his songwriting. He composed hit songs for Tina Turner, *What's Love Got To Do With It* and Michael Jackson, *Just Good Friends.*
15 Apr 76	9	1	1. I WANNA STAY WITH YOU *A&M AMS 7211*
15 Jul 76	4	4	2. HEART ON MY SLEEVE *A&M AMS 7227*
24 Feb 77	5	3	3. EVERY LITTLE TEARDROP *A&M AMS 57274*
			Patsy GALLANT — ***2 Weeks***
			Born on August 15, 1948 in Campbellton, New Brunswick, Canada. Made her entry into the music business singing with her sisters under the name, The Gallant Sisters. Left her siblings in 1967 to pursue a solo career. Made her first recordings in 1967. Has recorded in both the English and French languages.
20 Oct 77	5	2	1. FROM NEW YORK TO L.A. *EMI 2620*
			James GALWAY — ***7 Weeks***
			Born on December 8, 1939 in Belfast, N Ireland. Began playing the tin whistle as a young child before switching to the flute. Studied at the Royal College of Music and also at the Guildhall School of Music and Drama in London. Also studied at the Paris Conservatory. Began his musical career at the Sadlers Wells Opera and Royal Opera, Covent Garden. Played piccolo with the BBC Symphony Orchestra. Held position of principal flute with the London Symphony Orchestra and also with the Royal Philharmonic Orchestra. In 1969 joined the Berlin Philharmonic where he was principal flute for six years. In 1975 launched his career as a soloist. Received a Knighthood in 2001 for his services to music.
01 Jun 78	1(1)	7	• 1. ANNIE'S SONG • *RCA RB 5085*

Date	Pos	Wks	ARTIST / Record Title *Label & Number*

Art GARFUNKEL — *15 Weeks*

Born October 13, 1942 in Forest Hills, New York City USA. In 1957 teamed up with schoolfriend, Paul Simon. Made their disc debut, *Hey Schoolgirl*, under the name Tom and Jerry. Art recorded solo as Artie Garr. Achieved a Bachelor of Arts Degree at Columbia University. Met up again with Paul Simon in 1962. 1962. Started performing as Simon and Garfunkel in late 1963. Split in 1970. Starred in the films *Catch-22* (1970) and *Carnal Knowledge* (1971).

Date	Pos	Wks	ARTIST / Record Title *Label & Number*
09 Oct 75	2	5	1. I ONLY HAVE EYES FOR YOU *CBS 3575*
05 Apr 79	1(5)	10	•2. BRIGHT EYES *CBS SCBS 6947*

See also Simon and Garfunkel

Lief GARRETT — *3 Weeks*

Born Leif Per Nervik on November 8, 1961 in Hollywood, California USA. A child actor he got his first taste of acting in the 1969 film, *Bob And Carol And Ted And Alice*. Other film appearances include *Walking Tall* (1973), *The Outsiders* (1983) and *The Whispering* (1996). Also appeared in several TV series' including *Cannon* and *Gunsmoke*. In 1977, was signed to Scotti Brothers Record company by Michael Lloyd. Disc debut: *Surfin' USA* (1977). Retired from the music business in 1980 to concentrate on his acting career.

Date	Pos	Wks	ARTIST / Record Title *Label & Number*
22 Feb 79	5	3	1. I WAS MADE FOR DANCIN' *Scotti Brothers K 11202*

David GARRICK — *6 Weeks*

Born Philip Darryl Core in 1945 in Liverpool, England. A member of the Birkenhead Operatic Society in 1961. Spent two years in Italy training to be an opera singer. Discovered by Robert Wace, who was part of the Kinks management team. Signed with Pye Records. Disc debut: *Go* (1965). Left Pye in September 1969 and signed with Columbia. *Dear Mrs Applebee* originally recorded by its composer, Billy Meshel.

Date	Pos	Wks	ARTIST / Record Title *Label & Number*
10 Oct 66	2	6	1. DEAR MRS. APPLEBEE *Pye 7N 35335*

Date	Pos	Wks	ARTIST / Record Title *Label & Number*

GARY'S GANG — *1 Weeks*

Disco group formed in Queens, New York USA. Personnel: Eric Matthews (lead vocals/guitar), Al Lauricella (keyboards), Rino Minetti (keyboards), Bill Castalano (percussion), Bob Forman (saxophone), Jay Leon (trombone) and Gary Turnier (drums).

29 Mar 79	10	1	1. KEEP ON DANCIN' *CBS SCBS 7109*

Marvin GAYE — *3 Weeks*

Born Marvin Pentz Gaye Jr. on April 2, 1939 in Washington, D.C., USA. In the late 1950's teamed up with Harvey Fuqua in the re-formed doo wop group The Moonglows. Moved to Detroit in 1960 and secured work as a session singer at Motown. Recorded a series of successful duets with Mary Wells, Diana Ross, Tammy Terrell and Kim Weston. Debut hit: *Stubborn Kind Of Fellow* (1962). Shot to death by his father on April 1, 1984. Inducted into the Rock and Roll Hall of Fame in 1987.

10 Apr 69	7	3	1. I HEARD IT THROUGH THE GRAPEVINE *Tamla Motown TMG(I) 686*

Crystal GAYLE — *11 Weeks*

Born Brenda Gail Web on January 9, 1951 in Paintsville, Kentucky, USA. Family moved to Wabash, Indiana when she was young. Sister of country music legend Loretta Lynn. Began her professional singing career in her sisters road show. Disc debut in 1970. Signed with United Artists in 1974. In 1979 became the first country artist to tour China.

12 Jan 78	4	6	1. DON'T IT MAKE MY BROWN EYES BLUE *UA UP 36307*
14 Sep 78	5	5	2. TALKING IN YOUR SLEEP *UA UP 36422*

Gloria GAYNOR — *12 Weeks*

Born Gloria Fowles on September 7, 1949 in Newark, New Jersey, USA. Started her music career with jazz/pop group the Soul Satisfiers.

continues over

Date	Pos	Wks	ARTIST / Record Title *Label & Number*
			Disc debut: *She'll Be Sorry* (1965). Signed with CBS in 1970. Her autobiography, *I Will Survive*, was published in 1997.
23 Jan 75	3	4	1. NEVER CAN SAY GOODBYE *MGM 2006 463*
08 Mar 79	1(4)	8	•2. I WILL SURVIVE *Polydor 2095 017*

G-CLEFS — *6 Weeks*

Vocal group formed in Roxbury, Massachusetts, USA, in 1955. Personnel: brothers, Teddy, Chris, Arnold and Tim Scott, plus Ray Gibson. First hit: *Ka-Ding-Dong* (1956).Relocated to New York in 1956. Disbanded in 1966. *I Understand* is an adaptation of the tune, *Auld Lang Syne*, and was originally a hit in 1954 for the Four Tunes.

Date	Pos	Wks	ARTIST / Record Title *Label & Number*
14 Dec 61	8	6	1. I UNDERSTAND *London HLU 9433*

GENESIS — *1 Weeks*

Formed at Charterhouse School in Godalming, England in 1967 as (New) Anon. Sent a demo to Jonathan King at Decca. Suitable impressed he signed them to Decca and renamed the group, Genesis. Personnel: Peter Gabriel (vocals), Mike Rutherford (guitar), Tony Banks (keyboards), Steve Hackett (guitar) and Phil Collins (drums). Peter Gabriel left group in 1975 to pursue a solo career. Phil Collins became lead singer. Collins left group in 1996 to focus on his solo career.

Date	Pos	Wks	ARTIST / Record Title *Label & Number*
11 May 78	10	1	1. FOLLOW YOU FOLLOW ME *Charisma CB 309*

Bobbie GENTRY — *13 Weeks*

Born Roberta Lee Streeter on July 27, 1944 in Chickasaw County, Mississippi, USA. Studied at the Los Angeles Conservatory of Music. Adopted her stage name from the 1953 film, *Ruby Gentry*. Won the 1967 Best New Artist Grammy Award.

Date	Pos	Wks	ARTIST / Record Title *Label & Number*
19 Oct 67	6	4	1. ODE TO BILLY JOE *Capitol CL(I) 15511*
25 Sep 69	1(2)	9	•2. I'LL NEVER FALL IN LOVE AGAIN *Capitol CL(I) 15606*

Date	Pos	Wks	ARTIST / Record Title *Label & Number*

Bobbie GENTRY and Glen CAMPBELL 6 Weeks

Male/female vocal duo. Bobbie Gentry born on July 27, 1944 in Chickasaw County, Mississippi, USA. Glen Campbell born on April 22, 1936 in Billstown. Arkansas, USA.

08 Jan 70	2	6	1. ALL I HAVE TO DO IS DREAM *Capitol CL 15619*

GERALDINE 6 Weeks

Born Geraldine Brannigan in 1954 in Dublin, Ireland. With her brothers, Donal and Declan, performed on the cabaret scene as The Brannigans. Spotted by songwriter/producer Phil Coulter while appearing on RTE television. Represented Luxembourg at the 1975 Eurovision Song Contest, performing *Toi*, finishing in fifth position. Split from her brothers in 1975, to pursue a solo career. Debut solo disc: *Toi* (1975). Rejoined her brothers in April 1979 and under the name, The GB Band, concentrated on the ballroom circuit. Married songwriter Phil Coulter in 1998. Made a return to live performance in 2007.

08 Sep 77	4	4	1. ROMANO *CBS CBS 5534*
09 Feb 78	9	1	2. WONDERFUL *CBS CBS 5920*
24 Aug 78	7	1	3. SUNDAY SCHOOL TO BROADWAY *CBS CBS 6488*

Danyel GERARD 4 Weeks

Born Gerard Daniel Kherlakian on March 7, 1939 in Paris, France. Made disc debut in 1958.

21 Oct 71	5	4	1. BUTTERFLY *CBS 7454*

GERRY and the PACEMAKERS 33 Weeks

Group formed by Gerry Marsden in 1958 in Liverpool, England as the Mars Bars. Changed name to Pacemakers in 1959. Personnel: Gerry Marsden (born September 24, 1942 in Liverpool) (vocals), Leslie Maguire (piano), Les Chadwick (bass), and Freddie Marsden (drums). Appeared in the 1964 film *Ferry Cross The Mersey*.

continues over

Date	Pos	Wks	ARTIST / Record Title *Label & Number*
			Group broke up in 1967 with Gerry going on to star in the London West End stage musical, *Charlie Girl. How Do You Do It* was originally offered to the Beatles, who rejected it as unsuitable. *You'll Never Walk Alone* was later adopted as the anthem of Liverpool Football club. Freddie Marsden died from lung cancer on December 9, 2006.
13 May 63	4	3	1. HOW DO YOU DO IT? *Columbia DB(I) 4987*
10 Jun 63	1(4)	11	• 2. I LIKE IT *Columbia DB(I) 7041*
28 Oct 63	1(6)	10	• 3. YOU'LL NEVER WALK ALONE *Columbia DB(I) 7126*
27 Jan 64	3	9	4. I'M THE ONE *Columbia DB(I) 7189*

Andy GIBB — *3 Weeks*

Born Andrew Roy Gibb on March 5, 1958 in Manchester, England. Family moved to Australia when he was six months old. Made decision to pursue a musical career with encouragement from his brothers Maurice, Robin and Barry (of the Bee Gees). Disc debut: *I Just Want To Be Your Everything* (1977). Died from a heart virus on March 10, 1988.

Date	Pos	Wks	ARTIST / Record Title *Label & Number*
17 Aug 78	4	3	1. AN EVERLASTING LOVE *RSO 015*

Robin GIBB — *9 Weeks*

Born on December 22, 1949 in Douglas, Isle of Man. Twin brother of Bee Gee, Maurice Gibb. Left Bee Gees in March 1969 to pursue a brief solo career. He returned to the Bee Gees lineup in August 1971.

Date	Pos	Wks	ARTIST / Record Title *Label & Number*
07 Aug 69	1(3)	9	• 1. SAVED BY THE BELL *Polydor 56337*

Georgia GIBBS — *1 Weeks*

Born Frieda Lipschitz on August 17, 1919 in Worcester, Massachusetts, USA. Began singing in Boston ballrooms as a teenager under the name Fredda Gibson. In 1943 changed her name to Georgia Gibbs. Resident on the 'Lucky Strikes' radio programme from 1937 to 1939. Toured as vocalist with Artie Shaw Band.

continues over

Date	Pos	Wks	ARTIST / Record Title *Label & Number*
			Radio show host, Garry Moore, dubbed her with the title, *Her Nibs, Miss Georgia Gibbs*. Died from cancer on December 9, 2006.
21 Aug 56	-	1	1. ROCK RIGHT *Mercury MT 110*

Don GIBSON *7 Weeks*

Born Donald Eugene Gibson on April 3, 1928 in Shelby, North Carolina, USA. Made his first recordings with The Sons Of The Soil in 1949. Formed his own band The King Cotton Kinfolks in 1950. In 1955 Wesley Rose signed him to a songwriting contract with Acuff-Rose. Signed to RCA Records in 1957. Composed many classic songs including *I Can't Stop Loving You* and *Oh Lonesome Me*. Died of natural causes on November 17, 2003.

Date	Pos	Wks	ARTIST / Record Title *Label & Number*
12 Oct 61	6	5	1. SEA OF HEARTBREAK *RCA ERC 1243*
01 Mar 62	8	1	2. LONESOME NUMBER ONE *RCA ERC 1272*
26 Jul 62	8	1	3. I CAN MEND YOUR BROKEN HEART *RCA ERC 1297*

Terry GILKYSON and the Easy Riders *2 Weeks*

Born Hamilton Henry Gilykson 111 on June 17, 1916 in Mont Clare, Pennyslvania, USA. Relocated to California in 1947 to try and promote his songs and start a career as a folk singer. Performed with The Weavers in the early 1950's. Teamed up with the Easy Riders (Frank Miller and Richard Dehr) in 1953. Songwriter credits include *Cry Of The Wild Goose*, *Fast Freight*, *Memories Are Made Of This* and *Love Is A Golden Ring*. Left the Easy Riders in the 1962 to work on providing music for animated and motion pictures for the Walt Disney Studios. In 1968, received an Academy award nomination for the song, *The Bare Necessities* from the film, *Jungle Book*. Died on October 15, 1999. *Marianne* is an adaptation of a Bahamian folk song. Richard Dehr is featured vocals on *Marianne*.

Date	Pos	Wks	ARTIST / Record Title *Label & Number*
26 Mar 57	-	2	1. MARIANNE *Philips EPB 670*

Date	Pos	Wks	ARTIST / Record Title *Label & Number*

James GILREATH — *13 Weeks*

Vocalist/guitarist/songwriter. Born on November 14, 1939 in Una Community, near Prairie, Mississippi, USA. Began his musical career in 1961 as a member of a local group, The Nite-Liters. Disc debut: *I Need It* (1962). Died on September 7, 2003. John Mihelic is the featured trumpet player on *Little Band Of Gold*.

Date	Pos	Wks	ARTIST / Record Title *Label & Number*
06 May 63	3	13	1. LITTLE BAND OF GOLD *Pye Int. 7N 25190*

Jim GILSTRAP — *1 Weeks*

Born in Pittsburg, Texas, USA. Moved to California while in his teens. Noted session singer was also a member of several groups including Side Effect and The Reason Why. Also a member of Stevie Wonder's band, Wonderlove.

Date	Pos	Wks	ARTIST / Record Title *Label & Number*
01 May 75	10	1	1. SWING YOUR DADDY *Polydor 2005 021*

GINA, Dale HAZE and the CHAMPIONS — *11 Weeks*

Irish showband formed in 1971, as The Herdsmen. Changed name to The Champions, in September 1973. Personnel: Gina (born Mary Hurley in Middleton, Co. Cork, vocals), Dale Haze (born Jeremiah Mackey in Kilmacthomas, Co. Waterford, vocals), Mossie Walsh (organ), Eddie Fitzgerald (bass), Pat Walsh (guitar) and Tony Hornibrook (drums). Disc debut: *Paper Mansions* (1973) as 'Gina and the Herdsmen'.

Date	Pos	Wks	ARTIST / Record Title *Label & Number*
06 Mar 75	5	3	1. MINNIE MINNIE MINNIE *Release RL 763*
07 Jul 77	2	3	2. DO YOU WANT TO DO IT *Release RL 874*
22 Sep 77	8	3	3. I'VE BEEN WAITING FOR YOU *Release RL 871*
05 Apr 79	10	1	4. YOU'RE THE GREATEST LOVER *Release RL 950*
22 Nov 79	7	1	5. WHO DO YOU WANNA BE *Spider WEB 015*

Will GLAHE and his MUSIK — *1 Weeks*

Accordionist / pianist / bandleader. Born on February 12, 1902 in Elberfeld, Germany. Worked as a pianist in cafes and silent film cinemas while studying at Cologne Conservatory.

continues over

Date	Pos	Wks	ARTIST / Record Title *Label & Number*
			In 1929 was pianist with the Dajos Bela Orchestra. Formed his own orchestra in 1932. Died on November 21, 1989.
04 Feb 58	-	1	1. LIECHTENSTEINER POLKA • *Decca F 10961*
			John GLENN and the MAINLINERS 12 Weeks
			Born John Hanratty on March 22, 1952 in Crossmaglen, Co. Armagh. N Ireland Started out in showbusinness with local group, The Gamblers. Replaced Big Tom as lead singer with the Mainliners in May 1975. Disc debut: *Sunny Side Of The Mountain*. Left Mainliners in 1978, to form The Wranglers.
17 Jul 75	5	3	1. SUNNY SIDE OF THE MOUNTAIN *Denver DMC 1015*
13 May 76	8	5	2. CALL ME DARLING *Misty MYS 102*
21 Apr 77	6	4	3. A LITTLE COUNTRY TOWN IN IRELAND *Misty MYS 104*
			Gary GLITTER 43 Weeks
			Born Paul Gadd on May 8, 1940 in Banbury, Oxon, England. Entered showbiz at a young age performing with local groups. Made his disc debut, *Alone At Night*, in 1960, on the Decca label under the name Paul Raven. Also recorded under the names Paul Monday and Rubber Bucket. Changed his name to Gary Glitter in 1971. In November 1999 he was convicted in Britain of possessing child pornography and jailed for four months for offences of downloading indecent photographs of children onto his computer. He served two months before being released. In March 2006, he was convicted of committing "obscene acts with children" in Vietnam, and given a three year jail sentence.
20 Jul 72	4	4	1. ROCK AND ROLL PART 2 *Bell BELL 1216*
12 Oct 72	7	3	2. I DIDN'T KNOW I LOVED YOU (TILL I SAW YOU ROCK 'N' ROLL) *Bell BELL 1259*
08 Feb 73	9	1	3. DO YOU WANNA TOUCH ME? (OH YEAH) *Bell BELL 1280*
26 Apr 73	2	5	4. HELLO! HELLO! I'M BACK AGAIN *Bell BELL 1299*
26 Jul 73	2	6	5. I'M THE LEADER OF THE GANG (I AM) *Bell BELL 1321*
22 Nov 73	2	7	6. I LOVE YOU LOVE ME LOVE *Bell BELL 1337*

continues over

Date	Pos	Wks	ARTIST / Record Title *Label & Number*
11 Apr 74	9	2	7. REMEMBER ME THIS WAY *Bell BELL 1349*
20 Jun 74	1(2)	3	• 8. ALWAYS YOURS *Bell BELL 1359*
05 Dec 74	1(2)	8	• 9. OH YES YOU'RE BEAUTIFUL *Bell BELL 1391*
03 Jul 75	3	4	10. DOING ALL RIGHT WITH THE BOYS *Bell BELL 1429*

The GLITTER BAND — *5 Weeks*

Started life as backing musicians for Gary Glitter in 1972. The following year having provided the backing on several of Gary Glitter's hits the band approached Mike Leander and requested that the band be given a shot at becoming an act in their own right. Leander agreed and The Glitter Band made their debut at The Aquarius Club, London in 1973. Personnel: Gerry Shephard (vocals, lead guitar), John Springate (vocals, bass), John Rossall (leader, saxophone, trombone, MD), Harvey Ellison (tenor saxophone), Pete Phipps (drums, keyboards) and Tony Leonard (drums). Disc debut: *Angel Face* (1974). John Rossall left in late 1974 to pursue a solo career. Group continued as a five piece. Appeared in the film, *Never Too Young To Rock*, which had its premiere in Dublin on May 20, 1975. In early 1976 broke the ties with Gary Glitter when he decided to retire, changed their name to the G Band. Band split in 1977 with Harvey and Tony returning to Gary Glitter who had decided to come out of retirement. John Springate lead vocal on *Goodbye My Love.* Gerry Shephard died from cancer on May 6, 2003.

Date	Pos	Wks	ARTIST / Record Title *Label & Number*
06 Feb 75	4	4	1. GOODBYE MY LOVE *Bell BELL 1395*
15 May 75	7	1	2. THE TEARS I CRIED *Bell BELL 1416*

GLORIA — *56 Weeks*

Born Gloria Smith on May 25, 1946 in Bailieboro, Co. Cavan, Ireland. Began playing piano and accordion at an early age. While still attending primary school she made a number of appearances on radio and television. After leaving school, Gloria worked as a hotel receptionist while playing part time with her fathers band.

continues over

Date	Pos	Wks	ARTIST / Record Title *Label & Number*
			In 1968, she accepted a position as piano player and vocalist with the Maurice Lynch Showband. Made her recording debut with the Maurice Lynch Band, contributing three tracks to their 1971 album, *Let's Keep It Country*. In 1971, she was invited to become lead vocalist with the newly formed Cascades Showband. Moved to the Johnny McEvoy Band in July 1972, left in May 1976. Launched her own band, Mississippi, in June 1976.
18 Aug 77	5	7	1. ONE DAY AT A TIME *Release RL 873*
10 Sep 78	1(2)	21	• 2. ONE DAY AT A TIME (re-entry) *Release RL 873*
08 Mar 79	10	1	3. ONE DAY AT A TIME (2nd re-entry) *Release RL 873*
12 Jul 79	3	27	4. ONE DAY AT A TIME (3rd re-entry) *Release RL 873*

The GO LUCKY FOUR — *8 Weeks*

Ballad/folk group formed in 1964 in Belfast, Ireland. Personnel: Gerry Burns (lead vocals), Eamon McGirr (vocals, guitar), John Sullivan (vocals, bass) and Finbarr Carolan (vocals, guitar). Met up at St Thomas' School, Belfast, where all were teachers. Debut disc: *Up Went Nelson*. John Sullivan left when the group went professional in 1967, replaced by Brian McCann. Group broke up in early 1970's. Eamon McGirr died on June 14, 2004. Gerry Burns died in June 2007. *Up Went Nelson* was composed by Billy McBurney, following the blowing up of Nelson's Pillar in Dublin, by subversives, on March 8, 1966.

Date	Pos	Wks	ARTIST / Record Title *Label & Number*
18 Apr 66	2	8	1. UP WENT NELSON *Emerald MD 1040*

Andrew GOLD — *6 Weeks*

Born on August 2, 1951 in Burbank, California, USA. Son of Ernest Gold (composer of "Exodus") and Marni Nixon (the singing voice of Deborah Kerr (King And I), Audrey Hepburn (My Fair Lady) and Natalie Wood (West Side Story). Began writing songs at the age of thirteen. By the early 1970's was working as a session musician.

continues over

Date	Pos	Wks	ARTIST / Record Title *Label & Number*
			In 1973, joined the Linda Ronstadt band and by 1976 while still a member of the band, was also opening the show. Began recording solo in 1975. Disc debut: *Heartaches In Heartaches* (1975). In 1984 formed a duo, Common Knowledge, with 10cc's Graham Gouldman. Changed name to Wax later that same year. Andrew's song, *Thank You For Being A Friend*,was used as the theme for *The Golden Girls* television series.
27 Apr 78	2	6	1. NEVER LET HER SLIP AWAY *Asylum K 13112*
			GOLDIE ***2 Weeks***
			British group formed in Blyth Town, Northumberland, England in 1976 by ex-members of Kestrel, Pete McDonald (vocals) and Dave Black (lead guitar), Disbanded in 1980.
29 Jun 78	4	2	1. MAKING UP AGAIN *Bronze BRO 50*
			Bobby GOLDSBORO ***17 Weeks***
			Born on January 18, 1941 in Marianna, Florida, USA. Formed his own band, The Webbs, while still attending high school. In the autumn of 1962, Bobby and his group, The Webbs, became Roy Orbisons backing band. Signed to Laurie Records in 1962. Went solo in 1964. Formed publishing firm, House of Gold Music in 1975. In early 80's gave up performing and to concentrate on writing and producing children's stories.
23 May 68	1(4)	11	• 1. HONEY *United Artists UP 2215*
17 Apr 75	4	6	2. HONEY (re-issue) *United Artists UP 35633*
			Ron GOODWIN ***1 Weeks***
			Born on February 17, 1925 in Plymouth, Devon, England. Relocated with his family to London in 1934. Learned to play piano as a child. Played trumpet in school band. In 1939, age 14, formed his own dance band, The Woodchoppers. Worked for music publishers Campbell Connolly as a copyist. Got job as arranger with Norrie Paramor and Harry Gold.

continues over

Date	Pos	Wks	ARTIST / Record Title *Label & Number*

While working with music publisher Edward Kassner did arrangements for Stanley Black, Ted Heath and Geraldo. In 1949 took up job as musical director with newly formed Polygon Record company. Composed the scores for several successful films including *Village Of The Dammed* (1960), *Day Of The Triffids* (1962), *633 Squadron* (1964) and *Where Eagles Dare* (1968). Died on January 8, 2003, from complications due to asthma.

24 Apr 56	-	1	1. SUMMERTIME IN VENICE • *Parlophone DIP 216*

Eydie GORME — *6 Weeks*

Born Edith Gormezano on August 16, 1931 in New York City, USA. Vocalist with Tommy Tucker band in 1950 for two months before teaming up with Tex Beneke. Signed to Coral Records in 1952. Disc debut: *That Night Of Heaven*. Met Steve Lawrence on the *Tonight* TV show in 1953. Married Steve Lawrence on December 29, 1957. Recorded as the duo Steve and Eydie in 1963 and as Parker and Penny in 1979. *Blame It On The Bossa Nova* was originally written for Bobby Rydell, who passed on it. Eydie's recording of the song features the Cookies on backing vocals and Barry Mann on piano.

12 Jul 62	4	5	1. YES MY DARLING DAUGHTER *CBS EAAG 105*
04 Mar 63	9	1	2. BLAME IT ON THE BOSSA *Nov* A *CBS EAAG 131*

See also Steve Lawrence; Steve and Eydie

Brendan GRACE — *40 Weeks*

Born on April 1, 1951 in Dublin, Ireland. Left school at fifteen and formed a folk group called the Gingermen. Turned to comedy as a result of his chat between songs getting laughs. Went solo in early 1972. Married Eileen Doyle in 1973. Created several comedy characters for his live act, the most popular one being, *Bottler*, the smart alec bearded schoolboy. Hosted RTE television series, *That's Showbiz*, in 1981-82.

continues over

Date	Pos	Wks	ARTIST / Record Title *Label & Number*
			Appeared in the 1995 film, *Moondance*. Now resides in Florida, USA. *The Combine Harvester,* is a parody of Melanie's hit song, *Brand New Key*.
25 Jan 73	3	8	1. CUSHY BUTTERFIELD *Solo SOLO 106*
10 Jan 74	5	4	2. LIBERTY BOY *Solo SOLO 122*
13 Jun 74	4	4	3. PADDY THE PEDLAR *Solo SOLO 129*
19 Dec 74	3	4	4. A VISIT TO SANTA *Solo SOLO 132*
19 Jun 75	6	6	5. DELILAH *Solo SOLO 135*
30 Oct 75	1(1)	7	• 6. THE COMBINE HARVESTER *Solo SOLO 139*
28 Jul 77	1(2)	6	• 7. WHEN BENJY WRAPPED HIS TRACTOR ROUND THE OAK TREE *Solo SOLO 148*
26 Aug 76	9	1	8. WHERE HAVE THEY GONE *Solo SOLO 144*

Charlie GRACIE — *2 Weeks*

Born Charles Anthony Graci on May 14, 1936 in South Philadelphia, USA. At the age of ten his father bought him a guitar. Following some radio performances came to the attention of the owner of Cadillac Records. Disc debut: *I'm Gonna Sit Right Down And Write Myself A Letter* (1951). Signed to Cameo Records in 1956 and hit the #1 slot in the USA with his first single for the label. *Butterfly* spent two weeks at number one on the Billboard chart. Appeared in the 1957 film *Jamboree*. Toured the UK in 1957.

Date	Pos	Wks	ARTIST / Record Title *Label & Number*
21 May 57	-	1	1. BUTTERFLY *Parlophone DIP 272*
23 Oct 57	-	1	2. WANDERING EYES *London HLU 8467*

GRANNY'S INTENTIONS — *4 Weeks*

Beat group formed in Limerick, Ireland in mid 1965. Played local clubs and ballrooms and built up a reputation as one of the most exciting groups on the Irish scene. Moved to London in 1967. Signed to Deram Records. Debut disc: *The Story of David* (1967). Personnel: Johnny Duhan (vocals), John Ryan (keyboards), John Hockedy (lead guitar), Jack Costello (bass) and Greg Donaghy (drums).

continues over

Date	Pos	Wks	ARTIST / Record Title *Label & Number*
			Several changes in personnel from 1968–1970 with Duhan and Ryan the only ever present members. Group disbanded in late 1970. Johnny Duhan now a much respected singer/songwriter.
21 Nov 68	6	4	1. NEVER AN EVERYDAY THING *Deram DM(I) 214*

Norman GREENBAUM — *9 Weeks*

Born on November 20, 1942 in Malden, Massachusetts, USA. While attending Boston University played guitar and sang in coffee houses. Moved to Los Angeles in 1965 and formed Dr. West's Medicine Show and Junk Band, who had a minor hit in 1966 with *The Eggplant That Ate Chicago*. Group broke up in 1967 and Norman pursued a solo career, signing to Reprise Records. Retired from music business in 1981. *Spirit In The Sky* was also a number one hit for Doctor and The Medics (1986) and Gareth Gates (2003).

Date	Pos	Wks	ARTIST / Record Title *Label & Number*
23 Apr 70	1(1)	9	• 1. SPIRIT IN THE SKY *Pye RS 20885*

GREGORY and the CADETS — *11 Weeks*

Irish showband. Gregory was born Gregory Donaghy on March 12, 1946 in Sion Mills, County Tyrone, N. Ireland. Vocalist with the Drumbeats and the Polka Dots before joining the Cadets in April 1966. When the Cadets disbanded in April 1970, Gregory went on to front the Nashville Ramblers. Following the demise of the Nashville Ramblers, formed the Gregory Trio and performed on the cabaret scene. In 1976 was invited to Canada to join the Carlton Showband as lead singer. Stayed with the band until 1996 when he left to pursue a solo career. He now resides in Canada.

Date	Pos	Wks	ARTIST / Record Title *Label & Number*
11 Jul 66	1(3)	8	• 1. MORE THAN YESTERDAY *Pye 7N 17128*
24 Oct 66	9	1	2. AT THE CLOSE OF A LONG LONG DAY Pye 7N *17167*
03 Aug 67	9	2	3. LAND OF GINGERBREAD *Pye 7N 17349*

See also Eileen Reid and the Cadets

Date	Pos	Wks	ARTIST / Record Title *Label & Number*

GREYHOUND — *1 Weeks*

Formed in Jamaica in 1965 as the Rudies. Also operated under the names Tilermen and the Des All Stars before changing name to Greyhound in 1970. Personnel: Danny Smith, Glenroy Oakley, Slim Smith, Lloyd Charmers and Jimmy Riley. Disbanded in 1975.

Date	Pos	Wks	ARTIST / Record Title *Label & Number*
05 Aug 71	10	1	1. BLACK AND WHITE *TroJan TR 7820*

GUYS and DOLLS — *5 Weeks*

Formed in London, England in November, 1974. Personnel: Dominic Grant, Paul Griggs, David Van Day, Thereze Bazar, Martine Howard and Julie Forsythe. In July 1977, David Van Day and Tereze Bazar, left the group. They went on to form Dollar. Guys and Dolls continued as a four piece. Disbanded in December 1985. Julie Forsythe is a daughter of entertainer Bruce Forsythe. The groups debut disc, *There's A Whole Lot Of Loving*, was recorded by session singers and no member of the group was featured on it.

Date	Pos	Wks	ARTIST / Record Title *Label & Number*
27 Mar 75	2	5	1. THERE'S A WHOLE LOT OF LOVING *Magnet MAG 20*

Date	Pos	Wks	ARTIST / Record Title *Label & Number*

H

Bill HALEY and his COMETS **_11 Weeks_**

Born William John Clifton Haley on July 6, 1925 in Detroit, Michigan, USA. Grew up in Chester, Pennsylvania. In 1944 joined Shorty Cook's Downhomers with whom he toured the north and midwest. Formed his own group, the Four Aces of Swing who in a short time had a name change to the Saddlemen. Disc debut: *Rocket 88* (1951). In 1952, changed name of the group to The Comets. Signed to Decca in 1954. Film appearances include *Rock Around The Clock* (1956) and *Don't Knock The Rock* (1956). The Comets lineup (1956): Rudy Pompilli (tenor sax), Al Rex (bass), Ralph Jones (drums), Franny Beecher (lead guitar), Billy Williamson (steel guitar) and Johnny Grande (piano, accordion). Rudy Pompelli died in February 1976. Johnny Grande died on June 2, 2006. Bill Haley died of heart failure on February 9, 1981. Inducted into the Rock and Roll Hall of Fame in 1987. Session musician Danny Cedrone played lead guitar solo on Rock Around The Clock.

Date	Pos	Wks	ARTIST / Record Title *Label & Number*
15 Feb 55	-	1	1. SHAKE RATTLE AND ROLL *Brunswick 05338*
22 Nov 55	-	2	2. ROCK AROUND THE CLOCK *Brunswick 05317*
19 Jun 56	-	5	3. THE SAINTS ROCK 'N' ROLL *Brunswick 05565*
18 Sep 56	-	1	4. ROCKIN' THROUGH THE RYE *Brunswick 05582*
27 Nov 56	-	1	5. RIP IT UP *Brunswick 05615*
12 Feb 57	-	1	6. HOOK LINE AND SINKER *Brunswick 05641*

Roy HAMILTON **_1 Weeks_**

Born on April 16, 1929 in Leesburg, Georgia, USA. Moved to Jersey City at age fourteen. Fought as an amateur heavyweight boxer in his mid teens. In 1948 joined the Searchlight Singers. Spotted singing in a night club in Newark, New Jersey by DJ Bill Cook who arranged an audition with Epic Records.

continues over

Date	Pos	Wks	ARTIST / Record Title *Label & Number*
			Disc debut: *You'll Never Walk Alone* (1954). Topped bill for week July 16, 1955 at Top Hat, Dun Laoghaire, Co. Dublin. Died of a stroke on July 20, 1969.
05 Jul 55	-	1	1. UNCHAINED MELODY *Philips PB 448*

Steve HARLEY and COCKNEY REBEL 6 Weeks

Born Steven Nice on February 27, 1951 in Deptford, London, England. Began his singing career in the London folk clubs. Joined folk band Odin. After leaving school worked as a trainee journalist on the East London Advertiser. Formed Cockney Rebel in 1972. Signed to EMI. Personnel: Jim Cregan (guitar), Duncan Mackay (keyboards), George Ford (bass) and Stuart Elliott (drums). Disc debut: *The Human Menagerie* L.P. (1973). Disbanded in 1977. Presented *Sounds Of The Seventies* on BBC Radio 2 from 2000 - March 2008.

Date	Pos	Wks	ARTIST / Record Title *Label & Number*
27 Feb 75	1(2)	5	• 1. MAKE ME SMILE (Come Up And See Me) *EMI EMI 2263*
02 Sep 76	10	1	2. HERE COMES THE SUN *EMI EMI 2505*

Jet HARRIS 1 Weeks

Bass guitarist. Born Terence Harris on July 6, 1939 in Kingsbury, Middlesex, England. A member of Cliff Richard's backing group, The Shadows, 1959-62. Left Shadows in April 1962 to pursue a solo career.

Date	Pos	Wks	ARTIST / Record Title *Label & Number*
27 Sep 62	9	1	1. MAIN TITLE THEME (from The Man With The Golden Arm)• *Decca F 11488*

See also Jet Harris and Tony Meehan; The Shadows

Jet HARRIS and Tony MEEHAN 12 Weeks

Male instrumental duo. Formed in latter part of 1962. Jet Harris (born July 6, 1939 in Kingsbury, Middlesex, bass) and Tony Meehan (born on March 2, 1943 in London, drums) were colleagues in the Shadows. Duo broke up in late 1963. Tony Meehan composed music for both film and television. Composed score for the Ruth Rendall Mysteries television series.

continues over

Date	Pos	Wks	ARTIST / Record Title *Label & Number*

Tony Meehan died on November 28, 2005, from head injuries sustained in a fall at his home.

Date	Pos	Wks	ARTIST / Record Title *Label & Number*
28 Jan 63	1(1)	7	• 1. DIAMONDS • *Decca F 11563*
27 May 63	7	2	2. SCARLETT O'HARA • *Decca F 11644*
30 Sep 63	5	3	3. APPLEJACK • *Decca F 11710*

See also Jet Harris; The Shadows

Richard HARRIS — *3 Weeks*

Actor/singer. Born on October 1, 1930 in Limerick, Ireland. Attended the Royal Academy of Dramatic Art in London, England. Earned Academy Award nominations for his performance in the films *This Sporting Life* (1962) and *The Field* (1990). His other films include *Mutiny On The Bounty, Guns Of Navarone* (1961), *Mutiny On The Bounty* (1962) and *Camelot* (1967). In January 1968, Harris was chosen by American songwriter Jim Webb to record an album of Webb's songs. The resultant album, *A Tramp Shining*, included *Macarthur Park*. Directed the 1971 film, *Bloomfield* and produced, *The Return Of A Man Called Horse* (1976). Played the role of Albus Dumbledore in the Harry Potter films. Died of Hodgkin's disease on October 25, 2002.

Date	Pos	Wks	ARTIST / Record Title *Label & Number*
08 Aug 68	9	3	1. MACARTHUR PARK *RCA Victor ERC 1699*

Rolf HARRIS — *17 Weeks*

Singer/cartoonist/sculptor/composer. Born on March 30, 1930 in Perth, Australia. Moved to England in 1952 to attend London Art School, however the lure of showbiz proved to be too strong. Became a top television presenter of children's programmes such as *Rolf's Cartoon Club* and *Hey Presto–It's Rolf*. In 1993, Rolf released his version of the Led Zeppelin classic rock anthem, *Stairway To Heaven. Two Little Boys* was originally composed in 1903

Date	Pos	Wks	ARTIST / Record Title *Label & Number*
15 Sep 60	9	3	1. TIE ME KANGAROO DOWN SPORT *Columbia DB(I) 4483*
18 Dec 69	1(7)	14	• 2. TWO LITTLE BOYS *Columbia DB(I) 8630*

Date	Pos	Wks	ARTIST / Record Title *Label & Number*

George HARRISON — *12 Weeks*

Born on February 24, 1943 in Liverpool, England. Formed his first group, The Rebels, at age of 13. Teamed up with John Lennon and Paul McCartney in the Quarrymen in 1958. The group subsequently became The Beatles. Following the breakup of The Beatles he embarked on a successful solo career. Following the success of *My Sweet Lord* he was sued by the publishers of the Chiffons hit song *He's So Fine*, who maintained he had copied their song. George was ultimately found guilty of "unconscious plagiarism". In 1971, George organized the Concert for Bangladesh, an all star benefit in New York's Madison Square Garden, for flood and famine relief in Bangladesh. Proceeds from the concert, soundtrack album and documentary film, raised over thirteen million dollars. In 1988, teamed up with Roy Orbison, Bob Dylan, Tom Petty and Jeff Lynne, under the name The Traveling Wilburys. Died from cancer on November 29, 2001. Inducted into the Rock and Roll Hall of Fame in 2004.

Date	Pos	Wks	ARTIST / Record Title *Label & Number*
04 Feb 71	1(7)	11	•1. MY SWEET LORD *Apple DIP 516*
28 Jun 73	10	1	2. GIVE ME LOVE (Give Me Peace On Earth) *Parlophone R 5988*

See also The Beatles

Edwin HAWKINS SINGERS — *4 Weeks*

Gospel choir formed in 1967 as the Northern California State Youth Choir. The choir director, Edwin Hawkins, was born on August 4, 1943 in Oakland, California, USA. Buddah Records decided on a name change to the Edwin Hawkins Singers. The female soloist on *Oh Happy Day* is Dorothy Coombs Morrison.

Date	Pos	Wks	ARTIST / Record Title *Label & Number*
26 Jun 69	2	4	1. OH HAPPY DAY *Buddah 201048*

Bill HAYES — *1 Weeks*

Singer/actor. Born William Foster Hayes 111 on June 5, 1935 in Harvey, Illinois, USA. Vocalist with Dave Simpson and the Thorntoneers.

continues over

Date	Pos	Wks	ARTIST / Record Title *Label & Number*

Made his professional debut in 1947 in the stage musical, *Carousel*, in the city of Chicago. In 1950 became resident singer on the television programme *Your Show Of Shows*. Left in 1953 to make his Broadway debut in the musical, *Me And Juliet*. In 1965, he was offered the role of, Doug Williams, in a daytime television soap, *Days Of Our Lives*. Stayed with the soap until 1984. Film appearances include *Stop You're Killing Me* (1952) and *The Cardinal* (1963).

Date	Pos	Wks	ARTIST / Record Title *Label & Number*
17 Jan 56	-	1	1. THE BALLAD OF DAVY CROCKETT *London HL 8220*

Justin HAYWARD — *5 Weeks*

Born David Justin Hayward on October 14, 1946 in Swindon, England. Interest in music started at the age of seven when he had his first piano lesson. By his early teens was playing in local groups in Swindon. After replying to an advert in the Melody Maker he found himself a member of the Wilde Three with Marty Wilde and his wife Joyce. Disc debut as solo artist: *London Is Behind Me* (1965). Joined the Moody Blues in 1966. *Forever Autumn* is taken from Jeff Wayne's, *War Of The World's* album.

Date	Pos	Wks	ARTIST / Record Title *Label & Number*
03 Aug 78	3	5	1. FOREVER AUTUMN *CBS 6368*

Lee HAZLEWOOD – See Nancy and Lee

Ted HEATH and his MUSIC — *2 Weeks*

Born on March 30, 1902 in Wandsworth, London, England. His father taught him to play the tenor saxophone at age of six. At age fourteen he switched to trombone. In 1928 joined Bert Ambrose Orchestra, where he stayed until 1935. While a member of Geraldo's Orchestra in 1940 Ted and his wife Moira composed *That Lovely Weekend* and the royalties from the song helped Ted to form his own band in 1944. Made first American tour in 1956. Theme song *Listen To My Music*. Died on November 18, 1969.

continues over

Date	Pos	Wks	ARTIST / Record Title *Label & Number*
			The Ted Heath Orchestra continued under the direction of trombonist Don Lusher, until their final gig on December 4, 2000 at London's Royal Festival Hall.
01 May 58	-	2	1. SWINGING SHEPHERD BLUES • *Decca* F *11000*

HEATWAVE — *4 Weeks*

Formed by two American service men Johnnie Wilder and his brother Keith while serving in Germany. After their discharge from service moved to Britain. Personnel: Johnnie Wilder (born July 3, 1949 in Dayton, Ohio, lead vocals), Keith Wilder (vocals), Rod Temperton (keyboards), Mario Mantese (bass), Roy Carter (rhythm guitar), Eric Johns (guitar) and Ernest Berger (drums). Disc debut: *Ain't No Half Steppin'* (1976). Johnnie Wilder involved in a traffic accident in 1979 that left him paralysed from the neck down. Group disbanded in 1983. Reformed in 1989. Johnnie Wilder died on May 13, 2006.

Date	Pos	Wks	ARTIST / Record Title *Label & Number*
23 Feb 78	5	4	1. THE GROOVELINE *GTO GT 115*

Dermot HEGARTY and the PLAINSMEN — *47 Weeks*

Vocalist/organist born on October 6, 1940 in Longford, Ireland. Spotted by Mick Clerkin (director of King Records) playing a cabaret date at the Longford Arms Hotel, Longford. Impressed by Dermot's performance and rapore with the audience he signed him to King Records. Disc debut: *Shores Of Amerikay* (1967). In April 1969 launched his own showband, the Plainsmen. Personnel: Roger Farrell (guitar), Seamus Roddy (bass), Tony Farrell (drums), Frank McKenna (guitar), Francis Middleton (trumpet), Vincent Summers (tenor sax) and Brendan McCusker (tenor sax/fiddle). Wrote stage musical, *A Song To Remember*, and starred in it with The Plainsmen at the Temperance Hall, Longford, in March 1972. Left the band in April 1973 to return to the cabaret scene. The Plainsmen continued until 1977 with Brian Harkin as lead singer.

continues over

Date	Pos	Wks	ARTIST / Record Title *Label & Number*
26 Oct 67	4	2	1. THE SHORES OF AMERIKAY *King KG 1064*
14 May 70	1(5)	29	• 2. TWENTY ONE YEARS *Release RL 533*
27 Jan 72	7	3	3. LOVE IS TEASING *Release RL 604*
13 Apr 72	5	3	4. FOUR GREEN FIELDS *Release RL 626*
05 Oct 72	9	1	5. AFTER TWENTY ONE YEARS *Release RL 644*
05 Sep 74	1(3)	9	• 6. NINETEEN MEN *Release RL 744*

HEINZ — *1 Weeks*

Born Heinz Burt on July 24, 1942 in Hargin, Germany. Came to Britain in 1945. A member of the Tornados, he left the group in 1962. Launched as a solo singer by Joe Meek in early 1963. Disc debut: *Dreams Do Come True* (1963). Appeared in the film *Farewell Performance* (1962). Died from motor neurone disease on April 7, 2000. *Just Like Eddie* is a tribute to the rock 'n' roll legend, Eddie Cochran.

Date	Pos	Wks	ARTIST / Record Title *Label & Number*
23 Sep 63	10	1	1. JUST LIKE EDDIE *Decca F 11693*

HELLO — *2 Weeks*

Formed in London, England in 1971 under the name The Age. Spotted by David Blaylock who offered to become their manager. His first managerial decision was to change their name to Hello. Personnel: Bob Bradbury (vocals, guitar), Keith Marshall (guitar), Vic Faulkner (bass) and Jeff Allen (drums). Disc debut: *You Move Me* (1972). Very successful in Germany where they enjoyed nine hits in two years. Band broke up in 1979. Russ Ballard, former member of the Zombies, composed *New York Groove*. Keith Marshall enjoyed a top twenty hit in 1981 with *Only Crying*.

Date	Pos	Wks	ARTIST / Record Title *Label & Number*
13 Nov 75	6	2	1. NEW YORK GROOVE *Bell BELL 1438*

Joe Mr. Piano HENDERSON — *3 Weeks*

Born on May 2, 1920 in Glasgow, Scotland. Learned to play piano at a young age, turning pro at the age of fifteen. In the mid 1940's started working for London music publisher, Peter Maurice.

Date	Pos	Wks	ARTIST / Record Title *Label & Number*

In 1947 met singer Peula Clark and for the next ten years worked as her musical accompanist. Disc debut: *Sing It With Joe* (1955). Died of a heart attack on May 4, 1980.

Date	Pos	Wks	ARTIST / Record Title *Label & Number*
27 Mar 56	-	3	1. THEME FROM THE THREEPENNY OPERA • *Nixa N 15044*

Jimi HENDRIX EXPERIENCE 1 Weeks

Born on November 27, 1942 in Seattle, USA. Began musical career as a studio guitarist. Formed his own group, Jimmy James and the Blue Flames, in 1965. Discovered by ex Animal Hilton Valentine who brought him to Britain where he formed the Jimi Hendrix Experience (Jimi (lead guitar), Noel Redding (bass) and Mitch Mitchell (drums)). Died of a drug overdose on September 18, 1970. Noel Redding died on May 11, 2003. Mitch Mitchell died November 12, 2008.

Date	Pos	Wks	ARTIST / Record Title *Label & Number*
03 Dec 70	10	1	1. VOODOO CHILE *Track 2095 001*

Clarence 'Frogman' HENRY 15 Weeks

Born on March 19, 1937 in Algiers, Louisiana, USA. Played piano with Bobby Mitchell and The Toppers from 1952 to 1955. Nicknamed "Frogman" by New Orleans DJ Poppa Stoppa. because of the way he imitated frog noises on his 1957 American hit, *Ain't Got No Home.*

Date	Pos	Wks	ARTIST / Record Title *Label & Number*
29 Jun 61	2	12	• 1. BUT I DO *Pye Int. 7N 25078*
17 Aug 61	4	3	2. YOU ALWAYS HURT THE ONE YOU LOVE *Pye Int.7N 25089*

Dermot HENRY and the VIRGINIANS 48 Weeks

Born in Ballymote, Co. Sligo, Ireland. Spotted by Johnny Kelly (ex Capitol Showband) performing at a cabaret function. Invited to join the Virginians as lead vocalist. Disc debut: *My Lovely Irish Rose.* Left the Virginians in November 1974, to front The Entertainers. In April 75, decided to move to the USA.

continues over

Date	Pos	Wks	ARTIST / Record Title *Label & Number*
			Daddy What If was in fact a duet by Dermot Henry and Michael Landers (born on May 20, 1965 in Kilcullen, Co. Kildare), even though Michael is not credited on the record.
29 Oct 70	8	2	1. MY LOVELY IRISH ROSE *Ruby RUB 109*
10 Dec 70	1(6)	13	• 2. IF THOSE LIPS COULD ONLY SPEAK *Ruby RUB 115*
20 May 71	8	4	3. WHAT'S THE REASON DADDY *Ruby RUB 125*
02 Sep 71	3	10	4. BALLYHOE *Ruby RUB 134*
06 Jan 72	8	2	5. DADDY WHAT IF *Ruby RUB 146*
03 Aug 72	1(2)	12	• 6. THE GYPSY *Columbia IDB 813*
05 Apr 73	5	5	7. THE OLD DUNGARVAN OAK *Columbia IDB 827*

The HERD — *4 Weeks*

Group formed in Bromley, Kent, England in 1966. Personnel: Peter Frampton, (born April 22, 1950 in Beckenham, vocals, guitar), Andy Bown (organ), Gary Taylor (bass), and Andrew Steele (drums). Peter Frampton quit in 1969 to form Humble Pie. Andrew Steele died from cancer on April 18, 2005.

Date	Pos	Wks	ARTIST / Record Title *Label & Number*
30 May 68	5	4	1. I DON'T WANT OUR LOVING TO DIE *Fontana ETF 925*

See also Humble Pie

HERMAN'S HERMITS — *44 Weeks*

Formed in Manchester, England in 1963 as Pete Novak and the Heartbeats. The caretaker at one of the pubs the group played said Pete looked like Sherman from the children's cartoon series The Bullwinkle Show, and that the rest of the group looked like hermits, so they changed their name to Herman's Hermits. Personnel: Herman (born Peter Noone on November 5, 1947 in Manchester, vocals.), Derek Leckenby (lead guitar), Keith Hopwood (rhythm guitar), Karl Green (bass), and Barry Whitwam (drums). Discovered by producer Mickie Most. Appeared in films *When The Boys Meet The Girls* (1965), *Hold On* (1966) and *Mrs Brown You've Got A Lovely Daughter* (1968).

continues over

Date	Pos	Wks	ARTIST / Record Title *Label & Number*
			Peter Noone, who played the role of Len Fairclough's son, Stanley, in *Coronation Street* (1961), left the group in 1971 to pursue a solo career. Derek Leckenby died on June 4, 1996.
28 Sep 64	1(1)	6	• 1. I'M INTO SOMETHING GOOD *Columbia DB(I) 7338*
15 Mar 65	5	4	2. SILHOUETTES *Columbia DB(I) 7475*
07 Nov 66	7	3	3. NO MILK TODAY *Columbia DB(I) 8012*
23 Mar 67	7	3	4. THERE'S A KIND OF HUSH *Columbia DB(I) 8123*
06 Jun 68	9	1	5. SLEEPY JOE *Columbia DB(I) 8404*
08 Aug 68	3	7	6. SUNSHINE GIRL *Columbia DB(I) 8446*
23 Jan 69	5	7	7. SOMETHING'S HAPPENING *Columbia DB(I) 8504*
15 May 69	2	7	8. MY SENTIMENTAL FRIEND *Columbia DB(I) 8563*
26 Feb 70	5	6	9. YEARS MAY COME, YEARS MAY GO *Columbia DB(I) 8656*

Colin HICKS and the CABIN BOYS — *1 Weeks*

Younger brother of Tommy Steele. Born in March 1942 in Cornwall, England. Discovered singing at the famous 2I's coffee bar in Soho, London by John Kennedy (Tommy Steele's manager). Signed to Pye Records. Disc debut: *Wild Eyes and Tender Lips* (1957). Cabin Boys lineup: Jimmie Nicol (drums), Mike O'Neill (piano), Dave Tick (lead guitar) and Rod Slade (bass). Split with group in 1963, while on a tour of Italy.

Date	Pos	Wks	ARTIST / Record Title *Label & Number*
07 Jan 58	-	1	1. WILD EYES AND TENDER LIPS *Nixa N 15114*

The HIGHWAYMEN — *5 Weeks*

Folk group that had its birth at Wesleyen University in Middletown, Connecticut, USA, in late 1958. Originally named the Clansmen. Their manager, Ken Greengrass, suggested the name change, to the Highwaymen, after the title of the Alfred Noyes poem. Personnel: Dave Fisher, Bob Burnet, Steve Trott, Chan Daniels and Steve Butts. Signed with United Artists in 1959. Disc debut: *The Highwaymen* L.P. (1959). Disbanded in late 1964. Have been several reunions over the years. Chan Daniels died on August 2, 1975.

Date	Pos	Wks	ARTIST / Record Title *Label & Number*
12 Oct 61	2	5	1. MICHAEL *HMV POP(I) 910*

Date	Pos	Wks	ARTIST / Record Title *Label & Number*

Benny HILL — 3 Weeks

Born Alfred Hawthorne Hill on January 21, 1924 in Southampton, England. Entered showbusiness at an early age. Moved to London at the age of sixteen. Made his stage debut in *Stars In Battledress* in 1941. Own TV show on BBC in 1953. Moved to Thames Television in 1969. Slated by the critics for his saucy brand of humour, he became a victim of political correctness and eventually Thames TV bowed to the critics and in 1989 took his show of the schedules. A comedian who also wrote his own comedy routines and developed a talent for writing and performing comedy songs. Disc debut: *I Can't Tell A Waltz From A Tango* (1955). Starred in the 1955 film *Who Done It?*. Died of a heart attack on April 20, 1992.

Date	Pos	Wks	ARTIST / Record Title *Label & Number*
23 Dec 71	5	3	1. ERNIE (THE FASTEST MILKMAN IN THE WEST) *Columbia DB(I) 8833*

Dan HILL — *5 Weeks*

Born on June 3, 1954 in Toronto, Canada. Grew up listening to Frank Sinatra, Ella Fitzgerald and Count Basie. Began writing songs at age of fourteen.. Signed to GRT Records in Canada in 1973. His songs have been recorded by many artists including Tammy Wynnette, Rod Stewart and Barry Manilow. Received a Grammy Award nomination for Male Vocalist on *Sometimes When We Touch*. In 1996, received a Grammy Award for Producer of Celine Dion album, *Falling Into You*. Wrote best selling novel, *Comeback*.

Date	Pos	Wks	ARTIST / Record Title *Label & Number*
13 Apr 78	6	5	1. SOMETIMES WHEN WE TOUCH *20th Century BTC 2355*

The HILLTOPPERS — *3 Weeks*

Vocal group formed at Western Kentucky State College in Bowling Green, Kentucky, USA in 1952. Named after the Hilltoppers basketball team of Bowling Green.

continues over

Date	Pos	Wks	ARTIST / Record Title *Label & Number*
			Personnel: Jimmy Sacca (born on July 26, 1929 in Lockport, New York, lead), Eddie Crowe, Seymore Spiegelman and Don McGuire (bass). Disc debut: *Trying* (1952). Disbanded in 1960. Billy Vaughn who went to become MD at Dot Records was an original founder member. He died on September 26, 1991. Seymour Spiegelman died on February 13, 1987.
09 Apr 57	-	2	1. MARIANNE *London HL 8381*
21 Jan 58	-	1	2. THE JOKER *London HLD 8528*

Ronnie HILTON — *9 Weeks*

Born Adrian Hill on January 26, 1926 in Hull, Yorkshire, England. Family moved to Leeds. Took his first steps to stardom singing with his three brothers as The Singing Hills. In 1951, entered and won a local talent contest, the prize, a year's contract to sing with the local Johnnie Addlestone Band. Spotted by HMV A&R man, Wally Ridley, while performing at the Starlight Roof, Leeds Made his stage debut as Ronnie Hilton in July 1954 at the Dudley Hippodrome. Disc debut: *I Live For You* (1954). Suffered a Stroke in January 1993 but continued to entertain until he suffered a second Stroke in July 1999. Died on February 20, 2001.

Date	Pos	Wks	ARTIST / Record Title *Label & Number*
11 Oct 55	-	2	1. THE YELLOW ROSE OF TEXAS *HMV IP 1045*
03 Jul 56	-	2	2. NO OTHER LOVE *HMV IP 1099*
04 Sep 56	-	1	3. GIVE ME MY RANCH *HMV IP 1117*
04 Jun 57	-	3	4. AROUND THE WORLD *HMV IP 1240*
23 Jul 58	-	1	5. ON THE STREET WHERE YOU LIVE *HMV POP(I) 479*

Edmund HOCKRIDGE — *11 Weeks*

Born on August 9, 1919 in Vancouver, Canada. Spent five years in Britain during WW11 with the Royal Canadian Air Force. During this time made several broadcasts on BBC radio. Remained in Britain following his demob in 1945. Began to sing regularly on the BBC with the Queen's Hall Light Orchestra, George Melachrino and Geraldo.

continues over

Date	Pos	Wks	ARTIST / Record Title *Label & Number*
			An offer to host his own radio show in Canada saw him return to his native land. Returned to Britain in 1950 and successfully auditioned for leading role in stage musical *Carousel*. Disc debut: *I Leave My Heart In An English Garden*. Died on March 15, 2009.
14 Feb 56	-	3	1. YOUNG AND FOOLISH *Nixa N 15039*
08 May 56	-	4	2. NO OTHER LOVE *Nixa N 15048*
04 Sep 56	-	2	3. BY THE FOUNTAINS OF ROME *Nixa N 15063*
02 Oct 56	-	1	4. A WOMAN IN LOVE *Nixa N 15067*
03 Dec 57	-	1	5. ALL AT ONCE YOU LOVE HER *Nixa N 15107*

Larry HOGAN — *1 Weeks*

Born in 1939 in Limerick, Ireland. Had a difficult childhood due to illness. Attended art school. Went to Germany on a scholarship and studied techniques of film making. Returned to Dublin in 1962, as manager of a German film company. In 1967, formed the folk group, We Four. Group broke up in 1970 and Larry went to London. While living there, he composed a collection of songs based on the Gospel. He recorded the songs on the album, *Simple Song Of Love*. In the 1970's, presented the Radio Eireann programme, *Sounds Religious*. Died of heart failure on October 31, 1998.

Date	Pos	Wks	ARTIST / Record Title *Label & Number*
05 Dec 74	9	1	1. SIMPLE SONG OF LOVE *Polydor 2078 050*

Michael HOLLIDAY — *16 Weeks*

Born Norman Milne on November 26, 1924 in Liverpool, England. Joined Eric Winstone Band as vocalist in March 1953. Signed to Columbia Records in August 1955. Disc debut: *The Yellow Rose Of Texas* (1955). Described as 'Britain's Bing Crosby'. Appeared in the 1960 film *Life Is A Circus*. Own TV show, *Relax With Michael Holliday* (1958). Died on October 29, 1963 from an overdose of sleeping tablets. Biography The *Man Who Would Be Bing* published in 2004.

Date	Pos	Wks	ARTIST / Record Title *Label & Number*
07 May 57	-	1	1. MY HOUSE IS YOUR HOUSE *Columbia IDB 704*
04 Feb 58	-	4	2. THE STORY OF MY LIFE *Columbia DB (I) 4058*
16 Apr 58	-	1	3. ROONEY *Columbia DB(I) 4087*

continues over

Date	Pos	Wks	ARTIST / Record Title *Label & Number*
11 Jun 58	-	2	4. STAIRWAY OF LOVE *Columbia DB(I) 4121*
21 Jan 60	3	8	5. STARRY EYED *Columbia DB(I) 4378*

The HOLLIES — *63 Weeks*

Formed in November 1963 in Manchester, England. Personnel: Allan Clarke (born April 5, 1942 in Salford, lead vocals), Graham Nash (vocals, rhythm guitar), Tony Hicks (lead guitar), Bobby Elliott (drums) and Eric Haydock (bass). Haydock left in 1966, replaced by Bernie Calvert. Nash departed in 1968 (to form Crosby, Stills and Nash). Replaced by Terry Sylvester. Allan Clarke left for a brief period in 1972, replaced by Mikael Rickfors. Allan Clarke retired from the group in February 2000. Carl Wayne (ex Move) took over as lead singer. Carl Wayne died of cancer on August 31, 2004. Peter Howart replaced Wayne as lead vocalist.

Date	Pos	Wks	ARTIST / Record Title *Label & Number*
30 Mar 64	6	5	1. JUST ONE LOOK *Parlophone R(I) 5104*
28 Jun 65	1(1)	6	• 2. I'M ALIVE *Parlophone R(I) 5287*
20 Sep 65	3	6	3. LOOK THROUGH ANY WINDOW *Parlophone R(I) 5322*
21 Mar 66	3	4	4. I CAN'T LET GO *Parlophone R(I) 5409*
04 Jul 66	4	5	5. BUS STOP *Parlophone R(I) 5469*
31 Oct 66	5	3	6. STOP STOP STOP *Parlophone R(I) 5508*
16 Mar 67	5	4	7. ON A CAROUSEL *Parlophone R(I) 5562*
29 Jun 67	4	5	8. CARRIE ANNE *Parlophone R(I) 5602*
18 Apr 68	7	4	9. JENNIFER ECCLES *Parlophone R(I) 5680*
31 Oct 68	5	5	10. LISTEN TO ME *Parlophone R(I) 5733*
03 Apr 69	4	6	11. SORRY SUZANNE *Parlophone R(I) 5765*
16 Oct 69	3	7	12. HE AIN'T HEAVY, HE'S MY BROTHER *Parlophone R(I) 5806*
28 May 70	8	1	13. I CAN'T TELL THE BOTTOM FROM THE TOP *Parlophone R(I) 5837*
07 Mar 74	6	2	14. THE AIR THAT I BREATHE *Polydor 2058 435*

Buddy HOLLY — *29 Weeks*

Born Charles Hardin Holley on September 7, 1936 in Lubbock, Texas, USA. Disc debut: *Blue Days Black Nights* (1956). Formed the Crickets in 1957. Married Maria Elena Santiago in August 1958.

continues over

Date	Pos	Wks	ARTIST / Record Title *Label & Number*
			Split with Crickets in October 1958 and moved to New York. Killed in a plane crash on February 3, 1959 along with Ritchie Valens, the Big Bopper (J. P. Richardson) and the pilot Roger Peterson. Inducted into the Rock and Roll Hall of Fame in 1986.
19 Mar 59	1(7)	19	• 1. **IT DOESN'T MATTER ANYMORE** *Coral EQ 72360*
31 Aug 61	4	2	2. **BABY I DON'T CARE** *Coral EQ 72432*
15 Apr 63	3	8	3. **BROWN EYED HANDSOME MAN** *Coral EQ 72459*
			See also The Crickets

Eddie HOLMAN — *4 Weeks*

Born on June 3, 1946 in Norfolk, Virginia, USA. Began playing piano and guitar as a child. Made his disc debut in 1962. Signed to ABC Records in 1968. *Hey There Lonely Girl* originally recorded in 1963 by Ruby and The Romantics as *Hey There Lonely Boy*.

Date	Pos	Wks	ARTIST / Record Title *Label & Number*
21 Nov 74	5	4	1. **(HEY THERE) LONELY GIRL** *ABC ABC 4012*

John HOLT — *2 Weeks*

Born on July 11,1947 in Kingston, Jamaica. Made his music business debut performing on numerous talent shows. As a result of winning one such talent contest in 1962 made his disc debut *Forever I'll Stay*. Joined vocal group Paragons in 1964. Came to UK in 1974, returned to Jamaica in 1976.

Date	Pos	Wks	ARTIST / Record Title *Label & Number*
30 Jan 75	8	2	1. **HELP ME MAKE IT THROUGH THE NIGHT** *TroJan TR 7909*

The HONEYCOMBS — *7 Weeks*

Formed in London, England in 1963 as The Sheritons. Changed name to Honeycombs in 1964. Spotted playing at the Mildmay Tavern in Stoke Newington, N. London, by songwriting team, Ken Howard and Alan Blakley. Personnel: Denis D'ell (born Denis Dalziel on October 10, 1943 in London, lead vocals), Martin Murray (rhythm guitar), Alan Ward (lead guitar), John Lantree (bass), and Honey (Ann) Lantree (John's sister) (drums). Group broke up in 1967. Denis D'ell died from cancer on July 6, 2005.

Date	Pos	Wks	ARTIST / Record Title *Label & Number*
31 Aug 64	3	7	1. **HAVE I THE RIGHT** *Pye 7N 15664*

Date	Pos	Wks	ARTIST / Record Title *Label & Number*

Mary HOPKIN *26 Weeks*

Born on May 3, 1950 in Pontardawe, Wales. Spotted singing on television talent programme, *Opportunity Knocks*, by top model Twiggy who recommended her to Paul McCartney. He signed Mary to Apple Records. McCartney produced both of her first two singles. Represented the UK in the 1970 Eurovision Song Contest with, *Knock Knock*, finishing in second position.

Date	Pos	Wks	ARTIST / Record Title *Label & Number*
19 Sep 68	1(5)	10	• 1. THOSE WERE THE DAYS *Apple APPLE 2*
24 Apr 69	1(1)	7	• 2. GOODBYE *Apple APPLE 10*
19 Feb 70	3	2	3. TEMMA HARBOUR *Apple APPLE 22*
09 Apr 70	2	7	4. KNOCK KNOCK WHO'S THERE *Apple APPLE 26*

HORSLIPS *19 Weeks*

Irish rock group formed in Dublin in October 1970. Personnel: Charles O'Connor (mandolin/fiddle/concertina), Jim Lockhart (keyboards/flute), Eamon Carr (drums), Barry Devlin (rhythm guitar), Spud Murphy (lead guitar) and Gene Mulvanney (bass). In November, Spud Murphy left to join the rock music weekly, Sounds, to work as a photographer. Declan Sinnott was drafted in as replacement. First performance as a group happened on February 12, 1971, on the RTE television series, *Fonn*. Gene Mulvanney left group in April 1971. He was not replaced. Barry Devlin moved to bass. The groups performance at a star studded concert at the Dublin RDS, in September 1971, impressed promoter, Michael Deeny, who offered them a management deal. Released their debut single, *Johnny's Wedding*, in March 1972, on their own label, Oats. Declan Sinnott left group in June 1972. Replaced by Gus Guest (ex Mexicans Showband). In October 1972, the final personnel change occurred, when Johnny Fean replaced Gus Guest. Released their debut album, *Happy To Meet, Sorry To Part,* in November 1972. It went on to become Ireland's fastest selling album of the decade. Signed to Atlantic Records in 1973.

continues over

Date	Pos	Wks	ARTIST / Record Title *Label & Number*
			Successful tours of Ireland, Britain, Canada and the USA followed. Band members decided to split in 1980, and on May 1, played their final live gig, at Belfast's Whitla Hall. The band members went on to pursue successful solo careers in music, journalism and television.
30 Mar 72	10	1	1. JOHNNY'S WEDDING *Oats Moo 1*
24 May 73	8	3	2. DEARG DOOM *Oats Moo 4*
15 Aug 74	7	2	3. KING OF THE FAIRIES *Oats Moo 6*
14 Oct 76	4	6	4. DAYBREAK *Horslips Moo 11*
22 Dec 77	9	2	5. EXILES *Horslips MOO 16*
21 Sep 78	9	1	6. TOOR-A-LOOR-A-LOOR E.P. *Horslips Moo 16*
01 Nov 79	8	4	7. GUESTS OF THE NATION *Horslips Moo 18*

Tracks on **Toor-A-Loor-A-Loor EP**: Sure The Boy Was Green / Red River Rock // Trouble (with a capital T) / Bridge From Heart To Heart.

HOT BUTTER — *1 Weeks*

Nom de plume for keyboards player Stan Free. Recorded unsuccessfully during the 1960's. Was a member of The First Moog Quartet. *Popcorn* was originally written and recorded in 1969 and appeared on his album, *Music To Moog By*. The 1972 hit version is a different recording.

Date	Pos	Wks	ARTIST / Record Title *Label & Number*
07 Sep 72	8	1	1. POPCORN • *Pye 7N 25583*

HOT CHOCOLATE — *17 Weeks*

Formed in London, England in 1969. Personnel: Errol Brown (born on November 12, 1948 in Kingston, Jamaica, vocals), Tony Wilson (born on October 8, 1947 in Trinidad, vocals), Harvey Hinsley (guitar), Larry Ferguson (keyboards), Ian King (drums), and Patrick Olive (percussion). Disc debut: *Give Peace A Chance* (1969), as the Hot Chocolate Band. Brown and Wilson started out as songwriters for The Beatles Apple label. Composed hit songs for Mary Hopkin (*Think About Your Children*), Herman's Hermits (*Bet Yer Life I Do*) and Julie Felix (*Heaven Is Here*).

continues over

Date	Pos	Wks	ARTIST / Record Title *Label & Number*
			Band made their live debut at the Nevada Ballroom, Bolton in July 1970. Tony Wilson left in October 1975 to pursue a solo career. Group split in 1987. Errol Brown embarked on a solo career.
04 Apr 74	7	3	1. EMMA *Rak RAK 168*
18 Sep 75	6	2	2. A CHILD'S PRAYER *Rak RAK 212*
11 Dec 75	4	5	3. YOU SEXY THING *Rak RAK 221*
21 Jul 77	2	5	4. SO YOU WIN AGAIN *Rak RAK 259*
07 Dec 78	8	2	5. I'LL PUT YOU TOGETHER AGAIN *Rak RAK 286*

The HOT SHOTS — *1 Weeks*

British group formed in 1973 by Clive Crawley and Tony King.Their recording was a revival of the Royal Guardsmen's hit from 1966.

Date	Pos	Wks	ARTIST / Record Title *Label & Number*
05 Jul 73	10	1	1. SNOOPY VERSUS THE RED BARON *Mooncrest MOON 5*

Billy HOWARD — *4 Weeks*

Born in 1942 in Edgeware, London. England. Played trombone during his teens with semi-pro bands. In mid 1960's became a solo entertainer on the cabaret scene with a stage act that included trumpet, guitar, vocals and comedy impressions. In 1980, decided to give up showbusiness for a career in sales and marketing. Hit was based on Roger Miller's, *King Of The Road.* A parody with Billy impersonating the top TV cops of the period.

Date	Pos	Wks	ARTIST / Record Title *Label & Number*
05 Feb 76	5	4	1. KING OF THE COPS *Penny Farthing PEN 892*

The HUES CORPORATION — *1 Weeks*

Formed in Los Angeles, USA in 1969. Their name was intended as a pun on the Howard Hughes Corporation. Personnel: Fleming Williams, Bernard Henderson and H Ann Kelley. Disc debut: *Goodfootin'* (1970). Signed to RCA in 1973. Fleming Williams is lead vocal on *Rock The Boat.*

Date	Pos	Wks	ARTIST / Record Title *Label & Number*
05 Sep 74	9	1	1. ROCK THE BOAT *RCA APBO 0232*

Date	Pos	Wks	ARTIST / Record Title *Label & Number*

Tony HUGHES – See Tony and the Ventures

HUMBLE PIE *1 Weeks*

British super group formed in London in 1969. Personnel: Steve Marriott (born January 30, 1947 in London, guitar, vocals). Peter Frampton (born April 22, 1950 in Beckenham, guitar vocals), Greg Ridley (bass) and Jerry Shirley (drums). Frampton left to pursue a solo career in September 1971. Replaced by Dave Clempson. Group disbanded in 1975. Steve Marriott died in a house fire on April 20, 1991. Greg Ridley died on November 19, 2003.

25 Sep 69	6	1	1. NATURAL BORN BUGIE *Immediate IM 082*

Engelbert HUMPERDINCK *63 Weeks*

Born Arnold George Dorsey on May 2, 1936 in Madras, India. Moved to Leicester, England in 1946. Sang on a public stage for the first at the age of seventeen, in a pub talent contest. Started using the name Gerry Dorsey and worked in the night clubs around Britain. In 1954 was called up for National Service. Discharged in 1956 and resumed working the clubs. Made his disc debut, *Crazy Bells,* in February 1959, for Decca Records, under the name Gerry Dorsey. In 1961, was struck down with tuberculosis and had to give up his showbiz career for a period of time. In 1965, met up with Gordon Mills, manger of Tom Jones, who suggested a name change to Engelbert Humperdinck. A recording contract with Decca was arranged and in June 1966, the very first Engelbert Humperdinck recording, *Stay*, was released. In 1989, awarded a star on the Hollywood Walk of Fame, and received a Golden Globe Award for Entertainer of the Year. His autobiography, *Engelbert: What's In A Name?,* published in 2004.

02 Mar 67	1(3)	10	• 1. RELEASE ME *Decca F 12541*
15 Jun 67	2	10	2. THERE GOES MY EVERYTHING *Decca F 12610*
14 Sep 67	1(5)	12	• 3. THE LAST WALTZ *Decca F 12655*

continues over

Date	Pos	Wks	ARTIST / Record Title *Label & Number*
25 Jan 68	1(3)	7	•4. AM I THAT EASY TO FORGET *Decca F 12722*
09 May 68	1(2)	10	•5. A MAN WITHOUT LOVE *Decca F 12770*
17 Oct 68	5	4	6. LES BICYCLETTES DE BELSIZE *Decca F 12834*
20 Mar 69	6	3	7. THE WAY IT USED TO BE *Decca F 12879*
04 Dec 69	3	7	8. WINTER WORLD OF LOVE *Decca F 12980*

Tab HUNTER — *4 Weeks*

Born Arthur Kelm on July 11, 1931 in New York City, USA. Moved to San Francisco age two. In his early teens excelled as a sportsman, ice skater and horseman. Discovered by Dick Clayton who helped give him a new name. Made his film debut in *The Lawless* (1950). Other film appearances include *Island Of Desire* (1951), *Battle Cry* (1955) and *The Burning Hills* (1956). It was Chicago dj, Howard Miller, who pointed Tab in the direction of Dot Records and in 1957 Tab made his recording debut, *Young Love*. In 1958, signed to Warner Brothers. In 1959, embarked on his one and only pop tour with Sal Mineo and Everly Brothers in Australia. His autobiography, *Tab Hunter Confidential: The Making Of A Movie Star*, was published in 2005.

Date	Pos	Wks	ARTIST / Record Title *Label & Number*
27 Feb 57	-	3	1. YOUNG LOVE *London HL 8380*
21 May 57	-	1	2. NINETY NINE WAYS *London HL 8410*

Red HURLEY — *84 Weeks*

Born Brian Vincent Hurley on October 11, 1948 in Dublin, Ireland. Involved in a traffic accident in 1968 which led to his career as a drummer being put on hold. Following a successful audition he secured position as lead vocalist with The Colours Showband. Disc debut: *A Poor Man's Roses* (1969). Red next teamed up with ex members of The Airchords to form The Wheels. In 1971, Red was invited to front The Nevada Showband and with the band enjoyed a very successful run of hit records. Left the Nevada in April 1974 to form his own band who made their debut on August 8, 1974 in Tramore.

continues over

Date	Pos	Wks	ARTIST / Record Title *Label & Number*
			Represented Ireland in the 1976 Eurovision Song Contest with *When*, finishing in tenth position.
08 Jul 71	1(2)	13	• 1. SOMETIMES *Play PLAY 3*
11 Nov 71	1(2)	6	• 2. KISS ME GOODBYE *Play PLAY 6*
04 May 72	3	8	3. HOLD ME *Play PLAY 19*
08 Mar 73	2	7	4. ARKANSAS *Play PLAY 53*
08 Nov 73	5	5	5. I NEVER SAID GOODBYE *Play PLAY 63*
24 Oct 74	5	5	6. I KNOW *Release RL 741*
03 Apr 75	1(2)	9	• 7. LOVE IS ALL *Release RL 766*
19 Feb 76	7	4	8. BROKEN PROMISES *Release RL 801*
11 Mar 76	3	7	9. WHEN *Release RL 808*
26 Aug 76	8	3	10. TENNESSEE SPECIAL *Release RL 827*
17 Mar 77	3	7	11. IN SHAME LOVE IN SHAME *Release RL 855*
18 Aug 77	2	6	12. YOU'RE MY DAY YOU'RE MY NIGHT *Release RL 878*
12 Jul 79	9	1	13. YOU'RE SO GOOD TO ME / STEPPIN' ASIDE IS EASY *Spider WEB 003*
21 Dec 79	6	3	14. THE FUREY MAN *Spider WEB 016*

Brian HYLAND — *6 Weeks*

Born Bryan Francis Hyland on November 12, 1943 in Queens, New York, USA. Sang in church choir at age of nine. Learned to play clarinet and guitar. Formed his own vocal harmony group, the Delfis, at age of twelve. Signed with Kapp Records in 1959. Disc debut: *Rosemary* (1959).

Date	Pos	Wks	ARTIST / Record Title *Label & Number*
31 May 62	3	6	1. GINNY COME LATELY *HMV POP(I) 1013*

Date	Pos	Wks	ARTIST / Record Title *Label & Number*

I

Frank IFIELD ***39 Weeks***

Born on November 30, 1937 in Coventry, England. Moved to Australia in 1945. Disc debut: *Did You See My Daddy Over There* (1953). Returned to England in 1959 and signed to Columbia Records. Starred in the 1965 film, *Up Jumped A Swagman.* Now living and working in Australia. The harmonica player on *I Remember You*, Harry Pitch, also featured on the Mr Bloe 70's hit, *Groovin' With Mr Bloe.*

Date	Pos	Wks	ARTIST / Record Title *Label & Number*
02 Aug 62	1(5)	8	• 1. I REMEMBER YOU *Columbia DB(I) 4856*
05 Nov 62	1(4)	12	• 2. LOVESICK BLUES *Columbia DB(I) 4913*
04 Feb 63	3	7	3. THE WAYWARD WIND *Columbia DB(I) 4960*
29 Apr 63	2	5	4. NOBODY'S DARLIN' BUT MINE *Columbia DB(I) 7007*
15 Jul 63	1(1)	7	• 5. CONFESSIN' (That I Love You) *Columbia DB(I) 7062*

The IRISH ROVERS ***6 Weeks***

Irish folk group. Formed in Canada in 1963 when George Millar (guitar) and Jim Ferguson (vocals) met in Toronto at an Irish function. Performed as a duo until George's cousin Jim Millar (accordion) joined in 1964. Will Millar (accordion) (George's brother) joined up when they relocated to Alberta. Moved to the USA where they played the folk clubs in San Franciso area. Offered a recording contract by Decca Records. Disc debut: *The First Of The Irish Rovers* LP (1966). Wilcil McDowell (accordion) joined the group around this time. Hosted their own weekly series on Canadian TV. Will Millar retired in 1995. Jimmy Ferguson died in 1997. *The Unicorn* enjoyed top ten hit status in the USA in 1968. The group also hit the USA Top Forty singles chart in 1981, with *Wasn't That A Party.*

Date	Pos	Wks	ARTIST / Record Title *Label & Number*
23 May 68	5	6	1. THE UNICORN *MCA MU(I) 1011*

Date	Pos	Wks	ARTIST / Record Title *Label & Number*

Big Dee IRWIN **5 Weeks**

Born Difosca Erwin on August 4, 1939 in New York, USA. Formed the Pastels doo wop group in 1954. Recorded *Been So Long* with group in 1957. Went solo in 1959. Died of heart failure on August 27, 1995. *Swinging On A Star* was in fact a duet by Big Dee Irwin and Little Eva, even though Little Eva was not credited on record.

13 Jan 64	2	5	1. SWINGING ON A STAR *Colpix PX 11010*

Burl IVES **8 Weeks**

Actor/singer born on June 14, 1909 in Huntington Township, Illinois, USA. Made Broadway debut in 1938. Film debut in the 1946 film *Smoky*. Films include *East Of Eden* (1955), *Cat On A Hot Tin Roof* (1958), *The Big Country* (1958) and *Our Man In Havana* (1960). Won an Oscar (Best Supporting Actor) for his role in the film, *The Big Country*. Died from cancer on April 14, 1995.

15 Feb 62	3	8	1. A LITTLE BITTY TEAR *Brunswick 05863*

The IVY LEAGUE **7 Weeks**

Vocal group formed in August 1964 in London, England, purely to sing back up vocals on recording sessions. Did backing vocals on hit singles for The Who (*I Can't Explain*) and Tom Jones (*It's Not Unusual*). On the suggestion of Terry Kennedy the trio made a record. Disc debut: *What More Do You Want* (September 1964). Personnel: John Carter (born John Shakespeare on October 20, 1942 in Birmingham), Ken Lewis (born Kenneth Hawker on December 3, 1942 in Birmingham) and Perry Ford (born Bryan Pugh on December 30, 1940 in Lincoln). John Carter left group in July 1966. Replaced by Tony Burrows. Ken Lewis left January 1967. Replaced by Neil Landon. Burrows and Landon left in August 1967 to become the Flowerpot Men. Perry Ford kept the Ivy League name alive until 1979. Carter and Lewis wrote hits for many artists including Brenda Lee, Mike Sarne and Hermans Hermits.

12 Jul 65	2	7	1. TOSSING AND TURNING *Pye 7N 35251*

See also the Flowerpot Men

Date	Pos	Wks	ARTIST / Record Title *Label & Number*

J

Terry JACKS *6 Weeks*

Born on March 29, 1944 in Winnipeg, Manitoba, Canada. In early 60's joined The Chessmen with whom he made his recording debut, *The Way You Feel*, in 1965. During one of The Chessmen's many appearances on CBC-TV Music Hop, Terry met his wife to be, singer Susan Pesklevits. They formed The Poppy Family in 1968. The marriage and the Poppy Family broke up in 1973, with both moving on to concentrate on their solo careers. Terry retired from the music business in 1987. *Seasons In The Sun* originally recorded by the Kingston Trio, in 1964.

Date	Pos	Wks	ARTIST / Record Title *Label & Number*
11 Apr 74	1(1)	6	• 1. SEASONS IN THE SUN *Bell BELL 1344*

Dee D JACKSON *1 Weeks*

Born Deirdre Cozier on July 15, 1954 in Oxford, England. Moved to Germany in 1975. Signed to Jupiter Records in Munich. Disc debut: *Man Of Man* (1978). Following success of *Automatic Lover* she moved to Los Angeles. Returned to Europe in 1980. Now lives in Italy.

Date	Pos	Wks	ARTIST / Record Title *Label & Number*
25 May 78	6	1	1. AUTOMATIC LOVER *Mercury 6007 171*

Joe JACKSON *3 Weeks*

Born on August 11, 1954 in Burton-on-Trent, England. Grew up in Portsmouth. Took violin lessons at age eleven, but later switched to piano. Played with various groups on the local pub and club scene. Won a scholarship to study Composition at London's Royal Academy of Music. In 1978, some of his demo's were heard by producer, David Kershenbaum, who got Joe a recording contract with A&M Records. Disc debut: *Look Sharp* LP. (1978). His autobiography, *Cure For Sanity: A Musical Pilgrimage*, published in 1999.

Date	Pos	Wks	ARTIST / Record Title *Label & Number*
30 Aug 79	8	3	1. IS SHE REALLY GOING OUT WITH HIM *A&M AMS 7459*

Date	Pos	Wks	ARTIST / Record Title *Label & Number*

Michael JACKSON — *2 Weeks*

Born on August 29, 1958 in Gary, Indiana, USA. At the age of five was lead singer with his brothers in the Jackson 5. Embarked on a solo career in 1971. In 1985, purchased the ATV publishing company, controlling more than two hundred Lennon and McCartney compositions. Married Elvis Presley's daughter, Lisa Marie, in 1994. Divorced in 1996. Won Grammy award in 1983 for his album, *Thriller*. In 1994, faced child molestation charges, these were settled out of court. In 2003, faced further child molestation charges, he was subsequently charged. Charges were dismissed by court. Died June 25, 2009.

Date	Pos	Wks	ARTIST / Record Title *Label & Number*
18 Oct 79	10	2	1. DON'T STOP 'TIL YOU GET ENOUGH *Epic Sep C 7763*

See also The Jacksons

The JACKSONS — *11 Weeks*

Family group formed in 1966 in Gary, Indiana, USA by their father, Joe Jackson. Personnel: Jackie, Tito, Jermaine, Marlon and Michael Jackson. Disc debut: *Big Boy* on Steeltown (1967). Discovered in the summer of 1968, by Bobby Taylor who brought the group to Detroit where they signed with Tamla Motown. In 1976, moved from Motown to Epic. The move was due to Motown not allowing the group to choose their own songs, play instruments on record, choose producers or record songs that weren't from the Motown catalogue. As Motown owned the name Jackson 5, they made a name change to The Jacksons. Jermaine left the group in 1976 to record as a solo artist with Motown. Replaced by Randy Jackson.

Date	Pos	Wks	ARTIST / Record Title *Label & Number*
05 Mar 70	6	4	1. I WANT YOU BACK *Tamla Motown TMG(I) 724*
21 Jul 77	5	4	2. SHOW YOU THE WAY TO GO *Epic EPC 5266*
26 Apr 79	9	3	3. SHAKE YOUR BODY (Down To The Ground) *Epic Sep C 7181*

I Want You Back credit the Jackson Five.

See also Michael Jackson

Date	Pos	Wks	ARTIST / Record Title *Label & Number*
			Sonny JAMES ***4 Weeks***
			Born Jimmie Hugh Loden on May 1, 1929 in Hackleburg, Alabama, USA. Started out in showbusiness performing with his parents and sister as the Loden Family. Served with the US Army in Korea. In late 1953, headed for Nashville On the recommendation of Chet Atkins, was signed to Capitol Records and given a new name, Sonny James, by Capitol producer Ken Nelson. Disc debut: *Let's Go Bunny Huggin'* (1952).
27 Feb 57	-	4	1. YOUNG LOVE *Capitol CL(I) 14682*
			Tommy JAMES and the SHONDELLS ***7 Weeks***
			Born Thomas Jackson on April 29, 1947 in Dayton, Ohio, USA. In 1959, at the age of twelve, he formed his first group, The Tornadoes. Changed name to Shondells in 1963. Disc debut: *Hanky Panky* (1964). Shondells personnel: Ronnie Rosman, (organ), Mike Vale (bass), Vince Pietropaoli (drums) and George Magura (sax). Tommy James split from Shondells in 1970 to pursue a solo career. The title of song, *Mony Mony*, was created from the MONY (Mutual of New York) Insurance Company building whose logo could be seen from Tommy James' Manhatten apartment.
08 Aug 68	2	7	1. MONY MONY *Major Minor MM 567*
			Horst JANKOWSKI his Orchestra and Chorus **1 Weeks**
			Orchestra leader/pianist born on January 30, 1936 in Berlin, Germany. Trained as a classical concert pianist at the Berlin Music Conservatory. Composed *A Walk in The Black Forest* in 1962 under the title *Eine Schwarzwaldfahrt*. Died of lung cancer on June 29, 1998.
20 Sep 65	10	1	1. A WALK IN THE BLACK FOREST • *Mercury EMF 861*

Date	Pos	Wks	ARTIST / Record Title *Label & Number*

Jean-Michel JARRE — *1 Weeks*

Composer/producer/performer. Born August 24, 1948 in Lyon, France. Son of film composer/musician/conductor, Maurice Jarre, Studied piano at age of five. Disc debut: *Le Cage* (1971). Recorded the pioneering album *Oxygene* in 1976. On its release it proved to be an instant hit world wide and turned Jarre into an international star. In 1982, became the first western artist to tour China. The five concerts were recorded and issued on album. Is an UNESCO Goodwill Ambassador. Married actress, Charlotte Rampling in 1976. Divorced in 1996.

Date	Pos	Wks	ARTIST / Record Title *Label & Number*
06 Oct 77	7	1	1. OXYGENE • *Polydor 2001 721*

JETHRO TULL — *6 Weeks*

Progressive rock group formed in Luton, England in 1967. Personnel: Ian Anderson (born August 10, 1947 in Dunfermline, Scotland. vocals, flute), Mick Abrahams (guitar), Glen Cornick (bass), and Clive Bunker (drums). Disc debut: *Sunshine Day* (1968), which was erroneously credited to Jethro Toe. Mick Abrahams left in November 1968, replaced by Martin Barre. Numerous changes in personnel over the years.

Date	Pos	Wks	ARTIST / Record Title *Label & Number*
03 Jul 69	5	4	1. LIVING IN THE PAST *Island WIP-6056*
12 Feb 70	6	2	2. WITCH'S PROMISE *Chrysalis WIP 6077*

JIGSAW — *1 Weeks*

Formed in Coventry, England in 1966. Personnel: Des Dyer (lead vocals/drums) Barrie Bernard (bass), Tony Campbell (guitar), Clive Scott (keyboards), Tony Britnell (saxophone) and Barry Mahon (saxophone). Disc debut: *I Need Your Love* (1968). Disbanded in 1981. *Sky High* featured in the 1975 film, *The Man From Hong Kong*. Clive Scott died on May 10, 2009.

Date	Pos	Wks	ARTIST / Record Title *Label & Number*
27 Nov 75	9	1	1. SKY HIGH *Splash CPI 1*

Date	Pos	Wks	ARTIST / Record Title *Label & Number*
			Billy JOEL ***7 Weeks***
			Born William Martin Joel on May 9, 1949 in the Bronx, New York, USA. Formed his first band, The Echoes, in 1964. Released his first solo album, *Cold Spring Harbor*, in 1971. Signed to Columbia as a solo artist in 1973. Inducted into the Songwriters Hall of Fame in 1992. Inducted into the Rock and Roll Hall of Fame in 1999.
06 Apr 78	7	2	1. JUST THE WAY YOU ARE *CBS 5872*
25 Jan 79	3	5	2. MY LIFE *CBS 6821*
			Elton JOHN ***17 Weeks***
			Born Reginald Kenneth Dwight on March 25, 1947 in Pinner, Middlesex, England. Joined Bluesology in 1966. Worked as a session musician/vocalist re-creating the chart hits of the period for various budget record companies. Teamed up with lyricist Bernie Taupin as a result of an advert in the NME. Changed name to Elton John. Disc debut: *I've Been Loving You* (1968) on Philips. Signed with DJM in 1969. Formed Rocket Records in 1973 and played a role in relaunching the career of Neil Sedaka. His re-recording of *Candle In The Wind* (1997) is reputed to be the biggest selling single of all time.
25 May 72	6	3	1. ROCKET MAN *Pye DJX 501*
21 Dec 72	10	2	2. CROCODILE ROCK *Pye DJS 271*
08 Feb 73	4	4	3. DANIEL *Pye DJS 275*
01 Nov 73	4	3	4. GOODBYE YELLOW BRICK ROAD *Pye DJS 285*
28 Mar 74	8	1	5. CANDLE IN THE WIND *DJM DJS 297*
23 Dec 76	3	2	6. SORRY SEEMS TO BE THE SADDEST WORD *Rocket ROKN 517*
11 Jan 79	7	2	7. SONG FOR GUY *Rocket XPRES 5*
			Elton JOHN and Kiki DEE ***11 Weeks***
			Male/female vocal duo. Elton John, born Reginald Dwight on March 25, 1947 in Pinner, Middlesex, England. Kiki Dee, born Pauline Matthews on March 6, 1947 in Little Horton, Bradford,Yorkshire, England. Began her musical career singing with a local band in Bradford in the early 1960's. Disc debut: *I Was Only Kidding* on Fontana in 1963.

continues over

Date	Pos	Wks	ARTIST / Record Title *Label & Number*
			Signed to Elton John's record company Rocket in 1973. A successful solo artist, her vocal collaboration with Elton John resulted in chart topper for the duo in Ireland, Britain and the USA.
22 Jul 76	1(5)	11	• 1. DON'T GO BREAKIN' MY HEART *Rocket ROKN 512*

JILTED JOHN — *2 Weeks*

Born Graham Fellows in Manchester, England. The drama student was attending Manchester University when he recorded the self composed *Jilted John* for Tosh Records. Issued in April 1978, it was taken up by EMI and went on to sell over a quarter of a million copies in Britain. After his pop career went into decline Fellows returned to acting. Today, under the name, John Shuttleworth, he is regarded as one of Britains best comics.

Date	Pos	Wks	ARTIST / Record Title *Label & Number*
31 Aug 78	8	2	1. JILTED JOHN *EMI INT 567*

JOHNNY and the HURRICANES — *11 Weeks*

Instrumental group formed in Toledo, Ohio, USA in 1958 as The Orbits. Personnel: Johnny Paris (born John Pocisk on August 29, 1940 in Rossford, Ohio, tenor sax), Paul Tesluk (organ), Dave Yorko (guitar), Lionel Mattice (bass) and Bo Savich (drums). Disc debut: *Crossfire* (1959). Group split up in 1961. Johnny Paris formed the Attila Record Company in 1965. Bo Savich died on January 4, 2002. Johnny Paris died of pneumonia on May 1, 2006.

Date	Pos	Wks	ARTIST / Record Title *Label & Number*
24 Dec 59	5	1	1. RED RIVER ROCK • *London HL 8948*
28 Jul 60	6	2	2. DOWN YONDER • *London HLX 9134*
08 Dec 60	4	8	3. ROCKING GOOSE • *London HLX 9190*

Bryan JOHNSON — *5 Weeks*

Born on July 18, 1926 in London. England. Brother of singer Teddy Johnson. Represented Britain in 1960 Eurovision Song Contest with *Looking High High High*, finishing in second position. Died from cancer on October 18, 1995.

Date	Pos	Wks	ARTIST / Record Title *Label & Number*
31 Mar 60	8	5	1. LOOKING HIGH, HIGH, HIGH *Decca F 11213*

Date	Pos	Wks	ARTIST / Record Title *Label & Number*

Johnny JOHNSON and his BANDWAGON — *11 Weeks*

Johnny Johnson born on July 20, 1945 in Palm Beach, Florida, USA. Formed The Bandwagon in Rochester, New York, USA in 1966. Personnel: Johnny Johnson (lead vocals), Terry Lewis, Arthur Fulilove and Billy Bradley. Signed as The Bandwagon to Epic Records in 1967. Disc debut: *Baby Make Your Own Sweet Music* (1967). In April 1969 group renamed Johnny Johnson and his Bandwagon. Johnny Johnson relocated to Britain in late 1969. Signed with Bell Records. Gave up music business in mid 1970's.

Date	Pos	Wks	Title
21 Nov 68	5	6	1. BREAKIN' DOWN THE WALLS OF HEARTACHE *CBS 58-3670*
14 Jan 71	5	5	2. (BLAME IT) ON THE PONY EXPRESS *Bell BLL(I) 1128*

Breakin' Down The Walls Of Heartache credit to The Bandwagon.

Kevin JOHNSON — *1 Weeks*

Born on July 3, 1944 in Rockhampton, Queensland, Australia. It wasn't until his late teens that he became infatuated with the music of the day. Joined local group The Candymen. Started writing and performing his own songs and came to the notice of Col Joye, one of Australia's original rock stars, who signed Kevin to his publishing company. Disc debut: *Woman You Took My Life*. His songs have been recorded by many artists including Sonny Knowles, Des O'Connor and Val Doonican. Composed music for several films. Appeared in the 1992 film, *Fatal Bond*. RTE disc jockey, Val Joyce, has to be credited for the success of Kevin's recording, *Rock n Roll*, in Ireland. He was the first to play it on Irish radio, and continued to do so on a regular basis, on his *Airs And Races* programme until it struck a chord with the Irish record buying public.

Date	Pos	Wks	Title
04 Apr 74	8	1	1. ROCK N ROLL (I GAVE YOU THE BEST YEARS OF MY LIFE) *Pye MSS 304*

Date	Pos	Wks	ARTIST / Record Title *Label & Number*

Laurie JOHNSON ORCHESTRA — *3 Weeks*

Composer/ producer/ orchestra leader. Born on February 7, 1927 in Hampstead, London, England. Studied at the Royal College of Music in London. At the age of 19, began composing and arranging for the Ted Heath Band. In 1959 wrote music and acted as musical director for the London stage production of "Lock Up Your Daughters". One of the finest British composers of television themes and film scores. His credits include *No Hiding Place*, *The Avengers*, *The New Avengers* and *The Professionals.* His film scores include *The Moonraker* (1958), *East Of Sudan* (1966) and *Bitter Harvest* (1981). *Sucu Sucu* was the theme from the British Television series, *Top Secret.*

26 Oct 61	7	3	1. SUCU SUCU • *Pye 7N 15383*

Teddy JOHNSON and Pearl CARR — *4 Weeks*

Husband and wife vocal duo. Teddy born on September 4, 1920 in Surbiton, England. Pearl born on November 2, 1923 in Exmouth, Devon, England. Both started out as dance band singers. Met at a Stanley Black show in 1951. Married in 1955. Represented the UK at the 1959 Eurovision Song Contest with *Sing Little Birdie*, finishing in second position.

30 Apr 59	4	4	1. SING LITTLE BIRDIE *Columbia DB(I) 4275*

The JOHNSTON BROTHERS — *1 Weeks*

Vocal group formed in London, England in 1948 by Johnnie Johnston. Disc debut: *A Portrait Of Jenny* (1949). Personnel: Johnnie Johnston, Miff King, Eddie Lester and Frank Holmes. Johnnie Johnston compositions include *Don't Ringa* Da *Bell* and *The Wedding Of Lilli Marlene*. He died on June 10, 1998.

15 Feb 55	-	1	1. MAJORCA *Decca F 10451*

Date	Pos	Wks	ARTIST / Record Title *Label & Number*

The JOHNSTONS — *9 Weeks*

Family folk/ballad group formed in 1966 in Slane, County Meath, Ireland. Personnel: Adrienne and Lucy Johnston (vocals) with brother Michael Johnston (guitar). Debut disc: *The Travelling People*. Mick Moloney (vocals, guitar) joined in April 1967. Michael Johnston left in June 1967. Replaced by Paul Brady (vocals, guitar). Signed to Transatlantic Records in 1968. Lucy Johnston left group in November 1969. Group disbanded in 1973.

Date	Pos	Wks	ARTIST / Record Title *Label & Number*
01 Aug 66	1(1)	7	• 1. THE TRAVELLING PEOPLE *Pye 7N 17144*
01 Feb 68	8	2	2. I NEVER WILL MARRY *Target 7N 17430*

Jimmy JONES — *9 Weeks*

Born on June 2, 1937 in Birmingham, Alabama, USA. In 1955 joined a vocal group the Sparks Of Rhythm. Signed to MGM subsidiary Cub in 1959, and hit the jackpot with his first solo single, *Handy Man*.

Date	Pos	Wks	ARTIST / Record Title *Label & Number*
28 Apr 60	4	3	1. HANDY MAN *MGM MGM(I) 1051*
14 Jul 60	2	6	2. GOOD TIMIN' *MGM MGM(I) 1078*

Paul JONES — *1 Weeks*

Born Paul Pond on February 24, 1942 in Portsmouth, England. Joined Manfred Mann in 1962 when the group was operating under the name, the Mann-Hugg Blues Brothers. Departed in 1966 to pursue a solo career. *I've Been A Bad Bad Boy*, was featured in the 1967 film, *The Privilege*, which starred Paul Jones. Solo disc debut: *High Time* (1966).

Date	Pos	Wks	ARTIST / Record Title *Label & Number*
16 Feb 67	10	1	1. I'VE BEEN A BAD BAD BOY *HMV POP(I) 1576*

See also Manfred Mann

Sandie JONES and the DIXIES — *4 Weeks*

Born in 1950 in Crumlin, Dublin, Ireland. Made her first stage appearance with a song and dance routine at the age of six.

continues over

Date	Pos	Wks	ARTIST / Record Title *Label & Number*

Following an appearance in a local talent contest at Crumlin's Apollo Cinema a member of the audience Fr. Hillery invited her to join the Statesmen. Later sang with Monaco Showband. Began her showband career as lead vocalist with the Royal Earls. Disc debut: *Reflections Of You* (1969). Joined the Dixies as lead singer in 1972. Represented Ireland in the 1972 Eurovision Song Contest with a song in the Irish language, *Ceol An Ghra*, finishing in fifteenth position. Left the Dixies in October 1973 to form her own band, The Boyfriends. Quit the showband scene in April 1975 to concentrate on cabaret scene. Own television series, *Sandie Jones*, on RTE in 1978.

Date	Pos	Wks	ARTIST / Record Title *Label & Number*
09 Mar 72	1(1)	4	• 1. CEOL AN GHRA *Play PLAY 20*

See also Brendan O'Brien and The Dixies
See also Rory O'Connor and The Dixies

Sandie JONES, Joe O'TOOLE and DIXIES — *7 Weeks*

Female/male vocal duo. Sandie Jones born in 1950 in Crumlin, Dublin, Ireland. Sandie Jones left in October 1973. Joe O'Toole born in 1950 in Drimnagh, Dublin, Ireland. Before entering the music business worked as a tailor. Reached the finals of the RTE TV talent programme, *Reach For The Stars*, in August 1971. Turned professional shortly afterwards and formed the group *Apples*. Joined the Dixies in January 1972. Joe O'Toole left in 1975. Formed Flint in 1976. A talented songwriter his songs have been recorded by Red Hurley, Bill Ryan and D J Curtin. In 1993 made the Irish top ten with the song *We're Going To America*, which was released as Joe O'Toole and Skye. The Dixies personnel: Sandie Jones (vocals), Joe O'Toole (vocals), Steve Lynch (guitar), Chris O'Mahoney (bass), Mike Donovan (drums), Finbar O'Leary (organ), Sean Lucey (tenor sax) and Theo Cahill (tenor sax).

Date	Pos	Wks	ARTIST / Record Title *Label & Number*
27 Apr 72	1(1)	7	• 1. WHAT DO I DO *Play PLAY 21*

Date	Pos	Wks	ARTIST / Record Title *Label & Number*

Tammy JONES — *4 Weeks*

Born on March 12, 1943 in Tregarth near Bangor, North Wales. Began singing at an early age. Starred in her own Welsh TV series, *Tammy*. Trained for opera at the Guildhall School of Music, London. Disc debut: *Helen Wyn a Hebogiaid y Nos* (1965). In 1975 participated in the top rated television talent show, Opportunity Knocks, winning six weeks in succession. Signed by Epic Records. Was admitted to the Gorsedd of the Bards in 2005 for her substantial service to the Welsh nation, its language and culture. Now lives in New Zealand.

Date	Pos	Wks	ARTIST / Record Title *Label & Number*
15 May 75	4	4	1. LET ME TRY AGAIN *Epic Sep C 3211*

Tom JONES — *98 Weeks*

Born Thomas John Woodward on June 7, 1940 in Pontypridd, South Wales. Began his musical career singing in pubs, clubs and at parties. In 1963 he became frontman for local group Tommy Scott and The Senators. Recorded seven tracks for Joe Meek in early 1964. Following the success of, *It's Not Unusual*, four of those tracks were released in 1965, on two Columbia singles. Spotted by manager Gordon Mills (former lead vocals with the Viscounts) singing at a club, who renamed him Tom Jones and secured a recording contract with Decca. Disc debut: *Chills And Fever* (1964). In January 2006 Tom Jones was given an MBE in the Queen's New Year's Honours list.

Date	Pos	Wks	ARTIST / Record Title *Label & Number*
08 Mar 65	6	5	1. IT'S NOT UNUSUAL *Decca F 12062*
21 Nov 66	1(6)	14	• 2. GREEN GREEN GRASS OF HOME *Decca F 22511*
16 Mar 67	4	4	3. DETROIT CITY *Decca F 12555*
11 May 67	4	5	4. FUNNY FAMILIAR FORGOTTEN FEELINGS *Decca F 12599*
24 Aug 67	4	8	5. I'LL NEVER FALL IN LOVE AGAIN *Decca F 12639*
11 Jan 68	7	4	6. I'M COMING HOME *Decca F 12693*
07 Mar 68	1(3)	11	• 7. DELILAH *Decca F 12747*
01 Aug 68	1(3)	13	• 8. HELP YOURSELF *Decca F 12812*
12 Dec 68	4	8	9. A MINUTE OF YOUR TIME *Decca F 12854*
29 May 69	7	5	10. LOVE ME TONIGHT *Decca F 12924*

continues over

Date	Pos	Wks	ARTIST / Record Title *Label & Number*
25 Dec 69	7	6	11. WITHOUT LOVE *Decca F 12990*
30 Apr 70	3	9	12. DAUGHTER OF DARKNESS *Decca F 13013*
18 Nov 71	4	3	13. TILL *Decca F 13236*
06 Apr 72	7	3	14. THE YOUNG NEW MEXICAN PUPPETEER *Decca F 13298*

Jimmy JUSTICE — *11 Weeks*

Born James Anthony Bernard Little on December 15, 1939 in Bermondsey, London, England. Brought to Pye's attention by Emile Ford. Disc debut: *I Understand* (1960). Moved to Sweden in the mid 60's.

Date	Pos	Wks	ARTIST / Record Title *Label & Number*
12 Apr 62	4	7	1. WHEN MY LITTLE GIRL IS SMILING *Pye 7N 15421*
01 Oct 62	4	4	2. SPANISH HARLEM *Pye 7N 15457*

Bill JUSTIS — *1 Weeks*

Born on October 14, 1927 in Birmingham, Alabama, USA. Grew up in Memphis, playing trumpet in local jazz and dance bands. In 1957 Sam Philips hired Justis to work as musical director for his Sun Records label. Composed *Raunchy*, with guitarist Sid Manker. The number was originally titled *Backwoods*. Justis plays tenor saxophone on it. Discovered Charlie Rich in 1950's. Composed music score for the 1977 film, *Smokey And The Bandit*. Worked as producer, musical director and A&R man for several record companies including Sun and Mercury. Died of cancer on July 15, 1982.

Date	Pos	Wks	ARTIST / Record Title *Label & Number*
18 Feb 58	-	1	1. RAUNCHY • *London HLS 8517*

Date	Pos	Wks	ARTIST / Record Title *Label & Number*

K

Ernie K-DOE **3 Weeks**

Born Ernest Kador Jr on February 22, 1936 in New Orleans, USA. At the age of seven was singing in his father's choir. Joined the Blue Diamonds in 1954. Disc debut: *Do Baby Do* (1956) on Specialty Records. The bass man on *Mother-In-Law* is Benny Spellman. Died from liver failure on July 5, 2001.

Date	Pos	Wks	ARTIST / Record Title *Label & Number*
15 Jun 61	4	3	1. MOTHER-IN-LAW *London HLU 9330*

Eden KANE ***27 Weeks***

Born Richard Graham Sarstedt on March 29, 1942 in New Delhi, India. Relocated to London, England in March 1954. At school excelled in field sports cricket, soccer and hockey. After leaving school worked as a trainee architect. Formed a skiffle group, the Fabulous 5 and played coffee bars and youth clubs around London. In 1960 entered (and won) a talent contest sponsored by confectionery giant, Cadbury, at the Classic cinema, Kings Road, Chelsea. Signed by Pye Records and released single *Hot Chocolate Crazy* (1960). His brothers, Peter and Clive (Robin) Sarstedt also tasted chart success.

Date	Pos	Wks	ARTIST / Record Title *Label & Number*
27 Jul 61	1(5)	11	• 1. WELL I ASK YOU *Decca F 11353*
28 Sep 61	4	6	2. GET LOST *Decca F 11381*
01 Feb 62	6	5	3. FORGET ME NOT *Decca F 11418*
16 Mar 64	6	5	4. BOYS CRY *Fontana ETF 438*

Kitty KALLEN ***2 Weeks***

Born on May 25, 1921 in New Jersey, USA. At the age of twelve had her own programme *Kitty Kallen Calling* on Philadelphia radio station WCAU. In 1939 joined the newly formed Jack Teagarden Orchestra as vocalist. Made her disc debut in August 1939 with Teagarden.

continues over

Date	Pos	Wks	ARTIST / Record Title *Label & Number*

Left in 1942 to become a staff singer at NBC Studio in Hollywood. Replaced Helen O'Connell in the Jimmy Dorsey Orchestra in 1943. Joined Harry James in 1944. Left in December 1945 to pursue a solo career. Retired from showbusiness in the mid 1960's.

14 Sep 54	1(2)	2	• 1. LITTLE THINGS MEAN A LOT *Brunswick 05287*

The KAYE SISTERS — *6 Weeks*

Female vocal trio formed in 1954 by Carmen Kaye as the Three Kayes. Changed name to Kaye Sisters in 1956. Personnel: Sheila Jones (born on October 21, 1936 in London), Shirley (Shan) Palmer (born August 15, 1938 in Hull) and Carol Young (born on April 12, 1930 in Oldham). Sheila Jones left in 1975. Disbanded in 1976. Reformed in 1988 for a nation-wide tour of Britain. Carol Young died of cancer on August 20, 2006.

15 Sep 60	3	6	1. PAPER ROSES *Philips EPB 1024*

See also Frankie Vaughan and the Kaye Sisters

Tony KEARNEY — *2 Weeks*

Born in Belfast, N. Ireland. The song lyrics tell the story of the events of Sunday January 30, 1972 when thirteen civilians were killed by the British Army, during a civil rights march in Belfast.

20 Apr 72	2	2	1. BLOODY SUNDAY *Cuchulainn CCH 003*

Tony KEELING and the GRADUATES — *13 Weeks*

Tony Keeling born on September 18, 1945 in Skerries, County Dublin. Ireland. Disc debut: *Kelly* (1965). On the break up of the Graduates joined the Vibrations. Left music scene in 1973. The Graduates Showband formed in 1962. Personnel: Tony Keeling (lead vocals, guitar), George Hand (leader, organ), Colm McCormack (trombone), Gerry Bradley (tenor sax), Tommy Walsh (trumpet), Tommy Coleman (bass), Fergus O'Brien (guitar, trumpet) and Paddy Landy (drums). Disbanded in 1971. Paddy Landy died in July 2006.

continues over

Date	Pos	Wks	ARTIST / Record Title *Label & Number*
01 Mar 65	8	3	1. KELLY *King KG 1014*
13 Dec 65	10	1	2. ANYTHING THAT'S PART OF YOU Pye 7N *17008*
21 Nov 66	7	4	3. EDELWEISS *Pye 7N 17201*
07 Dec 67	7	5	4. THE CRYSTAL CHANDELIER *Pye 7N 17418*

Jerry KELLER *7 Weeks*

Born on June 20, 1937 in Fort Smith, Arkansas, USA. Relocated to Tulsa at age of six. Formed the Lads Of Note vocal quartet as a teenager. Worked as a disc jockey on KAKL radio in Tulsa. Following success in a talent contest took up position as vocalist with the Jack Dalton Orchestra. Moved to New York in 1956. Songwriting credits include *Almost There* and *Here Comes Summer.*

Date	Pos	Wks	ARTIST / Record Title *Label & Number*
01 Oct 59	3	7	1. HERE COMES SUMMER *London HLR 8890*

KELLEY and the NEVADA *8 Weeks*

Born Eileen Kelly on September 11, 1946 in Cork, Ireland. Sang with local group the Music Makers, while working as a secretary. T J Byrne, manager of the Royal Showband encouraged her to go into the music business full time. In early 1965 was signed by the Nevada Showband to replace Maisie McDaniel. Disc debut: *Be My Man* (1965). Left Nevada in September 1974 to join the Big 8. The following year joined the Las Vegas Band. Launched her own group, Kelley and Klass in November 1976 and opted to concentrate on the cabaret scene.

Date	Pos	Wks	ARTIST / Record Title *Label & Number*
14 Dec 72	3	6	1. HOW GREAT THOU ART *Play PLAY 44*
27 Jun 74	3	2	2. THE WEDDING SONG (There Is Love) *Desert SAND 501*

Des KELLY and the CAPITOL SHOWBAND *9 Weeks*

Born on February 1, 1936 in Turloughmore, County Galway, Ireland. Came from a musical background. Formed the Quicksilver Dance Orchestra in 1953 which enjoyed popularity in the local dance halls in Co. Galway.

continues over

Date	Pos	Wks	ARTIST / Record Title *Label & Number*

Moved to Dublin in the late 1950's to complete his agricultural science degree at UCD. In the winter of 1959 while at college Des met pianist Eamon Monaghan and trumpeter Paul Sweeney and decided to form a band. The Capitol Showband was launched at the Top Hat Ballroom in Dun Laoghaire. Left the Capitol in 1969. to go into management. Managed several artists, including Sweeney's Men and Planxty. Formed Ruby Records in 1970. Now a presenter with Galway Bay Radio. Capitol Showband formed in 1961 in Dublin. First Irish showband to release an LP, *Presenting The Capitol Showband* (1962). First Irish showband to appear on top British TV show, *Sunday Night At The London Palladium* (January 17, 1965). Personnel Butch Moore (vocals), Jimmy Hogan (lead guitar), Des Kelly (bass), Johnny Kelly (drums), Eamonn Monaghan (piano), Paddy Cole (tenor sax), Bram McCarthy (trumpet) and Don Long (trombone). Disbanded in 1971.

Date	Pos	Wks	ARTIST / Record Title *Label & Number*
02 Mar 67	3	9	1. THE STREETS OF BALTIMORE *Pye 7N 17257*

The Streets Of Baltimore credit Capitol Showband featuring Des Kelly

See also Johnny Kelly; Butch Moore and the Capitol Showband

Johnny KELLY — *20 Weeks*

Born on October 29, 1941 in Turloughmore, County Galway, Ireland. Younger brother of Des Kelly. Founder member of the Quicksilver Dance Orchestra. In late 1950's moved to Dublin to study medicine at UCD. Drummer/vocalist/founder member of the Capitol Showband. *Black Velvet Band* was the top selling record of 1967 in Ireland. He won the Billboard Award of 1967 for Top Native Artist. Left the Capitol Showband in late 1969. Died on October 25, 1987 in London.

Date	Pos	Wks	ARTIST / Record Title *Label & Number*
01 Jun 67	1(8)	20	• 1. BLACK VELVET BAND *Pye 7N 17322*

Date	Pos	Wks	ARTIST / Record Title *Label & Number*

KENNY — *11 Weeks*

Formed in Enfield, England in 1971 under the name Chufff. Got their break as a result of the decision by Irish born singer, Tony Kenny - who had scored two hits, *Heart Of Stone* and *Give It To Me Now,* under the name, Kenny - that he no longer wanted to be a pop star and had returned to Ireland. Bill Martin and Phil Coulter, two highly respected songwriters/producers were so convinced that the new Kenny single, *The Bump*, was going to be a hit that they needed a group to promote it, and so Chufff became Kenny. Personnel: Rick Driscoll (vocals), Yan Style (guitar), Chris Acklison (keyboards), Chris Redburn (bass) and Andy Walton (drums). Disbanded in 1978.

Date	Pos	Wks	ARTIST / Record Title *Label & Number*
23 Jan 75	2	5	1. THE BUMP *Rak RAK 186*
03 Apr 75	3	4	2. FANCY PANTS *Rak RAK 196*
10 Jul 75	9	1	3. BABY I LOVE YOU, OK! *Rak RAK 207*
11 Sep 75	10	1	4. JULIE ANN *Rak RAK 214*

Tony KENNY — *7 Weeks*

Born Anthony Kevin Kenny on April 14, 1946 in Dublin, Ireland. In 1964 joined the Mexicans Showband. Member of the Arran Showband for a brief period in 1965, leaving to join The Vampires beat group. Invited to join the newly formed Sands Showband as lead vocalist in September 1967. Left the Sands in 1973 to pursue a solo career. Signed by Bill Martin and Phil Coulter to record under the name Kenny. Enjoyed two international hit singles, *Heart Of Stone* and *Give It To Me Now*, but decided to abandon the pop music scene in favour of stage and cabaret work.

Date	Pos	Wks	ARTIST / Record Title *Label & Number*
08 Mar 73	4	6	1. HEART OF STONE *Rak RAK 144*
12 Jun 75	10	1	2. SOMEBODY DONE SOMEBODY WRONG SONG *Ram RMS 1014*

Heart Of Stone credit *Kenny*

See also The Sands

Date	Pos	Wks	ARTIST / Record Title *Label & Number*

John KERR — *7 Weeks*

Born in 1925 in Coolback, Fanad Peninsuala, Co. Donegal, Ireland. As a young man served his time as shoemaker. Relocated to Kerrykeel in the mid 1940's to work as a cobbler. Began his singing career at the age of twenty six with the Classic Dance Band. Disc debut: *Mulroy Bay* (1968). Performed at the Royal Albert Hall, London and Carnegie Hall, New York. Died on April 25, 2006, aged 80. John's recording of the *Three Leafed Shamrock*, first appeared on record as an album track in 1968.

Date	Pos	Wks	ARTIST / Record Title *Label & Number*
17 Feb 72	1(1)	7	• 1. THREE LEAFED SHAMROCK *Pye PMM 602*

Johnny KIDD and the PIRATES — *6 Weeks*

Born Frederick Albert Heath on November 23, 1935 in Willesden, London, England. Began his musical career as a member of the Nutters Skiffle Group, who, changed their name to the Pirates in 1959. Spotted by a local rep from EMI and signed to a recording contract with Parlophone. Disc debut: *Please Don't Touch* (1959). Split with the Pirates in 1966. Composer of rock classic *Shakin' All Over.* In 1976 the classic Pirates lineup of Frank Farley (drums), Johnny Spence (bass) and Mick Green (lead guitar) reformed. Session musician Joe Moretti is lead guitar on *Shakin' All Over.* Johnny Kidd died in a car crash on October 7, 1966.

Date	Pos	Wks	ARTIST / Record Title *Label & Number*
11 Aug 60	3	5	1. SHAKIN' ALL OVER *HMV POP(I) 753*
16 Sep 63	8	1	2. I'LL NEVER GET OVER YOU *HMV POP(I) 1173*

Andy KIM — *1 Weeks*

Born Andrew Joachim on December 5, 1946 in Montreal, Canada. Moved to New York while still in his teens. Met producer/songwriter Jeff Barry and after a deal of persuasion got a contract with Capitol Records. Disc debut: *How'd We Ever Get This Way* (1968). Co-wrote *Sugar Sugar* for the Archies.

Date	Pos	Wks	ARTIST / Record Title *Label & Number*
10 Oct 74	10	1	1. ROCK ME GENTLY *Capitol CL 15787*

Date	Pos	Wks	ARTIST / Record Title *Label & Number*

Carole KING ***2 Weeks***

Born Carole Klein on February 9, 1942 in Brooklyn, New York, USA. Played piano as a child. Began song-writing in 1958, teaming up with Gerry Goffin, who she later married. The duo wrote dozens of classic pop songs including *The Locomotion*, *Will You Love Me Tomorrow* and *Take Good Care Of My Baby*. Won four Grammys in 1971, including 'Record Of The Year' for *It's Too Late*. Inducted into the Rock and Roll Hall of Fame (with Gerry Goffin) in 1990.

Date	Pos	Wks	ARTIST / Record Title *Label & Number*
16 Sep 71	7	2	1. IT'S TOO LATE *A&M AMS 849*

Claude KING ***5 Weeks***

Born on February 5, 1923 near Keithville, Louisiana, USA. Spent his childhood on a farm. Bought his first guitar at the age of twelve. In 1942 joined U.S. Navy. On his discharge formed a band, the Rainbow Boys, with Buddy Attaway and Tillman Franks. Disc debut: *Flying Saucers* (1947). Joined the Louisiana Hayride in 1948.A talented songwriter, his songs recorded by artists including Webb Pierce, Kitty Wells and Johnny Horton. Signed to Columbia in 1961. Clifton Clowers, the subject of *Wolverton Mountain*, died in Morrilton, Arkansas on August 15, 1994. He was 102 and actually lived on Wolverton Mountain when the song was penned.

Date	Pos	Wks	ARTIST / Record Title *Label & Number*
20 Sep 62	2	5	1. WOLVERTON MOUNTAIN *CBS EAAG 108*

Dave KING ***9 Weeks***

Born on June 23, 1929 in Twickenham, London, England. Started his showbusiness career as a comedian. Member of the Morton Fraser Harmonica Gang. In 1953 hit out as solo act. Signed to Parlophone Records. Disc debut: *Sweet Kentucky Rose* (1955). In 1959, relocated to the USA to try his luck in the entertainment business. On his return to Britain in the early 1960's he turned to straight acting, appearing in several films and television dramas.

continues over

Date	Pos	Wks	ARTIST / Record Title *Label & Number*
			Film appearances include *Go To Blazes* (1962) and *The Long Good Friday* (1980). Played role of Jack Duckworth's rougish brother, Clifford, in the TV soap, *Coronation Street* (1994-95). Died on April 15, 2002.
14 Feb 56	-	4	1. MEMORIES ARE MADE OF THIS *Decca F 10684*
19 Jun 56	-	1	2. YOU CAN'T BE TRUE TO TWO *Decca F 10720*
09 Apr 57	-	2	3. LOVE IS A GOLDEN RING *Decca F 10865*
27 Aug 57	-	1	4. WITH ALL MY HEART *Decca F 10910*
05 Mar 58	-	1	5. THE STORY OF MY LIFE *Decca F 10973*

Jonathan KING — *2 Weeks*

Born Kenneth George King on December 6, 1944 in London, England. Singer, songwriter, pop columnist, producer and broadcaster. Discovered and produced the first album for Genesis. Founded UK Records in 1972. Enjoyed several hit records under various pseudonyms including Sakkarin, Weathermen, Bubblerock and One Hundred Ton And A Feather. In November 2000, was arrested and charged with various sexual offences against minors dating back to the early 70's. In 2001, he was found guilty and sentenced to seven years imprisonment.

Date	Pos	Wks	ARTIST / Record Title *Label & Number*
30 Aug 65	10	2	1. EVERYONE'S GONE TO THE MOON *Decca F 12187*

The KING BROTHERS — *3 Weeks*

Vocal/instrumental family trio. Brothers, Michael (born April 25, 1935, vocals, guitar), Tony (born January 31, 1937, vocals, bass) and Denis King (born July 25, 1939, vocals, piano) came from Hornchurch, Essex, England. Voted Britain's top vocal group of 1957 by readers of the NME. Broke up in late 1960's. Denis King went on to have a successful career as a composer of TV themes including *Galloping Home*, the theme from the *Black Beauty* television series. Denis King received an Ivor Novello Award - Best Theme from a Radio or TV Production - for *Galloping Home (Black Beauty)*, in 1973.

continues over

Date	Pos	Wks	ARTIST / Record Title *Label & Number*
			Standing On The Corner featured in the 1956 musical, *The Most Happy Fella*.
03 Dec 57	-	1	1. WAKE UP LITTLE SUSIE *Parlophone R(I) 4367*
02 Jun 60	3	2	2. STANDING ON THE CORNER *Parlophone R(I) 4639*

The KINKS — *38 Weeks*

Formed in London, England. Started out life in September 1961 as the Ray Davies Quartet, playing school dances and church functions. In April 1963 renamed The Ramrods. In September of the same year another change of name, to the Boll-Weevils. In September 1963, aspiring singer, Robert Wace meets up with the band and for a short period the group do a number of gigs billed as Robert Wace and The Boll-Weevils. In November 1963 a change of name to The Ravens and the group record a demo at Regent Sound. In January 1964 adopt the name, The Kinks. Personnel: Ray Davies (born 21 June 1944 in London, vocals, guitar), Dave Davies (lead guitar, vocals), Pete Quaife (bass) and Mick Avory (drums). Disc debut: *Long Tall Sally* (February 1964). Pete Quaife leaves the group in April 1969, replaced by John Dalton. Sign with RCA Records in 1971. Late 1973 formed their own record label, Konk, and open their own recording studios. In 1976 signed with Arista Records. Inducted into the Rock 'n Roll Hall of Fame in 1990. Ray Davies biography, *X-Ray*, published in 1994.

Date	Pos	Wks	ARTIST / Record Title *Label & Number*
14 Sep 64	6	3	1. YOU REALLY GOT ME *Pye 7N 15673*
01 Feb 65	3	5	2. TIRED OF WAITING FOR YOU *Pye 7N 15759*
21 Mar 66	3	6	3. DEDICATED FOLLOWER OF FASHION *Pye 7N 17064*
04 Jul 66	1(1)	5	• 4. SUNNY AFTERNOON *Pye 7N 17125*
12 Jan 67	7	3	5. DEAD END STREET *Pye 7N 17222*
08 Jun 67	3	6	6. WATERLOO SUNSET *Pye 7N 17321*
23 Jul 70	1(1)	9	• 7. LOLA *Pye 7N 17961*
28 Jan 71	10	1	8. APEMAN *Pye 7N 45016*

See also Dave Davies

Date	Pos	Wks	ARTIST / Record Title *Label & Number*

Kathy KIRBY *4 Weeks*

Born Kathleen O'Rourke on October 20, 1940 in Ilford, Essex, England. In 1956 recruited as featured vocalist with Ambrose and his Orchestra. Big break arrived in 1963 when she gained a residency in TV music series, *Stars And Garters*. In 1963-64 had her own television series, *The Kathy Kirby Show*, on BBC. Disc debut: *Love Can Be* (1960). Represented the UK in the 1965 Eurovision Song Contest with *I Belong*, finishing in second position. Made her last public performance in December 1983. Her biography, *Secrets, Loves And Lip Gloss*, by James Harman published in November 2005.

Date	Pos	Wks	ARTIST / Record Title *Label & Number*
02 Dec 63	7	4	1. SECRET LOVE *Decca F 11759*

Mac and Katie KISSOON *6 Weeks*

Brother and sister duo, born in Port-of-Spain, Trinidad. Moved to Britain in 1962. Mac Kissoon, born Gerald Farthing on November 11, 1943. Katie Kissoon, born Katherine Farthing on March 11, 1951. In 1965, were members of The Marionettes and Rag Dolls. Recorded the original version of *Chirpy Chirpy Cheep Cheep*, which was a top twenty hit for the duo in the USA. When the duo broke up, Mac and Katie worked, and continue to, as session singers. Katie with Van Morrison and Eric Clapton, and Mac with the James Last Orchestra.

Date	Pos	Wks	ARTIST / Record Title *Label & Number*
13 Feb 75	2	4	1. SUGAR CANDY KISSES *Polydor 2058 531*
29 May 75	7	2	2. DON'T DO IT BABY *State STAT 4*

Eartha KITT *2 Weeks*

Born Eartha Moe Kitt on January 17, 1927 in Columbia, South Carolina, USA. At eight years of age was given away by her mother and sent to live with an aunt in Harlem, New York. Auditioned successfully for the Katherine Dunham Dance troupe and toured the world as featured dancer and vocalist. Orson Wells called her the most exciting woman in the world.

continues over

Date	Pos	Wks	ARTIST / Record Title *Label & Number*
			Back in New York was spotted by a Broadway producer who put her into the revue, *New Faces of 1952*. It led to a recording contract with RCA. Films include *St Louis Blues* (1958). and *Anna Lucasta* (1958). Biography, *I'm Still Here* published in 1989. Died on December 25, 2008 of colon cancer.
29 Mar 55	-	2	**1. UNDER THE BRIDGES OF PARIS** *HMV IP 967*
			Gladys KNIGHT and the PIPS ***3 Weeks***
			Born on May 28, 1944 in Atlanta, Georgia, USA. Started singing at the age of four. Formed The Pips in 1952. Performed gospel songs at church functions. Personnel: Merald Knight, William Guest, Edward Patten and Langston George. Disc debut: *Whistle My Love* (1957). First billed as Gladys Knight and The Pips in 1962. Signed to Motown in 1966. Moved to Buddah in 1973. Pips disbanded in 1989. Inducted into the Rock and Roll Hall of Fame in 1996.
18 Sep 75	10	1	**1. BEST THING THAT EVER HAPPENED TO ME** *Buddah BDS 432*
04 Aug 77	7	2	**2. BABY DON'T CHANGE YOUR MIND** *Buddah BDS 458*
			Sonny KNOWLES ***26 Weeks***
			Saxophonist/vocalist. Born Thomas Knowles on November 2, 1932 in Dublin, Ireland. Studied clarinet and saxophone at the Dublin School of Music. Played with a number of bands including Johnny Butler, Neil Kearns and Earl Gill before joining the Pacific Showband in 1963. Disc Debut: *Mi Iomlain* (a pop song in the Irish language) in 1961. Left the Pacific in March 1968 and joined Dermot O'Brien's Clubmen. Embarked on a solo career in May 1970. Nickname: *The Singing Window Cleaner* (because of his trademark hand movements on stage). Received the National Entertainment Awards Hall of Fame Award in 1999.

continues over

Date	Pos	Wks	ARTIST / Record Title *Label & Number*
15 Mar 65	5	7	1. NO ONE WILL EVER KNOW *Pye 7N 15780*
02 Aug 65	6	3	2. WE COULD *Pye 7N 15903*
06 Jun 66	3	5	3. NO ONE KNOWS *Pye 7N 17115*
13 Dec 73	2	11	4. MUSIC FROM ACROSS THE WAY *Rex R 11085*

See also Sean Fagan; Sonny and Sean

Billy J. KRAMER with the DAKOTAS 15 Weeks

Born William Howard Ashton on August 19, 1943 in Bootle, Liverpool, England. Originally fronted a local group, the Coasters. Discovered by Beatles manager Brian Epstein, who teamed him up with Manchester group, The Dakotas. Formed in 1960, the Dakotas (Mike Maxfield, lead guitar), Ray Jones (bass), Robin McDonald (rhythm guitar) and Tony Mansfield (drums) signed a separate recording contract with Parlophone. Kramer embarked on a solo career in January 1967. Ray Jones died January 20, 2000.

Date	Pos	Wks	ARTIST / Record Title *Label & Number*
03 Jun 63	8	2	1. DO YOU WANT TO KNOW A SECRET? *Parlophone R(I) 5023*
26 Aug 63	3	5	2. BAD TO ME *Parlophone R(I) 5049*
16 Mar 64	2	8	3. LITTLE CHILDREN *Parlophone R(I) 5105*

Date	Pos	Wks	ARTIST / Record Title *Label & Number*

L

LA BELLE EPOQUE ***4 Weeks***

Female disco vocal trio, formed by Evelyne Lenton in Paris, France in 1977. Personnel: Evelyne Lenton (born on December 16, 1946 in Paris) lead vocal, Marcia Briscue and Judy Fortes. Disbanded in 1981, when Evelyne Lenton decided to return to her solo career.

Date	Pos	Wks	ARTIST / Record Title *Label & Number*
27 Oct 77	3	4	1. BLACK IS BLACK *Harvest HAR 5133*

Cleo LAINE ***5 Weeks***

Born Clementina Dinah Campbell on October 27, 1927 in Southhall, London. England Worked as an apprentice hairdressor and milliner before joining the Johnny Dankworth Seven in 1951. Made her disc debut in 1955 on the L.P. *Cleo Sings British*. In 1958 – the year she and Johnny Dankworth married –she quit the band. Signed as a solo artist with Fontana in 1960.

Date	Pos	Wks	ARTIST / Record Title *Label & Number*
19 Oct 61	3	5	1. YOU'LL ANSWER TO ME *Fontana EH 326*

Frankie LAINE ***16 Weeks***

Born Frank Paul LoVecchio on March 30, 1913 in Chicago, USA. At the age of seventeen, left home to try his luck as a marathon dancer. Frankie and his dancing partner, Ruth Smith, made the all-time marathon dance record in Atlantic City, New Jersey. They danced for a total of 3,501 hours over 145 consecutive days, and were rewarded with a prize of a thousand dollars for their efforts. Made disc debut in 1945 on Exclusive label with *In The Wee Small Hours*. Big break came in 1946 when songwriter Hoagy Carmichael heard him singing in Billy Berg's Jazz Club on Vine Street in Hollywood. A recording contract with Mercury Records followed. Moved to Columbia Records in 1951.

continues over

Date	Pos	Wks	ARTIST / Record Title *Label & Number*

Film appearances include *Sunny Side Of The Street* (1951), *Rainbow Round My Shoulder* (1952) and *Bring Your Smile Along* (1955). Performed the title song over the credits on several classic western films including *3.10 To Yuma* (1957), *Gunfight At O.K. Coral* (1957) and *Blazing Saddles* (1974). His autobiography, *That Lucky Old Son*, was published in 1993. Died of cardio-vascular disease on February 6, 2007, at the age of 93. His last public appearance was on the PBS television special, *Moments To Remember*, in 2005.

Date	Pos	Wks	ARTIST / Record Title *Label & Number*
19 Jul 55	-	5	1. COOL WATER *Philips PB 465*
02 Aug 55	-	2	2. STRANGE LADY IN TOWN *Philips PB 478*
03 Jan 56	-	1	3. HAWKEYE *Philips PB 519*
17 Jan 56	-	2	4. SIXTEEN TONS *Philips EPB 539*
17 Oct 56	-	3	5. A WOMAN IN LOVE *Philips EPB 617*
23 Apr 57	-	3	6. LOVE IS A GOLDEN RING *Philips EPB 676*

Frankie LAINE and Johnnie RAY — *1 Weeks*

Male vocal duo. Frankie Laine born on March 30, 1913 in Chicago, USA. Johnnie Ray born on January 10, 1927 in Hopewell, Oregon, USA. The idea of teaming up the two talents on record was the brainchild of Mitch Miller.

Date	Pos	Wks	ARTIST / Record Title *Label & Number*
23 Oct 57	-	1	1. UP ABOVE MY HEAD, I HEAR MUSIC IN THE AIR *Philips EPB 708*

The LANA SISTERS — *2 Weeks*

Female vocal trio formed in London, England in 1958. Personnel: Riss Chantelle, Lynne Abrams and Dusty Springfield. Disc debut: *Chimes Of Arcady* (1959). Dusty left in 1960 to join her brother Tom in the Springfields. Dusty Springfield died on March 2, 1999.

Date	Pos	Wks	ARTIST / Record Title *Label & Number*
07 Apr 60	5	2	1. YOU GOT WHAT IT TAKES *Fontana EH 235*

See also The Springfields; Dusty Springfield

Michael LANDERS – See Dermot Henry

Date	Pos	Wks	ARTIST / Record Title *Label & Number*
			Mario LANZA ***7 Weeks***
			Born Alfredo Cocozza on January 31, 1921 in Philadelphia, USA. He studied vocal training with Leonard Bernstein and later enrolled with Enrico Rosati, voice coach to Beniamino Gigli. Arrived at his stage name by using a variation of his mother's maiden name, Maria Lanza. Made screen debut in the 1949 film *That Midnight Kiss*. Other film appearances include *The Great Caruso* (1951), *Serenade* (1956) and *Seven Hills Of Rome* (1958). Died of a heart attack on October 7, 1959 while undergoing treatment at a Rome clinic.
21 Jun 55	-	7	1. I'll WALK WITH GOD *HMV IR 391*
			LARRY and MARGO ***3 Weeks***
			Irish male/female vocal duo. Personnel: Larry Cunningham born on February 13, 1935 in Granard, Co. Longford and Margo born Margaret O'Donnell on February 6, 1951 in Donegal Town. Formed in December 1975, when Margo teamed up with Larry Cunningham and his band the Country Blue Boys. Duo split in July 1976, with Larry and Margo pursuing their seperate solo careers.
05 Feb 76	6	3	1. YES MR. PETERS *Release RL 798*
			See also Larry Cunningham; Margo
			LAUREL and HARDY ***1 Weeks***
			Comedy Duo. Stan Laurel, born Arthur Stanley Jefferson on June 16, 1890 in Ulverston, Cumbria, England. Oliver Hardy, born Oliver Norville Hardy on January 18, 1892 in Harlem, Georgia, USA. Although their first cinematic meeting happened in a 1917 comedy short, *The Lucky Dog*, they didn't officially team up until 1927. Visited Ireland in 1952 and 1953. Performed for two weeks, commencing May 27, 1952, at the Olympia Theatre, Dublin. Also performed at the Grand Opera House Belfast the same year.

continues over

Date	Pos	Wks	ARTIST / Record Title *Label & Number*
			In 1953, Laurel and Hardy arrived in Ireland on the SS America and when the ship docked at the port of Cobh, Co. Cork, the bells of St. Colmans Cathedral began playing the duo's theme tune, *Dance of the Cuckoos.* On October 11, 1953 made a one night charity performance at Dublin's Olympia Theatre. Hardy died on August 7, 1957. Laurel died on February 23, 1965. *Trail Of The Lonesome Pine* was performed in the 1937 film, *Way Out West,* with musical help from The Avalon Boys featuring Chill Wills.
25 Dec 75	10	1	1. THE TRAIL OF THE LONESOME PINE *UA UP 36026*
			Steve LAWRENCE ***10 Weeks***
			Born Sidney Leibowitz on July 8, 1935 in Brooklyn, New York, USA. In 1951 was a winner on TV's Arthur Godfrey Talent Scouts show. In July 1953 was hired to sing on the TV talk show, *Tonight*, hosted by Steve Allen. First recorded for King in 1953. Married Eydie Gorme on December 29, 1957.
19 May 60	3	10	1. FOOTSTEPS *HMV POP(I) 726*
			See also Eydie Gorme; Steve and Eydie
			Vicky LEANDROS ***11 Weeks***
			Born Vasiliki Papathanasiou on August 23, 1952 in Corfu, Greece. In 1958 relocated with her family to Germany. Represented Luxembourg at the 1967 Eurovision Song Contest. Won 1972 Eurovision Song contest for Luxembourg with *Apres Toi.* Recorded the song in seven languages including English under the title, *Come What May.*
20 Apr 72	3	1	1. APRES TOI *Philips 6000 045*
27 Apr 72	2	8	2. COME WHAT MAY *Philips 6000 049*
08 Feb 73	6	2	3. THE LOVE IN YOUR EYES *Philips 6000 081*

Brenda LEE — *39 Weeks*

Born Brenda Mae Tarpley on December 11, 1944 in Atlanta, Georgia, USA. Professional singer since age of six. Renamed Brenda Lee by producer Sammy Barton while appearing on the Peach Blossom Special on WJAT-TV in Augusta in 1956. Signed to Decca Records on May 21, 1956. On her first recording session on July 30, 1956, she recorded seven songs. Disc debut: "Jambalaya" (September 1956) as Little Brenda Lee. Became known as *Little Miss Dynamite*. Made film debut in *The Two Little Bears* (1962). Also appeared in *Smokey And The Bandit II* (1980). Married Ronnie Shacklett on April 24, 1963. Has recorded in several languages including German, Italian, French and Japanese. Inducted into the Country Music Hall of Fame in 1997. Inducted into the Rockabilly Hall of Fame in 1999. Inducted into the Rock and Roll Hall of Fame in 2002. On October 3, 1987, in Lithonia, Georgia a street, Brenda Lee Lane, was named in her honour. *Speak To Me Pretty* was featured in the film *The Two Little Bears. Rockin' Around The Christmas Tree* was recorded on October 19, 1958 and on its release that year failed to make the chart. It is now Brenda Lee's second biggest selling record.

Date	Pos	Wks	ARTIST / Record Title *Label & Number*
28 Apr 60	2	11	1. SWEET NUTHIN'S *Brunswick 05819*
03 May 62	8	7	2. SPEAK TO ME PRETTY *Brunswick 05867*
17 Dec 62	4	4	3. ROCKIN AROUND THE CHRISTMAS TREE *Brunswick 05880*
11 Feb 63	5	8	4. ALL ALONE AM I *Brunswick 05882*
26 Aug 63	10	2	5. I WONDER *Brunswick 05891*
27 Jan 64	4	7	6. AS USUAL *Brunswick 05899*

Des LEE and the MIAMI — *2 Weeks*

Born Des McAlea on July 29, 1947 in Belfast, N. Ireland. Started playing music at age fourteen. Member of the following bands the Banshees, the Regal, and the Arrivals. Joined the Miami in September 1967. Changed his name to Des Lee. Disc debut: *Goody Goody Gumdrops* (1969).

continues over

Date	Pos	Wks	ARTIST / Record Title *Label & Number*
			Personnel: Des Lee (vocals, keyboards, tenor sax), Noel Ryan (organ), Norman Clifford (tenor sax, rhythm guitar), Ray Millar (drums), Steve Travers (bass) and Dessie O'Flaherty (guitar, vocals). Left the Miami in early 1978 to form Starband. In 1982 formed the Des Lee Band and shortly after emigrated to South Africa.
21 Oct 76	9	2	1. HOLD ON TO LOVE *Mint CHEW 14*

Peggy LEE — *1 Weeks*

Born Norma Jean Egstrom on May 26, 1920 in Jamestown, North Dakota, USA. Joined the Jack Wardlow band as vocalist in 1936. Member of Benny Goodman Orchestra 1941-43. Went solo in March 1943. Film appearances include *Mister Music* (1950), *The Jazz Singer* (1953) and *Pete Kelly's Blues* (1955). Nominated for an Academy Award for her performance in *Pete Kelly's Blues*. Co-wrote many songs including *Bella Notte*, *Manana*, *Johnny Guitar* and *It's A Good Day*. Won a Grammy award in 1969 for her recording of *Is That All There Is*. Made her Broadway debut, at the age of 62, in the auto-biographical musical *Peg*, in 1983. Inducted into the Big Band and Jazz Hall of Fame in 1992. Inducted into the Songwriters Hall of fame in 1999. Died on January 21, 2002.

Date	Pos	Wks	ARTIST / Record Title *Label & Number*
02 Jul 57	-	1	1. MR. WONDERFUL *Brunswick 05671*

John LENNON — *20 Weeks*

Born John Winston Lennon on October 9, 1940 in Woolton, Liverpool, England. Founding member of The Beatles. Married Cynthia Powell in 1962. Divorced in 1968. Met Yoko Ono in 1966 and married her in 1969. Involved in several solo projects while still a member of The Beatles including an appearance in the 1967 film *How I Won The War*, and his debut solo album, *Two Virgins* in 1968. Formed the Plastic Ono Band in 1969. Moved to New York City in 1971.

continues over

Date	Pos	Wks	ARTIST / Record Title *Label & Number*

Was shot dead outside his New York apartment by Mark Chapman on December 8, 1980.

Date	Pos	Wks	ARTIST / Record Title *Label & Number*
31 Jul 69	7	3	1. GIVE PEACE A CHANCE *Apple APPLE 13*
12 Mar 70	3	2	2. INSTANT KARMA *Apple APPLE 1003*
22 Apr 71	7	2	3. POWER TO THE PEOPLE *Apple R(I) 5892*
14 Dec 72	1(1)	5	• 4. HAPPY XMAS (War Is Over) *Parlophone R(I) 5970*
04 Dec 75	1(1)	8	• 5. IMAGINE *Apple DIP 521*

Give Peace A Chance credit: Plastic Ono Band. Instant Karma credit: Lennon, Ono and the Plastic Ono Band. Power To The People credit: John Lennon/Plastic Ono Band. Happy Xmas (War Is Over) credit: John and Yoko and the Plastic Ono Band with the Harlem Community Choir.

See also The Beatles

Ketty LESTER *6 Weeks*

Born Revoyda Frierson on August 16, 1934 in Hope, Arkansas, USA. Sang in both church and school choirs. Toured with the Cab Calloway Orchestra. Signed to RCA in 1964. Film appearances include *Just For Fun* (1963) and *Uptight* (1968). Lincoln Mayorga (Piltdown Men) responsible for the arrangement of and distinctive piano sound on *Love Letters*.

Date	Pos	Wks	ARTIST / Record Title *Label & Number*
17 May 62	4	6	1. LOVE LETTERS *London HLN 9257*

Jerry Lee LEWIS *6 Weeks*

Born on September 29, 1935 in Ferriday, Louisiana, USA. Nickname: *The Killer.* First recorded for Sun Records in 1956. Appeared in film *Disc Jockey Jamboree* in 1957. His early rock 'n' roll career documented in the 1989 film *Great Balls Of Fire*. His debut UK tour in 1958, was cut short when it was revealed in the media that he had married, his then thirteen-year-old cousin, while not divorced from his second wife. Lived in Ireland for a period of time during the 90's. Inducted into the Rock and Roll Hall of Fame in 1986.

Date	Pos	Wks	ARTIST / Record Title *Label & Number*
12 Feb 59	9	2	1. HIGH SCHOOL CONFIDENTIAL *London HLS 8780*
01 Jun 61	5	4	2. WHAT'D I SAY *London HLS 9335*

Date	Pos	Wks	ARTIST / Record Title *Label & Number*

Linda LEWIS **2 Weeks**

Born on September 27, 1950 in West Ham, London, England. During the late 1960's and early 1970's was a much in demand session singer. Spotted by producer Ian Samwell when she got up to sing at a John Lee Hooker gig in Southend. Disc debut: *You Turned My Bitter Into Sweet*. In 1970, replaced Marsha Hunt in the group, Ferris Wheel. Signed to Warner Reprise in 1971. Moved to Arista in 1975. Retired from the music business in 1985 and moved to the USA. Returned to UK in 1995.

14 Aug 75	9	2	1. IT'S IN HIS KISS *Arista 17*

John LEYTON **7 Weeks**

Actor/singer. Born John Dudley Leyton on February 17, 1939 in Frinton-on-Sea, Essex, England. Studied drama at the Actors Workshop. Starred in TV series 'Biggles' in 1960. Portrayed pop star, Johnny St. Cyr, in the TV soap *Harper's W.1.*. Performed *Johnny Remember Me* on the show, fans loved the song and the singer, and turned John Leyton into a teenage idol. Film appearances include *The Great Escape* (1963) *Von Ryans Express* (1965) and *Krakato East Of Java* (1969).

14 Sep 61	1(3)	6	• 1. JOHNNY REMEMBER ME *Top Rank JAR 577*
26 Oct 61	6	1	2. WILD WIND *Top Rank JAR 585*

LIEUTENANT PIGEON **7 Weeks**

Formed in Coventry, England in 1972. Personnel: Hilda Woodward (piano), Nigel Fletcher (drums), Rob Woodward (keyboards, whistles) and Steve Johnson (bass). Disc debut: *Mouldy Old Dough* (1972). Final gig: September 26, 1978. Hilda Woodward died in 1999. Rob and Nigel's joint autobiography, *When Show Business Is No Business*, was published in 2001.

19 Oct 72	1(1)	7	• 1. MOULDY OLD DOUGH • *Decca F 13278*

Date	Pos	Wks	ARTIST / Record Title *Label & Number*

The LIGHT BLUES — *4 Weeks*

Group of Irish session singers and musicians assembled by Hawk Records. Vocals John Keogh and Dave Pennyfeather. Song composed as a tribute to the Dublin Senior Gaelic football team and their manager, Kevin Heffernan.

05 Sep 74	9	4	1. HEFFO'S HEROS *Hawk HASP 351*

LINDISFARNE — *4 Weeks*

Formed in Newcastle –upon-Tyne, England in 1970 as Brethren. Signed to Charisma Records in 1970 where producer, John Anthony suggested a name change to Lindisfarne. Personnel: Ray Jackson (vocals, guitar, mandolin), Alan Hull (vocals, guitar, piano), Ray Laidlaw (drums), Rod Clements (bass, violin) and Simon Cowe (vocals, guitar, mandolin). Disc debut: *Clear White Light Part 2* (1970). In early 1973, Cowe, Clements and Laidlaw, split to form Jack The Lad, while Hull and Jackson continued as Lindisfarne eventually splitting in February 1975. The original Lindisfarne lineup got back together in late 1976 for two nights at Newcastle City Hall, before going their separate ways. A repeat performance but this time for five nights at Christmas 1977 led to the group deciding to reunite. Alan Hull died from a heart attack on November 17, 1995.

13 Jul 78	4	4	1. RUN FOR HOME *Mercury 6007 177*

LITTLE EVA — *6 Weeks*

Born Eva Narcissus Boyd on June 29, 1943 in Belhaven, North Carolina, USA. Discovered by songwriters Carole King and Gerry Goffin while babysitting their daughter Louise. She quit the music business in 1971. Died of cancer on April 10, 2003. Is featured uncredited on the Big Dee Irwin hit, *Swing On A Star.*

15 Oct 62	5	5	1. THE LOCO-MOTION *London HL 9581*
14 Sep 72	10	1	2. THE LOCO-MOTION *(re-issue) London HL 9581*

See also Big Dee Irwin

Date	Pos	Wks	ARTIST / Record Title *Label & Number*
			LITTLE RICHARD ***8 Weeks***
			Born Richard Wayne Penniman on December 5, 1932 in Macon, Georgia, USA. Talent contest win in 1951 led to recording contract with RCA. In 1955, he sent a demo tape to Specialty Records in Los Angeles who signed him to the label. Film appearances include *Don't Knock The Rock* (1956), *The Girl Can't Help It* (1956), *Mister Rock 'n' Roll* (1957) and *Down And Out In Beverly Hills* (1986). Following an Australian tour in 1957, he announced he was quitting the world of rock 'n' roll for religion. Returned to rock 'n' roll in 1962. Inducted into the Rock and Roll Hall of Fame in 1986.
07 Jan 58	-	1	1. KEEP A KNOCKIN' *London HL 8509*
12 Feb 59	3	6	2. BABY FACE *London HLU 8770*
16 Apr 59	9	1	3. BY THE LIGHT OF THE SILVERY MOON *London HLU 8831*
			LOBO ***5 Weeks***
			Born Roland Kent Lavoie on July 31, 1943 in Talahassee, Florida, USA. Started his musical career playing with a number of local groups including the Rumours. A member of The Legends with Gram Parsons.
22 Jun 71	6	4	1. ME AND YOU AND A DOG NAMED BOO *Philips 6073 801*
11 Jul 74	7	1	2. I'D LOVE YOU TO WANT ME *UK 68*
			Hank LOCKLIN ***17 Weeks***
			Born Lawrence Hankins Locklin on February 15, 1918 in McLellan, Florida, USA. In 1945 joined Jimmy Swan's band as lead guitarist, then moved to the Four Leaf Clover Boys. Signed to Four Star Records in 1949. Hank went to RCA Victor in 1955, staying with the label until 1973. Died on March 8, 2009.
15 Sep 60	1(2)	8	• 1. PLEASE HELP ME I'M FALLING *RCA ERC 1188*
08 Mar 62	5	5	2. FROM HERE TO THERE TO YOU *RCA ERC 1273*
24 Dec 62	8	4	3. WE'RE GONNA GO FISHIN' *RCA ERC 1305*

Date	Pos	Wks	ARTIST / Record Title *Label & Number*

Laurie LONDON — *1 Weeks*

Born Lawrence London on January 19, 1944 in London, England. Keen interest in music from a young age. Loved to sing and regularly performed for the benefit of visitors to the family home. Discovered in August 1957 at the annual Radio Show at London's Earls Court, when he got up on stage to sing. Came to the attention of song plugger, Harry Walters, who arranged an audition with EMI at the Abbey Road Studios. Producer Norman Newell was impressed and offered Laurie a recording contract with Parlophone. *He's Got The Whole World In His Hands*, Laurie's debut outing on disc, spent four weeks at number one in the USA. In the 1980's ran a hotel in West Sussex.

Date	Pos	Wks	ARTIST / Record Title *Label & Number*
07 Jan 58	-	1	1. HE'S GOT THE WHOLE WORLD IN HIS HANDS *Parlophone R(I) 4359*

Trini LOPEZ — *6 Weeks*

Born Trinidad Lopez III on May 15, 1937 in Dallas, Texas, USA. Disc debut: *The Right To Rock* (1955). Discovered by Don Costa while performing at PJ's nightclub in Los Angeles, who then brought Trini to the attention of Frank Sinatra, who immediately signed him to his own record label, Reprise Records. Film appearances include *Marriage On The Rocks* (1965), *The Dirty Dozen* (1967) and *Antonio* (1973).

Date	Pos	Wks	ARTIST / Record Title *Label & Number*
30 Sep 63	4	6	1. IF I HAD A HAMMER *Reprise R 20198*

LOS BRAVOS — *4 Weeks*

Formed in 1965 in Madrid, Spain from elements of two groups Los Sonor and The Runaways. Personnel: Mike Kogel (born 25, April 1945 in Berlin, Germany, lead vocals), Manolo Fernandez (keyboards), Pablo Samllehi (drums), Antonio Martinez (guitar) and Miguel Vicens Danus (bass).

Date	Pos	Wks	ARTIST / Record Title *Label & Number*
25 Jul 66	3	4	1. BLACK IS BLACK *Decca F 22419*

Date	Pos	Wks	ARTIST / Record Title *Label & Number*
			LOS INDIOS TABAJARAS ***9 Weeks***
			Brothers, Antenor Moreira Lima and Natalicio Moreira Lima. Born in Ceara, Brazil. Self taught musicians (guitar). Made first public appearance in 1945. *Maria Elena* is a Mexican tune from 1933.
25 Nov 63	5	9	1. MARIA ELENA • *RCA ERC 1365*
			LOUDEST WHISPER ***1 Weeks***
			Formed in Fermoy, Co. Cork, Ireland in 1964 as the Wizards by songwriter/guitarist Brian O'Reilly. Changed name to Loudest Whisper in late 1969. Personnel: Brian O'Reilly (vocals, guitar), John Aherne (bass), Paid O'Reilly (drums), Geraldine Dorgan (vocals). Disc debut: *Willam B* (1974). Brian O'Reilly composed a stage musical, *Children Of Lir*, based around the legend of Irish King, Lir. *The Children Of Lir* premiered on Jan 7, 1973 in Fermoy. Also staged at Cork Opera House. It was later released in album form by Polydor Records in Ireland and over the years has become one of the most collectable albums fetching prices of around 1000 Euros.
04 Nov 76	9	1	1. YOU AND I *Polydor 2078 071*
			The LOVE AFFAIR ***13 Weeks***
			Formed in London, England in 1966 as the Soul Survivors. Band management decided on a name change to Love Affair. Personnel: Steve Ellis (vocals), Lynton Guest (keyboards), Maurice Bacon (drums), Rex Brayley (lead guitar), Mike Jackson (bass). Disc debut: *She Smiled Sweetly* (1967). Lynton Guest left group in 1968 and Morgan Fisher was brought in as a replacement. Steve Ellis (born April 7, 1950 in London) was the only group member to feature on their hit singles. Ellis left in December 1969 to pursue a solo career.
25 Jan 68	2	7	1. EVERLASTING LOVE *CBS 3125*
13 Jun 68	6	4	2. RAINBOW VALLEY *CBS 3366*
31 Oct 68	9	2	3. A DAY WITHOUT LOVE *CBS 3674*

Date	Pos	Wks	ARTIST / Record Title *Label & Number*

Lene LOVICH *2 Weeks*

Born Lili-Marlene Premilovich on March 30, 1949 in Detroit, USA. Relocated to Hull, England at the age of thirteen. Started writing songs for several artists including Cerrone. Disc debut: *I Saw Mummy Kissing Santa Claus* (1976). Signed to Stiff Records in 1978. Retired from music business in 1982. Returned in 1990.

Date	Pos	Wks	ARTIST / Record Title *Label & Number*
29 Mar 79	7	2	1. LUCKY NUMBER *Stiff BUY 42*

The LOVIN' SPOONFUL *2 Weeks*

Formed in New York City, USA in early 1965. Personnel: John Sebastian (born March 17, 1944 in New York, lead vocals, songwriter, guitar), Zal Yanovsky (lead guitar), Steve Boone (bass) and Joe Butler (drums). Disc debut: 'Do You Believe In Magic' (1965). Zal Yanovsky left in mid 1967, replaced by Jerry Yester. In June 1968, John Sebastian left to pursue a solo career. Steve, Joe and Jerry went their separate ways in 1969. The trio got back together in 1991. Inducted into the Rock and Roll Hall of Fame in 2000. Zal Yanovsky died on December 13, 2002. John Sebastian inducted into the Songwriters Hall of Fame in 2008.

Date	Pos	Wks	ARTIST / Record Title *Label & Number*
16 May 66	7	2	1. DAYDREAM *Pye 7N 25361*

The LUDLOWS *15 Weeks*

Ballad/folk group formed in Dublin, Ireland in 1964 as the Ludlow Trio. Personnel: Margaret O'Brien (vocals), Sean Loughran (vocals, guitar) and Paddy Roche (vocals, guitar, banjo). Disc debut: *Kisses Sweeter Than Wine* (1965). Roche left in 1966, and was replaced by Jim McCann (guitar, vocals). Loughran left group in latter part of 1966 replaced by Gerry Cairns. Disbanded in September 1967. Reformed in July 1969 for a short period. Dominic Behan wrote their number one hit, *The Sea Around Us*.

Date	Pos	Wks	ARTIST / Record Title *Label & Number*
07 Mar 66	1(4)	10	• 1. THE SEA AROUND US *Pye 7N 17050*
27 Jun 66	8	3	2. THE WIND THRO' THE RAFTERS *Pye 7N 17123*
22 Jun 67	9	2	3. ENNISKILLEN DRAGOONS *Pye 7N 17319*

Date	Pos	Wks	ARTIST / Record Title *Label & Number*

LULU — 8 Weeks

Born Marie McDonald McLaughlin Lawrie on November 3, 1948 in Glasgow, Scotland. Joined local group The Gleneagles in 1963. Re-named Lulu and The Luvvers by their manager Marion Massey. Disc debut: *Shout* (1964). Appeared in 1967 film, *To Sir With Love*. Married Bee Gee Maurice Gibb in February 1969. They separated in 1973. Won the Eurovision Song Contest for Britain in 1969 with *Boom Bang-A-Bang*. In 1983, starred in the stage musical, *Song And Dance*. Her autobiography, *Lulu-Her Autobiography*, was published in 1986.

Date	Pos	Wks	ARTIST / Record Title *Label & Number*
16 Jan 69	8	1	1. I'M A TIGER *Columbia DB(I) 8500*
17 Apr 69	1(2)	6	• 2. BOOM BANG A BANG *Columbia DB(I) 8550*
21 Feb 74	8	1	3. THE MAN WHO SOLD THE WORLD *Polydor 2001 490*

Bob LUMAN — ***14 Weeks***

Born Robert Glynn Luman on April 15, 1937 in Blackjack, East Texas, USA. Joined the Louisiana Hayride in Shreveport in 1956. Disc debut: *All Night Long* (1957). Member of the Grand Ole Opry in 1965. Died of pneumonia on December 27, 1978.

Date	Pos	Wks	ARTIST / Record Title *Label & Number*
15 Sep 60	7	14	1. LET'S THINK ABOUT LIVING *Warner Bros. EWB 18*

Ray LYNAM and the HILLBILLIES — ***14 Weeks***

Born on November 29, 1950 in Moate, Co. Westmeath, Ireland. It was while a member of local group The Merrymen that fellow group member Kevin Sheerin persuaded him to front a new country band, The Hillbillies. Discovered by Mick Clerkin and Sean Reilly of Release Records. Signed to Release in November 1969. Disc debut: *Busted* (1970). Hillbillies formed in 1968. Personnel: Ray Lynam (vocals, guitar), Kevin Sheerin (lead guitar, steel guitar), Billy Condon (fiddle), Billy Burgoyne (drums), Mick Lube (rhythm guitar), John Ryan (piano) and John Lynam (bass). John Lynam died on August 21, 2007.

continues over

Date	Pos	Wks	ARTIST / Record Title *Label & Number*
27 Jun 72	6	5	1. BRAND NEW MR ME *Release RL 637*
11 Oct 73	8	1	2. BORROWED ANGEL *Release RL 688*
07 Feb 74	2	6	3. SECOND HAND FLOWERS *Release RL 711*
27 Feb 75	9	1	4. THE DOOR IS ALWAYS OPEN *Release RL 759*
12 Aug 76	10	1	5. YOU'RE THE ONE I SING MY LOVE SONGS TO *Release RL 818*

Ray LYNAM and Philomena BEGLEY 18 Weeks

Irish male/female vocal duo. Ray Lynam born on November 29, 1950 in Moate, Co. Westmeath. Philomena Begley born on October 20, 1939 in Pomeroy, Co. Tyrone. In early 1973, Michael Clerkin, managing director of Release Records, suggested Ray and Philomena team up for recording purposes. In 1974 Ray and Philomena Begley won the CMA Award for Best New Country Act in Europe. In 1975, voted Top Duet Act by the British Country Music Association. Shane McGowan paid tribute to the duo in his 1985 song, *A Pair Of Brown Eyes*, which includes the line, "while Ray and Philomena sang of my elusive dreams".

Date	Pos	Wks	ARTIST / Record Title *Label & Number*
24 May 73	5	12	1. YOU'RE THE ONE I CAN'T LIVE WITHOUT *Release RL 678*
01 Aug 74	3	6	2. MY ELUSIVE DREAMS *Release RL 733*

Pat LYNCH and the AIRCHORDS 35 Weeks

Born on December 2, 1934 in Bantry, County Cork, Ireland. Educated at the North Monastery, Cork. After leaving school took up an apprenticeship and qualified as a welder. Started singing part time with local band The Golden Eagles. On the invitation of band manager, George O'Reilly, joined the Clipper Carlton in 1964 as lead vocalist. Joined the Airchords as lead vocalist in April 1965. Debut single: *Are You Sincere* (October 1965). On March 3, 1968 performed *Kinsale* in the National Song Contest Final, finishing second (by one point) to Pat McGeegan and *Chance Of A Lifetime*. Represented Ireland at the 1968 Malta International Song Festival. On October 9, 1968 won the 'Straight

Date	Pos	Wks	ARTIST / Record Title *Label & Number*
			Songs Section' at the Castlebar International Song Contest, performing the Sean Sharkey/Eddie Masterson composition, *Reflections Of You*. Represented Ireland at the 1969 International Festival of Pop Song in Sopot, Poland. In March 1972, decides to drop the name Airchords and changes band name to The Tree Tops. In September 1973 left the band to pursue a solo career. Won the 'Pop Section' of the Castlebar International Song Contest on October 5, 1973, with the George Crosby/Jack Brierly song, *Time For Love*. Member of Sandie Jones and the Boyfriends, January 1974 to March 1975. Retired from the music business in 1977. The Airchords formed in 1960, by members of the Irish Air Corps. Turned professional in 1964. Disbanded in March 1972.
12 Dec 66	6	3	1. THE LEAVING OF LIVERPOOL *Pye 7N 17227*
13 Apr 67	3	11	2. THE IRISH SOLDIER *Pye 7N 17304*
30 Nov 67	1(4)	8	• 3. TREAT ME DAUGHTER KINDLY *Pye 7N 17421*
08 Apr 71	1(5)	13	• 4. WHEN WE WERE YOUNG *Ruby RUB 121*

Vera LYNN — *11 Weeks*

Born Vera Welch on March 20, 1917 in London, England. Began to sing in public from the age of seven. In 1931 she joined the Howard Baker Band as vocalist. She also performed with Billy Cotton, Charlie Kunz, Joe Loss and Ambrose. Disc debut: *The General's Fast Asleep* (1935). In 1941, was given a series of radio programmes, *Sincerely Yours*, by the BBC. It was at this point in her career she got the nickname, *The Forces Sweetheart*. Film appearances include *We'll Meet Again* (1942), *Rhythm Serenade* (1943) and *One Exciting Night* (1944). Married Harry Lewis in 1941, he later became her manager. Harry died in 1998. Topped the UK Album charts in 2009 at the age of 92.

Date	Pos	Wks	ARTIST / Record Title *Label & Number*
01 Mar 55	-	1	1. ADDIO AMORE *Decca F 10463*
05 Jul 55	-	7	2. DOONAREE *Decca F 10535*
21 Aug 56	-	2	3. WALK HAND IN HAND *Decca F 10737*
16 Jul 57	-	1	4. TRAVELLIN' HOME *Decca F 10903*

Date	Pos	Wks	ARTIST / Record Title *Label & Number*

M

M ***5 Weeks***

British singer/muli-instrumentalist born Robin Scott on April 1, 1947 in Croyden, London, England. Disc debut: *The Sailor* in 1969, as Robin Scott. Performed solo at folk clubs accompanying himself on guitar. Formed his own record company, Do It Records, in early 70's, and also recorded under the alias Comic Romance. In 1978, worked as producer for Barclay Records. *Pop Muzik* also features Julian Scott (bass), Wally Badarou (keyboards), John Lewis and Brigitte Vinchon (backing vocals).

10 May 79	2	5	1. **POP MUZIK** MCA *MCA 413*

CANON Sydney MacEWAN ***11 Weeks***

Born on October 19, 1908 in Glasgow, Scotland. Early interest in singing. While attending Glasgow University made a number of broadcasts on BBC Scotland. Following his graduation from University he enrolled at London's Royal Academy of Music. Spotted by Compton McKenzie who introduced him to John McCormack and Oscar Preus of Parlophone Records. Began recording for Parlophone in 1934. Decided to enter the priesthood and went to the Scots College in Rome. Ordained to priesthood on June 29, 1944. His superiors allowed him to continue his musical career alongside his priestly duties. Toured Britain, Ireland, Canada and North America up until 1956. Elevated to the rank of Canon in 1956. Was featured in BBC TV's *This Is Your Life* in 1963. His autobiography, *On The High C's (a light hearted journey),* was published in 1973. *Suffer Little Children*,a track from the album of Philip Green's Mass of Saint Francis, was featured at the opening of the 1972 Cork Film Festival, and issued as a single.

continues over

Date	Pos	Wks	ARTIST / Record Title *Label & Number*

Died on September 25, 1991. The Cork Children's Choir was an amalgamation of nine local Cork Choirs.

Date	Pos	Wks	ARTIST / Record Title *Label & Number*
09 Aug 73	3	11	1. SUFFER LITTLE CHILDREN *Columbia IDB 821*

Credit "Suffer Little Children" to Canon Sydney MacEwan and The Cork Children's Choir.

Eddie MACK & COLUMBIA SHOWBAND — *4 Weeks*

Born Eddie McElheron in Arklow, County Wicklow, Ireland. Disc debut: *Before This Day Ends* (1965). The Columbia Showband started out life in Arklow in 1959, as the Red Seven Showband. Changed name to the Columbia Showband in 1963. Personnel: Eddie Mack (lead vocals), Jim Tyrell (leader, piano), Pat Tyrell (tenor sax), Michael Tyrell (bass), Freddie Cutland (lead guitar), Pat McCarthy (trombone) and George Byrne (drums). Changed name to Columbia Boys in 1968. Disbanded 1969. Jim, Michael and George moving to the newly formed Ranchers Showband. Pat, Eddie and Freddie formed a local group, Family. Jim Tyrell died on May 14, 2007.

Date	Pos	Wks	ARTIST / Record Title *Label & Number*
03 Jan 66	6	4	1. WAY OUT OF REACH *Rex R 11018*

John MacNALLY — *1 Weeks*

Born in Dublin, Ireland. First success for singing was as a boy soprano at Feis Maitiu. Won silver bowl for Lieder singing at the 1961 Feis Ceoil. Educated at University College Dublin, Trinity College and the College of Technology. In 1961, qualified in Ophthalmic Optics and Dispensing Optics. In 1969, sold his opticians business to enter showbusiness as a full time occupation. Signed with CBS Records in 1969. Hosted his own show on RTE television in 1969. Now resides in Australia where he has hosted several radio and television shows including, *In Melbourne Tonight.* His autobiography, *Ireland's Own John MacNally: A Life In Song*, published in 1993.

Date	Pos	Wks	ARTIST / Record Title *Label & Number*
21 Aug 69	9	1	1. MARY IN THE MORNING *CBS 4356*

Date	Pos	Wks	ARTIST / Record Title *Label & Number*

MAGIC — *12 Weeks*

Born Kevin Walsh on August 30, 1953 in Clogherhead, Co. Louth, Ireland. In 1969, joined his first band, Bandy Blondy, who played relief at the Ashling Ballroom, Clogherhead. In 1974, joined Murphy and the Swallows as second vocalist. When Murphy left in August 1974, Kevin was given a new identity, *Magic*, and launched (complete with lit up suit) at the Old Sheiling Hotel, Dublin in September 1974. Disc debut: *Calendar Girl* (1974). In November 1974, The Swallows became the Magic Band. In April 1979, Magic decided to quit the music business. Magic #2 (Cornelius Ward) was drafted in and continued in this role until the band disbanded in 1982.

Date	Pos	Wks	ARTIST / Record Title *Label & Number*
03 Oct 74	4	5	1. CALENDAR GIRL *Play PLAY 78*
30 Jan 75	5	5	2. HAPPY BIRTHDAY SWEET SIXTEEN *Play PLAY 83*
28 Jul 77	9	1	3. REACHING OUT *Play PLAY 104*
05 Jan 78	6	1	4. LEND A HAND THIS CHRISTMAS *Play PLAY 108*

Terry MAHON & Jim FARLEY SHOWBAND — *5 Weeks*

Born on August 21, 1945 in Dublin, Ireland. Joined the Neptunes showband in 1963. Came to attention of band manager, Nelius O'Connell, who introduced her to bandleader, Jim Farley. Joined the Jim Farley Showband in March 1964. Disc debut: *If I Cried* (1966). Left Farley in December 1966 to form her own cabaret group, The Sensations. Rejoined Jim Farley in November 1967. Lead vocalist with the Nashville Ramblers 1970-72. Retired from the music business in September 1972. Jim Farley Showband personnel (1966): Jim Farley (leader, tenor sax), Terry Mahon (vocals), Roly Daniels (vocals), Danny Pearse (vocals, lead guitar), Joe McIntyre (trumpet), Michael Keane (organ), Kevin Gregan (bass) and Johnny Fennessy (drums).

Date	Pos	Wks	ARTIST / Record Title *Label & Number*
31 Jan 66	7	5	1. IF I CRIED *Columbia IDB 748*

Date	Pos	Wks	ARTIST / Record Title *Label & Number*

MAKEM and CLANCY — *18 Weeks*

Irish vocal duo formed in late 1975 by Tommy Makem (born on November 4, 1932 in Keady, Co. Armagh) and Liam Clancy (born on September 2, 1935 in Carrick-on-Suir, Co. Tipperary). First worked together in 1958 and were part of the highly successful folk/ballad group, The Clancy Brothers and Tommy Makem. Tommy left the group in 1969 to pursue a solo career. Liam left in 1972, initally to retire but the draw of the world of music was too great. He relocated to Canada. Makem came from a musical background. Played in a ceili band at 17. Emigrated in the 50's to USA where he worked briefly in a steel mill. Moved to New York where he met up with the Clancy Brothers. Has composed many songs including *Four Green Fields*. Clancy started out as an insurance clerk with ambitions to be an actor. Moved to New York. First met Makem in the 1950's in Tommy's home in Keady, when Liam arrived to collect songs from Tommy's mother, Sarah. Got together as a duo as a result of Liam inviting Tommy to appear on his television show. Their joint performance won the award for the Best Canadian Variety Show and it seemed the most natural thing in the world to re-unite. Disc debut as a duo: *Tommy Makem and Liam Clancy* L.P. (1976). The partnership split in March 1988. Tommy Makem died of lung cancer on August 1, 2007.

Date	Pos	Wks	ARTIST / Record Title *Label & Number*
13 Jan 77	1(3)	11	• 1. AND THE BAND PLAYED WALTZING MATILDA *Blackbird BB 101*
08 Mar 79	3	5	2. RED IS THE ROSE *Blackbird BB 106*
26 Jul 79	7	2	3. MORNING GLORY *Blackbird BB 107*

MAMA CASS — *2 Weeks*

Born Ellen Naomi Cohen on September 19, 1941 in Baltimore, USA. In 1963 formed a folk trio, The Triumvirate, with Tim Rose and John Brown. Became known as The Big Three when James Hendricks replaced Brown. Went solo in 1964.

continues over

Date	Pos	Wks	ARTIST / Record Title *Label & Number*
			Joined the Mamas And Papas in 1965. Split from the group in 1968 to pursue a solo career. Appeared in film, *Pufnstuf* (1970). Died of a heart attack on July 29, 1974, in London.
16 Oct 69	3	2	1. IT'S GETTING BETTER *Stateside SS(I) 8021*

The MAMAS and the PAPAS *12 Weeks*

Formed in New York City, USA in 1964 when members of the Mugwumps and the New Journeymen teamed up. Moved to California in 1965. Personnel: John Phillips, Michelle Phillips, Cass Elliott and Denny Doherty. Split in 1968, with Cass Elliott pursuing a solo career. Inducted into Rock and Roll Hall of Fame in 1998. Cass Elliott died of a heart attack on July 29, 1974. John Phillips died from heart failure on March 18, 2001. Denny Doherty died on January 19, 2007.

Date	Pos	Wks	ARTIST / Record Title *Label & Number*
06 Jun 66	4	7	1. MONDAY MONDAY *RCA ERC 1516*
18 May 67	7	5	2. DEDICATED TO THE ONE I LOVE *RCA ERC 1576*

MANFRED MANN *44 Weeks*

Formed in London, England in 1962 as the Mann-Hugg Blues Brothers. Changed name to Manfred Mann in 1963 and signed to HMV Records. Personnel: Manfred Mann, (keyboards) Paul Jones, (lead vocals), Mike Vickers (guitar), Mike Hugg (drums) and Tom McGuinness (bass). Disc debut *Why Should We Not* (1963). Wrote theme song, *5-4-3-2-1*, for top TV show, *Ready Steady Go* (1964). Paul Jones left in 1966 to pursue a solo career. Replaced by Mike D'Abo and group changed record companies leaving HMV for Fontana. Jack Bruce replaced Mike Vickers in 1965. Bruce left in 1966, replaced by Klaus Voorman. The group split up in June 1969. Manfred Mann formed Manfred Mann's Earth Band, in 1971. The HMV hits feature Paul Jones as lead vocalist while the Fontana hits feature Mike D'Abo.

Date	Pos	Wks	ARTIST / Record Title *Label & Number*
03 Aug 64	2	8	1. DO WAH DIDDY DIDDY *HMV POP(I) 1320*
09 Nov 64	4	4	2. SHA LA LA *HMV POP(I) 1346*

continues over

Date	Pos	Wks	ARTIST / Record Title *Label & Number*
15 Feb 65	10	1	3. COME TOMORROW *HMV POP(I) 1381*
04 Oct 65	4	5	4. IF YOU GOTTA GO, GO NOW *HMV POP(I) 1466*
02 May 66	1(4)	8	• 5. PRETTY FLAMINGO *HMV POP(I) 1523*
28 Nov 66	5	3	6. SEMI-DETACHED SURBURBAN MR. JAMES *Fontana ETF 757*
11 May 67	8	2	7. HA! HA! SAID THE CLOWN *Fontana ETF 812*
08 Feb 68	1(3)	7	• 8. MIGHTY QUINN *Fontana ETF 897*
30 Jan 69	2	5	9. FOX ON THE RUN *Fontana ETF 985*
26 Jun 69	10	1	10. RAGAMUFFIN MAN *Fontana* ETF *1013*

See also Paul Jones; Manfred Mann's Earthband

MANFRED MANN'S EARTH BAND *4 Weeks*

Formed in London, England in 1971 following the demise of Manfred Mann. Personnel: Manfred Mann (born Michael Lubowitz on October 21, 1940 in Johannesburg, South Africa, keyboards), Chris Thompson (lead vocals, guitar), Dave Flett (lead guitar), Colin Pattenden (bass) and Chris Slade (drums). Have been numerous personnel changes over the years.

Date	Pos	Wks	ARTIST / Record Title *Label & Number*
30 Sep 76	6	2	1. BLINDED BY THE LIGHT *Bronze BRO 29*
29 Jun 78	5	2	2. DAVY'S ON THE ROAD AGAIN *Bronze BRO 52*

MANHATTAN TRANSFER *9 Weeks*

Formed in New York City, USA in 1970 by Tim Hauser. Landed a recording deal with Capitol Records in 1971 and released the album *Junkin'*. In October 1972, a new revamped Manhattan Transfer was launched. Personnel: Tim Hauser, Laurel Masse, Janis Siegel and Alan Paul. Laurel Masse left the group in December 1978, following a serious car accident. Replaced by Cheryl Bentyne. In 1981, made history when became the first group to win Grammy Awards in both the Pop and Jazz categories in the same year with their album, *Mecca For Moderns*.

Date	Pos	Wks	ARTIST / Record Title *Label & Number*
03 Mar 77	1(3)	7	• 1. CHANSON D'AMOUR *Atlantic K 10886*
06 Apr 78	5	2	2. WALK IN LOVE *Atlantic K 11075*

Date	Pos	Wks	ARTIST / Record Title *Label & Number*

The MANHATTANS — *5 Weeks*

Vocal group formed in Jersey City, New Jersey, USA in 1962. Personnel: Gerald Alston (lead vocals), Edward Bivins, Winfred Lovett, Kenneth Kelly and Richard Taylor. Disc debut: *For The First Time* (1964). Gerald Alston left the group in 1988.

Date	Pos	Wks	ARTIST / Record Title *Label & Number*
05 Aug 76	10	2	1. KISS AND SAY GOODBYE *CBS 4317*
28 Oct 76	6	3	2. HURT *CBS 4562*

Barry MANILOW — *4 Weeks*

Born Barry Alan Pincus on June 17, 1946 in Brooklyn, New York City, USA. By the age of seven was taking accordion lessons and playing piano. Attended the New York College of Music and the Juilliard School of Music. In 1971, met Bette Midler and became her music director, arranger and pianist. In 1972, signed to Bell Records. Debut album, *Barry Manilow*, released in 1973. In 1974, Clive Davis took him to Arista Records. Has produced albums for Bette Midler, Nancy Wilson and Dionne Warwick. His autobiography, *Sweet Life: Adventures On The Way To Paradise*, was published in 1987.

Date	Pos	Wks	ARTIST / Record Title *Label & Number*
20 Mar 75	6	4	1. MANDY *Arista 1*

MANTOVANI and his ORCHESTRA — *2 Weeks*

Born Annunzio Paolo Mantovani on November 15, 1905 in Venice, Italy. Family relocated to London, England in 1912 where he studied piano and violin. In 1931 formed the Tipica Orchestra and quickly built up a reputation on the London hotel and cabaret circuit. In the mid 1930's formed his own Orchestra and signed to Columbia Records. In 1940 moved from Columbia to the Decca record company. Made international breakthrough in 1951, when Decca Records released his recording of *Charmaine*. The single climbed into the USA Top Ten and in the process sold over a million copies. Died on March 29, 1980.

Date	Pos	Wks	ARTIST / Record Title *Label & Number*
04 Jan 55	-	2	1. LONELY BALLERINA • *Decca F 10395*

Date	Pos	Wks	ARTIST / Record Title *Label & Number*

MANUEL & the MUSIC of the MOUNTAINS — *12 Weeks*

Orchestra leader/arranger/composer. Born Geoff Love on September 4, 1917 in Todmorden, Lanchashire, England. Learned to play the trombone in the local brass band. Joined Harry Gold's Pieces of Eight in 1946. Formed his own band in 1955 for the television show, *On The Town*, and started recording for EMI. In 1959 started to release recordings under the pseudonym, Manuel and his Music of the Mountains. Geoff Love died on July 8, 1991.

Date	Pos	Wks	ARTIST / Record Title *Label & Number*
22 Oct 59	8	2	1. THE HONEYMOON SONG • *Columbia DB(I) 4323*
10 Nov 60	5	6	2. NEVER ON A SUNDAY • *Columbia DB(I) 4515*
04 Mar 76	4	4	3. RODROGO'S GUITAR CONCERTO DE ARANJUEZ (Theme from 2nd Movement) • *EMI 2383*

MARBLES — *1 Weeks*

British male vocal duo formed in Skegness, Yorkshire by Trevor Gordon (born on May 5, 1948 in Skegness) and Graham Bonnett (born on December 12, 1947 in Skegness) in 1968. Childhood friends they sang together in a band called the Blue Sect. Barry Gibb of the Bee Gees came up with the name Marbles. He also produced all the duo's singles. Marbles split in 1970. Trevor embarked on a solo career. Graham joined Rainbow as lead vocalist in 1979, left in 1980.

Date	Pos	Wks	ARTIST / Record Title *Label & Number*
28 Nov 68	8	1	1. ONLY ONE WOMAN *Polydor 56272*

MARGO — *46 Weeks*

Born Margaret Catherine O'Donnell on February 6, 1951 in Donegal Town, Ireland Sister of country singer Daniel O'Donnell. Joined the Keynotes while still attending school. Disc debut: *Bonny Irish Boy* (1968). Left the Keynotes in late 1969 to form her own band, The Country Folk. Quit Country Folk in July, 1974. Made her debut with Country Pride on December 25, 1974.

continues over

Date	Pos	Wks	ARTIST / Record Title *Label & Number*
			Hosted her own six part colour TV series, *Country Folk,* on RTE in January 1975. Teamed up with Larry Cunningham and the Country Blue Boys in December 1975. Enjoyed chart success with Larry Cunningham under the name, Larry and Margo. Retired from music business in 1990's due to ill health.
07 Nov 68	10	1	1. BONNY IRISH BOY *Target 7N 17602*
06 Feb 69	2	7	2. THE ROAD BY THE RIVER *Target 7N 17677*
23 Apr 70	6	3	3. GRADH MO CHROI *Ruby RUB 102*
15 Oct 70	1(1)	17	• 4. I'LL FORGIVE AND I'LL TRY TO FORGET *Ruby RUB 113*
08 Mar 73	2	10	5. SHAMROCK FROM GLENORE *Ara 004*
09 Jan 74	6	4	6. THE GIRL FROM DONEGAL *IRL 224*
25 Nov 76	7	4	7. IRISH EYES *Release RL 838*
			See also Larry and Margo

MARIE — *1 Weeks*

Born in 1958 in Derry, N. Ireland. Discovered by Tony Johnston, who was Marie's teacher at Mallabuoy Primary School. Tony also discovered Dana. Disc debut: *Christmas Tree Angel* (1970).

Date	Pos	Wks	ARTIST / Record Title *Label & Number*
20 Apr 72	8	1	1. THE NICKEL SONG *Flame FLM 001*

Guy MARKS — *1 Weeks*

Born Mario Scarpa on October 31, 1923 in Philadelphia, USA. Worked on the night club circuit as a comedian/impressionist. Appeared in the 1975 film *Train Ride To Hollywood.* Originally recorded *Loving You Has Made Me Bananas* in 1968, parodying the music style and lyrics of the 1930's and 40's. Died on November 28, 1987.

Date	Pos	Wks	ARTIST / Record Title *Label & Number*
08 Jun 78	10	1	1. LOVING YOU HAS MADE ME BANANAS *ABC 4211*

The MARMALADE — *28 Weeks*

Formed in Glasgow, Scotland in 1961 as The Gaylords. Recorded for Columbia in 1964 as Dean Ford & The Gaylords. In 1966 on the suggestion of The Tremeloes manager Peter Walsh changed their name to the Marmalade.

Date	Pos	Wks	ARTIST / Record Title *Label & Number*
			Personnel: Dean Ford (born Thomas McAleese on September 5, 1946 in Glasgow, lead vocals), Alan Whitehead (drums), Graham Knight (bass), Junior Campbell (lead guitar) and Patrick Fairley (rhythm guitar). Signed to Decca in 1969. Junior Campbell left in June 1971 to pursue a solo career. Replaced by Hugh Nicholson. In 1971, Alan Whitehead was sacked and Dougie Henderson came in on drums. In November 1971, Pat Fairley announced his decision to quit, group continued as a four piece. In the Spring of 1972, Hugh Nicholson left. Down to a trio group signed to EMI in early 1973. Dean Ford left in 1975. Sandy Newman came into group as lead vocalist.
11 Jul 68	10	2	1. LOVIN' THINGS *CBS 3412*
02 Jan 69	1(1)	9	• 2. OB-LA-DI OB-LA-DA *CBS 3892*
31 Jul 69	6	3	3. BABY MAKE IT SOON *CBS 4287*
22 Jan 70	2	4	4. REFLECTIONS OF MY LIFE *Decca F 12982*
20 Aug 70	4	4	5. RAINBOW *Decca F 13035*
07 Oct 71	9	1	6. COUSIN NORMAN *Decca F 13214*
20 Apr 72	10	3	7. RADANCER *Decca F 13297*
29 Apr 76	8	2	8. FALLING APART AT THE SEAMS *Bullet TGT 105*

MARSHALL HAIN — *7 Weeks*

British male/female vocal/instrumental duo. Julian Marshall (keyboards) and Kit Hain (vocals) had known each other since their days at Dartington Hall School near Totnes, Devon, England. Went their separate ways, Marshall to the Royal College of Music in London and Hain to Durham University. Met up again London in 1976 and started performing and writing together. The duo split in 1980 Marshall went on to become a member of the Flying Lizards. Hain concentrated on songwriting and her solo recordings. Her songs have been recorded by Roger Daltrey, Kiki Dee and Barbra Dickson. Drummer on *Dancing In The City* is Peter Van Hook.

Date	Pos	Wks	ARTIST / Record Title *Label & Number*
06 Jul 78	2	7	1. DANCING IN THE CITY *Harvest HAR 5157*

Date	Pos	Wks	ARTIST / Record Title *Label & Number*

Dean MARTIN — *23 Weeks*

Born Dino Crocetti on June 7, 1917 in Steubenville, Ohio, USA. Moved to California in 1937. Teamed up with comedian Jerry Lewis in 1946. First film, *My Friend Irma* in 1949. Broke up in 1956 after sixteen movies together. Signed as a solo artist to Capitol Records in 1948. Left in 1963 for the Frank Sinatra owned Reprise label. Had his own variety show on NBC TV 1965-74. Starred in numerous films including *Rio Bravo* (1959), *Ocean's Eleven* (1960) and *Airport* (1970). In the late 1960's starred in a series of films as secret agent Matt Helm, *The Silencers* (1966), *Murder's Row* (1966), *The Ambushers* (1967) and *The Wrecking Crew* (1969). Died of emphysema on December 25, 1995.

Date	Pos	Wks	ARTIST / Record Title *Label & Number*
01 Feb 55	-	1	1. THE NAUGHTY LADY OF SHADY LANE *Capitol CL 14226*
10 May 55	-	1	2. UNDER THE BRIDGES OF PARIS *Capitol CL 14255*
28 Feb 56	-	2	3. MEMORIES ARE MADE OF THIS *Capitol CL 14523*
29 May 58	-	3	4. RETURN TO ME *Capitol CL(I) 14844*
21 May 59	5	5	5. IT TAKES SO LONG (TO SAY GOODBYE) *Capitol CL(I) 14990*
13 Mar 69	3	11	6. GENTLE ON MY MIND *Reprise RS 23343*

Tony MARTIN — *2 Weeks*

Born Alvin Morris on December 25, 1913 in Oakland, California, USA. Whilst attending college he took up the tenor saxophone and later formed his own band, Al Morris and his Four Red Peppers. In the 1930's began to make inroads into the acting profession. Made his film debut in *Follow The Fleet* (1936). Film appearances include *Sing Baby Sing* (1936), *You Can't Have Everything* (1937), *Ziegfeld Girl* (1941) and *Casbah* (1948). Married actress Cyd Charisse on May 15, 1948. She died on June 17, 2008.

Date	Pos	Wks	ARTIST / Record Title *Label & Number*
09 Nov 54	3	1	1. I REMEMBER PARIS *HMV POP 10771*
18 Sep 56	-	1	2. WALK HAND IN HAND *HMV IP 1152*

Date	Pos	Wks	ARTIST / Record Title *Label & Number*

Wink MARTINDALE *7 Weeks*

Born Winston Conrad Martindale on December 4, 1933 in Jackson, Tennessee, USA. Broke into radio in 1951 when at the age of seventeen he got a job with WPLI, Jackson. Moved to Memphis to work on WHBQ radio and TV station at age nineteen. Moved to California where he hosted radio and television programmes for KHJ. Randy Wood signed him to a recording contract with Dot Records. Hosted networked television game shows, *Tic-Tac-Dough*, *Trivial Pursuit*, *Gambit* and *What's This Song*. Honoured with a star on the Hollywood Walk of Fame in June 2006. *Deck of Cards* is a monologue telling the story of a soldier bringing out a pack of playing cards in church.

01 Jul 63	3	7	1. DECK OF CARDS *London HLD 8962*

Lee MARVIN *9 Weeks*

Born February 19, 1924 in New York, USA. Served with the U S Marine Corps in World War 2, wounded in the battle of Saipan in June 1944. On his discharged got involved in theatre work. Made Broadway debut in 1950. After a succession of small roles in TV productions he moved to Hollywood. Film appearances include: *The Wild Ones* (1953), *Cat Ballou* (1965), *The Dirty Dozen* (1967) and *Paint Your Wagon* (1969). Received Oscar for Best Actor for his dual role as a drunken gunfighter and his evil brother in *Cat Ballou*. Died from a heart attack on August 29, 1987. *Wanderin' Star* featured in the 1969 film, *Paint Your Wagon*.

26 Feb 70	1(2)	9	• 1. WAND'RIN' STAR *Paramount PARA 3004*

MARY LOU and HARVEST *1 Weeks*

Born Mary Coleman on June 29, 1957 in Coalisland, Co. Tyrone, N. Ireland.. First sang in public at age of eleven. Big break arrived as a result of winning a talent contest organised by Tony Loughman.

continues over

Date	Pos	Wks	ARTIST / Record Title *Label & Number*

Joined the Highwaymen. In 1972, she won the Pop Section in the Castlebar International Song Contest were she performed the song, *That's What Love Is Made.* Spotted by Connie Lynch, who signed her to front a new band. Made her debut with Harvest on March 22, 1973 in Drumshambo, Co. Leitrim. Harvest formed in Monaghan in March 1973. Personnel: Mary Lou (lead vocals), Tony Hughes, (guitar), Colm Hughes (drums), Pauric McElwaine (bass), John Chambers (piano), Des Flynn (guitar/vocals), Paddy Donnelly (trumpet) and Joe Corey (trombone). After leaving Harvest in June 1975 Mary Lou joined Music City in September 1975.

Date	Pos	Wks	ARTIST / Record Title *Label & Number*
12 Jul 73	10	1	1. TEDDY BEAR SONG *Release RL 681*

Johnny MATHIS — *13 Weeks*

Born John Royce Mathis on September 30, 1935 in Gilmer, Texas. USA. As a small boy the family moved to San Francisco. Sang in church choir, school functions, community events and amateur shows in the San Francisco area. Studied vocal techniques for six years under vocal coach, Connie Fox. A star athlete, he enrolled at San Francisco State College in 1954. While there, he set a high jump record of 6 foot 5½ inches, and was only two inches short of the Olympic Record of the time. In early 1955, landed a job singing weekends at Ann Dee's 440 Club. Spotted by George Avakian, then head of Jazz A&R at Columbia Records. In early 1956, was asked to attend trials for the 1956 USA Olympic teams that would travel to Melbourne, Australia, that summer. At the same time, Columbia Records requested that Johnny come to New York to start arrangements for his first recording sessions. On the advice of his father, he opted to travel to New York, to record his first album, *Johnny Mathis: A New Sound In Popular Music.*

Date	Pos	Wks	ARTIST / Record Title *Label & Number*
19 Nov 59	7	1	1. SOMEONE Fontana *EH 199*
11 Feb 60	7	4	2. MISTY *Fontana EH 219*
20 Mar 75	8	2	3. I'M STONE IN LOVE WITH YOU *CBS 2653*
23 Dec 76	1(2)	6	• 4. WHEN A CHILD IS BORN *CBS SCBS 4599*

Date	Pos	Wks	ARTIST / Record Title *Label & Number*

Johnny MATHIS and Denice WILLIAMS — *5 Weeks*

Male/female vocal duo. Johnny Mathis born on September 30, 1935 in Gilmer, Texas, USA. Denice Williams born June Denice Chandler on June 3, 1951 in Gary, Indiana, USA. Released an album of duets, *That's What Friends Are For*, in 1978.

Date	Pos	Wks	ARTIST / Record Title *Label & Number*
27 Apr 78	2	5	1. TOO MUCH, TOO LITTLE, TOO LATE *CBS SCBS 6164*

See also Denice Williams

Charlie MATTHEWS & ROYAL SHOWBAND — *7 Weeks*

Born on December 18, 1937 in Waterford, Ireland. Began his musical career with the local De La Salle School Boy Scouts Band. Founder member, drummer/vocalist of the Royal Showband. Disc debut: *Spanish Lace* (1964). The third member of the Royal Showband to secure a number one hit on the Irish Charts (Brendan Bowyer and Tom Dunphy also hit the jackpot). Charlie left the Royal in 1974.

Date	Pos	Wks	ARTIST / Record Title *Label & Number*
31 Oct 66	1(1)	7	• 1. SOMEWHERE MY LOVE *HMV IP 1305*

See also Brendan Bowyer; Tom Dunphy

MATTHEWS SOUTHERN COMFORT — *6 Weeks*

Formed in England in 1969. Personnel: Ian Matthews (born Ian Matthew McDonald on June 16, 1946 in Scunthorpe, England, vocals), Mark Griffiths (guitar), Carl Barnwell (guitar), Gordon Huntley (steel guitar), Andy Leigh (bass) and Ray Duffy (drums). Disbanded in 1972. *Woodstock* was composed by Joni Mitchell, as a tribute to the famous 1969 music festival, that she had been unable to attend.

Date	Pos	Wks	ARTIST / Record Title *Label & Number*
05 Nov 70	2	6	1. WOODSTOCK *UNI UNS 526*

Date	Pos	Wks	ARTIST / Record Title *Label & Number*
			Susan MAUGHAN ***6 Weeks***
			Born Marion Susan Maughan on July 1, 1942 in Consett, County Durham, England. After leaving school she joined the Ronnie Hancox Band. In 1961 was recruited as vocalist with the Ray Ellington Quartet. Starred in the 1962 film, *What A Crazy World*, with Joe Brown and Marty Wilde.
12 Nov 62	6	6	1. BOBBY'S GIRL *Philips 326544 EBF*
			Simon MAY ***7 Weeks***
			Orchestra leader/songwriter. Born in 1944 in Devizes, Wiltshire, England. Won a Choral Scholarship to Cambridge University where he took a degree in modern languages. Taught German and French for seven years at Kingston Grammar School before leaving to become a full time composer. In 1973 enjoyed commercial success with his first stage musical *Smike*. Composed the theme music for several successful television series including *Eastenders*, *Really Useful Show*, *Howards Way* and *El Dorado*. Composed several hit songs including *Born With A Smile On My Face* (Stephanie De Sykes), *More Than In Love* (Kate Robins) and *Every Loser Wins* (Nick Berry).
04 Nov 76	4	7	1. SUMMER OF MY LIFE *Pye 7N 45627*
			MAXI ***3 Weeks***
			Born Irene McCoubrey on February 28, 1949 in Dublin, Ireland. Nicknamed Maxi at school. Began her musical career while in her teens, with the Young Dublin Singers. Founder member of the vocal trio, Maxi, Dick and Twink. Represented Ireland in the 1973 Eurovision Song Contest with *Do I Dream*, finishing in tenth position. Joined Danny Doyle's Music Box in April 1972. Left in May 1974, to form own band Maxi and Company. In April 1978, formed female vocal trio, Sheeba, who represented Ireland in the 1981 Eurovision Song Contest with *Horoscopes*.

continues over

Date	Pos	Wks	ARTIST / Record Title *Label & Number*

Hosted the RTE television quiz show, *Rapid Roulette*. Presented *Late Date* programme on RTE Radio for eleven years. Currently presents the early morning radio show, *Risin' Time*, on RTE Radio 1.

12 Apr 73	7	3	1. DO I DREAM *Release RL 673*

Frankie McBRIDE — ***16 Weeks***

Born on February 14, 1943 in Omagh, County Tyrone, N. Ireland. Joined the Polka Dots Showband in the mid sixties. Disc debut: *One For The Road* (1966). In 1967, realised one of his ambitions when he made the UK singles chart with *Five Little Fingers*. It peaked at number 19. His debut album, *Frankie McBride Sings*, reached number 29 on British Album charts, in February 1968. Frankie departed from the ranks of the Polka Dots in 1970 and formed his own band, The Highwaymen.

17 Aug 67	2	16	1. FIVE LITTLE FINGERS *Emerald MD 1081*

C W McCALL — ***4 Weeks***

Born William Fries on November 15, 1928 in Audubon, Iowa, USA. Studied music and played in the school band while attending the University of Iowa. While working as the art director for an Omaha advertising agency in the early 60's, he created the character of a trucker called, *C W McCall*, as a selling tool for a local bakery. In 1974, Fries decided to cut a recording of a monologue, *Convoy*, under the name C W McCall. It's success influenced the 1978 film, *Convoy*.

18 Mar 76	8	4	1. CONVOY *MGM 2006 560*

Jim McCANN — ***1 Weeks***

Born on October 26, 1944 in Dublin, Ireland. While studying at University College Dublin he played guitar with various showbands including The Boston and the Bob Ormsby All Stars. Musical influences include Eddie Cochran and Buddy Holly. While working in Birmingham, England in 1964, developed an interest in folk music.

Date	Pos	Wks	ARTIST / Record Title *Label & Number*

On his return to Dublin in 1965, he was asked to replace Paddy Roche in the Ludlows ballad group. He left the group in 1967 to pursue a solo career. Solo disc debut: *Someday Soon* (1967). In 1973, played role of Peter in the first Irish stage production of *Jesus Christ Superstar*, at the Gaiety Theatre, Dublin. Joined the Dubliners in July 1974, as a temporary replacement for Ciaron Bourke. Made a full member in August 1974, when Ronnie Drew announced his decision to leave. Member of group until 1979.

22 Mar 79	10	1	1. HER FATHER DIDN'T LIKE ME ANYWAY *Hawk HASP 433*

Susan McCANN and the STORYTELLERS ***7 Weeks***

Born on February 26, 1950 in Forkhill, Co. Armagh, N. Ireland. As a teenager she sang with the local John Murphy Country Ceili Band. Following her marriage to band member, Dennis Heaney, they formed a their own band, The Fairylanders. In early 70's was approached by Tony Loughman, boss of Top Spin Records, to front a new band, The Storytellers. Disc debut: *Santa And The Kids* (1976). Storytellers personnel: Martin Campbell (guitar/trombone), Trevor Gibb (guitar/trumpet), Bill Conlon (bass), Dennis Heaney (piano/accordion), Tony McIlvanna (guitar) and Frankie Walker (drums). Susan McCann won the European Gold Star Award in 1982. In 1995, teamed up with singer Sean Wilson for a series of tours and an album, *King And Queen Of Irish Country Music*. In 2006, acquired control of her early recordings. Presents her own daily Country Music Show on Five FM radio.

19 May 77	1(2)	7	• 1. BIG TOM IS STILL THE KING *Top Spin TSS 70*

Paul McCARTNEY ***6 Weeks***

Born James Paul McCartney on June 18, 1942 in Liverpool, England. Founding member of The Beatles. Married Linda Eastman in 1969.

continues over

Date	Pos	Wks	ARTIST / Record Title *Label & Number*
			Released his first solo album, *McCartney*, in 1970. Formed Wings in 1971 with wife Linda on keyboards. The group officially disbanded in 1981. Linda died on April 17, 1998. Paul married model Heather Mills in June 2002. Split in May 2006.
18 Mar 71	1(1)	6	• 1. ANOTHER DAY *Apple R 5889*
			See also The Beatles; Wings

Marilyn McCOO and Billy DAVIS Jr — *3 Weeks*

Husband and wife vocal duo. Met up in 1966 when Billy joined the Fifth Dimension. Married in 1969. Spent ten years with the Fifth Dimension. After leaving the group in November 1975 Marilyn and Billy started recording and touring as a duo. Marilyn McCoo born on September 30, 1943 in Jersey City, USA. Billy Davis Jr born on June 26, 1939 in St. Louis, USA.

Date	Pos	Wks	ARTIST / Record Title *Label & Number*
05 May 77	5	3	1. YOU DON'T HAVE TO BE A STAR (To Be In My Show) *ABC 4147*

John McCORMACK — *4 Weeks*

Born John Francis McCormack on June 14, 1884 in Athlone, Co. Westmeath, Ireland. On leaving College his thoughts turned to a career in singing. Following a successful audition with Vincent O'Brien was offered a place in the Palestrina Choir of the Pro-Cathedral in Dublin. Won a gold medal in the tenor section at the 1903 Feis Ceoil in Dublin. Made his recording debut in 1904. In his early years made several recordings under the names Mr J F McCormack and John O'Reilly. Made his first appearance in opera in 1906 under the name Giovanni Foli. At 23, became the youngest tenor ever to sing a major role at the Royal Opera, Covent Garden, London when he sang role of Turiddu in Cavalleria Rusticana. Signed to Victor Records in USA in 1910. Starred in the 1929 film, *Song O' My Heart*, and appeared in the 1937 film, *Wings Of The Morning*.

continues over

Date	Pos	Wks	ARTIST / Record Title *Label & Number*
			In 1928, was raised to the Papal Peerage by Pope Pius XI in recognition of his unstinting work on behalf of charities. Made his final concert appearances on November 27, 1938 at the Royal Albert Hall, London. Made his last recording session on August 10, 1942. Died of pneumonia on September 16, 1945.
08 Nov 55	-	4	1. **JOHN COUNT McCORMACK E.P.** *HMV 7ER 5054*
			Tracks on **John Count McCormack EP**: Passing By / The Green Bushes / The Village That Nobody Knows / Maureen / The Lass With The Delicate Air.
			Van McCOY ***8 Weeks***
			Producer/songwriter/pianist. Born on January 6, 1944 in Washington D.C., USA. Began his musical adventure when he formed, and became lead singer, with vocal group, The Starlighters. Disc debut: *The Birdbeat* (1956). Moved to New York where he was hired by Florence Greenberg as a staff writer at Scepter Records. His song writing credits include *I Get The Sweetest Feeling*, *Getting Mighty Crowded* and *When You're Young And In Love*. Produced recordings by The Shirelles, Gladys Knight and The Stylistics. In the early 1970's formed his own orchestra, the Soul City Symphony. Died from heart attack on July 6, 1979. *The Hustle* won Grammy Award in 1975 for Best Pop Instrumental Performance.
26 Jun 75	5	5	1. **THE HUSTLE** *Philips 6105 037*
07 Jul 77	6	3	2. **THE SHUFFLE** *Avco 6105 076*
			George McCRAE ***5 Weeks***
			Born on October 19, 1944 in West Palm Beach, Florida, USA. Had first singing experience in church at the age of six. As a teenager sang with the Roosevelt High School Glee Club. Went on to form his own group, the Jivin' Jets. Married singer Gwen McCrae in 1964. Sang as a duo in the clubs and lounges around Florida.

continues over

Date	Pos	Wks	ARTIST / Record Title *Label & Number*
			Duo discovered by singer Betty Wright in 1967. Gwen signed solo contract with Columbia Records. The couple separated in 1976.
01 Aug 74	3	4	1. ROCK YOUR BABY *Jayboy BOY 85*
11 Sep 75	4	1	2. IT'S BEEN SO LONG *Jayboy BOY 100*

Gordon MacRAE ***1 Weeks***

Born Albert Gordon MacRae on March 12, 1921 in East Orange, New Jersey, USA. While attending high school took an interest in singing and acting. At age nineteen won a talent contest sponsored by Picture Magazine, the prize, a two week engagement at the New York World's Fair Outdoor Dancing Pavilion, singing with Harry James and Les Brown. Spotted by a Capitol Records executive in 1946 while appearing in the Broadway revue, *Three To Make Ready*. Film appearances include *Look For The Silver Lining* (1949), *Moonlight Bay* (1951), *By The Light Of The Silvery Moon* (1953), *Oklahoma* (1955) and *Carousel* (1956). Died from cancer on January 24, 1986.

Date	Pos	Wks	ARTIST / Record Title *Label & Number*
30 Oct 56	-	1	1. A WOMAN IN LOVE *Capitol CL(I) 14622*

Johnny McEVOY ***79 Weeks***

Born on April 24, 1945 in Banagher, County Offaly, Ireland. Moved to Dublin at age of eight. Teamed up with Mick Crotty in early sixties and performed under the name, *The Ramblers Two*. Signed to Pye Records and made their disc debut, *Today Is The Highway*, in 1965. Split with Crotty in 1966 and went out as solo performer under the name, *The Rambler*. Hit the jackpot with his second solo record, *Muirsheen Durkin*, issued under the name The Rambler (John McEvoy). Formed a country band in April 1970. Has appeared on all the major television and radio programmes in Ireland and has had his own TV series, *Sounds Like McEvoy*, on RTE and UTV.

continues over

Date	Pos	Wks	ARTIST / Record Title *Label & Number*
			Composed several successful songs including *Funny Man*, *You Seldom Come* to *See Me Anymore* and *Long Before Your Time*.
07 Nov 66	1(3)	16	• 1. MUIRSHEEN DURKIN *Pye 7N 17196*
04 May 67	1(3)	18	• 2. THE BOSTON BURGLAR *Pye 7N 17303*
31 Aug 67	10	2	3. FUNNY MAN *Pye 7N 17365*
15 Feb 68	1(1)	10	• 4. NORA *Target 7N 17472*
11 Mar 71	6	4	5. THREE SCORE AND TEN *Target 7N 45033*
02 Mar 72	8	2	6. GENTLE ANNIE *Target 7NX 7001*
12 Sep 74	6	5	7. ROSE OF MORAY *Hawk HASM 2001*
24 Apr 75	2	9	8. WHERE MY EILEEN IS WAITING *Hawk HASP 364*
11 Sep 75	6	3	9. ROSE OF ALLENDALE *Hawk HASP 371*
08 Jul 76	4	7	10. LONG BEFORE YOUR TIME *Hawk HASP 388*
18 Aug 77	7	3	11. NORA *Hawk HASP 405*
			Hawk HASP 405 features a different recording of *Nora*

McFADDEN and WHITEHEAD — *1 Weeks*

Duo formed in Philadelphia, USA in 1977 by Gene McFadden (born 1949 in Philadelphia) and John Whitehead (born 1948 in Philadelphia). Formed the Epsilons whilst still in their youth. Toured with Otis Redding. Wrote hit songs for the O'Jays (*Back Stabbers*) and for Harold Melvin and The Blue Notes (*Wake Up Everybody*). John Whitehead was shot dead while working on a car on May 11, 2004. Gene McFadden died from cancer on January 27, 2006.

Date	Pos	Wks	ARTIST / Record Title *Label & Number*
28 Jun 79	9	1	1. AIN'T NO STOPPIN' US NOW *Philadelphia Int. PIR 7365*

Pat McGEEGAN and the BIG FOUR — *14 Weeks*

Born Patrick McGuigan on February 10, 1935 in Clones, County Monaghan, Ireland. Started singing at an early age in local concerts. Moved to Britain in late 1950's. On his return joined the Dave Dixon Band. Made his disc debut *Gwievara Bay* in 1960 for Connoisseur Records. Formed the Big Four in 1961 and signed to Decca Records.

continues over

Date	Pos	Wks	ARTIST / Record Title *Label & Number*
			Personnel: Pat McGeegan (vocals/bass/flute/sax), Bill Davidson (lead gtr./vocals), Mike McGeady (alto/tenor/ clarinet/vocals) and Doug Stewart (drums/vibes/vocals). Member of Victors Showband (1964-66) and The Skyrockets (1966-69). Represented Ireland at the 1968 Eurovision Song Contest, finishing in fourth position with *Chance Of A Lifetime*. Father of former WBA world featherweight boxing champion Barry McGuigan, who annexed the title in 1985. Pat McGeegan died on June 27, 1987.
04 Nov 63	7	6	1. THE WEDDING / HAWAIIAN WEDDING SONG *Decca F11756*
11 Apr 68	1(1)	8	• 2. CHANCE OF A LIFETIME *Emerald MD 1096*
			Chance Of A Lifetime credit Pat McGeegan

Mary McGREGOR — *2 Weeks*

Born on May 6, 1948 in St Paul, Minnesota, USA. Studied classical piano from the age of six. At age fourteen, was singing professionally with a local band. Spotted by Peter Yarrow, of Peter Paul and Mary, who invited her to join him on a national tour, as a back up vocalist. Performed backing vocals on Peter Yarrow's *Love Songs* album. Her solo disc debut, *Torn Between Two Lovers*, was recorded in Muscle Shoals, Alabama.

Date	Pos	Wks	ARTIST / Record Title *Label & Number*
31 Mar 77	5	2	1. TORN BETWEEN TWO LOVERS *Ariola AA 111*

McGUINNESS FLINT — *6 Weeks*

Formed in London in 1969. Personnel: Tom McGuinness (guitar, vocals), Hughie Flint (drums), Dennis Coulson (keyboards), Benny Gallagher (guitar, vocals) and Graham Lyle (guitar, vocals). Gallagher and Lyle left in 1971 to pursue a career as a duo. Band broke up in late 1971. Reformed in 1973, before finally calling it a day in 1975.

Date	Pos	Wks	ARTIST / Record Title *Label & Number*
31 Dec 70	5	6	1. WHEN I'M DEAD AND GONE *Capitol CL(I) 15662*

Date	Pos	Wks	ARTIST / Record Title *Label & Number*

Barry McGUIRE — *7 Weeks*

Born on October 15, 1935 in Oklahoma City, USA. Joined the New Christy Minstrels in 1962. Left in 1965 to pursue a solo career. Composed *Green Back Dollar* for the Kingston Trio and *Green Green* for the New Christy Minstrels.

27 Sep 65	2	7	1. EVE OF DESTRUCTION *RCA ERC 1469*

The McGUIRE SISTERS — *1 Weeks*

Family vocal trio from Middletown, Ohio, USA. Personnel: Christine (born on July 30, 1929), Phyllis (born on February 14, 1931) and Dorothy McGuire (born on February 22, 1926). Began singing together as children in church choirs in their hometown. By 1949 were singing at military bases and church functions. Signed as vocalists with the Karl Taylor Band. In 1952, replaced Chordettes on Arthur Godfrey Show Talent Search and impressed so much they stayed for six years. Disc debut: *One, Two, Three, Four* (1952). Appeared in the 1963 film *Come Blow Your Horn*. Retired from public performances in 1968. Phyllis pursued a solo career. Inducted into the National Broadcasting Hall of Fame in 1994. Inducted into the Vocal Group Hall of fame in 2001.

21 May 59	7	1	1. MAY YOU ALWAYS *Coral EQ 72356*

Scott McKENZIE — *12 Weeks*

Born Philip Blondheim on January 10, 1939 in Jacksonville, Florida, USA. Teamed up with John Phillips (Mamas and Papas) in The Journeymen. Co-wrote the Beach Boys 1988 hit, *Kokomo*. John Phillips of the Mamas and Papas composed *San Francisco*, he also produced and played guitar on the recording. Member of the reformed Mamas and Papas 1986 to 1998. Now retired from music business.

03 Aug 67	1(1)	12	• 1. SAN FRANCISCO (Be Sure To Wear Some Flowers In Your Hair) *CBS 2816*

Date	Pos	Wks	ARTIST / Record Title *Label & Number*

Don McLEAN ***15 Weeks***

Born on October 2, 1945 in Rochelle, New York, USA. By the age of five had developed an interest in music. As a teenager purchased his first guitar. Started playing gigs in small clubs and coffee houses. In 1968, graduated from Iona College with a Bachelors Degree in Business Administration. Turned down a prestigious scholarship to Columbia University Graduates School in favour of becoming resident singer at Café Lena in New York. *American Pie*, inspired by the death of Buddy Holly, was recorded on May 26, 1971. McLean dedicated his first album, *American Pie*, to the memory of Buddy Holly. Composed *Vincent* as a tribute to the painter, Vincent Van Gogh.

Date	Pos	Wks	ARTIST / Record Title *Label & Number*
24 Feb 72	7	4	1. AMERICAN PIE *United Artists UP 35325*
08 Jun 72	1(2)	6	• 2. VINCENT *United Artists UP 35359*
15 Nov 73	2	5	3. MOUNTAINS OF MOURNE *United Artists UP 35607*

Ralph McTELL ***5 Weeks***

Born Ralph May on December 3, 1944 in Farnborough, Kent, England. Spent early years busking throughout Europe. Disc debut: *Eight Frames A Second* LP (1968). First recorded *Streets Of London* on his 1969 Transatlantic LP *Spiral Staircase*. Re-recorded the song for Reprise. Wrote the song after busking around Europe and witnessing poverty in Paris. When writing song decided to change the setting to London. *Streets Of London* earned him an Ivor Novello Award for Best Song in 1974.

Date	Pos	Wks	ARTIST / Record Title *Label & Number*
09 Jan 75	1(2)	5	• 1. STREETS OF LONDON *Reprise K 14380*

MECO ***4 Weeks***

Born Domenico Monardo on November 29, 1939 in Johnsonburg, Pennsylvania, USA. Learned to play trombone at the age of nine. Began his career as a session musician.

continues over

Date	Pos	Wks	ARTIST / Record Title *Label & Number*

During the period 1974-76 worked as a record producer and co-produced several hits including Gloria Gaynor's, *Never Can Say Goodbye* and Carol Douglas', *Doctors Orders*. In 1977, after watching the Star Wars movie, he got the idea to make a disco version of the film score by John Williams. The resulting album, *Star Wars And Other Galatic Funk*, proved successful and the hit single was taken from it.

27 Oct 77	3	4	1. STAR WARS THEME – CANTINA BAND • *RCA XB 1028*

MEDICINE HEAD — *1 Weeks*

Formed in Stafford, England in 1968 by John Fiddler (vocals/guitar) and Peter Hope-Evans (harmonica). Worked as a duo on college and club circuit. Signed by John Peel to his Dandelion record label. Disc debut: *His Guiding Hand* (1970). In 1973 added Roger Saunders (guitar), George Ford (bass) and Rob Townsend (drums) to the lineup. Peter Hope-Evans left for a short period in 1972, and ex Yardbirds member Keith Relf took his place. By 1976 had reduced back to a duo. Duo disbanded in 1977.

14 Jun 73	9	1	1. ONE AND ONE IS ONE *Polydor 2001 432*

MELANIE — *2 Weeks*

Born Melanie Safka on February 3, 1947 in Long Island, New York, USA. Started singing in the bars and folk clubs of Greenwich Village while still attending college. Made her solo recording debut, *My Beautiful People*, in 1967. Formed her own record label, Neighbourhood Records, in 1971.

27 Jan 72	8	2	1. BRAND NEW KEY *Buddah 2011 105*

The MEMORIES — *10 Weeks*

Vocal group formed in June 1963 in Dublin, Ireland, by Mike Swan, Daire Doyle, and Colm Harpur. Later that year, Ray Crowe and Jim Barry (lead vocals), invited to become members of group.

continues over

Date	Pos	Wks	ARTIST / Record Title *Label & Number*
			Operated on the cabaret and theatre circuit. Disc debut: *A Summer Song* (1967). In 1972, decided to take their talents onto the ballroom/showband circuit and added a drummer, Chris Heenan, to the lineup. Personnel (1974): Jim Barry (lead vocals), Mike Swan (keyboards), Daire Doyle (bass), Colm Harpur (guitar), Ray Crowe (guitar) and Chris Heenan (drums). In 1974, Daire Doyle was injured in an accident and Liam McKenna, was drafted in. When Daire Doyle returned, McKenna stayed and switched to guitar. Colm Harpur left in December 1974. In 1978, Ray Crowe left group, replaced by Dominic Greene. In 1981, Mike Swan, Daire Doyle and Dominic Greene split from Memories to form their own band, The Message. In late 1983, Mike and Daire returned to The Memories lineup.
29 Aug 68	10	1	1. OH NO! *Rex* R *11035*
20 Dec 73	7	5	2. DON'T PRETEND ANYMORE *Rex R 11809*
13 Jun 74	7	1	3. LAY IT ON ME *Rex R 11091*
12 Sep 74	7	3	4. THE LIKES OF HEFFO'S ARMY *Rex R 11093*

Bob MERRILL *1 Weeks*

Born Henry Lovan on May 17, 1921 in Atlantic City, New Jersey, USA. He worked as a night club singer and comedian in the early 1940's. Started writing songs in 1947. He couldn't read or write music and composed songs by tapping his melodies out on a toy xylophone. He had the names of the notes marked down on the xylophone. Wrote many of the top hits of the 1950's including *If I Knew You Were Coming, I'd Baked A Cake*, *How Much Is That Doggie In The Window*, *Mambo Italiano*, *Sparrow In The Treetop* and *Where Will The Dimple Be*. His songs have provided hits for dozens of artist including Guy Mitchell, Lita Roza, Patti Page, Rosemary Clooney, Georgia Gibbs and Barbra Streisand. Wrote scores for several Broadway productions including *New Girl In Town* (1957), *Carnival* (1961), *Funny Girl* (1964) and *Sugar* (1972). Worked as lyricist with Jule Styne, on the musical score of, *Funny Girl* (1964).

continues over

Date	Pos	Wks	ARTIST / Record Title *Label & Number*

Nominated for Broadway's Tony Award five times. He never won! Inducted into the Songwriters Hall of Fame in 1987. Died on February 17, 1998 from a self inflicted gunshot wound.

01 May 58	-	1	1. NAIROBI *Columbia DB(I) 4086*

The MERSEYBEATS — *1 Weeks*

Formed in Liverpool, England in 1961 as The Mavericks. Renamed The Merseybeats in April 1962 by Bob Woller, MC at the Cavern Club. Personnel: Billy Kinsley (vocals, bass), Tony Crane (vocals, lead guitar), Aaron Williams (rhythm guitar) and John Banks (drums). Disc debut: *It's Love That Really Counts* (1963). Kinsley left group for a short period in 1964, replaced by Johnny Gustafson. *I Think Of You* was voted a hit by the Beatles, on BBC TV's *Juke Box Jury*. Group folded in 1966. John Banks died on April 20, 1988. Billy Kinsley and Tony Crane reformed The Merseybeats in 1993.

16 Mar 64	10	1	1. I THINK OF YOU *Fontana ETF 431*

See also The Merseys

The MERSEYS — *4 Weeks*

Vocal duo formed in Liverpool in 1966 by ex-Merseybeats Tony Crane (born April 17, 1945 in Liverpool) and Billy Kinsley (born November 28, 1945 in Liverpool). Duo split in 1968. Kinsley went on to form Liverpool Express in the mid 70's.

06 Jun 66	7	4	1. SORROW *Fontana ETF 694*

See also The Merseybeats

The MIAMI featuring Charlie CHAPMAN — *1 Weeks*

Irish showband formed in Dublin in 1962. Numerous personnel changes over the years. On July 31, 1975 tragedy struck when three members of the band – Fran O'Toole, Brian McCoy and Tony Geraghty were murdered by terrorists at Newcastle while returning from a gig at the Castle Hotel, Banbridge, Co. Down.

continues over

Date	Pos	Wks	ARTIST / Record Title *Label & Number*
			Following the tragedy, The Miami was re-launched on October 26, 1975 in Salthill, Galway. Have been several lead vocalists with the band including Jimmy Harte, Dickie Rock and Fran O'Toole. Personnel: Charlie Chapman (lead vocals), P J Coyne (drums), Peter Eades (bass), Paul Duffy (trumpet), Mickey Joe Daly (keyboards) and Dessie O'Flaherty (lead guitar). Dublin born Charlie Chapman, a former male model, was vocalist with Flint before joining the Miami in 1978. Made his disc debut, *It's So Crazy*, with Flint in 1977.
24 Aug 78	10	1	1. I LIKE IT LIKE THAT *Mint CHEW 23*
			MIDDLE OF THE ROAD ***17 Weeks***
			Officially formed in Glasgow on April 1, 1970. The group was previously known as Los Caracas and prior to that in 1967 as Part Four. Ken Andrew came up with the name Middle of the Road. In 1968, Los Caracas, appeared four times on the popular British TV talent show, *Opportunity Knocks*. Personnel: Sally Carr (born Sally Young on March 28, 1945 in Glasgow, vocals), Eric McCredie (bass), Ian McCredie (guitar) and Ken Andrew (drums). Sally Carr left in 1977. Returned to lineup in 1991. Eric McCredie died on October 6, 2007.
24 Jun 71	1(3)	10	• 1. CHIRPY CHIRPY CHEEP CHEEP *RCA RCA 2047*
30 Sep 71	2	7	2. TWEEDLE DEE TWEEDLE DUM *RCA 2110*
			John MILES ***2 Weeks***
			Born John Errington on April 23, 1949 in Jarrow, County Durham, England. Introduced to music through piano classes. Later mastered the guitar and joined up with a local group, The Influence, whose lineup included members-to-be of Roxy Music and Geordie. Formed the John Miles Set in the late 1960's. Disc debut: *Jose* (1971).
06 May 76	9	2	1. MUSIC *Decca F 13627*

Date	Pos	Wks	ARTIST / Record Title *Label & Number*

MILK and HONEY featuring Gali ATARI — *5 Weeks*

Israel group who won 1979 Eurovision Song Contest with *Hallelujah*. Gali Atari (lead vocals) born in 1958 in Rehovot, Israel. Grew up in Tel Aviv. Made her first recordings in 1971. Milk and Honey had performed with different female singers before Gali Atari joined them for the Eurovision.

Date	Pos	Wks	Record
19 Apr 79	1(1)	5	• 1. HALLELUJAH *Polydor 2001 870*

Frankie MILLER — *11 Weeks*

Born on November 2, 1949 in Bridgeton, Glasgow, Scotland. Started writing songs at the age of nine, after being given a guitar by his parents. Began his musical career playing in various beat groups during the 60's. Moved to London in 1971, where he formed the rock group, Jude, with Robin Trower and Clive Bunker. After demise of Jude, signed a solo contract with Chrysalis in 1972. Released the album, *Once In A Blue Moon*, in 1973. Formed the Frankie Miller Band in 1975. Had lead role in the BBC TV play, *Just A Boy's Game*, in 1979. Suffered a massive brain hemorrhage in New York on August 25, 1994. Confounded the medical world and is now writing and hopes to release an album in the near future.

Date	Pos	Wks	Record
02 Nov 78	4	11	1. DARLIN' *Chrysalis CHS 2255*

Gary MILLER — *5 Weeks*

Born Neville Williams in 1924 in Blackpool, Lancashire, England. Spotted by producer, Norman Newell, who arranged a recording contract with EMI. Disc debut: *The Angels Are Lighting God's Little Candles* (1952). Died of a heart attack on June 15, 1968.

Date	Pos	Wks	Record
26 Oct 54	2	1	1. HOLD MY HAND *Philips PB 335*
12 Feb 57	-	1	2. THE GARDEN OF EDEN *Nixa N 15070*
13 Aug 57	-	2	3. WONDERFUL WONDERFUL *Nixa N 15094*
19 Nov 57	-	1	4. YEAR AFTER YEAR *Nixa N 15106*

Date	Pos	Wks	ARTIST / Record Title *Label & Number*

Mitch MILLER with his Orchestra & Chorus — *13 Weeks*

Born William Mitchell Miller on July 4, 1911 in Rochester, New York, USA. A child prodigy who could play a Bach concerto at age of six. Switched to oboe and by age of fifteen he was a member of the Rochester School Symphony Orchestra. Won a scholarship to the Eastman School of Music and after graduating in 1932, he moved to New York. Joined Keynote Records in 1947 to head the company's classical music division, he later moved on to head their popular records section. When Mercury took over Keynote his talents as A&R man producer guided Patti Page, Vic Damone and Frankie Laine to achieving record breaking sales figures. In 1950, he moved to Columbia Records as head of their pop music department and was instrumental in the recording success of Tony Bennett, Rosemary Clooney, Guy Mitchell and Doris Day. Also started recording, with his Orchestra and Chorus, a series of million selling sing-a-long albums.

Date	Pos	Wks	ARTIST / Record Title *Label & Number*
27 Sep 55	-	7	1. THE YELLOW ROSE OF TEXAS *Philips PB 505*
03 Jan 56	-	1	2. BONNIE BLUE GAL *Philips PB 525*
18 Feb 58	-	3	3. MARCH FROM BRIDGE ON RIVER KWAI *Philips EPB 777*
05 Mar 58	-	1	4. THE BOWERY GRENADIERS *Philips EPB 771*
19 Feb 59	8	1	5. THE CHILDREN'S MARCHING SONG (Nick Nack Paddy Whack) *Philips EPB 893*

Ned MILLER — *18 Weeks*

Born Henry Ned Miller on April 12, 1925 in Raines, Utah, USA. Made his recording debut in 1956 with *Roll O' Rolling Stone* on Fabor Records. Penned by Miller, *From a Jack To A King* was originally released in the USA in 1957. He also penned the hit songs *Dark Moon* and *Invisible Tears*. Miller severed all ties with the music business in the mid 1970's.

Date	Pos	Wks	ARTIST / Record Title *Label & Number*
25 Feb 63	1(9)	14	• 1. FROM A JACK TO A KING *London HL 9658*
08 Feb 65	8	4	2. DO WHAT YOU DO, DO WELL *London HL 9937*

Date	Pos	Wks	ARTIST / Record Title *Label & Number*

Roger MILLER — *4 Weeks*

Born Roger Dean Miller on January 2, 1936 in Fort Worth, Texas, USA. Disc debut: *Happy Child* (1957). Worked with Ray Price and Faron Young before going solo in 1960. Won six Grammy's in 1965 for *King Of The Road*. Wrote score for 1985 Broadway musical *Big River*. Died from lung cancer on October 25, 1992.

Date	Pos	Wks	ARTIST / Record Title *Label & Number*
17 May 65	5	4	1. KING OF THE ROAD *Philips EBF 1397*

MILLIE — *9 Weeks*

Born Millicent Small on October 6, 1946 in Clarendon, Jamaica. Her singing career began in the early 1960's with a win in the Vere Johns Opportunity Hour talent contest at the Palladium Theatre in Montego Bay, Jamaica. Made her disc debut, *We'll Meet*, as part of a duo, Roy and Millie. Discovered by Chris Blackwell (of Island Records) who brought her to England in late 1963. *My Boy Lollipop* originally recorded by Barbie Gaye, in 1956.

Date	Pos	Wks	ARTIST / Record Title *Label & Number*
04 May 64	1(2)	9	• 1. MY BOY LOLLIPOP *Fontana TF 449*

The MILLIONAIRES — *1 Weeks*

Irish showband formed in Dublin in 1964. Personnel: Joe Doherty (vocals, bass), Michael Conn (vocals, rhythm guitar), Gene Bannon (tenor sax), Michael O'Brien (drums), Billy Doyle (trombone), Jimmy Higgins (trumpet), and Fergie Burke (lead guitar). Disc debut: *The Merry Ploughboy* (1966). Joe Doherty (born October 6, 1943 in Belfast) and Michael Conn (born Michael Connolly in Coalisland, Co. Tyrone) are the featured vocalists on *Winter Winds*. The Millionaires disbanded in 1970. Michael Conn died on December 20, 2008.

Date	Pos	Wks	ARTIST / Record Title *Label & Number*
05 Dec 66	10	1	1. WINTER WINDS *Pye 7N 17208*

Date	Pos	Wks	ARTIST / Record Title *Label & Number*

Hayley MILLS — *3 Weeks*

Actress/singer. Born on April 18, 1946 in London. England. Daughter of English actor, John Mills. She starred in her first film, *Tiger Bay*, at age of 13. Signed to a five year contract by Walt Disney studios in 1960. Film appearances include *Pollyana* (1960), *The Parent Trap* (1961) and *Family Way* (1966). *Let's Get Together* is featured in the film, *The Parent Trap*.

23 Nov 61	6	3	1. LET'S GET TOGETHER *Decca F 21396*

The MINDBENDERS — *1 Weeks*

Group formed by Wayne Fontana in Manchester, England in 1963. Split with Wayne Fontana in October 1965. Personnel: Eric Steward (lead vocals, lead guitar), Bob Land (bass) and Ric Rothwell (drums). Graham Gouldman joined in 1968. Group called it a day in December 1968, with Stewart and Gouldman going on to form 10cc, with Kevin Godley and Lol Crème.

28 Mar 66	9	1	1. A GROOVY KIND OF LOVE *Fontana ETF 644*

See also Wayne Fontana and the Mindbenders

Sal MINEO — *2 Weeks*

Born Salvatore Mineo Jr on January 10, 1939 in The Bronx, New York, USA. Enrolled in stage school at an early age. Nominated for an Oscar as Best Supporting Actor for his performance in the 1955 film, *Rebel Without A Cause*. Other film appearances include *Gene Krupa Story* (1959) and *Exodus* (1960). In 1957, was launched as a pop star. Enjoyed a short but successful run as a teen idol. Continued with a successful acting career that embraced film, television and theatre. Was attacked and stabbed to death on the street on February 12, 1976.

16 Jul 57	-	2	1. START MOVIN' (In My Direction) *Philips EPB 707*

Date	Pos	Wks	ARTIST / Record Title *Label & Number*

Marcello MINERBI — *5 Weeks*

Orchestra leader/composer. Born on August 7, 1928 in Genoa, Italy. Composed the music score for the 1971 film, *Gunman Of One Hundred Crosses.*

Date	Pos	Wks	ARTIST / Record Title *Label & Number*
23 Aug 65	6	5	1. ZORBA'S DANCE • *Pye DRS 54001*

MR BLOE — *5 Weeks*

Group of British session musicians assembled by pianist/arranger Zack Lawrence. Features Harry Pitch on harmonica and Zack Lawrence on piano.

Date	Pos	Wks	ARTIST / Record Title *Label & Number*
25 Jun 70	8	5	1. GROOVIN' WITH MR BLOE • *Pye DJS 216*

Guy MITCHELL — *22 Weeks*

Born Albert Cernick on February 22, 1927 in Detroit, USA. After discharge from US Navy he joined Carmen Cavallaro's Orchestra as vocalist. Recorded under the names Al Cernick and Al Grant. Disc debut: *I Go In When The Moon Comes Out* in 1947 as Al Cernick. Signed to Columbia Records in 1950. Landed a movie contract with Paramount Pictures in 1953, made two films *Those Redheads From Seattle* (1953) and *Red Garters* (1954). Died following surgery on July 1, 1999.

Date	Pos	Wks	ARTIST / Record Title *Label & Number*
30 Aug 55	-	2	1. LET US BE SWEETHEARTS OVER AGAIN *Philips PB 487*
19 Jul 56	-	4	2. GREEN GROWS THE GRASS *Philips PB 456*
15 Jan 57	-	3	3. SINGING THE BLUES *Philips PB 650*
27 Feb 57	-	2	4. KNEE DEEP IN THE BLUES *Philips EPB 669*
21 May 57	-	1	5. ROCK A BILLY *Philips EPB 685*
23 Oct 57	-	4	6. CALL ROSIE ON THE PHONE *Philips EPB 743*
28 Jan 60	5	6	7. HEARTACHES BY THE NUMBER *Philips EPB 964*

The MIXTURES — *5 Weeks*

Formed in Melbourne, Australia in 1965. Personnel: Idris Jones (vocals), Mick Flinn (bass), Peter Williams (lead guitar), and Greg Cooke (drums). Disc debut: *Koko Joe* (1965). Relocated to England in January 1971. Returned to Australia at the end of 1971.

continues over

Date	Pos	Wks	ARTIST / Record Title *Label & Number*
			Mick Flinn quit group in 1972 and formed Springfield Revival with Donna Jones and Ray Martin. Idris Jones composed *Push Bike Song*. Numerous personnel changes during its lifespan. Disbanded in 1976.
11 Feb 71	3	5	1. THE PUSH BIKE SONG *Polydor 2058 083*
			The MOMENTS ***2 Weeks***
			Formed in Hackensack, New Jersey, USA in 1968. Personnel: William Brown, Al Goodman and Harry Ray. In 1979, operated as Ray, Goodman and Brown.
10 Mar 77	6	2	1. JACK IN THE BOX *All Platinum 6146 318*
			The MONKEES ***35 Weeks***
			Group formed in Los Angeles, California in 1965. Recruited from over four hundred applicants for a new comedy-fantasy TV series which debuted on American television on September 12, 1966. Personnel: Davy Jones (born December 30, 1945 in Manchester, England. (vocals), Micky Dolenz (born March 6, 1945 in Tarzana, California, drums, vocals), Michael Nesmith (born December 30, 1942 in Houston, Texas, guitar, vocals), and Peter Tork (born February 13, 1944 in Washington DC, bass, vocals). The Monkees TV series ran for a total of 58 episodes in 1966-1968. Group starred in the film *Head* (1968). Peter Tork left in 1968. Group disbanded in 1969. In 1986 three of the group reformed (minus Mike Nesmith) and enjoyed a hit record *That Was Then This Is Now*.
07 Nov 66	5	3	1. LAST TRAIN TO CLARKSVILLE *RCA ERC 1547*
19 Jan 67	1(5)	9	• 2. I'M A BELIEVER *RCA ERC 1560*
20 Apr 67	6	5	3. A LITTLE BIT ME, A LITTLE BIT YOU *RCA ERC 1580*
13 Jul 67	4	7	4. ALTERNATE TITLE *RCA ERC 1604*
07 Dec 67	1(2)	9	• 5. DAYDREAM BELIEVER *RCA ERC 1645*
18 Apr 68	8	2	6. VALLERI *RCA ERC 1673*

Date	Pos	Wks	ARTIST / Record Title *Label & Number*

Matt MONRO — *20 Weeks*

Born Terence Parsons on December 1, 1930 in Shoreditch, London, England. Worked as vocalist, under the name Al Jordan, with the Harry Leader Band. Came to the attention of popular pianist Winifred Atwell who suggested a name change and was instrumental in persuading Decca Records to sign him. Disc debut *Ev'rybody Falls In Love* on Decca (1956). Switched to Fontana in 1958. A Frank Sinatra parody (recorded under the name Fred Flange) for a Peter Sellers LP, *Songs For Swingin' Sellers*, resulted in George Martin signing Matt Monro to Parlophone. Represented UK in the 1964 Eurovision Song Contest, finishing in second position with *I Love The Little Things*. Died of liver cancer on February 7, 1985.

Date	Pos	Wks	ARTIST / Record Title *Label & Number*
26 Jan 61	2	6	1. PORTRAIT OF MY LOVE *Parlophone R(I) 4714*
30 Mar 61	5	3	2. MY KIND OF GIRL *Parlophone R(I) 4755*
15 Mar 62	9	2	3. SOFTLY AS I LEAVE YOU *Parlophone R(I) 4868*
26 Oct 64	3	7	4. WALK AWAY *Parlophone R(I) 5171*
08 Nov 65	8	2	5. YESTERDAY *Parlophone R(I) 5348*

Vaughn MONROE — *6 Weeks*

Born Vaughn Wilton Monroe on October 7, 1911 in Akron, Ohio, USA. Began playing trumpet aged eleven. In 1930 joined Gilly Lockhard's Jazz Orchestra. In 1931 enrolled at Carnegie Tech's School of Music in Pittsburg. A talented trumpeter, he also studied singing at the New England Conservatory Of Music. Made his recording debut, *Rain*, in 1934, while a member of the Larry Funk Orchestra. Joined the Jack Marshard Orchestra as both vocalist and trumpeter. In 1940, decided to form his own band and almost immediately was offered a recording contract by RCA Victor. Leader of his own Orchestra from 1940 until its demise in 1953. Film appearances include *Singing Guns* (1950) and *Toughest Man In Arizona* (1952). He continued to perform into the 70's. Re-recorded many of his hits for Dot records in the 1960's. Died on May 21, 1973.

continues over

Date	Pos	Wks	ARTIST / Record Title *Label & Number*
26 Oct 54	1(1)	2	• 1. THEY WERE DOING THE MAMBO *HMV IP 934*
16 Jul 59	4	4	2. BATTLE OF NEW ORLEANS *RCA ERC 1124*

Hugo MONTENEGRO his Orchestra & Chorus — *11 Weeks*

Orchestra leader/composer. Born on September 2, in 1925 in New York City, USA. Composed and conducted the soundtrack for films *Hurry Sundown* (1967) and *The Ambushers* (1967). Was arranger/conductor for Harry Belafonte. Died of emphysema on February 6, 1981. *The Good The Bad And The Ugly* features whistling by Muzzy Marcellino.

Date	Pos	Wks	ARTIST / Record Title *Label & Number*
31 Oct 68	1(4)	11	• 1. THE GOOD, THE BAD AND THE UGLY • *RCA ERC 1727*

Chris MONTEZ — *6 Weeks*

Born Ezekiel Christopher Montanez on January 17, 1943 in Los Angeles, USA. Began to sing and write songs at age of fifteen. Signed to Monogram Records in 1961. Disc debut: *All You Had To Do Was Tell Me* (1961).

Date	Pos	Wks	ARTIST / Record Title *Label & Number*
19 Nov 62	3	6	1. LET'S DANCE *London HLU 9596*

The MOODY BLUES — *7 Weeks*

Formed in Birmingham, England in May 1964 as the M&B 5 in the hope of attracting sponsorship from the local Mitchell & Butler brewery. Personnel: Denny Laine (vocals, guitar), Mike Pinder (keyboards), Graham Edge (drums), Ray Thomas (flute) and Clint Warwick (bass). Members had played with various groups in the Birmingham area. Laine and Warwick left in 1966. Replaced by Justin Hayward and John Lodge. Laine joined Wings in 1971. Patrick Moraz replaced Pinder in 1978. Clint Warwick died May 15, 2004.

Date	Pos	Wks	ARTIST / Record Title *Label & Number*
25 Jan 65	4	3	1. GO NOW *Decca F 12022*
28 May 70	1(1)	4	•2. QUESTION *Threshold TH(I) 4*

Date	Pos	Wks	ARTIST / Record Title *Label & Number*

Butch MOORE and CAPITOL SHOWBAND — *36 Weeks*

Born Seamus Moore on January 10, 1940 in Dublin, Ireland. Began his musical career with the Blue Clavons. Was singing with the Billy Carter Band in the National Ballroom when approached by the management of the Capitol Showband with a view to joining the band as lead singer. Joined the Capitol in 1960 as lead vocalist/ rhythm guitarist. Made recording debut on the Capitol's album *Presenting The Capitol Showband* (1962). Ireland's first representative in the Eurovision Song Contest, he sang *Walking The Streets In The Rain* into sixth position in Naples, Italy. Butch left the Capitol Showband in September 1966 to pursue a solo career. Joined the Kings Showband as lead vocalist from mid 1968 to April 1969. Moved to the USA in the early seventies. Died of a heart attack on April 3, 2001.

Date	Pos	Wks	ARTIST / Record Title *Label & Number*
10 Feb 64	3	6	1. FOOLIN' TIME *Piccadilly 7N 35170*
30 Nov 64	1(1)	8	•2. DOWN CAME THE RAIN *Pye 7N 15727*
01 Mar 65	1(2)	6	•3. BORN TO BE WITH YOU *Pye 7N 15789*
29 Mar 65	1(3)	8	•4. WALKING THE STREETS IN THE RAIN *Pye 7N 15832*
09 Aug 65	10	2	5. OUR LOVE WILL GO *Pye 7N 15910*
15 Nov 65	5	3	6. SO MANY WAYS *Pye 7N 15990*
20 Dec 65	5	3	7. A CHRISTMAS WISH E.P. *Pye NEP 24235*

A Christmas Wish EP credit Butch Moore and Capitol and the Choir of St. Mary's School and Home for the Blind, Merrion, Dublin. Tracks on **A Christmas Wish E.P**: Silver Bells / Santa Claus Is Coming To Town // What Child Is This / The Christmas Song.

Gary MOORE — *5 Weeks*

Born Robert William Gary Moore on April 4, 1952 in Belfast, N. Ireland. Learned to play guitar at a young age and involved with several local groups including The Beat Boys, Platform Three and The Substitutes. Moved to Dublin in 1968 and joined Brush Shiels in Skid Row. In 1973, formed the Gary Moore Band and released an album, *Grinding Stone*, on CBS.

continues over

Date	Pos	Wks	ARTIST / Record Title *Label & Number*
			Joined Thin Lizzy in January 1974. His stay was brief, he left in April. Member of Colosseum 11 1975-78. Filled in for Brian Robertson with Thin Lizzy for a US tour in 1977. In 1978, Moore rejoined Lizzy for the third time, replacing Brian Robertson. Left in 1979 to form G-Force. *Parisienne Walkways* features uncredited guest vocal by Phil Lynott.
17 May 79	5	5	1. **PARISIENNE WALKWAYS** MCA MCA *419*
			Jane MORGAN ***2 Weeks***
			Born Jane Currier on December 25, 1920 in Boston, USA. Brought up in Florida. Moved to New York where she studied at the Juilliard School of Music. While performing in New York night club was spotted by French impressario Bernard Hilda who offered her a singing contract to perform in France. Following success in Europe she returned to USA. Signed a recording deal with Kapp Records. Gilbert Becaud and Dick Manning composed *The Day The Rains Came*.
19 Feb 59	10	2	1. **THE DAY THE RAINS CAME** *London HLR 8751*
			Doretta MORROW and Richard KILEY ***3 Weeks***
			Female/male vocal duo. Doretta Morrow born Doretta Marano on January 27, 1928 in Brooklyn, New York, USA. The soprano starred in several Broadway musicals including *The King And I* (1950) and *Kismet* (1953). Co-starred with Mario Lanza in the 1952 film, *Because You're Mine*. Retired from showbusiness when she married. Cousin of singer, Vic Damone. Died of cancer on February 28, 1968. Richard Kiley born on March 31, 1922 in Chicago, USA. Made his musical debut in the Broadway production of *Kismet* in 1953. Appeared in the films *The Blackboard Jungle* (1955) and *The Little Prince* (1974). Won a Tony award as Best Actor (Musical) in 1959 for *Redhead*. Won a Tony Award for his role of Don Quixote in the 1966 stage production of *Man Of La Mancha*.

continues over

Date	Pos	Wks	ARTIST / Record Title *Label & Number*
			Died from bone marrow cancer on March 5, 1999. Doretta and Richard performed *Stranger In Paradise* in the Broadway musical, *Kismet.*
07 Jun 55	-	3	1. STRANGER IN PARADISE *Philips PB 435*
			The MOTORS ***4 Weeks***
			Formed in London, England in February 1977. Personnel: Nick Garvey (guitar), Andy McMaster (guitar), Bram Tchaikovsky (guitar), and Ricky Wernham (drums). Disc debut: *Dancing The Night Away* (1977). Disbanded in 1981.
22 Jun 78	8	3	1. AIRPORT *Virgin VS 219*
31 Aug 78	10	1	2. FORGET ABOUT YOU *Virgin VS 222*
			MOTT THE HOOPLE ***3 Weeks***
			Had their roots in Hereford, England as The Silence, were also known as the Doc Thomas Group at various times. In May 1969, auditioned for Island Records executive, Guy Stevens, who liked the band, but not the lead singer. An advert for a singer was placed in the Melody Maker, and Ian Hunter got the job. Guy Stevens, came up with the name, Mott The Hoople, after having read the novel by Willard Manus. Personnel: Ian Hunter (born on June 3, 1946 in Shrewsbury, England, lead vocals), Mick Ralphs (guitar), Overend Watts (bass), Verden Allen (keyboards) and Dale Griffin (drums). Band split in March 1972, but David Bowie persuaded the band to reform and offered one of his songs, *All The Young Dudes*, which the band duly recorded, with Bowie producing the session. Ian Hunter left in 1974. Remaining members continued under the name Mott. Disbanded in 1979.
07 Sep 72	4	3	1. ALL THE YOUNG DUDES *CBS 8271*

Date	Pos	Wks	ARTIST / Record Title *Label & Number*

Nana MOUSKOURI *1 Weeks*

Born Ioanna Mouskouri on October 13, 1934 in Chania, Crete, Greece. Moved to Athens at age of thirteen. Studied at the Musical Conserviatory in Athens. Disc debut: *Les Enfants Du Piree* (1958). Represented Luxembourg in the 1963 Eurovision Song Contest. Fluent in several languages including French, English, German, Spanish and Greek. Appointed a UNICEF Goodwill Ambassador in October 1993. Elected Member of the European Parliament 1994-1999.

04 May 72	8	1	1. FOUR AND TWENTY HOURS *Philips 6010 060*

MOUTH and MacNEAL *9 Weeks*

Dutch vocal duo formed in 1971 when producer Hans van Hemert brought together solo artists, Big Mouth (born Willem Duyn on March 31, 1937 in Haarlem) and Maggie MacNeal (born Sjoukje 't Spijker on May 5, 1950 in Krabbendan). Disc debut: *Hey You Love* (1971). Performed *I See A Star* at 1974 Eurovision Song Contest, finishing in third position. Duo split in December 1974.

09 May 74	1(2)	9	• 1. I SEE A STAR *Decca F 13504*

The MOVE *21 Weeks*

Formed in late 1965 from the cream of various groups on the Birmingham beat group scene. Personnel: Carl Wayne (vocals), Roy Wood (vocals, guitar), Bev Bevan (drums), Ace Kefford (bass), and Trevor Burton (guitar). Kefford left in April 1968. Trevor Burton departed in February 1969, replaced by Rick Price. Carl Wayne left in January 1970, replaced by Jeff Lynne. The groups debut disc, *Night of Fear*, was based on Tchaikovsky's *1812 Overture*. Harold Wilson, then Prime Minister of England, successfully sued the band over a postcard caricature designed to publicize their 1967 single, *Flowers In The Rain*. *Flowers* was the first record played on BBC Radio 1 on September 30, 1967.

continues over

Date	Pos	Wks	ARTIST / Record Title *Label & Number*

Group disbanded in 1972. Roy Wood and Jeff Lynne formed the Electric Light Orchestra and following his departure from ELO in late 1972 Roy Wood formed Wizzard. Roy Wood lead vocals on *Fire Brigade* and *Blackberry Way*. Carl Wayne died of cancer on August 31, 2004.

02 Feb 67	6	3	1. NIGHT OF FEAR *Deram DM(I) 109*
12 Oct 67	4	7	2. FLOWERS IN THE RAIN *Regal Zonophone RZ(I) 3001*
07 Mar 68	9	4	3. FIRE BRIGADE *Regal Zonophone RZ(I) 3005*
30 Jan 69	2	7	4. BLACKBERRY WAY *Regal Zonophone RZ(I) 3015*

MUD — *33 Weeks*

Formed in Mitcham, Surrey, England in 1963, when the Mourners decided on a name change to Mud. Personnel: Les Gray (born on April 9, 1946 in Carshalton, England,, lead vocals), Rob Davis (lead guitar), Ray Stiles (bass) and Pete Gray (drums). In 1967 offered a recording contract with CBS and decided to go pro, Pete was unwilling and Dave Mount brought in. First pro gig on March 31, 1968 at Marquee Club. Disc debut: Flower Power (Oct. 1967). Also recorded for Philips. In 1972, Mickie Most put the group in touch with songwriters/ producers Nicky Chinn and Mike Chapman and Mud signed a contract with RAK. Appeared in 1975 film, *You're Never Too Young To Rock*. In April 1975, split with Chinn and Chapman and Rak and signed to Private Stock. Around this time ex Candlewick Green keyboard player Andy Ball joined the group on stage and in the studio. In 1977, Les Gray signed to Warner Brothers as a solo artist. He left Mud in 1978. Margo Henderson (vocals) was brought in. Mud continued in various guises. Les Gray died from a heart attack on February 21, 2004. Dave Mount died on December 2, 2006.

22 Nov 73	9	1	1. DYNAMITE *Rak RAK 159*
24 Jan 74	1(2)	6	•2. TIGER FEET *Rak RAK 166*
25 Apr 74	5	2	3. THE CAT CREPT IN *Rak RAK 170*
15 Aug 74	7	2	4. ROCKET *Rak RAK 178*

Date	Pos	Wks	ARTIST / Record Title *Label & Number*
02 Jan 75	1(2)	3	• 5. LONELY THIS CHRISTMAS *Rak RAK 187*
27 Feb 75	3	3	6. THE SECRETS THAT YOU KEEP *Rak RAK 194*
01 May 75	1(3)	6	• 7. OH BOY *Rak RAK 201*
17 Jul 75	9	2	8. MOONSHINE SALLY *Rak RAK 208*
23 Oct 75	9	1	9. L'L'LUCY *Private Stock PVT 41*
01 Jan 76	2	7	10. SHOW ME YOU'RE A WOMAN *Private Stock PVT 45*

MUNGO JERRY — *21 Weeks*

Formed in London, England in 1969 by Ray Dorset.. Signed to Pye Records by in house producer, Barry Murray. Personnel: Ray Dorset (born Raymond Edward Dorset on March 21, 1946 in Ashford, Middlesex, England, vocals, harmonica, guitar), Colin Earl (piano), Mike Cole (bass) and Paul King (banjo). The group named after a character in T S Elliot's *Book Of Practical Cats*. Numerous personnel changes over the groups lifespan. John Godfrey replaced Mike Cole in 1971. King and Earl left in 1972. Ray Dorset composed all of the groups hits. He also composed, *Feels Like I'm In Love*, a UK chart-topper, for Kelly Marie, in 1980. In 1995, a reggae version of *In The Summertime* by Shaggy, complete with samples of Ray Dorset's vocal and guitar, made the top five in the UK and number one in the USA.

Date	Pos	Wks	ARTIST / Record Title *Label & Number*
25 Jun 70	1(3)	10	• 1. IN THE SUMMERTIME *Dawn DNX 2502*
11 Mar 71	5	3	2. BABY JUMP *Dawn DNX 2505*
24 Jun 71	6	4	3. LADY ROSE *Dawn DNX 2510*
26 Jul 73	4	4	4. ALRIGHT, ALRIGHT, ALRIGHT *Dawn DNS 1037*

The MUPPETS — *3 Weeks*

American puppet group created for television by Jim Henson. Henson was also creator of childrens TV series Sesame Street. The Muppets featured Kermit The Frog, Miss Piggy, Fozzie Bear, Animal and Gonzo. *Halfway Down The Stairs* was performed by Jerry Nelson (as Kermit's nephew Robin). Jim Henson died on May 16, 1990.

Date	Pos	Wks	ARTIST / Record Title *Label & Number*
30 Jun 77	6	3	1. HALFWAY DOWN THE STAIRS Pye *7N 45698*

Date	Pos	Wks	ARTIST / Record Title *Label & Number*

MURPHY and the SWALLOWS ***9 Weeks***

Born Margaret Murphy on February 3, 1953 in Glenamaddy, Co. Galway, Ireland. Discovered by Swallows manager, Noel Carty, playing bass and singing in a local group with her two brothers. Joined the Swallows in October 1971. Left band in August 1974. Married Sean Gorham in 1975. Relocated to London playing pubs and clubs. Returned to Ireland in 1989. The Swallows formed in 1970 by ex members of the Premier Aces. Personnel: Murphy (lead vocals/bass), Jimmy O'Neill (guitar/organ), Ronnie Creevey (lead guitar), Mickey Belton (drums), Sonny Ward (tenor saxophone), Michael Kane (tenor sax) and Johnny Carroll (trumpet).

Date	Pos	Wks	Title
06 Jan 72	3	4	1. DON'T TAKE ADVANTAGE OF ME *Play PLAY 9*
22 Jun 72	5	5	2. NED KELLY *Play PLAY 22*

Anne MURRAY ***5 Weeks***

Born Morna Anne Murray on June 20, 1945 in Springhill, Nova Scotia, Canada. Studied piano for six years. At age of fifteen, began taking classical voice lessons. Graduated from the University of New Brunswick with a degree in Physical Education. In 1966, auditioned successfully for *Sing Along Jubilee,* a regional Television programme. After spending a year teaching PE at a high school in Summerside, Prince Edward Island, she decided to give the music business a 'try'. Her first solo album, *What About Me*, released on Arc Records, in 1968. Signed with Capitol in 1969. *You Needed Me* won her a Grammy Award for Best Pop Vocal Performance in 1978. In 1989, following her involvement with Canada's Save The Children Fund the Springhill Anne Murray Center was opened in recognition of her tireless work for this charity.

Date	Pos	Wks	Title
25 Jan 79	7	5	1. YOU NEEDED ME *Capitol CL 16011*

Date	Pos	Wks	ARTIST / Record Title *Label & Number*

Ruby MURRAY — *21 Weeks*

Born on March 29, 1935 in Belfast, N. Ireland. Her hoarse singing voice was a result of a throat operation in early childhood. In 1954, following an appearance in the revue *Mrs Mulligan's Hotel* at the Metropolitan Theatre, Edgeware Road, London, was spotted by television producer, Richard Afton. He offered her a position as resident singer on the BBC TV series, *Quite Contrary*, replacing Joan Regan. Signed to Columbia Records by Ray Martin. Disc debut: *Heartbeat* (1954). On March 19, 1955 Ruby made chart history when five of her records had a placing in the Top Twenty of that week, *Softly Softly* (2), *Let Me Go Lover* (5), *Happy Days And Lonely Nights* (14), *Heartbeat* (15) and *If Anyone Finds This, I Love You* (17). Married Bernie Burgess (of the Jones Boys vocal group) in 1957. Starred in the 1956 film, *A Touch Of The Sun*. Wrote several songs with her pianist, Colin Keyes, including *I'm In Love With The Boy Next Door* and *Hurry Home*. Died on December 17, 1996. A plaque in her memory was unveiled on March 26, 2006 at the Ulster Hall in Belfast.

Date	Pos	Wks	ARTIST / Record Title *Label & Number*
15 Feb 55	-	7	1. SOFTLY SOFTLY *Columbia IDB 542*
30 Aug 55	-	1	2. EVERMORE *Columbia IDB 562*
11 Oct 55	-	3	3. I'LL COME WHEN YOU CALL *Columbia IDB 578*
09 Dec 55	-	2	4. THE VERY FIRST CHRISTMAS OF ALL *Columbia IDB 588*
03 Jan 56	-	1	5. SLOWLY WITH FEELING *Columbia IDB 588*
19 Jun 56	-	1	6. HONESTLY I DO *Columbia IDB 638*
17 Oct 56	-	1	7. YOU ARE MY FIRST LOVE *Columbia IDB 638*
04 Jun 57	-	1	8. MR. WONDERFUL *Columbia IDB 706*
25 Jun 59	6	4	9. GOODBYE JIMMY GOODBYE *Columbia DB(I) 4305*

Ruby MURRAY and Brendan O'DOWDA — *1 Weeks*

Irish female/male vocal duo. Ruby Murray born on March 29, 1935 in Belfast, Co. Antrim. Brendan O'Dowda born on October 1, 1925 in Dundalk, Co. Louth.

continues over

Date	Pos	Wks	ARTIST / Record Title *Label & Number*

It was orchestra leader/producer Norrie Paramor, who got the idea to team up Ruby and Brendan on record. Ruby and Brendan also recorded two other duets, *Eileen O'Grady* and *Doonaree,* which appeared on the 1964 album, *St Patricks Day.* Ruby Murray died on December 17, 1996. Brendan O'Dowda died on February 22, 2002. *A Pretty Irish Girl* was performed by Sean Connery and Janet Munro in the 1959 film, *Darby O'Gill And The Little People.*

02 Jul 59	8	1	1. A PRETTY IRISH GIRL *Columbia IDB 734*

MUSHROOM — *8 Weeks*

Formed in Dublin, Ireland in 1973. Personnel: Aonghas MacAnally (lead guitar/tin whistle/vocals), Pat Collins (violin/vocals), Alan Brown (bass /guitar/vocals), Colm 'Link' Lynch (drums/percussion/vocals) and Michael Power (organ/harpischord/vocals). Made debut on April 21, 1973 in Kilkenny. Disc debut: *Devil Among The Tailors* (1973). Issued their only album, *Early One Morning*, in 1973. It is now one of the most collectable Irish albums. Colm Lynch and Michael Power quit the group in August 1974. Group broke up in August 1975.

02 Aug 73	4	8	1. DEVIL AMONG THE TAILORS *Hawk HASP 320*

Date	Pos	Wks	ARTIST / Record Title *Label & Number*

N

NANCY and LEE ***9 Weeks***

Female/male vocal duo. Nancy Sinatra born on June 8, 1940 in Jersey City, New Jersey, USA. First child of Frank and Nancy Sinatra. Lee Hazlewood born Barton Lee Hazlewood on July 9, 1929 in Mannford, Oklahoma, USA. The songwriter/producer/disc jockey had his first song, *Four Bell Love Alarm*, registered with BMI in 1953. Made his disc debut, *Pretty Jane*, in 1958 under the name, Mark Robinson. While working as a dj at KCKY radio station in Coolige, Arizona, he met guitarist Duane Eddy and a historic musical partnership was formed. Composed the hit songs *The Fool* (Sandford Clark), *Houston* (Dean Martin) and *Boots* (Nancy Sinatra). Died of renal cancer on August 4, 2007.

Date	Pos	Wks	ARTIST / Record Title *Label & Number*
14 Oct 71	1(6)	9	• 1. DID YOU EVER? *Reprise K 14093*

See also Nancy Sinatra

Johnny NASH ***13 Weeks***

Born John Lester Nash on August 19, 1940 in Houston, Texas, USA. Discovered by Arthur Godfrey in 1957. Signed by ABC Paramount Records. Disc debut: *A Teenager Sings The Blues* (1957). Film appearances include *Take A Giant Step* (1958) and *Key Witness* (1960). Recorded *Hold Me Tight* at Byron Lee's Federal Studio in Jamaica.

Date	Pos	Wks	ARTIST / Record Title *Label & Number*
26 Sep 68	6	3	1. HOLD ME TIGHT *Regal* Zonophone *RZ(I) 3010*
31 Aug 72	9	1	2. I CAN SEE CLEARLY NOW *CBS 8113*
02 Nov 72	6	5	3. THERE ARE MORE QUESTIONS THAN ANSWERS *CBS 8351*
17 Jul 75	1(1)	4	• 4. TEARS ON MY PILLOW *CBS 3220*

Date	Pos	Wks	ARTIST / Record Title *Label & Number*
			Ricky NELSON ***19 Weeks***
			Born Eric Hilliard Nelson on May 8, 1940 in Teaneck, New Jersey, USA. Son of bandleader Ozzie Nelson. At the age of eight joined his parent's radio and TV show, *The Adventures Of Ozzie And Harriet*. Disc debut: *I'm Walking* (1957). Dropped the 'y' from his Christian name in 1961. Film appearances include *Here Come The Nelsons* (1952), *Rio Bravo* (1959) and The *Wackiest Ship In The Army* (1960). Formed the Stone Canyon Band in 1969. Inducted into the Rock and Roll Hall of Fame in 1987. Died in a plane crash in Dekalb, Texas, USA on December 31, 1985.
18 Feb 58	-	1	1. STOOD UP *London HLP 8542*
17 Sep 58	-	1	2. POOR LITTLE FOOL *London HLP 8670*
11 Jun 59	10	3	3. IT'S LATE *London HLP 8817*
27 Aug 59	8	1	4. NEVER BE ANYONE ELSE BUT YOU *London HLP 8817*
29 Oct 59	4	2	5. JUST A LITTLE TOO MUCH *London HLP 8927*
22 Jun 61	1(4)	11	•6. HELLO MARY LOU *London HLP 9347*
			Sandy NELSON ***6 Weeks***
			Drummer. Born Sander Nelson on December 1, 1938 in Santa Monica, California, USA. Attended High School with Jan Berry, Dean Torrence and Phil Spector. Started his career as drummer with the Kip Tyler Band. Started to play recording sessions in the late 1950's. In 1963, was involved in a motor cycle accident and as a result his right foot had to be amputated. He recovered and was able to continue as a session musician.
21 Jan 60	7	4	1. TEEN BEAT • *Top Rank JAR 197*
11 Jan 62	6	2	2. LET THERE BE DRUMS • *London HLP 9466*
			The NEW SEEKERS ***35 Weeks***
			Formed by ex-Seeker, Keith Podger, in London, England in June 1969, following the demise of the Seekers. Personnel: Eve Graham, Lyn Paul, Marty Kristian, Peter Doyle and Paul Layton. Disc debut: *Meet My Lord* (1969).

continues over

Date	Pos	Wks	ARTIST / Record Title *Label & Number*
			Represented the UK in the 1972 Eurovision Song contest with *Beg Steal Or Borrow*, finishing in second position. Peter Doyle left the group in May 1973, replaced by Peter Oliver. In May 1974, Eve and Lyn departed and the group disbanded. Group reformed in May 1976 with Eve Graham, Marty Kristian, Paul Leyton, Kathy Ann Rae and Danny Finn. Over the years have been many many personnel changes. In the current lineup, Paul Leyton is the only original member.Lyn Paul is lead vocals on *Beg Steal Or Borrow*, *You Won't Find Another Fool Like Me* and *I Get A Little Sentimental Over You*. Peter Doyle died of cancer on October 13, 2001.
12 Aug 71	1(3)	10	• 1. NEVER ENDING SONG OF LOVE *Philips 6006 125*
13 Jan 72	1(2)	7	• 2. I'D LIKE TO TEACH THE WORLD TO SING (in perfect harmony) *Philips 6006 184*
16 Mar 72	3	4	3. BEG STEAL OR BORROW *Philips 6006 202*
29 Jun 72	3	10	4. CIRCLES *Philips 6000 058*
24 Jan 74	1(1)	2	• 5. YOU WON'T FIND ANOTHER FOOL LIKE ME *Polydor 2058 421*
18 Apr 74	9	2	6. I GET A LITTLE SENTIMENTAL OVER YOU *Polydor 2058 439*

The NEW VAUDEVILLE BAND — *3 Weeks*

Formed by songwriter, Geoff Stephens in London, England in late 1966, following the chart success of *Winchester Cathedral*. John Carter (ex Ivy League) sang the lead vocal on the recording of *Winchester Cathedral*, with session musicians providing the musical backing. With a hit in the chart, Stephens now had to assemble a touring band to support the demand for New Vaudeville appearances. A chance meeting with singer/songwriter Alan Klein resulted in Klein becoming the front man of the New Vaudeville Band. Personnel: Alan Klein aka Tristram Seventh Earl of Cricklewood (lead vocals), Mick Wilsher (lead guitar), Bob Kerr (trumpet), Hugh Watts (trombone), Neil Korner (bass), Henri Harrison (drums) and Stan Haywood (piano).

continues over

Date	Pos	Wks	ARTIST / Record Title *Label & Number*
			Disbanded in late 1969. The song was originally titled *Westminster Cathedral.*
24 Oct 66	6	3	1. WINCHESTER CATHEDRAL *Fontana ETF 741*

NEW WORLD — *14 Weeks*

Formed in Brisbane, Australia in 1965 as the New World Trio. Disc debut: *Try To Remember* (1969). Relocated to Britain in early 1970. Signed with Decca Records. Personnel: John Lee (lead vocals), Mel Noonan and John Kane. Were in the process of returning to Australia when they got to appear on the top television talent show, *Opportunity Knocks.* They were an immediate success. Spotted by songwriters, Nicky Chinn and Mike Chapman who brought the group to the attention of RAK Records boss, Mickie Most. In late 1970, signed to RAK Records. In 1972, released the original version of *Living Next Door to Alice*, as their follow up to *Sister Jane.* It failed to chart. Four years later, a revamped version by Smokie climbed into the top five on both the British and Irish charts.

Date	Pos	Wks	ARTIST / Record Title *Label & Number*
22 Jul 71	3	8	1. TOM TOM TURN AROUND *Columbia IDB 788*
08 Jun 72	2	6	2. SISTER JANE *Columbia IDB 807*

Anthony NEWLEY — *28 Weeks*

Born Anthony George Newley on September 24, 1931 in Hackney, London, England. As a teenager, he played role of the *Artful Dodger*, in 1948 film version of *Oliver Twist.* In the 1959 film, *Idle On Parade*, he played the role of rock 'n' roll singer, Jeep Jackson. It launched his career as a singer. Songwriting credits include the theme to the James Bond movie *Goldfinger* and the successful stage musica, *I Stop The World, I Want To Get Off* (1961). Died from cancer on April 15, 1999.

Date	Pos	Wks	ARTIST / Record Title *Label & Number*
11 Feb 60	1(5)	9	• 1. WHY *Decca F 11194*
21 Apr 60	2	9	2. DO YOU MIND *Decca F 11220*
15 Sep 60	5	3	3. IF SHE SHOULD COME TO YOU *Decca F 11254*
22 Dec 60	5	4	4. STRAWBERRY FAIR *Decca F 11295*
13 Apr 61	7	3	5. AND THE HEAVENS CRIED *Decca F 11331*

Date	Pos	Wks	ARTIST / Record Title *Label & Number*

Olivia NEWTON-JOHN *24 Weeks*

Born on September 26, 1948 in Cambridge, England. Moved with her family to Australia at age of five. Returned to England in 1965 working as part of a female vocal duo, Pat and Olivia. Disc debut: *Till You Say You'll Be Mine* (1966). Joined the ill fated pop group Toomorrow in 1971., before signing as a solo artist to Pye International. Represented UK in 1974 Eurovision Song Contest performing *Long Live Love*, finishing in fourth position. Film appearances include: *Grease* (1978) and *Xanadu* (1980). Diagnosed with breast cancer in 1992, made a full recovery from surgery. Is now United Nations Ambassador for the Environment.

Date	Pos	Wks	ARTIST / Record Title *Label & Number*
22 Apr 71	6	3	1. IF NOT FOR YOU *Pye 7N 25543*
25 Nov 71	9	2	2. BANKS OF THE OHIO *Pye 7N 25568*
08 Mar 73	5	4	3. TAKE ME HOME COUNTRY ROADS *Pye 7N 25599*
28 Mar 74	9	1	4. LONG LIVE LOVE *Pye 7N 25638*
14 Jul 77	1(2)	5	• 5. SAM *EMI 2616*
02 Nov 78	1(1)	5	• 6. HOPELESSLY DEVOTED TO YOU *RSO RSO 017*
14 Dec 78	9	4	7. A LITTLE MORE LOVE *EMI EMI 2879*

See also John Travolta and Olivia Newton-John

Paul NICHOLAS *3 Weeks*

Born Paul Oscar Beuselinck on December 3, 1945 in Peterborough, England. Pop star who changed into a very successful actor. Starred in the popular TV sit-com *Just Good Friends* (1983). Film appearances include: *Stardust* (1974), *Yesterday's Hero* (1979) and *The Jazz Singer* (1980). Played the role of Rum Tum Tugger in the original London cast of the musical, Cats, in 1981.

Date	Pos	Wks	ARTIST / Record Title *Label & Number*
11 Nov 76	8	3	1. DANCING WITH THE CAPTAIN *RSO 2090 201*

NILSSON *11 Weeks*

Born Harry Edward Nilsson 111 on June 15, 1941 in Brooklyn, New York, USA. Dropped out of high school and moved to New York. While working as a computer programmer at a bank, began writing songs in his spare time.

continues over

Date	Pos	Wks	ARTIST / Record Title *Label & Number*

After having songs recorded by Glen Campbell and The Monkees, left the bank to work full time as a songwriter and singer. Signed with RCA in early 1967 and in October of that year released the album, *Pandemonium Shadow Show*. Won a Grammy Award in 1972 for *Without You*, in the category, Best Pop Vocal Performance Male. Died from a heart attack on January 15, 1994.

Date	Pos	Wks	ARTIST / Record Title *Label & Number*
24 Feb 72	1(2)	8	• 1. WITHOUT YOU *RCA RCA 2165*
18 Nov 76	5	3	2. WITHOUT YOU (re-issue) *RCA RCA 2733*

NINA and FREDERIK — *2 Weeks*

Husband and wife vocal duo. Nina Magdalene Moller born July 15, 1932 in Copenhagen, Denmark. Frederik born Frederik Jan Gustav Floris Baron van Pallandt on May 4, 1932 in Copenhagen, Denmark. Nina and Frederik made first professional appearance at Mon Coeur night club in Copenhagen in July 1, 1957. The couple separated in 1969, divorced in 1976. Frederik was shot dead at his home in Manila, Philippines on May 15, 1994.

Date	Pos	Wks	ARTIST / Record Title *Label & Number*
17 Dec 59	3	2	1. MARY'S BOY CHILD *Columbia DB(I) 4375*

1910 FRUITGUM CO. — *4 Weeks*

Formed in Lynden, New Jersey, USA in 1967. Spotted by producers Jeff Katz and Jerry Kasenetz while performing under the name Jeckell and The Hydes. Personnel: Mark Gutkowski (vocals, organ), Floyd Marcus (vocals, drums), Pat Karwan (vocals, lead guitar), Steve Mortkowitz (bass) and Frank Jeckell (vocals, rhythm guitar).

Date	Pos	Wks	ARTIST / Record Title *Label & Number*
25 Apr 68	5	4	1. SIMON SAYS *Pye 7N 25447*

Date	Pos	Wks	ARTIST / Record Title *Label & Number*
			Gary NUMAN ***9 Weeks***
			Born Gary Anthony James Webb on March 8, 1958 in London, England. Started his musical career as a member of the group, Meanstreet. Formed Tubeway Army in 1977. Personnel: Gary Numan (vocals), Paul Gardiner (bass) and Gerald Lidyard (drums). Signed with Beggars Banquet in 1978. Disc debut: *That's Too Bad*. Dropped the Tubeway Army tag in August 1979 and all subsequent record releases are credited to Gary Numan.
05 Jul 79	3	5	1. ARE FRIENDS ELECTRIC *Beggars Banquet BEG 18*
20 Sep 79	5	3	2. CARS *Beggars Banquet BEG 23*
07 Dec 79	9	1	3. COMPLEX *Beggars Banquet BEG 29*
			Are Friends Electric credit: *Tubeway Army*

Date	Pos	Wks	ARTIST / Record Title *Label & Number*

O

Brendan O'BRIEN and the DIXIES ***82 Weeks***

Born on July 23, 1941 in Cork. Ireland. In 1956, after watching the first Elvis Presley movie, *Love Me Tender*, traded in his trumpet and bought a guitar. Formed a skiffle group, the Comets Swing Group and when group disbanded joined the Johnny Burns Showband. Moved to London in 1960 to take up a position as a junior draughtsman. Returned to Cork in July 1961 to join Dixielanders (Dixies) as lead singer/rhythm guitarist. Disc debut: *It Depends On You* (1963). Dixies personnel: Brendan O'Brien (lead vocals/guitar), Steve Lynch (guitar), Chris O'Mahoney (bass), Joe McCarthy (drums), Finbar O'Leary (organ), Sean Lucey (tenor sax) and Theo Cahill (tenor sax/trombone). Brendan and Joe McCarthy departed from the Dixies in December 1971 to form their own band, Stage 2. On October 1, 1974, Brendan suffered serious injury (from electrical power surge), while on stage at a charity gig in the Stardust Ballroom, Cork. As a result was inactive on music scene for several years. Made the first of several comebacks in 1980. The Dixies broke up in 1976. Reformed on December 26, 1982, with their original lineup, minus Finbar O'Leary. The Dixies called it a day in mid 1990's. Theo Cahill died on July 23, 1988. Chris O'Mahoney died on July 10, 1990. Finbar O'Leary died on June 12, 2002. Brendan O'Brien died of a heart attack on April 3, 2008.

Date	Pos	Wks	ARTIST / Record Title *Label & Number*
23 Dec 63	10	1	1. CHRISTMAS TIME *Parlophone DIP 502*
20 Apr 64	6	4	2. I'M COUNTING ON YOU *Parlophone DIP 503*
10 Aug 64	4	5	3. IT'S ONLY MAKE BELIEVE *Parlophone DIP 504*
08 Feb 65	7	5	4. LOVE'S MADE A FOOL OF YOU Parlophone R*(I)* *5223*
07 Jun 65	10	1	5. HE'S GOT YOU *Pye 7N 15845*
08 Nov 65	2	10	6. I LOVE YOU MORE TODAY *Pye 7N 15975*

continues over

Date	Pos	Wks	ARTIST / Record Title *Label & Number*
24 Jan 66	4	5	7. TOGETHER AGAIN *Pye 7N 17005*
27 Jun 66	2	10	8. IT DOESN'T MATTER ANYMORE *Pye 7N 17121*
21 Nov 66	9	3	9. SAVE THE LAST DANCE FOR ME *Pye 7N 17200*
15 Aug 68	1(1)	13	• 10. LITTLE ARROWS *Pye 7N 17591*
28 Nov 68	2	8	11. KATIE'S KISSES *Pye 7N 17640*
21 Aug 69	4	12	12. THE JOYS OF LOVE *Honey COMB 5*
01 Jul 71	8	2	13. SALLY SUNSHINE *Play PLAY 002*
11 May 72	5	3	14. BEAUTIFUL SUNDAY *Dolphin DOS 97*

Christmas Time, I'm Counting On You, It's Only Make Believe credit: The Dixielanders featuring Brendan O'Brien. Love's Made A Fool Of You, He's Got You, Little Arrows, Katies Kisses, The Joys Of Love credit: The Dixies. Beautiful Sunday credit: Brendan O'Brien and Stage 2

Dermot O'BRIEN and his CLUBMEN 38 Weeks

Accordionist/pianist/trombonist/composer/vocalist born on October 24, 1932 in Ardee, County Louth, Ireland. A talented gaelic footballer, Dermot captained the Louth Senior Football team who captured the 1957 All Ireland Title. Formed his own ceili quartet in 1957. Changed to modern in 1962, when he launched his Clubmen. Achieved a number 46 position on the British Singles Chart in 1966 with The Merry Ploughboy. Left the showband circuit in 1972 to concentrate on the cabaret scene. Moved to the USA in the 1980's. Died of cancer on May 22, 2007.

Date	Pos	Wks	ARTIST / Record Title *Label & Number*
22 Aug 66	3	5	1. I WALK THE LINE *Envoy* ENV *013*
26 Sep 66	1(6)	10	• 2. THE MERRY PLOUGHBOY *Envoy ENV 016*
19 Jan 67	8	3	3. HOME BOYS HOME *Envoy ENV 020*
18 Nov 71	7	8	4. THE OLD CLADDAGH RING *Release RL 597*
30 May 74	3	8	5. SPANCIL HILL *Release RL 725*
04 Sep 75	8	3	6. THE BOYS OF KILLYBEGS *Release RL 779*
14 Oct 76	10	1	7. SKIBBEREEN *Release RL 835*

Date	Pos	Wks	ARTIST / Record Title *Label & Number*

Des O'CONNOR *11 Weeks*

Comedian/singer/TV chat show host. Born Bernard O'Connor on January 12, 1932 in Stepney, London. England. At the age of ten, moved to Northampton. Signed amateur forms with Northampton Football Club. Played for the Colts side for a couple of seasons. After completing his national service in the RAF, he worked as a Butlins Redcoat. In 1954 worked his first ever Summer season, sixteen weeks at the Arcadia, Lowestoft. Compere/comedian on the March 1958 tour of Britain by Buddy Holly and the Crickets. First came to national notice, when he appeared for six weeks, on the TV programme, *Spot The Tune*, during latter part of 1958. Disc debut in 1957 on Columbia with *Moonlight Swim*. In 1963, hosted his own television series, The Des O'Connor Show. Launched his own TV chat show, Des O'Connor Tonight, in 1977. His autobiography, *Bananas Can't Fly*, published in 2001. Hosted the Channel 4 TV quiz programme, *Countdown* (2006-2008).

Date	Pos	Wks	ARTIST / Record Title *Label & Number*
18 Jul 68	1(2)	10	• 1. I PRETEND *Columbia DB(I) 8397*
09 Jan 69	9	1	2. ONE, TWO, THREE, O'LEARY *Columbia DB(I) 8492*

Jim O'CONNOR and the NEVADA *4 Weeks*

Born on May 17, 1939 in Dublin, Ireland. Interested in music from an early age. Joined the Blue Clavons in late 1950's. Moved to the Jets Showband in early 1960's. In 1964, a revamped Jets became the Nevada Showband. Left the Nevada in 1978 to go into band management. The Nevada Showband formed in Dublin in 1964. Personnel: Jim O'Connor (bass, vocals), Red Hurley (vocals), Kelley (vocals), Val Kearney (trombone), Peter Hayden (drums), Bunty Hayden (tenor sax), Liam Hurley (guitar) and Willie Walsh (trumpet).

Date	Pos	Wks	ARTIST / Record Title *Label & Number*
17 Dec 70	6	4	1. CHRISTMAS TIME IN INNISFREE *Release RL 558*

Date	Pos	Wks	ARTIST / Record Title *Label & Number*
			***Rory O'CONNOR and the DIXIES* 5 Weeks**
			Born John O'Connor on March 19, 1948 in Waterford, Ireland. Started playing in showbands and groups from the age of fifteen. Moved to London in the 1960's where he played guitar and trombone with a number of bands including The Detroits, the houseband in the Hibernian Ballroom, Fulham. At the invitation of Dixies bandleader, Sean Lucey, joined the Cork band in September 1973. It was with the Dixies he was given the stage name 'Rory'. As a songwriter, he reached the finals of the Castlebar International Song Contest on two occasions. Disc debut: *Goodbye My Love Goodbye* (1974). Left the Dixies in June 1975. Formed his own band, The Rory O'Connor Chapter, concentrating on the cabaret scene. Quit the music business in the mid 1990's due to pressure of work with the newspaper, The Munster Express. In 2007, after being absent from the recording studio for over thirty years, Rory recorded one of his own songs, *From Deise's Shore*, and released it on CD.
28 Feb 74	6	5	1. GOODBYE MY LOVE GOODBYE *Play PLAY 71*
			***Cahir O'DOHERTY* 8 Weeks**
			Born Cahir Joseph O'Doherty on January 12, 1948 in Ballymena, Co. Antrim, N. Ireland. Started his musical career in 1963 as a member of the beat group, Gentry. Played role of Pontius Pilate in 1973 Dublin production of *Jesus Christ Superstar.* In 1974, played the role of Pharoah in the Dublin stage production of *Joseph and the Amazing Technicolour Dreamcoat.* Launched the Dazzle Band in May 1974. Emigrated to USA in 1980's. *Salute To Elvis* was only available as twelve inch single.
01 Aug 74	4	4	1. SONG OF THE KING *EMI EMD 4015*
17 Nov 77	6	4	2. SALUTE TO ELVIS *CBS 9221*

Date	Pos	Wks	ARTIST / Record Title *Label & Number*

Shaun O'DOWD and TOP LEAGUE *1 Weeks*

Born on July 31, 1944 in Carrick on Shannon, Co. Leitrim, Ireland. Started his musical career with a local group The Telstars. Was a member of the Kevin Woods Band for a period. Emigrated to London in early 60's where he joined Lee Lynch and The Blue Angels. Returned to Ireland in 1967 to joined the Donie Collins Showband. Disc debut: *Get Down With It* Left Collins in 1972 to join the newly formed Top League. After leaving Top League in September 1975 he formed his own band, Ding A Ling.

25 Jul 74	9	1	1. SILVER MOON *EMI EMD 4014*

Michael O'DUFFY *3 Weeks*

Born on November 29, 1928 in Derry, N.Ireland. Moved to Dublin in the 1940's to study music. Won the Golden Voice competition at the Adelphi Theatre. This win led to him broadcasting on Ireland's national radio station, Radio Eireann. His success led to tours in America, Australia and Russia. While living in USA he hosted his own very popular radio show on WOR in New York. Film appearances include *The Rising Of The Moon* (1957) and *Johnny Nobody* (1961). *Slattery's Mounted Fut* was featured in the 1957 John Ford film *The Rising Of The Moon*. Died on April 19, 2003.

18 Jun 57	-	3	1. SLATTERY'S MOUNTED FUT *Nixa N 15074*

ODYSSEY *1 Weeks*

Originally formed in New York, USA in 1968 as a family act, the Lopez Sisters. When Carmen Lopez dropped out in 1976, the remaining sisters decided to bring in a male singer and Odyssey was born. Personnel: Lillian Lopez (lead vocals), Louise Lopez and Tony Reynolds. Spotted by RCA executive, Tommy Mottola, who signed the group to the label. Following the success of *Native New Yorker*, Tony Reynolds was replaced by Billy McEachern.

26 Jan 78	7	1	1. NATIVE NEW YORKER *RCA PC 1129*

Date	Pos	Wks	ARTIST / Record Title *Label & Number*

Esther and Abi OFARIM ***5 Weeks***

Husband and wife vocal duo. Esther Ofarim born Esther Zaied on June 13, 1941 in Zafed, near Nazareth, Israel. Abi Ofarim born Abraham Reichstadt on October 5, 1937 in Tel Aviv, Israel. Came together in 1959 in the Hebrew 'Theatre Club'. Married in 1960. Divorced in 1970. Esther represented Switzerland in the 1963 Eurovision Song Contest with the song *T'en Va Pas*, finishing in second place.

14 Mar 68	5	5	1. CINDERELLA ROCKEFELLA *Philips EBF 1640*

Darby O'GILL ***7 Weeks***

Bandleader/trumpeter. Born Earl Gill on May 12, 1933 in Dublin, Ireland. Learned to play trumpet as a child. In late 1950's led the Earl Gill Orchestra who were resident in Dublin's Metropole Hotel. Formed Earl Gill Showband in 1960. Changed name to The Hoedowners in 1965 when bands residency on television programme, *Hoedown*. Adopted the pseudonym, Darby O'Gill (Tim Pat), as part of a publicity drive to launch the single, *Poor Poor Farmer*.

18 Feb 71	3	7	1. POOR POOR FARMER *Dolphin DOS 78*

Shay O'HARA and the ROYAL BLUES ***2 Weeks***

Born in Bagnalstown, County Carlow, Ireland. Moved to Dublin at age of ten. Joined Royal Blues in 1963. Disc debut: *Love's Gonna Live Here* (1965). Departed from the Royal Blues in March 1968 to join Premier Aces as lead singer. Split with Premier Aces in June 1969. Emigrated to Australia in early 1970's. Died on March 20, 2009.

19 Dec 66	8	2	1. SANTO NATALE *Pye 7N 17228*

OHIO EXPRESS ***3 Weeks***

Formed in Mansfield, Ohio, USA as Sir Timothy and The Royals. Personnel: Dale Powers (vocal, lead guitar), Doug Grassel (rhythm guitar), Jim Pfahler (organ), Tim Corwin (drums) and Dean Kastran (bass).

continues over

Date	Pos	Wks	ARTIST / Record Title *Label & Number*
			Songwriter, Joey Levine, is the vocalist on *Yummy Yummy Yummy*. Their final USA chart entry, *Sausalito* was recorded in England by the group that would become 10cc.
11 Jul 68	5	3	1. YUMMY YUMMY YUMMY *Pye 7N 25459*

Sean O'SE — *2 Weeks*

Born on January 16, 1936 in Cork, Ireland. In 1959, received a call from composer/musician Sean O'Riada to join Ceoltoiri Chualann. Came to the fore as a singer with songs such as *Puc Ar Buile* and *Maidirin Rua*. Continued to work as a teacher at the Cathedral School in Gurranebrahor, Cork during his musical career. Vocalist with the Blarney Ceili Band for a period. Sean was featured, singing a verse in Irish, on the 2004 number one hit record, *The Langer*, by Tim O'Riordan and Natural Gas.

Date	Pos	Wks	ARTIST / Record Title *Label & Number*
03 Feb 72	5	2	1. THE MANCHESTER RAMBLER *Play PLAY 11*

Gilbert O'SULLIVAN — *57 Weeks*

Born Raymond Edward O'Sullivan on December 1, 1946 in Waterford, Ireland. Family moved to Swindon, England when Raymond was age seven.. Worked as a postal clerk before his musical breakthrough. First public appearance at St Josephs Comprehensive School, Swindon in 1964. Began gigging around Swindon with various local bands. In 1967, he moved to London and began to do the rounds of the song publishing companies. Landed a writing contract with April Music and a recording contract with CBS. Disc debut: *Disappear* (1967) under the name Gilbert. After a disappointing start to his musical career he contacted Gordon Mills, manager of Tom Jones and Englebert Humperdinck and began sending him songs. Gordon signed up Raymond gave him a new image and signed him to MAM Records. In 1982, Gilbert took out a lawsuit against the MAM organisation over unpaid royalties and related matters.

continues over

Date	Pos	Wks	ARTIST / Record Title *Label & Number*

The matter was settled in 1985 with O'Sullivan winning control of his songs and all the masters of his recordings. *Alone Again (Naturally)*, was composed by Gilbert about the death of his father. *Clair* was inspired by his manager Gordon Mills three year old daughter. Gordon Mills played harmonica on the recording. Gilbert now lives in Jersey in the Channel Islands.

Date	Pos	Wks	ARTIST / Record Title *Label & Number*
17 Dec 70	2	8	1. NOTHING RHYMED *MAM 3*
13 Jan 72	7	2	2. NO MATTER HOW I TRY *MAM 53*
16 Mar 72	2	5	3. ALONE AGAIN (NATURALLY) *MAM 66*
06 Jul 72	1(2)	7	• 4. OOH-WAKKA-DOO-WAKKA-DAY *MAM 78*
19 Oct 72	1(5)	8	• 5. CLAIR *MAM 84*
29 Mar 73	1(3)	8	• 6. GET DOWN *Mam 96*
20 Sep 73	2	5	7. OOH BABY *Mam 107*
22 Nov 73	3	4	8. WHY, OH WHY, OH WHY *MAM 111*
28 Feb 74	4	2	9. HAPPINESS IS ME AND YOU *MAM 114*
19 Dec 74	5	5	10. CHRISTMAS SONG *MAM 124*
03 Jul 75	7	3	11. I DON'T LOVE YOU BUT I THINK I LIKE YOU *MAM 130*

Johnny OTIS SHOW — *4 Weeks*

Drummer/vocalist/pianist/impresario/disc jockey/bandleader. Born John Otis Veliotes on December 28, 1921 in Vallejo, California, USA. Began his musical career in 1939 as a drummer with Count Otis Matthews West Oakland House Rockers. In 1943, relocated to Los Angeles, where he joined Harlan Leonard's Rockets. Formed his own band in 1945. Disc debut: *Harlem Nocturne* (1945). In early 1950's began a successful career as a disc jockey, this led to a weekly variety show on television. *The Johbny Otis Show* was on TV in Los Angeles for eight years. Signed to Capitol Records in 1957. Inducted into the Rock and Roll Hall of Fame in 1994. *Ma (He's Making Eyes At Me For)* features Marie Adams and The Three Tons Of Joy (Sadie and Francine McKinley).

Date	Pos	Wks	ARTIST / Record Title *Label & Number*
07 Jan 58	-	4	1. MA (HE'S MAKING EYES AT ME) *Capitol CL(I) 13794*

Date	Pos	Wks	ARTIST / Record Title *Label & Number*

Fran O'TOOLE — *17 Weeks*

Born Francis O'Toole on February 8, 1947 in Bray, Co. Wicklow, Ireland. Started his musical career at the age of twelve, playing clarinet at Theatre Royal, Dublin. Formed his own group in mid 60's and soon after joined the Chosen Few. Following a split in the Miami Showband in September 1967, Fran was asked to join the band on keyboards and vocals. Disc debut: *Pledge Of Love* (1970). In August 1971, won the RTE television talent series, *Reach For the Stars.* In 1975, appeared on RTE TV series, *Me And My Music.* Died on July 31, 1975 at the hands of terrorists in Northern Ireland. The Miami Showband was returning to Dublin from a dance date in the Castle Ballroom, Banbridge, Co. Down, N. Ireland, when they were the victims of a sectarian ambush by the UVF. Three members of the Miami were murdered, Fran O'Toole, Tony Geraghty and Brian McCoy.

Date	Pos	Wks	ARTIST / Record Title *Label & Number*
17 Oct 74	8	7	1. CLAP YOUR HANDS AND STAMP YOUR FEET *Emerald MD 1179*
25 Sep 75	3	8	2. LOVE IS *Mint CHEW 1*
28 Jul 77	7	2	3. OUT THERE SINGING *Mint CHEW 17*

Joe O'TOOLE – See Sandie Jones and Joe O'Toole

Mike OLDFIELD — *7 Weeks*

Born Michael Gordon Oldfield on May 15, 1953 in Reading, England. Began composing music at the age of ten. After leaving school joined up with his sister Sally, in the group Sallyangie. For a period of time was bass player with Kevin Ayers and the Whole World. Began experimenting with sounds and instruments on his musical compositions, but was unable to place his original works with any record company. In 1973, was approached by Richard Branson, who was in the process of forming Virgin Records, and was offered a recording contract.

continues over

Date	Pos	Wks	ARTIST / Record Title *Label & Number*
			Oldfield's album, *Tubular Bells*, was Virgin's first release and its success helped establish Virgin as a record label. Oldfield left Virgin in 1992.
29 Jan 76	10	1	1. IN DULCE DUBILO • *Virgin VS 131*
06 Jan 77	2	6	2. PORTSMOUTH • *Virgin VS 163*
			OLIVER ***5 Weeks***
			Born William Swofford on February 22, 1945 in North Wilkesboro, North Carolina, USA. Founder member of the band Good Earth. Gave up the music business in 1982, to become a builder's representative. Died of cancer on February 12, 2000. *Good Morning Starshine* featured in the hit Broadway musical, *Hair.*
25 Sep 69	2	5	1. GOOD MORNING STARSHINE *CBS 4435*
			Roy ORBISON ***78 Weeks***
			Born Roy Kelton Orbison on April 23, 1936 in Vernon, Texas, USA. Formed his own band the Wink Westerners in 1949. Disc debut: *Ooby Dooby* (1956) on the Je-Wel label. In 1956 he signed to Sun Records. Moved to RCA Victor in 1958. Signed to Monument in 1959. Toured Britain with the Beatles in 1963. His wife, Claudette, killed in a motorcycle accident on June 7, 1966. His two sons died in a house fire in 1968. Inducted into the Rock 'n' Roll Hall of Fame in 1987. In the spring of 1988 teamed up with Bob Dylan, Jeff Lynne, Tom Petty and George Harrison to record an album under the name The Traveling Wilburys. Died of a heart attack on December 6, 1988 in Madison, Tennessee, USA.
06 Oct 60	1(2)	15	• 1. ONLY THE LONELY *London HLU 9149*
12 Jan 61	8	2	2. BLUE ANGEL *London HLU 9207*
05 Apr 62	1(1)	8	• 3. DREAM BABY *London HLU 9511*
22 Apr 63	1(2)	12	• 4. IN DREAMS *London HLU 9676*
17 Jun 63	8	2	5. FALLING *London HLU 9727*
14 Oct 63	1(1)	9	• 6. BLUE BAYOU / MEAN WOMAN BLUES *London HLU 9277*
23 Mar 64	9	1	7. BORNE ON THE WIND *London HLU 9845*
25 May 64	1(3)	10	• 8. IT'S OVER *London HLU 9882*

continues over

Date	Pos	Wks	ARTIST / Record Title *Label & Number*
05 Oct 64	1(1)	9	• 9. OH PRETTY WOMAN *London HLU 9919*
21 Dec 64	8	2	10. PRETTY PAPER *London HLU 9930*
18 Jul 66	8	2	11. LANA *London HLU 10051*
12 Sep 66	4	6	12. TOO SOON TO KNOW *London HLU 10067*

Donny OSMOND — *25 Weeks*

Born on December 9, 1957 in Ogden, Utah, USA. Seventh son of George and Olive Osmond. Teamed up with his brothers in the Osmonds family vocal group in 1963. First recorded solo in 1971. Signed to Capitol in 1988 and made a return to the US Charts.

Date	Pos	Wks	ARTIST / Record Title *Label & Number*
13 Jul 72	2	9	1. PUPPY LOVE *MGM 2006 104*
05 Oct 72	2	3	2. TOO YOUNG *MGM 2006 113*
23 Nov 72	4	3	3. WHY *MGM 2006 119*
05 Apr 73	3	4	4. TWELFTH OF NEVER *MGM 2006 199*
30 Aug 73	1(2)	5	• 5. YOUNG LOVE *MGM 2006 300*
06 Dec 73	10	1	6. WHEN I FALL IN LOVE *MGM 2006 365*

Donny and Marie OSMOND — *8 Weeks*

Brother and sister vocal duo. Donny born on December 9, 1957 in Ogden, Utah, USA. Marie born on October 13, 1959 in Ogden, Utah, USA. Hosted the Donny and Marie Show on American television 1976-78. Appeared in the 1978 film, *Goin' Coconuts*.

Date	Pos	Wks	ARTIST / Record Title *Label & Number*
05 Sep 74	3	4	1. I'M LEAVING IT ALL UP TO YOU *MGM 2006 446*
30 Jan 75	7	4	2. MORNING SIDE OF THE MOUNTAIN *MGM 2006 474*

Little Jimmy OSMOND — *15 Weeks*

Born on April 16, 1963 in Canoga Park, California, USA. Youngest member of the Osmond family. An accomplished artist and cartoonist, he published his first childrens book, *If Santa Were My Daddy*, in 1996.

Date	Pos	Wks	ARTIST / Record Title *Label & Number*
21 Dec 72	1(4)	11	• 1. LONG HAIRED LOVER FROM LIVERPOOL *MGM 2006 109*
12 Apr 73	6	4	2. TWEEDLEE DEE *MGM 2006 125*

Date	Pos	Wks	ARTIST / Record Title *Label & Number*

Marie OSMOND — *1 Weeks*

Born Olive Marie Osmond on October 13, 1959 in Ogden, Utah, USA. Began performing in concert with her brothers at age of fourteen. Co-hosted the TV series, *Ripley's Believe It Or Not*, from 1985 to 1986.

Date	Pos	Wks	ARTIST / Record Title *Label & Number*
13 Dec 73	6	1	1. **PAPER ROSES** *MGM 2006 315*

The OSMONDS — *13 Weeks*

Family vocal/instrumental group formed in Ogden, Utah, USA in 1957. In 1962, won a contract to appear on the weekly Andy Williams Show on American television. Spent seven years on the show. Donny joined the group in 1963. Personel: Alan (born June 22, 1949), Wayne (born August 28, 1951, Merrill (born on April 30, 1953), Jay (born March 2, 1955) and Donny (born on December 9, 1957). Merrill lead vocals on all groups major hits. Disbanded in 1980. All seven Osmonds appeared together on stage for the first time in twenty years on August 14, 2007, at the Orleans Casino in Las Vegas. The event was filmed for PBS.

Date	Pos	Wks	ARTIST / Record Title *Label & Number*
09 Aug 73	5	2	1. **GOIN' HOME** *MGM 2006 288*
15 Nov 73	7	1	2. **LET ME IN** *MGM 2006 321*
05 Sep 74	2	5	3. **LOVE ME FOR A REASON** *MGM 2006 458*
12 Jun 75	1(1)	5	• 4. **THE PROUD ONE** *MGM 2006 520*

OUR KID — *1 Weeks*

Male vocal quartet formed in Liverpool, England in 1976. Came to the attention of Polydor Records via a win on ITV's New Faces talent show in May 1976. Personnel: Kevin Rowan (lead vocal), Brian Farrell, Terry McCreith and Terry Baccino. Due to their young age (Kevin Rowan was only thirteen years old) performing restrictions by the Liverpool Education Committee led to the early demise of the group.

Date	Pos	Wks	ARTIST / Record Title *Label & Number*
29 Jul 76	7	1	1. **YOU JUST MIGHT SEE ME CRY** *Polydor 2058 729*

Date	Pos	Wks	ARTIST / Record Title *Label & Number*

OVERLANDERS — *2 Weeks*

British group formed in 1963 as a vocal trio. Personnel: Laurie Mason (vocals, piano), Peter Bartholomew (vocals, rhythm guitar), Paul Arnold (vocals, lead guitar). Disc debut: *Summer Skies And Golden Sands* (1963). In October 1965, two members added to lineup, Terry Widlake (bass) and David Walsh (drums). In August 1966, Paul Arnold quit group to pursue a solo career. Replaced by Ian Griffiths. Group disbanded in October 1967.

Date	Pos	Wks	ARTIST / Record Title *Label & Number*
31 Jan 66	5	2	1. MICHELLE *Pye 7N 17034*

Date	Pos	Wks	ARTIST / Record Title *Label & Number*

P

The PADDY WAGON ***5 Weeks***

Formed by the McGettigan brothers from San Francisco, USA who relocated to Ireland in September 1971 with the intention of forming a band. Personnel: Maurice McGettigan (bass), Hugie McGettigan (drums), Colm McGettigan (lead guitar), Patsy Frayne (guitar), Mike Mannion (fiddle) and Seamus Downey (tenor sax). Disc debut: *The Ghosts Of The Molly Maguires* (1972). The band split in mid 1972. *Sunday Bloody Sunday* was composed by Maurice McGettigan following the killing of thirteen civilians by British paratroopers in Derry city during a Civil Rights march on Sunday January 30, 1972.

13 Apr 72	1(1)	5	• 1. SUNDAY BLOODY SUNDAY *Columbia IDB 806*

Patti PAGE ***4 Weeks***

Born Clara Ann Fowler on November 8, 1927 in Claremore, Oklahoma, USA. Her father was a section hand on the MKT Railroad and the family moved around a lot. Performed with her sisters, Rema and Ruby, on radio in Muskogee. In 1938, the Fowlers settled in Tulsa. In 1943, Clara got a job on KTUL and performed as Ann Foster on *Melody And Stars* and under the name, Patti Page, hosted *Meet Patti Page*. Made her first recordings with Al Clauser Band for Okla Records in 1945. In the summer of 1946, she was heard singing on radio KTUL by Jack Rael of the Jimmy Joy Orchestra. In December of the same year she joined the band as vocalist. Signed to Mercury Records in July 1947 and debuted for the label with *Every So Often*. Appeared in the 1959 film *Elmer Gantry*. In 1962, left Mercury to sign for Columbia Records. Returned to Mercury in 1970. Also recorded for Epic, Avco and Plantation.

continues over

Date	Pos	Wks	ARTIST / Record Title *Label & Number*
17 Jul 56	-	1	1. TOO YOUNG TO GO STEADY *Mercury MT 104*
04 Sep 56	-	2	2. ALLEGHANY MOON *Mercury MT 112*
02 Oct 56	-	1	3. BORN TO BE WITH YOU *Mercury MT 116*

The PAPER DOLLS — *1 Weeks*

Formed in 1965 in Northampton, England as the Dolly Set. Personnel: Spyder (Pauline Bennett), Copper (Sue Marshall) and Tiger (Suzi Mathis). The girls had known each other since infant school. After leaving school began performing together under the name, the Dolly Set. Renamed the Paper Dolls in April 1968 by songwriter Tony Macauley. Spyder left group in 1970. Copper left in 1972. Replaced by Janet Cobb and Wendy Duckworth. Group disbanded in 1979.

Date	Pos	Wks	ARTIST / Record Title *Label & Number*
16 May 68	9	1	1. SOMETHING HERE IN MY HEART (Keeps A-Tellin' Me No) *Pye 7N 17456*

PAPER LACE — *11 Weeks*

Formed in Nottingham, England in 1969 as Music Box. Changed name in 1973. Personnel: Phil Wright (born April 19, 1948 in Nottingham, lead vocals, drums) Cliff Fish (bass, vocals), Michael Vaughan (guitar) and Chris Morris (guitar). Secured a residency at Tiffany cabaret club in Rochdale, Lancashire. In 1974 entered ITV talent show, Opportunity Knocks. Following their first appearance on show, the group were signed by songwriters, Mitch Murray and Peter Callander, to their Bus Stop record label.

Date	Pos	Wks	ARTIST / Record Title *Label & Number*
28 Mar 74	1(1)	5	• 1. BILLY DON'T BE A HERO *Bus Stop BUS 1014*
23 May 74	5	3	2. THE NIGHT CHICAGO DIED *Bus Stop BUS 1016*
26 Sep 74	7	3	3. BLACK EYED BOYS *Bus Stop BUS 1019*

Norrie PARAMOR — *1 Weeks*

Born on May 15, 1914 in London, England. Studied piano from age of seven. Formed dance band while still at school. Began his professional musical career as an accompanist.

continues over

Date	Pos	Wks	ARTIST / Record Title *Label & Number*

Worked as a pianist and arranger with several London bands including Harry Leader, Jack Harris and Maurice Winnick. Joined Harry Gold and his Pieces of Eight in 1944 and was their featured pianist for six years. Made his first recording, *Saloon Bar Rag*, in 1951. Appointed A&R manager with Columbia Records in 1952. Produced hit recordings for many artists including Eddie Calvert, Cliff Richard, Ruby Murray, Michael Holliday, Frank Ifield and The Shadows. Composed *Frightened City* and the music soundtrack for the 1960 film *Expresso Bongo*. In 1960, he arranged and conducted orchestra for Judy Garland's British recording sessions and was musical director for her London Palladium and concert appearances in Europe. Left EMI in late 1960's. Conductor of the BBC Midland Orchestra 1972-78. Died on September 9, 1979.

Date	Pos	Wks	ARTIST / Record Title *Label & Number*
24 Apr 56	-	1	1. THEME FROM THREEPENNY OPERA • *Columbia IDB 613*

Simon PARK ORCHESTRA — *4 Weeks*

Composer/arranger/conductor. Born in 1946 in Market Harborough, England. Studied piano at Winchester College. Composed music for BBC 2's *Hobby Horse* and mood music *Dawn To Dusk*, for Bounty Bars TV commercial. Also composed music under the pseudonym, Simon Haseley. *Eye Level* was originally produced for the De Wolfe Music Library and selected by Thames Television to be the theme music for the television series, *Van Der Valk*.

Date	Pos	Wks	ARTIST / Record Title *Label & Number*
11 Oct 73	3	4	1. EYE LEVEL • *Columbia DB(I) 8946*

Fess PARKER — *1 Weeks*

Born Fess Elisha Parker on August 16, 1924 in Fort Worth, Texas, USA. Graduated from the University of Texas in 1950 with a Degree in History. Moved to California where he achieved a Masters Degree in drama at the University of Southern California. Began acting professionally in 1951.

continues over

Date	Pos	Wks	ARTIST / Record Title *Label & Number*

In 1954, Walt Disney signed him to play the title role in the film *Davy Crockett King Of The Wild Frontier.* Other starring film roles include *Great Locomotive Chase* (1956), *Old Yeller* (1957) and *Hell Is For Heroes* (1962). During the years 1964-70 starred in and co-produced the network television series, *Daniel Boone.* In 1987, founded the Fess Parker Winery and Vineyard that now produces some of California's finest wines.

17 Jan 56	-	1	1. THE BALLAD OF DAVY CROCKETT *London HL 8220*

David PARTON — *5 Weeks*

Born in Newcastle-under-Lyne, England. Composed *Sad Sweet Dreamer* for Sweet Sensation. Legend has it that when the original singer booked for the *Isn't She Lovely* recording session was unable to do the gig, David Parton who was co-producing the session with Tony Hatch, sang the lead vocal. It was decided to release this version. *Isn't She Lovely* was a track on Stevie Wonder's 1976 album, *Songs In The Key Of Life.*

10 Feb 77	3	5	1. ISN'T SHE LOVELY *Pye 7N 45663*

Dolly PARTON — *4 Weeks*

Born Dolly Rebecca Parton on January 19, 1946 in Sevierville, Tennessee, USA. Made her first recordings in 1957 for Goldband. Moved to Nashville in 1964. Married Carl Dean on May 30, 1966. Spotted by Porter Waggoner in 1967, who signed her as a resident singer on his television programme, *The Porter Waggoner Show.* Dolly stayed for seven years. Signed a recording contract with RCA in 1967. In 1974, left Porter Waggoner to pursue a solo career. Film appearances include *9 to 5* (1980), *The Best Little Whorehouse In Texas* (1982) and *Steel Magnolia* (1989). Earned an Oscar nomination for composing the title song of her debut film, *Nine To Five.* In 1986, founded Dollywood, a Smokey Mountain area theme park in Pigeon Forge, Tennessee. Elected to the Country Music Hall of Fame in 1999.

08 Jul 76	6	4	1. JOLENE *RCA 2675*

Date	Pos	Wks	ARTIST / Record Title *Label & Number*

Don PARTRIDGE *7 Weeks*

Born on October 27, 1944 in Bournemouth, England. Travelled around Europe in the early 1960's as a solo entertainer. Discovered by Don Paul of the Viscounts, while busking as a one-man band on the streets of London. Formed the acoustic group, Accolade, in 1969. Gordon Giltrap was a member for a short period. Group disbanded in 1971. Went back to busking. Moved to Sweden in 1973. Returned to England in 1975. Released the album, *The Highwayman*, in 2004.

Date	Pos	Wks	ARTIST / Record Title *Label & Number*
04 Apr 68	8	1	1. ROSIE *Columbia DB(I) 8330*
27 Jun 68	1(3)	6	•2. BLUE EYES *Columbia DB(I) 8416*

The PARTRIDGE FAMILY *15 Weeks*

The Partridge Family was an American television sitcom with songs, about a family of five fatherless children, who form a band with their widowed mother and tour in a psychedelic van. The series was broadcast on ABC television from 1970 to 1974. Personnel: Shirley Jones (Shirley Partridge) vocals, David Cassidy (Keith Partridge) lead vocals/lead guitar, Danny Bonaduce (Danny Partridge) vocals/bass, Susan Dey (Laurie Partridge) vocals/piano/percussion, Suzanne Crough (Tracy Partridge) vocals/tambourine/percussion, Jeremy Gelbwaks (Chris Partridge 1970-71) drums and Brian Forster (Chris Partridge 1971-74) drums. Series inspired by the real life family pop group, the Cowsills. The Partridge Family musical sound was created by a group of studio musicians. David Cassidy (lead vocals) and Shirley Jones (backing vocals) were the only cast members featured on the recordings.

Date	Pos	Wks	ARTIST / Record Title *Label & Number*
11 Feb 71	2	8	1. I THINK I LOVE YOU *Bell BELL 1130*
10 Aug 72	2	7	2. BREAKING UP IS HARD TO DO *Bell MABEL 1*

See also David Cassidy

Date	Pos	Wks	ARTIST / Record Title *Label & Number*

The PATTERSONS — *4 Weeks*

Family folk vocal group formed in Letterkenny, Co. Donegal, Ireland in 1965. Made first public appearance at a local concert. Achieved sixth position at the 1967 Kilkenny Ballad Festival. Personnel: Dorothy, Christine, Billy and Ronnie Patterson. Disc debut: *Drill Ye Tarriers Drill* (1968). Had their own TV series, *The Patterson's People,* on BBC in 1969. Dorothy left in June 1969. Group broke up in 1973.

Date	Pos	Wks	ARTIST / Record Title *Label & Number*
21 Nov 68	2	4	1. I DON'T WANT TO BE A MEMORY *CBS 3749*

PAUL and PAULA — *3 Weeks*

Male/female vocal duo. Formed in 1962 by Paul (born Ray Hildebrand on December 21, 1940 in Joshua, Texas) and Paula (born Jill Jackson on May 20, 1942 in McCarney, Texas) whilst attending Howard Payne College in Brownwood, Texas, USA. Their debut single, *Hey Paula*, was originally released under the name, Jill and Ray, on LeCam Records. Shelby Singleton of Mercury Records heard the single and signed the duo to the Phillips label and changed their names to Paul and Paula. The duo split in 1965.

Date	Pos	Wks	ARTIST / Record Title *Label & Number*
10 Jun 63	10	3	1. YOUNG LOVERS *Philips 304016 EBF*

Freda PAYNE — *11 Weeks*

Born on September 19, 1945 in Detroit, USA. Her music career started when she won an amateur talent contest at the age of thirteen on WXYZ-TV in her home town. Tasted success on Ted Macks Amateur Hour. At the age of seventeen, Pearl Bailey gave Freda her first professional singing job. Moved to New York in 1963. Made her debut album, *After The Lights Go Down And Much More*, the same year. Signed to Invictus Records in 1969. In 1981, hosted her own television talk show, *Today's Black Woman*. Film appearances include *Book Of Numbers* (1973) and *Private Obsessions* (1995).

Date	Pos	Wks	ARTIST / Record Title *Label & Number*
17 Sep 70	1(6)	11	• 1. BAND OF GOLD *Columbia IDB 767*

Date	Pos	Wks	ARTIST / Record Title *Label & Number*

PEACHES and HERB — *5 Weeks*

Female/male vocal duo formed in Washington, D.C., USA in 1965. Made their record debut, *We're In This Thing Together*, in 1967. The original Peaches, Francine Hurd Barker left in late 1967. Replaced by Marlene Mack. Duo broke up in 1970 with Herb taking up a position as a law enforcement officer. In 1976, Herb, with a new Peaches, Linda Greene (born Washington D.C.), reformed the duo. The duo enjoyed many successes including *Reunited*. Went their separate ways in 1983. Herb Fame (born Herbert Feemster on October 1, 1942 in Washington D.C., USA). Peaches #1 (Francine Hurd Barker) died on August 13, 2005.

Date	Pos	Wks	ARTIST / Record Title *Label & Number*
24 May 79	3	5	1. REUNITED *Polydor POSP 43*

Donald PEERS — *4 Weeks*

Born Donald Rhys Hubert Peers on July 10, 1908 in Ammanford, Dyfed, Wales. The former house painter and decorator made his professional debut as a singer in 1927. In 1949, was given his own BBC radio show, *Cavalier Of Song*. Film appearances include *The Balloon Goes Up* (1942) and *Sing Along WithMe* (1952). Signature tune: *In A Shady Nook By A Babbling Brook*. His autobiography, *Pathway*, published in 1951. The song, *Please Don't Go,* is based on the Barcarolle from Offenbach's, *The Tales Of Hoffman*. Died on August 9, 1973.

Date	Pos	Wks	ARTIST / Record Title *Label & Number*
27 Feb 69	3	4	1. PLEASE DON'T GO *Columbia DB(I) 8502*

Maria PERILLI — *2 Weeks*

Soprano. Born in 1928 near Rome, Italy. Relocated to England with her parents as a child. Educated at the Convent of Notre Dame, Worthing where she was a member of the school choir. Made her concert debut at age of fifteen at the Pier Pavilion, Worthing. Spotted by comedian Max Miller.

continues over

Date	Pos	Wks	ARTIST / Record Title *Label & Number*
			Made her operatic debut in Arthur Benjamin's, *Prima Donna*, at the Fortune Theatre, London.
18 Mar 58	-	2	1. ONE FINE DAY *Philips EPB 791*

PETER and GORDON *17 Weeks*

Male vocal duo, formed in London in 1963 by Peter Asher (born June 22, 1944 1944 in London) and Gordon Waller (born June 4, 1945 in Braemar, Scotland) Met while attending Westminster School for Boys in London. Discovered by EMI A&R man Norman Newell singing at the Pickwick Club in London. Signed to Columbia Records in October 1963. At this time Peter Asher's sister, actress Jane Asher, was dating Paul McCartney, and Paul wrote the duo's first two hits. The duo broke up in 1967. Asher moved to Los Angeles and got involved in record production. Produced hit recordings for several artists including Linda Ronstadt and James Taylor. Gordon made a number of solo recordings. In 1970 was signed to play the part of the Pharoah in the musical *Joseph and His Amazing Technicolour Dreamcoat*. Toured UK and Australia with the production. Peter and Gordon reunited in 2005. Gordon died on July 17, 2009.

Date	Pos	Wks	ARTIST / Record Title *Label & Number*
13 Apr 64	1(2)	6	• 1. A WORLD WITHOUT LOVE *Columbia DB(I) 7225*
06 Jul y 64	8	1	2. NOBODY I KNOW *Columbia DB(I) 7292*
10 May 65	4	7	3. TRUE LOVE WAYS *Columbia DB(I) 7524*
12 Jul 65	5	3	4. TO KNOW YOU IS TO LOVE YOU *Columbia DB(I) 7617*

PETER PAUL and MARY *6 Weeks*

Folk trio. Formed in New York, USA. Made debut at Greenwich Village's Bitter End in late 1961. Signed to Warner Brothers Records. Disc debut: *Peter*, *Paul and Mary* LP (1962). Personnel: Peter Yarrow (born May 31, 1938 in New York City), Noel Paul Stookey (born December 30, 1937 in Baltimore) and Mary Travers (born on November 9, 1936 in Louisville.

continues over

Date	Pos	Wks	ARTIST / Record Title *Label & Number*
			Died September 16, 2009). Disbanded in 1970 to pursue individual interests. Reunited in 1978.
05 Feb 70	2	6	1. LEAVING ON A JET PLANE *Warner Bros* WB *73400*

PETERS and LEE — *13 Weeks*

Male/female vocal duo. Met up in 1969 and formed Peters and Lee in 1970. Toured clubs, pubs and holiday camps for a couple of years. Auditioned for Opportunity Knocks in February 1973. Made seven successive appearances on top rated TV talent show. As a result of their success were signed by Philips Records. Lennie Peters was born Leonard Sergeant in 1939 in London, England. Blinded in an accident at the age of sixteen. Played piano and sang in London pubs. Made a solo single, *Let Tears Begin*, in 1963. Dianne Lee, born Dianne Littlehales in 1950 in Sheffield. Duo broke up in 1980 to pursue solo careers. Reunited in 1986. Lennie died of cancer on October 10, 1992.

Date	Pos	Wks	ARTIST / Record Title *Label & Number*
05 Jul 73	1(5)	11	• 1. WELCOME HOME *Philips 6006 307*
16 May 74	5	2	2. DON'T STAY AWAY TOO LONG *Philips 6006 388*

Ray PETERSON — *10 Weeks*

Born Raymond August Krah on April 23, 1935 in Denton, Texas, USA. As a young child his parents divorced and his mother remarried. His stepfather, Harry Peterson, adopted him and he was raised as Ray Peterson. Began singing in his teens whilst undergoing treatment for polio at Warm Springs Foundation Hospital in Texas. Signed to RCA in 1957. Disc debut: *Fever.* Formed his own label, Dunes Records, named after the Las Vegas Dunes Hotel. His first record for the label, *Corrine Corrina*, was produced by a then relatively unknown, Phil Spector. Died from cancer on January 25, 2005.

Date	Pos	Wks	ARTIST / Record Title *Label & Number*
03 Sep 59	2	8	1. THE WONDER OF YOU *RCA ERC 1131*
06 Oct 60	7	2	2. TELL LAURA I LOVE HER *RCA ERC 1195*

Date	Pos	Wks	ARTIST / Record Title *Label & Number*

Esther PHILLIPS — *2 Weeks*

Born Esther Mae Washington on December 23, 1935 in Galveston, Texas, USA. Moved to Los Angeles in 1940. Spotted by band leader, Johnny Otis, and joined his Revue in 1949. Recorded and toured with the Johnny Otis Orchestra as Little Esther from 1949 until 1954. In 1964, too old to be called Little Esther, she re-christened herself, Esther Phillips. Died from kidney and liver failure on August 7, 1984.

Date	Pos	Wks	ARTIST / Record Title *Label & Number*
06 Nov 75	8	2	1. WHAT A DIFFERENCE A DAY MAKES *Polydor KUDU 925*

Bobby Boris PICKETT and the Crypt Kickers — *2 Weeks*

Born on February 11, 1938 in Somerville, Massachusetts, USA. A member of the Cordials and the Stompers before leaving to pursue an acting career.The Crypt Kickers consisted of Chuck Hamilton (bass), Billy Lee Riley (guitar), Jesse Sailes (drums), Gary Paxton (piano, hammond, backing vocals), Johnny MacRae and Ricki Page (backing vocals). As an actor appeared in TV series *T J Hooker*, *Dr Kildare* and *The Beverly Hillbillies*. Died of leukemia on April 25, 2007.

Date	Pos	Wks	ARTIST / Record Title *Label & Number*
04 Oct 73	5	2	1. MONSTER MASH *London HLU 10320*

PICKETTYWITCH — *3 Weeks*

Formed in London in 1969. Personnel: Polly Brown (vocals), Chris Warren (vocals), Martin Bridges (guitar), Mike Tomich (bass), Keith Hall (drums) and Bob Brittain (keyboards). Group got their name from a modern village just outside Yeovil in Somerset. Disc debut: *You Got Me So I Don't Know* (1969). Several personnel changes took place over the years. Polly Brown left the group on September 2, 1972. *That Same Old Feeling* was originally recorded by The Foundations in 1969.

Date	Pos	Wks	ARTIST / Record Title *Label & Number*
09 Apr 70	6	3	1. THAT SAME OLD FEELING *Pye 7N 17887*

Date	Pos	Wks	ARTIST / Record Title *Label & Number*
			The PIGLETS ***3 Weeks***
			Studio group assembled by producer Jonathan King. Lead vocals by session singers Adrianne Posta and Barbara Kay. *Johnny Reggae* composed by King.
02 Dec 71	6	3	1. JOHNNY REGGAE *Bell BELL 1180*
			PILOT ***8 Weeks***
			Formed in Edinburgh, Scotland in 1974. Personnel: David Paton (vocals, bass), Billy Lyall (keyboards), Stuart Tosh (drums) and Ian Bairnson (guitar). Disc debut: *Just A Smile* (1974). Did their first nationwide tour as headliners in 1975 when they were supported by Smokey. Billy Lyall left group in 1975 to pursue a solo career. Stuart Tosh departed in 1976 and teamed up with 10cc. The group disbanded in 1977. Billy Lyall died in 1989.
28 Nov 74	6	2	1. MAGIC *EMI 2217*
06 Feb 75	1(4)	6	•2. JANUARY *EMI 2255*
			PINK FLOYD ***9 Weeks***
			Progressive rock band formed in England in 1965. Personnel: Syd Barrett (born Roger Keith Barrett on January 6, 1946 in Cambridge, vocals, lead guitar), Roger Waters (bass), Nick Mason (drums), and Rick Wright (keyboards). Originally named Pink Floyd Sound. Barrett named the group after a record he owned by the Georgia bluesmen, Pink Anderson and Floyd Council. Disc debut: *See Emily Play* (1967). David Gilmour (guitar) joined in February 1968. Syd Barrett left group in April 1968. Syd Barrett died on July 7, 2006 from complications arising from diabetes. Richard Wright died on September 15, 2008.
10 Aug 67	10	1	1. SEE EMILY PLAY *Columbia DB(I) 8214*
14 Dec 79	1(4)	8	•2. ANOTHER BRICK IN THE WALL *Harvest HAR 5194*

Date	Pos	Wks	ARTIST / Record Title *Label & Number*

The PIPKINS ***2 Weeks***

Male vocal duo formed in London, England in 1970. Personnel: Roger Greenaway (born on August 19, 1940 in Bristol) and Tony Burrows (born on April 14, 1942 in Exeter, England).

Date	Pos	Wks	ARTIST / Record Title *Label & Number*
30 Apr 70	7	2	1. GIMME DAT DING *Columbia DB(I) 8662*

Gene PITNEY ***27 Weeks***

Born on February 17, 1940 in Hartford, Connecticut, USA. Studied music at school and sang in the church choir. In 1958, formed a group, Gene and the Genials. Disc debut: *Snuggle Up Baby* (1959), a duet with Ginny Mazarro, under the names, Jamie and Jane. Also recorded solo under the name Billy Bryan. In 1960, had first disc issued under his own name, *I'll Find You*. Composed hit songs *Hello Mary Lou* (Ricky Nelson), *He's A Rebel* (The Crystals) and *Rubber Ball* (Bobby Vee). Died from a heart attack on April 5, 2006. He had performed in concert at St. David's Hall, Cardiff, Wales on the previous night (April 4).

Date	Pos	Wks	ARTIST / Record Title *Label & Number*
20 Jan 64	5	6	1. TWENTY FOUR HOURS FROM TULSA *U.A. UP(I) 1035*
07 Dec 64	6	5	2. I'M GONNA BE STRONG *Stateside SS(I) 358*
28 Jun 65	5	5	3. LOOKING THRU THE EYES OF LOVE *Stateside SS(I) 420*
07 Mar 66	5	6	4. BACKSTAGE *Stateside SS(I) 490*
04 Jul 66	2	5	5. NOBODY NEEDS YOUR LOVE *Stateside SS(I) 518*

PLANXTY ***5 Weeks***

Formed in Dublin, Ireland in 1973. Made debut on RTE TV programme, *Capital Folk*. Disc debut: *Three Drunken Maidens* (1972). Personnel: Christy Moore (born Kildare, vocals, guitar), Donal Lunny (guitar, bouzuki), Andy Irvine (mandolin, guitar, harmonica) and Liam Og Flynn (uileann Pipes). Donal Lunny left in October 1973 replaced by Johnny Moynihan. Christy Moore left in September 1974. Replaced by Paul Brady. Disbanded in 1983. Reformed in late 2004 for a series of concerts.

Date	Pos	Wks	ARTIST / Record Title *Label & Number*
18 Jan 72	8	5	1. CLIFFS OF DOONEEN *Polydor 2078 023*

Date	Pos	Wks	ARTIST / Record Title *Label & Number*

PLASTIC BERTRAND *2 Weeks*

Born Roger Jouret on February 24, 1954 in Brussels, Belgium. At the age of nine was singer and drummer with the Buffalo Scouts Band. In 1973 formed the Hubble Bubble Band. Released album in 1975. Starts solo career as Plastic Bertrand in 1977. Represented Luxembourg in the 1987 Eurovision Song contest performing, *Amour Amour,* finishing in twenty first position.

15 Jun 78	4	2	1. CA PLANE POUR MOI *Philips 6078 616*

PLASTIC ONO BAND - See John Lennon

The PLATTERS *38 Weeks*

Formed in 1953 by students attending Jefferson High School in Los Angeles, California, USA as The Flamingos. Founder member Herb Reed came up with the name Platters. Personnel: Tony Williams (lead), David Lynch (second tenor), Paul Robi (baritone), Herb Reed (bass) and Zola Taylor. Disc debut: *Hey Now* (1953) on Federal label. Signed to Mercury in 1953. Tony Williams left in 1960 to pursue a solo career. Replaced by Sonny Turner. Zola Taylor left in 1964. Robi left in 1965. Reed left in 1969. Inducted into the Rock And Roll Hall of Fame in 1990. Inducted into the Vocal Group Hall of Fame in 1998. David Lynch died on January 2, 1981. Paul Robi died on February 1, 1989. Tony Williams died on August 14, 1992. Zola Taylor died on April 30, 2007. In 1997 Herb Reed awarded the exclusive rights to tour as The Platters.

17 Oct 56	-	6	1. ONLY YOU *Mercury MT 117*
15 Jan 57	-	3	2. MY PRAYER *Mercury MT 120*
27 Feb 57	-	5	3. IT ISN'T RIGHT *Mercury MT 130*
07 May 57	-	2	4. ON MY WORD OF HONOUR *Mercury MT 143*
04 Jun 57	-	1	5. ONE IN A MILLION *Mercury MT 145*
18 Jun 57	-	2	6. I'M SORRY *Mercury MT 145*
23 Oct 57	-	2	7. MY DREAM *Mercury MT 156*
29 May 58	-	5	8. TWILIGHT TIME *Mercury MT 214*
12 Feb 59	3	12	9. SMOKE GETS IN YOUR EYES *Mercury AMT(I) 1016*

Date	Pos	Wks	ARTIST / Record Title *Label & Number*

The POLICE *14 Weeks*

Formed in London, England in 1977. Personnel: Sting (vocals/bass), Stewart Copeland (drums) and Henri Padovani (guitar). Disc debut: *Fallout* (1977). In July 1977, Andy Summers was brought into the group and Padovani left in August. Signed to A&M in 1978. Disbanded following a gig on June 11, 1986. Sting (born Gordon Sumner on October 2, 1951 in Wallsend, Tyne & Wear) embarked on solo career. Group inducted into Rock and Roll Hall of Fame in 2003. Group reformed in 2007.

Date	Pos	Wks	ARTIST / Record Title *Label & Number*
09 Aug 79	7	3	1. CAN'T STAND LOSING YOU *A&M AMS 7381*
04 Oct 79	1(1)	5	• 2. MESSAGE IN A BOTTLE *A&M AMS 7474*
07 Dec 79	1(1)	6	• 3. WALKING ON THE MOON *A&M AMS 7494*

Brian POOLE and the TREMELOES *32 Weeks*

Brian Poole born on November 2, 1941 in Dagenham, Essex, England. Formed the Tremeloes in 1959. Personnel: Brian Poole (lead vocals), Ricky West (lead guitar), Alan Blakely (rhythm guitar), Alan Howard (bass) and Dave Munden (drums). Appeared in the *film Just For Fun* (1963). Brian Poole left in 1966 to pursue a solo career. The Tremeloes went on to enjoy a successful career. Alan Blakely died of cancer on June 10, 1996.

Date	Pos	Wks	ARTIST / Record Title *Label & Number*
05 Aug 63	3	7	1. TWIST AND SHOUT *Decca F 11694*
30 Sep 63	1(1)	10	• 2. DO YOU LOVE ME *Decca F 11739*
17 Feb 64	8	5	3. CANDY MAN *Decca F 11823*
08 Jun 64	2	10	4. SOMEONE SOMEONE *Decca F 11893*

See also The Tremeloes

The POPPY FAMILY *7 Weeks*

Formed by Terry Jacks (guitar) and his wife Susan (lead vocals) in Montreal, Canada in 1968. First met when Terry was a member of The Chessmen. Began to play small clubs as a duo. Added Craig McCaw (guitar) and Satwant Singh (percussion) and became The Poppy Family.

continues over

Date	Pos	Wks	ARTIST / Record Title *Label & Number*
			Disc debut: *Beyond The Clouds* (1968). The group, and Terry and Susan's marriage, broke up in July 1973. Both went on to pursue solo careers.
17 Sep 70	1(1)	7	• 1. WHICH WAY YOU GOING BILLY *Decca F 22976*

The POUND HOUNDS *1 Weeks*

Non de plume for The Mellomen. Formed in 1948, the Mellomen provided vocal backing on many of the top hits of the 1950's including *Mambo Italiano*, *This Ole House*, *Where Will The Dimple Be* and *Cool Water*. Personnel: Bill Lee, Bob Stevens, Mat Smith, and Thurl Ravenscroft. Thurl was the voice of *Tony the Tiger* in the television commercial for Kellogs Rice Krispies. The Mellomen appeared in the films *Glenn Miller Story* (1953) and *Trouble With Girls* (1969). Recorded under the name Big John and the Buzzards in 1954. Bob Stevens died in 1961. Bill Lee died on November 15, 1980, Max Smith died on July 23, 1999. Thurl Ravenscroft died on May 22, 2005. *Home Sweet Home* featured in the 1955 Walt Disney animated film, *The Lady And The Tramp*.

Date	Pos	Wks	ARTIST / Record Title *Label & Number*
08 Nov 55	-	1	1. HOME SWEET HOME *Brunswick 05484*

Cozy POWELL *3 Weeks*

Born Colin Flooks on December 29, 1947 in Cirencester, Gloucestershire, England. Started playing drums while still at school. A member of the Jeff Beck Group and the Ace Kefford Stand. Session drummer for Rak Records. Formed Cozy Powell's Hammer in 1974. Joined Rainbow in 1976. Died in a car crash on April 5, 1998.

Date	Pos	Wks	ARTIST / Record Title *Label & Number*
24 Jan 74	7	1	1. DANCE WITH THE DEVIL • *Rak RAK 164*
12 Sep 74	10	2	2. NA NA NA *Rak RAK 180*

Perez 'Prez' PRADO and his Orchestra *4 Weeks*

Born Damaco Perez Prado on December 11, 1916 in Mantanzas, Cuba. Studied classical piano and as a young man played organ and piano in local clubs and cinemas.

continues over

Date	Pos	Wks	ARTIST / Record Title *Label & Number*
			Relocated to Havana in 1942, where he worked with several different bands as pianist and arranger. In 1947 he left Cuba and embarked on a tour of South America. Settled in Mexico City in 1948, where he formed his own band. The following year signed with the international arm of RCA Records. Made his first USA performance in 1951. Died on September 14, 1989.
27 Apr 55	-	4	1. CHERRY PINK AND APPLE BLOSSOM WHITE • *HMV IP 978*
			Trumpet solo on 'Cherry Pink' by Billy Regis.

Elvis PRESLEY — *286 Weeks*

Born Elvis Aaron Presley on January 8, 1935 in Tupelo, Mississippi, USA. Moved with family to Memphis, Tennessee in 1948. Worked as theatre usher and truck driver. Made a private recording of *My Happiness*, for his mother's birthday. This attracted the attention of Sam Phillips head of Sun Records who signed him to the label.. Disc debut: *That's All Right Mama* backed with *Blue Moon Of Kentucky* (July 1954). Signed to RCA Records on November 22, 1955, who bought his contract from Sun, along with his original Sun recordings for 35,000 dollars. On February 10, 1956, Elvis made his first recordings for RCA - *Heartbreak Hotel* and *I Was the One*. First film: *Love Me Tender* in 1956. Served in Germany with US Army from March 24, 1958 to March 5, 1960. Married Priscilla Beaulieu on May 1, 1967. Divorced on October 2, 1973. Their only child, Lisa Marie, was born on February 1, 1968. Elvis's last live performance was in Indianapolis on June 26, 1977. Died in Memphis on August 16, 1977 (age 42) of heart failure caused by prescription drug abuse. Won the Lifetime Achievement Grammy in 1971. Inducted into the Rock 'n' Roll Hall of Fame in 1986.

Date	Pos	Wks	ARTIST / Record Title *Label & Number*
31 Jul 56	-	1	1. HEARTBREAK HOTEL *HMV IP 1114*
12 Feb 57	-	1	2. MYSTERY TRAIN *HMV IP 1217*
16 Jul 57	-	5	3. ALL SHOOK UP *HMV IP 1248*
10 Sep 57	-	3	4. PARALYZED *HMV IP 1255*

Date	Pos	Wks	ARTIST / Record Title *Label & Number*
12 Feb 59	1(1)	10	• 5. ONE NIGHT / I GOT STUNG *RCA ERC 1100*
30 Apr 59	3	8	6. I NEED YOUR LOVE TONIGHT *RCA ERC 1113*
14 May 59	2	16	7. A FOOL SUCH AS I *RCA ERC 1113*
13 Aug 59	5	6	8. A BIG HUNK O' LOVE RCA *ERC 1136*
05 May 60	3	6	9. STUCK ON YOU *RCA ERC 1187*
11 Aug 60	1(3)	10	• 10. A MESS OF BLUES *RCA ERC 1194*
06 Oct 60	4	5	11. THE GIRL OF MY BEST FRIEND *RCA ERC 1194*
03 Nov 60	1(9)	14	• 12. IT'S NOW OR NEVER *RCA ERC 1207*
19 Jan 61	1(6)	10	• 13. ARE YOU LONESOME TONIGHT *RCA ERC 1216*
16 Mar 61	1(7)	11	• 14. WOODEN HEART *RCA ERC 1226*
20 Apr 61	1(8)	14	• 15. SURRENDER *RCA ERC 1227*
14 Sep 61	1(1)	5	• 16. WILD IN THE COUNTRY *RCA ERC 1244*
09 Nov 61	1(5)	9	• 17. HIS LATEST FLAME *RCA ERC 1258*
25 Jan 62	1(6)	14	• 18. ROCK-A-HULA BABY *RCA ERC 1270*
03 May 62	1(10)	15	• 19. GOOD LUCK CHARM *RCA ERC 1280*
19 Jul 62	2	7	20. FOLLOW THAT DREAM E.P. *RCA ERCX 211*
06 Sep 62	1(7)	10	• 21. SHE'S NOT YOU *RCA ERC 1303*
10 Dec 62	1(4)	11	• 22. RETURN TO SENDER *RCA ERC 1320*
11 Mar 63	5	4	23. ONE BROKEN HEART FOR SALE *RCA ERC 1337*
15 Jul 63	1(3)	8	• 24. (You're The) DEVIL IN DISGUISE *RCA ERC 1355*
30 Mar 64	8	2	25. VIVA LAS VEGAS *RCA ERC 1390*
06 Jul 64	6	4	26. KISSIN' COUSINS *RCA ERC 1404*
14 Sep 64	9	3	27. SUCH A NIGHT RCA *ERC 1411*
16 Nov 64	5	2	28. AIN'T THAT LOVING YOU BABY *RCA ERC 1422*
14 Jun 65	1(3)	7	• 29. CRYING IN THE CHAPEL *RCA ERC 1455*
25 Jul 66	7	1	30. LOVE LETTERS *RCA 1526*
19 Dec 66	9	2	31. IF EVERY DAY WAS LIKE CHRISTMAS *RCA ERC 1557*
10 Jul 69	1(4)	9	• 32. IN THE GHETTO *RCA RCA 1831*
11 Dec 69	2	9	33. SUSPICIOUS MINDS *RCA RCA 1900*
19 Mar 70	4	5	34. DON'T CRY DADDY *RCA 1916*
30 Jul 70	1(4)	10	35. THE WONDER OF YOU *RCA 1974*
26 Oct 72	4	2	36. BURNING LOVE *RCA 2267*
18 Jan 73	9	3	37. ALWAYS ON MY MIN*D RCA 2304*
30 Aug 73	7	2	38. FOOL *RCA 2393*
12 Dec 74	4	7	39. MY BOY *RCA 2458*
06 Feb 75	7	3	40. PROMISED LAND *RCA 10074*
21 Oct 76	8	1	41. THE GIRL OF MY BEST FRIEND *(re-issue)* RCA *2729*

Date	Pos	Wks	ARTIST / Record Title *Label & Number*
12 May 77	6	4	42. MOODY BLUE *RCA PB 0857*
08 Sep 77	1(2)	5	• 43. WAY DOWN *RCA PB 0998*
12 Jan 78	6	2	44. MY WAY *RCA PB 1165*

Tracks on **Follow That Dream EP**: Follow That Dream / Angel / What A Wonderful Life / I'm Not The Marrying Kind.

Johnny PRESTON — *9 Weeks*

Born John Preston Courville on August 18, 1939 in Port Arthur. Texas, USA. Formed the Shades while attending Lamar State College of Technology in Beaumont, Texas. Discovered by JP Richardson aka The Big Bopper whilst performing at the Twilight Club in Port Naches. The Big Bopper and country singer, George Jones supplied the Indian yells on *Running Bear*.

Date	Pos	Wks	ARTIST / Record Title *Label & Number*
25 Feb 60	1(2)	9	• 1. RUNNING BEAR *Mercury AMT(I) 1079*

Mike PRESTON — *4 Weeks*

Born Jack Davis on May 14, 1938 in Clapton, East London, England. A keen sportsman he excelled in soccer, swimming, cricket, athletics and boxing. In 1958 Decca Records offered him a recording contract and he cut his debut disc, *A House A Car And A Wedding Ring*. Emigrated to Australia in the 1960's where he worked as a night club singer, TV host and actor.

Date	Pos	Wks	ARTIST / Record Title *Label & Number*
19 Nov 59	2	4	1. MR BLUE *Decca F 11167*

Alan PRICE — *2 Weeks*

Born April 19, 1941 in Fairfield, County Durham, England. Founder member of The Animals. Left the group in 1965. Formed the Alan Price Set in 1965. Disbanded Set in 1968 to pursue a solo career. Teamed up with Georgie Fame in 1971, under the name Fame and Price Together. Composed the music score for the 1973 film, *O Lucky Man*.

Date	Pos	Wks	ARTIST / Record Title *Label & Number*
04 Jul 74	5	2	1. JARROW SONG *Warner Bros. K 16372*

See also the Animals

Date	Pos	Wks	ARTIST / Record Title *Label & Number*

Lloyd PRICE *8 Weeks*

Born on March 9, 1933 in New Orleans, USA. Formed a band with his brother Leo, playing locally at parties and night clubs. A & R man Dave Bartholomew brought Lloyd to the attention of Art Rupe of Specialty Records. For his first recording session Lloyd cut a song, *Lawdy Miss Clawdy*. The title was a saying a local dj Okey-Dokey Smith used as a catch phrase. The year 1952. After leaving US Army formed his own record label KRC Records. In the late 1960's disillusioned with the music business he moved to Africa. Partnered boxing promoter Don King in staging the legendary 'Rumble In The Jungle' which pitted Mohammed Ali against George Foreman in Zaire on October 30, 1974. In the early 1980's, Price formed a corporation developing low-income housing in urban areas.

Date	Pos	Wks	ARTIST / Record Title *Label & Number*
25 Jun 59	3	8	1. PERSONALITY *HMV POP(I) 626*

PRINCE VINCE and the KINGS SHOWBAND *3 Weeks*

Prince Vince, born Frank McEnhill in Dunloe, Co.Donegal, Ireland. In 1957, he entered the Irish Army School of Music in Dublin. Invited to join the Kings Showband in 1962, as lead vocalist. Left in 1967, and moved to London where he joined Chris Lamb and The Universals. In the mid 1970's was resident singer at London's Hilton Hotel. The Kings Showband formed in Naas, Co. Kildare in 1962. Personnel: Prince Vince (lead vocals), Pat Braiden (lead guitar), Ronnie Reynolds (drums), Billy Hopkins (bass), Tommy Lundy (guitar), Dusty Young (trombone), Barry Cluskey (tenor sax) and Brendan McEnhill (tenor sax). Disbanded in 1970.

Date	Pos	Wks	ARTIST / Record Title *Label & Number*
31 Jan 66	4	3	1. BEAUTIFUL DREAMER *Columbia IDB 749*

Date	Pos	Wks	ARTIST / Record Title *Label & Number*

P.J. PROBY — *1 Weeks*

Born James Marcus Smith on November 6, 1938 in Houston, Texas, USA. After graduating in 1957 from Western Military in Alton, Illinoise he moved to Hollywood, where he recorded under the name Jett Powers and cut demos for Elvis Presley. Songwriter Sharon Sheeley suggested a name change to P.J. Proby and he signed to Liberty Records. Disc debut as PJ Proby, *Try To Forget Her* (1961). Invited to England in 1964, by television producer Jack Good, to appear on a Beatles TV special, *Around The Beatles*. Decca signed him to a recording contract unaware that he was under contract to Liberty.

Date	Pos	Wks	ARTIST / Record Title *Label & Number*
20 Jul 64	10	1	1. HOLD ME *Decca F 11904*

PROCOL HARUM — *10 Weeks*

Began life in 1959 in Southend, England as The Paramounts. Broke up in September 1966. In April 1967 Gary Brooker teamed up with lyricist Keith Reid and they formed Procul Harum. Personnel: Gary Brooker (vocals, piano), Matthew Fisher (organ), Ray Royer (guitar), Dave Knights (bass) and Bobby Harrison (drums). Following the success of *Pale*, Royer and Harrison were sacked and ex Paramounts Robin Trower and B J Wilson joined. Session drummer Bill Eyden played on hit recording of *A Whiter Shade Of Pale*. The song was based on Bach's, *Air On A G String*. In 1969, Fisher and Knights left the group with Chris Copping coming in on bass and organ. Group disbanded in 1977. B J Wilson died of pneumonia in October 1990.

Date	Pos	Wks	ARTIST / Record Title *Label & Number*
15 Jun 67	1(4)	8	• 1. A WHITER SHADE OF PALE *Deram DM(I) 126*
09 Nov 67	4	2	2. HOMBURG *Regal Zonophone RZ(I) 3003*

Gary PUCKETT – See The Union Gap

Date	Pos	Wks	ARTIST / Record Title *Label & Number*

PUSSYCAT — *12 Weeks*

Formed in 1963 by the three Kowalczyk sisters, Marianne, Betty and Tonny, in Limburg, Holland as Sweet Reaction. Changed name to Pussycat in 1975. Personnel: Toni Willie (vocals), Marianne Hensen (vocals), Betty Dragstra (vocals), Lou Willie (guitar, vocals), Theo Wetzels (bass), John Theunissen (guitar) and Theo Coumans (drums). Disbanded in 1985.

Date	Pos	Wks	ARTIST / Record Title *Label & Number*
30 Sep 76	1(4)	12	• 1. **MISSISSIPPI** *EMI IEMI 5042*

PYTHON LEE JACKSON — *2 Weeks*

Australian rock group formed in Melbourne in 1965. In October 1968, relocated to London, England. Personnel: David Bently (vocals/keyboards), David Montgomery (drums), Mick Liber (guitar) and Jamie Byrne (bass). In April 1969, the group recorded some tracks with Rod Stewart on vocals. Stewart was brought in when David Bently informed his fellow band members that he didn't think his voice was right for the song, *In A Broken Dream*. Stewart only received a session fee for his performance of the song.

Date	Pos	Wks	ARTIST / Record Title *Label & Number*
09 Nov 72	6	2	1. **IN A BROKEN DREAM** *Young Blood YB 1002*

Date	Pos	Wks	ARTIST / Record Title *Label & Number*

Q

Suzi QUATRO — ***19 Weeks***

Born Susan Kay Quatro on June 3, 1950 in Detroit, Michigan, USA. Her professional career started in mid 60's when she became a TV Go-Go dancer. She later formed the Pleasure Seekers with her two sisters. Spotted playing at a Detroit club by record producer, Mickie Most, who signed her to the RAK Record label. She relocated to London in 1970. Disc debut: *Rolling Stone* (1972). As her chart career came to an end she moved into television appearing in the cult series, *Happy Days*. She also starred in the London West End revival of the musical, *Annie Get Your Gun*. Has also hosted her own series on BBC radio. Her autobiography, *Suzi Quatro Unzipped*, published in August 2007.

Date	Pos	Wks	ARTIST / Record Title *Label & Number*
07 Jun 73	5	4	1. CAN THE CAN *Rak RAK 150*
23 Aug 73	6	1	2. 48 CRASH *Rak RAK 158*
21 Feb 74	1(1)	5	• 3. DEVIL GATE DRIVE *Rak RAK 167*
20 Apr 78	2	5	4. IF YOU CAN'T GIVE ME LOVE *Rak RAK 271*
08 Nov79	5	4	5. SHE'S IN LOVE WITH YOU *Rak RAK 299*

QUEEN — ***41 Weeks***

Formed in London, England in 1972. Personnel: Freddie Mercury (born Fred Bulsara on September 5, 1946 in Zanzibar, vocals), Brian May (guitar), John Deacon (bass) and Roger Taylor (drums). Mercury had recorded under the name Larry Lurex, before forming Queen. Composed soundtrack for the 1980 film, *Flash Gordon*. Mercury died of AIDS on November 24, 1991.

Date	Pos	Wks	ARTIST / Record Title *Label & Number*
14 Nov 74	2	5	1. KILLER QUEEN *EMI 2229*
04 Dec 75	1(6)	13	2. BOHEMIAN RHAPSODY *EMI 2375*
12 Aug 76	5	1	3. YOU'RE MY BEST FRIEND *EMI 2494*
23 Dec 76	6	3	4. SOMEBODY TO LOVE *EMI 2565*
17 Nov 77	3	9	5. WE ARE THE CHAMPIONS *EMI 2708*
07 Dec 78	10	1	6. BICYCLE RACE / FAT BOTTOMED GIRLS *EMI 2870*

continues over

Date	Pos	Wks	ARTIST / Record Title *Label & Number*
12 Apr 79	10	1	7. DON'T STOP ME NOW *EMI 2910*
08 Nov79	2	8	8. CRAZY LITTLE THING CALLED LOVE *EMI 5001*

Brendan QUINN — *16 Weeks*

Born on December 19, 1946 in Magherfelt, Co. Derry, N. Ireland. Joined the Breakaways as lead guitarist/vocalist in 1969. When the bands lead singer, Robin Averill decided to leave, Brendan was elevated to lead vocalist. Disc debut: *Help Me Make It Through The Night* (1970). In 1972, Brendan decided to change name of the band to Cades County. In December 1974, joined Mighty Avons as lead singer. After leaving the Avons in February 1976 formed his own band, the Bluebirds. He picked the name from from a range of Datsun cars. In 1981, relocated to Canada where he stayed for four years.

Date	Pos	Wks	ARTIST / Record Title *Label & Number*
28 Sep 72	5	4	1. FOUR IN THE MORNING *Velvet VE 018*
11 Apr 74	4	6	2. BEHIND CLOSED DOORS *Hawk HASP 337*
28 Jul 77	1(1)	6	• 3. DADDY'S LITTLE GIRL *Emerald MD 1196*

Clem QUINN — *4 Weeks*

Born William (Liam) Quinn on November 6, 1942 in Dublin. Ireland. Member of the Downbeats Quartet. Lead guitarist and founder member of the Miami Showband. Disc debut: *Buck's Polka*. Left the Miami in July 1974. Died in October 1996.

Date	Pos	Wks	ARTIST / Record Title *Label & Number*
06 Dec 65	8	4	1. BUCKS POLKA • *Pye 7N 17006*

See also Dickie Rock and the Miami Showband; Murty Quinn

Murty QUINN — *6 Weeks*

Trombonist/vocalist. Born Martin Quinn on February 5, 1944 in Dublin. Ireland. Started his showbusiness career as a member of the Three Sons. Joined the Chris Lamb Showband in 1961. Disc debut: *Tell Me Darling*. Invited to join the Miami Showband in 1962. Split from the Miami, with three other band members, in September 1967 to form the Sands Showband.

Date	Pos	Wks	ARTIST / Record Title *Label & Number*
17 Jan 66	3	6	1. ONE KISS FOR OLD TIMES SAKE *Pye 7N 17028*

Date	Pos	Wks	ARTIST / Record Title *Label & Number*

R

Date	Pos	Wks	ARTIST / Record Title *Label & Number*
			RACEY ***18 Weeks***
			Formed in Weston-Super-Mare, England in 1977. Spotted by producer Mickie Most playing at the Three Queens pub in their home town. Signed to Rak Records. Personnel: Richard Gower (lead vocals/keyboards), Clive Wilson (drums), Phil Fursdon (guitar) and Pete Miller (drums). Disc debut: *Baby It's You* (1978). Split in 1985.
14 Dec 78	2	8	1. LAY YOUR LOVE ON ME *Rak RAK 284*
05 Apr 79	2	8	2. SOME GIRLS *Rak RAK 291*
20 Sep 79	9	2	3. BOY OH BOY *Rak RAK 297*
			Gerry RAFFERTY ***8 Weeks***
			Born on April 16, 1947 in Paisley, Scotland. Member of Humblebums (with Billy Connolly) 1968-70. First solo album, *Can I Have My Money Back*, released in 1971. Formed Stealers Wheel with Joe Egan in 1972. Left in 1975 to embark on a solo career. Signed to United Artists in in 1978.
23 Mar 78	3	4	1. BAKER STREET *United Artists UP 36346*
05 Jul 79	5	4	2. NIGHT OWL *United Artists UP 36512*
			RAINBOW ***3 Weeks***
			Formed in London, England in May 1975 by Ritchie Blackmore. Personnel: Ritchie Blackmore (guitar),Cozy Powell (drums), Don Airey (keyboards), Graham Bonnet (vocals) and Roger Glover (bass). Bonnet and Powell left in August 1980. Airey left in 1981. Group disbanded in 1984. Reformed in 1994. Cozy Powell died in car accident on April 5, 1998.
18 Oct 79	5	3	1. SINCE YOU'VE BEEN GONE *Polydor POSP 70*

Date	Pos	Wks	ARTIST / Record Title *Label & Number*
			RAM JAM ***2 Weeks***
			Formed in New York, USA in mid 1977. Personnel: Myke Scavone (vocals, percussion), Bill Bartlett (lead guitar, vocals), Howie Blauvett (bass, vocals) and Peter Charles (drums).
10 Nov 77	8	2	1. BLACK BETTY *Epic EPC 5492*
			The RAMRODS ***4 Weeks***
			Instrumental group formed in Connecticut, USA in 1956. Personnel: Vincent Bell Lee (lead guitar), Eugene Moore (bass), Richard Lane (tenor sax) and Claire Lane (drums). The group were unusual for the era in that the lineup featured a female drummer. Group disbanded in 1963. Eugene Moore died in June 1990.
09 Mar 61	5	4	1. RIDERS IN THE SKY • *London HLU 9282*
			Johnnie RAY ***13 Weeks***
			Born John Alvin Ray on January 10, 1927 in Hopewell, Oregon, USA. Lost fifty per cent of his hearing at age thirteen while at a Boy Scout Jamboree in Dallas, Oregon. During a blanket toss Johnnie was thrown up into the air, the boys holding the blanket lost their grip and Johnnie slammed hard onto the ground, ramming a dry, stiff straw into his left ear. No first aid was given and Johnnie didn't mention it to his parents. In 1941, aged fourteen, Johnnie got his first hearing aid. Moved to Detroit in 1950. Spotted singing at the Flame Showbar by Columbia/Okeh Records rhythm and blues chief, Danny Kessler, who signed Johnnie to Okeh Records. Disc debut: *Whiskey And Gin* (1951). In October 1951 recorded *Cry* and *The Little White Cloud That Cried*. Produced by Mitch Miller with backing vocals by the Four Lads, it launched Johnnie as a major star. Appeared in the 1954 film, *There's No Business Like Showbusiness*. Died from liver failure on February 25, 1990.

continues over

Date	Pos	Wks	ARTIST / Record Title *Label & Number*
27 Apr 55	-	2	1. PATHS OF PARADISE *Philips PB 441*
30 Oct 56	-	4	2. JUST WALKING IN THE RAIN *Philips EPB 624*
04 Jun 57	-	4	3. YES TONIGHT JOSEPHINE *Philips EPB 686*
10 Sep 57	-	3	4. BUILD YOUR LOVE (on a strong foundation) *Philips EPB 721*
			See also Frankie Laine and Johnnie Ray

RAYDIO — *1 Weeks*

Formed in New York, USA in 1977. Personnel: Ray Parker Jr (vocals/ guitar), Arnell Carmichael (keyboards), Jerry Knight (bass/vocals) Charles Fearing (guitar), Larry Tolbert (drums) and Darren Carmichael (keyboards). By 1980 were billed as Ray Parker Jr and Raydio. Parker left group in 1981 to pursue a solo career. Jerry Knight is the featured vocalist on *Jack And Jill.*

Date	Pos	Wks	ARTIST / Record Title *Label & Number*
01 Jun 78	8	1	1. JACK AND JILL *Arista 161*

The REAL McCOY — *27 Weeks*

Showband formed in Dublin, Ireland in July 1968. Personnel: Mike O'Brien (born on January 24, 1949 in Dublin, lead vocals), Dave Coady (born on March 6, 1948 in Waterford, vocals, trumpet), Liam McKenna (bass), Eddie Campbell (lead guitar), Dave Pennyfeather (drums), Keith McAlea (organ) and Keith Donald (tenor sax). Mike O'Brien lead vocal on all hits except *Many The Memories*, which features Dave Coady and *I Don't Know How To Love Him* which features Tina. Mike O'Brien left in 1971. Replaced by Tina in October 1971. After numerous personnel changes, the Real McCoy disbanded in 1973.

Date	Pos	Wks	ARTIST / Record Title *Label & Number*
10 Oct 68	10	2	1. I GET SO EXCITED *Target 7N 17618*
02 Jan 69	1(2)	10	• 2. QUICK JOEY SMALL *Target 7N 17669*
20 Mar 69	9	2	3. ROUND THE GUM TREE *Target 7N 17704*
04 Dec 69	4	6	4. MANY THE MEMORIES *Target 7N 17850*
09 Dec 71	1(1)	7	5. I DON'T KNOW HOW TO LOVE HIM *Ruby RUB 142*
			See also Tina

Date	Pos	Wks	ARTIST / Record Title *Label & Number*
			The REAL THING ***9 Weeks***
			Formed in Liverpool, England. Personnel: Chris Amoo, Ray Lake, Dave Smith and Eddie Amoo. An appearance on TV talent show, *Opportunity Knocks*, led to a recording contract with Bell Records. Moved to Pye in 1975. In 1986, remixed versions of their two early hits, made the British top ten.
29 Jul 76	6	3	1. YOU TO ME ARE EVERYTHING *Pye Int. 25709*
23 Sep 76	2	6	2. CAN'T GET BY WITHOUT YOU *Pye 7N 45618*
			REDBONE ***4 Weeks***
			Formed in Los Angeles, California, USA in 1968. Signed to Epic Records in 1970. Disc debut: *Maggie* (1971). Personnel: Lolly Vegas (guitar, vocals), Pat Vegas (bass), Anthony Bellamy (guitar) and Peter De Poe (drums).
28 Oct 71	7	4	1. THE WITCH QUEEN OF NEW ORLEANS *CBS EPC 7351*
			Helen REDDY ***3 Weeks***
			Born on October 25, 1942 in Melbourne, Australia. Made her first appearance on stage at the age of four. Relocated to USA in 1966. Signed to Capitol Records in 1970. Film appearances include *Pete's Dragon* (1977) and *Airport'75* (1974). First Australian to win a Grammy Award. Did so in 1972 when she won the category, Best Pop Vocal Performance, with her own song, *I Am Woman*. Retired from live performances in 2002 and now practices as a clinical hypnotherapist in her native Australia. Her autobiography, *The Woman I Am*, was published in 2006.
20 Feb 75	5	3	1. ANGIE BABY *Capitol CL 15799*
			Jim REEVES ***122 Weeks***
			Born James Travis Reeves on August 20, 1923 in Galloway, Panola County, Texas, USA. Won a baseball Scholarship to the University of Texas in Austin. Played baseball in minor leagues in several states. In 1947, a leg injury ended his baseball career.

continues over

Date	Pos	Wks	ARTIST / Record Title *Label & Number*

For a period was a member of Moon Mulligan's band and worked as a d.j. and announcer with local radio stations. His musical break arrived while working as an announcer on KWKH Radio in Shreveport, Louisiana. Singer Sleepy La Beef could not make it on time for a performance on the *Louisiana Hayride*, and Jim Reeves was asked to stand in. Made his first recordings in 1949 for the Macy label in Houston. Signed for Abbott Records in 1952. Had his first country hit, *Mexican Joe*, in 1953. Signed to RCA Records in 1955. Starred in the 1963 film, *Kimberley Jim*, which was shot in South Africa. Toured Ireland in May/June of 1963. Died on July 31, 1964 when a small plane carrying Reeves and his manager Dean Manuel from Arkansas to Nashville flew into heavy rain four miles from Nashville and plunged into thick foliage killing all the occupants. Elected posthumously to the Country Music Hall of Fame in 1967. Inducted into the Texas Country Music Hall of Fame in 1998.

Date	Pos	Wks	ARTIST / Record Title *Label & Number*
17 Mar 60	1(3)	28	• 1. HE'LL HAVE TO GO *RCA ERC 1168*
07 Dec 61	2	4	2. YOU'RE THE ONLY GOOD THING (That Happened To Me) *RCA ERC 1261*
28 Jun 62	4	14	3. ADIOS AMIGO *RCA ERC 1293*
27 May 63	1(3)	12	• 4. WELCOME TO MY WORLD *RCA ERC 1342*
04 Nov 63	6	7	5. GUILTY *RCA ERC 1364*
02 Mar 64	1(3)	14	• 6. I LOVE YOU BECAUSE *RCA ERC 1385*
22 Jun 64	1(8)	19	• 7. I WON'T FORGET YOU *RCA ERC 1400*
09 Nov 64	10	1	8. THIS WORLD IS NOT MY HOME *RCA ERC 1412*
16 Nov 64	3	8	9. THERE'S A HEARTACHE FOLLOWING ME *RCA ERC 1423*
22 Feb 65	10	1	10. IT HURTS SO MUCH (To See You Go) *RCA ERC 1437*
10 May 65	6	7	11. NOT UNTIL THE NEXT TIME *RCA ERC 1446*
19 Sep 66	3	7	12. DISTANT DRUMS *RCA ERC 1537*

REFORM — *1 Weeks*

Irish rock group formed in Limerick, in 1968. The original line-up featured Don O'Connor (drums/vocals), Noel Casey (bass), Joe Mulcahy (rhythm guitar) and Willie Browne (vocals/lead guitar).

continues over

Date	Pos	Wks	ARTIST / Record Title *Label & Number*
			Noel Casey left in 1972 and Joe Mulcahy switched to bass guitar. Big break happened in February 1973 when a band composition, *I'm Gonna Get You*, won the Originality Spot on the RTE television programme, *Spin Off*. A recording contract with CBS followed and in September 1973 the group released their debut single, *I'm Gonna Get You*. In 1978, performed a band composition, *You Gotta Get Up*, in the National Song contest to find Ireland's representative for Eurovision. Were pipped by Colm Wilkinson and his song, *Born To Sing*. Disbanded in 1984. Don O'Connor went onto form Celtic Fusion.
25 May 78	9	1	1. YOU GOTTA GET UP *CBS CBS 6326*
			Eileen REID and the CADETS ***25 Weeks***
			Born on January 2 1943 in Dublin, Ireland. Disc debut: *Hello Trouble* on Decca Records in 1963. The first Irish female artist to achieve a number one hit in Ireland. Made the British Singles Chart in June 1965 with *Jealous Heart* (peaked at number 42). Left the Cadets in June 1968 to marry fellow Cadet, Jimmy Day. During the 1980's, Eileen and Jimmy enjoyed success as songwriters/performers. Their song *The Saddest Show On Earth* made it to the National Song Contest Final. Made her debut as an actress in March 1989 in *The Plough And The Stars* at Dublin's Gaiety Theatre. The Cadets Showband were formed in Dublin in 1961. Turned professional in April 1963. Personnel; Eileen Reid (lead vocals), Pat Murphy (leader, harmonica), Brendan O'Connell (lead guitar), Noel McGann (bass), Willie Devey (drums), Jerry Hayes (piano), Jimmy Day (tenor sax), Paddy Burns (trumpet) and Jas Fagan (trombone). In April 1966 added a male vocalist, Gregory Donaghy, to the ranks. The Cadets disbanded in early 1970. Reformed in June 1987 for a short Irish tour. Willie Devey died on May 22, 2004.
27 Apr 64	1(1)	8	• 1. FALLEN STAR *Columbia IDB 740*
05 Oct 64	4	7	2. I GAVE MY WEDDING DRESS AWAY *Pye 7N 15693*

continues over

Date	Pos	Wks	ARTIST / Record Title *Label & Number*
24 May 65	7	6	3. RIGHT OR WRONG *Pye 7N 15852*
07 Feb 66	4	4	4. IF I HAD MY LIFE TO LIVE OVER *Pye 7N 17024*

Neil REID — *2 Weeks*

Born in 1960 in Scotland. Discovered singing at a Christmas party for old age pensioners in 1968. For the next three years spent his school holidays singing in local clubs. Three winning appearances on British television's top talent show *Opportunity Knocks* in 1971, led to a recording contract with Decca Records. Became the youngest artist to top the British album chart, when his debut album, *Neil Reid*, reached number one in 1972.

Date	Pos	Wks	ARTIST / Record Title *Label & Number*
10 Feb 72	8	2	1. MOTHER OF MINE *Decca F 13264*

Paddy REILLY — *8 Weeks*

Born on October 18, 1939 in Dublin, Ireland. In the early 60's while working as a machinist in the paper mills in Saggart he was invited by Mick McCarthy (the owner of the famous ballad pub, The Embankment) to perform in the lounge. Started singing professionally in 1964. Paddy made his disc debut in 1967, with his recording of *The Curragh Of Kildare*, a track on the LP *Live At The Embankment*. Member of the Dubliners 1996-2005.

Date	Pos	Wks	ARTIST / Record Title *Label & Number*
02 Mar 74	5	4	1. THE TOWN I LOVED SO WELL *Dolphin DOS 117*
07 Aug 75	6	4	2. THE TOWN I LOVED SO WELL (re-entry) *Dolphin DOS 117*

RENAISSANCE — *1 Weeks*

Formed in London, England in 1969 by ex Yardbirds Keith Relf and Jim McCarty. Numerous personnel changes throughout groups lifespan. Personnel (1978): Annie Haslam (vocals), John Tout (keyboards), Terry Sullivan (drums), Michael Dunford (guitar), and Jon Camp (bass/vocals). Disbanded in 1987. Reunited in 1998. Northern Lights first appeared on the album, *A Song For All Seasons* (1978).

Date	Pos	Wks	ARTIST / Record Title *Label & Number*
24 Aug 78	9	1	1. NORTHERN LIGHTS *Warner Bros K17177*

Date	Pos	Wks	ARTIST / Record Title *Label & Number*

Gerry REYNOLDS and the HI-LOWS *1 Weeks*

Born on August 7, 1950 in Dromod, Co. Leitrim, Ireland. Joined the Hi-Lows in April 1971. Died of cancer on July 5, 2002. The Hi Lows formed in 1960 as the Grafton Showband, but had to undergo a name change due to the existence of another band called the Grafton. Des Tighe came up with the name Hi-Lows. Personnel: Gerry Reynolds (vocals, guitar), John Tighe (vocals, lead guitar), Des Tighe (organ, fiddle), Gerry Davis (bass), Mickey Hughes (tenor sax) and Jet Calders (drums). Disbanded in November 1979. John Tighe died on April 23, 2000.

Date	Pos	Wks	ARTIST / Record Title *Label & Number*
22 Jun 72	8	1	1. 100 CHILDREN *Release RL 627*

Charlie RICH *7 Weeks*

Born on December 14, 1932 in Colt, Arkansas, USA. Following a period of service in the U.S. Airforce began his professional musical career, performing in clubs around the Memphis area. Started working at Sun Studios as a piano player/singer/songwriter/arranger. Signed to Phillips International label. Disc debut: *Whirlwind* (1956). Had his first hit with, *Lonely Weekends*, in 1960. Over the next seven years recorded for several labels including Groove, Smash and Hi. In 1967, on the recommendation of producer, Billy Sherrill, he was signed by Epic Records and the hits soon started to flow. In 1973 won a Grammy for Best Country Vocal Performance for his recording of *Behind Closed Doors*. The following year was voted CMA Entertainer of the Year. In 1981 went into semi retirement. Died from a blood clot on his lung on July 24, 1995. Nickname: 'The Silver Fox'.

Date	Pos	Wks	ARTIST / Record Title *Label & Number*
14 Mar 74	2	5	1. THE MOST BEAUTIFUL GIRL *CBS 1897*
02 May74	9	2	2. BEHIND CLOSED DOORS *Epic EPC 1539*

Cliff RICHARD *254 Weeks*

Born Harry Roger Webb on October 14, 1940 in Lucknow, India. Relocated to England in 1948. Formed the Drifters in 1958.

continues over

Date	Pos	Wks	ARTIST / Record Title *Label & Number*
			Changed their name to the Shadows in 1960, to avoid confusion with the American vocal group of the same name. Showbiz agent George Canjou saw Cliff and the Drifters performing at Shepherds Bush Gaumount in London and fixed a recording test. Signed to Columbia Records. Debut disc: *Move It* (1958). Made his TV debut in September 1958 and started his first major one-night tour of the UK in October 1958 with America's Kalin Twins. Appeared in several films including *Serious Charge* (1959), *Expresso Bongo* (1960), *The Young Ones* (1961) and *Summer Holiday* (1963). Awarded an MBE in 1999.
30 Jul 59	1(7)	13	• 1. LIVING DOLL *Columbia DB(I) 4306*
29 Oct 59	1(1)	11	• 2. TRAVELLIN' LIGHT *Columbia DB(I) 4351*
04 Feb 60	1(1)	7	• 3. A VOICE IN THE WILDERNESS *Columbia DB(I) 4398*
07 Apr 60	2	14	4. FALL IN LOVE WITH YOU *Columbia DB(I) 4431*
07 Jul 60	1(5)	15	• 5. PLEASE DON'T TEASE *Columbia DB(I) 4479*
20 Oct 60	3	9	6. NINE TIMES OUT OF TEN *Columbia DB(I) 4506*
22 Dec 60	4	9	7. I LOVE YOU *Columbia DB(I) 4547*
30 Mar 61	4	8	8. THEME FOR A DREAM *Columbia DB(I) 4593*
11 May61	3	7	9. GEE WHIZ IT'S YOU *Columbia DC(I) 756*
06 Jul 61	4	7	10. A GIRL LIKE YOU *Columbia DB(I) 4667*
26 Oct 61	2	5	11. WHEN THE GIRL IN YOUR ARMS IS THE GIRL IN YOUR HEART *Columbia DB(I) 4716*
25 Jan 62	1(4)	9	• 12. THE YOUNG ONES *Columbia DB(I) 4761*
10 May62	2	12	13. I'M LOOKIN' OUT THE WINDOW *Columbia DB(I) 4828*
13 Sep 62	2	4	14. IT'LL BE ME *Columbia DB(I) 4886*
24 Dec 62	1(4)	10	• 15. THE NEXT TIME / BACHELOR BOY *Columbia DB(I) 4950*
04 Mar 63	2	10	16. SUMMER HOLIDAY *Columbia DB(I) 4977*
27 May63	1(1)	10	• 17. LUCKY LIPS *Columbia DB(I) 7034*
09 Sep 63	2	5	18. IT'S ALL IN THE GAME *Columbia DB(I) 7089*
25 Nov 63	1(1)	8	• 19. DON'T TALK TO HIM *Columbia DB(I) 7150*
24 Feb 64	9	2	20. I'M THE LONELY ONE *Columbia DB(I) 7203*
08 Jun 64	8	1	21. CONSTANTLY *Columbia DB(I) 7272*
03 Aug 64	6	4	22. ON THE BEACH *Columbia DB(I) 7305*
11 Jan 65	8	4	23. I COULD EASILY FALL *Columbia DB(I) 7420*
12 Apr 65	2	6	24. THE MINUTE YOU'RE GONE *Columbia DB(I) 7496*

continues over

Date	Pos	Wks	ARTIST / Record Title *Label & Number*
13 Dec 65	5	6	25. WIND ME UP (Let Me Go) *Columbia DB(I) 7745*
08 Aug 66	9	5	26. VISIONS *Columbia DB(I) 7968*
05 Jan 67	3	5	27. IN THE COUNTRY *Columbia DB(I) 8094*
05 Oct 67	10	1	28. THE DAY I MET MARIE *Columbia DB(I) 8245*
14 Dec 67	8	4	29. ALL MY LOVE *Columbia DB(I) 8293*
11 Apr 68	1(2)	7	• 30. CONGRATULATIONS *Columbia DB(I) 8376*
03 Apr 69	9	3	31. GOOD TIMES (BETTER TIMES) *Columbia DB(I) 8548*
03 Jul 69	8	1	32. BIG SHIP *Columbia DB(I) 8581*
09 Oct 69	8	2	33. THROW DOWN A LINE *Columbia DB(I) 8615*
25 Jun 70	1(1)	9	• 34. GOODBYE SAM, HELLO SAMANTHA *Columbia DB(I) 8685*
28 Sep 72	10	1	35. LIVING IN HARMONY *Columbia DB(I) 8917*
05 Apr 73	2	7	36. POWER TO ALL OUR FRIENDS *EMI 2012*
08 Apr 76	6	3	37. MISS YOU NIGHTS *EMI EMI 2376*
17 Jun 76	10	1	38. DEVIL WOMAN *EMI 2458*
30 Sep 76	7	1	39. I CAN'T ASK FOR ANYTHING MORE *EMI 2499*
16 Aug 79	1(4)	8	• 40. WE DON'T TALK ANYMORE *EMI EMI 2975*

Living Doll credit: Cliff Richard and the Drifters. Numbers: 3-11; 13-18; 20-21; 23-24 credit: Cliff Richard and The Shadows. Throw Down A Line: Cliff and Hank. **See also The Shadows**

The RIGHTEOUS BROTHERS — *5 Weeks*

Male vocal duo. Bill Medley (born on September 19, 1940 in Santa Ana, California, USA), and Bobby Hatfield (born on August 10, 1940 in Beaver Dam, Wisconsin, USA). First sang together in 1962 at a small country club in Orange County, California. Split in 1968. Teamed up again in 1974. Bobby Hatfield was found dead in a hotel room in Kalamazoo, Michigan on November 5, 2003, just before the duo were due to go out on stage.

Date	Pos	Wks	ARTIST / Record Title *Label & Number*
01 Feb 65	2	5	1. YOU'VE LOST THAT LOVIN' FEELIN' *London HLU 9943*

The DONAL RING SOUND with Paul O'Leary — *3 Weeks*

Formed in Cork, Ireland in 1958. Made debut in the Glen Hall in Blackpool, Cork. Donal Ring born in 1935 in Rathduff, Co. Cork. From a musical family.

continues over

Date	Pos	Wks	ARTIST / Record Title *Label & Number*

Greatly influenced by his father who played melodeon and accordion. Started playing accordion at an early age. Joined his first band at age sixteen. In 1961, Donal and band won the All Ireland Hohner Championship. Cork born vocalist, Paul O'Leary, joined the Donal Ring Sound in 1971. Left the band in 1972.

04 May 72	4	3	1. BEAUTIFUL CITY *Pye 7N 60011*

Waldo de los RIOS — *6 Weeks*

Pianist/composer/conductor/arranger. Born Osvaldo Ferrara on September 7, 1934 in Buenos Aires, Argentina. Relocated to USA in 1958. Moved to Spain in 1962. Composed music for several films including *Savage Pampas* (1966) and *Bad Man's River* (1971). Died of a self inflicted gunshot wound on March 28, 1977.

29 Apr 71	3	6	1. MOZART SYMPHONY No. 40 IN G MINOR K550 1ST MOVEMENT (ALLEGRO MOLTO) • *Pye AMS 836*

Minnie RIPPERTON — *2 Weeks*

Born on November 8, 1947 in Chicago, USA. As a youth studied music, drama and dance at the Lincoln Center, Chicago. Pop career began in 1961 when she joined the girl group, the Gems. Recorded for Chess Records under the name Andrea Davis. Disc debut: *Lonely Girl* (1966). In 1968, joined the group Rotary Connection. Toured with Stevie Wonder in 1970 as a member of his backing band, Wonderlove. Diagnosed with breast cancer in 1976. Died on July 12, 1979. *Loving You* was co-produced by Stevie Wonder.

15 May75	3	2	1. LOVING YOU *Epic EPC 3121*

Tex RITTER — *2 Weeks*

Born Woodward Maurice Ritter on January 12, 1905 in Murvaul, Panola County, Texas, USA. The youngest of six children he showed an early interest in singing. During his undergraduate years he was introduced to cowboy songs, and was greatly influenced by John A. Lomax.

Date	Pos	Wks	ARTIST / Record Title *Label & Number*

In late 1930 was offered the role of Cord Elam in the Theatre Guild production of *Green Grow The Lilacs*, in which he got to sing four cowboy songs. Disc debut: *Rye Whiskey* (1933). Film debut: *Song Of The Gringo* (1936). Singing cowboy star of 'B' westerns during the years 1936-45. Performed the title song in classic western film, *High Noon* (1952). Inducted into the Country Music Hall of Fame in 1964. Member of the Grand Ole Opry in 1965. Died of a heart attack on January 2, 1974.

Date	Pos	Wks	ARTIST / Record Title *Label & Number*
31 Jul 56	-	2	1. **THE WAYWARD WIND** *Capitol CL(I) 14581*

Marty ROBBINS — *22 Weeks*

Born Martin David Robinson on September 26, 1925 near Glendale, Arizona, USA. Joined the US Navy at the age of 17. Following his discharge from the navy he started performing regularly in local clubs. Because his mother disapproved, he briefly worked under the name Jack Robinson. First recorded for Columbia Records in 1951. In 1953, made a member of *Grand Ole Opry*. Film appearances include *Ballad Of A Gunfighter* (1964) and *Guns Of A Stranger* (1973). Parted with the Columbia in 1972 to sign with MCA. Returned to Columbia in 1975. Died of a heart attack on December 8, 1982.

Date	Pos	Wks	ARTIST / Record Title *Label & Number*
18 Jun 57	-	3	1. **A WHITE SPORT COAT** *Philips EPB 696*
05 Nov 57	-	1	2. **PLEASE DON'T BLAME ME** *Philips EPB 741*
19 Nov 57	-	1	3. **TEENAGE DREAM** *Philips EPB 741*
24 Mar 60	9	2	4. **EL PASO** *Fontana EH 233*
22 Oct 62	2	15	5. **DEVIL WOMAN** *CBS EAAG 114*

B A ROBERTSON — *5 Weeks*

Born Brian Alexander Robertson in 1952 in Glasgow, Scotland. Attended the Royal Scottish Academy of Music. Professional music career began aged twenty one, when he was signed by Steve Morris. Disc debut: *Wringing Applause* L.P. (1973). Has composed hits, *Carrie* and *Wired For Sound* (Cliff Richard), *Silent Running* and *The Living Years* (Mike and the Mechanics). Hosted his own television music series, *B A In Music.*

continues over

Date	Pos	Wks	ARTIST / Record Title *Label & Number*
06 Sep 79	5	3	1. BANG BANG *Asylum K 13152*
22 Nov 79	8	2	2. KNOCKED IT OFF *Asylum K 12396*

Smokey ROBINSON and the MIRACLES — *7 Weeks*

Born William Robinson on February 19, 1940 in Detroit, USA. In 1954 formed his first vocal group, the Matadors, while attending the Northern High School, Detroit. At the suggestion of Berry Gordy, changed the group name to the Miracles, in 1957. Personnel: Smokey Robinson (lead vocals), Claudette Rogers, Bobby Rogers, Warren Moore and Ronnie White. Disc debut: *Get A Job* (1958). Married Claudette Rogers in 1962. She stopped touring with Miracles in 1965. Smokey left the group in July 1972 to pursue a solo career. Composed hit songs and produced numerous other Motown artists including Mary Wells, Temptations, Marvin Gaye and the Marvelettes. Described by Bob Dylan as 'America's greatest living poet'. His autobiography, *Inside My Life*, published in 1989. Inducted into the Rock and Roll Hall of Fame in 1987.

Date	Pos	Wks	ARTIST / Record Title *Label & Number*
03 Sep 70	3	7	1. TEARS OF A CLOWN *Tamla Motown TMG(I) 745*

Dickie ROCK and The MIAMI SHOWBAND — *95 Weeks*

Born Richard Rock on September 10, 1940 in Dublin. Member of his local church choir. Joined the Casino Players, an amateur variety group who entertained at various hospitals around Dublin City. Later lead vocalist with the Mellochords and the Echoes. Made a big impression on the bill of the Cliff Richard Show at the National Stadium, Dublin in January 1962. Replaced Jimmy Harte as lead vocalist in the Miami Showband later that same year. Disc Debut: *There's Always Me* (1963). Represented Ireland in 1966 Eurovision Song Contest with *Come Back To Stay*, finishing in joint fourth position. Married Judy Murray on June 20, 1966.

Date	Pos	Wks	ARTIST / Record Title *Label & Number*
			Dickie Rock departed from the ranks of the Miami in December 1972 to form his own band. His autobiography, *Always Me*, published in 2007.
09 Dec 63	1(4)	11	• 1. THERE'S ALWAYS ME *Piccadilly 7N 35154*
11 May64	1(1)	5	• 2. I'M YOURS *Piccadilly 7N 35185*
19 Oct 64	1(6)	9	• 3. FROM THE CANDY STORE ON THE CORNER TO THE CHAPEL ON THE HILL *Piccadilly 7N 35202*
21 Dec 64	2	4	4. JUST FOR OLD TIMES SAKE *Pye 7N 15729*
18 Jan 65	2	6	5. ROUND AND AROUND *Pye 7N 15750*
24 May65	1(3)	10	• 6. EVERY STEP OF THE WAY *Pye 7N 15855*
23 Aug 65	4	4	7. (I Left My Heart) IN SAN FRANCISCO *Pye 7N 15891*
08 Nov 65	1(2)	9	• 8. WISHING IT WAS YOU *Pye 7N 15977*
21 Feb 66	1(4)	9	• 9. COME BACK TO STAY *Pye 7N 17063*
12 Dec 66	4	3	10. DARLING I LOVE YOU *Pye 7N 17206*
23 Feb 67	7	2	11. WHEN YOU CRY *Pye 7N 17253*
25 Apr 68	1(1)	10	• 12. SIMON SAYS *Pye 7N 17527*
02 Jan 69	10	1	13. CHRISTMAS TIME AND YOU *United Artists UP 2256*
10 Jun 71	7	2	14. MY HEART KEEPS TELLING ME (I Love Melanie So) *Pye 7N 45062*
17 Feb 72	9	1	15. TILL *Pye PMM 601*
09 Jun 77	1(4)	9	• 16. BACK HOME *Solo SOLO 147*
			Come Back To Stay; Christmas Time And You; My Heart Keeps Telling Me (I Love Melanie So); Till; Back Home. Credit: Dickie Rock.

ROCKY TOPS – See Pat ELY

The ROCKIN' BERRIES *1 Weeks*

Formed in Birmingham, England, in 1959 as the Bobcats. Personnel: Clive Lea (lead vocals), Geoff Turton (lead vocals-falsetto, guitar), Roy Austin (bass), Chuck Botfield (lead guitar) and Terry Bond (drums). Disc debut: *Wah Wah Whoo* (1963) on Decca. Signed to Piccadilly in 1964. Geoff Turton departed in 1968, to pursue a solo career. He enjoyed chart success under the name Jefferson. Joined the Fortunes for a short period of time in August 2005.

Date	Pos	Wks	ARTIST / Record Title *Label & Number*
23 Nov 64	9	1	1. HE'S IN TOWN *Piccadilly 7N 35203*

Date	Pos	Wks	ARTIST / Record Title *Label & Number*

Clodagh RODGERS — *14 Weeks*

Born on March 5, 1947 in Ballymena, County Antrim. N. Ireland. Big break came about in 1957, when she got to sing on same bill as Michael Holliday. Signed by Decca Records in 1961. Disc debut (as Cloda Rodgers): *Believe Me I'm No Fool* (1962). Appeared in the films *Just For Fun* (1963) and *It's All Over Town* (1964). Moved to Columbia Records in 1965. Signed to RCA Records in 1968. Represented the UK in the 1971 Eurovision Song Contest with *Jack in the Box* finishing in fourth position. Toured Britain in the stage production of *Blood Brothers*, 1995-98.

Date	Pos	Wks	ARTIST / Record Title *Label & Number*
08 May 69	2	6	1. COME BACK AND SHAKE ME *RCA ERC 1792*
14 Aug 69	7	4	2. GOODNIGHT MIDNIGHT *RCA RCA 1852*
15 Apr 71	5	4	3. JACK IN THE BOX *RCA RCA 2066*

Jimmie RODGERS — *3 Weeks*

Born James Frederick Rodgers on September 18, 1933 in Canas, Washington, USA. Formed the Rhythm Kings while serving in Korea with the US Air Force. Disc debut: *Honeycomb* (1957). In 1959 hosted his own weekly NBC TV music and variety series, *The Jimmie Rodgers Show*.

Date	Pos	Wks	ARTIST / Record Title *Label & Number*
19 Jul 62	7	3	1. ENGLISH COUNTRY GARDEN *Columbia DB(I) 4847*

Tommy ROE — *20 Weeks*

Born on May 9, 1943 in Atlanta, Georgia, USA. Formed the Satins while still at high school. Disc debut: *I Got A Girl* (1959). Originally recorded *Sheila* in 1960, for Judd Records. Signed to ABC in 1962 for whom he re-recorded *Sheila*. In 1991, Vic Reeves had a UK number one with *Dizzy*.

Date	Pos	Wks	ARTIST / Record Title *Label & Number*
01 Oct 62	3	9	1. SHEILA *HMV POP(I) 1060*
15 Apr 63	9	2	2. THE FOLK SINGER *HMV POP(I) 1138*
05 Jun 69	2	8	3. DIZZY *Stateside SS(I) 2143*
11 Sep 69	9	1	4. HEATHER HONEY *Stateside SS(I) 2152*

Date	Pos	Wks	ARTIST / Record Title *Label & Number*
			Julie ROGERS ***1 Weeks***
			Born Julie Rolls on April 6, 1943 in Bermondsey, London, England.. Spotted by Philips Records A&R executive Johnny Franz whilst vocalist with bandleader Teddy Foster. Signed to Mercury Records in 1964. *The Wedding*, was also a Top Ten hit in the USA.
19 Oct 64	10	1	1. THE WEDDING *Mercury EMF 820*
			Kenny ROGERS and the First Edition ***15 Weeks***
			Born Kenneth Donald Rogers on August 21, 1938 in Houston, Texas, USA. In 1966 joined the New Christy Minstrels. Formed the First Edition in 1967. Personnel: Kenny Rogers (bass, vocals), Thelma Camacho (vocals), Mike Settle (rhythm guitar), Terry Williams (lead guitar) and Mickey Jones (drums). In 1969, Mary Arnold replaced Thelma Camacho and Mickey Hart replaced Mickey Jones. Group disbanded in 1974, with Kenny Rogers embarking on a solo career.
04 Dec 69	4	8	1. RUBY (don't take your love to town) *Pye RS 20829*
16 Apr 70	10	1	2. SOMETHINGS BURNING *Pye RS 20888*
16 Jun 77	2	6	3. LUCILLE *United Artists UP 36242*
			Tommy ROGERS and his Ballroom Orchestra ***1 Weeks***
			British born Orchestra leader. Orchestra directed by Harry Gold.
03 Jul 56	-	1	1. SEPTEMBER LOVE *Parlophone R(I) 4167*
			The ROLLING STONES ***92 Weeks***
			Formed in London, England in June 1962. Group took their name from a Muddy Waters song. Personnel: Mick Jagger (lead vocals), Keith Richards (lead guitar), Brian Jones (guitar), Dick Taylor (bass), Ian Stewart (piano) and Tony Chapman (drums). First gig July 1962. In December 1962, Bill Wyman replaces Dick Taylor. In January 1963 Charlie Watts replaced Tony Chapman.

continues over

Date	Pos	Wks	ARTIST / Record Title *Label & Number*
			In May 1963, the members of the group decided that Ian Stewart be removed from the front line. The group get a residency at the Crawdaddy Club at the Station Hotel, Richmond. In May 1963, acting on the advice of Beatle, George Harrison, Decca's Dick Rowe goes to the Crawdaddy Club to see the Stones perform. He signs the group to Decca Records. Disc debut: *Come On* (June 1963). Brian Jones left group in 1969. Replaced by Mick Taylor. In 1970 the group form their own record company Rolling Stones Records. In 1975, Ron Wood ex Small Faces replaced Taylor. Bill Wyman left group in 1994. Group won Lifetime Achievement Award in 1986. Inducted into Rock n Roll Hall of Fame in 1989. Have been described by many as the 'greatest rock and roll band in the world'. Brian Jones was found drowned in his swimming pool on July 3, 1969. Ian Stewart died in December 1985.
13 Apr 64	5	3	1. NOT FADE AWAY *Decca F 11845*
20 Jul 64	2	8	2. IT'S ALL OVER NOW *Decca F 11934*
30 Nov 64	4	3	3. LITTLE RED ROOSTER *Decca F 12014*
22 Mar 65	2	7	4. THE LAST TIME *Decca F 12104*
23 Aug 65	1(4)	9	• 5. (I CAN'T GET NO) SATISFACTION *Decca F 12220*
01 Nov 65	2	6	6. GET OFF MY CLOUD *Decca F 12263*
14 Feb 66	2	5	7. NINETEENTH NERVOUS BREAKDOWN *Decca F 12331*
23 May66	2	7	8. PAINT IT BLACK *Decca F 12395*
03 Oct 66	5	3	9. HAVE YOU SEEN YOUR MOTHER BABY STANDING IN THE SHADOW *Decca F 12497*
16 Feb 67	6	4	10. RUBY TUESDAY *Decca F 12546*
06 Jun 68	3	9	11. JUMPING JACK FLASH *Decca F 12782*
31 Jul 69	1(1)	9	• 12. HONKY TONK WOMEN *Decca F 12952*
20 May 71	2	5	13. BROWN SUGAR *Rolling Stones RS 19100*
27 Sep 73	9	2	14. ANGIE *Rolling Stones RS 19105*
22 Aug 74	6	2	15. IT'S ONLY ROCK AND ROLL *Rolling Stones RS 19114*
17 Jun 76	5	6	16. FOOL TO CRY *Rolling Stones RS 19131*
15 Jun 78	2	4	17. MISS YOU *Rolling Stones RS 2861*

Date	Pos	Wks	ARTIST / Record Title *Label & Number*
			Don RONDO **1 Weeks**
			Born in Springfield, Massachusetts, USA. Disc debut: *In Chi Chi Chihuahua.*
24 Sep 57	-	1	1. WHITE SILVER SANDS *London HL 8466*
			Pat ROPER and the SPOTLIGHTS **9 Weeks**
			Born in Glasgow, Scotland of a Scottish mother and an Irish father (County Donegal). Invited to Ireland to front the Spotlights Showband. The Spotlights formed in May 1970, started out as the Cabaret All Stars. Personnel: Pat Roper (lead vocals), Jimmy Hogan (lead guitar), Mike Shortt (bass), Kevin Brady (drums), Eamonn Monahan (piano), Jim Clarke (trombone) and Ken Aust (tenor saxophone). In January 1972, the Spotlights changed their musical identity to a Scottish style dance band, complete with kilts, and were renamed, The Tartans. After a short period reverted back to the name Spotlights, but disbanded shortly after. Pat Roper moved to the USA in 1973.
25 Feb 71	3	9	1. THE RING YOUR MOTHER WORE *Release RL 568*
			ROSE ROYCE **2 Weeks**
			Formed in Los Angeles, USA in 1972 as The Total Concept Unlimited. Changed name to Rose Royce in 1975. Personnel: Gwen Dickey (vocals), Kenji Chiba Brown (guitar), Michael Nash (keyboards), Duke Jobe (bass), Kenny Copeland (trumpet), Freddie Dunn (trumpet), Michael Moore (tenor sax) and Terral Santiel (congas).
05 Oct 78	7	2	1. LOVE DON'T LIVE HERE ANYMORE *Whitfield K 17234*
			Diana ROSS **13 Weeks**
			Born Diane Ross on March 26, 1944 in Detroit, USA. Lead singer of The Supremes 1961-69. Went solo in late 1969. Film appearances include *Lady Sings The Blues* (1972), *Mahogany* (1975) and *The Wiz* (1978). Oscar nominee for film, *Lady Sings The Blues.*

continues over

Date	Pos	Wks	ARTIST / Record Title *Label & Number*
26 Aug 71	1(1)	7	• 1. I'M STILL WAITING *Tamla Motown TMG(I) 781*
06 May76	4	6	2. DO YOU KNOW WHERE YOU'RE GOING TO *Tamla Motown TMG(I) 1010*

Diana ROSS and the SUPREMES and the TEMPTATIONS — *2 Weeks*

Born Diane Ross on March 26, 1944 in Detroit, USA. Lead singer of The Supremes 1961-69. Went solo in late 1969. The Supremes: Diana Ross, Mary Wilson and Cindy Birdsong. Formed in 1959 as The Primettes. The Temptations formed in Detroit in 1960, as The Elgins. Changed name on signing to Motown in 1961. Personnel: Dennis Edwards, Eddie Kendricks, Paul Williams, Melvin Franklin, and Otis Williams. Disc debut: *Oh Mother Of Mine* (1961). Paul Williams died on August 17, 1974.

Date	Pos	Wks	ARTIST / Record Title *Label & Number*
06 Mar 69	5	2	1. I'M GONNA MAKE YOU LOVE ME *Tamla Motown TMG(I) 685*

See also Diana Ross; The Supremes

Nini ROSSO — *4 Weeks*

Trumpeter/composer. Born Celeste Rosso on September 19, 1926 in Turin, Italy. Formed a small orchestra in 1940's and toured all over Italy. Wrote *Concerto Disperato* in 1963. It became the theme for Stewart Granger's film, *The Legion's Last Patrol. Il Silenzio* a variation of *The Last Post* was written by Rosso and Gaglielmo Brezza.

Date	Pos	Wks	ARTIST / Record Title *Label & Number*
04 Oct 65	7	4	1. IL SILENZIO • *Pye DRS 54000*

Demis ROUSSOS — *10 Weeks*

Born Artemios Roussos on June 15, 1946 in Alexandria, Egypt. At the age of ten he learned to play the trumpet. Due to the Suez crisis, moved with his parents to Greece, at the age of fifteen. Started his musical career, playing trumpet, at various clubs in Athens. In 1963, joined the rock band, The Idols, as bassist. Moved on to join We Five, as lead singer.

continues over

Date	Pos	Wks	ARTIST / Record Title *Label & Number*
			In 1968 met Vangelis, and they formed Aphrodite's Child. They enjoyed international success with their recordings including a hit single, *Rain And Tears.* Split from Aphrodite's Child and in 1971 he made his first solo recording, *We Shall Dance.* In the 1980's co-wrote a best selling book, *A Question Of Weight.* On June 14, 1985, Demis was one of the passengers on board an aircraft, flying from Athens to Rome, which was hijacked by armed men, and forced to land at Beriut Airport.
19 Sep 74	8	1	1. MY FRIEND THE WIND *Philips 6009 534*
15 Jan 76	7	3	2. HAPPY TO BE ON AN ISLAND IN THE SUN *Philips 6042 033*
12 Aug 76	4	2	3. THE ROUSSOS PHENOMENON EP *Philips DEMU 001*
28 Oct 76	3	4	4. WHEN FOREVER HAS GONE *Philips 6042 186*
			Tracks on Roussos Phenomenon EP: Forever And Ever / Sing An Ode To Love / So Dreamy / My Friend The Wind.
			John ROWLES ***7 Weeks***
			Born on March 26, 1947 in Whakatane, New Zealand. Moved to Australia in 1963. Disc debut: *The End Of The Rainbow* (1966) The record was released under the name, JA-AR (The Secret). In 1967, was brought to England by Eric Jury, after being spotted in Australia by Peter Gormley (Cliff Richard's manager). Signed to MCA Records.
25 Apr 68	6	3	1. IF I ONLY HAD TIME *MCA MU(I) 1000*
11 Jul 68	8	4	2. HUSH NOT A WORD TO MARY *MCA MU(I) 1023*
			ROXY MUSIC ***8 Weeks***
			Formed in London, England in November 1970. Disc debut: *Roxy Music* LP (June 1972). In June 1976 band members went their separate ways. Reformed in August 1978. Personnel: Bryan Ferry (vocals), Andy Mackay (tenor sax), Phil Manzanera (guitar), Paul Thompson (drums), Gary Tibbs (bass) and David Skinner (keyboards). Bryan Ferry born on September 26, 1945 in Washington, Co. Durham, England. Moved to London in 1968. Issued his first solo album in 1973.
24 May 79	1(1)	8	• 1. DANCE AWAY *Polydor POSP 44*

Date	Pos	Wks	ARTIST / Record Title *Label & Number*

Pipes and Drums and Military Band of the ROYAL SCOTS DRAGOON GUARDS *4 Weeks*

The regiment was formed in 1971 from the union of two famous regiments, the 3rd Carabiniers and the Royal Scots Greys. The pipes and drums of the Royal Scots Dragoon Guards have their origins in the small pipe band which came to the Scots Grays in 1946 as a result of demobilisation of certain Scottish Territorial Armoured Corps units. Band members are all regular soldiers who crew tanks as well as play instruments. *Amazing Grace* was first played on the amalgamation Parade of the Regiment and was the first time Military band music had been incorporated with pipe music.

Date	Pos	Wks	ARTIST / Record Title *Label & Number*
27 Apr 72	1(1)	4	• 1. AMAZING GRACE • *RCA RCA 2191*

Lita ROZA *2 Weeks*

Born Lilian Patricia Roza on March 14, 1926 in Liverpool, England. At the age of sixteen Lita secured her first professional engagement, singing in a Southport restaurant, The New Yorker. Relocated to London where she joined the Harry Roy Band. Married at the age of eighteen, moved to the USA to live. Returned to England in 1950 and joined the Ted Heath Band. Disc debut: *Allentown Jail* (1952). In May 1954 left the Ted Heath Band to pursue a solo career. Died on August 14, 2008.

Date	Pos	Wks	ARTIST / Record Title *Label & Number*
09 Nov 54	1(1)	1	• 1. THE MAMA DOLL SONG *Decca F 10393*
17 Sep 58	-	1	2. NEL BLU DE PINTO DE BLUE (VOLARE) *Nixa N 15155*

RUBBISH *7 Weeks*

Formed in Dublin, Ireland in late 1976, by Dave Pennyfeather and Shay Healy. Dave Pennyfeather was drummer with chart topping showband, the Real McCoy. Songwriter/performer Shay Healy composed hits for Johnny Dawson and Brendan Grace. Also composed Ireland's 1980 Eurovision winning song, *What's Another Year. Hey C'Mere* is a parody of Abba's hit song, *Mama Mia.*

Date	Pos	Wks	ARTIST / Record Title *Label & Number*
06 Jan 77	4	7	1. HEY C'MERE *Blackbird BB 102*

Date	Pos	Wks	ARTIST / Record Title *Label & Number*

The RUBETTES — *13 Weeks*

Formed in London in the autumn of 1973, when Wayne Bickerton A&R chief at Polydor Records teamed up with several top session musicians and singers at Landsdown Studios in Holland Park, London, to record four songs. Convinced of the hit potential of one of the songs, Polydor decided to release it. The people who participated on the session were asked to become the Rubettes Personnel: Paul Da Vinci (lead vocals), Alan Williams (vocals, guitar), John Richardson (drums), Pete Arnesen (keyboards), Mick Clarke (bass), Bill Hurd (keyboards) and Tony Thorpe (guitar). Following the release of *Sugar Baby Love*, Paul Da Vinci decided to leave the group to pursue a solo career. Alan Williams took over as lead vocalist. Group disbanded in 1979. In 1983, Alan Williams, Mick Clarke and Bill Hurd reformed the Rubettes with Alex Bines on drums completing the lineup. In 1999, Bill and Alex left group, original drummer, John Richardson, rejoined the group.

Date	Pos	Wks	ARTIST / Record Title *Label & Number*
23 May 74	3	4	1. SUGAR BABY LOVE *Polydor 2058 442*
12 Dec 74	3	7	2. JUKE BOX JIVE *Polydor 2058 529*
03 Apr 75	5	2	3. I CAN DO IT *State STAT 1*

Barry RYAN — *6 Weeks*

Born Barry Sapherson on October 24, 1948 in Leeds, England. Son of British 1950's singing star, Marion Ryan. Began performing with his twin brother, Paul, at the age of fifteen. In 1965 Paul and Barry Ryan, signed with Decca Records and enjoyed several hit singles during the years 1965-67. In 1968, the duo split with Paul concentrating on songwriting. Barry stopped performing in the early 1980's. Returned to live performance in the 1990's..

Date	Pos	Wks	ARTIST / Record Title *Label & Number*
21 Nov 68	2	6	1. ELOISE *MGM MGM(I) 1442*

Date	Pos	Wks	ARTIST / Record Title *Label & Number*

Bill RYAN and BUCKSHOT *3 Weeks*

Born Bernard O'Boyle on June 25, 1947 in Burtonport, Co. Donegal, Ireland. Emigrated to England. Sang in pubs and clubs. Cousin of Margo (O'Donnell). Returned to Ireland in 1970 and joined The Hootnannys. Disc debut: *Mighty Lonesome* (1970). Buckshot formed in Dublin in September 1972. Personnel: Bill Ryan (lead vocals), Tommy Kinsella (bass), Martin McGregor (drums), Alan Loughnane (fiddle), Bobby Smith (trumpet), Michael O'Connor (tenor sax), Buddy Boland (lead guitar). Disbanded in 1980.

Date	Pos	Wks	ARTIST / Record Title *Label & Number*
07 Dec 72	7	2	1. THE KEYS IN THE MAILBOX *Play PLAY 39*
11 Jul 74	8	1	2. MAMA I'M NOT THE BOY I USED TO BE *Release RL 726*

Declan RYAN and the REGAL SHOWBAND *7 Weeks*

Born on July 24, 1942 in Cork City, Ireland. Started his musical career with the Dolly Butler Band. Signed by the Jack Brierly Band as lead vocalist. Joined the Regal Showband in 1961. Personnel: Declan Ryan (lead vocals), Mick Ahearn (lead guitar), Paddy O'Sullivan (bass), Benno Haussman (drums), John Minehane (tenor sax/trombone), Kevin Lynch (alto, tenor, baritone sax), Des McAlea (tenor sax) and Gordon Hanley (organ/trumpet). Disc debut: *Love Me* (1964). Left Regal in November 1965, with colleagues, Benno Haussman, Des McAlea and Mick Ahearne, and formed the Arrivals. Declan left the Arrivals in mid 1967. Rejoined Regal for a short period in 1968. Still active on the Irish music scene.

Date	Pos	Wks	ARTIST / Record Title *Label & Number*
26 Jul 65	6	7	1. I NEED YOU *Emerald MD 1014*

Date	Pos	Wks	ARTIST / Record Title *Label & Number*

Marion RYAN *5 Weeks*

Born on February 4, 1931 in Leeds, England. Sang in the school choir. Worked in a variety of jobs before joing the Ray Ellington Quartet in 1953. Made her recording debut in 1954, duetting with Ray Ellington on *All's Going Well.* Signed as a solo artist in 1955 by the new Nixa Record label. Her debut disc *Sailor Boys Have to Talk To Me In English,* issued the same year. Her twin sons, Paul and Barry Ryan, achieved pop success in the 1960's. Died of heart failure on January 15, 1999.

Date	Pos	Wks	ARTIST / Record Title *Label & Number*
18 Mar 58	-	2	1. LOVE ME FOREVER *Nixa N 15121*
16 Apr 58	-	3	2. ALWAYS AND FOREVER *Nixa N 15130*

Bobby RYDELL *2 Weeks*

Born Robert Ridarelli on April 26, 1942 in Philadelphia, USA. Disc debut: *Fatty Patty.* Appeared in films *Bye Bye Birdie* (1962) and *The Lady From Peking* (1970). Was honoured by the City of Philadelphia in October 1995, when the 2400 Block of S. 11th Street in Philadelphia was renamed, Bobby Rydell Boulevard.

Date	Pos	Wks	ARTIST / Record Title *Label & Number*
29 Jul 63	8	2	1. FORGET HIM *Cameo Parkway C 108*

Date	Pos	Wks	ARTIST / Record Title *Label & Number*

S

SAD CAFE ***2 Weeks***

Formed in Manchester, England in 1976, when some members of two rival Manchester bands decided to form a new group. The group took its name from the Carson McCullers book, *The Ballad Of The Sad Café*. Personnel: Paul Young (lead vocals), Ashley Mulford (lead guitar), Ian Wilson (rhythm guitar), Vic Emerson (keyboards), John Stimpson (bass) and Dave Irving (drums). Disc debut: *Black Rose* (1977). Paul Young died on July 17, 2000.

08 Nov 79	9	2	1. EVERY DAY HURTS *RCA PB 5180*

SAILOR ***6 Weeks***

Formed in 1973 in London, England. Personnel: Georg Kajanus (vocals/guitar), Henry Marsh (keyboards), Grant Serpell (drums) and Phil Pickett (keyboards). Signed to Epic Records in 1974. Disc debut: "Traffic Jam" (1974). Phil Pickett went on to work with Culture Club. He co-wrote *Karma Chameleon*. He also played on Sakkarin's hit single, *Sugar Sugar*.

29 Jan 76	2	6	1. A GLASS OF CHAMPAGNE *Epic SEPC 3770*

Crispian ST. PETERS ***5 Weeks***

Born Robin Peter Smith on April 5, 1939 in Swanley, Kent, England. Interested in music from an early age. Formed the duo, Hard Travellers, in 1956. Spotted by EMI employee, David Nicolson, who became his manager. He gave Robin a new name and obtained a recording contract with Decca Records. Disc debut: *At This Moment* (1965). Suffered a major stroke in 1995. Announced his full retirement in 2001 due to constant and worsening ill health.

21 Feb 66	6	3	1. YOU WERE ON MY MIND *Decca F 12287*
23 May66	9	2	2. PIED PIPER *Decca F 12359*

Date	Pos	Wks	ARTIST / Record Title *Label & Number*

Buffy SAINTE MARIE — *5 Weeks*

Born on February 20, 1941 on Piapot Reserve, Saskatchewan, Canada. Daughter of Cree Indian parents. Came to the public's attention during the folk period of the late 1960's. *Soldier Blue* featured in the 1970 film of same name.

Date	Pos	Wks	ARTIST / Record Title *Label & Number*
02 Sep 71	4	5	1. SOLDIER BLUE *RCA 2081*

SAN JOSE featuring Rodriguez ARGENTINA — *2 Weeks*

Instrumental group fronted by Rodriguez Argentina aka ex- Zombies /Argent keyboards player, Rod Argent. Born on June 14, 1945 in St. Albans, Hertfordshire, England. *Agentine Melody* composed by Andrew Lloyd Webber was the official BBC TV 1978 World Cup Theme.

Date	Pos	Wks	ARTIST / Record Title *Label & Number*
29 Jun 78	7	2	1. ARGENTINE MELODY (Cancion De Argentina) • *MCA 369*

The SANDPIPERS — *2 Weeks*

Male vocal trio formed in Los Angeles, USA. Personnel: Jim Brady, Michael Piano and Richard Shoff. Were members of the California based Mitchell Boys Choir before forming a vocal group named the Four Seasons. On discovering that a group of the same name already existed, they became the Grads. Introduced to Herb Alpert who signed the trio to A&M records.

Date	Pos	Wks	ARTIST / Record Title *Label & Number*
24 Oct 66	3	2	1. GUANTANAMERA *Pye 7N 25380*

The SANDS — *26 Weeks*

Irish showband. Formed in Dublin in September 1967 by four ex members of the Miami Showband. Personnel: Tony Kenny (vocals), Murty Quinn (vocals/ trombone), Martin Phelan (tenor sax), Tommy O'Rourke (trumpet), Denis Murray (bass), Bobby Kelly (lead guitar/vocals) and Fran Byrne (drums). Disc debut: *Help Me Rhonda* (1968).

continues over

Date	Pos	Wks	ARTIST / Record Title *Label & Number*

After scoring several hits on Tribune, Hit and Release, the Sands teamed up with producers/songwriters, Phil Coulter and Bill Martin, and signed to RCA Records in November 1971. In August 1972, Tony Kenny, Bobby Kelly and Fran Byrne left the band. The Sands continued, with several personnel changes, until they disbanded in 1978.

Date	Pos	Wks	ARTIST / Record Title *Label & Number*
22 Feb 68	9	2	1. HELP ME RHONDA *Tribune TRS 114*
18 Jul 68	6	4	2. YUMMY YUMMY YUMMY *Tribune TRS 120*
21 Nov 68	4	3	3. DANCE DANCE DANCE *Tribune TRS 122*
10 Jul 69	6	3	4. BUBBLEGUM MUSIC *Tribune TRS 129*
11 Feb 71	6	5	5. CANDIDA *Release RL 553*
15 Apr 71	5	6	6. KNOCK THREE TIMES *Hit HIT 1*
02 Dec 71	5	3	7. LEND A HELPING HAND *RCA RCA 2136*

Candida; Knock Three Times credit: Tony Kenny and The Sands

See also Tony Kenny

Samantha SANG — *2 Weeks*

Born Cheryl Sang on August 5, 1953 in Melbourne, Australia. Made radio debut at the age of eight. Disc debut: *You Made Me What I Am* (1966), under the name Cheryl Gray. Changed her name to, Samantha Sang, in the mid 1970's. Barry Gibb wrote, produced and sang on *Emotions*.

Date	Pos	Wks	ARTIST / Record Title *Label & Number*
30 Mar 78	9	2	1. EMOTIONS *Private Stock PVT 128*

SANTANA — *4 Weeks*

Latin rock group formed by Carlos Santana in San Francisco, USA in 1966. Carlos Santana born on July 20, 1947 in Autlan de Navarro, Mexico. Took up the violin at age of five. When family moved to Tijuana, started to play the guitar. Moved to San Francisco in 1961. Formed the Santana Blues Band in 1965. Personnel (1977): Carlos Santana (vocals, guitar), Tom Coster (keyboards), Graham Lear (drums), David Morgan (bass), Pete Escovedo (bongos, congas, percussion), Armundo Peroza (bongos, congas, percussion).

continues over

Date	Pos	Wks	ARTIST / Record Title *Label & Number*

Paul Rekow (congas, percussion) and Greg Walker (vocals). In 1998, with his wife, Deborah, founded the Milagro Foundation, which supports organizations promoting the welfare of underserved children in areas of health, education and the arts. Has awarded over 1.8 million dollars in grants to date. Inducted into the Rock and Roll Hall of Fame in 1998.

15 Dec 77	4	4	1. SHE'S NOT THERE *CBS 5671*

Mike SARNE — *6 Weeks*

Born Michael Scheuer on August 6, 1940 in Paddington, London. England. Prior to his pop success had minor roles in several films including *No Kidding* (1960). An audition for Robert Stigwood resulted in Mike embarking on a pop career. *Come Outside* featured actress Wendy Richard (Pauline Fowler in the BBC TV soap *Eastenders*). For his follow up single, *Will I What*, Mike teamed up with singer, *Billie Davis*. Starred in films *A Place To Go* (1964) and *Everyday's A Holiday* (1965). After his pop career finished in 1965 moved into photography. Directed several films including *Road To St. Tropez* (1966) and *Myra Breckinridge* (1970). Wendy Richard died on February 26, 2009.

21 Jun 62	4	5	1. COME OUTSIDE *Parlophone R(I) 4902*
13 Sep 62	6	1	2. WILL I WHAT *Parlophone R(I) 4932*

Peter SARSTEDT — *8 Weeks*

Born on December 10, 1943 in Delihi, India. Moved to England in 1954. In the early 60's played bass in Eden Kane's backing group. Disc debut: *I Am A Cathederal* (1968). *Where Do You Go To My Lovely* won the Ivor Novello Award in 1969 (shared it with David Bowie's *Space Oddity*). Peter's two brothers Richard (Eden Kane) and Clive (Robin Sarstedt) have also enjoyed successful careers in pop music.

13 Mar 69	1(2)	8	• 1. WHERE DO YOU GO TO (MY LOVELY) *United Artists UP 2262*

Date	Pos	Wks	ARTIST / Record Title *Label & Number*

Telly SAVALAS *5 Weeks*

Born Aristotle Savalas on January 21, 1924 in Garden City, New York, USA. In his teens worked as a lifeguard at Jones Beach. Joined US Army in 1941. Received a Purple Heart for his services in World War Two. Released from Army service in 1943 after suffering serious injuries in a car accident. Enrolled at Columbia University, studying in psychology, radio and English. Made his film debut in the 1961 film *The Young Savages*. Received an Academy Award nomination as Best Supporting Actor for his role as prisoner, Feto Gomez, in the 1962 film, *The Birdman Of Alcatraz*. Other film appearances include *The Dirty Dozen* (1967), *On Her Majesty's Secret Service* (1969) and *Kelly's Heroes* (1970). In 1973 landed the role of a tough talking New York detective in the television movie, *The Marcus Nelson Murders*. His portrayal of Lieutenant Theo Kojak was so popular that a spin off series resulted. *Kojak* ran until 1978, and resulted in the catch phrase, 'who loves ya, baby'. Died from complications of bladder cancer on January 22, 1994.

06 Mar 75	1(1)	5	• 1. IF *MCA MCA 174*

Leo SAYER *35 Weeks*

Born Gerard Hugh Sayer on May 21, 1948 in Shoreham-by-Sea, Sussex, England. In the late 1960's formed the group, Patches, playing gigs all over the south coast of England. Following an advert in the Brighton local newspaper, the Evening Argus, the band entered the Melody Maker 'Battle of the Bands' contest. The audition took place place at Brighton's Pavilion Theatre, where Leo met the promoter, David Courtney. Leo and Courtney started writing together and put down some demos. Adam Faith got to hear the demos and suitably impressed arranged a recording session. In 1972, Leo and Patches had their first record release, *Living In America*, issued by Warner Bros.

continues over

Date	Pos	Wks	ARTIST / Record Title *Label & Number*
17 Jan 74	3	3	1. THE SHOW MUST GO ON *Chrysalis CHS 2023*
11 Jul 74	5	3	2. ONE MAN BAND *Chrysalis CHS 2045*
03 Oct 74	4	4	3. LONG TALL GLASSES *Chrysalis CHS 2052*
11 Sep 75	1(2)	5	• 4. MOONLIGHTIN' *Chrysalis CHS 2076*
18 Nov 76	5	4	5. YOU MAKE ME FEEL LIKE DANCING *Chrysalis CHS 2119*
17 Feb 77	1(3)	7	• 6. WHEN I NEED YOU *Chrysalis CHS 2127*
02 Jun 77	4	4	7. HOW MUCH LOVE *Chrysalis CHS 2140*
28 Sep 78	5	5	8. I CAN'T STOP LOVING YOU (Though I Try) *Chrysalis CHS 2240*

The SCAFFOLD — *11 Weeks*

Formed in Liverpool, England in 1963. Personnel: John Gorman, Roger McGough and Mike McGear. Disc debut: *2 Day's Monday* (1966). Mike McGear is Paul McCartney's younger brother. Wrote and performed the theme for the hit TV show, *The Liver Birds*. Jack Bruce (Cream) and Graham Nash (Hollies) are featured on *Lily The Pink*.

Date	Pos	Wks	ARTIST / Record Title *Label & Number*
05 Dec 68	1(3)	11	• 1. LILY THE PINK *Parlophone R(I) 5734*

Jack SCOTT — *1 Weeks*

Born Giovanni Dominic Scafone on January 28, 1936 in Windsor, Ontario, Canada. In 1954, formed his own group The Southern Drifters. Disc debut: *Baby She's Gone* for ABC Paramount in 1957.

Date	Pos	Wks	ARTIST / Record Title *Label & Number*
21 Apr 60	10	1	1. WHAT IN THE WORLD'S COME OVER YOU *Top Rank JAR 280*

Linda SCOTT — *1 Weeks*

Born Linda Joy Sampson on June 1, 1945 in Queens, New York, USA. Disc debut: *In-Between Teens* (1960). In 1961 A&R man Gerry Granahan signed Linda to Canadian-American Records and changed her surname to Scott. She appeared in the 1962 film, *Don't Knock The Twist*. Retired in 1969.

Date	Pos	Wks	ARTIST / Record Title *Label & Number*
29 Jun 61	9	1	1. I'VE TOLD EVERY LITTLE STAR *Columbia DB(I) 4638*

Date	Pos	Wks	ARTIST / Record Title *Label & Number*

The SEARCHERS *30 Weeks*

Formed in Liverpool, England in 1960. Took their name from the 1956 John Wayne film, *The Searchers*. Signed by Tony Hatch to Pye Records in 1963. Personnel: Chris Curtis (drums), Mike Pender (born March 3, 1942 in Liverpool, vocals, lead guitar), John McNally (rhythm guitar) and Tony Jackson (born July 16, 1940 in Liverpool, lead vocals, bass). Jackson left the group in mid 1964 to pursue a solo career. Replaced by Frank Allen. Chris Curtis left in 1969, replaced by Billy Adamson. Mike Pender left in 1985 - now leads the Mike Pender Searchers. Tony Jackson is lead vocals on *Sweets* and *Sugar.* Mike Pender is lead vocals on all other hits. Tony Jackson died on August 20, 2003. Chris Curtis died on February 28, 2005.

Date	Pos	Wks	ARTIST / Record Title *Label & Number*
12 Aug 63	1(1)	5	• 1. SWEETS FOR MY SWEET *Pye 7N 15533*
11 Nov 63	6	3	2. SUGAR AND SPICE *Pye 7N 15566*
03 Feb 64	1(4)	8	• 3. NEEDLES AND PINS *Pye 7N 15594*
20 Apr 64	1(1)	8	• 4. DON'T THROW YOUR LOVE AWAY *Pye 7N 15630*
26 Oct 64	4	3	5. WHEN YOU WALK IN THE ROOM *Pye 7N 15694*
22 Mar 65	7	3	6. GOODBYE MY LOVE *Pye 7N 15794*

Neil SEDAKA *22 Weeks*

Born on March 13, 1939 in Brooklyn, New York, USA. Intended to become a concert pianist and studied both piano and composition. Won a scholarship to the famous Juilliard School of Music. Formed songwriting team with lyricist Howard Greenfield while both attended Abraham Lincoln High School. The partnership lasted over twenty years. Composed hits for many artists including Connie Francis, Clyde McPhatter and Captain & Tennille. Recorded with the Tokens in 1956. Signed as a solo artist to RCA Victor in 1958. Career revived in 1974 after signing with Elton John's newly formed Rocket Records label.

Date	Pos	Wks	ARTIST / Record Title *Label & Number*
04 Feb 60	8	3	1. OH CAROL *RCA ERC 1152*
09 Mar 61	2	4	2. CALENDAR GIRL *RCA ERC 1220*

continues over

Date	Pos	Wks	ARTIST / Record Title *Label & Number*
15 Jun 61	6	7	3. LITTLE DEVIL *RCA ERC 1236*
11 Jan 62	7	4	4. HAPPY BIRTHDAY SWEET SIXTEEN *RCA ERC 1266*
16 Aug 62	4	4	5. BREAKING UP IS HARD TO DO *RCA ERC 1298*

The SEEKERS *38 Weeks*

Formed in Australia in 1962 when Judith Durham (born Judith Cock on July 3, 1943 in Melbourne) met up with Keith Podger (guitar), Bruce Woodley (guitar) and Athol Guy (double bass). Moved to Britain in May 1964. Met up with ex Springfields leader Tom Springfield who produced and wrote many of their hits. Disbanded in 1968. Reformed in 1992. Keith Potger formed the New Seekers in 1970.

Date	Pos	Wks	ARTIST / Record Title *Label & Number*
01 Mar 65	2	9	1. I'LL NEVER FIND ANOTHER YOU *Columbia DB(I) 7431*
10 May 65	2	9	2. A WORLD OF OUR OWN *Columbia DB(I) 7532*
15 Nov 65	1(2)	10	• 3. THE CARNIVAL IS OVER *Columbia DB(I) 7711*
19 Dec 66	2	8	4. MORNINGTOWN RIDE *Columbia DB(I) 8060*
30 Mar 67	10	1	5. GEORGY GIRL *Columbia DB(I) 8134*
02 Nov 67	10	1	6. WHEN WILL THE GOOD APPLES FALL *Columbia DB(I) 8273*

Peter SELLERS and Sophia LOREN *7 Weeks*

Peter Sellers, born Richard Henry Sellers on September 8, 1925 in Southsea, England. Made his radio debut, as a comedian, in 1948. In 1949, met up with Harry Secombe and Spike Milligan. On May 28, 1951, *The Goon Show*, with Peter, Harry, Spike and Michael Bentine, made its radio debut under the title *Crazy People*. On June 22, 1952, it was re-christened, The Goon Show. Film appearances include *The Ladykillers* (1955), *I'm Allright Jack* (1959) and a series of Pink Panther films in which Sellers played the role of the bungling detective, Inspector Clouseau. Disc debut: *Jakka And The Flying Saucers* in 1953. Died of a heart attack on July 24, 1980. Sophia Loren, was born Sofia Scicolone, on September 20, 1934 in Naples, Italy. Made her film debut in 1950 as an extra.

continues over

Date	Pos	Wks	ARTIST / Record Title *Label & Number*

Won Oscar for her performance in the 1960 film, *Two Women*. Sellers and Loren starred in the 1960 film, *The Millionairess*.

Date	Pos	Wks	ARTIST / Record Title *Label & Number*
22 Dec 60	5	7	1. GOODNESS GRACIOUS ME *Parlophone R(I) 4702*

SEVERINE — *5 Weeks*

Born Josiane Grizeau on October 10, 1948 in Paris, France. Musical career started at the age of fourteen in band called Les Murators. Represented Monaco in the 1971 Eurovision Song Contest winning with *Un Banc, Un Arbre, Une Rue*. Since 2002 has worked as a singing teacher in Paris.

Date	Pos	Wks	ARTIST / Record Title *Label & Number*
13 May 71	3	5	1. UN BANC, UN ARBRE, UNE RUE *Philips 6009 135*

The SEX PISTOLS — *3 Weeks*

Formed in London, England. Played their first gig on November 6, 1975 and their final one on January 14, 1978. Personnel: Johnny Rotten (vocals), Steve Jones (guitar), Glen Matlock (bass) and Paul Cook (drums). Sid Vicious replaced Matlock in February 1977. Disc debut: *Anarchy In The UK* (1976). From day one group attracted media headlines and controversy. Dropped by EMI shortly after their first single was released. Signed, and almost immediately dropped, by A&M. They wound up on Virgin Records, and released a series of classic singles including *God Save The Queen* and *Pretty Vacant*. Johnny Rotten, (born John Lydon on January 31, 1956 in London) went on to form the group Public Image Ltd. Sid Vicious (born John Simon Ritchie on May 10, 1957 in London) died from a drug overdose on February 2, 1979, whilst on bail on a charge of murdering his girlfriend, Nancy Spungen.

Date	Pos	Wks	ARTIST / Record Title *Label & Number*
15 May 79	8	2	1. SOMETHING ELSE / FRIGGIN' IN THE RIGGIN' *Virgin VS 240*
19 Jul 79	10	1	2. C'MON EVERYBODY *Virgin VS 272*

Date	Pos	Wks	ARTIST / Record Title *Label & Number*

The SHADOWS — *70 Weeks*

Formed in 1958 in London as The Drifters. Changed name to Shadows in July 1960 when American vocal group the Drifters obtained an injunction preventing the group from using their name in USA. Personnel: Hank B Marvin (lead guitar), Bruce Welch (rhythm guitar), Jet Harris (bass) and Tony Meehan (drums). Disc debut (as Shadows) : *Saturday Dance* (1960). Tony Meehan left in late 1961, replaced by Brian Bennett. Jet Harris left in April 1962, replaced by Brian Locking, who in turn was replaced in 1963 by John Rostill. Disbanded in 1968. Reformed in 1973. Represented the UK in the 1975 Eurovision Song Contest with *Let Me Be The One*, finishing in second position. John Rostill died on November 26, 1973. He was accidentally electrocuted while playing guitar in his home studio. Tony Meehan died on November 28, 2005

Date	Pos	Wks	ARTIST / Record Title *Label & Number*
25 Aug 60	1(2)	11	• 1. APACHE • *Columbia DB(I) 4484*
01 Jun 61	7	5	2. FRIGHTENED CITY • *Columbia DB(I) 4637*
15 Mar 62	1(4)	11	• 3. WONDERFUL LAND • *Columbia DB(I) 4790*
16 Aug 62	3	7	4. GUITAR TANGO • *Columbia DB(I) 4870*
31 Dec 62	1(2)	9	• 5. DANCE ON • *Columbia DB(I) 4948*
11 Mar 63	2	8	6. FOOT TAPPER • *Columbia DB(I) 4984*
08 Jul 63	3	7	7. ATLANTIS • *Columbia DB(I) 7047*
21 Oct 63	7	3	8. SHINDIG • *Columbia DB(I) 7106*
17 Apr 75	10	1	9. LET ME BE THE ONE *EMI 2269*
25 Jan 79	7	4	10. DON'T CRY FOR ME ARGENTINA • *EMI EMI 2890*
24 May79	8	4	11. THEME FROM 'THE DEERHUNTER' (Cavatina) • *EMI EMI 2939*

See also Cliff Richard

SHAG — *1 Weeks*

British singer/songwriter/producer Jonathan King, under a nom de plum.

Date	Pos	Wks	ARTIST / Record Title *Label & Number*
23 Nov 72	4	1	1. LOOP DI LOVE *UK 7*

Date	Pos	Wks	ARTIST / Record Title *Label & Number*

SHAM 69 — *2 Weeks*

Formed in Hersham, Surrey, England in 1975. Personnel: Jimmy Pursey (vocals), Dave Parsons (guitar), Dave Tregenna (bass) and Mark Cain (drums). Disc debut: *I Don't Wanna* (1977). Disbanded in 1980. Reformed with Pursey and Parsons in 1987.

Date	Pos	Wks	ARTIST / Record Title *Label & Number*
17 Aug 78	6	1	1. IF THE KIDS ARE UNITED *Polydor 2059 050*
30 Aug 79	9	1	2. HERSHAM BOYS *Polydor POSP 64*

The SHANGRI-LAS — *3 Weeks*

Formed in Queens, New York, USA in 1963. Personnel: Mary and Elizabeth (Betty) Weiss and the Ganser twins, Margie and Mary Ann. Began singing together while still students at Andrew Jackson High School. Started performing at local dances. Came to the attention of producer, George "Shadow" Morton. Took their name from a restaurant, The Shangri-la, in Long Island. Disc debut: *Simon Says* (1963) on Smash. Signed to Red Bird in 1964. Toured UK in March 1965. Broke up in 1968. Mary Ann Ganser died on March 14, 1970. Margie Ganser died of lung cancer on July 28, 1996. Mary Weiss, lead vocals, on hit recordings.

Date	Pos	Wks	ARTIST / Record Title *Label & Number*
23 Nov 72	10	1	1. LEADER OF THE PACK *Kama Sutra 2013 024*
29 Jul 76	9	2	2. LEADER OF THE PACK (re-issue) *Charley CS 1009*

Del SHANNON — *50 Weeks*

Born Charles Weedon Westover on December 30, 1934 in Grand Rapids, Michigan, USA. Taught to play the ukulele by his mother as a young child. Playing guitar by the age of fourteen. Drafted into US Army in 1956 and was stationed in Stuttgart, Germany. Discharged in 1958. Returned to the USA and settled in Battle Creek. Changed his name to Del Shannon. Discovered by disc jockey Ollie McLaughlin, who introduced Del to Irving Micahnik and Harry Balk. Signed with Big Top records in 1961. Debut disc: *Runaway*.

continues over

Date	Pos	Wks	ARTIST / Record Title *Label & Number*

While on tour in England in 1963, heard The Beatles rehearsing *From Me To You* at London's Royal Albert Hall. On his return to the USA he recorded the song and in doing so became the first American artist to cover a Beatles song. Del's version peaked at number sixty seven in July 1963. Moved from Big Top to Amy in 1964. Composed *I Go To Pieces* which was a top ten hit in the USA for Peter and Gordon. Produced US top five hits for Brian Hyland (*Gypsy Woman*) (1970) and Smith (*Baby It's You*) (1969). Died on February 8, 1990 of a self inflicted gunshot wound.

Date	Pos	Wks	ARTIST / Record Title *Label & Number*
25 May 61	2	13	1. RUNAWAY *London HLX 9317*
02 Nov 61	4	2	2. HATS OFF TO LARRY *London HLX 9402*
11 Jan 62	9	3	3. SO LONG BABY *London HLX 9462*
05 Apr 62	2	6	4. HEY LITLE GIRL *London HLK 9515*
29 Oct 62	3	12	5. THE SWISS MAID *London HLX 9609*
28 Jan 63	1(1)	9	• 6. LITLE TOWN FLIRT *London HLX 9653*
13 May63	9	2	7. TWO KINDS OF TEARDROPS *London HLX 9710*
11 Feb 65	6	3	8. KEEP SEARCHIN' (We'll Follow The Sun) *Stateside SS 368*

Helen SHAPIRO — *34 Weeks*

Born on September 28, 1946 in Bethnal Green, London, England. As a thirteen year old attended the Maurice Burman School of Modern Pop Singing. Auditioned for John Barry, who turned her down. Signed to Columbia Records by Norrie Paramor. Starred in the 1962 film *It's Trad Dad*. Played role of Nancy in the 1979 stage production of *Oliver*. Played role of hairdresser, Viv Harker, in the 1986 TV soap, *Albion Market*. Her autobiography, *Walking Back To Happiness*, published in 1993.

Date	Pos	Wks	ARTIST / Record Title *Label & Number*
18 May 61	6	4	1. DON'T TREAT ME LIKE A CHILD *Columbia DB(I) 4589*
03 Aug 61	1(2)	10	• 2. YOU DON'T KNOW *Columbia DB(I) 4670*
12 Oct 61	1(2)	10	• 3. WALKIN' BACK TO HAPPINESS *Columbia DB(I) 4715*
29 Mar 62	3	6	4. TELL ME WHAT HE SAID *Columbia DB(I) 4782*
02 Aug 62	7	4	5. LITTLE MISS LONELY *Columbia DB(I) 4869*

Date	Pos	Wks	ARTIST / Record Title *Label & Number*

Sandie SHAW — *24 Weeks*

Born Sandra Goodrich on February 26, 1947 in Dagenham, Essex, England. In early 1964 entered a talent contest at the Ilford Palais, coming second. As a result got the opportunity to appear on the same bill with Adam Faith at a charity gig on March 1, 1964 at the Commodore Theatre, Hammersmith, London. Adam Faith was impressed and a management and recording contract quickly followed together with a stage name of Sandie Shaw. Disc debut: *As Long As You're Happy* (1964). In 1967 was chosen to perform Britain's entry for the Eurovision Song Contest. *Puppet On A String* not only won the Eurovision title but also topped the charts in Britain and Ireland. In the late 1960's got involved in the fashion business and designed a range of clothing and shoes for the Sandie Shaw label. Enjoyed a return to the charts in 1984 when she teamed up with The Smiths on the single *Hand In Glove*. Her autobiography, *The World At My Feet* published in 1992. Qualified as a Psychotherapist in 1994. In 2002, regained all the rights to her record catalogue.

Date	Pos	Wks	ARTIST / Record Title *Label & Number*
09 Nov 64	7	2	1. (THERE'S) ALWAYS SOMETHING THERE TO REMIND ME *Pye 7N 15704*
24 May 65	1(2)	9	• 2. LONG LIVE LOVE *Pye 7N 15841*
18 Oct 65	8	2	3. MESSAGE UNDERSTOOD *Pye 7N 15940*
06 Apr 67	1(3)	9	• 4. PUPPET ON A STRING *Pye 7N 17272*
20 Mar 69	9	2	5. MONSIEUR DUPONT *Pye 7N 17675*

Gary SHEARSON — *1 Weeks*

Born in 1939 in Inverell, New South Wales, Australia. Moved to Sydney at age of eleven. His mother introduced him to the world of music via her piano playing. Professional singer at age nineteen. Signed to Leedon (Festival) Records in 1962. Disc debut: *The Ballad Of Thunderbolt* (1963). One of his songs *Sometime Lovin'* was recorded by Peter Paul and Mary. Relocated to USA in 1968. In 1972, moved to London.

continues over

Date	Pos	Wks	ARTIST / Record Title *Label & Number*

Had a novel, *Balkenna*, published in 1989. Ordained a church minister in 1992. Today he is an Anglican Church minister in rural Australia.

07 Nov 74	10	1	1. I GET A KICK OUT OF YOU *Charisma CB 234*

Doug SHELDON — *1 Weeks*

Actor/singer. Born Douglas Sheldon in 1936 in Stepney, London, England. Spotted singing on the TV show *Something Old Something New* by showbiz manager Bunny Lewis, who got him a recording contract with Decca. Disc debut: *Book Of Love* (1961). As his recording career ended Doug concentrated on acting and writing. In 1975 his novel, *The Rainbow Man*, was published.

30 Nov 61	8	1	1. RUNAROUND SUE *Decca F 11398*

Peter SHELLEY — *6 Weeks*

Born in London, England. Music was his first love, but worked at various occupations before getting a job in 1965 as record-plugger at Chappell's Ltd. Moved on to join Norman Newell at EMI. Took a position at Decca, as a talent scout, before setting up as an independent producer. Formed a song writing partnership with Ben Findon. Formed Tiger Music, with Marty Wilde, Peter Callander and Mitch Murray. In 1973, co-founded Magnet Records and helped to re-launch 1960's pop star, Shane Fenton, under the name Alvin Stardust.

17 Oct 74	8	2	1. GEE BABY *Magnet MAG 12*
17 Apr 75	4	4	2. LOVE ME LOVE MY DOG *Magnet MAG 22*

Anne SHELTON — *12 Weeks*

Born Patricia Sibley on November 10, 1928 in Dulwich, South London. Vocalist with Ambrose for six years. In 1944 did six shows with the Glenn Miller Orchestra in England. Film appearances include *King Arthur Was A Gentleman* (1942), *Miss London Ltd* (1943), *Bees In Paradise* (1944) and *Come Dance With Me* (1950).

continues over

Date	Pos	Wks	ARTIST / Record Title *Label & Number*
			In 1951 did a three month tour of USA. She received OBE in 1990, for her charity work. Last public performance on July 27, 1994. Died in her sleep on July 31, 1994.
21 Aug 56	-	5	1. LAY DOWN YOUR ARMS *Philips EPB 616*
07 May 57	-	1	2. ABSENT FRIENDS *Philips EPB 679*
17 Dec 59	3	6	3. VILLAGE OF ST. BERNADETTE *Philips EPB 969*
			Pauline SHEPHERD ***3 Weeks***
			Born on September 19, 1938 in London, England. Made her TV debut at the age of sixteen, as a singer, on the BBC programme *Quite Contrary*. Film appearances include *Operation Cupid* (1960).
26 Mar 57	-	3	1. BY YOU, BY YOU, BY YOU *Nixa N 15084*
			SHERBET ***3 Weeks***
			Formed in Sydney, Australia in early 1969. Personnel: Daryl Braithwaite (vocals), Harvey James (guitar), Tony Mitchell (bass), Garth Porter (keyboards) and Alan Sandow (drums). Disc debut: *Crimson Ships* (1970). Changed name to Highway in 1979. Regrouped in the 1980's as the Sherbs, before calling it a day in 1984.
28 Oct 76	5	3	1. HOWZAT *Epic EPC 4574*
			Brendan SHINE ***123 Weeks***
			Born on June 2, 1940 in Portarlington, Co. Laois, Ireland. Moved to Kielty near Athlone in South Roscommon at a young age. A talented musician, he began playing the organ at his local church in Drum at the age of eleven. In the mid 1960's teamed up with the Ciaran Kelly Ceili Band. Disc debut: *Treat My Daughter Kindly* (1967). Formed his own country dance band in March 1968. Big break occurred when promoter Noel Carty went to see the band and and agreed to manage Brendan and the band. Hosted own television programme on RTE television.

continues over

Date	Pos	Wks	ARTIST / Record Title *Label & Number*
23 Oct 70	6	9	1. A BUNCH OF VIOLETS BLUE *Release RL 545*
13 May71	8	2	2. SAILOR BOY *Release RL 578*
10 Jun 71	1(3)	15	• 3. O'BRIEN HAS NO PLACE TO GO *Play PLAY 1*
03 Feb 72	4	3	4. YOU'LL NEVER MISS YOUR MOTHER TIL SHE'S GONE *Play PLAY 13*
03 Aug 72	4	8	5. FAR TOO YOUNG *Play PLAY 27*
14 Jun 73	1(2)	18	• 6. WHERE THE THREE COUNTIES MEET *Play PLAY 56*
11 Jul 74	1(3)	10	• 7. ABBEYSHRULE *Play PLAY 75*
19 Dec 74	5	3	8. CHRISTMAS TIME IN IRELAND *Play PLAY 81*
10 Apr 75	10	1	9. I'LL BE HOME *Play PLAY 84*
10 Jul 75	6	3	10. DUN LAOGHAIRE *Play PLAY 86*
05 Feb 76	1(3)	9	• 11. TURN OUT THE LIGHT *Play PLAY 90*
27 May76	4	6	12. WRONG ROAD AGAIN *Play PLAY 93*
12 Aug 76	6	6	13. ALL MY ROADS *Play PLAY 96*
03 Mar 77	3	5	14. HOW MUCH TIME (Does It Take) *Play PLAY 99*
19 May 77	5	5	15. SOME BROKEN HEARTS NEVER MEND *Play PLAY 102*
05 Jan 78	8	1	16. CHRISTMAS TIME IN IRELAND (re-entry) *Play PLAY 81*
31 May79	1(4)	19	• 17. DO YOU WANT YOUR LOBBY WASHED DOWN *Play PLAY 122*

The BRENDAN SHINE SUPERBAND *6 Weeks*

Launched on July 23, 1972. Personnel: Brendan Shine (leader, accordion), Seamus Shannon (trombone, accordion), Frankie Carroll (bass), Jimmy Hogan (guitar), Louis Burgoyne (drums), Emmet Wynne (trumpet), Owen Shine (organ) and Johnny Dawson (percussion).

Date	Pos	Wks	ARTIST / Record Title *Label & Number*
07 Dec 72	8	6	1. MARCH OF THE HIGH KINGS • *Play PLAY 40*

The SHIRELLES *1 Weeks*

Female vocal group formed in Passiac, New Jersey, USA in 1957 as The Poquellos. Signed to Tiara records by Florence Greenberg who changed their name to The Shirelles. Personnel: Shirley Owens (lead vocal), Addie 'Micki' Harris, Doris Coley and Beverly Lee. Disc debut: *I Met Him On A Sunday* (1958). Shirley Owens-Alston left group in 1975 to pursue a solo career. Inducted into the Rock 'n' Roll Hall of Fame in 1996.

continues over

Date	Pos	Wks	ARTIST / Record Title *Label & Number*

Addie Harris died of a heart attack on June 10, 1982. Doris Coley Kenner-Jackson died of breast cancer on February 4, 2000.

20 Apr 61	9	1	1. WILL YOU LOVE ME TOMORROW *Top Rank JAR 540*

SHOCKING BLUE — *1 Weeks*

Formed in the Hague, Holland in 1967. Personnel: Mariska Veres (vocals), Robbie van Leeuwen (guitar), Klaasje van der Wal (bass) and Cornelis van der Beck (drums). Disc debut: *Lucy Brown Is Back In Town* (1968). Broke up in 1974 when Mariska left to pursue a solo career. Mariska Veres (born October 1, 1947) died from cancer on December 2, 2006.

05 Mar 70	10	1	1. VENUS *Penny Farthing PEN 702*

Troy SHONDELL — *1 Weeks*

Born Gary Shelton on May 14, 1944 in Fort Wayne, Indiana, USA. Discovered at a High School Talent show in 1956 in Fort Wayne. A recording contract in 1958 led to his first record release, *My Hero*, on Smash Records.

30 Nov 61	7	1	1. THIS TIME *London HLG 9432*

SHOWADDYWADDY — *37 Weeks*

Formed at the Fosseway Pub in Leicester, England in 1973, when members of two local bands, Choise and The Golden Hammers decided to amalgamate. Made debut as Showaddywaddy on September 1, 1973 at the Dreamland Ballroom, Margate. Made television debut in late 1973 on talent show, *New Faces*, they won one programme and finished runners up in the All Winners Final. This led to interest from several record companies, but they had by this time, signed to Bell Records. Personnel: Dave Bartram (vocals), Romeo Challenger (drums), Rod Deas (bass), Al James (bass), Trevor Oakes (guitar), Malcolm Allured (drums), Russ Field (lead guitar) and Bill 'Buddy' Gask (vocals, rhythm guitar).

continues over

Date	Pos	Wks	ARTIST / Record Title *Label & Number*
			Disc debut: *Hey Rock n Roll* (1974). Malcolm Allured left group in 1984. Russ Feld left in 1985. Bill Gask left in 1995.
20 Jun 74	5	3	1. HEY ROCK N ROLL *Bell BELL 1357*
29 May75	1(1)	7	• 2. THREE STEPS TO HEAVEN *Bell BELL 1426*
18 Sep 75	5	4	3. HEARTBEAT *Bell BELL 1450*
18 Nov76	3	3	4. UNDER THE MOON OF LOVE *Bell BELL 1495*
07 Apr 77	7	3	5. WHEN *Arista 91*
22 Dec 77	6	2	6. DANCING PARTY *Arista 149*
04 May78	10	1	7. I WONDER WHY *Arista 174*
13 Jul 78	2	5	8. A LITTLE BIT OF SOAP *Arista 191*
09 Nov78	2	4	9. PRETTY LITTLE ANGEL EYES *Arista 222*
12 Apr 79	7	3	10. REMEMBER THEN *Arista ARIST 278*
23 Aug 79	9	2	11. SWEET LITTLE ROCK N ROLLER *Arista ARIST 278*

Labi SIFFRE — *2 Weeks*

Born on June 25, 1945 in London, England. Became seriously interested in music through his older brother's record collection. Bought a guitar at age sixteen. Started writing songs two years later. Played with a number of groups up until 1969 when he decided to embark on a solo career. His song, *Something Inside So Strong* won the 1986 Ivor Novello Award for best song, musically and lyrically. Has had three poetry collections published. Madness recorded and scored a top five hit in 1981 with Labi's composition, *It Must Be Love*.

Date	Pos	Wks	ARTIST / Record Title *Label & Number*
20 Apr 72	7	2	1. CRYING LAUGHING LOVING LYING *Pye Int. 7N 25576*

Carly SIMON — *8 Weeks*

Born on June 25, 1945 in New York City, USA. Teamed up with her sister, Lucy, and gigged as the Simon Sisters. Signed to Kapp Records and issued a single, *Winking Blink And Nod* in 1964. Carly was lead singer with the group, Elephants Memory, for a short period in 1968. Married to James Taylor 1972-83. Signed to Elektra Records in 1985.

continues over

Date	Pos	Wks	ARTIST / Record Title *Label & Number*
			In the late 1980's started writing books for children and to date has five published including *Midnight Farm* (1987) and *Amy The Dancing Bear* (1989). Mick Jagger is featured on backing vocals on *You're So Vain*. *Nobody Does It Better* featured in the 1977 James Bond film, *The Spy Who Loved Me*.
18 Jan 73	4	4	1. YOU'RE SO VAIN *Elektra K 12077*
08 Sep 77	1(1)	4	• 2. NOBODY DOES IT BETTER *Elektra K 12261*

Paul SIMON — *1 Weeks*

Born on October 13, 1941 in Newark, New Jersey, USA. First recorded and released singles as a solo artist in the years 1958-62, under a series of names, Jerry Landes, True Taylor and Paul Kane. Teamed up with Art Garfunkel at high school. Following the split with Garfunkel in 1971, embarked on a solo career. Issued his first solo album, *The Paul Simon Songbook*, in 1965. In 1980, wrote and directed the film, *One Trick Pony*.

Date	Pos	Wks	ARTIST / Record Title *Label & Number*
19 Jul 73	10	1	1. TAKE ME TO THE MARDI GRAS *CBS 1578*

SIMON and GARFUNKEL — *28 Weeks*

Folk/rock duo. Paul Simon born on October 13, 1941 in Newark, New Jersey and Art Garfunkel born on November 5, 1941 in Forest Hills, New York. Became friends in school and started singing together. Made their record debut in 1957 with *Hey Schoolgirl*, under the name Tom and Jerry. Went their separate ways after high school. Teamed up again in 1963, as Simon and Garfunkel, and recorded the album *Wednesday Morning 3 AM*. Due to poor sales the duo split, with Art returning to study at Columbia University and Paul embarking on a tour of England. Reformed in 1965. Stayed together until 1971, when both decided to resume their solo careers. Have reunited for several concerts and tours including a 1982 concert in Central Park and their Old Friends world tour in 2003-2004.

continues over

Date	Pos	Wks	ARTIST / Record Title *Label & Number*
08 Aug 68	6	5	1. **MRS ROBINSON** *CBS 3443*
20 Feb 69	5	5	2. **MRS ROBINSON E.P.** *CBS EP 6400*
22 May 69	7	7	3. **THE BOXER** *CBS 4162*
12 Mar 70	2	11	4. **BRIDGE OVER TROUBLED WATER** *CBS S 54790*

Tracks on **Mrs. Robinson E.P**: Mrs. Robinson / April Come She Will // Scarborough Fair-Canticle / The Sound Of Silence.

See also **Art Garfunkel; Paul Simon**

Nina SIMONE — *2 Weeks*

Born Eurice Kathleen Waymon on February 21, 1933 in Tyron, South Carolina, USA. Made her recording debut in 1959, on Bethlehem record label with the album, *Little Girl Blue*. Left the USA in 1973 to live abroad. Her autobiography, *I Put A Spell On You*, published in 1991. Died April 21, 2003.

Date	Pos	Wks	ARTIST / Record Title *Label & Number*
02 Jan 69	9	2	1. **AIN'T GOT NO - I GOT LIFE** *RCA ERC 1743*

Frank SINATRA — *43 Weeks*

Born Francis Albert Sinatra on December 12, 1915 in Hoboken, New Jersey, USA. Worked as a helper on a delivery truck for the Jersey Observer newspaper 1933-36. With Harry James Orchestra 1939-40. With Tommy Dorsey Orchestra 1940-42. Went solo in 1942. Made film debut as singer with Tommy Dorsey Band in *Las Vegas Nights* (1941). Won an Oscar for Best Supporting Actor in the 1953 film *From Here To Eternity*. Was originally signed to play Billy Bigelow in the 1956 musical, *Carousel*, but walked off the set when he learned they were going to shoot each scene twice. Formed Reprise record company in 1961. Sold it to Warner Brothers in 1963. Won the Lifetime Achievement Grammy in 1965. Announced his retirement in 1970, but made a come back in 1973. Inducted into the Big Band Hall of Fame in 1980. Regarded by many as the greatest popular singer of the 20th century. Nicknames include Ol' Blue Eyes, The Guvnor and Chairman of the Board. Died on May 14, 1998.

continues over

Date	Pos	Wks	ARTIST / Record Title *Label & Number*
14 Sep 54	2	2	1. THREE COINS IN A FOUNTAIN *Capitol CL 14120*
19 Jul 55	-	3	2. LEARNING THE BLUES *Capitol CL 14396*
18 Feb 58	-	2	3. CHICAGO *Capitol CL(I) 14800*
16 Apr 58	-	1	4. ALL THE WAY *Capitol CL(I) 14800*
29 Oct 59	1(2)	7	• 5. HIGH HOPES *Capitol CL(I) 15052*
28 Jul 60	2	4	6. RIVER STAY 'WAY FROM MY DOOR *Capitol CL(I) 15135*
02 Nov 61	9	1	7. GRANADA *Reprise R 20010*
30 May 66	1(2)	8	• 8. STRANGERS IN THE NIGHT *Pye R 23052*
08 May 69	4	10	9. MY WAY *Reprise RS 20817*
06 Nov 69	5	5	10. LOVE'S BEEN GOOD TO ME *Pye RS 20852*

Nancy SINATRA *7 Weeks*

Born on June 8, 1940 in Jersey City, New Jersey, USA. First child of Frank and Nancy Sinatra. Made her national TV debut with her father and Elvis Presley in 1959. Married rock 'n' roll singer Tommy Sands on September 11, 1960. Divorced in 1965. Appeared in several films including *Last Of The Secret Agents* (1966) and *Speedway* (1968) with Elvis Presley.

Date	Pos	Wks	ARTIST / Record Title *Label & Number*
14 Feb 66	1(1)	7	• 1. THESE BOOTS ARE MADE FOR WALKIN' *Pye R 20432*

See also Nancy and Lee

NANCY SINATRA and FRANK SINATRA *7 Weeks*

Father and daughter vocal duo. *Something Stupid* was recorded at the end of a session that Nancy's dad was cutting with Antonio Carlos Jobim. The song was recorded in two take. It would have been done in one, except that during the first take, Frank kept making strange noises trying to break Nancy up. *Something Stupid* topped the singles charts in Ireland, UK and USA.

Date	Pos	Wks	ARTIST / Record Title *Label & Number*
13 Apr 67	1(1)	7	• 1. SOMETHING STUPID *Reprise RS 23166*

The SINGING NUN (Soeur Sourire) *5 Weeks*

Born Jeannine Deckers on October 17, 1933 in Belgium. After a brief period as a teacher she entered the Dominican Order at Fichermont Convent in Wavre, near Brussels in 1959. Took the name Sister Luc-Gabrielle.

continues over

Date	Pos	Wks	ARTIST / Record Title *Label & Number*

On October 24, 1961 she recorded *Dominique* at the Phillips recording studio in Brussels. In 1962, *Dominique* topped the USA singles chart for four weeks. She left the convent in July 1966. Committed suicide on March 29, 1985 along with her friend Annie Pecher. A biography, *Music From The Soul: The Singing Nun Story* by D.A. Chadwick was published in 2005.

23 Dec 63	4	5	1. DOMINIQUE *Philips EBF 1293*

SIOUXIE and the BANSHEES — *1 Weeks*

Formed in London, England in 1976. Personnel: Siouxie Sioux (born Susan Dallion on May 27, 1958 in Bromley, England, vocals), Steven Severin (bass), John McKay (guitar) and Kenny Morris (drums). Disc debut: *Hong Kong Garden*. Disbanded in 1996. Siouxie continued under the name The Creatures.

21 Sep 78	10	1	1. HONG KONG GARDEN *Polydor 2059 052*

Peter SKELLERN — *2 Weeks*

Born on March 14, 1947 in Bury, Lancashire, England. Played organ at his local church and became choirmaster. Studied piano and graduated from the Guildhall School of Music in 1968. Joined local group Harlan County. Group broke up shortly after completing their first album. Wrote the lyrics of *You're A Lady* while working as a hotel porter in Shaftesbury, Dorset. In 1984, formed the group Oasis, with Julian Lloyd Webber, Mary Hopkin and Bill Lovelady.

02 Nov 72	7	2	1. YOU'RE A LADY *Decca F 13333*

The SKIDS — *1 Weeks*

Formed in Dunfermline, Scotland in 1977. Personnel: Richard Jobson (vocals), Stuart Adamson (guitar), Willie Simpson (bass) and Tom Kellichan (drums). Signed by Virgin Records in 1978. Disc debut: *Reasons* (1978). Disbanded in 1982.

continues over

Date	Pos	Wks	ARTIST / Record Title *Label & Number*
			Stuart Adamson left group in 1980. Formed Big Country in 1982. Died on December 16, 2001.
28 Jun 79	6	1	1. MASQUERADE *Virgin VS 262*

SLADE — *54 Weeks*

Formed in Wolverhampton, England in 1966 as the 'N Betweens. Released a single, *You Better Run* on Columbia. In 1968, changed their name to Ambrose Slade. Signed to Fontana Records and issued a single, *Genesis*, and an LP. Spotted by Animals bassist, Chas Chandler, who became their manager. Suggested they shorten their name to Slade. Issued their first record as Slade, *Wild Winds Are Blowing*, in October 1969. Personnel: Noddy Holder (born Neville John Holder on June 15, 1946 in Walsall, vocals), Dave Hill (guitar), Jim Lea (bass) and Don Powell (drums). Starred in the 1975 film, *Slade In Flame.* Played their final concert, in March 1984, at the Cow Palace, San Francisco, USA. Don Powell reformed the group in 1993. Noddy Holder's autobiography *Who's Crazee Now? My Autobiography*, published in 2000.

Date	Pos	Wks	ARTIST / Record Title *Label & Number*
25 Nov 71	1(1)	6	• 1. COZ I LUV YOU *Polydor 2058 155*
17 Feb 72	6	1	2. LOOK WOT YOU DUN *Polydor 2058 195*
29 Jun 72	4	4	3. TAKE ME BACK 'OME *Polydor 2058 231*
14 Sep 72	1(2)	4	• 4. MAMA WEER ALL CRAZEE NOW *Polydor 2058 274*
30 Nov 72	2	7	5. GUDBUY T'JANE *Polydor 2058 312*
22 Feb 73	1(2)	5	• 6. CUM ON FEEL THE NOIZE *Polydor 2058 339*
05 Jul 73	1(1)	5	• 7. SKWEEZE ME PLEEZE ME *Polydor 2058 377*
11 Oct 73	1(3)	6	• 8. MY FRIEND STAN *Polydor 2058 407*
20 Dec 73	1(3)	4	• 9. MERRY XMAS EVERYBODY *Polydor 2058 422*
11 Apr 74	4	3	10. EVERYDAY *Polydor 2058 453*
18 Jul 74	3	1	11. THE BANGIN' MAN *Polydor 2058 492*
31 Oct 74	2	5	12. FAR FAR AWAY *Polydor 2058 522*
29 May 75	3	3	13. THANKS FOR THE MEMORY (Wham Bam Thank You Mam) *Polydor 2058 585*

Date	Pos	Wks	ARTIST / Record Title *Label & Number*

SLIK — *7 Weeks*

Formed in Scotland in 1972 under the name Salvation. Changed name to Slik in 1974. Personnel: Midge Ure (born on October 10, 1953 in Gambusland Scotland, vocals, guitar), Jim McGinlay (bass), Kenny Hyslop (drums) and Billy McIsaac (keyboards). Came to the attention of songwriting/producers Bill Martin and Phil Coulter who became closely involved with the group. Disc debut: *Boogiest Band In Town* (1975). The band split in 1977. Midge Ure went on to enjoy success with the Rich Kids and Ultravox and as a solo artist. Teamed up with Bob Geldof in 1985 to organize Live Aid Concert, on July 13, 1985, to raise funds for famine relief in Ethiopia. *Forever And Ever* was originally recorded by Kenny on their LP, *The Sound Of Super K*.

Date	Pos	Wks	ARTIST / Record Title *Label & Number*
05 Feb 76	2	7	1. FOR EVER AND EVER *Bell BELL 1464*

The SMALL FACES — *10 Weeks*

Formed in London, England in 1965. Personnel: Steve Marriott (born January 30, 1947 in London, vocals, guitar), Ronnie Lane (bass), Kenny Jones (drums) and Ian McLagan (organ). Their original keyboard player Jimmy Winston, was replaced by McLagan shortly after signing for Decca. Disc debut: *What'cha Gonna Do About It* (1965). Marriott left in 1969 to form Humble Pie. Remaining members teamed up with Rod Stewart and Ron Wood in 1969 and became the Faces. Steve Marriott died in a house fire on April 20, 1991. Ronnie Lane died from multiple sclerosis on June 4, 1997.

Date	Pos	Wks	ARTIST / Record Title *Label & Number*
05 Sep 66	3	5	1. ALL OR NOTHING *Decca F 12470*
12 Jan 67	8	1	2. MY MIND'S EYE *Decca F 12500*
23 May68	5	3	3. LAZY SUNDAY *Immediate IM 064*
29 Jan 76	9	1	4. ITCHYCOO PARK (re-issue) *Immediate IMS 102*

See also Humble Pie

Date	Pos	Wks	ARTIST / Record Title *Label & Number*

O.C. SMITH — *8 Weeks*

Born Ocie Lee Smith on June 21, 1932 in Mansfield, Louisiana USA. On his discharge from US Air Force in July 1955 he decided to go for a career in entertainment. Worked with Sy Oliver Band and Art Mooney Orchestra. Disc debut: *Tutti Frutti* (1955). Replaced Joe Williams as vocalist with Count Basie from 1961 to 1963. Died of a heart attack on November 23, 2001.

Date	Pos	Wks	ARTIST / Record Title *Label & Number*
04 Jul 68	2	8	1. THE SON OF HICKORY HOLLER'S TRAMP *CBS 3343*

Hurricane SMITH — *2 Weeks*

Producer/sound engineer/songwriter/singer. Born Norman Smith on February 22, 1923 in London, England. Played in several jazz groups before being hired by the Abbey Road Studios as a tape operator in 1959. Was engineer on all of the Beatles recordings up until 1965, when EMI promoted him from engineer to producer. Produced early Pink Floyd albums including *Piper At The Gates Of Dawn*. Produced the Pretty Things concept rock opera album, *S F Sorrow*. Published his memoirs, *John Lennon Called Me Normal*, in 2007. Died on March 3, 2008.

Date	Pos	Wks	ARTIST / Record Title *Label & Number*
15 Jul 71	8	1	1. DON'T LET IT DIE *Columbia DB(I) 8785*
15 Jun 72	10	1	2. OH BABE WHAT WOULD YOU SAY *Columbia DB(I) 8878*

Patti SMITH GROUP — *2 Weeks*

Formed in Chicago, USA in 1974. Personnel: Patti Smith (born on December 31, 1946 in Chicago. vocals), Lenny Kaye (guitar), Richard Sohl (piano), Ivan Kral (bass) and J D Daugherty (drums). Disc debut: *Hey Joe* (1974). Co-wrote *Because The Night* with Bruce Springsteen.

Date	Pos	Wks	ARTIST / Record Title *Label & Number*
01 Jun 78	4	2	1. BECAUSE THE NIGHT *Arista 181*

Whistling Jack SMITH — *1 Weeks*

Studio session production by the Mike Sammes Singers. Producer Ivor Raymond provided the whistling.

continues over

Date	Pos	Wks	ARTIST / Record Title *Label & Number*

When the disc hit the charts, Billy Moeller was given the name of Whistling Jack Smith to promote the disc on tours throughout Britain. Composed by Roger Cook and Roger Greenaway, the tune was originally titled, *Too Much Bird Seed.*

13 Apr 67	9	1	1. I WAS KAISER BILL'S BATMAN • *Deram DM(I) 112*

Des SMYTH — *1 Weeks*

Born in Dublin., Ireland. Made first public singing appearance with the Catholic Boys Brigade Choir. Formed a vocal group, The Smyth Brothers, with his two brothers Frank and Jimmy. Made their first radio broadcast in 1955 with the Radio Eireann Light orchestra from the Phoenix Hall, Dublin. Discovered by Fred O'Donovan, the group were booked for radio series, *Odd Noises.* Did a season at Butlins Holiday Camp in Mosney. When the group broke up Des worked as a Redcoat at Butlins in 1958 and 1959. Vocalist with the Pete Cusack Orchestra at Mosney in the early 1960's. Joined the Collegemen as lead vocalist in 1962. Disc debut: *The Pillow That Whispers* (1965). Teamed up with the Victors Showband in June 1967. Departed in June 1968 to join Jim Doherty at Dublin's Intercontinental Hotel. Over the years has appeared on more radio and television shows than any other Irish artist. A leading session singer he has provided vocal backing on numerous hit records for other stars. Wrote scripts for RTE television series, *Mike Murphy Show.* A member of vocal group, Family Pride, for a short period in the 1970's. In 1975, won the Overall Title at the Castlebar International Song Contest performing the song, *Roulette.* In 2002, a short film, *Just A Little Bit Of Love – A Tribute To Des Smyth,* starring Claire McGary (girl) and Peter Vollebregt (as Des Smyth), won Awards at Film Festivals in the USA and the Philippines.

continues over

Date	Pos	Wks	ARTIST / Record Title *Label & Number*
			The storyline: A young girl, tired of waiting for the Man of her dreams, decides to build herself one instead, modeling him on her favourite showband singer, Des Smyth. *Rag And Bone Man*, composed by Des and guitarist Jerry Hughes.
16 Aug 73	8	1	1. RAG AND BONE MAN *EMI EMD 4001*
			See also Family Pride

Pat SMYTH & Johnny FLYNN SHOWBAND — *10 Weeks*

Born Patrick Smyth in Dublin, Ireland. Joined band in 1964. The Johnny Flynn Showband was formed in 1956 in Tuam, Co. Galway. Band recorded for a number of record companies during its lifetime including Pye, Emerald, Decca, Hawk and Talisman. Personnel: Johnny Flynn (piano), Frank Flynn (bass), Frankie Hannon (drums), Jim Dalton (lead guitar), Billy Kelly (trumpet) Danny Kelly (trombone), Joe McIntyre (tenor sax) and Pete Creighton (guitar). Johnny Flynn died on November 26, 1996. Frankie Hannon died on August 16, 1975. Jim Dalton died in May 2004.

Date	Pos	Wks	ARTIST / Record Title *Label & Number*
14 Mar 66	1(2)	10	• 1. THE BLACK AND TAN GUN *Emerald MD 1033*

SMOKIE — *44 Weeks*

Formed in Bradford, Yorkshire, England in 1965 as The Elizabethans. In late 1969, had a change of name to Kindness, signing a record contract with RCA After one single release the group were dropped. A move to Decca in 1972, resulted in three single releases, all unsuccessful. In 1974, were spotted by Mike Chapman (of the Chinn and Chapman songwriting team) and were signed to Mickie Most's Rak Records. The group were renamed Smokey. Made their disc debut in February 1975 with the release of their album, *Pass It Around*. Personnel: Chris Norman (lead vocals, guitar), Alan Silson (lead guitar), Terry Uttley (bass) and Pete Spencer (drums).

continues over

Date	Pos	Wks	ARTIST / Record Title *Label & Number*
			In November 1975, Smokey changed the spelling of their name to Smokie. Group disbanded in 1982 with Chris Norman, (born on October 25, 1950 in Redcar), embarking on a solo career. In 1985, the original lineup were asked to reform for a one off gig to raise funds for the Bradford City Football Club disaster fund. Following the gig they decided to go back on road. Chris Norman's solo career was taking off and he left the group in 1986. Alan Barton was drafted as lead singer. In 1995, while on tour in Germany the group were involved in a road accident and as a result of his injuries Alan Barton died on March 23, 1995. Mike Croft was brought in as the bands new lead vocalist. The group enjoyed a return to the British and Irish charts in 1995,with a re-recording of, *Living Next Door To Alice (Who the F*** Is Alice?)*. Terry Uttley is now the only original member in the group lineup.
07 Aug 75	2	5	1. IF YOU THINK YOU KNOW HOW TO LOVE ME *Rak RAK 206*
23 Oct 75	7	3	2. DON'T PLAY YOUR ROCK N ROLL TO ME *Rak RAK 217*
04 Nov 76	3	7	3. I'LL MEET YOU AT MIDNIGHT *Rak RAK 241*
23 Dec 76	3	7	4. LIVING NEXT DOOR TO ALICE *Rak RAK 244*
14 Apr 77	5	4	5. LAY BACK IN THE ARMS OF SOMEONE *Rak RAK 251*
11 Aug 77	6	2	6. IT'S YOUR LIFE *Rak RAK 260*
10 Nov 77	3	5	7. NEEDLES AND PINS *Rak RAK 263*
01 Jun 78	2	6	8. OH CAROL *Rak RAK 276*
21 Sep 78	4	5	9. MEXICAN GIRL *Rak RAK 283*

SONNY and CHER — *6 Weeks*

Husband and wife vocal duo. Sonny, born Salvatore Bono on February 16, 1935 in Detroit, USA. Cher, born Cherilyn LaPierre on May 20, 1946 in El Centro, California. Met up in 1962 at a Ronnettes recording session. First recorded together in 1963 as Caesar and Cleo. Married in 1963. Divorced in 1974. Sonny and Cher performed together from 1965 to 1973. Both recorded solo during their careers.

continues over

Date	Pos	Wks	ARTIST / Record Title *Label & Number*
			Sonny was elected Mayor of Palm Springs, California in 1988. Sonny died on January 5, 1998 when he crashed into a tree whilst snow skiing near Lake Tahoe, along the Nevada – California State line.
06 Sep 65	2	6	1. I GOT YOU BABE *Atlantic AT 4035*
			See also Cher
			SONNY and SEAN — ***4 Weeks***
			Irish male vocal duo. Members of the Pacific Showband. Sonny Knowles born November 2, 1932 in Dublin. Sean Fagan born July 11, 1937 in Dublin.
05 Sep 66	4	4	1. I ONLY CAME TO DANCE WITH YOU *Pye 7N 17165*
			See also Sean Fagan; Sonny Knowles
			David SOUL — ***23 Weeks***
			Born David Solberg on in Chicago, USA. Started his career as a folk singer after dropping out of college in the Sixties. A contract with the New York based William Morris theatrical agency saw him give up music for an acting career. Hit the big time with a starring role in the TV cop series, *Starsky And Hutch.* Played role of Hutch. At the age of thirty three, decided to return to music, and signed to Private Stock records. Returned to acting in late Seventies and his film appearances include *Salem's Lot* (1979).
13 Jan 77	1(2)	5	• 1. DON'T GIVE UP ON US *Private Stock PVT 84*
05 May 77	7	1	2. GOING IN WITH MY EYES OPEN *Private Stock PVT 99*
15 Sep 77	1(4)	9	• 3. SILVER LADY *Private Stock PVT 115*
05 Jan 78	5	4	4. LET'S HAVE A QUIET NIGHT IN *Private Stock PVT 130*
01 Jun 78	6	4	5. IT SURE BRINGS OUT THE LOVE IN YOUR EYES *Private Stock PVT 137*
			Joe SOUTH — ***5 Weeks***
			Born Joe Souter on February 28, 1940 in Atlanta, Georgia, USA Began his career as a country musician. Joined the Pete Drake Band in 1957. Disc debut: *The Purple People Eater Meets The Witch Doctor* (1958).

continues over

Date	Pos	Wks	ARTIST / Record Title *Label & Number*

His songs have provided hits for Deep Purple (*Hush*) (1968), Billy Joe Royal (*Down In The Boondocks*) (1965) and Lynn Anderson (*Rose Garden*) (1970).

Date	Pos	Wks	ARTIST / Record Title *Label & Number*
17 Apr 69	4	5	1. **GAMES PEOPLE PLAY** *Capitol CL(I) 15579*

The SOUTHLANDERS — *1 Weeks*

Formed in London, England in 1953 by Jamaica born singer, Vernon Nesbeth, as The Caribbeans. Changed name to the South Londoners, this was shortened to the Southeners before finally settling on The Southlanders in 1954. Spotted by George Martin who signed the group to Parlophone Records. Disc debut: *Crazy Otto Rag / Earth Angel* (1955). Switched to Decca in 1957. Personnel: Vernon Nesbeth, Frank Mannah, Alan and Harry Wilmot. Are best remembered for their 1958 recording of the novelty song *The Mole In The Hole*. Harry Wilmott died in 1961. Frank Mannah died in 1991. Vernon Nesbeth still fronts the group.

Date	Pos	Wks	ARTIST / Record Title *Label & Number*
03 Dec 57	-	1	1. **ALONE** *Decca F 10946*

SPACE — *5 Weeks*

French electronic music group formed in 1977 by pianist/vocalist/composer, Didier Marouani. Marouani was born on July 14, 1950 in Monaco. At the age of five began his classical music studies in piano, notation and harmonics. At age of fifteen he entered Paris Conservatoire of Music. Had his first album, as a singer, released in 1974.

Date	Pos	Wks	ARTIST / Record Title *Label & Number*
29 Sep 77	3	5	1. **MAGIC FLY** *Pye 7N 25746*

SPARKS — *2 Weeks*

Began life in Los Angeles, California, USA in 1970, under the name Halfnelson. Following an unsuccessful album release, a change of name was decided upon. Sparks was born in 1971. Relocated to England in 1974 and signed to Island Records. Returned to USA in 1975.

continues over

Date	Pos	Wks	ARTIST / Record Title *Label & Number*

Teamed up with producer Giorgio Moroder for hit single, *Number One Song In Heaven*. Personnel: Russell Mael (born on October 5, 1953 in Santa Monica, California, vocals), Ron Mael (born born on August 12, 1947 in Culver City, California. keyboards), Keith Forsey (drums), Dan Wyman (syntheiser, programming), Giorgio Moroder (syntheiser), Chris Bennett (backing vocals) Jack Monan (backing Vocals) and Denis Young (backing vocals).

Date	Pos	Wks	ARTIST / Record Title *Label & Number*
21 Jun 79	5	2	1. NUMBER ONE SONG IN HEAVEN *Virgin VS 244*

Billie Jo SPEARS — *5 Weeks*

Born on January 14, 1937 in Beaumont, Texas, USA. Discovered by songwriter Jack Rhodes. In 1952 made her disc debut, *Too Old For Toys, Too Young For Boys* under the name Billie Jo Moore. Moved to Nashville in 1964, where she obtained a recording contract with United Artists. Signed to Capitol in 1966. Returned to United Artists in 1975.

Date	Pos	Wks	ARTIST / Record Title *Label & Number*
04 Sep 75	9	1	1. BLANKET ON THE GROUND *United Artists UP 35805*
16 Sep 76	4	4	2. WHAT I'VE GOT IN MIND *United Artists UP 36118*

Dusty SPRINGFIELD — *15 Weeks*

Born Mary Isabel Catherine O'Brien on April 16, 1939 in Hampstead, London, England. Had the name Dusty since childhood. As a teenager performed folk songs at a small London club. In 1958, she joined a vocal trio, the Lana Sisters. In 1960, she accepted the invitation of her brother Tom to join him and a friend Tim Field, in what was to become The Springfields. Dusty left the Springfields in 1963 to pursue a solo career. In 1964, she was voted Best Female Vocalist in the NME Pop Poll, a feat she would repeat in 1965, 1966, 1967 and 1969. She relocated to Los Angeles in 1973 and signed to ABC- Dunhill Records. Diagnosed with breast cancer in 1994. At her final recording session in Autumn of 1995 she recorded *Someone To Watch Over Me*.

continues over

Date	Pos	Wks	ARTIST / Record Title *Label & Number*
			Died from breast cancer on March 2, 1999. Inducted into the Rock and Roll Hall of Fame in 1999 (the ceremony was held eleven days after she died).
06 Jan 64	7	4	1. I ONLY WANT TO BE WITH YOU *Philips EBF 1292*
03 Aug 64	5	3	2. I JUST DON'T KNOW WHAT TO DO WITH MYSELF *Philips EBF 1348*
26 Jul 65	8	1	3. IN THE MIDDLE OF NOWHERE *Philips EBF 1418*
02 May 66	4	4	4. YOU DON'T HAVE TO SAY YOU LOVE ME *Philips EBF 1482*
22 Aug 68	6	3	5. I CLOSE MY EYES AND COUNT TO TEN *Philips EBF 1682*

See also The Springfields
See also The Lana Sisters

The SPRINGFIELDS — *10 Weeks*

Pop/folk trio formed in London, England in 1960. Personnel: Tom Springfield (Dion O'Brien), his sister Dusty Springfield (Mary O'Brien) and Tim Field. Disc debut: *Dear John* (1961). Voted Best British Vocal Group of 1961 and 1963 by readers of the New Musical Express. Tim Field left in 1963, replaced by Mike Hurst. Appeared in 1963 film, *Just For Fun.* The Springfields made their final appearance together as a group on October 6, 1963. Dusty going on to pursue a solo career. Tom to concentrate on songwriting. Mike Hurst went on to discover and produce, Cat Stevens. Dusty Springfield died on March 2, 1999.

Date	Pos	Wks	ARTIST / Record Title *Label & Number*
11 Feb 63	2	10	1. ISLAND OF DREAMS *Philips 326557 EBF*

SPRINGWATER — *1 Weeks*

Pseudonym for multi instrumentalist Phil Cordell. Born on July 17, 1947 in Enfield, England. In 1963 joined Steve Douglas and the Challengers. In 1965, formed the group Tuesdays Children. Left in the summer of 1967 to pursue a solo career. Solo disc debut: *Red Lady* (1969). Composed and played all the musical instruments on the recording of *I Will Return.* In 1974, issued an album under the name, *Dan The Banjo Man.* Died on March 31, 2007.

Date	Pos	Wks	ARTIST / Record Title *Label & Number*
02 Dec 71	6	1	1. I WILL RETURN *Polydor 2058 141*

Date	Pos	Wks	ARTIST / Record Title *Label & Number*

SPUD — *5 Weeks*

Formed in Dublin, Ireland in January 1973 by breakaway members of folk group, Thatch. Personnel: Dermot O'Connor (guitar/ mandolin/vocals), Austin Kenny (mandolin/ banjo), Michael 'Smithy' Smith (bass), and Don Knox (fiddle /harmonica/ whistle/ vocals). Disc debut: *Blackleg Miner* (1974). Dermot O'Connor left in 1977, replaced by Ken Wilson and Dave Gaynor (drums). Group disbanded in 1978.

Date	Pos	Wks	ARTIST / Record Title *Label & Number*
19 Dec 74	5	5	1. THE WIND IN THE WILLOWS *Philips 6156 007*

SQUEEZE — *3 Weeks*

Formed in London, England in 1975. Personnel: Chris Difford (vocals/guitar), Glenn Tilbrook (keyboards/vocals), Gilson Lavis (drums), Jools Holland (keyboards/ vocals) and Harry Kakoulli (bass). Disc debut: *Packet Of Three* E.P (1977). Kakoulli left in late 1979. Replaced by John Bently. Jools Holland left in 1980. Replaced by Paul Carrack. Disbanded in 1982. Reformed in 1985 for a charity gig and decided to continue as a working band.

Date	Pos	Wks	ARTIST / Record Title *Label & Number*
19 Apr 79	8	2	1. COOL FOR CATS *A&M AMS 7426*
28 Jun 79	10	1	2. UP THE JUNCTION *A&M AMS 7444*

Dorothy SQUIRES — *1 Weeks*

Born Edna May Squires on March 25, 1915 in Carmarthenshire, Wales. Her earliest professional shows were in the Llanelli area, performing with a local dance band, The Denza Players. At age of eighteen moved to London to pursue her musical ambitions. Made her first radio broadcast in 1936. Signed by Billy Reid and his Accordion Band as vocalist. Disc debut: *When The Poppies Bloom Again* (1936). Married actor Roger Moore in July 1953, they broke up in 1961. Film appearances include *Stars In Your Eyes* (1956). In 1970 she hired the London Palladium, at a personal cost of £5,000, for a concert to be staged on December 6.

continues over

Date	Pos	Wks	ARTIST / Record Title *Label & Number*

Within hours she sold out all 2,300 seats. Declared bankrupt in 1986. Gave last stage performance on March 17, 1990 at Brighton's Dome Theatre. Diagnosed with cancer in 1996. Died on April 14, 1998.

14 Feb 56	-	1	1. WHEN YOU LOSE THE ONE YOU LOVE *Nixa N 15010*

Jo STAFFORD — *2 Weeks*

Born Jo Elizabeth Stafford on November 12, 1917 in Coalinga, California, USA. As a young girl studied classical music, intending to become a classical singer. Teamed up with her sisters, Pauline and Christine, in the vocal trio, the Stafford Sisters. When the trio broke up, Jo joined the Pied Pipers vocal group. In 1939 Tommy Dorsey, signed the Pied Pipers as featured vocalists with his orchestra. Jo left the Dorsey band in 1943 to sign with Capitol Records. The following year she left the Pied Pipers to embark on a solo career. In 1950 Jo left Capitol to sign with Columbia Records. Stayed with Columbia until 1961, when she returned to Capitol. Married Orchestra leader Paul Weston in 1952. Recorded with Red Ingle under the name Cinderella G Stump. Won the Downbeat Award for Top Singer of 1943 and 1945. Went into semi-retirement in 1966 and by 1975 had retired from the music business. Died July 16, 2008.

27 Mar 56	-	2	1. IT'S ALMOST TOMORROW *Philips PB 557*

Cyril STAPLETON and his ORCHESTRA — *2 Weeks*

Born on December 3, 1914 in Mapperley, Nottingham, England. Began learning to play the violin at the age of seven. By the time he was twelve he had made his first radio broadcast from the local radio station in Nottingham. At age seventeen won a scholarship to London's Trinity College of Music. While there spotted a newspaper report that Henry Hall was forming a dance band at the BBC.

continues over

Date	Pos	Wks	ARTIST / Record Title *Label & Number*

Cyril successfully auditioned for membership. In October 1952, the BBC Dance Orchestra had a change of name to the BBC Show Band, and Cyril was appointed as its conductor. The Show Band continued to broadcast three times weekly until June 1957. In the mid 1960's was appointed A&R manager at Pye Records. Died on February 25, 1974.

30 Jul 57	-	1	1. FORGOTTEN DREAMS • *Decca F 10912*
12 Feb 59	8	1	2. NICK NACK PADDY WHACK (The Children's Marching Song) *Decca F 11094*

Alvin STARDUST — *16 Weeks*

Born Bernard William Jewry on September 27, 1942 in Muswell Hill, London, England. Moved with his family to Mansfield, where he grew up. First tasted chart success in the early 1960's under the name Shane Fenton. In late 1973 teamed up with songwriter/producer and co-founder of Magnet Records, Peter Shelley, who relaunched him as Alvin Stardust. Made his debut as Alvin Stardust on *Top Of The Pops* on November 15, 1973. The voice on the recording of *My Coo Ca Choo* was that of Peter Shelley and had actually been released prior to Shane Fenton's appointment as Alvin Stardust. He only assumed the identity of Alvin a few days before *My Coo Ca Choo* was due to performed on *Top Of The Pops*. Peter Shelley also did the vocal on the middle-eight sections of *Jealous Mind*.

13 Dec 73	3	9	1. MY COO CA CHOO *Magnet MAG 1*
28 Feb 74	1(2)	5	• 2. JEALOUS MIND *Magnet MAG 5*
03 Oct 74	5	2	3. YOU YOU YOU *Magnet MAG 13*

The STARGAZERS — *1 Weeks*

Male/female vocal group. Formed in London, England in 1950 when vocalist Dick James suggested to Cliff Adams that they should form a vocal group. Signed to Decca Records. Disc debut: *The Cry Of The Wild Goose* (1950).

continues over

Date	Pos	Wks	ARTIST / Record Title *Label & Number*
			Provided vocal accompaniment on record for many solo singers including Dennis Lotis, Jimmy Young and Dickie Valentine. Voted Best UK Vocal Group for years 1954-56, in the NME Readers Poll. Several personnel changes over the years. Personnel: Bob Brown, Cliff Adams, Dave Carey, Fred Datchler and Eula Parker. Disbanded in 1961.
08 Nov 55	-	1	1. TWENTY TINY FINGERS *Decca F 10626*
			Edwin STARR ***4 Weeks***
			Born Charles Edwin Hatcher on January 21, 1942 in Nashville, Tennessee, USA. Raised and educated in Cleveland, Ohio. In 1962 moved to Detroit. He changed his surname to *Starr* on the suggestion of Don Briggs, the manager of the Bill Doggett combo. Died following a heart attack on April 2, 2003.
12 Nov 70	5	3	1. WAR *Tamla Motown TMG(I) 754*
01 Mar 79	8	1	2. CONTACT *20th Century BTC 2396*
			Kay STARR ***1 Weeks***
			Born Katheryn LaVerne Starks on July 21, 1922 in Dougherty, Oklahoma, USA It was while working at radio station WREC in Memphis that she adopted the name Kay Starr. In 1936 she joined the Joe Venuti Orchestra. When the band broke up she joined Bob Crosby. Signed to Capitol Records in 1947. Left to join RCA in 1955. Resigned to Capitol in July 1959.
27 Mar 56	-	1	1. ROCK AND ROLL WALTZ *HMV IP 1091*
			Ringo STARR ***10 Weeks***
			Born Richard Starkey on July 7, 1940 in Liverpool, England. Built up a reputation as a drummer with local group, Rory Storm and the Hurricanes. In 1962 replaced Pete Best as drummer in the Beatles. Had his first solo album, *Sentimental Journey*, released before the Beatles disbanded. Debut solo single: *It Don't Come Easy*. Solo film appearances include *Candy* (1969), and *That'll Be The Day* (1973).

continues over

Date	Pos	Wks	ARTIST / Record Title *Label & Number*

Narrator of award winning children's television series *Thomas The Tank Engine*. Married actress Barbara Bach in 1981.

Date	Pos	Wks	ARTIST / Record Title *Label & Number*
06 May 71	4	5	1. IT DON'T COME EASY *Apple R(I) 5898*
07 Mar 74	2	5	2. YOU'RE SIXTEEN *Apple R 5995*

See also The Beatles

Candi STATON — *4 Weeks*

Born Canzetta Maria Staton on March 13, 1943 in Hanceville, Alabama, USA. Moved with her mother to Cleveland, Ohio at the age of ten. Member of church choir. With her older sister, Maggie, and Naoimi Harrison formed the Jewel Gospel Trio. Recorded for Nashboro Records. Her big break arrived when she won an amateur night talent show at the 27/28 Club in Birmingham, Alabama. The prize, to open at the club for singer Clarence Carter. She later married Carter.

Date	Pos	Wks	ARTIST / Record Title *Label & Number*
22 Sep 77	4	4	1. NIGHTS ON BROADWAY *Warner Bros K 16972*

STATUS QUO — *16 Weeks*

Formed in London, England in 1962 by Francis Rossi and Alan Lancaster under the name the Scorpions. Changed name later that year to the Spectres. In July 1966, signed to Piccadilly Records and issued single *I (Who Have Nothing)*. The following year, changed group name to Traffic, this was quickly amended to The Traffic Jam, to avoid confusion with Stevie Winwood's group, Traffic. In July 1967, another name change to The Status Quo. Disc debut as Status Quo *Pictures Of Matchstick Men* (1968). Personnel: Francis Rossi (vocals/guitar), Rick Parfitt (guitar/vocals), Alan Lancaster (bass) and John Coghlan (drums). Andrew Bown (keyboards) joined Quo officially in 1976. John Coghlan left in 1982. Alan Lancaster left in 1985.

Date	Pos	Wks	ARTIST / Record Title *Label & Number*
23 Jan 75	2	2	1. DOWN DOWN *Philips 6059 114*
25 Mar 76	6	4	2. RAIN *Vertigo 6059 133*
24 Nov 77	1(1)	6	• 3. ROCKIN' ALL OVER THE WORLD *Vertigo 6059 184*

continues over

Date	Pos	Wks	ARTIST / Record Title *Label & Number*
07 Sep 78	5	1	4. AGAIN AND AGAIN *Vertigo QUO 1*
11 Oct 79	5	3	5. WHATEVER YOU WANT *Vertigo 6059 242*

Tommy STEELE and the Steelemen *9 Weeks*

Born Thomas Hicks on December 17, 1936 in Bermondsey, London, England. Joined the Merchant Navy in April 1952. Discovered in September 1956 singing at the 2 I's Coffee Bar on Old Compton Road, in Soho by entrepreneur John Kennedy, who invited Hugh Mendl of Decca Records to hear Tommy sing. Introduced to Larry Parnes and with a new name, Tommy Steele, and a recording contract with Decca Records was on his way to becoming Britain's first rock 'n' roll star. Disc debut: *Rock With The Caveman* (1956). Made film debut in *Kill Me Tomorrow* (1957). Married Ann Donoughue on June 18, 1960. Starred in several films including *Tommy Steele Story* (1957), *Duke Wore Jeans* (1958), *Tommy The Toreador* (1959), *The Happiest Millionaire* (1967) and *Finians Rainbow* (1968). Appeared on stage on Broadway, New York and London's West End in the production of *Half A Sixpence. Little White Bull* was featured in Tommy's 1959 film, *Tommy The Toreador.* Regarded as one of Britain's finest all round entertainers. His autobiography, *Bermondsey Boy: Memories Of A Forgotten World*, published in 2006. Mike Sammes provided the whistling on *Singing The Blues.*

Date	Pos	Wks	ARTIST / Record Title *Label & Number*
15 Jan 57	-	2	1. SINGING THE BLUES *Decca F 10819*
08 Oct 57	-	1	2. A HANDFUL OF SONGS *Decca F 10923*
19 Nov 57	-	1	3. HEY YOU *Decca F 10941*
16 Apr 58	-	1	4. NAIROBI *Decca F 10991*
14 Jan 60	3	4	5. LITTLE WHITE BULL *Decca F 11177*

Little White Bull credit Tommy Steele

STEELEYE SPAN *6 Weeks*

English folk group formed in London, England in 1969. Disc debut: *Hark The Village Wait* LP (1970). The name 'Steeleye Span' is taken from a character in the Lincolnshire ballad, *Horkstow Grange.*

continues over

Date	Pos	Wks	ARTIST / Record Title *Label & Number*

Personnel: Maddy Prior (vocals), Tim Hart (guitar/vocals), Peter Knight (fiddle), Bob Johnson (guitar), Rick Kemp (bass) and Nigel Pegrum (drums). *All Around My Hat* was produced by Mike Batt.

18 Dec 75	3	6	1. ALL AROUND MY HAT *Chrysalis CHS 2078*

STEVE and EYDIE — *6 Weeks*

Husband and wife vocal duo. Steve Lawrence born Sidney Lelbowitz on July 8, 1935 in Brooklyn, New York, USA. Eydie Gorme born Edith Gormezano on August 16, 1931 in New York City. Steve and Eydie married on August 29, 1957. Performed in Ireland on the Frank Sinatra Show in 1992.

16 Sep 63	3	6	1. I WANT TO STAY HERE *CBS EAAG 163*

See also Eydie Gorme; Steve Lawrence

Cat STEVENS — *8 Weeks*

Born Steven Demetre Georgiou on July 21, 1948 in London, England. Discovered by ex-Springfield member and producer Mike Hurst. Signed to Deram in 1966, moving to Island in 1970. Disc debut: *I Love My Dog* (1966). Dropped out of the music business in 1981 following his conversion to the Islamic faith. Took the name Yusef Islam. Returned to the singles charts in late 2004 when he combined with Ronan Keating on *Father And Son*.

02 Feb 67	3	6	1. MATTHEW AND SON *Deram DM(I) 110*
03 Feb 72	6	1	2. MORNING HAS BROKEN *Island WIP 6121*
15 Feb 73	10	1	3. CAN'T KEEP IT IN *Island WIP 6152*

Connie STEVENS — *6 Weeks*

Born Conceta Anna Ingolia on April 8, 1938 in Brooklyn, New York, USA. Started her singing career with a group called the Three Debs. Played role of Cricket Blake in the TV series *Hawaiian Eye* from 1959 to 1963.

continues over

Date	Pos	Wks	ARTIST / Record Title *Label & Number*
			Her film appearances include *Young And Dangerous* (1957), *Palm Springs Weekend* (1963) and *Grease 2* (1982). Married to Eddie Fisher 1967-1969.
16 Jun 60	5	6	1. SIXTEEN REASONS *Warner Bros. EWB 3*
			Ray STEVENS ***21 Weeks***
			Born Harold Ray Ragsdale on January 24, 1939 in Clarksdale, Georgia, USA. Started taking piano lessons at the age of seven.In 1954 formed the Barons while attending High School. Moved to Atlanta in 1956. Enrolled at Georgia State University to study classical piano and music theory. Disc debut: *Silver Bracelet* (1957). In 1962 joined Mercury Records in Nashville as assistant A&R man. Also worked and recorded for Monoument, Barnaby, RCA and MCA. Won a Grammy Award - Best Contemporary Vocal Performance – in 1970 for *Everything Is Beautiful.* Achieved a second Grammy Award, Best Arrangement, in 1975 for *Misty.*
11 Jun 70	3	6	1. EVERYTHING IS BEAUTIFUL *CBS 4953*
08 Apr 71	3	6	2. BRIDGET THE MIDGET *CBS 7070*
20 Jun 74	2	3	3. THE STREAK *Philips 6146 201*
10 Jul 75	2	6	4. MISTY *Philips 6146 204*
			Rod STEWART ***63 Weeks***
			Born on January 10, 1945 in Highgate, London, England. Discoved by Long John Baldry. Vocalist with several groups including Soul Agents, Steampacket and Jeff Beck Group. Disc debut (as solo artist): *Good Morning Little Schoolgirl* on Decca in 1964. Joined The Faces in 1969. Signed a solo deal with Mercury. Inducted into the Rock and Roll Hall of Fame in 1994.
07 Oct 71	2	10	1. MAGGIE MAY *Mercury 6052 097*
14 Sep 72	2	3	2. YOU WEAR IT WELL *Mercury 6052 171*
04 Oct 73	8	1	3. OH! NO NOT MY BABY *Mercury 6052 371*
28 Aug 75	1(1)	9	• 4. SAILING *Warner Bros K 16600*
27 Nov 75	3	8	5. THIS OLD HEART OF MINE *Riva 1*
24 Jun 76	4	6	6. TONIGHT'S THE NIGHT *Riva 3*
23 Sep 76	3	3	7. KILLING OF GEORGIE *Riva 4*

continues over

Date	Pos	Wks	ARTIST / Record Title *Label & Number*
14 Oct 76	5	4	8. SAILING (re-entry) *Warner Bros K 16600*
16 Jun 77	4	5	9. I DON'T WANT TO TALK ABOUT IT *Riva 7*
27 Oct 77	2	3	10. YOU'RE IN MY HEART *Riva 11*
16 Feb 78	4	5	11. HOT LEGS *Riva 10*
08 Jun 78	8	1	12. OLE OLE *Riva 15*
23 Nov 78	5	3	13. DO YA THINK I'M SEXY *Riva 17*
22 Feb 79	5	2	14. AIN'T LOVE A BITCH *Riva 18*

See also The Faces; Python Lee Jackson

Morris STOLOFF and his ORCHESTRA 1 Weeks

Born on August 1, 1898 in Philadelphia, USA. A child prodigy on the violin Joined the Los Angeles Philharmonic Orchestra in 1915. Musical Director at Columbia Pictures for the period 1936-1962. Began recording under his own name in the late 1940's. Won three Oscars for Best film Musical Scores *Cover Girl* (1944), *The Jolson Story* (1946) and *Song Without End* (1960). When Frank Sinatra founded Reprise Records in the early 1960's he hired Stoloff as Musical Director. Died on April 16, 1980.

Date	Pos	Wks	ARTIST / Record Title *Label & Number*
04 Sep 56	-	1	1. MOONGLOW AND THEME FROM PICNIC • *Brunswick 05553*

Jamie STONE 8 Weeks

Born Carl Corcoran in 1948 in Clontarf, Dublin, Ireland. Had piano lessons as a boy, also learned guitar. Studied music at UCD. Discovered singing traditional songs on an a Crehan Family album, *The Green Hills Of Clare.* Signed to EMI by Guy Robinson. Record producer, John Drummond, came up with his stage name. First gig as Jamie Stone, November 18, 1974 at Carlton Cinema, Dublin. Won RMI (Recorded Music Industry Award) in November 1974 for his debut album, *New Day*, and Best All Irish Record Award for his debut single, *Gulliver.* In 1978 relocated to the USA. Returned to Dublin in 1998 and worked with RTE Radio 1, under his own name, Carl Corcoran. Now a respected presenter, with Lyric FM radio.

Date	Pos	Wks	ARTIST / Record Title *Label & Number*
02 Dec 76	4	8	1. I BELIEVE IN LOVE *EMI IEMI 5052*

Date	Pos	Wks	ARTIST / Record Title *Label & Number*

R and J STONE — *1 Weeks*

Husband and wife vocal duo. Russell Stone and Joanne Williams met while working as vocalists with the James Last Orchestra. Russell Stone born 1946 in Norwich, England. Entered showbusiness in 1964 as a chorus boy with the Black and White Minstrels. Member of Brotherhood of Man in 1971. Joanne Stone died of a tumour in 1979. Today, Russell is a professional counsellar and psychotherapist.

Date	Pos	Wks	ARTIST / Record Title *Label & Number*
04 Mar 76	9	1	1. WE DO IT *RCA 2616*

Gale STORM — *1 Weeks*

Born Josephine Cottle on April 5, 1922 in Bloomington, Texas, USA. Became active in acting after performing at High School Dramatics. Won a local radio talent search contest in 1939 which resulted in a trip to Hollywood and a win in the National final. Signed to RKO Pictures. Film appearances include *Tom Brown's Schooldays* (1940) and *Dude Goes West* (1948). In 1952-55 starred in the TV sit-com *My Little Margie*. Launched own TV series in 1956. Signed recording contract with Dot Records. Her autobiography, *I Ain't Down Yet*, published in 1981. Died on June 27, 2009.

Date	Pos	Wks	ARTIST / Record Title *Label & Number*
13 Aug 57	-	1	1. DARK MOON *London HL 8424*

Wally STOTT and his ORCHESTRA — *1 Weeks*

Born Walter Stott on March 10, 1924 in Leeds, Yorkshire, England. Principal saxophonist with the Oscar Rabin Band and the Geraldo Orchestra in the 1940's. Conductor of the BBC Radio Orchestra in the 70's. Influenced and encouraged by Robert Farnon. Employed as producer by Philips Records and responsible for production on recordings by artists such as Diana Dors and Dusty Springfield. In 1972, underwent a sex reassignment surgery and changed name to Angela Morley. Received three Emmy Awards for her work in television musical scoring. Died on January 15, 2009.

Date	Pos	Wks	ARTIST / Record Title *Label & Number*
23 Nov 54	1(1)	1	• 1. THE CAT FROM COOS BAY • *Philips PB 351*

Date	Pos	Wks	ARTIST / Record Title *Label & Number*

The STRANGERS — *5 Weeks*

Irish beat group formed in Balbriggan, Co. Dublin in 1963. Personnel: Jimmy Fanning (born on March 14, 1945 in Dublin. lead vocals), Len Guest (lead guitar), Maxie McEvoy (bass), Tommy Caffrey (rhythm guitar) and Vic McNamara (drums). Disc debut: *Look Out (Here Comes Tomorrow)*. Vic McNamara left in January 1968 to join Derrick and the Sounds. Len Guest departed in May 1969 to join The Lions. In July 1969, the group augmented to a seven piece and joined the showband ranks for a short period. Split in early 1970's. Vic McNamara died in October 2005.

Date	Pos	Wks	ARTIST / Record Title *Label & Number*
13 Apr 67	6	5	1. LOOK OUT (HERE COMES TOMORROW) *Pye 7N 17274*

The STRAWBS — *1 Weeks*

Formed in London, England in 1967 as the Strawberry Hill Boys. In June 1967, formally renamed The Strawbs. Disc debut: *Oh How She Changed*, in June 1968 on A&M Records. Personnel: Dave Cousins (guitar), John Ford (bass), Richard Hudson (drums), Blue Weaver (keyboards), and Dave Lambert (guitar). Following a U.S. tour in mid 1973, Ford, Hudson and Weaver split from group, going to form Hudson-Ford. *Part Of The Union* composed by John Ford and Richard Hudson.

Date	Pos	Wks	ARTIST / Record Title *Label & Number*
01 Mar 73	10	1	1. PART OF THE UNION *A&M AMS 7047*

Gary STREET and the FAIRWAYS — *1 Weeks*

Irish showband. Gary Street was born Joe Conway on July 31, 1947 in Nuneaton, Warwickshire, England. In 1962, formed a group called The Tartans. Relocated to Ireland in 1965. Joined The Agents in mid 1967. Changed name to The Fairways in January 1968. With fellow member of the Fairways, Mick Bryan, composed the bulk of the Fairways recorded output. Left Fairways in December 1969. Joined the Tom Kelly Sound who evolved into the New Fairways. Died on July 5, 2003.

continues over

Date	Pos	Wks	ARTIST / Record Title *Label & Number*

The Fairways Showband were formed in 1965 in Edenderry, County Offaly. Ireland, as The Agents. Personnel: Gary Street (lead vocals), Mick Bryan (lead guitar), Ollie Kennedy (bass), Danny Slevin (trombone), Michael Moore (tenor sax), Bobby Clark (trumpet), P.J. Walsh (drums) and Pat Cleary (organ). Disbanded in December 1969. The rhythm section joined Larry Cunningham's County Blue Boys. In 1969, Gary Street and The Fairways won the Pop Songs Section at the Castlebar International Song Contest performing the song, *Jodi.* Mick Bryan died on April 25, 1970. Gary Street died on July 5, 2003.

Date	Pos	Wks	ARTIST / Record Title *Label & Number*
14 Mar 68	10	1	1. FLIPIDDY FLOP *King KG 1071*

Barbra STREISAND — *4 Weeks*

Born Barbara Joan Streisand on April 24, 1942 in Brooklyn, New York City, USA. Began her showbiz career as an actress making her Broadway debut in the 1962 production of *I Can Get It For You Wholesale.* Film debut: *Funny Girl* (1968) for which she won Oscar for Best actress. Also starred in *Hello Dolly* (1969), *A Star Is Born* (1976) and *Meet The Fockers* (2004). Received an Academy award for co-writing (with Paul Williams) the song *Evergreen.*

Date	Pos	Wks	ARTIST / Record Title *Label & Number*
30 Jun 77	4	4	1. LOVE THEME FROM 'A STAR IS BORN' (EVERGREEN) *CBS 4855*

See also Barbra and Neil
See also Donna Summer and Barbra Streisand

The STRING-A-LONGS — *6 Weeks*

Formed in Plainview, Texas, USA in 1955 as the Patio Kids. The group recorded as the Leen Teens before their manager, Norman Petty, changed their name to the String-A-Longs, and launched them as an instrumental group. Disc debut: *I Think It's Really Love* (1956) as the Leen Teens.

continues over

Date	Pos	Wks	ARTIST / Record Title *Label & Number*
			Personnel: Jimmy Torres (lead guitar), Aubrey Lee de Cordova (bass), Richard Stephens (lead guitar), Keith McCormack (rhythm guitar), and Don Allen (drums).
09 Mar 61	4	6	1. WHEELS • *London HLU 9278*

Gene STUART and the MIGHTY AVONS — *30 Weeks*

Born on May 16, 1943 in Lisnagleer, Dungannon, Co. Tyrone, N. Ireland. Member of school choir. Joined local group the Dynamic Sounds before moving to the Ken Kennedy Band. Worked with the Dungannon Observer newspaper as a freelance photographer. Signed by the Mighty Avons as replacement for Larry Cunningham. Made his debut on September 18, 1969. Mighty Avons personnel: Gene Stuart (lead vocals), Jimmy Smith (leader, tenor sax), Paddy Smith (trumpet), Peter Smith (tenor sax), Mickey Brady (lead guitar), Gerry Walsh (bass) and Brian Finlay (drums). In July 1972, Gene was struck down with a serious illness and spent six months off the bandstand. Brian Harkin filled in for him. Gene returned in January 1973. He left the Mighty Avons in December 1974, to form his own band, The Homesteaders.

Date	Pos	Wks	ARTIST / Record Title *Label & Number*
22 Jan 70	3	9	1. BEFORE THE NEXT TEARDROP FALLS *Dolphin DOS 53*
16 Jul 70	5	10	2. I'M JUST LUCKY I GUESS *Dolphin DOS 67*
09 Sep 71	8	5	3. DON'T GO *Velvet VE 009*
13 Apr 72	6	3	4. KISS AN ANGEL GOOD MORNING *Velvet VE 014*
03 Jan 74	2	3	5. CHRISTMAS IN MY HOMETOWN *Hawk HASP 331*

The STYLISTICS — *18 Weeks*

Formed in Philadelphia, USA in 1968 when two competing groups, The Monarchs and The Percussions, met at a talent contest and decided to amalgamate and The Stylistics were born. Personnel: Russell Thompkins Jr.(lead vocals), Airrion Love, James Smith, James Dunn and Herb Murrell. Disc debut: *You're A Big Girl Now* (1969). James Dunn left group in 1980.

continues over

Date	Pos	Wks	ARTIST / Record Title *Label & Number*
			James Smith left in 1981, replaced by Raymond Johnson, who left in 1985. Russell Thompkins Jr left in 2000. In 2004 he formed The New Stylistics.
27 Feb 75	8	1	1. STAR ON A TV SHOW *Avco 6105 035*
05 Jun 75	5	3	2. SING BABY SING *Avco 6105 036*
14 Aug 75	1(3)	7	• 3. CAN'T GIVE YOU ANYTHING (But My Love) *Avco 6105 039*
27 Nov 75	3	6	4. NA NA IS THE SADDEST WORD *Avco 6105 059*
23 Sep 76	9	1	5. SIXTEEN BARS *H&L STYL 6105 059*

Donna SUMMER — *9 Weeks*

Born Donna Adrian Gaines on December 31, 1948 in Boston, Massachusetts, USA. Sang in the local church choir. Member of rock band The Crow. On their breakup moved to New York. Auditioned for a role in the Broadway production of *Hair*. Hired for a touring US production, she was assigned to the musical's German cast and relocated to Germany. In 1973 Donna met producer and writer Giorgio Moroder who went on to produce her hits. Her autobiography, *Ordinary Girl The Journey*, published in 2004.

Date	Pos	Wks	ARTIST / Record Title *Label & Number*
11 Aug 77	9	2	1. I FEEL LOVE *GTO GT 100*
05 Jan 78	2	5	2. LOVE'S UNKIND *GTO GT 113*
02 Nov 78	7	2	3. MACARTHUR PARK *Casablanca CAN 131*

Donna SUMMER and Barbra STREISAND — *2 Weeks*

Female vocal duo. Donna Summer born Donna Adrian Gaines on December 31, 1948 in Boston, Massachusetts, USA. Barbra Streisand born on April 24, 1942 in Brooklyn New York City, USA. Record originally released by both the artists record companies, Casablanca and CBS, at the same time. Track produced by Gary Klein and Georgio Moroder.

Date	Pos	Wks	ARTIST / Record Title *Label & Number*
29 Nov 79	7	2	1. NO MORE TEARS (Enough Is Enough) *Casablanca CAN 174 / CBS 8000*

Date	Pos	Wks	ARTIST / Record Title *Label & Number*
			SUNNY ***3 Weeks***
			Sunny Leslie born Heather Weetman in 1948 in Madras, India. Relocated to Britain at a young age. At the age of fifteen teamed up with her sister, Sue (Yvonne Weetman), and they recorded together under several names including The Myrtelles, Sue and Sunshine and Sue and Sunny. The sisters were also original members of Brotherhood of Man. Sunny embarked on a solo career in early 1970's.
02 May74	4	3	1. DOCTORS ORDERS *CBS 2068*
			The Monty SUNSHINE QUARTET ***1 Weeks***
			Part of the Chris Barber Jazzband. Personnel: Monty Sunshine (clarinet), Eddie Smith (banjo), Dick Smith (bass) and Ron Bowden (drums). Monty Sunshine born on April 8, 1928 in London, England. Started to play the clarinet while a student at Camberwell School of Art. Formed the Crane River Jazz Band in 1949. Founding member of the Chris Barber Jazzband, made their debut on May 31, 1954. Left the Barber band at the end of 1960 and in March 1961 launched the Monty Sunshine Jazz Band. *The Old Rugged Cross* was recorded while Monty was a member of Chris Barber Jazzband.
18 Feb 58	-	1	1. THE OLD RUGGED CROSS • *Nixa NJ 2020*
			See also the Chris Barber Jazzband
			SUPERTRAMP ***6 Weeks***
			Formed in London, England in 1969 when Dutch millionaire, Stanley August Micsegaes, gave Richard Davies, the money to form his own band. Personnel: Richard Davies (vocals, keyboards), Roger Hodgson (lead guitar), Dougie Thompson (bass), John Helliwell (saxophone) and Bob Siedenberg (drums). Disbanded in 1971. Reformed in 1973.
03 May79	6	3	1. THE LOGICAL SONG *A&M AMS 7427*
26 Jul 79	6	3	2. BREAKFAST IN AMERICA *A&M AMS 7451*

Date	Pos	Wks	ARTIST / Record Title *Label & Number*

Art SUPPLE and the VICTORS — *4 Weeks*

Irish showband. Art Supple born on December 21, 1942 in Youghal, County Cork, Ireland. Started his musical career as vocalist with local band, the Pat Irwin All Stars. Joined Victors in May 1963. Nickname: *Mr Personality*. Disc debut: *Showbands On Parade*. Art moved to the Brendan Shine Superband in July 1974. Left in April 1977 to join Stage Two. In 1979 formed his own band The Showstoppers. In 1999 entered local politics and was elected to Cork County Council. The Victors Showband formed in Cork in 1963. Personnel: Art Supple (lead vocals, bass), Pat McGeegan (lead vocals, rhythm guitar), Chris St Leger (leader, tenor sax), Tony Erangey (drums), Len McCarthy (tenor sax), Mickey Brennan (trombone) and Wolfgang Nordt (lead guitar). Many personnel changes over the years. The Victors disbanded in 1974.

Date	Pos	Wks	ARTIST / Record Title *Label & Number*
02 Aug 65	9	3	1. SHOWBANDS ON PARADE *Rex R 11008*
13 Jun 66	8	1	2. SAFELY IN LOVE AGAIN *Emerald MD 1043*

The SUPREMES — *8 Weeks*

Female vocal group formed in 1959 in Detroit, USA, as the Primettes. Personnel: Mary Wilson, Florence Ballard and Betty McGlown. Diana Ross (born March 26, 1944 in Detroit) joined the group later the same year. Recorded for Lupine in 1960. In 1961 after McGlown and her replacement Barbara Martin left the group, the Primettes signed a recording contract with Motown Records, and changed their name to the Supremes. In July 1967, Florence Ballard was dismissed from the group and replaced by Cindy Birdsong. Group then billed as Diana Ross and the Supremes. Ross left in 1970 to pursue a solo career. Jean Terrell replaced Ross. Supremes broke up in 1977. Inducted into Rock 'n Roll Hall of Fame in 1988. Florence Ballard died of a heart attack on February 22, 1976.

continues over

Date	Pos	Wks	ARTIST / Record Title *Label & Number*
05 Nov 64	3	1	1. WHERE DID OUR LOVE GO *Stateside SS(I) 327*
16 Nov 64	2	5	2. BABY LOVE *Stateside SS(I) 350*
22 Jun 67	10	2	3. THE HAPPENING *Tamla Motown TMG(I) 607*

See also Diana Ross and the Supremes and the Temptation

The SUTHERLAND BROTHERS and QUIVER *9 Weeks*

Formed in London, England in 1972. Personnel: Iain Sutherland (vocals, guitar), Gavin Sutherland (bass, vocals), Tim Renwick (guitar), Pete Wood (keyboards), Bruce Thomas (bass) and Willie Nelson (drums). Disbanded in 1977. The Sutherland brothers composed *Sailing*, a million seller for Rod Stewart.

Date	Pos	Wks	ARTIST / Record Title *Label & Number*
20 May76	2	9	1. ARMS OF MARY *CBS 4001*

The SWARBRIGGS *29 Weeks*

Irish showband formed in Mullingar, Co. Westmeath in October 1975, around the musical and songwriting talents of brothers, Tommy and Jimmy Swarbrigg. Tommy Swarbrigg born Thomas Sheridan Swarbrigg on May 18, 1942 in Castlerea, Co. Roscommon. Member of the Jordanaires Showband 1961-63. Joined Joe Dolan and The Drifters Showband, as trumpeter, in 1963. Made his solo vocal disc debut in 1966, when, *Minutes To Midnight*, was featured on Joe Dolan and Drifters Showband E.P., *Two Of A Kind*. Left the Drifters Showband in 1969, to team up with brother, Jimmy, and together with three ex Drifters, formed the Times Showband. Jimmy Swarbrigg born John James Swarbrigg on October 20, 1943 in Castlerea, Co. Roscommon. Moved to London in early 1960's. Member of Lee Hunter and The Falcons (1963-65) and the Saints And Sinners Showband (1965-69). The Swarbriggs personnel: Tommy Swarbrigg (vocals), Jimmy Swarbrigg (vocals), James Delaney (keyboards), Mickey O'Neill (drums), Sean Kenny (lead guitar) and Tommy Moore (bass).

continues over

Date	Pos	Wks	ARTIST / Record Title *Label & Number*
			Numerous changes in personnel occurred over the band's lifespan. For a short period in 1978, were known as Winter, an attempt by their record company EMI, to break the group on the international market. Tommy Swarbrigg retired from the music business in 1981. Jimmy continued for a short period before retiring from the performing side of the music business.
13 Mar 75	2	7	1. THAT'S WHAT FRIENDS ARE FOR *EMI IEMI 5013*
13 Nov 75	2	7	2. FUNNY *EMI IEMI 5031*
19 Aug 76	4	6	3. JOANNE *EMI IEMI 5047*
06 Jan 77	5	6	4. SOMEONE ELSES'S LAND *EMI IEMI 5054*
20 Apr 78	9	3	5. ROCK N ROLL KISSES *EMI IEMI 5079*
			See also The Times

The SWARBRIGGS Plus 2 — *10 Weeks*

Formed in early 1977, on the suggestion of RTE producer, Tom McGrath, to participate in the National Song Contest of that year. The group won the National Song Contest, with a Tommy and Jimmy Swarbrigg composition, *It's Nice To Be In Love Again.* Represented Ireland in the Eurovision Song Contest, finishing in third position. Personnel: Tommy Swarbrigg, Jimmy Swarbrigg, Alma Carroll and Nicola Kerr. The group only made about a dozen live public appearances before disbanding. Tommy and Jimmy Swarbrigg returned to the Swarbriggs band. Alma Carroll (born in Dublin) resumed her solo career and Nicola Kerr (born in Lurgan, Co. Armagh) joined the New Seekers.

Date	Pos	Wks	ARTIST / Record Title *Label & Number*
07 Apr 77	1(2)	10	• 1. IT'S NICE TO BE IN LOVE AGAIN *EMI IEMI 5059*

SWEENEYS MEN — *13 Weeks*

Folk/ballad group formed in 1966 in Galway, Ireland. Personnel: Johnny Moynihan (born Dublin, fiddle, bouzouki), Andy Irvine (born London, guitar) and Joe Dolan (born Galway, guitar). Disc debut: "Old Maid In A Garret" (1967). Andy Irvine lead vocals on *Old Maid In A Garret.*

continues over

Date	Pos	Wks	ARTIST / Record Title *Label & Number*
			Johnny Moynihan lead vocals on *Waxies Dargle*. Joe Dolan left in June 1967, was replaced by Dublin born Terry Woods. Andy Irvine left in May 1968, replaced by Henry McCullough (born Portsteward, Co. Antrim). Group signed to Transatlantic Records in 1968. Disbanded in 1969. Terry Woods went on to form the Woods Band. In 1980's he teamed up with The Pogues. Henry McCullough went on to join Paul McCartney in Wings. Joe Dolan died in January 2008.
25 May 67	6	6	1. OLD MAID IN A GARRET *Pye 7N 17312*
15 Feb 68	5	7	2. WAXIES DARGLE *Pye 7N 17459*
			The SWEET ***47 Weeks***
			Formed in London in 1966 under the name Sweetshop. Personnel: Brian Connolly (born October 5, 1945 in Hamilton, Scotland, vocals), Mick Tucker (drums), Steve Priest (bass) and Frank Torpey (guitar). A change of name to Sweet and a recording contract with Fontana followed. Disc debut: *Slow Motion* (1968). After a number of unsuccessful singles with Fontana and Parlophone Frank Torpey was replaced by Mick Stewart who in turn was replaced by Andy Scott. The group were introduced to Nicky Chinn and Mike Chapman and signed to RCA. Brian Connolly died on February 9, 1997. Mick Tucker died from luekaemia on February 14, 2002.
13 May 71	7	2	1. FUNNY FUNNY *RCA 2051*
08 Jul 71	3	7	2. CO-CO *RCA 2087*
06 Jul 72	9	2	3. LITTLE WILLY *RCA 2225*
05 Oct 72	4	4	4. WIG WAM BAM *RCA 2260*
25 Jan 73	1(2)	9	• 5. BLOCKBUSTER *RCA 2305*
10 May 73	2	4	6. HELL RAISER *RCA 2357*
27 Sep 73	1(3)	5	• 7. BALLROOM BLITZ *RCA 2403*
31 Jan 74	1(2)	5	• 8. TEENAGE RAMPAGE *RCA LPBO 5004*
10 Apr 75	2	5	9. FOX ON THE RUN *RCA RCA 2524*
07 Aug 75	7	2	10. ACTION *RCA 2578*
16 Mar 78	8	2	11. LOVE IS LIKE OXYGEN *Polydor POSP 001*

Date	Pos	Wks	ARTIST / Record Title *Label & Number*
			SWEET SENSATION ***2 Weeks***
			Formed in Manchester, England in 1973. Following their win on TV talent show, New Faces, the group were signed to Pye Records. Personnel: Marcel King (lead vocals), St. Clair Palmer, Vincent James, Junior Day plus musicians Leroy Smith (piano), Gary Shaughnessy (guitar), Barry Johnson (bass) and Roy Flowers (drums). Leroy Smith died on January 15, 2009.
10 Oct 74	6	2	1. **SAD SWEET DREAMER** *Pye 7N 45385*
			The SWINGING BLUE JEANS ***7 Weeks***
			Formed in Liverpool, England in 1959 as the Blue-Genes. Changed name to the Swinging Blue Jeans in 1962. Disc debut: *It's Too Late Now* (June 1963). Personnel: Ray Ennis (born on May 26, 1940 in Huyton, Liverpool, lead vocals, guitar), Les Braid (bass), Ralph Ellis (guitar vocals) and Norman Kuhlke (drums). Ellis left in January 1966, replaced by Terry Sylvester. In December 1968, Terry Sylvester left to join The Hollies. Replaced by Colin Manley. Norman Kuhlke left group in 1969. Colin Manley died on April 9, 1999. Les Braid died of cancer on July 31, 2005.
20 Jan 64	2	7	1. **HIPPY HIPPY SHAKE** *HMV POP(I) 1242*
			SYLVIA ***2 Weeks***
			Born Sylvia Vrethammer on August 22, 1945 in Uddevalla, Gotalands Ian, Sweden.
26 Sep 74	6	2	1. **VIVA ESPANA** *Sonet SON 2037*

Date	Pos	Wks	ARTIST / Record Title *Label & Number*

T

T REX — *38 Weeks*

Formed in London, England in 1970 by Marc Bolan. Personnel: Marc Bolan (vocals, guitar), Mickey Finn (percussion), Steve Currie (bass) and Bill Legend (drums). Disc debut: *Ride A White Swan* (1970). Marc Bolan was born Marc Feld on September 30, 1947 in Hackney, London, England. Changed his name to Bolan in 1965. Signed to Decca Records and made his solo disc debut, *The Wizard* (1965). In March 1967 joined the group, John's Children. When the group broke up, Bolan and Steve Peregrin Took formed Tyrannosaurus Rex Rex, a folk rock acoustic duo. Signed with Regal Zonophone. Took left in late 1969. Mickey Finn replaced him, they shortened the group name and T Rex was born. In 1977, Marc Bolan fronted a six part television series, *Marc*, on ITV. Marc Bolan died when a car driven by his then girlfriend, Gloria Jones, hit a tree on September 16, 1977. Steve Currie died in a road crash on April 28, 1981. Mickey Finn died on January 11, 2003.

Date	Pos	Wks	ARTIST / Record Title *Label & Number*
25 Mar 71	1(3)	10	• 1. HOT LOVE *Fly BUG 6*
29 Jul 71	1(2)	6	• 2. GET IT ON *Fly BUG 10*
09 Dec 71	2	5	3. JEEPSTER *Fly BUG 16*
10 Feb 72	1(1)	3	• 4. TELEGRAM SAM *T Rex 101*
01 Jun 72	1(1)	5	• 5. METAL GURU *T Rex MARC 1*
28 Sep 72	1(2)	4	• 6. CHILDREN OF THE REVOLUTION *T Rex MARC 2*
14 Dec 72	4	5	7. SOLID GOLD EASY ACTION *T Rex MARC 3*

The TAMS — *5 Weeks*

Formed in Atlanta, Georgia, USA in 1952 as the Four Dots. Changed name to Tams in 1960. Personnel: Joseph Pope (lead vocals), Charles Pope, Robert Smith, Floyd Ashton and Horace Key.

continues over

Date	Pos	Wks	ARTIST / Record Title *Label & Number*

Ashton left in 1964, replaced by Albert Cottle. Horace Kay died in 1991. Joseph Pope died on March 16, 1996. *Hey Girl Don't Bother Me* was originally released in the USA in 1964.

23 Sep 71	1(1)	5	• 1. HEY GIRL DON'T BOTHER ME *Probe PRO 532*

The TARRIERS — *1 Weeks*

Formed in New York, USA in 1955 as The Tunetellers. Personnel: Bob Carey (bass, guitar), Erik Darling (tenor, banjo) and Alan Arkin (baritone, guitar). Made their first recording with balladeer Vince Martin on *Cindy Oh Cindy*. Toured Europe in 1957. Alan Arkin left the group after the tour to pursue his acting career. Replaced by Clarence Cooper. In 1959, Erik Darling replaced Pete Seeger in the Weavers. Eric Darling left the Weavers in June 1962 to form the Rooftop Singers. The Tarriers disbanded in April 1964. Erik Darling died on August 2, 2008 of Burkitt's lymphoma.

27 Feb 57	-	1	1. BANANA BOAT SONG *Columbia IDB 697*

A TASTE OF HONEY — *2 Weeks*

Formed in Los Angeles, California, USA in 1972. Personnel: Janice Marie Johnson (guitar, vocals), Hazel Payne (vocals, bass), Perry Kimble (keyboards) and Donald Johnson (drums). Won the 1978 Best New Artist Grammy Award.

20 Jul 78	9	2	1. BOOGIE OOGIE OOGIE *Capitol CL 15988*

TAVARES — *6 Weeks*

Formed in New Bedford, Massachusetts, USA in 1964 as Chubby and The Turnpikes. In 1969 decided on a name change to Tavares. Personnel: Brothers, Ralph, Antone, Feliciano, Arthur and Perry Lee Tavares.

19 Aug 76	7	2	1. HEAVEN MUST BE MISSING AN ANGEL *Capitol CL 15876*
11 Nov 76	5	4	2. DON'T TAKE AWAY THE MUSIC *Capitol CL 15886*

Date	Pos	Wks	ARTIST / Record Title *Label & Number*

James TAYLOR — *6 Weeks*

Born James Vernon Taylor on March 12, 1948 in Boston, USA. Relocated to Chapel Hill, North Carolina in 1951. Moved to New York in 1965 where he formed The Flying Machine in 1966. Release one single, *Night Owl*. In 1968, decided to move to London, England where he was signed to Apple Records. In November 1968 his debut solo album, *James Taylor*, issued. After one album he returned to the USA where he signed to Warner Brothers. In 1972, won Grammy for Best Pop Male Vocal Performance for his recording of *You've Got A Friend*. Married Carly Simon in in 1972 and was divorced in 1983. Inducted into the Rock and Roll Hall of Fame in 2000.

Date	Pos	Wks	ARTIST / Record Title *Label & Number*
14 Oct 71	3	6	1. YOU'VE GOT A FRIEND *Warner Bros. WB 16085*

R Dean TAYLOR — *5 Weeks*

Born in 1939 in Toronto, Canada. At the age of twelve started singing at various country and western shows in the Toronto area. Disc debut: *At The High School Dance* (1960). In 1962, travelled to New York to cut some tracks for release on Amy. In 1963, met with Brian Holland and Lamont Dozier of Motown and was signed as a songwriter and artist for the label. Songwriting credits include *Love Child* and *I'm Living In Shame* by The Supremes, *All I Need* by The Temptations, *I'll Turn To Stone* by The Four Tops and *Just Look What You've Done* by Brenda Holloway. Was inspired to write *Indiana Wants Me* after seeing the film, *Bonnie And Clyde*.

Date	Pos	Wks	ARTIST / Record Title *Label & Number*
03 Jun 71	2	5	1. INDIANA WANTS ME *Tamla Motown TMG(I) 763*

Roy TAYLOR and the NEVADA — *5 Weeks*

Roy Taylor born on April 24, 1957 in Crumlin, Dublin, Ireland. Worked with several local groups. Big break happened when he sent a demo tape to promoter and manager of the Nevada Showband, Tommy Hayden.

continues over

Date	Pos	Wks	ARTIST / Record Title *Label & Number*

Replaced Ronnie Medford as lead singer with The Nevada in 1977. Disc debut: *I'll Never Forget Your Name* (1977). Left the Nevada in the early 1980's. A member of Jump The Gun who represented Ireland in the 1988 Eurovision Song Contest with *Take Him Home*, finishing in eight position. Formed the Absolutelys in 1991.

09 Feb 78	7	5	1. DON'T STOP THE CAROUSEL *Release RL 906*

TEACH IN — *2 Weeks*

Formed in Enschede, Holland in 1967. Personnel: Gettie Kaspers (vocals), Chris de Wolde (guitar), Ard Weenink (bass), Koos Versteeg (keyboards), John Gaasbeek (keyboards) and Ruud Nijhuis (drums). Disc debut: *Spoke The Lord Creator* (1971). Won the 1975 Eurovision Song Contest with *Ding A Dong*. Split up in 1978.

01 May 75	8	2	1. DING A DONG *Polydor 2058 570*

The TEDDY BEARS — *3 Weeks*

Formed in Los Angeles, USA in 1958. Personnel: Annette Kleinbard (lead vocals), Phil Spector and Marshall Leib. When group broke up in 1960, Spector moved to New York where he laid the foundation for his groundbreaking career as a record producer. Annette Kleinbard changed her name to Carol Connors and achieved success as a songwriter. Marshall Leib died on March 15, 2002. Phil Spector was inducted into the Rock and Roll Hall of Fame as a 'non-performer' in 1989. The title of the groups hit song came from an inscription on Spector's fathers gravestone.

12 Feb 59	4	3	1. TO KNOW HIM IS TO LOVE HIM *London HL 8733*

The TEENAGERS featuring Frankie LYMON — *2 Weeks*

Formed in 1954 by students at Edward W Scott Junior High School, Harlem, New York. Worked as The Ermines, Coupe de Villes and the Premiers.

continues over

Date	Pos	Wks	ARTIST / Record Title *Label & Number*

Introduced by Richard Barrett (of The Valentines) to George Goldner of Gee Records, who changed their name to The Teenagers. Personnel: Frankie Lymon (born Franklin Joseph Lymon on September 30, 1942), Jimmy Merchant (first tenor), Sherman Garnes (bass), Joe Negroni (baritone) and Herman Santiago (second tenor). Played a week's engagement at Dublin's Theatre Royal in May 1957. Film appearances: *Rock Rock Rock* (1956) and *Mr. Rock And Roll* (1957). In August 1957, at the behest of record label chiefs, George Goldner and Morris Levy, Frankie Lymon left the Teenagers to pursue (what turned out to be an unsuccessful) solo career. The Teenagers broke up in 1961. Inducted into the Rock and Roll Hall of Fame in 1993. Inducted into the Vocal Group Hall of Fame in 2000. In 1998 a film loosely based on Lymon's life, *Why Do Fools Fall In Love*, was released. Frankie Lymon died from a heroin overdose on February 27, 1968. Sherman Garnes died on February 26, 1977. Joe Negroni died on September 5, 1978.

04 Sep 56	-	2	1. WHY DO FOOLS FALL IN LOVE *Columbia IDB 642*

The TEMPERANCE SEVEN ***16 Weeks***

Formed in 1955 by John RT Davies aka Sheik Haroun Wadi el Yoadouinir, at the Royal College of Art, London. England. They were a tongue-in-cheek attempt to recreate Twenties white dance band music. Personnel: Whispering Paul McDowell (vocals), Sheik Haroun Wadi el Yoadouinir (trombone/saxophone), Captain Cephas Howard (trumpet/euphonium), Alan Swainston-Cooper (clarinet), Philip "Fingers" Harrison (saxophone), Canon Colin Bowles (piano), Brian Innes (drums), Dr John Grieves-Watson (banjo) and Frank Paverty (sousaphone). Split in the late 1960's.

27 Apr 61	2	8	1. YOU'RE DRIVING ME CRAZY *Parlophone R(I) 4757*
13 Jul 61	7	8	2. PASADENA *Parlophone R(I) 4781*

Date	Pos	Wks	ARTIST / Record Title *Label & Number*

TEMPTATIONS – See Diana Ross and the Supremes and the Temptations

10cc — *43 Weeks*

Formed in Manchester, England in 1972. Personnel: Eric Stewart (guitar, vocals), Graham Gouldman (bass, vocals), Lol Crème (bass, keyboards, vocals) and Kevin Godley (drums, vocals). Had previousley worked together under the name Hotlegs and scored a number two hit in Britain with *Neanderthal Man* (1970). Signed to Jonathan King's UK label in 1972. King renamed the group 10cc. When Godley and Crème left in 1976, the group continued with Stewart and Gouldman drafting in replacements.

Date	Pos	Wks	ARTIST / Record Title *Label & Number*
02 Nov 72	2	4	1. DONNA *UK 6*
07 Jun 73	1(2)	7	• 2. RUBBER BULLETS *UK UK 36*
06 Sep 73	1(1)	4	• 3. THE DEAN AND I *UK UK 48*
11 Jul 74	9	1	4. WALL STREET SHUFFLE *UK UK 69*
01 May75	7	2	5. LIFE IS A MINESTRONE *Mercury 6008 010*
19 Jun 75	1(3)	7	• 6. I'M NOT IN LOVE *Mercury 6008 014*
01 Jan 76	4	7	7. ART FOR ART'S SAKE *Mercury 6008 017*
29 Apr 76	6	4	8. I'M MANDY FLY ME *Mercury 6008 019*
17 Aug 78	2	7	9. DREADLOCK HOLIDAY *Mercury 6008 025*

Joe TEX — *6 Weeks*

Born Joseph Arrington Jr on August 3, 1933 in Rogers, Texas, USA. Started singing gospel songs at the local Baptist church. In 1954, shortly after winning a talent contest in Houston, started using the stage name, Joe Tex. Spotted by singer Arthur Prystock, while performing at the Celebrity Club in Freeport, Long Island. Prystock arranged a recording deal with King Records. Relocated to Nashville in 1961 where he met Buddy Killen, who signed Joe to his label, Dial Records. They hit the jackpot in 1964 with *Hold What You Got.*

continues over

Date	Pos	Wks	ARTIST / Record Title *Label & Number*
			Converted to the Muslim faith in 1972 and took the name Yusef Hazziez. Died of a heart attack on August 13, 1982.
23 Jun 77	3	6	1. AIN'T GONNA BUMP NO MORE (with no big fat woman) *Epic EPC 5035*

THEM ***7 Weeks***

Formed in 1963 in Belfast, N. Ireland, from elements of the Monarchs. Secured a residency at Belfast's Maritime Hotel. Recorded some tracks in Belfast in 1964, which remained unreleased until after the group made their chart breakthrough. Moved to London in 1964 and signed to Decca Records. Disc debut: *Don't Start Crying Now* (1964). Personnel: Van Morrison (born George Ivan Morrison on August 31, 1945 in Belfast; lead vocals), Alan Henderson (bass), John McAuley (organ), Pat McAuley (drums), and Billy Harrison (lead guitar). There were many personnel changes in the group both before and after the above 1965 lineup. Morrison left Them in June 1966. Relocated to the USA. Signed by Bert Berns to Bang Records as a solo artist. His first solo release, *Brown Eyed Girl* (1967) made the USA top ten. Them continued with different lineups for a number of years.

Date	Pos	Wks	ARTIST / Record Title *Label & Number*
12 Apr 65	2	7	1. HERE COMES THE NIGHT *Decca F 12094*

THIN LIZZY ***39 Weeks***

Formed in Dublin,Ireland in January 1970. Personnel: Phil Lynott (born August 20, 1949 in West Bromwich, England, vocals, bass), Eric Bell (lead guitar), Brian Downey (drums) and Eric Wrixon (keyboards). Wrixon left the group after a few months. Disc debut: *The Farmer* (1970). Relocated to London in November 1970 and signed with Decca Records. Their debut album, *Thin Lizzy*, released in April 1971, was championed by Radio Luxembourg dj Kid Jensen, and this helped to launch group.

continues over

Date	Pos	Wks	ARTIST / Record Title *Label & Number*
			Eric Bell quit band after the 1973 New Years Eve concert in Belfast. In January 1974, Gary Moore joined, he left in April. In June 1974, Scott Gorham and Brian Robertson joined Phil's first book of poetry, *Songs For While I'm Away*, is published in October 1974. In January 1977, Gary Moore fills in for Brian Robertson, who injured his hand. Brian Robertson returns in September 1977. In August 1978, Brian Robertson is dismissed by Phil, and Gary Moore returns for the third time. Gary stays until 1979 when he is replaced by Snowy White. Darren Wharton (keyboards) joins in 1981. In mid 1982, Snowy departs and John Sykes takes his place. Thin Lizzy disband in late 1983. Phil Lynott died on January 4, 1986.
07 Dec 72	1(3)	14	• 1. WHISKEY IN THE JAR *Decca F 13355*
01 Jul 76	1(2)	9	• 2. THE BOYS ARE BACK IN TOWN *Vertigo 6059139*
17 Feb 77	2	7	3. DON'T BELIEVE A WORD *Vertigo LIZZY 001*
25 Aug 77	4	6	4. DANCIN' IN THE MOONLIGHT (IT'S CAUGHT ME IN ITS SPOTLIGHT) *Vertigo 6059 177*
15 Mar 79	6	3	5. WAITING FOR AN ALIBI *Vertigo LIZZY 3*

B J THOMAS — *1 Weeks*

Born Billy Joe Thomas on August 7, 1942 in Hugo, Oklahoma, USA. In 1957 joined a Houston, Texas band, The Triumphs. Disc debut: *Billy And Sue* (1964). It was Dionne Warwick who recommended B.J., to her friends Burt Bacharach and Hal David, as having the perfect voice to sing their song, *Raindrops Keep Fallin' On My Head*, on the film soundtrack of the 1969 film, *Butch Cassidy And The Sundance Kid*. A committed Christian B.J. released his first all-gospel album, *Home Where I Belong*, in 1977. His autobiography, *Home Where I Belong*, published in 1978.

Date	Pos	Wks	ARTIST / Record Title *Label & Number*
05 Mar 70	9	1	1. RAINDROPS KEEP FALLIN' ON MY HEAD *Wand WN 1*

Date	Pos	Wks	ARTIST / Record Title *Label & Number*
			Ken THORNE and his ORCHESTRA 5 Weeks
			Orchestra leader/pianist/ composer. Born January 29, 1924 in East Dereham, Norfolk, England. A member of the Vic Lewis Orchestra. Composed film score for *Superman 11* and *Superman 111.* Nini Rosso wrote *Concerto Disperato,* in 1963, it became the theme for the Stewart Granger film, *The Legion's Last Patrol.* Ray Davies is the trumpet player featured on the Ken Thorne recording of *Theme From Film 'The Legion's Last Patrol'.*
09 Sep 63	4	5	1. THEME FROM FILM 'THE LEGION'S LAST PATROL' ⊠ *HMV POP(I) 1176*
			The THREE DEGREES 11 Weeks
			Formed in Philadelphia, USA in 1963. Discovered by producer/songwriter Richard Barrett. Disc debut: *Gee Baby (I'm Sorry).* Personnel: Sheila Ferguson, Fayette Pinkney and Valerie Holiday. Pinkney left in 1976, replaced by original member Helen Scott. Sheila Ferguson left group in 1986.
15 Aug 74	2	5	1. WHEN WILL I SEE YOU AGAIN *Philadelphia Int. PIR 2073*
08 May75	8	2	2. TAKE GOOD CARE OF YOURSELF *Philadelphia Int PIR 3177*
01 Feb 79	6	4	3. WOMAN IN LOVE *Ariola ARO 141*
			THREE DOG NIGHT 5 Weeks
			Formed in Los Angeles, California, USA in 1968. They almost signed to The Beach Boys label, Brother Records, under the name Redwood. Personnel: Danny Hutton (vocals), Cory Wells (vocals), Chuck Negron (vocals), Jimmy Greenspoon (keyboards), Michael Allsup (guitar), Joe Schermie (bass) and Floyd Sneed (drums). Group officially disbanded in 1977. Re-formed minus Chuck Negron in 1981. Cory Wells is lead vocal on *Mama Told Me (Not To Come).*
10 Sep 70	6	5	1. MAMA TOLD ME (NOT TO COME) *Stateside SS(I) 8052*

Date	Pos	Wks	ARTIST / Record Title *Label & Number*

THUNDERCLAP NEWMAN — *6 Weeks*

Formed in London, England in 1969. Discovered by Pete Townshend of The Who. Personnel: Andy 'Thunderclap' Newman (piano), Jimmy McCullough (lead guitar), and Speedy Keen (vocals, drums). Broke up in 1970. Jimmy McCullough went on to join Stone The Crows and later Wings. McCullough died from heart failure on September 27, 1979. John 'Speedy' Keen died in March 21, 2002.

Date	Pos	Wks	ARTIST / Record Title *Label & Number*
10 Jul 69	2	6	1. SOMETHING IN THE AIR *Track 604031*

Johnny TILLOTSON — *14 Weeks*

Born on April 20, 1939 in Jacksonville, Florida, USA. In 1957 a local DJ submitted a tape of Johnny's singing to the National Pet Milk Talent Contest. Johnny was chosen as one of the six national winners, which gave him the opportunity to broadcast on WSM radio in Nashville. Music publisher Lee Rosenburg heard him and brought Johnny to the attention of Archie Bleyer of Cadence Records. Disc debut: *Well I'm Your Man* (1958). In late 1963, moved from Cadence to MGM. Has composed several hit songs including *It Keeps Right On A-Hurtin'* and *Out of My Mind.*

Date	Pos	Wks	ARTIST / Record Title *Label & Number*
22 Dec 60	1(1)	11	• 1. POETRY IN MOTION *London HLA 9231*
08 Oct 62	7	3	2. SEND ME THE PILLOW YOU DREAM ON *London HLA 9598*

The TIMES — *22 Weeks*

Irish showband formed in Mullingar, County Westmeath, in 1968 by breakaway members of the Drifters Showband. Personnel: Tommy Swarbrigg (lead vocals), Joey Gilheaney (trombone), Des Doherty (piano), Sid Aughey (drums) and Jimmy Horan (bass) (all ex members of Joe Dolan and the Drifters Showband) plus Jimmy Swarbrigg (lead vocals), Gene Bannon (tenor sax) and Sean Kenny (lead guitar). Disc debut: *What Made Milwaukee Famous* (1968).

continues over

Date	Pos	Wks	ARTIST / Record Title *Label & Number*
			First Irish showband to record an album of original compositions, *Looking Through The Eyes Of The Times* (1971). Tommy and Jimmy Swarbrigg represented Ireland in the 1975 and 1977 Eurovision Song contests with their own songs, *That's What Friends Are For* (ninth position) and *It's Nice To Be In Love Again* (third position). Tommy and Jimmy Swarbrigg left the Times in October, 1975 to form the Swarbriggs Band. The Times drafted in replacements and continued on the dance hall circuit until they disbanded in 1982.
29 May 69	9	1	1. DOZIE *Dolphin DOS 29*
27 Nov 69	7	1	2. HITCHIN' TO MIAMI *Dolphin DOS 46*
06 Aug 70	7	5	3. LOOKIN' THRU THE EYES OF A BEAUTIFUL GIRL *Parlophone R(I) 5855*
12 Oct 72	4	4	4. THE ENTERTAINER *Parlophone DIP 523*
03 May73	6	3	5. IT ALL DEPENDS ON YOU *Parlophone DIP 524*
18 Jul 74	1(4)	8	• 6. IF MA COULD SEE ME NOW *EMI EMD 2178*

Hitchin' To Miami credit *The Times featuring Jim Swarbrigg*

See also The Swarbriggs; The Swarbriggs plus Two

TINA — *17 Weeks*

Born Philomena Quinn on April 21, 1945 in Greystones, Co. Wicklow, Ireland. Relocated to England in 1964. She entered and won a talent contest at Butlins Holiday Camp in Skegness. The story of her win was featured in her local newspaper, The Wicklow People and caught the attention of Tom Cranny, then manager of The Mexicans Showband. Tom brought her back to Ireland to become lead vocalist with The Mexicans. Disc debut: *One Love Two* (1967) In late 1968, teamed up with Jim Farley and The Top Hatters. Returned to the Mexicans in July 1969. Left Mexicans in mid 1971 for cabaret scene. Offered position of lead singer with the Real McCoy in October 1971. In July 1973 involved in a serious road accident and did not return to Real McCoy.

continues over

Date	Pos	Wks	ARTIST / Record Title *Label & Number*

Represented Ireland at the 1974 Eurovision Song contest with *Cross Your Heart*, finishing in jointh fifth position. Joined the Nevada Showband in mid 1974. In 1977 was involved in a car accident while on road with Nevada and in 1978 decided to retire from showband scene.

Date	Pos	Wks	ARTIST / Record Title *Label & Number*
09 Dec 71	1(1)	7	• 1. I DON'T KNOW HOW TO LOVE HIM *Ruby RUB 142*
14 Mar 74	1(3)	6	• 2. CROSS YOUR HEART *Polydor 2058 449*
10 Feb 77	7	4	3. I'LL DO IT ALL AGAIN *Release RL 848*

I Don't Know How To Love Him credit : the *Real McCoy featuring Tina*

Jim TOBIN and the FIREHOUSE *17 Weeks*

Born in 1946 in Dunshaughlin, Co. Meath, Ireland. Started out as vocalist with a local group, The Craftsmen. Des Doherty of the Times showband advised him that the Firehouse were auditioning for a lead singer, Jim applied and got the job. Disc debut: *This Is It* (1969). The Firehouse formed in Castlepollard, Co. Westmeath in the mid 1960's. Personnel: Donie Cassidy, P J Kennedy, Larry Kennedy, Eddie Newcombe, Noel Masterson and Vinny Baker. Disbanded in the early 1980's.

Date	Pos	Wks	ARTIST / Record Title *Label & Number*
19 Feb 70	5	5	1. THIS IS IT *Honey COMB 15*
24 Nov 77	5	8	2. THE RHYTHM OF LOVE *Hawk HASP 412*
27 Sep 79	1(2)	4	• 3. WELCOME JOHN PAUL *CMR CM 005*

TONY and the VENTURES *1 Weeks*

Tony born Anthony Hughes on June 13, 1946 in Monaghan, Ireland. Joined The Ventures Showband in 1966. Disc debut: *The Little Windup Doll* (1967). The Ventures Showband formed in Monaghan in 1965. Personnel: Tony Hughes (vocals, guitar), Bill Rice (rhythm guitar, vocals), Shay Turbett (trumpet), Sean McKenna (bass), Peadar McDonald (organ, tenor sax), Brendan Sherlock (trombone), Porrie McElwaine (lead guitar) and Colm Hughes (drums).

continues over

Date	Pos	Wks	ARTIST / Record Title *Label & Number*

On the advice of Mighty Avons keyboard player, Ronnie Griffith, the Ventures turned professional in 1968,. In March 1973, Tony Hughes, Colm Hughes and Porrie McElwaine left band to form Harvest. The Ventures continued with Bill Rice as lead vocalist. Disbanded in 1976. *Happy Anniversary* was originally intended as an album track. Bill Rice died on March 16, 1998. Porrie McElwaine died on December 7, 1999.

09 Mar 72	7	1	1. **HAPPY ANNIVERSARY** *Release RL 607*

The TORNADOS — *11 Weeks*

Instrumental group formed in late 1961 as house band for record producer Joe Meek. In February 1962 the Tornados became Billy Fury's backing group. Personnel: Alan Caddy (lead guitar), Heinz Burt (bass), George Bellamy (guitar), Norman Hale (keyboards) and Clem Cattini (drums). Disc debut: *Love And Fury* (1962). Shortly after first record release Norman Hale was replaced by Roger LaVern. Heinz Burt departed in 1963 to pursue a solo career. He died on April 7, 2000. Joe Meek was inspired to compose *Telstar* as a tribute to the Telstar communications satellite, which broadcast the first television pictures across the Atlantic on July 11, 1962. Songwriter Geoff Goddard played the melody line on *Telstar* using the clavioline, tinkled the piano during the guitar breaks and added vocal backing on the track. The Tornados appeared in the film *Just For Fun* (1963). By early 1964, drummer Clem Cattini was the sole surviving original member in the group. He left in 1965.

27 Sep 62	1(2)	11	• 1. **TELSTAR** • *Decca F 11494*

See also HEINZ

Mitchell TOROK — *3 Weeks*

Born on October 28, 1929 in Houston, Texas, USA. Took an interest in country music and the guitar at the age of twelve. After he graduated from college he decided to make music his career.

continues over

Date	Pos	Wks	ARTIST / Record Title *Label & Number*

Big break arrived when Fabor Robinson of Abbott Records heard him performing one his own songs, *Mexican Joe*. Made first recordings in 1948. Toured UK and Ireland in 1957. A talented painter, he has one of his paintings on display at the Elvis Presley Museum in Nashville.

Date	Pos	Wks	ARTIST / Record Title *Label & Number*
11 Oct 55	-	1	1. CARIBBEAN *London HL 8004*
30 Oct 56	-	2	2. WHEN MEXICO GAVE UP THE RHUMBA *Brunswick 05586*

TRAFFIC — *5 Weeks*

Formed in 1967. Personnel: Stevie Winwood (born on May 12, 1948 in Birmingham, England. vocals, keyboards), Dave Mason (guitar, vocals), Jim Capaldi (drums, vocals) and Chris Wood (flute, tenor sax). Debut single: *Paper Sun* (1967). Dave Mason left in late 1967, returned in early 1968. Stevie Winwood left in 1969 to join Blind Faith. Rejoined Traffic in 1970. Group disbanded in 1974. Chris Wood died of liver failure on July 12, 1983. Jim Capaldi died from cancer on January 28, 2005. *Hole In My Shoe* written and sung by Dave Mason. Inducted into Rock and Roll Hall of Fame in 2004.

Date	Pos	Wks	ARTIST / Record Title *Label & Number*
19 Oct 67	7	5	1. HOLE IN MY SHOE *Island WIP 6017*

See also Spencer Davis Group

John TRAVOLTA — *12 Weeks*

Born on February 18, 1954 in Englewood, New Jersey, USA. First gained fame in the television series *Welcome Back Kotter* (1975). However it was his appearance in the 1978 film, *Saturday Night Fever*, that brought him international recognition. Film appearances include: *Grease* (1978) and *Look Who's Talking* (1989). Nominated for an Oscar for his role as a hit man in the 1994 film, *Pulp Fiction*.

Date	Pos	Wks	ARTIST / Record Title *Label & Number*
12 Oct 78	1(2)	6	• 1. SANDY *Polydor POSP 6*
07 Dec 78	8	6	2. GREASED LIGHTNING *Polydor POSP 14*

Date	Pos	Wks	ARTIST / Record Title *Label & Number*

John TRAVOLTA & Olivia NEWTON-JOHN — *26 Weeks*

Male/female vocal duo. John Travolta born on February 18, 1954 in Englewood, New Jersey, USA. Olivia Newton-John born on September 26, 1948 in Cambridge, England. John and Olivia starred in the 1978 film, *Saturday Night Fever.* Both hits featured in the film.

Date	Pos	Wks	ARTIST / Record Title *Label & Number*
01 Jun 78	1(9)	15	• 1. YOU'RE THE ONE THAT I WANT *RSO RSO 006*
21 Sep 78	1(3)	11	• 2. SUMMER NIGHTS *RSO RSO 18*

See also Olivia Newton-John

The TREMELOES — *44 Weeks*

Formed by Brian Poole in 1958. Poole left group in 1966 to pursue a solo career. Personnel: Len 'Chip' Hawkes (born November 11, 1946 in London, lead vocals, bass), Rick West (lead guitar), Alan Blakely (rhythm guitar), and Dave Munden (drums). First 'solo' recording: *Blessed* (1966) on Decca. Signed to CBS in 1967. Chip Hawkes left in 1974 to pursue a solo career. He rejoined group in 1979, left again in 1989. The Tremeloes still continue to perform with original members Dave Munden and Rick West in the lineup. Alan Blakely died from cancer on June 10, 1996. Reunited with Brian Poole for a British and Irish tour in October/November 2006.

Date	Pos	Wks	ARTIST / Record Title *Label & Number*
16 Mar 67	8	2	1. HERE COMES MY BABY *CBS 202519*
25 May 67	1(1)	8	• 2. SILENCE IS GOLDEN *CBS 2723*
07 Sep 67	7	5	3. EVEN THE BAD TIMES ARE GOOD *CBS 2930*
08 Feb 68	9	4	4. SUDDENLY YOU LOVE ME *CBS 3234*
10 Oct 68	1(1)	8	• 5. MY LITTLE LADY *CBS 3680*
20 Nov 69	2	9	6. (CALL ME) NUMBER ONE *CBS 4582*
08 Oct 70	2	8	7. ME AND MY LIFE *CBS CBS S 5139*

See also Brian Poole and the Tremeloes

The TROGGS — *11 Weeks*

Formed in Andover, Hampshire, England in 1965, when members of two local groups, the Troglodytes and the Ten Feet High amalgamated.

continues over

Date	Pos	Wks	ARTIST / Record Title *Label & Number*

Personnel: Reg Presley (born Reginald Ball on June 6, 1943 in Andover, vocals), Ronnie Bond (drums), Pete Staples (bass) and Chris Britton (lead guitar). Disc debut: *Lost Girl* (1966). Ronnie Bond died on November 13, 1992. Reg Presley composed *Love Is All Around* (a hit for the Troggs in 1967) which provided a number one hit single for Wet Wet Wet in 1994, spending fifteen weeks at number one in Britain.

27 Jun 66	5	1	1. WILD THING *Fontana ETF 689*
01 Aug 66	2	7	2. WITH A GIRL LIKE YOU *Fontana ETF 717*
31 Oct 66	3	3	3. I CAN'T CONTROL MYSELF *Page One POF 001*

The TURTLES — *10 Weeks*

Formed in Los Angeles, USA in 1962 as The Nightriders. Met while members of the Westchester High Acappella Choir. In 1963, changed their name to the Crossfires. They became The Turtles upon signing with White Whale Records in 1965. Personnel: Howard Kaylan (lead vocals), Mark Volman (vocals), Al Nichol (guitar), Jim Pons (bass) and John Barbata (drums). Disbanded in 1970. Kaylan and Volman went on to achieve further success under the name The Phlorescent Leech & Eddie, later shortened to Flo and Eddie.

13 Jul 67	3	6	1. SHE'D RATHER BE WITH ME *London HL 10135*
05 Dec 68	6	4	2. ELENORE *London HL 10223*

Conway TWITTY — *1 Weeks*

Born Harold Lloyd Jenkins on September 1, 1933 in Friars Point, Mississippi, USA. Formed his first band, the Phillips County Ramblers, when he was ten, following the family move to Helena, Arkansas. In 1956, recorded some tracks at Sun Studios in Memphis, but none were released. Composed *Rock House*, a minor hit for Roy Orbison. At the beginning of 1957 signed to Mercury Records. Disc debut: *I Need Your Lovin'*. Took his professional name from two American towns, Conway in Arkansas and Twitty in Texas.

continues over

Date	Pos	Wks	ARTIST / Record Title *Label & Number*

Composed *It's Only Make Believe* with band member, Jack Nance, between sets while performing at the Flamingo Lounge in Toronto. Signed to MGM Records in 1958. Film appearances include *Kittens Go To College*, *Platinum High School* and *College Confidential* (all 1960). Signed by legendary producer, Owen Bradley, to Decca in 1965, an event that was to change his musical direction from Rock 'n' Roll to Country. In 1982, opened *Twitty City*, a nine acre tourist complex and theme park, in Hendersonville, Tennessee. Inducted into the Country Music Hall of Fame in 1999. Died on June 5, 1993.

14 Apr 60	9	1	1. LONELY BLUE BOY *MGM MGM(I) 1056*

TWO'S COMPANY — *7 Weeks*

Male/female vocal duo. Formed in 1968. First public appearance: The Embankment, Tallaght, County Dublin. Personnel: Mary Darcy born on December 9, 1948 in Rathvilly County Carlow. Played accordion with Slieve Bloom Ceili Band and was lead singer with resident group at Four Provinces, Kings Heath, Birmingham, England and Eamonn McRory born on January 10, 1942 in Dungannon, County Tyrone. Played rhythm guitar with a number of showbands including the Grafton and the Polka Dots. Two's Company represented Ireland at the Eurovision Gold Star Awards in Holland in 1983. Disc debut: *Eileen McManus* (1969). In 1992, they decided to augment the group with a rhythm section and became a five piece operating under the name, Two's Company Five. Disbanded in 1994.

28 Aug 69	10	1	1. EILEEN McMANUS *Honey COMB 4*
23 Oct 75	5	6	2. YOU'RE MY BEST FRIEND *Release RL 784*

Date	Pos	Wks	ARTIST / Record Title *Label & Number*

Bonnie TYLER — *4 Weeks*

Born Gaynor Hopkins on June 8, 1951 in Skewen, near Swansea, Wales. In 1968 changed her name to Sherene Davis. While fronting The Imaginations was spotted by talent scout Dave Mackay who introduced her to the management and production team of Ronnie Scott and Steve Wolfe. A change of name to Bonnie Tyler and a recording contract with RCA followed. Disc debut: *My, My Honeycomb* (1976). In 1979, won the Yamaha World Popular song contest in Tokyo with *Sitting On The Edge Of The Ocean*. In 1980 Bonnie moved to CBS records.

Date	Pos	Wks	ARTIST / Record Title *Label & Number*
12 Jan 78	3	4	1. **IT'S A HEARTACHE** *RCA PB 5057*

The TYMES — *3 Weeks*

Formed in Philadelphia, USA in 1956 as The Latineers. Personnel: George Williams (lead vocal), Donald Banks, Norman Burnett, Terri Gonzalez and Melanie Moore. George Williams died on July 28, 2004.

Date	Pos	Wks	ARTIST / Record Title *Label & Number*
30 Jan 75	1(1)	3	• 1. **Ms GRACE** *RCA RCA 2493*

TYPICALLY TROPICAL — *6 Weeks*

British session musicians assembled by Jeffrey Calvert and Max West. Jeffrey and Max met while working at Morgan Studios doing reggae recordings for Trojan Records. Gerraint Hughes and Jeff Calvert penned the hit song *I Lost My Heart To A Starship Trooper* and decided to write a reggae song following Calvert's holiday in Jamaica, *Barbados* was the result. Personnel: Max West (vocals), Chris Spedding (guitar), Roger Coulam (keyboards), Vic Flick (guitar) and Clem Cattini (drums).

Date	Pos	Wks	ARTIST / Record Title *Label & Number*
31 Jul 75	1(2)	6	• 1. **BARBADOS** *Gull GULS 14*

Date	Pos	Wks	ARTIST / Record Title *Label & Number*

U

The UNION GAP featuring Gary Puckett — *13 Weeks*

Formed in San Diego, California, USA in 1967. Group named after the town of Union Gap, Washington. Personnel: Gary Puckett (born on October 1, 1942 in Hibbing, Minnesota, lead vocals), Kerry Chater (bass), Paul Wheatbread (drums), Dwight Bement (tenor sax) and Gary Withern (keyboards). Gary Puckett left group in 1971 to pursue a solo career. Kerry Chater scored a minor hit in the USA in 1977 with *Part Time Love*.

Date	Pos	Wks	ARTIST / Record Title *Label & Number*
23 May 68	1(2)	10	• 1. YOUNG GIRL *CBS 3365*
18 Jul 74	5	3	2. YOUNG GIRL (re-issue) *CBS 8202*

UNIT FOUR PLUS TWO — *5 Weeks*

Formed in Hertfordshire, England in 1963 as Unit Four. Later that year two additional members brought in and a name change to Unit 4 + 2. Personnel: Tommy Moeller (lead vocals, guitar), Howard Lubin (piano), David Meikle (guitar/vocals), Pete Moules (guitar/vocals), Rod Garwood (bass), and Hugh Halliday (drums). Disc debut: *Green Fields* (1964). In 1967 left Decca and signed to Fontana. That same year Russ Ballard and Bob Henrit replaced Rod Garwood and Hugh Halliday. Group broke up in 1969.

Date	Pos	Wks	ARTIST / Record Title *Label & Number*
05 Apr 65	4	5	1. CONCRETE AND CLAY *Decca F 12071*

Date	Pos	Wks	ARTIST / Record Title *Label & Number*

V

Ricky VALANCE *7 Weeks*

Born David Spencer on April 10, 1939 in Ynysddu, South Wales. Signed to Columbia Records in 1960. Hit the number one spot in Britain for three weeks with his debut single *Tell Laura I Love Her.* Relocated to Ireland in late 1966, to front the Chessmen Showband. Made one record with the Chessmen, a remake of *Tell Laura I Love Her* (1967). Living in Spain since 2002.

Date	Pos	Wks	ARTIST / Record Title *Label & Number*
20 Oct 60	7	7	1. TELL LAURA I LOVE HER *Columbia DB(I) 4493*

Dickie VALENTINE *15 Weeks*

Born Richard Bryce on November 4, 1929 in Camden Town, London, England. From the age of ten wanted to be a singer. Worked as a theatre call boy at the Palace Theatre, Manchester and later at the London Palladium. Big break came in 1949, when Ted Heath heard him singing and signed him up as one of the band's featured vocalists. In 1954 decided to leave the Ted Heath band to pursue a solo career. Moved from Decca Records to Pye in early 1959. Died on May 6, 1971 following his involvement in a car accident.

Date	Pos	Wks	ARTIST / Record Title *Label & Number*
01 Feb 55	-	1	1. THE FINGER OF SUSPICION *Decca F 10394*
09 Dec 55	-	2	2. CHRISTMAS ALPHABET *Decca F 10628*
30 Apr 59	6	1	3. VENUS *Pye Nixa 7N 15192*
02 Jul 59	7	2	4. A TEENAGER IN LOVE *Pye Nixa 7N 15202*
08 Oct 59	5	9	5. ONE MORE SUNRISE (Morgen) *Pye Nixa 7N 15221*

Frankie VALLI *9 Weeks*

Born Francis Castellucio on May 3, 1934 in Newark, New Jersey, USA. Originally a solo singer under the name Frank Valley. Joined the Variatones in 1954.

continues over

Date	Pos	Wks	ARTIST / Record Title *Label & Number*

Although he was lead singer with the Four Seasons, he also began a solo career. Made his first solo recording *(You're Gonna) Hurt Yourself* in 1965.

Date	Pos	Wks	ARTIST / Record Title *Label & Number*
06 Mar 75	4	2	1. MY EYES ADORED YOU *Private Stock PVT 1*
22 May 75	8	1	2. THE NIGHT *Mowest MW 3024*
14 Sep 78	3	6	3. GREASE *RSO RSO 012*

See also Four Seasons

Leroy VAN DYKE — *10 Weeks*

Born on October 4, 1929 near Spring Fork, Pettis County, Missouri, USA. Interested in singing from a very young age. Sang in the church choir and in the University of Missouri Men's Glee Club. In 1952, graduated from the University of Missouri with a Bachelor of Science in Agriculture and a major in journalism. Attended the Reppert's School of Auctioneering in Decatur, Indiana. Drafted into the US Army in 1952. Served in Korea and while in the service composed a song, *The Auctioneer*, as a tribute to his cousin Ray Sims, a livestock auctioneer. Released on Dot Records in October 1956, the songs sold over a million copies. Signed to Mercury Records in January 1961. Recorded *Walk On By* in May 1961. Hank Sugarfoot Garland is lead guitar on the record. Starred in the 1967 film *What Am I Bid.*

Date	Pos	Wks	ARTIST / Record Title *Label & Number*
25 Jan 62	3	10	1. WALK ON BY *Mercury AMT(I) 1166*

Randy VANWARMER — *2 Weeks*

Born Randall Van Wormer on March 30, 1955 in Indian Hills, Colorado, USA. Relocated to Cornwall, England in 1970. Began writing songs and playing local folk clubs. Returned to USA in 1978. Died from leukemia on January 12, 2004.

Date	Pos	Wks	ARTIST / Record Title *Label & Number*
04 Oct 79	5	2	1. JUST WHEN I NEEDED YOU MOST *Bearsville WIP 6516*

Date	Pos	Wks	ARTIST / Record Title *Label & Number*
			VARIOUS ARTISTS ***8 Weeks***
			Four track singles featuring some of the Release record labels top selling artists and their biggest hits for the company.
24 Aug 72	4	7	1. FOUR GREAT IRISH HITS *Release MRL 1001*
09 Nov 72	10	1	2. FOUR GREAT IRISH HITS Vol. 2 *Release MRL 1002*
			Tracks on **Four Great Irish Hits**: Four Green Fields (Dermot Hegarty) / Old Claddagh Ring (Dermot O'Brien) / Slaney Valley (Larry Cunningham) / These Are My Mountains (Brian Coll). Tracks on **Four Great Irish Hits Vol. 2**: Give An Irish Girl To Me (Brian Coll) / Twenty One Years (Dermot Hegarty) / The Galway Shawl (Dermot O'Brien) / James Connolly (Larry Cunningham).
			Frankie VAUGHAN ***30 Weeks***
			Born Francis Abelson on February 3, 1928 in Liverpool, England. Got his break following a performance in a college revue at the Leeds College of Art. Disc debut: *Too Marvellous For Words* (1953). Film appearances include *Ramsbottom Rides Again* (1956), *These Dangerous Years* (1957), *Lady Is A Square* (1959) and *Let's Make Love* with Marilyn Monroe, in 1960. Signature tune: *Give Me The Moonlight*. In 1985, starred in the London West End stage production of, *42nd Street*. Died on September 17, 1999.
27 Nov 56	-	2	1. GREEN DOOR *Philips EPB 640*
12 Feb 57	-	1	2. THE GARDEN OF EDEN *Philips EPB 660*
08 Oct 57	-	1	3. MAN ON FIRE *Philips EPB 729*
21 Jan 58	-	3	4. KISSES SWEETER THAN WINE *Philips EPB 775*
18 Mar 58	-	1	5. CAN'T GET ALONG WITHOUT YOU *Philips EPB 793*
13 Aug 59	3	11	6. THE HEART OF A MAN *Philips EPB 930*
30 Nov 61	1(4)	8	• 7. TOWER OF STRENGTH *Philips EPB 1195*
25 Feb 63	9	3	8. LOOP-DE-LOOP *Philips 326566 EBF*

Date	Pos	Wks	ARTIST / Record Title *Label & Number*

Frankie VAUGHAN and the KAYE SISTERS — *2 Weeks*

Male vocalist/female vocal trio. Frankie Vaughan born on February 3, 1928 in Liverpool, England. Kaye Sisters: Sheila Jones, Shan Palmer and Carole Young.

Date	Pos	Wks	ARTIST / Record Title *Label & Number*
03 Dec 57	-	2	1. GOTTA HAVE SOMETHING IN THE BANK, FRANK *Philips EPB 751*

See also the Kaye Sisters

Malcolm VAUGHAN — *3 Weeks*

Born Malcolm Thomas on March 22, 1929 in Troedyrhiw, Near Merthyr, Wales. In early 1944, whilst staying with an aunt in Reading, he auditioned and was accepted to play the role of a Welsh boy in a new play, *The Druid's Nest*, by Emlyn Williams. In October 1944 obtained a role in the stage musical, *Jenny Jones*, at the London Hippodrome. Variety, summer seasons and straight plays followed. In March 1954, formed a comedy-vocal act with Kenneth Earle. The partnership was to last eighteen years. It was during the early days of their partnership that Malcolm Thomas became Malcolm Vaughan. Spotted by radio personality, Jack Jackson,, who was so impressed with the quality of Malcolm's voice, that he persuaded the A&R man at HMV Records, Walter Ridley, to come and hear him. Suitably impressed, Wally Ridley signed Malcolm to a recording contract. Disc debut: *Mama / Every Day Of My Life*. In 1972, Malcolm and Kenneth Earle dissolved their showbusiness partnership. Malcolm continued his solo career into the 1990's. His biography, *The Reluctant Star* published in 2009.

Date	Pos	Wks	ARTIST / Record Title *Label & Number*
13 Nov 56	-	2	1. ST. THERESE OF THE ROSES *HMV IP 1186*
07 May 57	-	1	2. CHAPEL OF THE ROSES *HMV IP 1233*

Date	Pos	Wks	ARTIST / Record Title *Label & Number*

Sarah VAUGHAN — *3 Weeks*

Born Sarah Lois Vaughan on March 27, 1924 in Newark, New Jersey, USA. Studied piano from an early age. Organist and choir soloist at the Mount Zion Bapist Church. In 1942 she won first prize at the famed Amateur Contest at the Apollo Theatre in Harlem. Among the audience was singer Billy Eckstine. Some months later Sarah was invited to join Eckstine in the Earl Hines Big Band. Vaughan went solo in 1945. Recorded for Columbia 1949-53, Mercury 1953-60, Roulette 1960-64, Mercury 1963-67. Died of cancer on April 3, 1990.

Date	Pos	Wks	ARTIST / Record Title *Label & Number*
26 Nov 59	5	3	1. BROKEN HEARTED MELODY *Mercury AMT(I) 1057*

Billy VAUGHN and his Orchestra — *9 Weeks*

Born Richard Vaughn on April 12, 1919 in Glasgow, Kentucky, USA. Started out as a vocalist with The Dinning Brothers. Founder member of The Hilltoppers vocal group. Left the group in 1955 to become Musical Director at Dot Records. Formed a studio orchestra to provide musical accompaniment to Dot recording artists such as Fontane Sisters and Gale Storm. Recorded a series of very popular instrumental orchestral recordings featuring two tenor saxophones playing in close harmony. The hits continued for the orchestra until 1966. When he left Dot in 1968 he took the opportunity to tour Japan. Died on September 26, 1991.

Date	Pos	Wks	ARTIST / Record Title *Label & Number*
09 Dec 55	-	3	1. SHIFTING WHISPERING SANDS *London HL 8205*
18 Mar 58	-	1	2. RAUNCHY • *London HL 8522*
01 Apr 58	-	1	3. SAIL ALONG SILVERY MOON • *London HL 8680*
19 Nov 59	2	4	4. MORGEN (One More Sunrise) • *London HLD 8952*

Bobby VEE — *20 Weeks*

Born Robert Thomas Velline on April 30, 1943 in Fargo, North Dakota, USA. His first claim to fame was that he and his brother were members of the group (The Shadows) who deputized for air crash victim Buddy Holly at a gig in Moorhead, Minnesota on the night of February 3, 1959.

continues over

Date	Pos	Wks	ARTIST / Record Title *Label & Number*
			Disc debut: *Susie Baby* (1959) on Soma Records. Signed to Liberty Records in Autumn of 1959. Film appearances include *Swingin' Along* (1962), *Play It Cool* (1962) and *Just For Fun* (1963).
09 Feb 61	2	7	1. RUBBER BALL *London HLG 9255*
01 Jun 61	3	4	2. MORE THAN I CAN SAY *London HLG 9316*
16 Nov 61	2	8	3. TAKE GOOD CARE OF MY BABY *London HLG 9438*
08 Apr 63	9	1	4. THE NIGHT HAS A THOUSAND EYES *Liberty LIB(I) 10069*

The VENTURES — *3 Weeks*

Instrumental group formed in Seattle, Washington, USA in 1959 by Don Wilson and Bob Bogle. Don and Bob bought fifteen dollar guitars at a pawnshop. Began playing part time in taverns, while holding down day jobs in the construction industry. Unable to get a record company interested in signing the group, Don Wilson's mother put up the money to form their own record label, Blue Horizon. Disc debut: *Cookies And Coke*. Personnel: Don Wilson (rhythm guitar), Bob Bogle (lead guitar), Nokie Edwards (bass), and Howie Johnson (drums). Edwards left in 1968. Howie Johnston died in 1988. Inducted into the Rock and Roll Hall of Fame in 2008. Bob Bogle died on June 14, 2009.

Date	Pos	Wks	ARTIST / Record Title *Label & Number*
19 Jan 61	5	3	1. PERFIDIA • *London HLG 9232*

VILLAGE PEOPLE — *14 Weeks*

Formed in New York, USA in 1978 by producer composer Jacques Morali. Personnel: Victor Willis (Cop, lead vocals), Randy Jones (Cowboy), David Hodo (Construction Worker), Felipe Rose (native American Indian), Glenn Hughes (Biker) and Alexander Briley (G.I). In late 1979 Willis was replaced by Ray Simpson. Glenn Hughes died from lung cancer on March 14, 2001. He requested to be buried wearing his leather biker outfit.

Date	Pos	Wks	ARTIST / Record Title *Label & Number*
14 Dec 78	1(4)	10	• 1. YMCA *Mercury 6007 192*
29 Mar 79	2	4	2. IN THE NAVY *Mercury 6007 209*

Date	Pos	Wks	ARTIST / Record Title *Label & Number*

Bobby VINTON ***5 Weeks***

Born Stanley Robert Vinton on April 16, 1935 in Canonsburg, Pennsylvania, USA. Formed his own band while in High School. Played saxophone, trumpet, oboe, drums and clarinet. Studied music at Duquesne University and graduated with a degree in Musical Composition. Appearances on Guy Lombardo's 'TV Talent Scouts' show, landed him a contract with Epic Records. Composed hit songs *Mr Lonely* and *L-O-N-E-L-Y.* His autobiography, *Polish Prince*, published in 1978. Hit the UK and Irish charts in 1990 with a reissue of his 1963 USA hit, *Blue Velvet.* In May 2005, Akon took Bobby's song *Mr Lonely* to the number one slot on the singles chart in Ireland and the UK.

16 Aug 62	2	5	1. ROSES ARE RED (My Love) *Columbia DB(I) 4878*

The VIPERS SKIFFLE GROUP ***1 Weeks***

Formed in London, England in 1956. Discovered while performing at the 2 I's Coffee Bar in London. Personnel: Wally Whyton (guitar, vocals), Johnny Martyn (guitar, vocals), Jan Van der Bosch (guitar), Tony Tolhurst (double bass) and John Pilgrim (washboard). Disc debut: *Pick A Bale Of Cotton* (1956). At one time Hank Marvin, Jet Harris and Bruce Welch were members.Wally Whyton died from lung cancer on January 22, 1997. Johnny Martyn died on March 19, 2007.

26 Mar 57	-	1	1. DON'T YOU ROCK ME DADDY-O *Parlophone DIP 271*

Date	Pos	Wks	ARTIST / Record Title *Label & Number*

Adam WADE — *1 Weeks*

Born on March 17, 1937 in Pittsburgh, USA. After graduating from Virginia State University took up a position as a biochemist at the Dr. Jonas Salk Polio Research Center at the University of Pittsburgh. Film appearances include *Wanderlove* (1970), Claudine (1974) and *Kiss Me Goodbye* (1982).

Date	Pos	Wks	Record
21 Sep 61	9	1	1. TAKE GOOD CARE OF HER *HMV POP(I) 843*

Johnny WAKELIN — *6 Weeks*

Born in 1939 in Brighton, England. Started singing on the cabaret and club scene in Sussex during the 1960's. Discovered by Pye Records producer Robin Blanchflower. Both his hit singles were tributes to World Champion Heavyweight boxer Muhammad Ali (Cassius Clay).

Date	Pos	Wks	Record
20 Feb 75	9	1	1. BLACK SUPERMAN (Mohammad Ali) *Pye 7N 45420*
26 Aug 76	3	5	2. IN ZAIRE *Pye 7N 45545*

The WALKER BROTHERS — *11 Weeks*

Formed in Hollywood, California, USA in 1964. Personnel: Scott Walker (born Scott Engel on January 9, 1944 in Hamilton, Ohio, lead vocals, bass), John Walker (born John Maus, guitar, vocals) and Gary Walker (born Gary Leeds, drums). Arrived in the UK in February 1965. Signed to Philips Records. Disc debut: *Pretty Girls Everywhere*. Split in 1967. Scott Walker enjoyed some hits as a solo artist in late 1960's. Group reformed in 1976. Enjoyed chart success with a revival of the Tom Rush song, *No Regrets*.

Date	Pos	Wks	Record
20 Sep 65	3	3	1. MAKE IT EASY ON YOURSELF *Philips EBF 1428*
28 Mar 66	5	5	2. THE SUN AIN'T GONNA SHINE ANYMORE *Philips EBF 1473*
26 Feb 76	9	3	3. NO REGRETS *GTO GT 42*

Date	Pos	Wks	ARTIST / Record Title *Label & Number*

Caitriona WALSH *8 Weeks*

Born in Dublin, Ireland. Studied Music at University College Dublin qualifying in 1978 with a teaching diploma. Joined New Seekers in 1979, left group in August 1980. During her time with the New Seekers, recorded a solo single, *Viva Il Papa*, to celebrate the visit to Ireland by Pope Paul IV in September 1979. In 1982, starred in the Dublin production of *The Pirates Of Penzance*. In 1983 relocated to London. In 1987 was appointed General Adminstrator of London Chamber Orchestra. Returned to Dublin in 1995 and was appointed Chief Executive with Irish Film Orchestra in Dublin.

13 Sep 79	1(1)	8	• 1. VIVA IL PAPA *Release RL 981*

WAR *4 Weeks*

Formed in Los Angeles, California in 1962 as The Creators. Changed name to Night Shift in 1968. Spotted by Jerry Goldstein who introduced them to Eric Burdon. Toured with Burdon as his backing band until 1971. Personnel: Howard Scott (guitar, vocals), Harold Brown (percussion, vocals), Lonnie Jordan (keyboards), B. B. Dickerson (bass, vocals), Charles Miller (flute, saxophone), Papa Lee Allen (keyboards, vocals) and Lee Oskar (harmonica, percussion, vocals). Charles Miller died in 1980.

02 Feb 78	5	4	1. GALAXY *MCA 339*

Anita WARD *5 Weeks*

Born on December 20, 1956 in Memphis, Tennessee, USA. Sang in church choir as a child. While attending Rust College in Memphis she joined the College Acappella Choir. Obtained a degree in Psychology and worked as a teacher. Discovered by producer/songwriter, Frederick Knight. Disc debut: *Spoiled By Love* (1978).

21 Jun 79	2	5	1. RING MY BELL *TK STKR 7543*

Date	Pos	Wks	ARTIST / Record Title *Label & Number*

Dionne WARWICK ***1 Weeks***

Born Marie Dionne Warrick on December 12, 1940 in East Orange, New Jersey, USA. As a teenager formed a group, The Gospelaires, with her sister Dee Dee and her aunt Cissy Houston (later to be mother of Whitney Houston). Came to the attention of Burt Bacharach while doing backing vocals at a Drifters recording session (*Mexican Divorce*) in 1961. Disc debut: *Don't Make Me Over* (1962). When the record was released, a typing mistake led to the performer credit reading Dionne Warwick instead of Dionne Warrick and she kept the new name. Her recording of, *Do You Know The Way To San Jose*, won Dionne a 1968 Grammy Award for Best Female Solo Vocal Performance.

04 Jul 68	8	1	1. DO YOU KNOW THE WAY TO SAN JOSE *Pye 7N 25457*

Joan WEBER ***3 Weeks***

Born on December 12, 1936 in Paulsboro, New Jersey, USA. Relocated to New York City in 1954. Came to the attention of Charles Randolph Green who introduced her to the A&R chief at Columbia Records. Mitch Miller signed her to the label. Her only chart entry, *Let Me Go Lover* hit the number one spot in the USA on both the Cashbox and Billboard chart. Died on May 13, 1981.

01 Feb 55	-	3	1. LET ME GO LOVER *Philips PB 389*

Houston WELLS and the PREMIER ACES ***13 Weeks***

Born Andrew Smith in 1938 in Northumberland, England. After a spell singing in the clubs around Tyneside, he teamed up with a group from the south of England, the Coasters. A successful audition for producer Joe Meek led to a recording contract with EMI. A change of name came at this juncture. The Coasters became the Marksmen while EMI's Tony Palmer gave Andrew a new stage name, Houston Wells.

continues over

Date	Pos	Wks	ARTIST / Record Title *Label & Number*
			Disc debut: *This Song Is Just For You* (1962). In 1964, following a period of dissent, the Marksmen and Houston went their separate ways. He moved to Ireland in April 1965 to take up the position of lead singer with the Premier Aces Showband from Ballintubber, Co. Roscommon. Personnel: Houston Wells (vocals), Paddy Malone (alto sax), Johnny Carroll (trumpet), Sonny Ward (tenor sax), Jimmy O'Neill (rhythm guitar), Larry Carolan (bass), Billy Ryan (lead guitar), Michael Slyman (trombone) and Andy Malone (drums). Houston Wells left the Premier Aces in 1968 to form his own showband, the Tridents. In December 1973 decided to emigrate to New Zealand.
09 Sep 63	7	6	1. ONLY THE HEARTACHES *Parlophone R(I) 5031*
28 Feb 66	6	7	2. ABOVE AND BEYOND *Parlophone DIP 509*
			Only The Heartaches credit: Houston Wells and the Marksmen.

Mary WELLS — *1 Weeks*

Born Mary Esther Wells on May 13, 1943 in Detroit, USA. Originally auditioned by Motown boss Berry Gordy as a songwriter, but instead received a contract as a performer. Disc debut: *Bye Bye Baby* (1961). The Beatles declared Mary Wells to be their favourite American female singer. Diagnosed with cancer of the larynx in 1990. Died on July 26, 1992.

Date	Pos	Wks	ARTIST / Record Title *Label & Number*
13 Jul 64	9	1	1. MY GUY *Stateside SS(I) 288*

Keith WEST — *6 Weeks*

Born Keith Hopkins on December 6, 1943 in Dagenham, Essex, England. Originally a member of The In Crowd and the cult group Tomorrow, who issued the classic psychedelic single, *My White Bicycle* (1967). Embarked on a solo career while still a member of Tomorrow.

Date	Pos	Wks	ARTIST / Record Title *Label & Number*
21 Sep 67	2	6	1. EXCERPT FROM A 'TEENAGE OPERA' *Parlophone R(I) 5623*

Date	Pos	Wks	ARTIST / Record Title *Label & Number*

Barry WHITE **4 Weeks**

Born Barry Eugene Carter on September 12, 1944 in Galveston, Texas, USA. Raised in Los Angeles. He made his first recordings with the Upfronts vocal group in 1960. Made several recordings during the 1960's as Barry Lee. Formed Love Unlimited, a female vocal trio, in 1969. Recorded as Barry White from 1973. Died from kidney failure on July 4, 2003.

Date	Pos	Wks	ARTIST / Record Title *Label & Number*
12 Dec 74	6	4	1. YOU'RE THE FIRST, THE LAST, MY EVERYTHING *20th Century BTC 2133*

WHITE PLAINS **4 Weeks**

Formed in London, England in 1969 as a studio project by songwriters, Roger Cook and Roger Greenaway. Personnel: Tony Burrows (vocals), Roger Greenaway (vocals), Pete Nelson (piano), Robin Shaw (bass), Ricky Wolff (guitar/keyboards), Robin Box (lead guitar) and Roger Hills (drums). Tony Burrows and Roger Greenaway, left shortly after *My Baby Loves Lovin'* was recorded, to join Brotherhood of Man. Replaced by Robin Box and Roger Hills. Ricky Wolff left in 1974. Replaced by Ron Reynolds. Group disbanded in 1976.

Date	Pos	Wks	ARTIST / Record Title *Label & Number*
02 Apr 70	9	1	1. MY BABY LOVES LOVIN' *Deram DM(I) 280*
03 Dec 70	8	2	2. JULIE DO YA LOVE ME *Deram DM(I) 315*
22 Mar 73	9	1	3. STEP INTO A DREAM *Deram DM(I) 371*

David WHITFIELD **6 Weeks**

Born on February 2, 1926 in Kingston-upon-Hull, Yorkshire, England. As a child became a choirboy in St. Peter's Church. At age seventeen joined the British Royal Navy. After his demob in 1950 worked at various labouring jobs. Sang part time in local working men's clubs. In May 1950, made it to the final of the Radio Luxembourg talent show, *Opportunity Knocks*. The shows host, Hughie Green, arranged a booking for David at the Criterion in London. This led to a residency at the Washington Hotel in London's West End.

continues over

Date	Pos	Wks	ARTIST / Record Title *Label & Number*
			Spotted by Decca Records executive, Bunny Lewis, who signed him to the label. Disc debut: *Marta* (1953). Died of a brain haemorrhage on January 16, 1980.
14 Sep 54	3	2	1. CARA MIA *Decca F 10327*
07 Jun 55	-	1	2. MAMA *Decca F 10515*
22 Nov 55	-	1	3. WHEN YOU LOSE THE ONE YOU LOVE *Decca F 10627*
12 Feb 57	-	1	4. THE ADORATION WALTZ *Decca F 10833*
11 Jun 58	-	1	5. ON THE STREET WHERE YOU LIVE *Decca F 11018*

Slim WHITMAN — *9 Weeks*

Born Otis Dewey Whitman Jr on January 20, 1924 in Tampa, Florida, USA. Enlisted in the US Navy during the Second World War. It was during his naval career that he began playing the guitar and singing. Spotted by Colonel Tom Parker who heard him singing on the radio. Signed to RCA in 1948. Moved to Imperial Records in 1952. Stayed with label until 1970. Joined the Grand Ole Opry in 1955. Appeared in the 1957 film, *Jamboree*.

Date	Pos	Wks	ARTIST / Record Title *Label & Number*
02 Aug 55	-	2	1. ROSE MARIE *London HL 8061*
25 Oct 55	-	1	2. INDIAN LOVE CALL *London HL 1149*
17 Jul 56	-	2	3. SERENADE *London HL 8287*
07 May 57	-	1	4. I'LL TAKE YOU HOME AGAIN KATHLEEN *London HL 8403*
10 Sep 57	-	1	5. LOVESICK BLUES *London HL 8459*
05 Nov 57	-	1	6. CURTAIN OF TEARS *London HL 8416*
07 Jan 58	-	1	7. UNCHAIN MY HEART *London HL 8518*

Roger WHITTAKER — *29 Weeks*

Born on March 22, 1936 in Nairobi, Kenya. In 1954 drafted into the Kenya Army. Following his demob in 1956, enrolled at University of Cape Town, South Africa, to study medicine. After eighteen months left to try teaching. During this period began to sing and entertain in local clubs. Relocated to Britain in 1959 where he enrolled at the University of Bangor, Wales, where for three years studied zoology, biochemistry and marine biology, ending up with a B.Sc.

continues over

Date	Pos	Wks	ARTIST / Record Title *Label & Number*

Had by now started to write his own songs and as a result of performing some of the songs in the University Rag Week, a demo of his songs reached a music publisher. Signed to Fontana Records, he made his disc debut in 1962 with *The Charge Of The Light Brigade.* His autobiography, *So Far So Good*, published in 1986. The lyrics of, *The Last Farewell*, were written by a silversmith in Birmingham, England, who entered a contest in which the best lyric or poem sent to Roger Whittaker, would be put to music and recorded by Roger. The song originally appeared on an album.

Date	Pos	Wks	ARTIST / Record Title *Label & Number*
07 May 70	4	10	1. I DON'T BELIEVE IN IF ANYMORE *Columbia DB(I) 8664*
05 Nov 70	1(3)	10	• 2. NEW WORLD IN THE MORNING *Columbia DB(I) 8718*
21 Aug 75	2	9	3. THE LAST FAREWELL *EMI EMI 2294*

The WHO — *5 Weeks*

Formed in Shepherds Bush, London, England in 1962. Group evolved out of a local youth club band, the Detours. In early February 1964 the Detours became The Who. Manager/publicist Peter Meadon took over the group and changed group name to the High Numbers. Made disc debut (as High Numbers) with *I'm The Face,* in July 1964. Kit Lambert and Chris Stamp then took over as managers and renamed the group, The Who. Personnel: Roger Daltrey (born April 1, 1944 in London, vocals), Pete Townshend (lead guitar), John Entwistle (bass) and Keith Moon (drums). Their first single as The Who, *I Can't Explain* was issued in 1965. Released the concept album, *Tommy,* in 1969. Six years later it was turned into a film. Following Keith Moon's death in 1978, Kenney Jones, ex-Small Faces/Faces drummer, was drafted into the lineup. Disbanded in 1982. Have been many reunion tours. Inducted into the Rock 'n' Roll Hall of Fame in 1990. Keith Moon died of a drug overdose on September 7, 1978 after attending the West End film premiere of *The Buddy Holly Story.* John Entwistle died of a heart attack on June 27, 2002.

continues over

Date	Pos	Wks	ARTIST / Record Title *Label & Number*
06 Dec 65	7	2	1. MY GENERATION *Brunswick 05944*
17 Oct 66	7	2	2. I'M A BOY *Reaction 591004*
26 Jan 67	8	1	3. HAPPY JACK *Reaction 591010*

See also Roger Daltrey

Marty WILDE — *3 Weeks*

Born Reginald Smith on April 15, 1936 in London, England. Discovered by Larry Parnes who renamed him Marty Wilde. Disc debut: *Honeycomb* (1957). Hosted television pop music show *Boy Meets Girl* (1959). Starred in the 1961 London West End production of *Bye Bye Birdie*. In 1963 starred in the film *What A Crazy World*. Formed the Wilde Three with his wife Joyce and future Moody Blues vocalist, Justin Hayward. Composed hits for Status Quo, (*Ice In The Sun*), The Freshmen, (*Half-way To Where*), The Casuals (*Jesamine*) and his daughter, Kim Wilde (*Kids In America*).

Date	Pos	Wks	ARTIST / Record Title *Label & Number*
30 Apr 59	5	2	1. DONNA *Philips EPB 902*
10 Dec 59	8	1	2. SEA OF LOVE *Philips EPB 959*

Colm C.T. WILKINSON — *7 Weeks*

Born on June 5, 1944 in Dublin, Ireland. At age sixteen joined the Chris Lamb Band. Member of The Action beat group in mid 1960's. Later joined the Jim Doherty Band. In the late 1960's joined the Witnessess Showband. Left in 1971 to pursue a solo career. Offered the role of Judas in the first Irish production of *Jesus Christ Superstar* at Dublin's Gaiety Theatre in March 1973. Moved to England in January 1974, to sing role of Judas in the London production at the Palace Theatre. Disc debut: *Kick The Can*, a track on the soundtrack album of *Demolition Man* (1975). First solo single, *My Happiness*, issued on DJM in April 1976. Represented Ireland at the 1978 Eurovision Song contest with his own composition, *Born To Sing*, finishing in fifth position. In 1976, invited by Andrew Lloyd Webber and Tim Rice to sing the part of Che on the concept album for the musical, *Evita*.

Date	Pos	Wks	ARTIST / Record Title *Label & Number*

Received critical acclaim for his performances as Jean Valjean in the 1985 London production and the 1987 Broadway production of *Les Miserables*. Relocated to Canada in 1989 to star in the Toronto production of *The Phantom Of The Opera*.

Date	Pos	Wks	ARTIST / Record Title *Label & Number*
17 Mar 77	2	6	1. THERE WAS A DREAM *Release RL 862*
04 May 78	8	1	2. BORN TO SING *Polydor 2090 287*

Andy WILLIAMS *29 Weeks*

Born Howard Andrew Williams on December 3, 1927 in Wall Lake, Iowa, USA. Began singing with his three brothers in a local Presbyterian Church choir. Made his professional singing debut at the age of eight as part of the Williams Brothers Quartet. Became regulars on radio station WHO's *Iowa Barn Dance Show*. Made their first professional recording, *Swinging On A Star*, with Bing Crosby in 1944. Group disbanded in 1951, Andy chose to move to New York to pursue a solo career. Made his first solo recordings for the RCA subsidiary label "X". Signed to Cadence Records in 1955. He switched to Columbia in 1961. Own NBC-TV variety series in USA from 1962-67 and 1969-71. Introduced the Osmonds to the world of popular music via his weekly TV show in the 1960's. Opened the Andy Williams Moon River Theatre in Branson, Missouri on May 1, 1992.

Date	Pos	Wks	ARTIST / Record Title *Label & Number*
07 May 57	-	4	1. BUTTERFLY *London HLA 8399*
13 May 63	6	6	2. CAN'T GET USED TO LOSING YOU *CBS EAAG 138*
11 Oct 65	5	4	3. ALMOST THERE *CBS 201813*
16 May 68	8	2	4. CAN'T TAKE MY EYES OFF YOU *CBS 3298*
16 Apr 70	4	4	5. CAN'T HELP FALLING IN LOVE *CBS 4818*
21 Jan 71	10	1	6. HOME LOVIN' MAN *CBS 5267*
29 Apr 71	7	2	7. (WHERE DO I BEGIN) LOVE STORY *CBS 7020*
07 Sep 72	6	3	8. LOVE THEME FROM'THE GODFATHER' (SPEAK SOFTLY LOVE) *CBS 8166*
14 Feb 74	3	3	9. SOLITAIRE *CBS 1824*

Date	Pos	Wks	ARTIST / Record Title *Label & Number*

Danny WILLIAMS — *12 Weeks*

Born on January 7, 1942 in Port Elizabeth, South Africa. Started as a boy soprano in a local church choir. At the age of fourteen won an talent contest and got the opportunity to work on the touring show *Golden City Dixies*. He toured with the show for three years. In March 1959, the revue came to London, where his performances came to the attention of Norman Newell, who arranged a recording contract with EMI. Disc debut: *Tall As A Tree* (1959). Recorded with many prominent arrangers including Geoff Love and Nelson Riddle. In 1994, began touring a Nat King Cole Tribute Show. Died from lung cancer on December 6, 2005.

Date	Pos	Wks	ARTIST / Record Title *Label & Number*
07 Dec 61	2	8	1. MOON RIVER *HMV POP(I) 932*
22 Feb 62	9	1	2. JEANNIE *HMV POP(I) 968*
31 May62	7	3	3. THE WONDERFUL WORLD OF THE YOUNG *HMV POP(I) 1002*

Denice WILLIAMS — *1 Weeks*

Born June Deniece Chandler on June 3, 1951 in Gary, Indiana, USA. During her childhood sang in a Pentecostal Gospel Choir. In the late 1960's recorded for the Toddlin' Town label under the name Denice Chandler. Disc debut: *Love Is Tears* (1969). In 1972 discovered by Stevie Wonder, who hired her as a member of his Wonderlove vocal backing group. Left in 1976 to pursue a solo career. Signed to Columbia Records.

Date	Pos	Wks	ARTIST / Record Title *Label & Number*
02 Jun 77	8	1	1. FREE *CBS 4978*

See also Johnny Mathis and Denice Williams

Larry WILLIAMS — *1 Weeks*

Born Lawrence Williams on May 10, 1935 in New Orleans, USA. Learned to play the piano as a child. In 1954 Lloyd Price employed Larry as his pianist and valet until Price was drafted for military service. Signed to Specialty Records. Disc debut: *Just Because* (1957).

continues over

Date	Pos	Wks	ARTIST / Record Title *Label & Number*
			Song writing credits include *Short Fat Fannie*, *Dizzy Miss Lizzy*, *Boney Moronie* and *Slow Down*. Dropped by Specialty in 1959. Moved to Chess and later had a spell as A&R man at Okeh Records. Teamed up with Johnny 'Guitar' Watson for a number of record releases and a tour of UK. Committed suicide on January 7, 1980.
18 Mar 58	-	1	1. BONY MORONIE *London HLU 8532*
			Meri WILSON ***1 Weeks***
			Born on June 15, 1949 in Nagoya, Japan. Raised in Marietta, Georgia, USA. In the 1970's moved to Dallas and worked as a singer and a model. In 1999 she re-recorded *Telephone Man* under the title, *Internet Man*. Died in a car crash in Americus, Georgia, USA on December 28, 2002.
20 Oct 77	9	1	1. TELEPHONE MAN *Pye International 7N 25747*
			Robert WILSON ***7 Weeks***
			Born on January 2, 1907 in Cambuslang, Glasgow, Scotland. Started singing in Glasgow halls before becoming a professional singer with the Rothesay Entertainers. A member of the famous D'Oyly Carte Opera Company from April 1931 to July 1937. In 1939 embarked on a solo career as a concert singer. Recorded for Parlophone and HMV. Died on September 22, 1964.
19 Jul 55	-	7	1. DOONAREE *HMV IP 1007*
			WINGS ***42 Weeks***
			Formed in London, England in August 1971 by ex Beatle Paul McCartney. Disc debut: *Wild Life* LP (1971). Personnel: Paul McCartney (vocals, bass), Linda McCartney (vocals, keyboards), Denny Laine (vocals, guitar), Henry McCullough (lead Guitar) and Denny Seiwell (drums). Seiwell and McCullough left in late 1973, replaced by Jimmy McCulloch and Geoff Britton.

continues over

Date	Pos	Wks	ARTIST / Record Title *Label & Number*

In November 1974, Britton departed and Joe English joined band. In late 1977, McCulloch and English left, replaced by Laurence Juber and Steve Holly. On April 27, 1981, Denny Laine gave in his notice and shortly afterwards Wings disbanded.

Date	Pos	Wks	ARTIST / Record Title *Label & Number*
02 Mar 72	1(1)	4	• 1. GIVE IRELAND BACK TO THE IRISH *Apple R 5936*
25 Jul 74	7	2	2. BAND ON THE RUN *Apple R 5997*
26 Jun 75	4	3	3. LISTEN TO WHAT THE MAN SAID *Capitol R 6014*
17 Jun 76	1(2)	7	• 4. SILLY LOVE SONGS *Parlophone R 6014*
02 Sep 76	2	6	5. LET 'EM IN *Parlophone R 6015*
01 Dec 77	1(10)	13	• 6. MULL OF KINTYRE *Parlophone R 6018*
13 Apr 78	3	5	7. WITH A LITTLE LUCK *Parlophone R 6019*
30 Nov 78	10	1	8. MULL OF KINTYRE (re-entry) *Parlophone R 6018*
12 Apr 79	9	1	9. GOODNIGHT TONIGHT *Parlophone R 6023*

See also Paul McCartney

WIZZARD *15 Weeks*

Formed in Birmingham, England in 1972 by Roy Wood following his departure from the Electric Light Orchestra. Personnel: Roy Wood (born Ulysses Adrian Wood on November 8, 1946 in Birmingham, England, lead vocals, guitar), Rick Price (bass), Hugh McDowell (cello), Nick Pentelow (saxophone), Mike Burney (saxophone), Bill Hunt (keyboards), Keith Smart (drums) and Charlie Grima (drums). Disbanded in 1975.

Date	Pos	Wks	ARTIST / Record Title *Label & Number*
25 Jan 73	8	1	1. BALL PARK INCIDENT *Harvest HAR 5062*
17 May 73	1(1)	7	• 2. SEE MY BABY JIVE *Harvest HAR 5070*
20 Sep 73	7	3	3. ANGEL FINGERS *Harvest HAR 5076*
20 Dec 73	6	3	4. I WISH IT COULD BE CHRISTMAS EVERY DAY *Harvest HAR 5079*
30 Jan 75	10	1	5. ARE YOU READY TO ROCK *Warner Bros K 16479*

See also The Move

WOLFHOUND *2 Weeks*

Ballad/folk group formed in Belfast, N. Ireland in August 1970. Personnel: Danny Burns, Ray McAreavey, Gogie McCullough, Malcolm Rodgers and Billy Tierney.

Date	Pos	Wks	ARTIST / Record Title *Label & Number*

Disc debut: *Boys Of The Old Brigade* (1971). Billy Tierney left group in 1973, replaced by Kieran Manning. Malcolm Rodgers departed in 1973. The group disbanded in 1976. Danny Burns died on May 7, 2002. The song, *Over The Wall*, composed by Danny Burns, is about nine internees who escaped to freedom by climbing over the wall of Crumlin Road Jail in Belfast, during a football match in the excerise yard, on November 17, 1971.

06 Apr 72	8	2	1. OVER THE WALL *R&O RO 1002*

The WOLFE TONES — *12 Weeks*

Ballad/folk group formed in Inchicore, Dublin, Ireland in 1963 by brothers Derek and Brian Warfield and Noel Nagle. Started playing around the Fleadhs (traditional music festivals) throughout Ireland. In July 1964, they met Tommy Byrne at a fleadh ceoil in Elphin, Co. Roscommon. Impressed by his guitar playing the trio invited Tommy to join the group. He accepted and in November 1964 they decided to pack up the day job and go professional. Won the Festival of Kerry Ballad Competition in Tralee in 1964. Disc debut: *Spanish Lady* (1965). Derek Warfield left the group in 2000. *The Helicopter Song* was composed to mark the event of October 31, 1973, when three leading IRA members escaped from Mountjoy Prison, Dublin, via a helicopter that landed in the exercise yard of the prison.

02 Mar 72	7	1	1. SNOWY BREASTED PEARL *Dolphin DOS 92*
22 Nov 73	1(4)	7	• 2. UP AND AWAY (The Helicopter Song) *Dolphin DOS 112*
05 Jul 79	4	4	3. PADRAIC PEARSE *Triskel TRS 4*

The WOMBLES — *4 Weeks*

The Wombles originated as fictional characters in a set of stories created by Elizabeth Beresford and published as children's novels in 1968. In 1973, the stories were adapted for television and turned into a childrens TV series.

continues over

Date	Pos	Wks	ARTIST / Record Title *Label & Number*
			Mike Batt (born on February 6, 1950 in Southampton, England), was hired to write the music for the teleevision series. The Wombles recordings featured lead vocals by Mike Batt, with top session musicians including Clem Cattini (drums) and Chris Spedding (lead guitar) providing the musical backing.
02 May 74	6	3	1. **REMEMBER YOU'RE A WOMBLE** *CBS SCBS 2241*
25 Jul 74	10	1	2. **BANANA ROCK** *CBS 2465*
			See also Mike Batt

Stevie WONDER — *12 Weeks*

Born Steveland Judkins on May 13, 1950 in Saginaw, Michigan, USA. Was blinded soon after birth due to too much oxygen being pumped into his incubator. Family moved to Detroit in 1954. Began to play piano at the age of seven. In 1961 he was discovered by Ronnie White of The Miracles, who arranged an audition with Motown Records. Berry Gordy signed Steveland and renamed him Little Stevie Wonder. 'The Little' part of his name was dropped in 1964. Disc debut: *Fingertips Pt. 2* (1963). Inducted into Rock and Roll Hall of Fame in 1989.

Date	Pos	Wks	ARTIST / Record Title *Label & Number*
21 Aug 69	9	4	1. **MY CHERIE AMOUR** *Tamla Motown TMG(I) 690*
04 Dec 69	3	8	2. **YESTER-ME, YESTER-YOU, YESTERDAY** *Tamla Motown TMG(I) 717*

Sheb WOOLEY — *2 Weeks*

Actor/singer/songwriter. Born Shelby Wooley on April 10, 1921 near Erick, Oklahoma, USA. Moved to Nashville in 1945, where he made his disc debut For the Bullet label. Signed to MGM in 1948. Played the role of cook, Pete Nolan, in the TV western series, Rawhide, which starred a young Clint Eastwood. Also recorded under the name Ben Colder. Film appearances include *High Noon* (1952) and *Giant* (1955). Died on September 16, 2003.

Date	Pos	Wks	ARTIST / Record Title *Label & Number*
09 Jul 58	-	2	1. **PURPLE PEOPLE EATER** *MGM MGM(I) 981*

Date	Pos	Wks	ARTIST / Record Title *Label & Number*

Tammy WYNETTE — *7 Weeks*

Born Virginia Wynette Pugh on May 5, 1942 in Itawamba County, Mississippi, USA. Daughter of a local musician who died when she was eight months old. Married at the age of seventeen. Her musical career started in 1965, when she began performing on a Birmingham television programme, *The Country Boy Eddie Show*. Moved to Nashville in 1966. Discovered by producer Billy Sherrill who signed her to Epic Records. Disc debut: *Apartment #9* (1966). Married to country singer George Jones from 1969-1975. Her autobiography, *Stand By Your Man*, was published in 1979. Died on April 6, 1998.

Date	Pos	Wks	ARTIST / Record Title *Label & Number*
15 May 75	1(3)	7	• 1. STAND BY YOUR MAN *Epic EPC 7137*

Mark WYNTER — *12 Weeks*

Born Terry Lewis on January 29, 1943 in Woking, Surrey, England. Made his disc debut, *Image Of A Girl*, for Decca in 1960. Had a few minor hits with Decca before Tony Hatch signed him to Pye. Starred in the 1963 film, *Just For Fun*. In the late 1960's, with his pop idol days behind him, he turned his attention to the theatre. Has since starred in many stage productions including *Phil The Fluter*, *P.T.* Barnum, *Cats*, *Conduct Unbecoming*, *Side By Side* and *Charleys Aunt*. *Venus In Blue Jeans* was originally recorded by Bruce Bruno of The Orchids on Roulette in late 1961.

Date	Pos	Wks	ARTIST / Record Title *Label & Number*
15 Oct 62	5	7	1. VENUS IN BLUE JEANS *Pye 7N 15466*
21 Jan 63	8	5	2. GO AWAY LITTLE GIRL *Pye 7N 15482*

Date	Pos	Wks	ARTIST / Record Title *Label & Number*

The YARDBIRDS — *8 Weeks*

Formed in Kingston, Surrey, England in 1963. Took over the Rolling Stones residency at the Crawdaddy, Station Hotel, in Richmond, Surrey. Personnel: Keith Relf (born March 22, 1943 in Richmond, Surrey, vocals, harmonica), Eric Clapton (lead guitar), Chris Dreja (rhythm guitar), Paul Samwell-Smith (bass), and Jim McCarty (drums). Clapton left in 1965 and was replaced by Jeff Beck. Jimmy Page joined in 1966. Group disbanded in July 1968 with Page forming the New Yardbirds, which evolved into Led Zeppelin. Keith Relf died on May 14, 1976, electrocuted while playing his guitar at home.

Date	Pos	Wks	ARTIST / Record Title *Label & Number*
12 Apr 65	10	2	1. FOR YOUR LOVE *Columbia DB(I) 7499*
19 Jul 65	3	3	2. HEART FULL OF SOUL *Columbia DB(I) 7594*
25 Oct 65	6	3	3. EVIL HEARTED YOU *Columbia DB(I) 7706*

YELLOW DOG — *2 Weeks*

Formed in London, England in 1978 by ex members of the group Fox. Personnel: Kenny Young (vocals, guitar), Herbie Armstrong (guitar), Jim Gannon (guitar), Gary Roberts (guitar), Gary Taylor (bass) and Gerry Conway (drums).

Date	Pos	Wks	ARTIST / Record Title *Label & Number*
23 Mar 78	10	2	1. JUST ONE MORE NIGHT *Virgin VS 195*

YES — *3 Weeks*

Formed in London, England in 1968. Personnel: Jon Anderson (born on October 25, 1944 in Accrington, England, vocals), Peter Banks (guitar), Tony Kaye (keyboards), Chris Squire (bass) and Bill Bruford (drums). Disc debut: *Yes* L.P. (1969). Peter Banks left in 1971 to be replaced by Steve Howe. Tony Kaye departed in 1971. Replaced by Rick Wakeman.

continues over

Date	Pos	Wks	ARTIST / Record Title *Label & Number*

Bill Bruford left in late 1972 to be replaced by Alan White. Group disbanded in 1980, but reformed three years later.

20 Oct 77	6	3	1. WONDEROUS STORIES *Atlantic K 10999*

Faron YOUNG — *4 Weeks*

Born on February 25, 1932 in Shreveport, Louisiana, USA. Grew up on his father's dairy farm. By the time he left high school he was singing in a country band. Joined the Louisiana Hayride as a resident performer. In 1951, recorded *Have I Waited Too Long*. In 1952 signed to Capitol Records. Served in Korea with the U S Army Special Services Division. Discharged in November 1954. Film appearances include *Hidden Guns* (1956), *Daniel Boone Trailblazer* (1956) and *Raiders Of Old California* (1957). Nickname: *The Singing Sheriff*. Founder of country music magazine, *Music City News*. In 1962 signed with Mercury. Switched to MCA in 1979. Depressed by his poor health, he shot himself on December 9, 1996, he died the next day. Elected to Country Music Hall Of Fame in 2000.

21 Sep 72	5	4	1. FOUR IN THE MORNING *Mercury 6052 140*

Jimmy YOUNG — *5 Weeks*

Born Leslie Ronald Young on September 21, 1923 in Cinderford, Gloucestershire, England. As a young man he excelled at sport and played rugby for Bath and Wigan. Joined the RAF in 1942. In August 1949 made his first broadcast as a singer on BBC radio. Signed to Polygon Records in 1950. On the Decca roster 1952-58. Joined Columbia in 1958. A two week engagement on the BBC Light Programme's, presenting *Housewives Choice*, in 1960 led to more radio work as a disc jockey and compere. With the launch of BBC Radio's 1 and 2 in 1967, Jimmy got his own morning radio show. It ran until December 2002.

continues over

Date	Pos	Wks	ARTIST / Record Title *Label & Number*
			Published two volumes of his autobiography, *J. Y.: The Autobiography of Jimmy Young*, in 1973 and 1982. Received a Knighthood in 2002.
24 May 55	-	3	1. UNCHAINED MELODY *Decca F 10502*
11 Oct 55	-	2	2. THE MAN FROM LARAMIE *Decca F 10597*

John Paul YOUNG — *4 Weeks*

Born on June 21, 1950 in Glasgow, Scotland. Moved to Sydney, Australia as a child. In the 70's was lead singer with rock group, Elm Tree. In 1972 was a member of Australian production of *Jesus Christ Superstar*. Spotted by producer Simon Napier-Bell who signed him as a solo artist. Disc debut: *Pasadena* (1972). On November 4, 1994, became a naturalized Australian. Sang at the closing ceremony of the 2000 Sydney Olympic Games.

Date	Pos	Wks	ARTIST / Record Title *Label & Number*
01 Jun 78	3	4	1. LOVE IS IN THE AIR *Arista ARO 117*

Karen YOUNG — *1 Weeks*

Born in 1946 in Sheffield, England. In 1964 joined local beat group the Counterbeats. Spotted singing at a Northern Club by the Bachelors who introduced her to their managers, Dorothy and Phil Solomon. Disc debut: *Are You Kidding* (1965).

Date	Pos	Wks	ARTIST / Record Title *Label & Number*
27 Nov 69	10	1	1. NOBODY'S CHILD *Major Minor MM 625*

Date	Pos	Wks	ARTIST / Record Title *Label & Number*

Z

Helmut ZACHARIAS and his ORCHESTRA — *1 Weeks*

Orchestra leader/violinist. Born on January 27, 1920 in Berlin, Germany. *Tokyo Melody* was the theme to the 1964 Tokyo Olympics. Died on February 28, 2002.

Date	Pos	Wks	ARTIST / Record Title *Label & Number*
23 Nov 64	8	1	1. TOKYO MELODY • *Polydor NH 52341*

ZAGER and EVANS — *6 Weeks*

Denny Zager (born February 15, 1944 in Wymore, Nebraska, USA) and Rick Evans (born January 20, 1943 in Lincoln, Nebraska). In 1962 played together in a group called the Eccentrics. Went their separate ways when the group split up. Met up again in 1968 in Lincoln, Nebraska. Recorded a song, *In The Year 2525*, which Evans had written in 1964. Issued on their own label, Truth Records, it was picked up by RCA, who gave it a national release in June 1969. The duo split up shortly after the success of the record.

Date	Pos	Wks	ARTIST / Record Title *Label & Number*
28 Aug 69	1(2)	6	• 1. IN THE YEAR 2525 (Exordium & Terminus) *RCA RCA 1860*

Michael ZAGER BAND — *1 Weeks*

Studio group formed by multi-instrumentalist/songwriter/ Michael Zager. Born on January 3, 1943 in Passaic, Jersey City, New York, USA. Graduated from Miami University with a degree in Communication. Entered Mames College of Music majoring in composition. Member of group Ten Wheel Drive from 1968 to 1973. Produced recordings for Whitney Houston, Gladys Knight, Herb Alpert and Luther Vandross.

Date	Pos	Wks	ARTIST / Record Title *Label & Number*
25 May 78	8	1	1. LET'S ALL CHANT *Private Stock PVT 143*

RAMBLING MAN
Philomena Begley & Rambling Men
The second top ten hit for the lady from Pomeroy Co. Tyrone. Prior to Philomena deciding on a full time career in the music business she worked in Fishers hat factory in Cookstown.

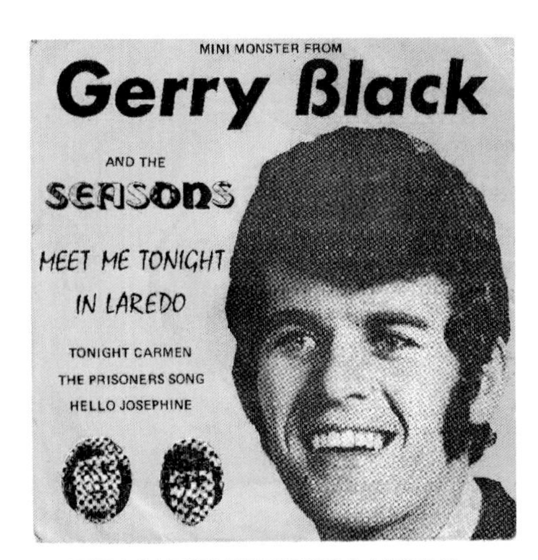

MEET ME TONIGHT IN LAREDO
Gerry Black and Seasons
Castleblaney, Co. Monaghan based showband, Gerry Black and The Seasons, tasted their one and only top ten hit with their version of the Marty Robbins song, "*Meet Me Tonight In Laredo*".

O HOLY NIGHT
Tommy Drennan and Monarchs
Composed in 1847 by Adolphe Adam "*O Holy Night*" was translated into English in 1855. Tommy Drennan's number one hit recording of the song is unique as it features the voice of Tommy Drennan as a 12 year old boy soprano and as an adult vocalist circa 1971.

EILEEN O'GRADY
Hugo Duncan and Tall Men
Affectionately known as The Wee Man from Strabane, Hugo Duncan is now a much respected broadcaster with BBC Radio Ulster. "*Eileen O'Grady*" peaked at number ten in July 1972.

A BUNCH OF THYME
Foster and Allen
Vocal instrumental duo Mick Foster and Tony Allen caused a stir when they appeared on the BBC TV programme *Top Of The Pops* in March 1982 dressed in leprechaun suits.

MINNIE MINNIE
Gina, Dale Haze & Champions
Originally a hit in Europe for Dutch vocal duo, Mouth and MacNeal. "*Minnie Minnie*" provided Gina, Dale Haze and the Champions with the first of their many Top Ten hits.

LOVE IS TEASING
Dermot Hegarty & Plainsmen
Traditional Irish song given the showband treatment by Longford singer Dermot Hegarty. Dermot a founder member of Release Records formed the Plainsmen Showband in April 1969.

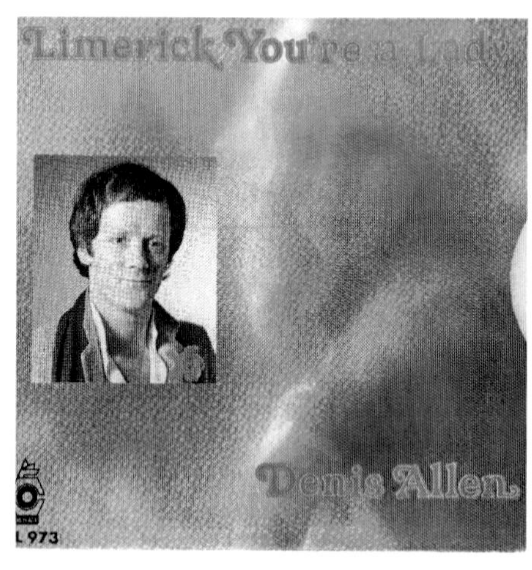

LIMERICK YOU'RE A LADY
Dennis Allen
Composed by Denis Allen, for the 1979 Limerick Lady Festival. It is now regarded as the unofficial anthem of Limerick city.

LOVE IS ALL
Red Hurley
Dublin born Brian Vincent Hurley received his stage name of 'Red' when he joined the Colours Showband as lead singer in 1969. "*Love Is All*" was Red's third number one hit, spending two weeks at the top.

MY ELUSIVE DREAMS
Ray Lynam & Phil Begley
A classic country song recorded originally in 1967 by Tammy Wynnette and David Houston. Ray and Phil teamed up on record at the suggestion of Release Records boss Mick Clerkin.

HOW GREAT THOU ART
Kelley and the Nevada
Composed originally in 1891, "*How Great Thou Art*" is one of the great uplifting hymns of all time. Having heard the song on a Dolly Parton album, Eileen Kelly adopted "*How Great Thou Art*" as her party piece. Members of the Nevada Showband came around to Kelley's idea that that this song would be a great choice for her as a single.

BORROWED ANGEL
Ray Lynam and the Hillbillies
In late 1969 Ray Lynam was persuaded by his friend Kevin Sheerin, to forsake pop and concentrate on country music. Ray is now regarded by his contemporaries as one of Ireland's greatest male country singers. "*Borrowed Angel*" provided Ray Lynam and the Hillbillies with their second top ten hit.

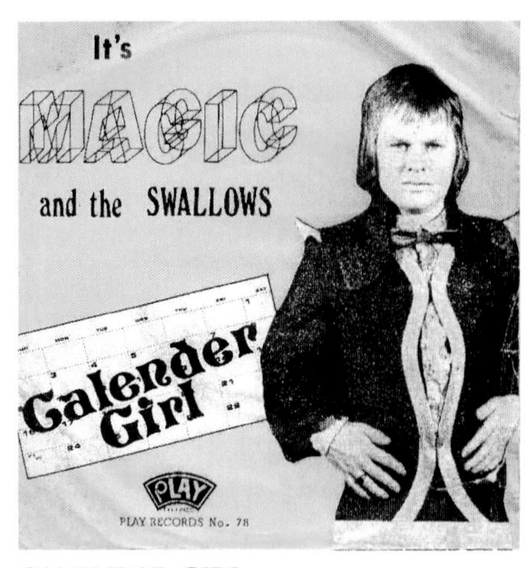

CALENDAR GIRL
Magic
The song writing magic of Neil Sedaka provided Co. Louth born singer Magic with his first top ten hit and launched him on a successful career.

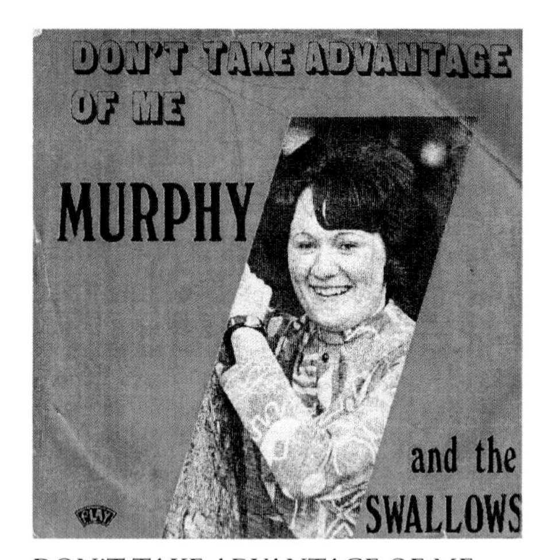

DON'T TAKE ADVANTAGE OF ME
Murphy and the Swallows
Discovered by showbiz promoter Noel Carty, Margaret Murphy's debut single *"Don't Take Advantage Of Me"* peaked at number three on Irelands Top Ten in January 1972.

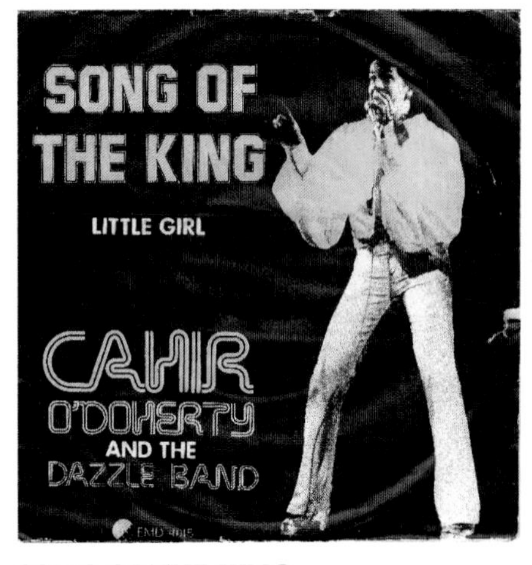

SONG OF THE KING
Cahir O'Doherty
Composed by Andrew Lloyd Webber and Tim Rice *"Song Of The King"* featured in the musical *'Joseph and the Amazing Technicolour Dreamcoat'*. Cahir O'Doherty appeared in the role of Pharaoh in the 1974 Dublin production of the stage musical.

O'BRIEN HAS NO PLACE TO GO
Brendan Shine
A chart topper for three weeks in June/July 1971. In May 1974 Eamonn Andrews presented Brendan Shine with a Silver Disc for sales of the record in excess of 25,000.

YOU GAVE ME A MOUNTAIN
Brendan Bowyer and the Big 8
Marty Robbins wrote "*You Gave Me A Mountain*" in late 1968. Brendan Bowyer's recording of the song hit the number six slot on Irelands Top Ten in November 1971.

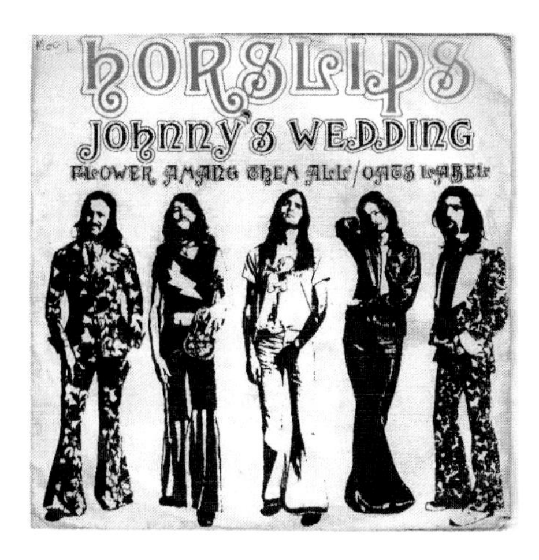

JOHNNY'S WEDDING
Horslips
Issued on their own record label, Oats, and released on St. Patricks Day 1972, the debut disc from Irish Celtic rock group Horslips sparked a remarkable run of Top Ten hits for the group

MANCHESTER RAMBLER
Sean O'Se
A top five hit for the Cork born singer/ teacher who was invited by Sean O'Riada to join Ceoltoiri Cualann in 1959.

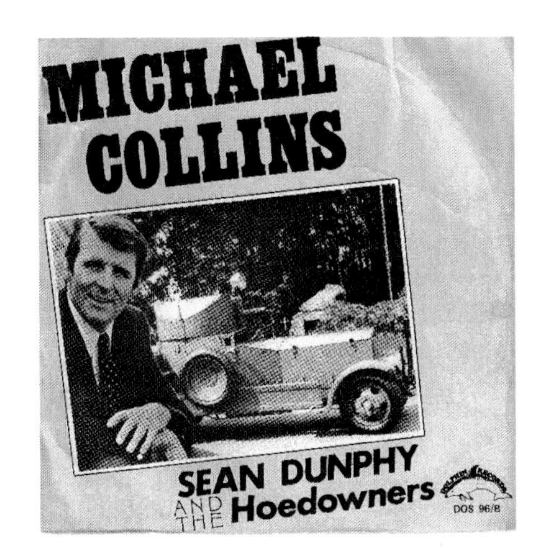

MICHAEL COLLINS
Sean Dunphy and the Hoedowners
Tribute in song to legendary Irish politician and revolutionary, Michael Collins. He was shot and killed on 22 August 1922 at Beal na mBlath, Co. Cork.

THE KEYS IN THE MAILBOX
Bill Ryan
Former singer with the Hootenannys, Bill Ryan helped to form Dublin based band Buckshot in 1972. Written by Buck Owens *"The Keys In The Mailbox"* peaked at number seven. Bill is a cousin of Margo and Daniel O'Donnell.

THESE ARE MY MOUNTAINS
Brian Coll
"These Are My Mountains" proved to be Brian Coll's most successful recording, peaking at number three in 1971. Brian Coll was winner of the 1989 Country and Irish RTE Guide Hall of Fame Award.

MEET THE COTTONS
Cotton Mill Boys
A 4 track single that provided the band with their debut top ten hit and showcased the vocal and instrumental talents of band members Gerry Madigan, Tony Hughes, Mike Scott and Mick McManus.

A DAISY A DAY
Danny Doyle
Composed by American singer/songwriter Jud Strunk. *"Daisy A Day"* provided Danny Doyle with his second number one hit, spending three weeks in the top spot.

MILK AND ALCOHOL
Dr Feelgood
"*Milk And Alcohol*" was written by Nick Lowe and band member John 'Gypie' Mayo. The song first appeared on Dr Feelgood's 1978 album, "*Private Practice*".

COOL FOR CATS
Squeeze
British group whose line-up included keyboard player/vocalist Jools Holland. Band member Chris Difford provided the lead vocal on "*Cool For Cats*".

HAPPY MAN
Cathal Dunne
Singer/songwriter, who represented Ireland, with his own song, "*Happy Man*", at the 1979 Eurovision Song Contest, finishing in fifth position. Cathal Dunne is the nephew of the former Taoiseach of Ireland, Jack Lynch. Lynch was Taoiseach for two periods 1966-1973 and 1977- 1979

TWO OF A KIND EP
Joe Dolan and the Drifters
Five track EP featuring the vocal talents of Drifters Joe Dolan, Ben Dolan and Tommy Swarbrigg. Tommy Swarbrigg's songwriting talent also gets an airing on the EP with "*I'll Sit On Your Doorstep*" and "*Minutes to Midnight*".

THAT'S WHAT FRIENDS ARE FOR
The Swarbriggs
Brothers Tommy and Jimmy Swarbrigg represented Ireland at the 1975 Eurovision Song Contest in Stockholm, Sweden. "*That's What Friends Are For*" composed by the two brothers finished in ninth position.

SPACE ODDITY
David Bowie
Classic song from the pen of David Bowie. It tells the story of Major Tom, a fictional astronaut. The song won an Ivor Novello Award in 1969. Bowie was inducted into the Rock and Roll Hall of Fame in 1996

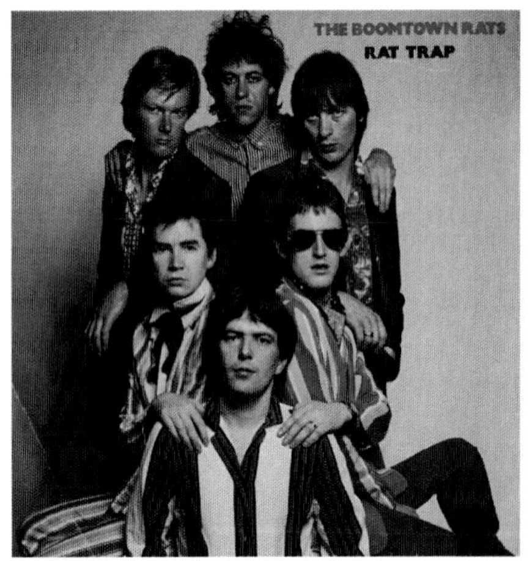

RAT TRAP
Boomtown Rats
(Punk) rock group from Dublin fronted by Bob Geldof. Relocated to London in 1976 and signed to Ensign Records. Geldof received an honorary knighthood in 2006 from Queen Elizabeth II in recognition for his work for charitable causes. *Rat Trap* was number one in the UK for two weeks. It peaked at number two in Ireland

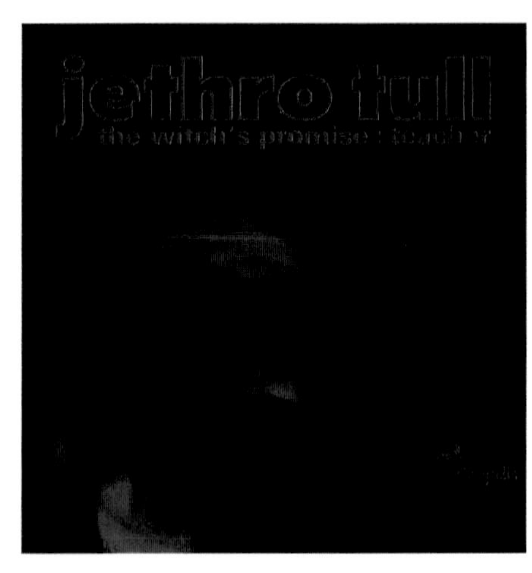

THE WITCH'S PROMISE
Jethro Tull
Widely recognized as the man who introduced the flute to rock music, Ian Anderson formed Jethro Tull in 1968. Ian was awarded an MBE for services to music in 2008. "*The Witch's Promise*" reached number six on Ireand's Top Ten.

Part Two

The Irish Hit Singles:

ALPHABETICALLY BY TITLE

Where there is no letter in brackets after the title, all hit recordings are of just one number. Individual titles of songs or tunes on L.P.'s and E.P.'s which made the singles chart are not included here, with the obvious exception of titles that are actually part of the overall title of the hit L.P. or E.P.

The recording act named alongside each song title is exactly as listed on the record. The year of chart entry column contains the year in which each disc made its very first appearance on the chart. Position in parenthesis is highest chart position attained.

Title – *Act* (Position) Year of Chart Entry

ABBEYSHRULE – *Brendan Shine* (1) 1974
ABOVE AND BEYOND – *Houston Wells and the Premier Aces* (6) 1966
ABSENT FRIENDS – *Anne Shelton* (-) 1957
ACAPULCO 1922 • – *Kenny Ball and his Jazzmen* (8) 1963
ACHING BREAKING HEART – *Joe Dolan and the Drifters* (2) 1965
ACTION – *Sweet* (7) 1975
ADDIO AMORE – *Vera Lynn* (-) 1955
ADIOS AMIGO – *Jim Reeves* (4) 1962
ADORATION WALTZ – *David Whitfield* (-) 1957
AFTER THE LOVE HAS GONE – *Earth Wind and Fire* (8) 1979
AFTER TWENTY ONE YEARS – *Dermot Hegarty and the Plainsmen* (9) 1972
AGAIN AND AGAIN – *Status Quo* (5) 1978
AIN'T GONNA BUMP NO MORE (With No Big Fat Woman) – *Joe Tex* (3) 1977
AIN'T GOT NO-I GOT LIFE – *Nina Simone* (9) 1969
AIN'T LOVE A BITCH – *Rod Stewart* (5) 1979
AIN'T NO STOPPIN' US NOW – *McFadden and Whitehead* (9) 1979
AIN'T THAT LOVING YOU BABY – *Elvis Presley* (5) 1964
THE AIR THAT I BREATHE – *The Hollies* (6) 1974
AIRPORT – *The Motors* (8) 1978
ALBATROSS • – *Fleetwood Mac* (5) 1969
ALLEGHANY MOON – *Patti Page* (-) 1956
ALL ALONE AM I – *Brenda Lee* (5) 1963
ALL AROUND MY HAT – *Steeleye Span* (3) 1975
ALL AT ONCE YOU LOVE HER – *Edmund Hockridge* (-) 1957
ALL FOR ME GROG – *The Dubliners* (10) 1967
ALL I HAVE TO DO IS DREAM – *Everly Brothers* (-) 1958
ALL I HAVE TO DO IS DREAM – *Bobbie Gentry and Glen Campbell* (2) 1970
ALL I HAVE TO OFFER YOU IS ME – *Rocky Tops* (9) 1972
ALL I REALLY WANT TO DO – *The Byrds* (8) 1965
ALL KINDS OF EVERYTHING – *Dana* (1) 1970
ALL MY LOVE – *Cliff Richard* (8) 1967
ALL MY ROADS – *Brendan Shine* (6) 1976
ALL OF ME LOVES ALL OF YOU – *Bay City Rollers* (5) 1974
ALL OR NOTHING – *Small Faces* (3) 1966
ALL RIGHT NOW – *Free* (5) 1970
ALL SHOOK UP – *Elvis Presley* (-) 1957
ALL THE WAY – *Frank Sinatra* (-) 1958

Title – *Act* (Position) Year of Chart Entry

ALL THE YOUNG DUDES – Mott The Hoople (4) 1972
ALL YOU NEED IS LOVE – *The Beatles* (1) 1967
ALMOST PERSUADED – *D J Curtin and The Kerry Blues* (3) 1973
ALMOST THERE – *Andy Williams* (5) 1965
ALONE – *Petula Clark* (-) 1957
ALONE – *The Southlanders* (-) 1957
ALONE AGAIN (Naturally) – *Gilbert O'Sullivan* (2) 1972
ALRIGHT ALRIGHT ALRIGHT – *Mungo Jerry* (4) 1973
ALTERNATE TITLE – *The Monkees* (4) 1967
ALWAYS AND FOREVER – *Marion Ryan* (-) 1958
ALWAYS ON MY MIND – *Elvis Presley* (9) 1973
ALWAYS YOURS – *Gary Glitter* (1) 1974
AM I THAT EASY TO FORGET – *Engelbert Humperdinck* (1) 1968
AMAZING GRACE • – *Pipes and Drums and Military Band of the Royal Scots Dragoon Guards* (1). 1972
AMERICAN PIE – *Don McLean* (7) 1972
AMONG THE WICKLOW HILLS – *Larry Cunningham and Mighty Avons* (2) 1966
AN AFFAIR TO REMEMBER – *Vic Damone* (-) 1958
AN EVERLASTING LOVE – *Andy Gibb* (4) 1978
AN OLD LOG CABIN FOR SALE – *Big Tom and the Mainliners* (4) 1967
AND I LOVE YOU SO – *Perry Como* (2) 1973
AND THE BAND PLAYED WALTZING MATILDA – *Makem & Clancy* (1) 1977
AND THE HEAVENS CRIED – *Anthony Newley* (7) 1961
ANGEL FINGERS – *Wizzard* (7) 1973
ANGEL SHE WAS LOVE – *Roly Daniels* (10) 1969
ANGEL EYES – *Abba* (3) 1979
ANGELA JONES – *Johnny Ferguson* (6) 1960
ANGELO – *Brotherhood Of Man* (1) 1977
ANGIE – *Rolling Stones* (9) 1973
ANGIE BABY – *Helen Reddy* (5) 1975
ANNAGHDOWN – *Larry Cunningham* (9) 1976
ANNIE'S SONG – *John Denver* (1) 1974
ANNIE'S SONG • – *James Galway* (1) 1978
ANOTHER BRICK IN THE WALL – *Pink Floyd* (1) 1979
ANOTHER DAY – *Paul McCartney* (1) 1971
THE ANSWER TO EVERYTHING – *Joe Dolan and the Drifters* (4) 1964
ANY DREAM WILL DO – *Joe Cuddy* (1) 1974
ANYONE WHO HAD A HEART – *Cilla Black* (1) 1964

Title – *Act* (Position) Year of Chart Entry

ANYTHING THAT'S PART OF YOU – *Tony Keeling* (10)....1965
ANY TIPPERARY TOWN – *The Rocky Tops featuring Pat Ely* (9)....1974
APACHE ♦ – *The Shadows* (1)....1960
APEMAN – *The Kinks* (10)....1971
APPLEJACK ♦ – *Jet Harris and Tony Meehan* (5)....1963
APRES TOI – *Vicki Leandros* (3)....1972
APRIL LOVE – *Pat Boone* (-)....1958
ARE FRIENDS ELECTRIC – *Tubeway Army* (3)....1979
ARE YOU LONESOME TONIGHT – *Elvis Presley* (1)....1961
ARE YOU READY TO ROCK – *Wizzard* (10)....1975
ARE YOU SURE – *The Allisons* (2)....1961
ARGENTINE MELODY (Cancion De Argentina) ♦ – *San Jose featuring Rodriguez Argentina* (7)....1978
ARIA ♦ – *Acker Bilk* (9)....1976
ARKANSAS – *Red Hurley and the Nevada* (2)....1973
ARMS OF MARY – *Sutherland Brothers and Quiver* (2)....1976
AROUND THE WORLD – *Bing Crosby* (-)....1957
AROUND THE WORLD – *Gracie Fields* (-)....1957
AROUND THE WORLD – *Ronnie Hilton* (-)....1957
ART FOR ART'S SAKE – *10CC* (4)....1976
AS I LOVE YOU – *Shirley Bassey* (5)....1959
AS TEARS GO BY – *Marianne Faithfull* (9)....1964
AS USUAL – *Brenda Lee* (4)....1964
AS YOU LIKE IT – *Adam Faith* (4)....1962
AT THE CLOSE OF A LONG LONG DAY – *Cadets featuring Gregory* (9)....1966
ATLANTIS ♦ – *The Shadows* (3)....1963
AUTOMATIC LOVER – *Dee D Jackson* (6)....1978

BABY COME BACK – *The Equals* (2)....1968
BABY DON'T CHANGE YOUR MIND – *Gladys Knight and The Pips* (7)....1975
BABY FACE – *Little Richard* (3)....1959
BABY I DON'T CARE – *Buddy Holly* (4)....1961
BABY I LOVE YOU – *Dave Edmunds* (6)....1973
BABY I LOVE YOU, OK! – *Kenny* (9)....1975
BABY JUMP – *Mungo Jerry* (5)....1971
BABY LOVE – *The Supremes* (2)....1964
BABY LOVER – *Petula Clark* (-)....1958
BABY MAKE IT SOON – *The Marmalade* (6)....1969

Title – *Act* (Position) Year of Chart Entry

BABY NOW THAT I'VE FOUND YOU – *The Foundations* (3) 1967
BABY STOP CRYING – *Bob Dylan* (5) 1978
BACHELOR BOY – *Cliff Richard and the Shadows* (1) 1962
BACK HOME (a) – *England World Cup Squad* (2) 1970
BACK HOME (b) – *Dickie Rock* (1) 1977
BACKSTAGE – *Gene Pitney* (5) 1966
BAD MOON RISING – *Creedence Clearwater Revival* (1) 1969
BAD TO ME – *Billy J Kramer with the Dakotas* (3) 1963
BAIDIN FHEIDLIMI – *Emmet Spiceland* (6) 1968
BAKER STREET – *Gerry Rafferty* (3) 1978
BALL PARK INCIDENT – *Wizzard* (8) 1973
THE BALLAD OF BONNIE AND CLYDE – *Georgie Fame* (4) 1968
BALLAD OF JAMES CONNOLLY – *Larry Cunningham* (10) 1969
THE BALLAD OF JOHN AND YOKO – *The Beatles* (1) 1969
BALLAD OF PALADIN • – *Duane Eddy* (3) 1962
THE BALLAD OF DAVY CROCKETT – *Bill Hayes* (-) 1956
THE BALLAD OF DAVY CROCKETT – *Fess Parker* (-) 1956
BALLROOM BLITZ – *Sweet* (1) 1973
BALLYHOE – *Dermot Henry and The Virginians* (3) 1971
BANANA BOAT SONG – *Shirley Bassey* (-) 1957
BANANA BOAT SONG (DAY-O) – *Harry Belafonte* (-) 1957
BANANA BOAT SONG – *The Tarriers* (-) 1957
BANANA ROCK – *The Wombles* (10) 1974
BAND OF GOLD – *Don Cherry* (-) 1956
BAND OF GOLD – *Freda Payne* (1) 1970
BAND ON THE RUN – *Paul McCartney and Wings* (7) 1974
BANG BANG – *B A Robertson* (5) 1979
BANG BANG (MY BABY SHOT ME DOWN) – *Cher* (3) 1966
THE BANGIN' MAN – *Slade* (3) 1974
BANKS OF THE OHIO – *Olivia Newton John* (9) 1971
BANNER MAN – *Blue Mink* (3) 1971
BARBADOS – *Typically Tropical* (1) 1975
BARBARA ANN – *The Beach Boys* (7) 1966
BATTLE OF NEW ORLEANS – *Lonnie Donegan and his Skiffle Group* (1) 1959
BATTLE OF NEW ORLEANS – *Vaughn Monroe* (4) 1959
BE MY GUEST – *Fats Domino* (2) 1959
BEAUTIFUL CITY – Donal Ring Sound with Paul O'Leary (4) 1972

Title – *Act* (Position) Year of Chart Entry

BEAUTIFUL DREAMER – *Kings Showband featuring Prince Vince* (4) 1966
BEAUTIFUL LOVER – *Brotherhood Of Man* (6) 1978
BEAUTIFUL NOISE – *Neil Diamond* (6) 1976
BEAUTIFUL PEACE – *Tommy Drennan and Top League* (2) 1973
BEAUTIFUL SUNDAY – *Brendan O'Brien and Stage 2* (5) 1972
BECAUSE THE NIGHT – *Patti Smith Group* (4) 1978
BECAUSE THEY'RE YOUNG • – *Duane Eddy and the Rebels* (3) 1960
BEFORE THE NEXT TEARDROP FALLS – *Gene Stuart & Mighty Avons* (3) 1970
BEHIND CLOSED DOORS – *Brendan Quinn* (4) 1974
BEHIND CLOSED DOORS – *Charlie Rich* (9) 1974
BEG STEAL OR BORROW – *New Seekers* (3) 1972
BELFAST – *Boney M* (1) 1977
BEND IT! – *Dave Dee, Dozy, Beaky, Mick and Tich* (3) 1966
BEND ME SHAPE ME – *Amen Corner* (5) 1968
BEST THING THAT EVER HAPPENED TO ME – *Gladys Knight and The Pips* (7) 1977
BICYCLE RACE – Queen (10) 1978
BIG BAD JOHN – *Jimmy Dean* (2) 1961
A BIG HUNK O' LOVE – *Elvis Presley* (5) 1959
BIG SHIP – *Cliff Richard* (8) 1969
BIG TOM IS STILL THE KING – *Susan McCann and the Storytellers* (1) 1977
BILLY DON'T BE A HERO – *Paper Lace* (1) 1974
BITS AND PIECES – *Dave Clark Five* (1) 1964
THE BLACK AND TAN GUN – *Pat Smyth and Johnny Flynn Showband* (1) 1966
BLACK AND WHITE – *Greyhound* (10) 1971
BLACK BETTY – Ram Jam (8) 1977
THE BLACK EYED BOYS – *Paper Lace* (7) 1974
BLACK IS BLACK – *Los Bravos* (3) 1966
BLACK IS BLACK – *La Belle Epoque* (3) 1977
BLACK NIGHT – *Deep Purple* (4) 1970
BLACK SUPERMAN (Muhammad Ali) – *Johnny Wakelin and the Kinshasa Band* (9) 1975
BLACK VELVET BAND – *The Dubliners* (4) 1967
BLACK VELVET BAND – *Johnny Kelly* (1) 1967
BLACKBERRY WAY – *The Move* (2) 1969
BLAME IT ON THE BOSSA NOVA – *Eydie Gorme* (9) 1963
(BLAME IT ON THE) PONY EXPRESS – *Johnny Johnson and the Bandwagon* (5) 1971
BLANKET ON THE GROUND – *Philomena Begley and the Rambling Men* (5) 1975
BLANKET ON THE GROUND – *Billie Jo Spears* (9) 1975

Title – *Act* (Position) Year of Chart Entry

BLESS YOU (FOR BEING AN ANGEL) – *Royal Showband featuring Brendan Bowyer* (1) 1964
BLINDED BY THE LIGHT – *Manfred Mann's Earthband* (6) 1976
BLOCKBUSTER – *Sweet* (1) 1973
BLOODY SUNDAY – *Tony Kearney* (2) 1972
BLUE ANGEL – *Roy Orbison* (2) 1961
BLUE BAYOU – *Roy Orbison* (1) 1963
BLUE EYES – *Don Partridge* (1) 1968
BLUE IS THE COLOUR – *Chelsea F.C.* (8) 1972
BLUEBELLS OF BROADWAY – *Doris Day* (-) 1955
BLUEBERRY HILL – *Fats Domino* (-) 1957
BOBBY'S GIRL – *Susan Maughan* (6) 1962
BOHEMIAN RHAPSODY – *Queen* (1) 1975
BONNIE BLUE GAL – *Mitch Miller* (-) 1956
BONNY IRISH BOY – *Margo and the Keynotes* (10) 1968
BONY MORONIE – *Larry Williams* (-) 1958
BOOGIE OOGIE OOGIE – *A Taste Of Honey* (9) 1978
BOOGIE WONDERLAND – *Earth Wind and Fire* (5) 1979
BOOM BANG-A-BANG – *Lulu* (1) 1969
BORN TO BE WITH YOU – *Beverly Sisters* (-) 1956
BORN TO BE WITH YOU – *The Capitol Showband* (1) 1965
BORN TO BE WITH YOU – *The Chordettes* (-) 1956
BORN TO BE WITH YOU – *Patti Page* (-) 1956
BORN TO SING – *Colm C. T. Wilkinson* (8) 1978
BORN WITH A SMILE ON MY FACE – *Stephanie De Sykes* (6) 1974
BORNE ON THE WIND – *Roy Orbison* (9) 1964
BORROWED ANGEL – *Ray Lynam and The Hillbillies* (8) 1973
THE BOSTON BURGLAR – *Johnny McEvoy* (1) 1967
BOULAVOGUE – *Tommy Drennan and the Monarchs* (4) 1964
THE BOWERY GRENADIERS – *Mitch Miller* (-) 1958
THE BOXER – *Simon and Garfunkel* (7) 1969
THE BOY FROM NEW YORK CITY – *Darts* (3) 1978
A BOY NAMED SUE – *Johnny Cash* (3) 1969
BOY OH BOY – *Racey* (9) 1979
THE BOYS ARE BACK IN TOWN – *Thin Lizzy* (1) 1976
BOYS CRY – *Eden Kane* (6) 1964
THE BOYS FROM THE COUNTY ARMAGH – *Bridie Gallagher* (-) 1958
THE BOYS OF KILLYBEGS – *Dermot O'Brien* (8) 1975

Title – *Act* (Position) Year of Chart Entry

BRAND NEW KEY – *Melanie* (8) 1972
BRAND NEW MR ME – *Ray Lynam and The Hillbillies* (6) 1972
BREAK AWAY – *The Beach Boys* (10) 1969
BREAKFAST IN AMERICA – *Supertramp* (6) 1979
BREAKIN' DOWN THE WALLS OF HEARTACHE – *The Bandwagon* (5) 1968
BREAKIN' IN A BRAND NEW BROKEN HEART – *Connie Francis* (5) 1961
BREAKING UP IS HARD TO DO – *Neil Sedaka* (4) 1962
BREAKING UP IS HARD TO DO – *Partridge Family* (2) 1972
BRIDGE OVER TROUBLED WATER – *Simon and Garfunkel* (2) 1970
BRIDGET THE MIDGET – *Ray Stevens* (3) 1971
BRIGHT EYES – *Art Garfunkel* (1) 1979
BRING IT ON HOME TO ME – *The Animals* (6) 1965
BRING THEM HOME – *Barleycorn* (4) 1974
BROKEN HEARTED MELODY – *Sarah Vaughan* (5) 1959
BROKEN MARRIAGE VOWS – *Big Tom and The Mainliners* (1) 1972
BROKEN PROMISES – *Red Hurley* (7) 1976
BROWN EYED HANDSOME MAN – *Buddy Holly* (3) 1963
BROWN GIRL IN THE RING – *Boney M* (1) 1978
BROWN SUGAR – *Rolling Stones* (2) 1971
BUBBLEGUM MUSIC – *The Sands* (6) 1969
BUCKS POLKA – *Clem Quinn* (8) 1965
BUILD ME UP BUTTERCUP – *The Foundations* (3) 1968
BUILD YOUR LOVE (ON A STRONG FOUNDATION) – *Johnnie Ray* (-) 1957
THE BUMP – *Kenny* (2) 1975
A BUNCH OF THYME – *Foster and Allen* (8) 1979
A BUNCH OF VIOLETS BLUE – *Brendan Shine* (6) 1970
BUNCLODY – *Emmet Spiceland* (8) 1968
BUONA SERA – *Mr Acker Bilk and his Paramount Jazz Band* (6) 1961
BURNING LOVE – *Elvis Presley* (4) 1972
BUS STOP – *The Hollies* (4) 1966
BUT I DO – *Clarence 'Frogman' Henry* (2) 1961
BUTTERFLY (a) – *Charlie Gracie* (-) 1957
BUTTERFLY (a) – *Andy Williams* (-) 1957
BUTTERFLY (b) – *Danyel Gerard* (5) 1971
BY THE FOUNTAINS OF ROME – *Edmund Hockridge* (-) 1956
BY THE LIGHT OF THE SILVERY MOON – *Little Richard* (9) 1959
BY YOU, BY YOU, BY YOU – *Pauline Shepherd* (-) 1957

Title – *Act* (Position) Year of Chart Entry

Title – *Act* (Position) Year of Chart Entry

CHANSON D'AMOUR – *Manhattan Transfer* (1) 1977
CHAPEL OF THE ROSES – *Malcolm Vaughan* (-) 1957
CHARLIE BROWN – *The Coasters* (6) 1959
CHARMAINE – *The Bachelors* (8) 1963
CHERRY PINK AND APPLE BLOSSOM WHITE ♦ – *Eddie Calvert* (-) 1955
CHERRY PINK AND APPLE BLOSSOM WHITE ♦ – *Perez Prado* (-) 1955
CHICAGO – *Frank Sinatra* (-) 1957
CHILDREN OF THE REVOLUTION – *T Rex* (1) 1972
A CHILD'S PRAYER – *Hot Chocolate* (6) 1975
THE CHILDREN'S MARCHING SONG (Nick Nack Paddy Whack)
– *Mitch Miller with his Orchestra and Chorus* (8) 1959
A CHILDREN'S WINTER – *Blackthorn* (8) 1979
CHINA TEA ♦ – *Russ Conway* (1) 1959
CHIQUITITA – *Abba* (1) 1979
CHIRPY CHIRPY CHEEP CHEEP – *Middle Of The Road* (1) 1971
THE CHOSEN FEW – *The Dooleys* (4) 1979
CHRISTMAS – *Rosemary Clooney* (-) 1955
CHRISTMAS ALPHABET – *Dickie Valentine* (-) 1955
CHRISTMAS IN MY HOME TOWN – *Gene Stuart and the Mighty Avons* (2) 1974
CHRISTMAS POLKA – *Sean Dunphy and the Hoedowners* (2) 1968
CHRISTMAS SONG – *Gilbert O'Sullivan* (5) 1974
CHRISTMAS TIME – *The Dixielanders featuring Brendan O'Brien* (10) 1963
CHRISTMAS TIME AND YOU – *Dickie Rock* (10) 1969
CHRISTMAS TIME IN INNISFREE –*The Nevada featuring Jim O'Connor* (6) 1970
CHRISTMAS TIME IN IRELAND – *Brendan Shine* (5) 1974
A CHRISTMAS WISH E.P. – *Butch Moore and the Capitols* (5) 1965
CINDERELLA – *Billy Brown* (3) 1977
CINDY, OH CINDY – *Eddie Fisher* (-) 1956
CINDERELLA ROCKAFELLA – *Esther and Abi Ofarim* (5) 1968
CINDY INCIDENTALLY – *The Faces* (8) 1973
CIRCLES – *New Seekers* (3) 1972
CLAIR – *Gilbert O'Sullivan* (1) 1972
CLAP YOUR HANDS AND STAMP YOUR FEET –*Fran O'Toole and the Miami* (8) 1974
THE CLIFFS OF DOONEEN – *Planxty* (8) 1972
THE CLOUDS WILL SOON ROLL BY – *Tony Brent* (-) 1958
C'MON EVERYBODY – *Sex Pistols* (10) 1979
COCKLES AND MUSSELS ♦ – *Eric Delaney* (-) 1956

Title – *Act* (Position) Year of Chart Entry

CO-CO – *Sweet* (3) 1971
COLOURS – *Donovan* (10) 1965
THE COMBINE HARVESTER – *Brendan Grace* (1) 1975
COME AND GET IT – *Badfinger* (5) 1970
COME BACK AND SHAKE ME – *Clodagh Rodgers* (2) 1969
COME BACK MY LOVE – *Darts* (7) 1978
COME BACK TO STAY – *Dickie Rock* (1) 1966
COME DOWN THE MOUNTAIN KATIE DALY – *The Royal Showband featuring Tom Dunphy* (8)...1962
COME OUTSIDE – *Mike Sarne* (4) 1962
COME SOFTLY TO ME – *The Fleetwoods* (4) 1959
COME TOMORROW – *Manfred Mann* (10) 1965
COME WHAT MAY – *Vicki Leandros* (2) 1972
COMPLEX – *Gary Numan* (9) 1979
CONCRETE AND CLAY – *Unit Four Plus Two* (4) 1965
CONFESSIN' (THAT I LOVE YOU) – *Frank Ifield* (1) 1963
CONGRATULATIONS – *Cliff Richard* (1) 1968
CONSTANTLY – *Cliff Richard* (8) 1964
CONTACT – *Edwin Starr* (8) 1979
CONVERSATIONS – *Cilla Black* (5) 1969
CONVOY – *C W McCall* (8) 1976
COOL FOR CATS – *Squeeze* (8) 1979
COOL WATER – *Frankie Laine* (-) 1955
COTTAGE IN OLD DONEGAL – *Mattie Fox and the Grassroots* (10) 1974
COTTONFIELDS – *Beach Boys* (3) 1970
COULD IT BE FOREVER – *David Cassidy* (3) 1972
COUNT YOUR BLESSINGS INSTEAD OF SHEEP – *Bing Crosby* (-) 1955
COUNTRY BOY – *Fats Domino* (6) 1960
COUNTRY BOY (You Got Your Feet In L.A.) – *Glen Campbell* (5) 1976
COUSIN NORMAN – *Marmalade* (9) 1971
COZ I LUV YOU – *Slade* (1) 1971
CRACKLIN' ROSIE – *Neil Diamond* (2) 1970
CRAZY LITTLE THING CALLED LOVE – *Queen* (2) 1979
CROCODILE ROCK – *Elton John* (10) 1972
CROSS YOUR HEART – *Tina* (1) 1974
CRY CRY AGAIN – *Hugo Duncan and The Tall Men* (8) 1972
THE CRYING GAME – *Dave Berry* (7) 1965
CRYING IN THE CHAPEL – *Elvis Presley* (1) 1965

Title – *Act* (Position) Year of Chart Entry

CRYING IN THE RAIN – *The Everly Brothers* (3) 1962
CRYING LAUGHING LOVING LYING – *Labi Siffre* (7) 1972
THE CRYSTAL CHANDELIER – *Tony Keeling and the Graduates* (7) 1967
CUM ON FEEL THE NOIZE – *Slade* (1) 1973
CUMBERLAND GAP – *Lonnie Donegan and his Skiffle Group* (-) 1957
CUPID – *Sam Cooke* (9) 1961
CURTAIN OF TEARS – *Slim Whitman* (-) 1957
CUSHY BUTTERFIELD – *Brendan Grace* (3) 1973

DA DOO RON RON – *The Crystals* (3) 1963
DA DUM DA DUM I LOVE YOU SO – *Dennis Allen* (7) 1977
DADDY COOL -THE GIRL CAN'T HELP IT – *Darts* (10) 1977
DADDY WHAT IF – *Dermot Henry* (8) 1972
DADDY'S LITTLE GIRL – *Brendan Quinn and The Bluebirds* (1) 1977
DAISY A DAY – *Danny Doyle* (1) 1973
DANCE AWAY – *Roxy Music* (1) 1979
DANCE DANCE DANCE – *The Sands* (4) 1968
DANCE ON • – *The Shadows* (1) 1963
DANCE LITTLE LADY DANCE – *Tina Charles* (4) 1976
DANCE WITH THE DEVIL • – *Cozy Powell* (7) 1974
(DANCE WITH THE) GUITAR MAN – *Duane Eddy and The Rebelettes* (4) 1962
DANCIN' IN THE MOONLIGHT (It's Caught Me In Its Spotlight) – *Thin Lizzy* (4) 1977
DANCIN' PARTY – *Showaddywaddy* (6) 1977
DANCING IN THE CITY – *Marshall Hain* (2) 1978
DANCIN' (ON A SATURDAY NIGHT) – *Barry Blue* (4) 1973
DANCING QUEEN – *Abba* (1) 1976
DANCING WITH THE CAPTAIN – *Paul Nicholas* (8) 1976
DANIEL – *Elton John* (4) 1973
DARK MOON – *Tony Brent* (-) 1957
DARK MOON – *Gale Storm* (-) 1957
DARLIN' – Frankie Miller (4) 1978
DARLING I LOVE YOU – *Dickie Rock and the Miami* (4) 1966
DAUGHTER OF DARKNESS – *Tom Jones* (3) 1970
DAVY'S ON THE ROAD AGAIN – *Manfred Mann's Earthband* (5) 1978
THE DAY I MET MARIE – *Cliff Richard* (10) 1967
THE DAY THE RAINS CAME – *Jane Morgan* (10) 1959
DAY TRIPPER – *The Beatles* (1) 1965

Title – *Act* (Position) Year of Chart Entry

A DAY WITHOUT LOVE – *Love Affair* (9) 1968
DAYBREAK – *Horslips* (4) 1976
DAYDREAM – Lovin' Spoonful (7) 1966
DAYDREAM BELIEVER – *The Monkees* (1) 1967
DAYDREAMER – *David Cassidy* (3) 1973
DEAD END STREET – *The Kinks* (7) 1967
DEAD OR ALIVE – *Lonnie Donegan and his Skiffle Group* (-) 1956
THE DEAN AND I – *10cc* (1) 1973
DEAR GOD – *Hugo Duncan and the Tall Men* (3) 1971
DEAR MRS APPLEBEE – *David Garrick* (2) 1966
DEARG DOOM – *Horslips* (8) 1973
DEATH OF A CLOWN – *Dave Davies* (6) 1967
DECEMBER '63 (Oh What A Night) – *Four Seasons* (3) 1976
DECK OF CARDS – *Wink Martindale* (3) 1963
DEDICATED FOLLOWER OF FASHION – *The Kinks* (3) 1966
DEDICATED TO THE ONE I LOVE – *Mamas and Papas* (7) 1967
DELAWARE – *Perry Como* (2) 1960
DELILAH – *Tom Jones* (1) 1968
DELILAH – *Brendan Grace* (6) 1975
DENIS – *Blondie* (3) 1978
DESIDERATA – *Les Crane* (9) 1972
DESIREE – *Neil Diamond* (6) 1978
DETROIT CITY – *Tom Jones* (4) 1967
DEVIL AMONG THE TAILORS – *Mushroom* (4) 1973
DEVIL GATE DRIVE – *Suzi Quatro* (1) 1974
DEVIL WOMAN (a) – Marty Robbins (2) 1962
DEVIL WOMAN (b) – *Cliff Richard* (10) 1976
DEVIL'S ANSWER – *Atomic Rooster* (9) 1971
DIAMOND SMILES – *Boomtown Rats* (3) 1979
DIAMONDS • – *Jet Harris and Tony Meehan* (1) 1963
DIANA – *Paul Anka* (-) 1957
DIANE – *The Bachelors* (2) 1964
DIARY OF HORACE WIMP – *Electric Light Orchestra* (10) 1979
DID YOU EVER – *Nancy and Lee* (1) 1971
DING A DONG – *Teach In* (8) 1975
DIRTY OLD TOWN – *The Dubliners* (10) 1968
DISCO DUCK – *Rick Dees and his Cast Of Idiots* (10) 1976

Title – *Act* (Position) Year of Chart Entry

DISTANT DRUMS – *Pacific Showband* (5)........ 1964
DISTANT DRUMS – *Jim Reeves* (3)........ 1966
D.I.V.O.R.C.E. – *Billy Connolly* (6)........ 1975
DIZZY – *Tommy Roe* (2)........ 1969
DO I DREAM – Maxi (7)........ 1973
DO IT AGAIN – *The Beach Boys* (5)........ 1968
DO IT, DO IT AGAIN – *Raffaella Carra* (9)........ 1978
DO WAH DIDDY DIDDY – *Manfred Mann* (2)........ 1964
DO WHAT YOU DO, DO WELL – *Ned Miller* (8)........ 1965
DO YOU KNOW THE WAY TO SAN JOSE – *Dionne Warwick* (8)........ 1968
DO YOU LOVE ME – *Brian Poole and The Tremeloes* (1)........ 1963
DO YOU MIND – *Anthony Newley* (2)........ 1960
DO YOU KNOW WHERE YOU'RE GOING TO – *Diana Ross* (4)........ 1976
DO YOU WANNA TOUCH ME? (OH YEAH) – *Gary Glitter* (9)........ 1973
DO YOU WANT TO DO IT – *Gina, Dale Haze and The Champions* (2)........ 1977
DO YOU WANT TO KNOW A SECRET – *Billy J Kramer with the Dakotas* (8)........ 1963
DO YOU WANT YOUR LOBBY WASHED DOWN – *Brendan Shine* (1)........ 1979
DO YA THINK I'M SEXY – *Rod Stewart* (5)........ 1978
DOCTOR KISS KISS – *5000 Volts* (9)........ 1976
DOCTOR'S ORDERS – *Sunny* (4)........ 1974
DOES MY RING HURT YOUR FINGER – *Mattie Fox and the Country Blue Boys* (5)........ 1972
DOES YOUR CHEWING GUM LOSE ITS FLAVOUR (ON THE BEDPOST OVERNIGHT)
– *Lonnie Donegan and his Skiffle Group* (5)........ 1959
DOES YOUR MOTHER KNOW – *Abba* (3)........ 1979
DOING ALRIGHT WITH THE BOYS – *Gary Glitter* (3)........ 1975
DOMINIQUE – *The Singing Nun* (4)........ 1963
DONNA (a) *Marty Wilde* (5)........ 1959
DONNA (b) – *10cc* (2)........ 1972
DON'T BELIEVE A WORD – *Thin Lizzy* (2)........ 1977
DON'T BRING ME DOWN (a) – *The Animals* (7)........ 1966
DON'T BRING ME DOWN (b) – *Electric Light Orchestra* (6)........ 1979
DON'T CRY DADDY – *Elvis Presley* (4)........ 1970
DON'T CRY FOR ME ARGENTINA – *Julie Covington* (2)........ 1977
DON'T CRY FOR ME ARGENTINA • – *The Shadows* (7)........ 1979
DON'T DO IT BABY – *Mac and Katie Kissoon* (7)........ 1975
DON'T EVER CHANGE – *The Crickets* (9)........ 1962
DON'T FORGET TO REMEMBER – *Bee Gees* (1)........ 1969

Title – *Act* (Position) Year of Chart Entry

DON'T FORGET TO SAY I LOVE YOU – *Roly Daniels* (6) 1972
DON'T FORBID ME – *Pat Boone* (-) 1957
DON'T GIVE UP ON US BABY – *David Soul* (1) 1977
DON'T GO – *Gene Stuart and the Mighty Avons* (8) 1971
DON'T GO BREAKING MY HEART – *Elton John and Kiki Dee* (1) 1976
DON'T GO DOWN TO RENO – *Tony Christie* (8) 1972
DON'T IT MAKE MY BROWN EYES BLUE – *Crystal Gayle* (4) 1978
DON'T LET IT DIE – *Hurricane Smith* (8) 1971
DON'T LET LIFE GET YOU DOWN – *Joe Cuddy* (2) 1976
DON'T LET ME BE MISUNDERSTOOD – *The Animals* (7) 1965
DON'T LET ME CROSS OVER – *Larry Cunningham & Country Blue Boys* (7) 1970
DON'T LOOK BACK – *Boston* (8) 1978
DON'T LOSE YOUR HUCKLEBUCK SHOES – *Royal Showband featuring Brendan Bowyer* (1) 1965
DON'T PLAY YOUR ROCK YOUR ROCK 'N' ROLL TO ME – *Smokie* (7) 1975
DON'T PRETEND ANYMORE – *The Memories* (7) 1973
DON'T STAY AWAY TOO LONG – *Peters and Lee* (5) 1974
DON'T STOP ME NOW – *Queen* (10) 1979
DON'T STOP THE CAROUSEL – *Roy Taylor and the Nevada* (7) 1978
DON'T STOP 'TIL YOU GET ENOUGH – *Michael Jackson* (10) 1979
DON'T TAKE ADVANTAGE OF ME – *Murphy and The Swallows* (3) 1972
DON'T TAKE AWAY THE MUSIC – *Tavares* (5) 1976
DON'T TALK TO HIM – *Cliff Richard and The Shadows* (1) 1963
DON'T THROW YOUR LOVE AWAY – *The Searchers* (1) 1964
DON'T TREAT ME LIKE A CHILD – *Helen Shapiro* (6) 1961
DON'T YOU KNOW IT – *Adam Faith* (2) 1961
DON'T YOU ROCK ME DADDY-O – *Lonnie Donegan & his Skiffle Group* (-) 1957
DON'T YOU ROCK ME DADDY-O – *The Vipers Skiffle Group* (-) 1957
DOONAREE – *Vera Lynn* (-) 1955
DOONAREE – *Robert Wilson* (-) 1955
THE DOOR IS ALWAYS OPEN – *Ray Lynam and The Hillbillies* (9) 1975
DOUBLE BARREL – *Dave and Ansil Collins* (10) 1971
DOWN CAME THE RAIN – *Butch Moore and the Capitol Showband* (1) 1964
DOWN DOWN – *Status Quo* (2) 1975
DOWN ON THE BEACH TONIGHT – *The Drifters* (4) 1974
DOWN YONDER • – *Johnny and the Hurricanes* (6) 1960
DOWNTOWN – *Petula Clark* (2) 1965
DOZIE – *The Times* (9) 1969

Title – *Act* (Position) Year of Chart Entry

DREADLOCK HOLIDAY – *10cc* (2) 1978
DREAM BABY – *Roy Orbison* (1) 1962
DREAMIN' – *Johnny Burnette* (3) 1960
DREAM LOVER – *Bobby Darin* (1) 1959
DREAMBOAT – *DeMarco Sisters* (-) 1955
DREAMING – *Blondie* (3) 1979
DREAMING MY DREAMS – *Marianne Faithfull* (1) 1976
DUKE OF EARL – *Darts* (10) 1979
DUN LAOGHAIRE – *Brendan Shine* (6) 1975
DYNAMITE – *Mud* (9) 1973

EBONY EYES – *Everly Brothers* (1) 1961
EDELWEISS – *Tony and the Graduates* (7) 1966
EIGHTEEN YELLOW ROSES – *Bobby Darin* (10) 1963
EILEEN McMANUS – *Two's Company* (10) 1969
EILEEN O'GRADY – *Hugo Duncan and the Tall Men* (10) 1972
EL BIMBO • – *Bimbo Jet* (4) 1975
EL PASO – *Marty Robbins* (9) 1960
ELEANOR RIGBY – *The Beatles* (1) 1966
ELECTED – *Alice Cooper* (8) 1972
ELENORE – *The Turtles* (6) 1968
ELOISE – *Barry Ryan* (2) 1968
ELUSIVE BUTTERFLY – *Val Doonican* (3) 1966
THE EMMIGRANT – *Larry Cunningham and the Mighty Avons* (10) 1968
EMMA – *Hot Chocolate* (7) 1974
EMOTIONS – *Samantha Sang* (9) 1978
ENGLISH COUNRY GARDEN – *Jimmie Rodgers* (7) 1962
ENNISKILLEN DRAGOONS – *The Ludlows* (9) 1967
THE ENTERTAINER – *The Times* (4) 1972
ERNIE (The Fastest Milkman In The West) – *Benny Hill* (5) 1971
EVE OF DESTRUCTION – *Barry McGuire* (2) 1965
EVEN THE BAD TIMES ARE GOOD – *The Tremeloes* (7) 1967
EVERLASTING LOVE – *Love Affair* (2) 1968
EVERMORE – *Ruby Murray* (-) 1955
EVERY DAY HURTS – *Sad Café* (9) 1979
EVERY LITTLE TEARDROP – *Gallagher and Lyle* (5) 1977
EVERY STEP OF THE WAY – *Dickie Rock and the Miami* (1) 1965

Title – *Act* (Position) Year of Chart Entry

EVERYBODY DANCE – *Chic* (6) 1978
EVERYBODY KNOWS – *Dave Clark Five* (6) 1968
EVERYBODY'S SOMEBODY'S FOOL – *Connie Fancis* (9) 1960
EVERYDAY – *Slade* (4) 1974
EVERYONE'S GONE TO THE MOON – *Jonathan King* (10) 1965
EVERYTHING I OWN – *Ken Boothe* (1) 1974
EVERYTHING IS BEAUTIFUL – *Ray Stevens* (3) 1970
EVIL HEARTED YOU – *The Yardbirds* (6) 1965
EXCERPT FROM 'A TEENAGE OPERA' – *Keith West* (2) 1967
EXILES – *Horslips* (9) 1977
EXODUS (Theme from 'Exodus) • – *Ferrante and Teicher* (3) 1961
EXPERIMENTS WITH MICE • – *Johnny Dankworth and his Orchestra*(-) 1956
EYE LEVEL • – *Simon Park Orchestra* (3) 1973

FALL IN LOVE WITH YOU – *Cliff Richard and The Shadows* (2) 1960
FALLEN STAR – *The Cadets (vocalist Eileen Reid)* (1) 1964
FALLING – *Roy Orbison* (8) 1963
FALLING APART AT THE SEAMS – *Marmalade* (8) 1976
FANCY PANTS – *Kenny* (3) 1975
FANTASY – *Earth Wind and Fire* (4) 1978
FAR AWAY FROM YOU – *Doc Carroll and The Royal Blues* (8) 1966
FAR FAR AWAY – *Slade* (2) 1974
FAR TOO YOUNG – *Brendan Shine* (4) 1972
FAREWELL TO NANCY – *Blackthorn* (8) 1979
FAT BOTTOMED GIRLS – *Queen* (10) 1978
FEELINGS – *Morris Albert* (9) 1975
FERNANDO – *Abba* (1) 1976
FIGARO – *Brotherhood Of Man* (1) 1978
FINGER OF SUSPICION – *Dickie Valentine* (-) 1954
FINGS AIN'T WOT THEY USED T'BE – *Max Bygraves* (3) 1960
FIRE – *Crazy World Of Arthur Brown* (8) 1968
FIRE BRIGADE – *The Move* (9) 1968
FIRST OF MAY – *Bee Gees* (4) 1969
FIVE LITTLE FINGERS – *Frankie McBride* (2) 1967
5-7-0-5 – *City Boy* (6) 1978
FLIPIDDY FLOP – *Gary Street and the Fairways* (10) 1968
FLOAT ON – *The Floaters* (5) 1977

Title – *Act* (Position)	Year of Chart Entry
THE FLORAL DANCE – *Brighouse and Rastrick Brass Band* (2)	1978
FLOWERS IN THE RAIN – *The Move* (4)	1967
THE FLY – *Brendan Bowyer with the Royal Showband* (6)	1966
THE FOLK SINGER – *Tommy Roe* (9)	1963
FOLLOW THAT DREAM E.P. – *Elvis Presley* (2)	1962
FOLLOW YOU FOLLOW ME – *Genesis* (10)	1978
FOOL – *Elvis Presley* (7)	1973
A FOOL SUCH AS I – *Elvis Presley* (2)	1959
FOOL TO CRY – *Rolling Stones* (5)	1976
FOOLIN' TIME – *Butch Moore and the Capitol Showband* (3)	1964
FOOLS PARADISE – *Larry Cunningham and the Mighty Avons* (5)	1967
FOOT TAPPER • – *The Shadows* (2)	1963
FOOTSTEPS – *Steve Lawrence* (3)	1960
FOR A PENNY – *Pat Boone* (9)	1959
FOR EVER AND EVER – *Slik* (2)	1976
FOR THE FIRST TIME IN A LONG TIME – *Philomena Begley and the Ramblin' Men* (5)	1977
FOR THE GOOD TIMES – *Perry Como* (1)	1973
FOR YOUR LOVE – *The Yardbirds* (10)	1965
FOREVER AUTUMN – *Justin Hayward* (3)	1978
FOREVER IN BLUE JEANS – *Neil Diamond* (4)	1979
FORGET ABOUT YOU – *Motors* (10)	1978
FORGET HIM – *Bobby Rydell* (8)	1963
FORGET ME NOT – *Eden Kane* (4)	1962
FORGOTTEN DREAMS • – *Leroy Anderson and his Pop Concert Orchestra* (-)	1957
FORGOTTEN DREAMS • – *Cyril Stapleton and his Orchestra* (-)	1957
48 CRASH – *Suzi Quatro* (6)	1973
FOUR AND TWENTY HOURS – *Nana Mouskouri* (8)	1972
FOUR GREAT IRISH HITS – *Various Artists* (4)	1972
FOUR GREAT IRISH HITS Vol. 2 – *Various Artist* (10)	1972
FOUR GREEN FIELDS – *Flying Column* (6)	1972
FOUR GREEN FIELDS – *Dermot Hegarty and the Plainsmen* (5)	1972
FOUR IN THE MORNING – Brendan Quinn and Cades County (5)	1972
FOUR IN THE MORNING – *Faron Young* (5)	1972
FOX ON THE RUN (a) – *Manfred Mann* (2)	1969
FOX ON THE RUN (b) – *Sweet* (2)	1975
FREE – *Denice Williams* (8)	1977
FREE THE PEOPLE – *The Dubliners* (7)	1971

Title – *Act* (Position) Year of Chart Entry

FREEDOM COME FREEDOM GO – *The Fortunes* (5) 1971
FRIDAY ON MY MIND – *The Easybeats* (7) 1967
FRIENDS – *Arrival* (8) 1970
FRIGGIN' IN THE RIGGIN' – *Sex Pistols* (8) 1979
FRIGHTENED CITY • – *The Shadows* (3) 1961
FROM A JACK TO A KING – *Ned Miller* (1) 1963
FROM HERE TO THERE TO YOU – *Hank Locklin* (10) 1962
FROM ME TO YOU – *The Beatles* (1) 1963
FROM NEW YORK TO L.A. – *Patsy Gallant* (5) 1977
FROM THE CANDY STORE ON THE CORNER TO THE CHAPEL ON THE HILL
– *Dickie Rock and the Miami Showband* (1) 1964
FUNNY – *The Swarbriggs* (2) 1975
FUNNY FACE – *Roly Daniels* (4) 1973
FUNNY FAMILIAR FORGOTTEN FEELINGS – *Tom Jones* (4) 1967
FUNNY FUNNY – *Sweet* (7) 1971
FUNNY MAN – *Johnny McEvoy* (10) 1967
THE FUREY MAN – *Red Hurley* (6) 1979

GALAXY – *War* (5) 1978
GALVESTON – *Glen Campbell* (9) 1969
GAMBLIN' MAN – *Lonnie Donegan and his Skiffle Group* (-) 1957
GAME OF LOVE – *Wayne Fontana and the Mindbenders* (10) 1965
GAMES PEOPLE PLAY – *Joe South* (4) 1969
THE GARDEN OF EDEN – *Gary Miller* (-) 1957
THE GARDEN OF EDEN – *Frankie Vaughan* (-) 1957
GEE BABY – *Peter Shelley* (8) 1974
GEE WHIZ IT'S YOU – *Cliff Richard and the Shadows* (5) 1961
GENTLE ANNIE – *Johnny McEvoy* (8) 1972
GENTLE MOTHER – *Big Tom McBride and the Mainliners* (7) 1967
GENTLE ON MY MIND – *Dean Martin* (3) 1969
GEORGY GIRL – *The Seekers* (10) 1967
GET AWAY – *Georgie Fame and the Blue Flames* (6) 1966
GET BACK – *The Beatles with Billy Preston* (1) 1969
GET DOWN – *Gilbert O'Sullivan* (1) 1973
GET IT – *Darts* (9) 1979
GET IT ON – *T. Rex* (1) 1971
GET LOST – *Eden Kane* (8) 1961

Title – *Act* (Position) Year of Chart Entry

GET OFF MY CLOUD – *Rolling Stones* (2) 1965
GIDDY UP A DING DONG – *Freddie Bell and the Bell Boys* (-) 1956
GIGI – *Vic Damone* (7) 1959
GIGI – *Billy Eckstine* (5) 1959
GILLY GILLY OSSENFEFFER KATZEN BOGEN BY THE SEA – *Max Bygraves* (-) 1954
GIMME DAT DING – *Pipkins* (7) 1970
GIMME GIMME GIMME (A Man After Midnight) – *Abba* (1) 1979
GIMME SOME LOVING – *Spencer Davis Group* (7) 1966
GINNY COME LATELY – *Brian Hyland* (3) 1962
THE GIRL FROM DONEGAL L.P. – *Bridie Gallagher* (-) 1958
THE GIRL FROM DONEGAL – *Margo* (6) 1974
A GIRL LIKE YOU – *Cliff Richard and the Shadows* (2) 1961
THE GIRL OF MY BEST FRIEND – *Elvis Presley* (4) 1960
GIVE A LITTLE LOVE – *Bay City Rollers* (1) 1975
GIVE AN IRISH GIRL TO ME – *Brian Coll* (7) 1970
GIVE IRELAND BACK TO THE IRISH – *Wings* (1) 1972
GIVE ME JUST A LITTLE MORE TIME – *Chairmen Of The Board* (5) 1970
GIVE ME LOVE (Give Me Peace On Earth) – *George Harrison* (10) 1973
GIVE ME MY RANCH – *Ronnie Hilton* (-) 1956
GIVE ME YOUR HAND – *Family Pride* (5) 1972
GIVE ME YOUR WORD – *Tennessee Ernie Ford* (-) 1955
GIVE PEACE A CHANCE – *Plastic Ono Band* (7) 1969
GIVING IT ALL AWAY – *Roger Daltrey* (10) 1973
GLAD ALL OVER – *Dave Clark Five* (1) 1964
A GLASS OF CHAMPAGNE – *Sailor* (2) 1976
GLENDORA – *Perry Como* (-) 1956
GLITTER AND GLEAM – *Branagan Brothers* (10) 1977
GO (Before You Break My Heart) – *Gigliola Cinquetti* (9) 1974
GO AWAY LITTLE GIRL – *Mark Wynter* (8) 1963
GO NOW – *Moody Blues* (4) 1965
GOD ONLY KNOWS – *Beach Boys* (6) 1966
GOIN' HOME – *The Osmonds* (5) 1973
GOING IN WITH MY EYES OPEN – *David Soul* (7) 1977
GOLDEN YEARS – *David Bowie* (9) 1976
GONNA MAKE YOU A STAR – *David Essex* (1) 1974
GOOD LUCK CHARM – *Elvis Presley* (1) 1962
GOOD MORNING FREEDOM – *Blue Mink* (10) 1970

Title – *Act* (Position) Year of Chart Entry

GOOD MORNING STARSHINE – *Oliver* (2) 1969
GOOD OLD ROCK 'N' ROLL – *Dave Clark Five* (10)....1970
THE GOOD, THE BAD AND THE UGLY • – *Hugo Montenegro, His Orchestra and Chorus* (1)....1968
GOOD TIMES (BETTER TIMES) – *Cliff Richard* (9) 1969
GOOD TIMIN' – *Jimmy Jones* (2) 1960
GOOD VIBRATIONS – *Beach Boys* (3)....1966
GOODBYE – *Mary Hopkin* (1) 1969
GOODBYE COMES HARD TO ME – *Larry Cunningham* (5)....1973
GOODBYE GOODBYE – *Chips* (2) 1977
GOODBYE JIMMY GOODBYE – *Ruby Murray* (6) 1959
GOODBYE MY LOVE (a) – *The Searchers* (7)....1965
GOODBYE MY LOVE (b) – *Glitter Band* (4) 1975
GOODBYE MY LOVE GOODBYE – *The Dixies featuring Rory O'Connor* (6)....1974
GOODBYE SAM HELLO SAMANTHA – *Cliff Richard* (1)....1970
GOODBYE YELLOW BRICK ROAD – *Elton John* (4) 1973
GOODNESS GRACIOUS ME – *Peter Sellers and Sophia Loren* (2)....1960
GOODNIGHT MIDNIGHT – *Clodagh Rodgers* (7) 1969
GOODNIGHT TONIGHT – *Wings* (9) 1979
GOTTA HAVE SOMETHING IN THE BANK, FRANK – *Frankie Vaughan and the Kaye Sisters* (-)....1957
GRADH MO CHROI – *Margo and the Country Folk* (6)....1970
GRANADA – *Frank Sinatra* (7) 1961
THE GRAND COOLIE DAM – *Lonnie Donegan and his Skiffle Group* (-)....1958
GRANDAD – *Clive Dunn* (6) 1971
GREASE – *Frankie Valli* (3) 1978
GREASED LIGHTNING – *John Travolta* (8) 1978
GREEN DOOR – *Frankie Vaughan* (-) 1956
GREEN FIELDS OF FRANCE – *Furey Brothers and Davy Arthur* (1)....1979
GREEN GREEN GRASS OF HOME – *Tom Jones* (1) 1966
GREEN GROWS THE GRASS – *Guy Mitchell* (-) 1956
THE GREEN LEAVES OF SUMMER • – *Kenny Ball and his Jazzmen* (7) 1962
THE GROOVE LINE – *Heatwave* (5) 1978
GROOVIN' WITH MR BLOE • – *Mr Bloe* (8)....1970
A GROOVY KIND OF LOVE – *The Mindbenders* (9)....1966
GUANTANAMERA – *The Sandpipers* (3) 1966
GUDBUY T' JANE – *Slade* (2) 1972
GUESTS OF THE NATION – *Horslips* (8) 1979
GUILTY – *Jim Reeves* (6) 1963

Title – *Act* (Position)	Year of Chart Entry
GUITAR TANGO • – *The Shadows* (3)	1962
THE GYPSY – *Dermot Henry* (1)	1972
GYPSYS TRAMPS AND THIEVES – *Cher* (3)	1971
HA! HA! SAID THE CLOWN – *Manfred Mann* (8)	1967
HALFWAY DOWN THE STAIRS – *The Muppets* (6)	1977
HALFWAY TO PARADISE – *Billy Fury* (5)	1961
HALFWAY TO WHERE – *The Freshmen* (10)	1970
HALLELUJAH – *Milk and Honey featuring Gali Atari* (1)	1979
HAMMER HORROR – *Kate Bush* (10)	1978
HAND ME DOWN MY BIBLE – *The Dubliners* (7)	1971
A HANDFUL OF SONGS – *Tommy Steele* (-)	1957
HANDY MAN – *Jimmy Jones* (4)	1960
THE HAPPENING – *The Supremes* (10)	1967
HAPPINESS IS ME AND YOU – *Gilbert O'Sullivan* (4)	1974
HAPPY ANNIVERSARY – *Tony and The Ventures* (7)	1972
HAPPY BIRTHDAY SWEET SIXTEEN – *Neil Sedaka* (4)	1962
HAPPY BIRTHDAY SWEET SIXTEEN – *Magic* (5)	1975
HAPPY JACK – *The Who* (8)	1967
HAPPY MAN – *Cathal Dunne* (3)	1979
HAPPY TO BE ON AN ISLAND IN THE SUN – *Demis Roussos* (7)	1975
HAPPY XMAS (War Is Over) – *John and Yoko and The Plastic Ono Band* (1)	1972
A HARD DAY'S NIGHT– *The Beatles* (1)	1964
HATS OFF TO LARRY – *Del Shannon* (4)	1961
HAVE A DRINK ON ME – *Lonnie Donegan and his Group* (3)	1961
HAVE I THE RIGHT – *The Honeycombs* (3)	1964
HAVE I THE RIGHT – *Dead End Kids* (1)	1977
HAVE YOU SEEN YOUR MOTHER BABY, STANDING IN THE SHADOW – *Rolling Stones* (5)	1966
HAWAIIAN WEDDING SONG – *Pat McGeegan and the Big Four* (7)	1963
HAWKEYE – *Frankie Laine* (-)	1956
HE AIN'T HEAVY, HE'S MY BROTHER – *The Hollies* (3)	1969
HEART FULL OF SOUL – *The Yardbirds* (3)	1965
THE HEART OF A MAN – *Frankie Vaughan* (3)	1959
HEART OF GLASS – *Blondie* (2)	1979
HEART OF STONE – *Kenny* (4)	1973
HEART ON MY SLEEVE – *Gallagher and Lyle* (4)	1976
HEARTACHE TONIGHT – *The Eagles* (10)	1979

Title – *Act* (Position) Year of Chart Entry

HEARTACHES BY THE NUMBER – *Guy Mitchell* (5)..........1960
HEARTBEAT – *Showaddywaddy* (5)..........1975
HEARTBREAK HOTEL – *Stan Freberg* (-)..........1956
HEARTBREAK HOTEL – *Elvis Presley* (-)..........1956
HEARTS OF STONE – *Fontane Sisters* (-)..........1955
HEATHER HONEY – *Tommy Roe* (9)..........1969
HEAVEN MUST BE MISSING AN ANGEL – *Tavares* (7)..........1976
HE'LL HAVE TO GO – *Jim Reeves* (1)..........1960
HE'LL HAVE TO STAY – *Jeanne Black* (4)..........1960
HEFFO'S HEROES – *Light Blues* (9)..........1974
HELL RAISER – *Sweet* (2)..........1973
HELLO DARLING – *Roly Daniels* (2)..........1972
HELLO DOLLY – *Louis Armstrong and The All Stars* (5)..........1964
HELLO GOODBYE – *The Beatles* (2)..........1967
HELLO! HELLO! I'M BACK AGAIN – *Gary Glitter* (2)..........1973
HELLO MARY LOU – *Ricky Nelson* (1)..........1961
HELLO SUSIE – *Amen Corner* (7)..........1969
HELLO THIS IS JOANNIE (The Telephone Answering Machine Song) – *Paul Evans* (2)..........1979
HELP! – *The Beatles* (1)..........1965
HELP ME MAKE IT THROUGH THE NIGHT – *John Holt* (8)..........1975
HELP ME RHONDA – *The Sands Showband* (9)..........1968
HELP YOURSELF – *Tom Jones* (1)..........1968
HER FATHER DIDN'T LIKE ME ANYWAY – *Jim McCann* (10)..........1979
HERE COMES MY BABY – *The Tremeloes* (8)..........1967
HERE COMES SUMMER – *Jerry Keller* (3)..........1959
HERE COMES THE NIGHT – *Them* (2)..........1965
HERE COMES THE SUN – *Steve Harley* (10)..........1976
HERE IT COMES AGAIN – *The Fortunes* (5)..........1965
HERE TODAY AND GONE TOMORROW – *Philomena Begley and Country Flavour* (7)..........1971
HEROES – *David Bowie* (8)..........1977
HERSHAM BOYS – *Sham 69* (9)..........1979
HE'S GOT THE WHOLE WORLD IN HIS HANDS – *Laurie London* (-)..........1958
HE'S GOT YOU – *The Dixies* (10)..........1965
HE'S IN TOWN – *Rockin' Berries* (9)..........1964
HEY BABY – *Bruce Channel* (3)..........1962
HEY C'MERE – *Rubbish* (4)..........1977
HEY GIRL DON'T BOTHER ME – *The Tams* (1)..........1971

Title – *Act* (Position) Year of Chart Entry

HEY JUDE – *The Beatles* (1)........1968
HEY LITTLE GIRL – *Del Shannon* (2)........1962
HEY ROCK AND ROLL – *Showaddywaddy* (5)........1974
HEY THERE – *Rosemary Clooney* (-)........1955
(HEY THERE) LONELY GIRL – *Eddie Holman* (5)........1974
HEY YOU – *Tommy Steele* (-)........1957
HIAWATHA • – *Mike Daniels* (10)........1959
HIDEAWAY – *Dave Dee, Dozy, Beaky, Mick & Tich* (10)........1966
HIGH HOPES – *Frank Sinatra* (1)........1959
HIGH IN THE SKY – *Amen Corner* (9)........1968
HIGH SCHOOL CONFIDENTIAL – *Jerry Lee Lewis* (9)........1959
HIPPY HIPPY SHAKE – *Swinging Blue Jeans* (2)........1964
HIS LATEST FLAME – *Elvis Presley* (1)........1961
HIT ME WITH YOUR RHYTHM STICK – *Ian Dury and the Blockheads* (3)........1979
HITCHIN' TO MIAMI – *The Times featuring Jim Swarbrigg* (7)........1969
HOLD ME(a) – *P J Proby* (10)........1964
HOLD ME (b) – *Red Hurley and the Nevada* (3)........1972
HOLD ME CLOSE – *David Essex* (1)........1975
HOLD ME TIGHT – *Johnny Nash* (6)........1968
HOLD MY HAND – *Don Cornell* (-)........1954
HOLD MY HAND – *Gary Miller* (-)........1954
HOLD ON TO LOVE – *Des Lee* (9)........1976
HOLE IN MY SHOE – *Traffic* (7)........1967
THE HOLY CITY – *Brendan Bowyer and the Royal Showband* (7)........1967
HOMBURG – *Procul Harum* (4)........1967
HOME BOYS HOME – *Dermot O'Brien and his Clubmen* (8)........1967
HOME LOVIN' MAN – *Andy Williams* (10)........1971
HOME SWEET HOME – *The Pound Hounds* (-)........1955
HOMELY GIRL – *The Chi-Lites* (10)........1974
HOMETOWN ON THE FOYLE – *Brian Coll* (5)........1974
HONESTLY I DO – *Ruby Murray* (-)........1956
HONEY – *Bobby Goldsboro* (1)........1968
HONEY CHILE – *Fats Domino* (-)........1957
HONEY COME BACK – *Glen Campbell* (2)........1970
THE HONEYMOON SONG • – *Manuel and the Music of the Mountains* (8)........1959
HONKY TONK WOMEN – *Rolling Stones* (1)........1969
HONG KONG GARDEN – *Sioux and The Banshees* (10)........1978

Title – *Act* (Position) Year of Chart Entry

HOOK LINE AND SINKER – *Bill Haley and his Comets* (-) 1957
HOORAY HOORAY, IT'S A HOLI-HOLIDAY – *Boney M* (5) 1979
HOPELESSLY DEVOTED TO YOU – *Olivia Newton John* (1) 1978
A HORSE WITH NO NAME – *America* (4) 1972
HOT DIGGITY (DOG ZIGGITY BOOM) – *Perry Como* (-) 1956
HOT LOVE – *T. Rex* (1) 1971
HOT LEGS – *Rod Stewart* (4) 1978
THE HOUSE OF THE RISING SUN – *The Animals* (10) 1964
THE HOUSE OF THE RISING SUN – *Frijid Pink* (7) 1970
THE HOUSE WITH THE WHITE WASHED GABLE – *Joe Dolan and the Drifters* (1) 1967
HOW CAN I BE SURE – *David Cassidy* (1) 1972
HOW CAN I MEET HER – *Everly Brothers* (4) 1962
HOW DEEP IS YOUR LOVE – *Bee Gees* (2) 1977
HOW DO YOU DO IT – *Gerry and the Pacemakers* (4) 1963
HOW GREAT THOU ART – *Kelley and the Nevada* (3) 1972
HOW MUCH LOVE – *Leo Sayer* (4) 1977
HOW MUCH TIME (Does It Take) – *Brendan Shine* (3) 1977
HOWZAT – *Sherbet* (5) 1976
HUCKLEBUCK – *Brendan Bowyer and Royal Showband* (1) 1965
HURDY GURDY MAN – *Donovan* (5) 1968
HURT – *The Manhattans* (6) 1976
HUSH NOT A WORD TO MARY – *John Rowles* (8) 1968
THE HUSTLE – *Van McCoy* (5) 1975

I AM – *Angela Farrell* (9) 1972
I AM I SAID – *Neil Diamond* (1) 1971
I BELIEVE – *The Bachelors* (2) 1964
I BELIEVE IN LOVE – *Jamie Stone* (4) 1976
I CAN DO IT – *The Rubettes* (5) 1975
I CAN MEND YOUR BROKEN HEART – *Don Gibson* (8) 1962
I CAN SEE CLEARLY NOW – *Johnny Nash* (9) 1972
I CAN'T ASK FOR ANYTHING MORE – *Cliff Richard* (7) 1976
I CAN'T CONTROL MYSELF – *The Troggs* (3) 1966
(I CAN'T GET NO) SATISFACTION – *Rolling Stones* (1) 1965
(I CAN'T GET NO) SATISFACTION – *Bubblerock* (9) 1974
I CAN'T GET YOU OUT OF MY HEART – *Brendan Bowyer of the Royal Showband* (4) 1966
I CAN'T LET GO – *The Hollies* (3) 1966

Title – *Act* (Position)	Year of Chart Entry
I CAN'T STAND THE RAIN – *Eruption* (6)	1978
I CAN'T STOP LOVIN' YOU (Though I Try) – *Leo Sayer* (5)	1978
I CAN'T STOP LOVING YOU – *Ray Charles* (1)	1962
I CAN'T TELL A WALTZ FROM A TANGO – *Alma Cogan* (-)	1954
I CAN'T TELL THE BOTTOM FROM THE TOP – *The Hollies* (8)	1970
I CLOSE MY EYES AND COUNT TO TEN – *Dusty Springfield* (6)	1968
I COULD EASILY FALL – *Cliff Richard and the Shadows* (8)	1965
I COULD HAVE DANCED ALL NIGHT – *Julie Andrews* (-)	1958
I COULD HAVE DANCED ALL NIGHT – *Rosemary Clooney* (-)	1958
I DID WHAT I DID FOR MARIA – *Tony Christie* (2)	1971
I DIDN'T KNOW I LOVED YOU (TILL I SAW YOU ROCK 'N' ROLL) – *Gary Glitter* (7)	1972
I DON'T BELIEVE IN IF ANYMORE – *Roger Whittaker* (4)	1972
I DON'T KNOW HOW TO LOVE HIM – *Tina and the Real McCoy* (1)	1971
I DON'T LIKE MONDAYS – *Boomtown Rats* (1)	1979
I DON'T LOVE YOU BUT I THINK I LIKE YOU – *Gilbert O'Sullivan* (7)	1975
I DON'T WANT OUR LOVING TO DIE – *The Herd* (5)	1968
I DON'T WANT TO BE A MEMORY – *The Pattersons* (2)	1968
I DON'T WANT TO PUT A HOLD ON YOU – *Berni Flint* (4)	1977
I DON'T WANT TO TALK ABOUT IT – *Rod Stewart* (4)	1977
I DREAMED – *Billie Anthony* (-)	1957
I FEEL FINE – *The Beatles* (1)	1964
I FEEL LOVE – *Donna Summer* (9)	1977
I GAVE MY WEDDING DRESS AWAY – *Cadets featuring Eileen Reid* (4)	1964
I GET A KICK OUT OF YOU – *Gary Shearson* (10)	1974
I GET A LITTLE SENTIMENTAL OVER YOU – *New Seekers* (9)	1974
I GET SO EXCITED – *Real McCoy* (10)	1968
I GOT STUNG – *Elvis Presley* (1)	1959
I GOT YOU BABE – *Sonny and Cher* (2)	1965
I GUESS I'M CRAZY – *Larry Cunningham and the Mighty Avons* (4)	1965
I HAVE A DREAM – *Abba* (2)	1979
I HEAR YOU KNOCKING – *Dave Edmunds Rockpile* (1)	1970
I HEARD IT THROUGH THE GRAPEVINE – *Marvin Gaye* (7)	1969
I JUST DON'T KNOW WHAT TO DO WITH MYSELF – *Dusty Springfield* (5)	1964
I KNOW (a) – *Perry Como* (7)	1959
I KNOW (b) – *Red Hurley* (5)	1974
(I Left My Heart) IN SAN FRANCISCO – *Dickie Rock, Miami and Strings* (4)	1965
I LIKE IT – *Gerry and the Pacemakers* (1)	1963

Title – *Act* (Position) Year of Chart Entry

I LIKE IT LIKE THAT – *The Miami featuring Charlie Chapman* (10)....1978
I LOST MY HEART TO A STARSHIP TROOPER – *Sarah Brightman and Hot Gossip* (5)....1978
I LOVE TO LOVE – *Tina Charles* (2)....1976
I LOVE YOU – *Cliff Richard and the Shadows* (2)....1960
I LOVE YOU BABY – *Paul Anka* (-)....1957
I LOVE YOU BECAUSE – *Jim Reeves* (1)....1964
I LOVE YOU LOVE ME LOVE – *Gary Glitter* (2)....1973
I LOVE YOU MORE AND MORE EACH DAY – *Joe Dolan & the Drifters* (3)....1965
I LOVE YOU MORE TODAY – *Brendan O'Brien and the Dixies* (2)....1965
I LOVE YOU STILL – *Big Tom and the Mainliners* (1)....1973
I MAY NEVER PASS THIS WAY AGAIN – *Robert Earl* (-)....1958
I NEED YOU (a) – *Declan Ryan and the Regal Showband* (6)....1965
I NEED YOU (b) – *Joe Dolan* (1)....1977
I NEED YOUR LOVE TONIGHT – *Elvis Presley* (3)....1959
I NEVER SAID GOODBYE – *Red Hurley and the Nevada* (5)....1973
I NEVER WILL MARRY – *The Johnstons* (8)....1968
I ONLY CAME TO DANCE WITH YOU – *Sonny and Sean* (4)....1966
I ONLY HAVE EYES FOR YOU – *Art Garfunkel* (2)....1975
I ONLY WANNA BE WITH YOU – *Bay City Rollers* (4)....1976
I ONLY WANT TO BE WITH YOU – *Dusty Springfield* (7)....1964
I PRETEND – *Des O'Connor* (1)....1968
I RAN ALL THE WAY HOME – *The Royal Showband featuring Brendan Bowyer* (1)....1964
I REMEMBER PARIS – *Tony Martin* (-)....1954
I REMEMBER YOU – *Frank Ifield* (1)....1962
I SEE A STAR – *Mouth and MacNeal* (1)....1974
I THINK I LOVE YOU – *Partridge Family* (2)....1971
I THINK OF YOU – *The Merseybeats* (10)....1964
I UNDERSTAND – *The G-Clefs* (10)....1961
I WALK THE LINE – *Dermot O'Brien and his Clubmen* (3)....1966
I WANNA GO HOME – *Lonnie Donegan* (8)....1960
I WANNA STAY WITH YOU – *Gallagher and Lyle* (9)....1976
I WANT TO GIVE – *Perry Como* (6)....1974
I WANT TO HOLD YOUR HAND – *The Beatles* (2)....1963
I WANT TO STAY HERE – *Steve and Eydie* (3)....1963
I WANT TO WALK YOU HOME – *Fats Domino* (6)....1959
I WANT YOU BACK – *Jackson 5* (6)....1970
I WAS KAISER BILL'S BATMAN • – *Whistling Jack Smith* (9)....1967

Title – *Act* (Position) Year of Chart Entry

I WAS MADE FOR DANCIN' – *Leif Garrett* (5) 1979
I (WHO HAVE NOTHING) – *Shirley Bassey* (10) 1963
I WILL RETURN – *Springwater* (6) 1971
I WILL SURVIVE – *Gloria Gaynor* (1) 1979
I WISH IT COULD BE CHRISTMAS EVERY DAY – *Wizzard* (6) 1973
I WONDER – *Brenda Lee* (10) 1963
I WONDER WHY – *Showaddywaddy* (10) 1978
I WON'T FORGET YOU – *Jim Reeves* (1) 1964
I WOULDN'T TRADE YOU FOR THE WORLD – *The Bachelors* (1) 1964
I'D LIKE TO TEACH THE WORLD TO SING (In Perfect Harmony) – *The New Seekers* (1) 1972
I'D NEVER FIND ANOTHER YOU – *Billy Fury* (9) 1962
I'D LOVE YOU TO WANT ME – *Glen Curtin* (7) 1974
I'D LOVE YOU TO WANT ME – *Lobo* (7) 1974
IF – *Telly Savalas* (1) 1975
IF DREAMS CAME TRUE – *Pat Boone* (-) 1958
IF EVERY DAY WAS LIKE CHRISTMAS – *Elvis Presley* (9) 1966
IF I CAN HELP SOMEBODY – *Billy Eckstine* (-) 1958
IF I CAN'T HAVE YOU – *Yvonne Elliman* (9) 1978
IF I COULD CHOOSE – *Sean Dunphy* (2) 1967
IF I CRIED – *Terry Mahon and the Jim Farley Showband* (7) 1966
IF I DIDN'T HAVE A DIME (To Play The Jukebox) – *Tom Dunphy with the Royal Showband* (1) 1965
IF I GIVE MY HEART TO YOU – *Doris Day* (-) 1955
IF I HAD A HAMMER – *Trini Lopez* (4) 1963
IF I HAD MY LIFE TO LIVE OVER – *Cadets featuring Eileen Reid* (4) 1966
IF I HAD WORDS – *Scott Fitzgerald and Yvonne Keeley* (9) 1978
IF I ONLY HAD TIME – *John Rowles* (6) 1968
IF I SAID YOU HAD A BEAUTIFUL BODY (WOULD YOU HOLD IT AGAINST ME)
– *Bellamy Brothers* (8) 1979
IF I WERE A CARPENTER – *The Four Tops* (6) 1968
IF MA COULD SEE ME NOW – *The Times* (1) 1974
IF NOT FOR YOU – *Olivia Newton John* (6) 1971
IF NOT YOU – *Dr Hook* (4) 1976
(IF PARADISE IS) HALF AS NICE – *Amen Corner* (4) 1969
IF SHE SHOULD COME TO YOU – *Anthony Newley* (5) 1960
IF THE KIDS ARE UNITED – *Sham 69* (6) 1978
IF THE WHOLE WORLD STOPPED LOVIN' – *Val Doonican* (2) 1967
IF THOSE LIPS COULD ONLY SPEAK – *Dermot Henry & Virginians* (1) 1970

Title – *Act* (Position) Year of Chart Entry

IF YOU CAN'T GIVE ME LOVE – *Suzi Quatro* (2)....1978
IF YOU GOTTA GO, GO NOW – *Manfred Mann* (4)....1965
IF YOU LEAVE ME NOW – *Chicago* (1)....1976
IF YOU THINK YOU KNOW HOW TO LOVE ME – *Smokie* (2)....1975
IL SILENZIO • – *Nini Rosso* (7)....1965
I'LL BE HOME – *Pat Boone* (-)....1956
I'LL BE HOME – *Brendan Shine* (10)....1975
I'LL COME WHEN YOU CALL – *Ruby Murray* (-)....1955
I'LL DO IT ALL AGAIN – *Tina* (7)....1977
I'LL FORGIVE AND I'LL TRY TO FORGET – *Margo & Country Folk* (1)....1970
I'LL KEEP YOU SATISFIED – *Billy J Kramer with the Dakotas* (8)....1963
I'LL MEET YOU AT MIDNIGHT – *Smokie* (3)....1976
I'LL NEVER FALL IN LOVE AGAIN [a] – *Bobby Gentry* (1)....1969
I'LL NEVER FALL IN LOVE AGAIN [b] – *Tom Jones* (4)....1967
I'LL NEVER FIND ANOTHER YOU – *The Seekers* (2)....1965
I'LL NEVER GET OVER YOU – *Johnny Kidd and the Pirates* (8)....1963
I'LL PUT YOU TOGETHER AGAIN – *Hot Chocolate* (8)....1978
I'LL REMEMBER TONIGHT – *Pat Boone* (3)....1959
I'LL TAKE YOU HOME AGAIN KATHLEEN – *Slim Whitman* (-)....1957
I'LL WALK WITH GOD – *Mario Lanza* (-)....1955
I'M A BELIEVER – *The Monkees* (1)....1967
I'M A BOY – *The Who* (7)....1966
I'M A CLOWN – *David Cassidy* (9)....1973
I'M ALIVE – *The Hollies* (1)....1965
I'M A TIGER – *Lulu* (8)....1969
I'M COMING HOME – *Tom Jones* (7)....1968
I'M COUNTING ON YOU – *The Dixielanders (vocalist Brendan O'Brien)* (6)....1964
I'M GONNA BE STRONG – *Gene Pitney* (6)....1964
I'M GONNA MAKE IT – *Joe Cuddy* (1)....1973
I'M GONNA MAKE YOU LOVE ME – *Diana Ross, the Supremes and the Temptations* (5)....1969
I'M GONNA MAKE YOU MINE – *Lou Christie* (4)....1969
I'M INTO SOMETHING GOOD – *Herman Hermits* (1)....1964
I'M JUST LUCKY I GUESS – *Gene Stuart and the Mighty Avons* (5)....1970
I'M LEAVING IT ALL UP TO YOU – *Donny and Marie* (3)....1974
I'M LITTLE BUT THERE'S LOTS OF ME TO LOVE – *Brendan Shine Superband featuring Johnny Dawson* (5)....1974
I'M LOOKING OUT THE WINDOW – *Cliff Richard* (2)....1962

Title – *Act* (Position) Year of Chart Entry

I'M MANDY FLY ME – *10cc* (6)........1976
I'M NOT IN LOVE – *10cc* (1)........1975
I'M ON FIRE – *5000 Volts* (9)........1975
I'M SORRY – *The Platters* (-)........1957
I'M STILL WAITING – Diana Ross (1)........1971
I'M STONE IN LOVE WITH YOU – *Johnny Mathis* (8)........1975
I'M THE LEADER OF THE GANG (I AM) – *Gary Glitter* (2)........1973
I'M THE LONELY ONE – *Cliff Richard and the Shadows* (9)........1964
I'M THE ONE – *Gerry and the Pacemakers* (3)........1964
I'M YOURS – *Dickie Rock and the Miamis* (1)........1964
IMAGINE – *John Lennon* (1)........1975
IN A BROKEN DREAM – *Python Lee Jackson* (6)........1972
IN DREAMS – *Roy Orbison* (1)........1963
IN DULCE JUBILO • – *Mike Oldfield* (10)........1976
IN SHAME LOVE IN SHAME – *Red Hurley* (3)........1977
IN SUMMER – *Billy Fury* (4)........1963
IN THE BAD BAD OLD DAYS – *The Foundations* (7)........1969
IN THE COUNTRY – *Cliff Richard and The Shadows* (3)........1967
IN THE GHETTO – *Elvis Presley* (1)........1969
IN THE MIDDLE OF AN ISLAND – *Tony Bennett* (-)........1957
IN THE MIDDLE OF NOWHERE – *Dusty Springfield* (8)........1965
IN THE NAVY – *Village People* (2)........1979
IN THE SUMMERTIME – Mungo Jerry (1)........1970
IN THE YEAR 2525 – *Zager and Evans* (1)........1969
IN ZAIRE – *Johnny Wakelin* (3)........1976
INDIAN LOVE CALL – *Slim Whitman* (-)........1955
INDIAN RESERVATION – *Don Fardon* (5)........1970
INDIANA WANTS ME – *R Dean Taylor* (2)........1971
INSTANT KARMA – *Lennon/Ono and The Plastic Ono Band* (3)........1970
THE IRELAND OF TOMORROW – *Denis Bowler and Sun Valley Boys* (6)........1972
IRISH EYES – *Margo* (7)........1976
THE IRISH SOLDIER – *Pat Lynch and the Airchords* (3)........1967
THE IRISH SOLDIER LADDIE – *Danny Doyle* (9)........1967
IS SHE REALLY GOING OUT WITH HIM – *Joe Jackson* (8)........1979
(IS THIS THE WAY TO) AMARILLO – *Tony Christie* (3)........1971
ISLAND IN THE SUN – *Harry Belafonte* (-)........1957
ISLAND OF DREAMS – *The Springfields* (2)........1963

Title – *Act* (Position) Year of Chart Entry

ISN'T SHE LOVELY – *David Parton* (3) 1977
ISRAELITES – *Desmond Dekker and the Aces* (7) 1969
IT ALL DEPENDS ON YOU – *The Times* (6) 1973
IT DOESN'T MATTER ANYMORE – *Buddy Holly* (1) 1959
IT DOESN'T MATTER ANYMORE – *Brendan O'Brien and the Dixies* (2) 1966
IT DON'T COME EASY – *Ringo Starr* (4) 1971
IT HURTS SO MUCH (TO SEE YOU GO) – *Jim Reeves* (10) 1965
IT ISN'T RIGHT – *The Platters* (-) 1956
IT ONLY TOOK A MINUTE – *Joe Brown and the Bruvvers* (8) 1963
IT SURE BRINGS OUT THE LOVE IN YOUR EYES – *David Soul* (6) 1978
IT TAKES SO LONG (TO SAY GOODBYE) – *Dean Martin* (5) 1959
ITCHYCOO PARK – *Small Faces* (9) 1976
IT'LL BE ME – *Cliff Richard and the Shadows* (2) 1962
IT'S A GAME – *Bay City Rollers* (6) 1977
IT'S A HEARTACHE – *Bonnie Tyler* (3) 1978
IT'S A WEARY WEARY WORLD – *Big Tom and The Travellers* (10) 1976
IT'S ALL IN THE GAME – *Cliff Richard* (2) 1963
IT'S ALL OVER NOW – *Rolling Stones* (2) 1964
IT'S ALMOST TOMORROW – *The Dreamweavers* (-) 1956
IT'S ALMOST TOMORROW – *Jo Stafford* (-) 1956
IT'S BEEN SO LONG – *George McCrae* (4) 1975
IT'S GETTING BETTER – *Mama Cass* (3) 1969
IT'S GONNA BE A COLD COLD CHRISTMAS – *Dana* (3) 1976
IT'S IMPOSSIBLE – *Perry Como* (6) 1971
IT'S IN HIS KISS – *Linda Lewis* (9) 1975
IT'S LATE – *Ricky Nelson* (10) 1959
IT'S MY LIFE – *The Animals* (9) 1965
IT'S NICE TO BE IN LOVE AGAIN – *The Swarbriggs plus 2* (1) 1977
IT'S NOT UNUSUAL – *Tom Jones* (6) 1965
IT'S NOW OR NEVER – *Elvis Presley* (1) 1960
IT'S ONLY MAKE BELIEVE – *The Dixielanders* (4) 1964
IT'S ONLY MAKE BELIEVE – *Billy Fury* (7) 1964
IT'S ONLY MAKE BELIEVE – *Glen Campbell* (3) 1970
IT'S ONLY MAKE BELIEVE – *Child* (7) 1978
IT'S ONLY ROCK AND ROLL – *Rolling Stones* (6) 1974
IT'S OVER – *Roy Orbison* (1) 1964
IT'S RAINING – *Darts* (2) 1978

Title – *Act* (Position)	Year of Chart Entry
IT'S TOO LATE – *Carole King* (7)	1971
IT'S YOUR LIFE – *Smokie* (6)	1977
I'VE BEEN A BAD BAD BOY – *Paul Jones* (10)	1967
I'VE BEEN WAITING FOR YOU – *Gina Dale Haze and the Champions* (8)	1977
I'VE GOTTA GET A MESSAGE TO YOU – *The Bee Gees* (1)	1968
I'VE TOLD EVERY LITTLE STAR – *Linda Scott* (9)	1961
JACK AND JILL – *Raydio* (8)	1978
JACK IN THE BOX (a) – *Moments* (6)	1977
JACK IN THE BOX (b) – *Clodagh Rodgers* (5)	1971
JACK O' DIAMONDS – *Lonnie Donegan and his Skiffle Group* (-)	1957
JAMAICA FAREWELL – *Harry Belafonte* (-)	1957
JAMBALAYA – *Fats Domino* (7)	1962
JANUARY – *Pilot* (1)	1975
JARROW SONG – *Alan Price* (5)	1974
JE T'AIME MOI NON PLUS – *Jane Birkin and Serge Gainsbourg* (2)	1969
JEALOUS MIND – *Alvin Stardust* (1)	1974
JEALOUSY – *Billy Fury* (1)	1961
THE JEAN GENIE – *David Bowie* (3)	1973
JEANNIE – *Danny Williams* (9)	1962
JEANS ON – *David Dundas* (3)	1976
JEEPSTER – *T. Rex* (2)	1971
JENNIFER ECCLES – *The Hollies* (7)	1968
JENNIFER JUNIPER – *Donovan* (7)	1968
JESAMINE – *The Casuals* (3)	1968
JILTED JOHN – *Jilted John* (8)	1978
JINGLE BELL ROCK – *Max Bygraves* (5)	1959
JIVE TALKIN' – *Bee Gees* (5)	1975
JOANNE – *The Swarbriggs* (4)	1976
JOHN COUNT McCORMACK E.P. – *John McCormack* (-)	1955
JOHNNY REGGAE – *The Piglets* (6)	1971
JOHNNY REMEMBER ME – *John Leyton* (1)	1961
JOHNNY WILL – *Pat Boone* (2)	1961
JOHNNY'S WEDDING – *Horslips* (10)	1972
THE JOKER – *The Hilltoppers* (-)	1958
JOLENE – *Dolly Parton* (6)	1976
THE JOYS OF LOVE – *The Dixies* (4)	1969

Title – *Act* (Position) Year of Chart Entry

JUDY – *Cotton Mill Boys* (7) 1973
JUDY IN DISGUISE (WITH GLASSES) – *John Fred & his Playboy Band* (3) 1968
JUKE BOX BABY – *Perry Como* (-) 1956
JUKE BOX JIVE – *The Rubettes* (3) 1974
JULIE ANN – *Kenny* (10) 1975
JULIE DO YA LOVE ME – *White Plains* (8) 1970
JULIET – *The Four Pennies* (3) 1964
JUMPING JACK FLASH – *Rolling Stones* (3) 1968
JUST A LITTLE TOO MUCH – *Ricky Nelson* (4) 1959
JUST BEYOND THE MOON – *Smokey Mountain Ramblers* (8) 1971
JUST FOR OLD TIMES SAKE – *Dickie Rock and the Miami Showband* (2) 1964
JUST LIKE EDDIE – *Heinz* (10) 1963
JUST ONE LOOK – *The Hollies* (6) 1964
JUST ONE MORE NIGHT – *Yellow Dog* (10) 1978
JUST THE WAY YOU ARE – *Billy Joel* (7) 1978
JUST TO SEE YOU SMILE – *The Freshmen* (9) 1969
JUST WALKING IN THE RAIN – *Johnnie Ray* (-) 1956
JUST WHEN I NEEDED YOU MOST – *Randy Van Warmer* (5) 1979

KATIES KISSES – *The Dixies* (2) 1968
KEEP A KNOCKIN' – *Little Richard* (-) 1958
KEEP ON DANCIN' – *Gary's Gang* (10) 1979
KEEP ON RUNNING – *Spencer Davis Group* (3) 1966
KEEP SEARCHIN' – *Del Shannon* (6) 1965
KELLY – *Tony and the Graduates* (8) 1965
KEVIN BARRY – *Lonnie Donegan and his Skiffle Group* (5) 1959
KEY TO MY HEART – *Rosemary Clooney* (-) 1956
THE KEY'S IN THE MAILBOX – *Bill Ryan and Buckshot* (7) 1972
KILLER QUEEN – *Queen* (2) 1974
KILLING ME SOFTLY WITH HIS SONG – *Roberta Flack* (10) 1973
THE KILLING OF GEORGIE – *Rod Stewart* (3) 1976
KING OF THE COPS – *Billy Howard* (5) 1976
KING OF THE FAIRIES • – *Horslips* (7) 1974
KING OF THE ROAD – *Roger Miller* (5) 1965
KISS AN ANGEL GOOD MORNING – *Gene Stuart and the Mighty Avons* (6) 1972
KISS AND SAY GOODBYE – *The Manhattans* (10) 1976
KISS ME GOODBYE – *Red Hurley and the Nevada* (1) 1971

Title – *Act* (Position) Year of Chart Entry

KISS ME HONEY, HONEY KISS ME – *Shirley Bassey* (6) 1959
KISS ME QUICK – *Brendan Bowyer with the Royal Showband* (1) 1963
KISS YOU ALL OVER – *Exile* (7) 1978
KISSES SWEETER THAN WINE – *Frankie Vaughan* (-) 1957
KISSIN' COUSINS – *Elvis Presley* (6) 1964
KISSIN' IN THE BACK ROW OF THE MOVIES – *The Drifters* (2) 1974
KNEE DEEP IN THE BLUES – *Guy Mitchell* (-) 1957
KNOCK KNOCK WHO'S THERE – *Mary Hopkin* (2) 1970
KNOCK ON WOOD – *David Bowie* (4) 1974
KNOCK THREE TIMES – *Dawn* (3) 1971
KNOCK THREE TIMES – *Tony Kenny and The Sands* (5) 1971
KNOCKED IT OFF – *B. A. Robertson* (8) 1979
KNOCKIN' ON HEAVEN'S DOOR – *Bob Dylan* (9) 1973
KNOWING ME KNOWING YOU – *Abba* (1) 1977
KUNG FU FIGHTING – *Carl Douglas* (1) 1974

LA MER (BEYOND THE SEA) – *Bobby Darin* (5) 1960
LA YENKA – *Derek Dean and the Freshmen* (10) 1965
LADY LYNDA – *Beach Boys* (8) 1979
LADY MADONNA – *The Beatles* (3) 1968
LADY ROSE – *Mungo Jerry* (6) 1971
LADY WILLPOWER – *Brendan Bowyer and the Royals* (9) 1968
LANA – *Roy Orbison* (8) 1966
LAND OF BEAUTY – *The Diamonds* (-) 1958
LAND OF GINGERBREAD – *Gregory and the Cadets* (9) 1967
THE LAST FAREWELL – *Roger Whittaker* (2) 1975
LAST NIGHT WAS MADE FOR LOVE – *Billy Fury* (6) 1962
THE LAST TIME – *Rolling Stones* (2) 1965
LAST TRAIN TO CLARKSVILLE – *The Monkees* (5) 1966
LAST TRAIN TO SAN FERNANDO – *Johnny Duncan and the Blue Grass Boys* (-) 1957
THE LAST WALTZ – *Engelbert Humperdinck* (1) 1967
THE LAUGHING GNOME – *David Bowie* (5) 1973
LAY BACK IN THE ARMS OF SOMEONE – *Smokie* (5) 1977
LAY DOWN YOUR ARMS – *Billie Anthony* (-) 1956
LAY DOWN YOUR ARMS – *Anne Shelton* (-) 1956
LAY IT ON ME – *The Memories* (7) 1974
LAY YOUR LOVE ON ME – *Racey* (2) 1978

Title – *Act* (Position)	Year of Chart Entry
LAYLA – *Derek and The Dominoes* (10)	1972
LAZY RIVER – *Bobby Darin* (2)	1961
LAZY SUNDAY – *Small Faces* (5)	1968
LEAD US THROUGH – *Tommy Drennan and Top League* (6)	1973
LEADER OF THE PACK – *The Shangri-las* (9)	1976
LEARNING THE BLUES – *Frank Sinatra* (-)	1955
THE LEAVING OF LIVERPOOL – *Pat Lynch and the Airchords* (6)	1966
THE LEAVING OF LIVERPOOL – *Billy Brown* (5)	1974
LEAVING ON A JET PLANE – *Peter Paul & Mary* (2)	1970
LEAVING NANCY – *Furey Brothers and Davy Arthur* (5)	1979
THE LEGEND OF ZANADU – *Dave, Dee, Dozy, Beaky, Mick and Tich* (1)	1968
LEND A HAND THIS CHRISTMAS – *Magic and the Magic Band* (6)	1978
LEND A HELPING HAND – *The Sands* (5)	1971
LES BICYCLETTES DE BELSIZE – *Engelbert Humperdinck* (5)	1968
LET 'EM IN – *Wings* (2)	1976
LET IT BE – *The Beatles* (3)	1970
LET ME GO LOVER – *Joan Weber* (-)	1955
LET ME BE THE ONE – *The Shadows* (10)	1975
LET ME IN – *The Osmonds* (7)	1973
LET ME TRY AGAIN – *Tammy Jones* (4)	1975
LET THE HEARTACHES BEGIN – *Long John Baldry* (2)	1967
LET THERE BE DRUMS ♦ – *Sandy Nelson* (6)	1962
LET US BE SWEETHEARTS OVER AGAIN – *Guy Mitchell* (-)	1955
LET YOUR LOVE FLOW – *Bellamy Brothers* (3)	1976
LET'S ALL CHANT – *Michael Zager Band* (8)	1978
LET'S DANCE – *Chris Montez* (3)	1962
LET'S GET TOGETHER – *Hayley Mills* (6)	1961
LET'S GET TOGETHER No. 1 – *Big Ben Banjo Band* (-)	1955
LET'S GO TO SAN FRANCISCO – *Flowerpot Men* (8)	1967
LET'S HAVE ANOTHER PARTY ♦ – *Winifred Atwell* (-)	1954
LET'S HAVE A QUIET NIGHT IN – *David Soul* (5)	1978
LET'S THINK ABOUT LIVING – *Bob Luman* (5)	1960
LET'S TWIST AGAIN – *Chubby Checker* (2)	1962
LET'S WORK TOGETHER – *Canned Heat* (6)	1970
LIBERTY BOY – *Brendan Grace* (5)	1974
LIECHTENSTEINER POLKA – *Will Glahe and his Musik* (-)	1958
LIFE IS A MINESTRONE – *10cc* (7)	1975

Title – *Act* (Position) Year of Chart Entry

LIFE ON MARS – *David Bowie* (4)....1973
LIGHT IN THE WINDOW – *Philomena Begley* (7)....1973
LIKE A ROLLING STONE – *Bob Dylan* (9)....1965
LIKE CLOCKWORK – *Boomtown Rats* (5)....1978
LIKE I DO – *Maureen Evans* (4)....1963
LIKE I'VE NEVER BEEN GONE – *Billy Fury* (4)....1963
THE LIKES OF HEFFO'S ARMY – *The Memories* (7)....1974
LILAC WINE – *Elkie Brooks* (8)....1978
LILY THE PINK – *The Scaffold* (1)....1968
LIMBO ROCK – *Chubby Checker* (4)....1962
LIMERICK YOU'RE A LADY – *Dennis Allen* (2)....1979
LIPSTICK ON YOUR COLLAR – *Connie Francis* (2)....1959
LISTEN TO ME – *The Hollies* (5)....1968
LISTEN TO WHAT THE MAN SAID – *Wings* (4)....1975
LITTLE ARROWS – *The Dixies* (1)....1968
LITTLE BAND OF GOLD – *James Gilreath* (3)....1963
A LITTLE BIT ME, A LITTLE BIT YOU – *The Monkees* (6)....1967
A LITTLE BIT MORE – *Dr Hook* (2)....1976
A LITTLE BIT OF SOAP – *Showaddywaddy* (2)....1978
A LITTLE BITTY TEAR – *Burl Ives* (4)....1962
LITTLE BOY LOST – *Tommy Drennan and the Monarchs* (6)....1970
LITTLE CHILDREN – *Billy J Kramer with the Dakotas* (2).... 1964
A LITTLE COUNTRY TOWN IN IRELAND – *John Glenn and Mainliners* (6).... 1977
LITTLE DARLIN' – *The Diamonds* (-)....1957
LITTLE DEVIL – *Neil Sedaka* (4)....1961
LITTLE DONKEY – *Beverley Sisters* (7)....1959
LITTLE DONKEY – *Gracie Fields* (2)....1959
LITTLE DRUMMER BOY – *Beverley Sisters* (6)....1959
LITTLE DRUMMER BOY – *Michael Flanders* (2)....1959
A LITTLE LOVE AND UNDERSTANDING – *Gilbert Becaud* (9)....1975
LITTLE MISS LONELY – *Helen Shapiro* (7)....1962
A LITTLE MORE LOVE – *Olivia Newton John* (9)....1978
LITTLE RED ROOSTER – *Rolling Stones* (4).... 1964
LITTLE SISTER – *Elvis Presley* (1)....1961
LITTLE THINGS – *Dave Berry* (9)....1965
LITTLE THINGS MEAN A LOT – *Kitty Kallen* (-)....1954
LITTLE THINGS – *Dave Berry* (9)....1965

Title – *Act* (Position) Year of Chart Entry

LITTLE TOWN FLIRT – *Del Shannon* (1) 1963
LITTLE WHITE BULL – *Tommy Steele* (3)....1960
LITTLE WILLY – *Sweet* (9)....1972
LIVELY – *Lonnie Donegan and his Group* (10)....1960
LIVERPOOL LOU – *Dominic Behan* (8)....1964
LIVIN' THING – *Electric Light Orchestra* (5)....1976
LIVING DOLL – *Cliff Richard and the Drifters* (1)....1959
LIVING IN HARMONY – *Cliff Richard* (10)....1972
LIVING IN THE PAST – *Jethro Tull* (5)....1969
LIVING NEXT DOOR TO ALICE – *Smokie* (3)....1976
L'L'LUCY – *Mud* (9)....1975
THE LOCO-MOTION – *Little Eva* (5)....1962
THE LOGICAL SONG – *Supertramp* (6)....1979
LOLA – *The Kinks* (1)....1970
LOLLIPOP – *The Chordettes* (-)....1958
LONELY BALLERINA • – *Mantovani* (-)....1955
LONELY BOY – *Paul Anka* (4)....1959
LONELY BLUE BOY – *Conway Twitty* (9)....1960
LONELY PUP (IN A CHRISTMAS SHOP) – *Adam Faith* (6)....1960
LONELY THIS CHRISTMAS – *Mud* (1)....1975
THE LONELY WOODS OF UPTON – *Sean Dunphy and the Hoedowners* (1)....1969
LONESOME – *Adam Faith* (5)....1962
LONESOME NUMBER ONE – *Don Gibson* (8)....1962
LONG BEFORE YOUR TIME – *Johnny McEvoy* (4)....1976
LONG HAIRED LOVER FROM LIVERPOOL – *Little Jimmy Osmond* (1)....1972
LONG LIVE LOVE (a) – *Sandie Shaw* (1)....1965
LONG LIVE LOVE (b) – *Olivia Newton John* (9)....1974
LONG TALL GLASSES – *Leo Sayer* (4)....1974
LONG TIME AGO – *The Bachelors* (9)....1964
LOOK OUT (HERE COMES TOMORROW) – *The Strangers* (6)....1967
LOOK THROUGH ANY WINDOW – *The Hollies* (3)....1965
LOOK WOT YOU DUN – *Slade* (6)....1972
LOOKING AFTER NO. 1 – *Boomtown Rats* (2)....1977
LOOKING HIGH HIGH HIGH – *Bryan Johnson* (8)....1960
LOOKING THRU THE EYES OF A BEAUTIFUL GIRL – *The Times* (7)....1970
LOOKING THRU THE EYES OF LOVE – *Gene Pitney* (5)....1965
LOOP-DE-LOOP – *Frankie Vaughan* (9)....1963

Title – *Act* (Position) Year of Chart Entry

LOOP DI LOVE – *Shag* (4) 1972
LOSING YOU (a) – *Tennessee Ernie Ford* (-) 1955
LOSING YOU (b) – *D J Curtin and The Kerry Blues* (7) 1974
LOST JOHN – *Lonnie Donegan Skiffle Group* (-) 1956
LOVE AND THE COUNTRY – *Tommy Drennan and Top League* (8) 1973
LOVE DON'T LIVE HERE ANYMORE – *Rose Royce* (7) 1978
LOVE GROWS (Where My Rosemary Goes) – *Edison Lighthouse* (1) 1970
LOVE HURTS – *Jim Capaldi* (8) 1975
THE LOVE IN YOUR EYES – *Vicky Leandros* (6) 1973
LOVE IS – *Fran O'Toole* (3) 1975
LOVE IS A GOLDEN RING – *Dave King* (-) 1957
LOVE IS A GOLDEN RING – *Frankie Laine* (-) 1957
LOVE IS A MANY SPLENDORED THING ♦ – *Eddie Calvert* (-) 1956
LOVE IS ALL – *Red Hurley* (1) 1975
LOVE IS IN THE AIR – *John Paul Young* (3) 1978
LOVE IS LIKE OXYGEN – *Sweet* (8) 1978
LOVE IS TEASING – *Dermot Hegarty and the Plainsmen* (7) 1972
LOVE LETTERS – *Ketty Lester* (4) 1962
LOVE LETTERS – *Elvis Presley* (7) 1966
LOVE LETTERS IN THE SAND – *Pat Boone* (-) 1957
LOVE MAKES THE WORLD GO ROUND – *Perry Como* (7) 1959
LOVE ME FOREVER – *Marion Ryan* (-) 1958
LOVE MATTERS – *Chips* (6) 1975
LOVE ME FOR A REASON – *The Osmonds* (2) 1974
LOVE ME LOVE MY DOG – *Peter Shelley* (4) 1975
LOVE ME LIKE I LOVE YOU – *Bay City Rollers* (3) 1976
LOVE ME TONIGHT – *Tom Jones* (7) 1969
LOVE OF THE COMMON PEOPLE – *Joe Dolan and the Drifters* (8) 1968
LOVE THEME FROM 'A STAR IS BORN' (EVERGREEN) – *Barbra Streisand* (4) 1977
LOVE THEME FROM 'THE GODFATHER' (SPEAK SOFTLY LOVE) – *Andy Williams* (6) 1972
LOVE YOU INSIDE OUT – *Bee Gees* (6) 1979
LOVELY LEITRIM – *Larry Cunningham and the Mighty Avons* (1) 1966
LOVE'S BEEN GOOD TO ME – *Frank Sinatra* (5) 1969
LOVE'S JUST A BROKEN HEART – *Cilla Black* (10) 1966
LOVE'S MADE A FOOL OF YOU – *The Dixies* (7) 1965
LOVE'S UNKIND – *Donna Summer* (2) 1978
LOVESICK BLUES – *Slim Whitman* (-) 1957

Title – *Act* (Position) Year of Chart Entry

LOVESICK BLUES – *Frank Ifield* (1) 1962
LOVIN' THINGS – *The Marmalade* (10) 1968
LOVING YOU – *Minnie Ripperton* (3) 1975
LOVING YOU HAS MADE ME BANANAS – *Guy Marks* (10) 1978
LUCILLE – *Cotton Mill Boys* (2) 1977
LUCILLE – *Kenny Rogers* (2) 1977
LUCKY LIPS – *Cliff Richard and the Shadows* (1) 1963
LUCKY NUMBER – *Lene Lovich* (7) 1979
LUCKY STARS – *Dean Friedman* (3) 1978
LYIN' EYES – *The Eagles* (5) 1975

MA BAKER – *Boney M* (4) 1977
MA (HE'S MAKING EYES AT ME) – *Johnny Otis Show* (-) 1958
MACARTHUR PARK – *Richard Harris* (9) 1968
MACARTHUR PARK – *Donna Summer* (7) 1978
MACK THE KNIFE – *Bobby Darin* (1) 1959
MAGGIE MAY – *Rod Stewart* (2) 1971
MAGIC – Pilot (6) 1974
MAGIC FLY • – Space (3) 1977
MAIN TITLE THEME (from The Man With The Golden Arm) • – *Jet Harris* (9) 1962
MAJORCA – *Johnston Brothers* (-) 1955
MAKE IT A PARTY • – *Winifred Atwell* (-) 1956
MAKE IT EASY ON YOURSELF – *Walker Brothers* (3) 1965
MAKE IT WITH YOU – *Bread* (10) 1970
MAKE ME AN ISLAND – *Joe Dolan* (2) 1969
MAKE ME SMILE (Come Up And See Me) –*Steve Harley & Cockney Rebel*(1) 1975
MAKING UP AGAIN – *Goldie* (4) 1978
MAMA (a) – *David Whitfield* (-) 1955
MAMA [a] – *Connie Francis* (10) 1960
MAMA [b] – *Dave Berry* (6) 1966
THE MAMA DOLL SONG – *Lita Roza* (-) 1954
MAMA I'M NOT THE BOY I USED TO BE – *Bill Ryan and Buckshot* (8) 1974
MAMA LOOK A BOO BOO – *Harry Belafonte* (-) 1957
MAMA TOLD ME (NOT TO COME) – *Three Dog Night* (6) 1970
MAMA WEER ALL CRAZEE NOW – *Slade* (1) 1972
MAMBO ITALIANO – *Rosemary Clooney* (-) 1955
MAMMA MIA – *Abba* (1) 1976

Title – *Act* (Position)	Year of Chart Entry
THE MAN FROM LARAMIE – *Jimmy Young* (-)	1955
MAN OF THE WORLD – *Fleetwood Mac* (5)	1969
MAN ON FIRE – *Frankie Vaughan* (-)	1957
THE MAN WHO SOLD THE WORLD – *Lulu* (8)	1974
THE MAN WITH THE CHILD IN HIS EYES – *Kate Bush* (3)	1978
A MAN WITHOUT LOVE – *Engelbert Humperdinck* (1)	1968
THE MANCHESTER RAMBLER – *Sean O'Se* (5)	1972
MANDOLINS IN THE MOONLIGHT – *Perry Como* (7)	1959
MANDY – *Barry Manilow* (6)	1975
MANY TEARS AGO – *Connie Francis* (8)	1961
MANY THE MEMORIES – *Real McCoy* (4)	1969
MARCH FROM BRIDGE ON THE RIVER KWAI – *Mitch Miller* (-)	1958
MARCH OF THE HIGH KINGS • – Brendan Shine Superband (8)	1972
MARCH OF THE SIAMESE CHILDREN • – *Kenny Ball and his Jazzmen* (3)	1962
MARCHETA – *Karl Denver* (9)	1961
MARIA ELENA • – *Los Indios Tabajaras* (5)	1963
MARIANNE – *Terry Gilkyson and Easy Riders* (-)	1957
MARIANNE – *The Hilltoppers* (-)	1957
MARY FROM DUNGLOE – *Emmet Spiceland* (1)	1968
MARY IN THE MORNING – *John MacNally* (9)	1969
MARY'S BOY CHILD – *Nina and Frederick* (3)	1959
MARY'S BOY CHILD – OH MY LORD – *Boney M* (1)	1978
MASQUERADE – Skids (6)	1979
MASSACHUSETTS – *Bee Gees* (2)	1967
MATCHSTALK MEN AND MATCHSTALK CATS AND DOGS – *Brian and Michael* (1)	1978
MATTHEW AND SON – *Cat Stevens* (3)	1967
MAY YOU ALWAYS – *McGuire Sisters* (7)	1959
ME AND MY LIFE – *The Tremeloes* (2)	1970
ME AND THE ELEPHANT – *Glen Curtin* (10)	1977
ME AND YOU AND A DOG NAMED BOO – *Lobo* (6)	1971
MEAN WOMAN BLUES – *Roy Orbison* (1)	1963
MEET ME TONIGHT IN LAREDO – *Gerry Black and The Seasons* (7)	1973
MEET THE COTTONS – *Cotton Mill Boys* (7)	1972
MELODY OF LOVE – *The Four Aces* (-)	1955
MEMORIES ARE MADE OF THIS – *Mindy Carson* (-)	1956
MEMORIES ARE MADE OF THIS – *Petula Clark* (-)	1956
MEMORIES ARE MADE OF THIS – *Dave King* (-)	1956

Title – *Act* (Position) Year of Chart Entry

MEMORIES ARE MADE OF THIS – *Dean Martin* (-) 1956
MEMPHIS TENNESSEE – *Chuck Berry* (3) 1963
MEMPHIS TENNESSEE – *Dave Berry and the Cruisers* (9) 1963
THE MEN BEHIND THE WIRE – *Barleycorn* (1) 1972
THE MERRY PLOUGHBOY – *Blarney Folk* (7) 1966
THE MERRY PLOUGHBOY – *Dermot O'Brien and his Clubmen* (1) 1966
MERRY XMAS EVERYBODY – Slade (1) 1973
A MESS OF BLUES – *Elvis Presley* (1) 1960
MESSAGE IN A BOTTLE – *Police* (1) 1979
MESSAGE UNDERSTOOD – *Sandie Shaw* (8) 1965
METAL GURU – *T Rex* (1) 1972
MEXICALI ROSE – *Karl Denver* (4) 1961
MEXICAN GIRL – *Smokie* (4) 1978
MICHAEL – *The Highwaymen* (1) 1961
MICHAEL COLLINS – *Sean Dunphy and the Hoedowners* (2) 1972
MICHAEL MURPHY'S BOY – *Alan Dee and the Chessmen* (5) 1966
MICHAEL ROW THE BOAT – *Lonnie Donegan and his Skiffle Group* (3) 1961
MICHELLE – *The Overlanders* (5) 1966
MIDNIGHT IN MOSCOW • – *Kenny Ball and his Jazzmen* (2) 1961
MIGHTY QUINN –*Manfred Mann* (1) 1968
MILK AND ALCOHOL – *Dr Feelgood* (8) 1979
MINNIE MINNIE MINNIE – *Gina Dale Haze and the Champions* (5) 1975
A MINUTE OF YOUR TIME – *Tom Jones* (4) 1968
THE MINUTE YOU'RE GONE – *Cliff Richard* (2) 1965
MISS YOU – *Rolling Stones* (2) 1978
MISS YOU NIGHTS – *Cliff Richard* (6) 1976
MISSISSIPPI – *Pussycat* (1) 1976
MR BLUE – *Mike Preston* (2) 1959
MR TAMBOURINE MAN – *The Byrds* (1) 1965
MR WONDERFUL – *Peggy Lee* (-) 1957
MR WONDERFUL – *Ruby Murray* (-) 1957
MISTY – *Johnny Mathis* (7) 1960
MISTY – *Ray Stevens* (2) 1975
MOLLY – *Tommy Drennan and the Monarchs* (9) 1965
MONDAY MONDAY – *Mamas and the Papas* (4) 1966
MONEY HONEY – *Bay City Rollers* (4) 1975
MONEY MONEY MONEY – *Abba* (2) 1976

Title – *Act* (Position) Year of Chart Entry

MONSIEUR DUPONT – *Sandie Shaw* (9)....................1968
MONSTER MASH – *Bobby 'Boris' Pickett and The Crypt Kickers* (5)....................1973
MONY MONY – *Tommy James and the Shondells* (2)....................1968
MOODY BLUE – *Elvis Presley* (6)....................1977
MOODY RIVER – *Pat Boone* (7)....................1961
MOON RIVER – *Danny Williams* (2)....................1961
MOONGLOW AND THEME FROM PICNIC • – *Morris Stoloff* (-)....................1956
MOONLIGHTING – *Leo Sayer* (1)....................1975
MOONSHINE SALLY – *Mud* (9)....................1975
MORE LIKE THE MOVIES – *Dr Hook* (5)....................1978
MORE THAN EVER – *Edmund Hockridge* (-)....................1958
MORE THAN I CAN SAY – *Bobby Vee* (5)....................1961
MORE THAN YESTERDAY – *The Cadets featuring Gregory* (1)....................1966
MORGEN (One More Sunrise) – *Billy Vaughn and his Orchestra* (2)....................1959
MORNING – *Val Doonican* (5)....................1972
MORNING GLORY – *Makem and Clancy* (7)....................1979
MORNING HAS BROKEN – *Cat Stevens* (6)....................1972
MORNING SIDE OF THE MOUNTAIN – *Donny and Marie* (7)....................1975
MORNINGTOWN RIDE – *The Seekers* (2)....................1966
THE MOST BEAUTIFUL GIRL – *Roly Daniels* (2)....................1974
THE MOST BEAUTIFUL GIRL – *Charlie Rich* (2)....................1974
MOTHER OF MINE – *Neil Reid* (8)....................1972
MOTHER-IN-LAW – *Ernie K-Doe* (4)....................1961
MOULDY OLD DOUGH • – *Lieutenant Pigeon* (1)....................1972
MOUNTAINS OF MOURNE – *Don McLean* (2)....................1973
MOZART SYMPHONY NO. 40 In G MINOR K550 1ST MOVEMENT (ALLEGRO MOLTO) •
– *Waldo de los Rios* (3)....................1971
MRS ROBINSON – *Simon and Garfunkel* (6)....................1968
MRS ROBINSON E.P – *Simon and Garfunkel* (5)....................1969
MS GRACE – *The Tymes* (1)....................1975
MULL OF KINTYRE – *Wings* (1)....................1977
MULTIPLICATION – *Bobby Darin* (6)....................1962
MUIRSHEEN DURKIN – *The Rambler (John McEvoy)* (1)....................1966
MUSIC – *John Miles* (9)....................1976
MUSIC FROM ACROSS THE WAY – *Sonny Knowles* (2)....................1973
MUSKRAT – *Everly Brothers* (8)....................1961
MY BABY LOVES LOVIN' – *White Plains* (9)....................1970

Title – *Act* (Position) Year of Chart Entry

MY BOY – *Elvis Presley* (4) 1974
MY BOY LOLLIPOP – *Millie* (1) 1964
MY CHERIE AMOUR – *Stevie Wonder* (9) 1969
MY COO CA CHOO – *Alvin Stardust* (3) 1973
MY DING-A-LING – *Chuck Berry* (1) 1972
MY DIXIE DARLING – *Lonnie Donegan and his Skiffle Group* (-) 1957
MY DREAM – *The Platters* (-) 1957
MY ELUSIVE DREAMS – *Ray Lynam and Philomena Begley* (3) 1974
MY EYES ADORED YOU – Frankie Valli (4) 1975
MY FRIEND STAN – Slade (1) 1973
MY FRIEND THE WIND – Demis Roussos (8) 1974
MY GENERATION – *The Who* (7) 1965
MY GUY – *Mary Wells* (9) 1964
MY HAPPINESS – *Connie Francis* (6) 1959
MY HEART KEEPS TELLING ME (I Love Melanie So) – *Dickie Rock* (7) 1971
MY HEART HAS A MIND OF ITS OWN – *Connie Francis* (4) 1960
MY HOUSE IS YOUR HOUSE – *Michael Holliday* (-) 1957
MY KATHLEEN – *Larry Cunningham* and the *Country Blue Boys* (3) 1975
MY KIND OF GIRL – *Matt Monro* (6) 1961
MY LIFE – Billy Joel (3) 1979
MY LITTLE LADY – *The Tremeloes* (1) 1968
MY LOVE – *Petula Clark* (6) 1966
MY LOVELY IRISH ROSE – *Dermot Henry and the Virginians* (8) 1970
MY LOVELY ROSE AND YOU – *Sean Fagan* (7) 1969
MY MIND'S EYE – *Small Faces* (8) 1967
MY OLD MAN'S A DUSTMAN – *Lonnie Donegan and his Group* (1) 1960
MY OWN PECULIAR WAY – *Joe Dolan and the Drifters Showband* (2) 1965
MY PRAYER – *The Platters* (-) 1956
MY SENTIMENTAL FRIEND – *Herman's Hermits* (2) 1969
MY SPECIAL ANGEL – *Robert Earl* (-) 1958
MY SWEET LORD – *George Harrison* (1) 1971
MY WAY – *Frank Sinatra* (4) 1969
MY WAY (b) – *Elvis Presley* (6) 1978
MYSTERY TRAIN – *Elvis Presley* (-) 1957

NA-NA IS THE SADDEST WORD – *The Stylistics* (3) 1975
NA NA NA – *Cozy Powell* (10) 1974

Title – *Act* (Position) Year of Chart Entry

NAIROBI – *Bob Merrill* (-) 1958
NAIROBI – *Tommy Steele* (-) 1958
THE NAME OF THE GAME – *Abba* (2) 1977
NATIVE NEW YORKER – *Odyssey* (7) 1978
NATURAL BORN BUGIE – *Humble Pie* (6) 1969
NATURAL SINNER – *Fair Weather* (9) 1970
THE NAUGHTY LADY OF SHADY LANE – *The Ames Brothers* (-) 1955
THE NAUGHTY LADY OF SHADY LANE – *Dean Martin* (-) 1955
NED KELLY – *Murphy and the Swallows* (5) 1972
NEL BLU DI PINTO DE BLU (VOLARE) – *Lita Roza* (-) 1954
NEEDLES AND PINS – *The Searchers* (1) 1964
NEEDLES AND PINS – *Smokie* (3) 1977
NELSON'S FAREWELL – *The Dubliners* (6) 1966
NEVER AN EVERYDAY THING – *Granny's Intentions* (6) 1968
NEVER BE ANYONE ELSE BUT YOU – *Ricky Nelson* (8) 1959
NEVER GOODYBYE – *Karl Denver* (7) 1962
NEVER CAN SAY GOODBYE – *Gloria Gaynor* (3) 1975
NEVER ENDING SONG OF LOVE – *New Seekers* (1) 1971
NEVER LET HER SLIP AWAY – *Andrew Gold* (2) 1978
NEVER ON A SUNDAY • – *Manuel and the Music of the Mountains* (5) 1960
NEW WORLD IN THE MORNING – *Roger Whittaker* (1) 1970
NEW YORK GROOVE – *Hello* (6) 1975
THE NEXT TIME – *Cliff Richard and the Shadows* (1) 1962
NICK NACK PADDY WACK (The Children's Marching Song) – *Cyril Stapleton and his Orchestra* (8) .. 1959
THE NICKEL SONG – *Marie* (8) 1972
THE NIGHT – *Frankie Valli and The Four Seasons* (8) 1975
THE NIGHT CHICAGO DIED – *Paper Lace* (5) 1974
NIGHT FEVER – *Bee Gees* (1) 1978
THE NIGHT HAS A THOUSAND EYES – *Bobby Vee* (9) 1963
NIGHT OF FEAR – *The Move* (6) 1967
NIGHT OWL – *Gerry Rafferty* (5) 1979
THE NIGHT THEY DROVE OLD DIXIE DOWN – *Joan Baez* (8) 1971
NIGHTS ON BROADWAY – *Candi Staton* (4) 1977
NINE TIMES OUT OF TEN – *Cliff Richard and the Shadows* (3) 1960
NINETEEN MEN – *Dermot Hegarty* (1) 1974
NINETEENTH NERVOUS BREAKDOWN – *Rolling Stones* (2) 1966
NINETY NINE WAYS – *Tab Hunter* (-) 1957

Title – *Act* (Position) Year of Chart Entry

NO ARMS CAN EVER HOLD YOU – *The Bachelors* (8) 1965
NO CHARGE – *J J Barrie* (5) 1976
NO MATTER HOW I TRY – *Gilbert O'Sullivan* (7) 1972
NO MATTER WHAT – *Badfinger* (7) 1971
NO MILK TODAY – *Herman's Hermits* (7) 1966
NO MORE – *Royal Showband featuring Brendan Bowyer* (1) 1963
NO MORE TEARS (Enough Is Enough) –*Donna Summer & Barbra Streisand* (7) 1979
NO ONE KNOWS – *Sonny Knowles and the Pacific Showband* (3) 1966
NO ONE WILL EVER KNOW – *Sonny Knowles and the Pacific Showband* (5) 1965
NO OTHER LOVE – *Ronnie Hilton* (-) 1956
NO OTHER LOVE – *Edmund Hockridge* (-) 1956
NO PARTICULAR PLACE TO GO – *Chuck Berry* (7) 1964
NO REGRETS – *Walker Brothers* (9) 1976
NOBODY DOES IT BETTER – *Carly Simon* (2) 1977
NOBODY I KNOW – *Peter and Gordon* (8) 1964
NOBODY LOVES LIKE AN IRISHMAN – *Lonnie Donegan* (-) 1958
NOBODY NEEDS YOUR LOVE – *Gene Pitney* (2) 1966
NOBODY'S CHILD – *Karen Young* (10) 1969
NOBODY'S DARLIN' BUT MINE – *Frank Ifield* (2) 1963
NON HO L'ETA PER AMARTI – *Gigliola Cinquetti* (4) 1964
NORA – *Johnny McEvoy* (1) 1968
NORA (re-recording) – *Johnny McEvoy* (7) 1977
NOREEN BAWN – *D J Curtin* (9) 1977
NORTHERN LIGHTS – *Renaissance* (9) 1978
NOT FADE AWAY – *Rolling Stones* (5) 1964
NOT UNTIL THE NEXT TIME – *Jim Reeves* (6) 1965
NOTHING RHYMED – *Gilbert O'Sullivan* (2) 1970
NOW YOU HAS JAZZ – *Bing Crosby and Louis Armstrong All Stars* (-) 1956
NUMBER ONE SONG IN HEAVEN – *Sparks* (5) 1979
NUT ROCKER • – *B Bumble and the Stingers* (2) 1962

O'BRIEN HAS NO PLACE TO GO – *Brendan Shine* (1) 1971
O HOLY NIGHT – *Tommy Drennan and the Monarchs* (1) 1971
OB-LA-DI OB-LA-DA – *The Marmalade* (1) 1969
ODE TO BILLY JOE – *Bobbie Gentry* (6) 1967
OH BABE WHAT WOULD YOU SAY – Hurricane Smith (10) 1972
OH BOY – *Mud* (1) 1975

Title – *Act* (Position) Year of Chart Entry

OH BOY (The Mood I'm In) – *Brotherhood Of Man* (6) 1977
OH CAROL (a) – *Neil Sedaka* (8) 1960
OH CAROL (b) – *Smokie* (2) 1978
OH HAPPY DAY – *Edwin Hawkins Singers* (2) 1969
OH LONESOME ME – *Craig Douglas* (7) 1962
OH MY LORD – *Boney M* (1) 1978
OH, NO! – *The Memories* (10) 1968
OH! NO NOT MY BABY – *Rod Stewart* (8) 1973
OH PRETTY WOMAN – *Roy Orbison* (1) 1964
OH WELL – *Fleetwood Mac* (5) 1969
OH WHAT A CIRCUS – *David Essex* (8) 1978
OH YES YOU'RE BEAUTIFUL – *Gary Glitter* (1) 1974
OKAY! – *Dave Dee, Dozy, Beaky, Mick and Tich* (7) 1967
THE OLD CLADDAGH RING – Dermot O'Brien (7) 1971
THE OLD DUNGARVAN OAK – *Dermot Henry and the Virginians* (5) 1973
THE OLD FENIAN GUN – *Sean Dunphy and the Hoedowners* (5) 1970
OLD LOVE LETTERS – *Big Tom and the Mainliners* (1) 1974
OLD MAID IN A GARRET – *Sweeney's Men* (6) 1967
OLD MAN TROUBLE – *Doc Carroll and the Royal Blues* (1) 1966
THE OLD RUGGED CROSS • – *Monty Sunshine Quartet* (-) 1958
OLE OLA – *Rod Stewart* (8) 1978
OLIVER'S ARMY – *Elvis Costello* (4) 1979
ON A CAROUSEL – *The Hollies* (5) 1967
ON A SLOW BOAT TO CHINA – *Emile Ford and the Checkmates* (4) 1960
ON THE BEACH – *Cliff Richard and the Shadows* (6) 1964
ON THE REBOUND • – *Floyd Cramer* (4) 1961
ON MY WORD OF HONOUR – *The Platters* (-) 1957
ON THE STREET WHERE YOU LIVE – *Vic Damone* (-) 1958
ON THE STREET WHERE YOU LIVE – *Ronnie Hilton* (-) 1958
ON THE STREET WHERE YOU LIVE – *David Whitfield* (-) 1958
ONCE AROUND THE DANCE FLOOR – *Philomena Begley and the Ramblin' Men* (3) 1976
ONE AND ONE ARE TWO – *Patricia Cahill* (6) 1968
ONE AND ONE IS ONE – Medicine Head (9) 1973
ONE BROKEN HEART FOR SALE – *Elvis Presley* (5) 1963
ONE DAY AT A TIME – *Gloria* (1) 1977
ONE DAY LOVE – *Angela Farrell* (4) 1971
ONE FINE DAY – *Maria Perilli (-)* 1958

Title – *Act* (Position) Year of Chart Entry

100 CHILDREN – *Gerry Reynolds and the Hi-Lows* (8) 1972
ONE IN A MILLION – *The Platters* (-) 1957
ONE KISS FOR OLD TIMES SAKE – *Murty Quinn* (3) 1966
ONE MAN BAND – *Leo Sayer* (5) 1974
ONE MORE SUNRISE (MORGEN) – *Dickie Valentine* (5) 1959
ONE NIGHT – *Elvis Presley* (1) 1959
1-2-3 – *Len Barry* (8) 1965
ONE, TWO, THREE O'LEARY – *Des O'Connor* (9) 1969
THE ONLY MAN ON THE ISLAND – *Vic Damone* (-) 1958
ONLY ONE WOMAN – *Marbles* (8) 1968
ONLY SIXTEEN – *Craig Douglas* (1) 1959
ONLY THE HEARTACHES – *Houston Wells and the Marksmen* (7) 1963
ONLY THE LONELY – *Roy Orbison* (1) 1960
ONLY YESTERDAY – *The Carpenters* (5) 1975
ONLY YOU – *The Platters* (-) 1956
ONLY YOU CAN – *Fox* (3) 1975
OOH BABY – *Gilbert O'Sullivan* (2) 1973
OOH-WAKKA-DOO-WAKKA-DAY – *Gilbert O'Sullivan* (1) 1972
OUR LOVE WILL GO ON – *Butch Moore and the Capitol Showband* (10) 1965
OUT THERE SINGING – *Fran O'Toole* (7) 1977
OVER THE WALL – *The Wolfhounds* (8) 1972
OXYGENE • – *Jean-Michel Jarre* (7) 1977

PADDY THE PEDLER – *Brendan Grace* (4) 1974
PADRAIC PEARSE – Wolfe Tones (4) 1979
PAINT IT BLACK – *Rolling Stones* (2) 1966
PAL OF MY CRADLE DAYS – *Sean Dunphy and the Hoedowners* (3) 1973
PAMELA PAMELA – *Wayne Fontana* (10) 1967
PAPA-OO-MOW-MOW – *The Freshmen* (7) 1968
PAPER KISSES – *Alma Cogan* (-) 1955
PAPER ROSES – *The Kaye Sisters* (3) 1960
PAPER ROSES – *Marie Osmond* (6) 1973
PAPERBACK WRITER – *The Beatles* (1) 1966
PARISIENNE WALKWAYS – *Gary Moore* (5) 1979
PARALYZED – *Elvis Presley* (-) 1957
PART OF THE UNION – *The Strawbs* (10) 1973
PASADENA – *The Temperance Seven* (9) 1961

Title – *Act* (Position)	Year of Chart Entry
PATCHES – *Clarence Carter* (4)	1970
PATHS OF PARADISE – *Johnnie Ray* (-)	1955
THE PAY OFF • – *Kenny Ball and his Jazzmen* (10)	1962
PEARL'S A SINGER – *Elkie Brooks* (9)	1977
PENNY LANE – *The Beatles* (2)	1967
PEPE • – *Duane Eddy* (4)	1961
PERFIDA • – *The Ventures* (4)	1961
PERSONALITY – *Lloyd Price* (3)	1959
PETITE FLEUR • – *Chris Barber Jazz Band* (1)	1959
PIANISSIMO – *Ken Dodd* (9)	1962
PICK A BALE OF COTTON – *Lonnie Donegan and his Group* (8)	1962
PICK UP THE PIECES – *Average White Band* (10)	1975
PICKIN' A-CHICKEN – *Eve Boswell* (-)	1956
A PICTURE OF YOU – *Joe Brown and the Bruvvers* (2)	1962
PIED PIPER – *Crispian St. Peters* (9)	1966
PLAY ME LIKE YOU PLAY YOUR GUITAR – *Duane Eddy* (5)	1975
PLEASE DON'T BLAME ME – *Marty Robbins* (-)	1957
PLEASE DON'T GO – *Donald Peers* (3)	1969
PLEASE DON'T TEASE – *Cliff Richard and the Shadows* (1)	1960
PLEASE HELP ME I'M FALLING – *Hank Locklin* (1)	1960
PLEASE MR. POSTMAN – *Carpenters* (2)	1975
PLEASE PLEASE ME – *The Beatles* (10)	1963
PLEASE TELL HIM THAT I SAID HELLO – *Dana* (7)	1974
POETRY IN MOTION – *Johnny Tillotson* (1)	1961
POOR LITTLE FOOL – *Ricky Nelson* (-)	1958
POOR ME – *Adam Faith* (3)	1960
POOR PEOPLE OF PARIS • – *Winifred Atwell* (-)	1956
THE POOR POOR FARMER – *Darby O'Gill (Tim Pat)* (3)	1971
POP GO THE WORKERS – *The Barron Knights* (7)	1965
POP MUZIK – *M* (2)	1979
POPCORN – *Hot Butter* (8)	1972
PORTRAIT OF MY LOVE – *Matt Monro* (4)	1961
PORTSMOUTH • – *Mike Oldfield* (2)	1977
POWER TO ALL OUR FRIENDS – *Cliff Richard* (2)	1973
POWER TO THE PEOPLE – *John Lennon/Plastic Ono Band* (7)	1971
PRETTY BLUE EYES – *Craig Douglas* (3)	1960
PRETTY BROWN EYES – *Joe Dolan and the Drifters* (1)	1966

Title – *Act* (Position) Year of Chart Entry

PRETTY FLAMINGO – *Manfred Mann* (1) 1966
A PRETTY IRISH GIRL – *Ruby Murray and Brendan O'Dowda* (8) 1959
PRETTY LITTLE ANGEL EYES – *Showaddywaddy* (2) 1978
PRETTY LITLE GIRL FROM OMAGH – *Larry Cunningham* (10) 1969
PRETTY PAPER – *Roy Orbison* (8) 1964
THE PRICE OF LOVE – *Everly Brothers* (3) 1965
PRIDE OF THE HERD – *Shaun Davey* (7) 1978
PROBLEMS – *The Everly Brothers* (8) 1959
THE PROMISE AND THE DREAM – *Tommy Drennan and Top League* (3) 1972
PROMISED LAND – *Elvis Presley* (7) 1975
THE PROUD ONE – *The Osmonds* (1) 1975
A PUB WITH NO BEER – *Slim Dusty* (1) 1959
PUPPET ON A STRING – *Sandie Shaw* (1) 1967
PUPPY LOVE – *Donny Osmond* (2) 1972
THE PUPPY SONG – *David Cassidy* (3) 1973
THE PURPLE PEOPLE EATER – *Sheb Wooley* (-) 1958
THE PUSHBIKE SONG – *The Mixtures* (3) 1971
PUSSYCAT – *The Ames Brothers* (9) 1959
PUT YOUR HEAD ON MY SHOULDER – *Paul Anka* (6) 1959
PUTTIN' ON THE STYLE – *Lonnie Donegan and his Skiffle Group* (-) 1957

QUESTION – *Moody Blues* (1) 1970
QUICK JOEY SMALL – *Real McCoy* (1) 1969

RADANCER – *Marmalade* (10) 1972
RAG AND BONE MAN – *Des Smyth* (8) 1973
RAG DOLL – *Four Seasons* (4) 1964
RAGAMUFFIN MAN – *Manfred Mann* (10) 1969
RAIN – *Status Quo* (6) 1976
RAINBOW – *Marmalade* (4) 1970
RAINBOW VALLEY – *Love Affair* (6) 1968
RAINDROPS KEEP FALLIN' ON MY HEAD – *B J Thomas* (9) 1970
RAINING IN MY HEART – *Cotton Mill Boys* (3) 1976
RAMBLIN' MAN – *Philomena Begley and Country Flavour* (9) 1972
RAMBLIN' ROSE – *Nat King Cole* (4) 1962
RAMONA – *The Bachelors* (6) 1964
THE RARE OLD TIMES – *Danny Doyle* (1) 1978

Title – *Act* (Position) Year of Chart Entry

RASPUTIN – *Boney M* (3) 1978

RAT TRAP – *Boomtown Rats* (2) 1978

RAUNCHY ♦ – *Bill Justis* (-) 1958

RAUNCHY ♦ – *Billy Vaughn* and his Orchestra (-) 1958

REACH FOR THE STARS – *Shirley Bassey* (8) 1961

REACH OUT I'LL BE THERE – *Four Tops* (4) 1966

REACHING OUT – *Magic* (9) 1977

REBEL REBEL – *David Bowie* (2) 1974

THE RED BALLOON – *Dave Clark Five* (5) 1968

RED IS THE ROSE – *Makem and Clancy* (3) 1979

RED RIVER ROCK ♦ – *Johnny and the Hurricanes* (5) 1959

REFLECTIONS OF MY LIFE – *Marmalade* (2) 1970

RELEASE ME – *Engelbert Humperdinck* (1) 1967

REMEMBER ME THIS WAY – *Gary Glitter* (10) 1974

REMEMBER THEN – *Showaddywaddy* (7) 1979

REMEMBER YOU'RE A WOMBLE – *The Wombles* (6) 1974

REMEMBER YOU'RE MINE – *Pat Boone* (-) 1957

RESURRECTION SHUFFLE – *Ashton, Gardner and Dyke* (6) 1971

RETURN TO ME – *Dean Martin* (-) 1958

RETURN TO SENDER – *Elvis Presley* (1) 1962

REUNITED – *Peaches and Herb* (3) 1979

RHINESTONE COWBOY – *Glen Campbell* (1) 1975

THE RHYTHM OF LOVE – *Jim Tobin and the Firehouse* (5) 1977

RHYTHM OF THE RAIN – *The Cascades* (1) 1963

RIDERS IN THE SKY ♦ – *The Ramrods* (7) 1961

RIGHT OR WRONG – *The Cadets featuring Eileen Reid* (7) 1965

RING MY BELL – *Anita Ward* (2) 1979

THE RING YOUR MOTHER WORE – *Pat Roper and The Spotlights* (3) 1971

RIP IT UP – *Bill Haley and the Comets* (-) 1956

THE RIVER – *Ken Dodd* (3) 1965

RIVER STAY 'WAY FROM MY DOOR – *Frank Sinatra* (2) 1960

RIVERS OF BABYLON – *Boney M* (1) 1978

THE ROAD BY THE RIVER – *Margo and the Keynotes* (2) 1969

ROBOT MAN – *Connie Francis* (3) 1960

ROCK AND ROLL Part 2 – *Gary Glitter* (4) 1972

ROCK AND ROLL WALTZ – *Kay Starr* (-) 1956

ROCK AROUND THE CLOCK – *Bill Haley and the Comets* (-) 1955

Title – *Act* (Position) Year of Chart Entry

ROCK BOTTOM – *Lynsey De Paul and Mike Moran* (7) 1977
ROCK ME GENTLY – *Andy Kim* (10) 1974
ROCK 'N' ROLL • – *Big Ben Accordion Band* (-) 1956
ROCK 'N' ROLL (I Gave You The Best Years Of My Life) –*Kevin Johnson* (8) 1974
ROCK 'N' ROLL KISSES – *The Swarbriggs* (9) 1978
ROCK RIGHT – *Georgia Gibbs* (-) 1956
ROCK THE BOAT – *Hues Corporation* (9) 1974
ROCK YOUR BABY – George McCrae (3) 1974
ROCK-A-BILLY – *Guy Mitchell* (-) 1957
ROCK-A-HULA BABY – *Elvis Presley* (1) 1962
ROCKET – *Mud* (7) 1974
ROCKET MAN – *Elton John* (6) 1972
ROCKIN' ALL OVER THE WORLD – *Status Quo* (1) 1977
ROCKIN' AROUND THE CHRISTMAS TREE – *Brenda Lee* (4) 1962
ROCKIN' GOOSE • – *Johnny and the Hurricanes* (4) 1960
ROCKIN' THROUGH THE RYE – *Bill Haley and the Comets* (-) 1956
RODRIGO'S GUITAR CONCERTO DE ARAN JUEZ (Theme From 2nd Movement) •
– *Manuel and The Music Of The Mountains* (4) 1976
ROMANO – *Geraldine* (4) 1977
ROMEO – *Petula Clark* (2) 1961
ROMPIN' AND STOMPIN' – *Freddie Bell and the Bell Boys* (-) 1957
ROONEY – *Michael Holliday* (-) 1958
ROSE GARDEN – *Lynn Anderson* (1) 1971
A ROSE HAS TO DIE – *The Dooleys* (9) 1978
ROSE MARIE – *Slim Whitman* (-) 1955
ROSE OF ALLENDALE – Johnny McEvoy (6) 1975
ROSE OF MORAY – *Johnny McEvoy* (6) 1974
ROSES ARE RED – *Ronnie Carroll* (7) 1962
ROSES ARE RED (My Love) – *Bobby Vinton* (2) 1962
ROSIE – *Don Partridge* (8) 1968
ROUND AND AROUND – *Dickie Rock and the Miami Showband* (2) 1965
ROUND THE GUM TREE – *Real McCoy* (9) 1969
ROULETTE • – *Russ Conway* (1) 1959
THE ROUSSOS PHENOMENON EP – *Demis Roussos* (4) 1976
RUBBER BALL – *Bobby Vee* (2) 1961
RUBBER BULLETS – *10cc* (1) 1973
RUBY (DON'T TAKE YOUR LOVE TO TOWN) – *Kenny Rogers and the First Edition* (4) 1969

Title – *Act* (Position) Year of Chart Entry

RUBY TUESDAY – *Rolling Stones* (6) 1967
RUN FOR HOME – *Lindisfarne* (4) 1978
RUN TO ME – *Bee Gees* (7) 1972
RUNAROUND SUE – *Doug Sheldon* (8) 1961
RUNAWAY – *Del Shannon* (2) 1961
RUNNING BEAR – *Johnny Preston* (1) 1960

SAD SWEET DREAMER – *Sweet Sensation* (3) 1974
SAFELY IN LOVE AGAIN – *Art Supple and the Victors* (8) 1966
SAIL ALONG SILVERY MOON • – *Billy Vaughn and his Orchestra* (-) 1958
SAIL ON – *The Commodores* (7) 1979
SAILING – *Rod Stewart* (1) 1975
SAILOR – *Petula Clark* (2) 1961
SAILOR BOY – *Brendan Shine* (8) 1971
ST THERESE OF THE ROSES – *Malcolm Vaughan* (-) 1956
THE SAINTS ROCK 'N' ROLL – *Bill Haley and the Comets* (-) 1956
SALLY SUNSHINE – *Brendan O'Brien and the Dixies* (8) 1971
SALUTE TO ELVIS – *Cahir O'Doherty* (6) 1977
SAM – *Olivia Newton John* (1) 1977
THE SAME OLD SONG – *Brendan Bowyer and the Royal Showband* (9) 1968
SAN BERNADINO – *Christie* (4) 1970
SAN FRANCISCO (BE SURE TO WEAR SOME FLOWERS IN YOUR HAIR) – *Scott McKenzie* (1) ... 1967
SANDY – *John Travolta* (1) 1978
SANTO NATALE – *Shay O'Hara and the Royal Blues* (8) 1966
SAVE ME – *Dave Dee, Dozy, Beaky, Mick and Tich* (4) 1967
SAVE THE LAST DANCE FOR ME – *The Drifters* (1) 1960
SAVE THE LAST DANCE FOR ME – *Brendan O'Brien and the Dixies* (9) 1966
SAVE YOUR KISSES FOR ME – *Brotherhood Of Man* (1) 1976
SAVED BY THE BELL – *Robin Gibb* (1) 1969
SAY, HAS ANYBODY SEEN MY SWEET GYPSY ROSE – *Dawn featuring Tony Orlando* (8) 1973
SAY WONDERFUL THINGS – *Ronnie Carroll* (6) 1963
SAY YOU DON'T MIND – *Colin Blunstone* (10) 1972
SCARLETT O'HARA • – *Jet Harris and Tony Meehan* (7) 1963
SCHOOL'S OUT – *Alice Cooper* (2) 1972
THE SEA AROUND US – *The Ludlows* (1) 1966
SEA OF HEARTBREAK – *Don Gibson* (6) 1961
SEA OF LOVE – *Marty Wilde* (8) 1959

Title – *Act* (Position) Year of Chart Entry

SEASONS IN THE SUN – *Terry Jacks* (1)....1974
SECOND HAND FLOWERS – *Ray Lynam and the Hillbillies* (2)....1974
SECRET LOVE – *Kathy Kirby* (7)....1963
THE SECRETS THAT YOU KEEP – *Mud* (3)....1975
SEE EMILY PLAY – *Pink Floyd* (10)....1967
SEE MY BABY JIVE – *Wizzard* (1)....1973
SEMI-DETACHED SURBURBAN MR JAMES – *Manfred Mann* (5)....1966
SEND IN THE CLOWNS – *Judy Collins* (3)....1975
SEND ME THE PILLOW YOU DREAM ON – *Johnny Tillotson* (7)....1962
SEPTEMBER – *Earth Wind & Fire* (8)....1979
SEPTEMBER LOVE • – *Tommy Rogers and his Ballroom Orchestra* (-)....1956
SERENADE – *Slim Whitman* (-)....1956
SEVEN DRUNKEN NIGHTS – *The Dubliners* (1)....1967
SEVEN LITTLE GIRLS SITTING IN THE BACK SEAT – *The Avons* (2)....1959
SHA LA LA – *Manfred Mann* (4).... 1964
SHAKE RATTLE AND ROLL – *Bill Haley and the Comets* (-)....1955
SHAKE YOUR BODY (Down To The Ground) – *Jacksons* (9)....1979
SHAKIN' ALL OVER – *Johnny Kidd and the Pirates* (3)....1960
SHAMROCK FROM GLENORE – *Margo and the Country Folk* (2)....1973
SHAZAM! • – *Duane Eddy* (3)....1960
SH-BOOM – *The Crewcuts* (-)....1954
SH-BOOM – *Stan Freberg* (-)....1954
SHE – *Charles Aznavour* (1)....1974
SHE LOVES YOU – *The Beatles* (2)....1963
SHE WEARS MY RING – *Sean Fagan and the Pacific Showband* (3).... 1964
SHE'D RATHER BE WITH ME – *The Turtles* (3)....1967
SHEILA – *Tommy Roe* (3)....1962
SHE'S IN LOVE WITH YOU – *Suzi Quatro* (5)....1979
SHE'S NOT THERE – *Santana* (4).... 1977
SHE'S NOT YOU – *Elvis Presley* (1)....1962
SHE'S SO MODERN – *Boomtown Rats* (10)....1978
THE SHIFTING WHISPERING SANDS – *Eamonn Andrews* (-)....1956
THE SHIFTING WHISPERING SANDS – *Billy Vaughn and his Orchestra* (-)....1955
SHINE A LITTLE LOVE – *Electric Light Orchestra* (4)....1979
SHINDIG • – *The Shadows* (7)....1963
THE SHORES OF AMERIKAY – *The Broadsiders* (7)....1967
THE SHORES OF AMERIKAY – *Dermot Hegarty* (4)....1967

Title – *Act* (Position) Year of Chart Entry

THE SHORES OF LOUGH BRAN – *Pat Ely and the Rocky Tops* (5) 1973
SHOW ME YOU'RE A WOMAN – *Mud* (2) 1976
THE SHOW MUST GO ON – *Leo Sayer* (3) 1974
SHOW YOU THE WAY TO GO – *The Jacksons* (5) 1977
SHOWBALL CRAZY – *The Hoedowners, Commentary by Michael O'Hehir* (2) 1966
SHOWBANDS ON PARADE – *Art Supple and the Victors* (9) 1965
THE SHUFFLE – *Van McCoy* (6) 1977
SIDE SADDLE • – *Russ Conway* (2) 1959
SILENCE IS GOLDEN – *The Tremeloes* (1) 1967
SILENT NIGHT – *Joe Dolan* (2) 1979
SILHOUETTES – *Herman's Hermits* (5) 1965
SILLY LOVE SONGS – *Wings* (1) 1976
SILVER LADY – *David Soul* (1) 1977
SILVER MOON – *Top League featuring Shaun O'Dowd* (9) 1974
SIMON SAYS – *1910 Fruitgum Company* (5) 1968
SIMON SAYS – *Dickie Rock and the Miami* (1) 1968
SIMPLE SONG OF LOVE – *Larry Hogan* (9) 1974
SINCE YOU'VE BEEN GONE – *Rainbow* (5) 1979
SING BABY SING – *The Stylistics* (5) 1975
SING LITTLE BIRDIE – *Teddy Johnson and Pearl Carr* (4) 1959
SING IRISHMEN SING – *Barleycorn* (4) 1973
SING ME – *The Brothers* (4) 1977
SINGING THE BLUES – *Guy Mitchell* (-) 1956
SINGING THE BLUES – *Tommy Steele* (-) 1957
SISTER JANE – *New World* (2) 1972
SISTER MARY – *Joe Dolan* (1) 1976
SIXTEEN BARS – *The Stylistics* (9) 1976
SIXTEEN REASONS – *Connie Stevens* (5) 1960
SIXTEEN TONS – *Frankie Laine* (-) 1956
SKWEEZE ME PLEEZE ME – *Slade* (1) 1973
SKIBBEREEN – *Dermot O'Brien* (10) 1976
SKY HIGH – *Jigsaw* (9) 1975
SLANEY VALLEY – *Larry Cunningham* (1) 1971
SLATTERY'S MOUNTED FUT – *Michael O'Duffy* (-) 1957
SLEEPY JOE – *Herman's Hermits* (9) 1968
SLOOP JOHN B – *The Beach Boys* (2) 1966
SLOWLY WITH FEELING – *Ruby Murray* (-) 1956

Title – *Act* (Position) Year of Chart Entry

SMILE – *Nat King Cole* (-)....1954
SMOKE GETS IN YOUR EYES – *The Platters* (3)....1959
THE SMURF SONG – *Father Abraham and The Smurfs* (5)....1978
SNOOPY VS THE RED BARON – *Hot Shots* (10)....1973
SNOWCOACH ♦ – *Russ Conway* (7)....1959
SNOWFLAKE – *Larry Cunningham and the Mighty Avons* (2)....1966
THE SNOWY BREASTED PEARL – Wolfe Tones (7).... 1972
SO DO I – *Kenny Ball and his Jazzmen* (10)....1962
SO LONG BABY – *Del Shannon* (9)....1962
SO MANY WAYS – *Butch Moore and the Capitols* (5)....1965
SO SAD (TO WATCH GOOD LOVE GO BAD) – *Everly Brothers* (3)....1960
SO YOU WIN AGAIN – *Hot Chocolate* (2).... 1977
SOFTLY AS I LEAVE YOU – *Matt Monro* (7)....1962
SOFTLY SOFTLY – *Ruby Murray* (-)....1955
SOFTLY WHISPERING I LOVE YOU – *Congregation* (7).... 1972
SOLDIER BLUE – Buffy Sainte Marie (4)....1971
SOLID GOLD EASY ACTION – *T Rex* (4).... 1972
SOLITAIRE – *Andy Williams* (3)....1974
SOME BROKEN HEARTS NEVER MEND – *Brendan Shine* (5).... 1977
SOME GIRLS – *Racey* (2)....1979
SOME KIND-A EARTHQUAKE ♦ – *Duane Eddy and the Rebels* (3)....1959
SOMEBODY DONE SOMEBODY WRONG SONG – *Tony Kenny* (10)....1975
SOMEBODY HELP ME – *Spencer Davis Group* (5)....1966
SOMEBODY TO LOVE – *Queen* (6)....1976
SOMEONE – *Johnny Mathis* (7)....1959
SOMEONE SOMEONE – *Brian Poole and the Tremeloes* (2).... 1964
SOMEONE ELSE'S LAND – *The Swarbriggs* (5).... 1977
SOMETHIN' STUPID – *Nancy Sinatra and Frank Sinatra* (1)....1967
SOMETHING – *The Beatles* (9)....1970
SOMETHING ELSE – *Sex Pistols* (8)....1979
SOMETHING HERE IN MY HEART (KEEPS A-TELLIN' ME NO) – *The Paper Dolls* (9)....1968
SOMETHING IN THE AIR – *Thunderclap Newman* (2)....1969
SOMETHING TELLS ME (Something Is Gonna Happen Tonight) – *Cilla Black* (3)....1971
SOMETHING'S BURNING – *Kenny Rogers and the First Edition* (10)....1970
SOMETHING'S HAPPENING – *Herman's Hermits* (5)....1969
SOMETIMES – *Red Hurley and the Nevada* (1)....1971
SOMETIMES WHEN WE TOUCH – *Dan Hill* (6)....1978

Title – *Act* (Position) Year of Chart Entry

SOMEWHERE MY LOVE – *Charlie Matthews and the Royal Showband* (1) 1966
SOMEWHERE SOMEBODY'S WAITING – *Danny Doyle* (8) 1976
THE SON OF HICKORY HOLLER'S TRAMP – *O. C. Smith* (2) 1968
SON OF MY FATHER – *Chickory Tip* (3) 1972
SONG FOR GUY – *Elton John* (7) 1979
SONG OF THE KING – *Cahir O'Doherty* (4) 1974
SORROW – *The Merseys* (7) 1966
SORROW – *David Bowie* (2) 1973
SORRY I'M A LADY – *Baccara* (4) 1978
SORRY SEEMS TO BE THE HARDEST WORD – *Elton John* (3) 1976
SORRY SUZANNE – *The Hollies* (4) 1969
S.O.S. – *Abba* (4) 1975
THE SOUND OF SILENCE – *The Bachelors* (9) 1966
SOUTHERN NIGHTS – *Glen Campbell* (2) 1977
SPACE ODDITY – *David Bowie* (3) 1975
A SPACEMAN CAME TRAVELLING – *Chris De Burgh* (3) 1977
SPANCIL HILL – *Dermot O'Brien* (3) 1974
SPANISH HARLEM – *Jimmy Justice* (4) 1962
SPEAK TO ME PRETTY – *Brenda Lee* (8) 1962
THE SPECIAL YEARS – *Val Doonican* (2) 1965
SPEEDY GONZALES – *Pat Boone* (4) 1962
THE SPINNING WHEEL – *Rose Brennan* (-) 1955
SPIRIT IN THE SKY – *Norman Greenbaum* (1) 1970
THE STAIRWAY OF LOVE – *Terry Dene* (-) 1958
THE STAIRWAY OF LOVE – *Michael Holliday* (-) 1958
STAND BY YOUR MAN – *Tammy Wynette* (1) 1975
STANDING ON THE CORNER – *The King Brothers* (3) 1960
STAR ON A TV SHOW – The Stylistics (8) 1975
STAR WARS THEME -CANTINA BAND • – *Meco* (3) 1977
STARDUST (a) – *Nat King Cole* (-) 1957
STARDUST (b) – *David Essex* (3) 1975
STARRY EYED – *Michael Holliday* (3) 1960
START MOVIN' (IN MY DIRECTION) – *Sal Mineo* (-) 1957
STAYIN' ALIVE – *Bee Gees* (4) 1978
A STEEL GUITAR AND A GLASS OF WINE – *Paul Anka* (9) 1962
STEP INTO A DREAM – *White Plains* (9) 1973
STEP IT OUT MARY – *Danny Doyle* (4) 1967

Title – *Act* (Position) Year of Chart Entry

STEPPING ASIDE IS EASY – *Red Hurley* (9) 1979
STILL (a) – *Karl Denver* (3) 1963
STILL (b) – *The Commodores* (3) 1979
STOOD UP – *Ricky Nelson* (-) 1958
STOP STOP STOP – *The Hollies* (5) 1966
STORM IN A TEACUP – *The Fortunes* (9) 1972
THE STORY OF MY LIFE – *Michael Holliday* (-) 1958
THE STORY OF MY LIFE – *Dave King* (-) 1958
STRANGE LADY IN TOWN – *Frankie Laine* (-) 1955
STRANGER IN PARADISE – *Tony Bennett* (-) 1955
STRANGER IN PARADISE – *Bing Crosby* (-) 1955
STRANGER IN PARADISE – *Doretta Morrow and Richard Kiley* (-) 1955
STRANGER ON THE SHORE • – *Mr Acker Bilk* (1) 1961
STRANGERS IN THE NIGHT – *Frank Sinatra* (1) 1966
STRAWBERRY FAIR – *Anthony Newley* (7) 1960
THE STREAK – *Ray Stevens* (2) 1974
STREETS OF BALTIMORE – *Capitol Showband featuring Des Kelly* (3) 1967
STREETS OF LONDON – *Ralph McTell* (1) 1975
STUCK ON YOU – *Elvis Presley* (3) 1960
SUBSTITUTE – *Clout* (1) 1978
SUCH A NIGHT – *Elvis Presley* (9) 1964
SUCU SUCU • – *Laurie Johnson Orchestra* (6) 1961
SUDDENLY YOU LOVE ME – *The Tremeloes* (9) 1968
SUFFER LITTLE CHILDREN – *Canon Sydney MacEwan and the Cork Children's Choir* (3) 1973
SUGAR AND SPICE – *The Searchers* (6) 1963
SUGAR BABY LOVE – *The Rubettes* (3) 1974
SUGAR CANDY KISSES – *Mac and Katie Kissoon* (2) 1975
SUGAR MOON – *Pat Boone* (-) 1958
SUGAR SUGAR – *The Archies* (1) 1969
SUGARTIME – *Alma Cogan* (-) 1958
SULTANS OF SWING – *Dire Straits* (6) 1979
SUMMER HOLIDAY – *Cliff Richard and the Shadows* (2) 1963
SUMMER NIGHT CITY – *Abba* (1) 1978
SUMMER NIGHTS – *John Travolta and Olivia Newton John* (1) 1978
SUMMER OF MY LIFE – *Simon May* (4) 1976
SUMMER SET • – *Mr Acker Bilk and his Paramount Jazz Band* (3) 1960
SUMMERLOVE SENSATION – *Bay City Rollers* (5) 1974

Title – *Act* (Position) Year of Chart Entry

SUMMERTIME CITY – *Mike Batt with The New Edition* (4) 1975
SUMMERTIME IN VENICE – *Rossano Brazzi* (-) 1956
SUMMERTIME IN VENICE • – *Ron Goodwin* (-) 1956
THE SUN AIN'T GONNA SHINE ANYMORE – *Walker Brothers* (5) 1966
SUNDAY BLOODY SUNDAY – *The Paddy Wagon* (1) 1972
SUNDAY GIRL – *Blondie* (1) 1979
SUNDAY MONDAY TUESDAY – *Dana* (4) 1973
SUNDAY SCHOOL TO BROADWAY – *Geraldine* (7) 1978
SUNNY – *Boney M* (4) 1977
SUNNY AFTERNOON – *The Kinks* (1) 1966
SUNNYSIDE OF THE MOUNTAIN – *John Glenn and the Mainliners* (5) 1975
SUNSET YEARS OF LIFE – *Big Tom and the Mainliners* (3) 1970
SUNSHINE AFTER THE RAIN – *Elkie Brooks* (7) 1977
SUNSHINE GIRL – *Herman's Hermits* (3) 1968
SUNSHINE SUPERMAN – *Donovan* (3) 1967
SURRENDER – *Elvis Presley* (1) 1961
SURROUND YOURSELF WITH SORROW – *Cilla Black* (5) 1969
SUSPICIOUS MINDS – *Elvis Presley* (2) 1969
SWEET CAROLINE – *Neil Diamond* (7) 1971
SWEET LITTLE ROCK 'N' ROLLER – *Showaddywaddy* (9) 1979
SWEET NUTHIN'S – *Brenda Lee* (2) 1960
SWEET TALKIN' WOMAN – *Electric Light Orchestra* (6) 1978
SWEETS FOR MY SWEET – *The Searchers* (1) 1963
SWING YOUR DADDY – *Jim Gilstrap* (10) 1975
SWINGIN' SHEPHERD BLUES • – *Ted Heath and his Music* (-) 1958
SWINGING ON A STAR – *Big Dee Irwin* (2) 1964
THE SWISS MAID – *Del Shannon* (3) 1962
SYLVIA – *Focus* (9) 1973
SYLVIA'S MOTHER – *Dr Hook and the Medicine Show* (1) 1972

TAKE A CHANCE ON ME – *Abba* (1) 1978
TAKE ME BAK 'OME – *Slade* (4) 1972
TAKE GOOD CARE OF HER – *Adam Wade* (9) 1961
TAKE GOOD CARE OF MY BABY – *Bobby Vee* (9) 1961
TAKE GOOD CARE OF YOURSELF – *Three Degrees* (8) 1975
TAKE ME HOME COUNTRY ROADS – *Olivia Newton John* (5) 1973
TAKE ME TO THE MARDI GRAS – *Paul Simon* (10) 1973

Title – *Act* (Position) Year of Chart Entry

TAKE THESE CHAINS FROM MY HEART – *Ray Charles* (2) 1963
TALKING IN MY SLEEP – *Crystal Gayle* (5) 1978
TAR AND CEMENT – *Joe Dolan* (3) 1967
TAXES BY THE SCORE – *Tommy Drennan and the Monarchs* (8) 1971
TEACHER'S PET – *Doris Day* (-) 1958
TEARS – *Ken Dodd* (1) 1965
THE TEARS I CRIED – *Glitter Band* (7) 1975
TEARS OF A CLOWN – Smokey Robinson and The Miracles (3) 1970
TEARS ON MY PILLOW – *Johnny Nash* (1) 1975
TEDDY BEAR SONG – *Mary Lou and Harvest* (10) 1973
TEEN BEAT • – *Sandy Nelson* (7) 1960
TEENAGE DREAM – *Marty Robbins* (-) 1957
TEENAGE RAMPAGE – *Sweet* (1) 1974
A TEENAGER IN LOVE – *Dion and the Belmonts* (1) 1959
A TEENAGER IN LOVE – *Dickie Valentine* (7) 1959
TELEGRAM SAM – *T Rex* (1) 1972
TELEPHONE MAN – *Meri Wilson* (9) 1977
TELL LAURA I LOVE HER – *Ray Peterson* (7) 1960
TELL LAURA I LOVE HER – *Ricky Valance* (7) 1960
TELL ME WHAT HE SAID – *Helen Shapiro* (2) 1962
TELSTAR • – *The Tornados* (1) 1962
TEMMA HARBOUR – *Mary Hopkin* (3) 1970
TEMPTATION – *Everly Brothers* (3) 1961
TENNESSEE SPECIAL – *Red Hurley* (8) 1976
TERESA – *Joe Dolan* (1) 1969
THANK YOU ELVIS – *Brendan Bowyer* (4) 1977
THANKS FOR THE MEMORIES – *Danny Doyle* (2) 1974
THANKS FOR THE MEMORY (WHAM BAM THANK YOU MAM) – *Slade* (3) 1975
THAT SAME OLD FEELING – *Pickettywitch* (6) 1970
THAT'S MY HOME – *Mr Acker Bilk and his Paramount Band* (10) 1961
THAT'S WHAT FRIENDS ARE FOR – *The Swarbriggs* (2) 1975
THAT'S WHAT LOVE WILL DO – *Joe Brown and the Bruvvers* (2) 1963
THEME FOR A DREAM – *Cliff Richard and the Shadows* (3) 1961
THEME FROM DIXIE • – *Duane Eddy* (4) 1961
THEME FROM 'THE DEERHUNTER' (CAVATINA) • – *The Shadows* (8) 1979
THEME FROM THE LEGION'S LAST PATROL • – *Ken Thorne Orchestra* (4) 1963
THEME FROM THE THREEPENNY OPERA – *Louis Armstrong* (-) 1956

Title – *Act* (Position) Year of Chart Entry

THEME FROM THE THREEPENNY OPERA • – *Joe Mr Piano Henderson* (-) 1956
THEME FROM THE THREEPENNY OPERA • – *Norrie Paramor* (-) 1956
THEN HE KISSED ME – *The Crystals* (3) 1963
THEN I KISSED HER – *The Beach Boys* (4) 1967
THERE ARE MORE QUESTIONS THAN ANSWERS – *Johnny Nash* (6) 1972
THERE GOES MY EVERYTHING – *Engelbert Humperdinck* (2) 1967
THERE GOES MY FIRST LOVE – *The Drifters* (2) 1975
THERE IS A MOUNTAIN – *Donovan* (9) 1967
THERE WAS A DREAM – *Colm Wilkinson* (2) 1977
THERE'S A GOLDMINE IN THE SKY – *Pat Boone* (-) 1957
THERE'S A HEARTACHE FOLLOWING ME – *Jim Reeves* (3) 1964
THERE'S A KIND OF HUSH – *Herman's Hermits* (7) 1967
THERE'S ALWAYS ME – *Dickie Rock and the Miami Showband* (1) 1963
(THERE'S) ALWAYS SOMETHING THERE TO REMIND ME – *Sandie Shaw* (7) 1964
THERE'S AN ISLAND IN THE SUN – *Sean Dunphy and Hoedowners* (10) 1972
THERE'S A WHOLE LOT OF LOVING – *Guys and Dolls* (2) 1975
THERE'S THAT SMILE AGAIN – *Larry Cunningham & the Mighty Avons* (5) 1965
THESE ARE MY MOUNTAINS – *Brian Coll* (3) 1971
THESE BOOTS ARE MADE FOR WALKIN' –*Nancy Sinatra* (1) 1966
(THEY LONG TO BE) CLOSE TO YOU – *The Carpenters* (6) 1970
THEY WERE DOING THE MAMBO – *Vaughn Monroe* (-) 1954
A THING CALLED LOVE – *Johnny Cash* (1) 1972
THINGS – *Bobby Darin* (2) 1962
THINKIN' OF A RENDEVOUZ – *Roly Daniels* (10) 1977
THIS GUY'S IN LOVE WITH YOU – *Herb Alpert and the Tijuana Brass* (8) 1968
THIS IS IT – *Jim Tobin and The Firehouse* (5) 1970
THIS LITTLE BIRD – *Marianne Faithfull* (9) 1965
THIS IS MY SONG – *Petula Clark* (1) 1967
THIS OLD HEART OF MINE – *Rod Stewart* (3) 1975
THIS OLE HOUSE – *Billie Anthony* (-) 1954
THIS OLE HOUSE – *Rosemary Clooney* (-) 1954
THIS TIME – *Troy Shondell* (7) 1961
THIS TIME OF THE YEAR – *Larry Cunningham* (3) 1974
THIS WORLD IS NOT MY HOME – *Jim Reeves* (10) 1964
THOSE WERE THE DAYS – *Mary Hopkin* (1) 1968
THE THREE BELLS – *The Browns* (2) 1959
THREE COINS IN A FOUNTAIN – *Frank Sinatra* (-) 1954

Title – *Act* (Position) Year of Chart Entry

THREE LEAF SHAMROCK – *Hugo Duncan and the Tall Men* (7) 1972
THREE LEAF SHAMROCK – *John Kerr* (1) 1972
THREE SCORE AND TEN – *Johnny McEvoy* (6) 1971
THREE STARS – *Tommy Dee and the Teen Tones* (5) 1959
THREE STEPS TO HEAVEN – *Eddie Cochran* (1) 1960
THREE STEPS TO HEAVEN – *Showaddywaddy* (1) 1975
THREE STEPS TO THE PHONE – *Larry Cunningham & the Mighty Avons* (8) 1967
THREE TIMES A LADY – *The Commodores* (1) 1978
THROW DOWN A LINE – *Cliff and Hank* (8) 1969
THROW A LITTLE LOVING – *Roly Daniels & the Jim Farley Showband* (9) 1966
TICKET TO RIDE – *The Beatles* (1) 1965
TIE A YELLOW RIBBON ROUND THE OLE OAK TREE – *Dawn featuring Tony Orlando* (1) 1973
TIE ME KANGAROO DOWN SPORT – *Rolf Harris* (9) 1960
TIGER FEET – *Mud* (1) 1974
('TIL) I KISSED YOU – *The Everly Brothers* (6) 1959
TILL – *Tom Jones* (4) 1971
TILL – *Dickie Rock* (9) 1972
THE TIME HAS COME – *Adam Faith* (2) 1961
TIRED OF WAITING FOR YOU – *The Kinks* (3) 1965
TO KNOW HIM IS TO LOVE HIM – *The Teddy Bears* (4) 1959
TO KNOW YOU IS TO LOVE YOU – *Peter and Gordon* (5) 1965
TO WHOM IT CONCERNS – *Chris Andrews* (9) 1966
TOGETHER – *Connie Francis* (7) 1961
TOGETHER AGAIN – *Brendan O'Brien and the Dixies* (4) 1966
TOKYO MELODY • – *Helmut Zacharias and his Orchestra* (8) 1964
TOM TOM TURN AROUND – *New World* (3) 1971
TOMBOY – *Perry Como* (8) 1959
TONIGHT'S THE NIGHT – *Rod Stewart* (4) 1976
TOO MUCH HEAVEN – *Bee Gees* (2) 1978
TOO MUCH, TOO LITTLE, TOO LATE – *Johnny Mathis and Denice Williams* (2) 1978
TOO SOON TO KNOW – *Roy Orbison* (4) 1966
TOO YOUNG – *Donny Osmond* (2) 1972
TOO YOUNG TO GO STEADY – *Patti Page* (-) 1956
TOOR-A-LOOR-A-LOOR E.P. – *Horslips* (9) 1978
TOP OF THE WORLD – *The Carpenters* (3) 1973
TORN BETWEEN TWO LOVERS – Mary McGregor (5) 1977
TOSSING AND TURNING – *The Ivy League* (2) 1965

Title – *Act* (Position) Year of Chart Entry

TOWER OF STRENGTH – *Frankie Vaughan* (1) 1961
THE TOWN I LOVED SO WELL – *Paddy Reilly* (5) 1974
TRACY – *The Cuff Links* (6) 1970
TRAGEDY – *Bee Gees* (1) 1979
THE TRAIL OF THE LONESOME PINE – *Laurel and Hardy with the Avalon Boys featuring Chill Wills* (10) 1975
TRAINS AND BOATS AND PLANES – *Burt Bacharach his Orchestra and Chorus* (7) 1965
TRAVELIN' BAND – *Creedence Clearwater Revival* (8) 1970
TRAVELLIN' HOME – *Vera Lynn* (-) 1957
TRAVELLIN' LIGHT – *Cliff Richard and the Shadows* (1) 1959
THE TRAVELLING PEOPLE – *The Johnstons* (1) 1966
TREAT ME DAUGHTER KINDLY – *Pat Lynch and the Airchords* (1) 1967
TRIBUTE TO JIM REEVES – *Larry Cunningham and the Mighty Avons* (9) 1965
TRUE LOVE – *Bing Crosby and Grace Kelly* (-) 1957
TRUE LOVE WAYS – *Peter and Gordon* (4) 1965
TURN OUT THE LIGHT – *Brendan Shine* (1) 1976
TWEEDLE DEE – *Little Jimmy Osmond* (6) 1973
TWEEDLE DEE TWEEDLE DUM – *Middle Of The Road* (2) 1971
THE TWELFTH OF NEVER – *Donny Osmond* (3) 1973
TWENTY FOUR HOURS FROM TULSA – *Gene Pitney* (5) 1964
TWENTY ONE YEARS – *Dermot Hegarty and the Plainsmen* (1) 1970
TWENTY TINY FINGERS – *The Stargazers* (-) 1955
TWILIGHT TIME – *The Platters* (-) 1958
TWIST AND SHOUT – *Brian Poole and the Tremeloes* (3) 1963
TWISTIN' THE NIGHT AWAY – *Sam Cooke* (6) 1962
TWO KINDS OF TEARDROPS – *Del Shannon* (9) 1963
TWO LITTLE BOYS – *Rolf Harris* (1) 1969
TWO LOVES – *Sean Dunphy and the Hoedowners* (2) 1968
TWO OF A KIND E.P. – *Joe Dolan and the Drifters* (10) 1966
TWO OF THE USUAL – *Hugo Duncan and the Tall Men* (10) 1973

UN BANC, UN ABRE, UNE RUE – *Severine* (3) 1971
UNCHAIN MY HEART – *Slim Whitman* (-) 1958
UNCHAINED MELODY – *Roy Hamilton* (-) 1955
UNCHAINED MELODY – *Jimmy Young* (-) 1955
UNDER THE BRIDGES OF PARIS – *Eartha Kitt* (-) 1955
UNDER THE BRIDGES OF PARIS – *Dean Martin* (-) 1955

Title – *Act* (Position) Year of Chart Entry

UNDER THE MOON OF LOVE – *Showaddywaddy* (6) 1976
THE UNICORN – *The Irish Rovers* (5) 1968
UP ABOVE MY HEAD, I HEAR MUSIC IN THE AIR – *Frankie Laine and Johnnie Ray* (-) 1957
UP AROUND THE BEND – *Creedence Clearwater Revival* (3) 1970
UP THE JUNCTION – *Squeeze* (10) 1979
UP TOWN TOP RANKING – *Althia and Donna* (2) 1978
UP AND AWAY (The Helicopter Song) – *Wolfe Tones* (1) 1973
UP WENT NELSON – *The Go Lucky Four* (2) 1966

VALLERI – *The Monkees* (8) 1968
VENUS (a) – *Frankie Avalon* (5) 1959
VENUS (a) – *Dickie Valentine* (6) 1959
VENUS (b) – *Shocking Blue* (10) 1970
VENUS IN BLUE JEANS – *Mark Wynter* (5) 1962
THE VERY FIRST CHRISTMAS OF ALL – *Ruby Murray* (-) 1955
VIDEO KILLED THE RADIO STAR – *Buggles* (1) 1979
VILLAGE OF ST BERNADETTE – *Anne Shelton* (3) 1959
VINCENT – *Don McLean* (1) 1972
VISIONS – *Cliff Richard* (9) 1966
A VISIT TO SANTA – *Brendan Grace* (3) 1974
VIVA BOBBY JOE – *The Equals* (3) 1969
VIVA ESPANA – *Sylvia* (6) 1974
VIVA IL PAPA – *Caitriona Walsh* (1) 1979
VIVA LAS VEGAS – *Elvis Presley* (8) 1964
A VOICE IN THE WILDERNESS – *Cliff Richard and the Shadows* (1) 1960
VOODOO CHILE – *Jimi Hendrix Experience* (10) 1970
VOULEZ VOUS – *Abba* (3) 1979

THE WAGES OF LOVE – *Muriel Day* (1) 1969
WAIT A LITTLE LONGER PLEASE JESUS – *Philomena Begley and the Ramblin' Men* (5) 1974
WAIT AND SEE – *Fats Domino* (-) 1958
WAITING FOR AN ALIBI – *Thin Lizzy* (6) 1979
WAKE UP LITTLE SUSIE – *The Everly Brothers* (-) 1957
WAKE UP LITTLE SUSIE – *The King Brothers* (-) 1957
WAGES OF LOVE – *Muriel Day* (1) 1969
WALK AWAY – *Matt Monro* (3) 1964
WALK AWAY RENEE – *The Four Tops* (5) 1968

Title – *Act* (Position) Year of Chart Entry

WALK DON'T RUN • – *The John Barry Seven* (8) 1960
WALK HAND IN HAND – *Vera Lynn* (-) 1956
WALK HAND IN HAND – *Tony Martin* (-) 1956
WALK IN LOVE – *Manhattan Transfer* (5) 1978
A WALK IN THE BLACK FOREST • – *Horst Jankowski his Orchestra and Chorus* (10) 1965
WALK ON BY – *Leroy Van Dyke* (3) 1962
WALK RIGHT BACK – *Everly Brothers* (2) 1961
WALK TALL – *Val Doonican* (2) 1964
WALKIN' BACK TO HAPPINESS – *Helen Shapiro* (1) 1961
WALKING ON THE MOON – *Police* (1) 1979
WALKING THE STREETS IN THE RAIN – *Butch Moore* (1) 1965
WALL STREET SHUFFLE – *10cc* (9) 1974
WANDERIN' EYES – *Charlie Gracie* (-) 1957
WAND'RIN' STAR – *Lee Marvin* (1) 1970
WANTED – *The Dooleys* (3) 1979
WAR – *Edwin Starr* (5) 1970
WATERLOO – *Abba* (1) 1974
WATERLOO SUNSET – *The Kinks* (3) 1967
WAXIES DARGLE – *Sweeney's Men* (5) 1968
WAY DOWN – *Elvis Presley* (1) 1977
WAY DOWN YONDER IN NEW ORLEANS – *Freddy Cannon* (3) 1960
THE WAY IT USED TO BE – *Engelbert Humperdinck* (6) 1969
A WAY OF LIFE – *Family Dogg* (6) 1969
WAY OUT OF REACH – *Eddie Mack and the Columbia Showband* (6) 1966
THE WAYWARD WIND – *Tex Ritter* (-) 1956
THE WAYWARD WIND – *Frank Ifield* (3) 1963
WE ARE THE CHAMPIONS – *Queen* (3) 1977
WE CAN WORK IT OUT – *The Beatles* (1) 1965
WE COULD – *Sonny Knowles and the Pacific Showband* (6) 1965
WE DO IT – *R and J Stone* (9) 1976
WE DON'T TALK ANYMORE – *Cliff Richard* (1) 1979
THE WEDDING – *Pat McGeegan and the Big Four* (7) 1963
THE WEDDING – *Julie Rogers* (10) 1964
THE WEDDING SONG – *Cotton Mill Boys* (9) 1976
THE WEDDING SONG – *Kelley and The Nevada* (3) 1974
WELCOME HOME – *Peters and Lee* (1) 1973
WELCOME JOHN PAUL – Jim Tobin (1) 1979

Title – *Act* (Position) Year of Chart Entry

WELCOME TO MY WORLD – *Jim Reeves* (1) 1963
WELL I ASK YOU – *Eden Kane* (1) 1961
WE'RE ALL ALONE – *Rita Coolidge* (6) 1977
WE'RE GONNA GO FISHIN' – *Hank Locklin* (8) 1962
WE'VE GOTTA GET OUT OF THIS PLACE – *The Animals* (5) 1965
WHAT A DIFFERENCE A DAY MAKES – *Esther Phillips* (8) 1975
WHAT A WONDERFUL WORLD – *Louis Armstrong* (2) 1968
WHAT ARE YOU DOING SUNDAY – *Dawn featuring Tony Orlando* (1) 1971
WHAT DO I DO – *The Dixies with Sandie and Joe* (1) 1972
WHAT DO YOU WANT? – *Adam Faith* (1) 1959
WHAT DO YOU WANT TO MAKE THOSE EYES AT ME FOR – *Emile Ford and the Checkmates* (1) .. 1959
WHAT I'VE GOT IN MIND – *Billie Jo Spears* (4) 1976
WHAT IN THE WORLD'S COME OVER YOU – *Jack Scott* (10) 1960
WHAT WOULD I BE – *Val Doonican* (3) 1966
WHAT'D I SAY – *Jerry Lee Lewis* (3) 1961
WHATEVER WILL BE WILL BE (Que Sera Sera) – *Doris Day* (-) 1956
WHATEVER YOU WANT – *Status Quo* (5) 1979
WHAT'S THE REASON DADDY – *Dermot Henry and the Virginians* (8) 1971
WHEELS • – *The String A Longs* (2) 1961
WHEN (a) – *Showaddywaddy* (7) 1977
WHEN (b) – *Red Hurley* (3) 1976
WHEN A CHILD IS BORN – *Johnny Mathis* (1) 1976
WHEN BENJY WRAPPED HIS TRACTOR ROUND THE OLD OAK TREE – *Brendan Grace* (1) 1977
WHEN FOREVER HAS GONE – *Demis Roussous* (3) 1976
WHEN I FALL IN LOVE – *Nat King Cole* (-) 1957
WHEN I FALL IN LOVE – *Donny Osmond* (10) 1973
WHEN I NEED YOU – *Leo Sayer* (1) 1977
WHEN I'M DEAD AND GONE – *McGuinness Flint* (5) 1970
WHEN MEXICO GAVE UP THE RHUMBA – *Mitchell Torok* (-) 1956
WHEN MY BLUE MOON TURNS TO GOLD – *Brian Coll* (8) 1972
WHEN MY LITTLE GIRL IS SMILING – *Jimmy Justice* (4) 1962
WHEN THE FIELDS ARE WHITE WITH DAISIES – *Sean Dunphy and the Hoedowners* (1) 1969
WHEN THE GIRL IN YOUR ARMS IS THE GIRL IN YOUR HEART – *Cliff Richard* (2) 1961
WHEN WE WERE YOUNG – *Pat Lynch and the Airchords* (1) 1971
WHEN WILL I BE LOVED – *Everly Brothers* (4) 1960
WHEN WILL I SEE YOU AGAIN – *Three Degrees* (2) 1974
WHEN WILL THE GOOD APPLES FALL – *The Seekers* (10) 1967

Title – *Act* (Position) Year of Chart Entry

WHEN WILL YOU SAY I LOVE YOU – *Billy Fury* (4) 1963
WHEN YOU CRY – *Dickie Rock and the Miami* (7) 1967
WHEN YOU LOSE THE ONE YOU LOVE – *Dorothy Squires* (-) 1956
WHEN YOU LOSE THE ONE YOU LOVE – *David Whitfield* (-) 1955
WHEN YOU WALK IN THE ROOM – *The Searchers* (4) 1964
WHEN YOU'RE IN LOVE WITH A BEAUTIFUL WOMAN – *Dr Hook* (1) 1979
(WHERE DO I BEGIN) LOVE STORY – *Andy Williams* (7) 1971
WHERE DID OUR LOVE GO – *The Supremes* (3) 1964
WHERE DO YOU GO TO (MY LOVELY) – *Peter Sarstedt* (1) 1969
WHERE HAVE THEY GONE – *Brendan Grace* (9) 1976
WHERE LOVE BEGINS – *Roly Daniels* (9) 1976
WHERE MY EILEEN IS WAITING – *Johnny McEvoy* (2) 1975
WHERE THE BOYS ARE – *Connie Francis* (2) 1961
WHERE THE THREE COUNTIES MEET – *Brendan Shine* (1) 1973
WHERE WILL THE DIMPLE BE? – *Rosemary Clooney* (-) 1955
WHICH WAY YOU GOING BILLY – *Poppy Family* (1) 1970
WHISKEY IN THE JAR – *Thin Lizzy* (1) 1972
WHISKEY ON A SUNDAY – *Danny Doyle* (1) 1967
WHISPERING GRASS – *Don Estelle and Windsor Davies* (4) 1975
WHITE SILVER SANDS – *Don Rondo* (-) 1957
A WHITE SPORT COAT – *Marty Robbins* (-) 1957
A WHITER SHADE OF PALE – *Procul Harum* (1) 1967
WHO AM I? – *Adam Faith* (6) 1961
WHO DO YOU WANNA BE – *Gina Dale Haze and the Champions* (7) 1979
WHO PUT THE LIGHTS OUT – *Dana* (5) 1971
WHO'S SORRY NOW – *Connie Francis* (-) 1958
WHY – *Frankie Avalon* (2) 1960
WHY – *Anthony Newley* (1) 1960
WHY – *Donny Osmond* (4) 1972
WHY DO FOOLS FALL IN LOVE – *The Teenagers featuring Frankie Lymon* (-) 1956
WHY, OH WHY, OH WHY – *Gilbert O'Sullivan* (3) 1973
WIDE EYED AND LEGLESS – *Andy Fairweather Low* (7) 1976
WIG WAM BAM – *Sweet* (4) 1972
WILD EYES AND TENDER LIPS – *Colin Hicks* (-) 1958
WILD IN THE COUNTRY – *Elvis Presley* (1) 1961
WILD THING – The *Troggs* (5) 1966
WILD WEST HERO – *Electric Light Orchestra* (9) 1978

Title – *Act* (Position) Year of Chart Entry

WILD WIND – *John Leyton* (6) 1961
WILL I WHAT – *Mike Sarne* (6) 1962
WILL YOU LOVE ME TOMORROW – *Mike Berry with the Outlaws* (6) 1961
WILL YOU LOVE ME TOMORROW – *The Shirelles* (7) 1961
WIMOWEH – *Karl Denver* (6) 1962
WINCHESTER CATHEDRAL – *New Vaudeville Band* (6) 1966
THE WIND IN THE WILLOWS – *Spud* (5) 1974
WIND ME UP (LET ME GO) – *Cliff Richard* (5) 1965
THE WIND THRO' THE RAFTERS – *The Ludlows* (8) 1966
WINTER WINDS – *The Millionaires* (10) 1966
WINTER WORLD OF LOVE – *Engelbert Humperdinck* (3) 1969
WISHING IT WAS YOU – *Dickie Rock and the Miami* (1) 1965
THE WITCH QUEEN OF NEW ORLEANS – *Redbone* (7) 1971
THE WITCH'S PROMISE – *Jethro Tull* (6) 1970
WITH A GIRL LIKE YOU – *The Troggs* (2) 1966
WITH A LITTLE HELP FROM MY FRIENDS – *Joe Cocker* (2) 1968
WITH A LITTLE LUCK – *Wings* (3) 1978
WITH ALL MY HEART – *Petula Clark* (-) 1957
WITH ALL MY HEART – *Dave King* (-) 1957
WITH THE WIND AND RAIN IN YOUR HAIR – *Pat Boone* (6) 1959
WITHOUT LOVE – *Tom Jones* (7) 1969
WITHOUT YOU – *Nilsson* (1) 1972
WOLVERTON MOUNTAIN – *Claude King* (2) 1962
A WOMAN IN LOVE – *The Four Aces* (-) 1956
A WOMAN IN LOVE – *Edmund Hockridge* (-) 1956
A WOMAN IN LOVE – *Frankie Laine* (-) 1956
A WOMAN IN LOVE – *Gordon MacRae* (-) 1956
WOMAN IN LOVE – *Three Degrees* (6) 1979
WOMAN WOMAN – *Brendan Bowyer and the Royals* (9) 1968
THE WONDER OF YOU – *Ray Peterson* (2) 1959
THE WONDER OF YOU – *Brendan Bowyer of the Royal Showband* (2) 1965
THE WONDER OF YOU – *Elvis Presley* (1) 1970
WONDERFUL – *Geraldine* (9) 1978
WONDERFUL DREAM – *Anne-Marie David* (3) 1973
WONDERFUL LAND • – *The Shadows* (1) 1962
A WONDERFUL TIME UP THERE – *Pat Boone* (-) 1958
WONDERFUL WONDERFUL – *Gary Miller* (-) 1957

Title – *Act* (Position) Year of Chart Entry

WONDERFUL WORLD OF THE YOUNG – *Danny Williams* (7)....1962
WONDERFUL WORLD OF MY DREAMS – *Sean Dunphy and and The Hoedowners* (5)....1966
WONDEROUS STORIES – *Yes* (6) 1977
WON'T SOMEBODY DANCE WITH ME – *Lynsey De Paul* (9) 1973
WOODEN HEART – *Elvis Presley* (1) 1961
WOODSTOCK – Matthews Southern Comfort (2)....1970
WORDS – *Rita Coolidge* (7) 1978
A WORLD OF OUR OWN – *The Seekers* (2) 1965
A WORLD WITHOUT LOVE – *Peter and Gordon* (1) 1964
WRONG ROAD AGAIN – *Marianne Faithfull* (6) 1976
WRONG ROAD AGAIN – *Brendan Shine* (4)....1976
WUTHERING HEIGHTS – *Kate Bush* (1) 1978

YEAR AFTER YEAR – Gary Miller (-) 1957
YEARS MAY COME, YEARS MAY GO – *Herman's Hermits* (5) 1970
YEH YEH – Georgie Fame and the Blue Flames (3) 1965
YELLOW RIVER – *Christie* (1)....1970
THE YELLOW ROSE OF TEXAS – *Ronnie Hilton* (-) 1955
THE YELLOW ROSE OF TEXAS – *Mitch Miller* (-)....1955
YELLOW SUBMARINE – *The Beatles* (1) 1966
YES MR PETERS – *Larry and Margo* (6) 1976
YES MY DARLING DAUGHTER – *Eydie Gorme* (4)....1962
YES SIR I CAN BOOGIE – *Baccara* (1).... 1977
YES TONIGHT JOSEPHINE – *Johnnie Ray* (-)....1957
YESTERDAY – *Matt Monro* (8) 1965
YESTERDAY – *The Beatles* (5)....1976
YESTERDAY HAS GONE – *Cupids Inspiration* (5) 1968
YESTERDAY MAN – Chris *Andrews* (1)....1965
YESTERDAY ONCE MORE – *The Carpenters* (8)....1973
YESTER-ME, YESTER-YOU, YESTERDAY – *Stevie Wonder* (3) 1969
Y.M.C.A. – *Village People* (1) 1978
YOU AIN'T SEEN NOTHING YET – *Bachman Turner Overdrive* (4)....1974
YOU ALWAYS HURT THE ONE YOU LOVE – *Clarence Frogman Henry* (3)....1961
YOU AND I – *Loudest Whisper* (9)....1976
YOU ARE MY DESTINY – *Paul Anka* (-)....1958
YOU ARE MY FIRST LOVE – *Ruby Murray* (-)....1956
YOU CAN GET IT IF YOU REALLY WANT IT – *Desmond Dekker* (4) 1970

Title – *Act* (Position) Year of Chart Entry

YOU CAN'T BE TRUE TO TWO – *Dave King* (-) 1956
YOU DON'T BRING ME FLOWERS – *Barbra and Neil* (4) 1978
YOU DON'T HAVE TO BE A BABY TO CRY – *The Caravelles* (8) 1963
YOU DON'T HAVE TO BE A STAR (To Be In My Show) – *Marilyn McCoo and Billy Davis Jr* (5) 1977
YOU DON'T HAVE TO SAY YOU LOVE ME – *Dusty Springfield* (4) 1966
YOU DON'T KNOW – *Helen Shapiro* (1) 1961
YOU DON'T KNOW ME – *Ray Charles* (2) 1962
YOU GAVE ME A MOUNTAIN – *Brendan Bowyer and the Big 8* (6) 1971
YOU GOT WHAT IT TAKES – *The Lana Sisters* (5) 1960
YOU GOTTA GET UP – *Reform* (9) 1978
YOU JUST MIGHT SEE ME CRY – *Our Kid* (7) 1976
YOU MAKE ME FEEL LIKE DANCING – *Leo Sayer* (5) 1976
YOU MUST HAVE BEEN A BEAUTIFUL BABY – *Bobby Darin* (8) 1961
YOU NEEDED ME – *Anne Murray* (7) 1979
YOU REALLY GOT ME – *The Kinks* (6) 1964
YOU SEXY THING – *Hot Chocolate* (4) 1975
YOU SHOULD BE DANCING – *Bee Gees* (4) 1976
YOU TO ME ARE EVERYTHING – *Real Thing* (6) 1976
YOU WEAR IT WELL – *Rod Stewart* (2) 1972
YOU WERE MADE FOR ME – *Freddie and the Dreamers* (10) 1963
YOU WERE ON MY MIND – *Crispian St. Peters* (6) 1966
YOU WON'T FIND ANOTHER FOOL LIKE ME – *New Seekers* (1) 1974
YOU YOU YOU – *Alvin Stardust* (5) 1974
YOU'LL ANSWER TO ME – *Cleo Laine* (2) 1961
YOU'LL NEVER KNOW – *Shirley Bassey* (5) 1961
YOU'LL NEVER MISS YOUR MOTHER TILL SHE'S GONE – *Brendan Shine* (4) 1972
YOU'LL NEVER WALK ALONE – *Gerry and the Pacemakers* (1) 1963
YOUNG AND FOOLISH – *Edmund Hockridge* (-) 1956
YOUNG GIRL – *Union Gap featuring Gary Puckett* (1) 1968
YOUNG LOVE – *Tab Hunter* (-) 1957
YOUNG LOVE – *Sonny James* (-) 1957
YOUNG LOVE – *Donie Collins Showband featuring Chris* (6) 1966
YOUNG LOVE – *Donny Osmond* (1) 1973
YOUNG LOVERS – *Paul and Paula* (10) 1963
THE YOUNG NEW MEXICAN PUPPETEER – *Tom Jones* (7) 1972
THE YOUNG ONES – *Cliff Richard and the Shadows* (1) 1962
YOU'RE A LADY – Peter Skellern (7) 1972

Title – *Act* (Position) Year of Chart Entry

YOU'RE DRIVING ME CRAZY – *The Temperance Seven* (3) 1961
(YOU'RE) HAVING MY BABY – *Paul Anka featuring Odia Coates* (4) 1974
YOU'RE IN MY HEART – *Rod Stewart* (2) 1977
YOU'RE MY BEST FRIEND (a) – *Queen* (5) 1976
YOU'RE MY BEST FRIEND (b) – *Two's Company* (5) 1975
YOU'RE MY DAY, YOU'RE MY NIGHT – *Red Hurley* (2) 1977
YOU'RE MY WORLD – *Cilla Black* (2) 1964
YOU'RE SIXTEEN – *Johnny Burnette* (2) 1961
YOU'RE SIXTEEN – *Ringo Starr* (2) 1974
YOU'RE SO GOOD TO ME – *Red Hurley* (9) 1979
YOU'RE SO VAIN – *Carly Simon* (4) 1973
YOU'RE STILL THE ONLY ONE – *Colm and The Sundowners* (10) 1973
YOU'RE SUCH A GOOD LOOKING WOMAN – *Joe Dolan* (4) 1970
(YOU'RE THE) DEVIL IN DISGUISE – *Elvis Presley* (1) 1963
YOU'RE THE FIRST, THE LAST, MY EVERYTHING – *Barry White* (6) 1974
YOU'RE THE GREATEST LOVER – *Gina Dale Haze & The Champions* (10) 1979
YOU'RE THE ONE I CAN'T LIVE WITHOUT – *Ray Lynam and Philomena Begley* (5) 1973
YOU'RE THE ONE I SING MY LOVE SONGS TO – *Ray Lynam and the Hillbillies* (10) 1976
YOU'RE THE ONE THAT I WANT – *John Travolta & Olivia Newton John* (1) 1978
YOU'RE THE ONLY GOOD THING (THAT HAPPENED TO ME) – *Jim Reeves* (4) 1961
YOU'VE GOT A FRIEND – *James Taylor* (3) 1971
YOU'VE GOT YOUR TROUBLES – *The Fortunes* (3) 1965
YOU'VE LOST THAT LOVIN' FEELIN' – *Righteous Brothers* (2) 1965
YOUR CHEATING HEART – *Ray Charles* (7) 1962
YUMMY YUMMY YUMMY – *The Ohio Express* (5) 1968
YUMMY YUMMY YUMMY – *The Sands Showband* (6) 1968

ZABADAK – *Dave Dee, Dozy, Beaky, Mick and Tich* (7) 1967
ZAMBESI • – *Lou Busch and his Orchestra* (-) 1956
ZORBA'S DANCE • –*Marcello Minerbi and his Orchestra* (6) 1965

Part Three

Facts And Feats

Date disc hit the #1 spot — Number of weeks at No. 1

THE NUMBER ONE HITS

1959

Date	Title / Artist (Label)	Weeks
12 Feb	ONE NIGHT / I GOT STUNG ... *Elvis Presley* (RCA)	1
19 Feb	A PUB WITH NO BEER ... *Slim Dusty* (Columbia)	6
02 Apr	PETITE FLEUR ... *Chris Barber Jazzband* (Pye Nixa)	5
07 May	IT DOESN'T MATTER ANYMORE ... *Buddy* Holly (Coral)	7
25 Jun	ROULETTE ... *Russ Conway* (Columbia)	2
09 Jul	BATTLE OF NEW ORLEANS ... *Lonnie Donegan* (Pye Nixa)	1
16 Jul	A TEENAGER IN LOVE ... *Dion and The Belmonts* (London)	1
23 Jul	DREAM LOVER ... *Bobby Darin* (London)	1
30 Jul	A TEENAGER IN LOVE ... *Dion and The Belmonts* (London)	1
06 Aug	DREAM LOVER ... *Bobby Darin* (London)	1
13 Aug	BATTLE OF NEW ORLEANS ... *Lonnie Donegan* (Pye)	1
20 Aug	LIVING DOLL ... *Cliff Richard and the Shadows* (Columbia)	7
08 Oct	CHINA TEA ... *Russ Conway* (Columbia)	1
15 Oct	ONLY SIXTEEN ... *Craig Douglas* (Top Rank)	2
29 Oct	HIGH HOPES ... *Frank Sinatra* (Capitol)	2
12 Nov	TRAVELLIN' LIGHT ... *Cliff Richard and the Shadows* (Columbia)	1
19 Nov	MACK THE KNIFE ... *Bobby Darin* (London)	3
10 Dec	WHAT DO YOU WANT TO MAKE THOSE EYES AT ME FOR? ... *Emile Ford and the Checkmates* (Pye)	3
31 Dec	WHAT DO YOU WANT? ... *Adam Faith* (Parlophone)	1

1960

Date	Title / Artist (Label)	Weeks
07 Jan	WHAT DO YOU WANT TO MAKE THOSE EYES AT ME FOR? ... *Emile Ford and the Checkmates* (Pye)	4
04 Feb	A VOICE IN THE WILDERNESS ... *Cliff Richard and the Shadows* (Columbia)	1
11 Feb	WHY ... *Anthony Newley* (Decca)	5
17 Mar	RUNNING BEAR ... *Johnny Preston* (Mercury)	2
31 Mar	HE'LL HAVE TO GO ... *Jim Reeves* (RCA)	3
21 Apr	MY OLD MAN'S A DUSTMAN ... *Lonnie Donegan* (Pye)	4
19 May	CATHY'S CLOWN ... *Everly Brothers* (Warner Brothers)	5
23 Jun	THREE STEPS TO HEAVEN ... *Eddie Cochran* (London)	5

Date disc hit the #1 spot		Number of weeks at No. 1
28 Jul	PLEASE DON'T TEASE ... *Cliff Richard and the Shadows* Columbia)	5
01 Sep	APACHE ... *The Shadows* (Columbia)	2
15 Sep	A MESS OF BLUES ... *Elvis Presley* (RCA)	3
06 Oct	PLEASE HELP ME I'M FALLING ... *Hank Locklin* (RCA)	2
20 Oct	ONLY THE LONELY ... *Roy Orbison* (London)	2
03 Nov	IT'S NOW OR NEVER ... *Elvis Presley* (RCA)	8
29 Dec	SAVE THE LAST DANCE FOR ME – *The Drifters* (London)	1

1961

05 Jan	IT'S NOW OR NEVER – *Elvis Presley* (RCA)	1
12 Jan	SAVE THE LAST DANCE FOR ME ... *The Drifters* (London)	1
19 Jan	POETRY IN MOTION ... *Johnny Tillotson* (London)	1
26 Jan	ARE YOU LONESOME TONIGHT ... *Elvis Presley* (RCA)	6
09 Mar	EBONY EYES ... *Everly Brothers* (Warner Brothers)	2
23 Mar	WOODEN HEART ... *Elvis Presley* (RCA)	7
11May	SURRENDER ... *Elvis Presley* (RCA)	8
06 Jul	HELLO MARY LOU ... *Ricky Nelson* (London)	4
03 Aug	WELL I ASK YOU ... *Eden Kane* (Decca)	3
24 Aug	YOU DON'T KNOW ... *Helen Shapiro* (Columbia)	2
07 Sep	WELL I ASK YOU ... *Eden Kane* (Decca)	2
21 Sep	JOHNNY REMEMBER ME ... *John Leyton* (Top Rank)	3
12 Oct	WILD IN THE COUNTRY ... *Elvis Presley* (RCA)	1
19 Oct	JEALOUSY ... *Billy Fury* (Decca)	1
26 Oct	WALKIN' BACK TO HAPPINESS ... *Helen Shapiro* (Columbia)	2
09 Nov	HIS LATEST FLAME ... *Elvis Presley* (RCA)	5
14 Dec	TOWER OF STRENGTH ... *Frankie Vaughan* (Philips)	4

1962

11 Jan	STRANGER ON THE SHORE ... *Mr Acker Bilk* (Columbia)	2
25 Jan	THE YOUNG ONES ... *Cliff Richard and the Shadows* (Columbia)	4
22 Feb	ROCK A HULA BABY ... *Elvis Presley* (RCA)	5
29 Mar	WONDERFUL LAND ... *The Shadows* (Columbia)	1
05 Apr	ROCK-A-HULA BABY ... *Elvis Presley* (RCA)	1

Date disc hit the #1 spot		Number of weeks at No. 1
12 Apr	WONDERFUL LAND ... *The Shadows* (Columbia)	3
03 May	DREAM BABY ... *Roy Orbison* (London)	1
10 May	WONDERFUL LAND ... *The Shadows* (Columbia)	1
17 May	GOOD LUCK CHARM ... *Elvis Presley* (RCA)	10
26 Jul	I CAN'T STOP LOVING YOU ... *Ray Charles* (HMV)	2
09 Aug	I REMEMBER YOU ... *Frank Ifield* (Columbia)	5
13 Sep	SHE'S NOT YOU ... *Elvis Presley* (RCA)	7
29 Oct	TELSTAR ... *The Tornados* (Decca)	2
12 Nov	LOVESICK BLUES ... *Frank Ifield* (Columbia)	4
10 Dec	RETURN TO SENDER ... *Elvis Presley* (RCA)	4

1963

07 Jan	BACHELOR BOY/ THE NEXT TIME ... *Cliff Richard and the Shadows* (Columbia)	4
04 Feb	DANCE ON ... *The Shadows* (Columbia)	2
18 Feb	DIAMONDS ... *Jet Harris and Tony Meehan* (Decca)	1
25 Feb	LITTLE TOWN FLIRT ... *Del Shannon* (London)	1
04 Mar	FROM A JACK TO A KING ... *Ned Miller* (London)	9
06 May	RHYTHM OF THE RAIN ... *The Cascades* (Warner Bros)	1
13 May	FROM ME TO YOU ... *The Beatles* (Parlophone)	1
20 May	IN DREAMS ... *Roy Orbison* (London)	2
03 Jun	LUCKY LIPS ... *Cliff Richard and the Shadows* (Columbia)	1
10 Jun	WELCOME TO MY WORLD ... *Jim Reeves* (RCA)	3
01 Jul	I LIKE IT ... *Gerry and the Pacemakers* (Columbia)	4
29 Jul	CONFESSIN' ... *Frank Ifield* (Columbia)	1
05 Aug	(YOU'RE THE) DEVIL IN DISGUISE ... *Elvis Presley* (RCA)	3
26 Aug	SWEETS FOR MY SWEET ... *The Searchers* (Pye)	1
02 Sep	KISS ME QUICK ... *Brendan Bowyer and Royal Showband* (HMV)	7
21 Oct	DO YOU LOVE ME? ... *Brian Poole and the Tremeloes* (Decca)	1
28 Oct	BLUE BAYOU / MEAN WOMAN BLUES ... *Roy Orbison* (London)	1
04 Nov	YOU'LL NEVER WALK ALONE ... *Gerry and the Pacemakers* (Columbia)	6
16 Dec	DON'T TALK TO HIM ... *Cliff Richard and the Shadows* (Columbia)	1
23 Dec	NO MORE ... *Royal Showband featuring Brendan Bowyer* (HMV)	1
30 Dec	THERE'S ALWAYS ME ... *Dickie Rock and the Miami* (Piccadilly)	4

Date disc hit the #1 spot		Number of weeks at No. 1

1964

27 Jan	GLAD ALL OVER ... *Dave Clark Five* (Columbia)	2
10 Feb	NEEDLES AND PINS ... *The Searchers* (Pye)	4
09 Mar	BITS AND PIECES ... *Dave Clark Five* (Columbia)	1
16 Mar	ANYONE WHO HAD A HEART ... *Cilla Black* (Parlophone)	1
23 Mar	I LOVE YOU BECAUSE ... *Jim Reeves* (RCA)	3
13 Apr	CAN'T BUY ME LOVE ... *The Beatles* (Parlophone)	3
04 May	A WORLD WITHOUT LOVE ... *Peter and Gordon* (Columbia)	2
18 May	DON'T THROW YOUR LOVE AWAY ... *The Searchers* (Pye)	1
25 May	FALLEN STAR ... *The Cadets vocalist Eileen Reid* (Columbia)	1
	I'M YOURS ... *Dickie Rock and the Miami* (Piccadilly)	1
01 Jun	MY BOY LOLLIPOP ... *Millie* (Fontana)	1
08 Jun	IT'S OVER ... *Roy Orbison* (London)	1
15 Jun	MY BOY LOLLIPOP ... *Millie* (Fontana)	1
22 Jun	IT'S OVER ... *Roy Orbison* (London)	1
29 Jun	BLESS YOU ... *Royal Showband featuring Brendan Bowyer* (HMV)	2
13 Jul	IT'S OVER ... *Roy Orbison* (London)	1
20 Jul	I WON'T FORGET YOU ... *Jim Reeves* (RCA)	2
03 Aug	A HARD DAY'S NIGHT ... *The Beatles* (Parlophone)	3
24 Aug	I WON'T FORGET YOU ... *Jim Reeves* (RCA)	6
05 Oct	I WOULDN'T TRADE YOU FOR THE WORLD ... *The Bachelors* (Decca)	1
12 Oct	I'M INTO SOMETHING GOOD ... *Herman's Hermits* (Columbia)	1
19 Oct	OH PRETTY WOMAN ... *Roy Orbison* (London)	1
26 Oct	FROM THE CANDY STORE ON THE CORNER TO THE CHAPEL ON THE HILL ... *Dickie Rock and the Miami* (Piccadilly)	6
07 Dec	DOWN CAME THE RAIN ... *Butch Moore and the Capitol* (Pye)	1
14 Dec	I FEEL FINE ... *The Beatles* (Parlophone)	5

1965

18 Jan	I RAN ALL THE WAY HOME / HUCKLEBUCK ... *Royal Showband featuring Brendan Bowyer* (HMV)	7
08 Mar	BORN TO BE WITH YOU ... *Capitol Showband* (Pye)	2
22 Mar	IF I DIDN'T HAVE A DIME ... *Tom Dunphy with the Royal Showband* (HMV)	2
05 Apr	WALKING THE STREETS IN THE RAIN ... *Butch Moore* (Pye)	3

Date disc hit the #1 spot		Number of weeks at No. 1
26 Apr	TICKET TO RIDE ... *The Beatles* (Parlophone)	4
24 May	EVERY STEP OF THE WAY ... *Dickie Rock* (Pye)	3
14 Jun	LONG LIVE LOVE ... *Sandie Shaw* (Pye)	2
28 Jun	CRYING IN THE CHAPEL ... *Elvis Presley* (RCA)	3
19 Jul	I'M ALIVE ... *The Hollies* (Parlophone)	1
26 Jul	MR TAMBOURINE MAN ... *The Byrds* (CBS)	1
02 Aug	HELP! ... *The Beatles* (Parlophone)	5
06 Sep	DON'T LOSE YOUR HUCKLEBUCK SHOES ... *Royal Showband featuring Brendan Bowyer* (HMV)	1
13 Sep	(I CAN'T GET NO) SATISFACTION ... *Rolling Stones* (Decca)	4
11 Oct	TEARS ... *Ken Dodd* (Columbia)	4
08 Nov	YESTERDAY MAN ... *Chris Andrews* (Decca)	2
22 Nov	WISHING IT WAS YOU ... *Dickie Rock and the Miami* (Pye)	2
06 Dec	THE CARNIVAL IS OVER ... *The Seekers* (Columbia)	2
20 Dec	DAY TRIPPER / WE CAN WORK IT OUT - *The Beatles* (Parlophone)	5

1966

24 Jan	LOVELY LEITRIM ... *Larry Cunningham and Mighty Avons* (King)	2
07 Feb	OLD MAN TROUBLE ... *Doc Carroll and the Royal Blues* (Parlophone)	2
21 Feb	THESE BOOTS ARE MADE FOR WALKIN' ... *Nancy Sinatra* (Pye)	1
28 Feb	COME BACK TO STAY ... *Dickie Rock* (Pye)	4
28 Mar	THE SEA AROUND US ... *The Ludlows* (Pye)	4
25 Apr	THE BLACK AND TAN GUN ... *Pat Smyth and the Johnny Flynn Showband* (Emerald)	2
09 May	PRETTY FLAMINGO ... *Manfred Mann* (HMV)	4
06 Jun	STRANGERS IN THE NIGHT ... *Frank Sinatra* (Pye)	2
20 Jun	PAPERBACK WRITER ... *The Beatles* (Parlophone)	4
18 Jul	SUNNY AFTERNOON ... *The Kinks* (Pye)	1
25 Jul	MORE THAN YESTERDAY ... *The Cadets featuring Gregory* (Pye)	3
15 Aug	THE TRAVELLING PEOPLE ... *The Johnstons* (Pye)	1
22 Aug	YELLOW SUBMARINE / ELEANOR RIGBY ... *The Beatles* (Parlophone)	2
05 Sep	PRETTY BROWN EYES ... *Joe Dolan and the Drifters* (Pye)	3
26 Sep	THE MERRY PLOUGHBOY ... *Dermot O'Brien and the Clubmen* (Envoy)	6
07 Nov	SOMEWHERE MY LOVE ... *Charlie Matthews and the Royal Showband* (HMV)	1
14 Nov	MUIRSHEEN DURKIN ... *The Rambler (John McEvoy)* (Pye)	3
05 Dec	GREEN GREEN GRASS OF HOME ... *Tom Jones* (Decca)	6

Date disc hit the #1 spot		Number of weeks at No. 1

1967

19 Jan	I'M A BELIEVER ... *The Monkees* (RCA)	5
23 Feb	THE HOUSE WITH THE WHITE WASHED GABLE ... *Joe Dolan and the Drifters* (Pye)	1
02 Mar	THIS IS MY SONG ... *Petula Clark* (Pye)	3
23 Mar	RELEASE ME ... *Engelbert Humperdinck* (Decca)	3
13 Apr	SOMETHING STUPID ... *Nancy and Frank Sinatra* (Reprise)	1
20 Apr	PUPPET ON A STRING ... *Sandie Shaw* (Pye)	3
11 May	SEVEN DRUNKEN NIGHTS ... *The Dubliners* (Major Minor)	1
18 May	THE BOSTON BURGLAR ... *Johnny McEvoy* (Pye)	3
08 Jun	SILENCE IS GOLDEN ... *The Tremeloes* (CBS)	1
15 Jun	BLACK VELVET BAND ... *Johnny Kelly* (Pye)	1
22 Jun	A WHITER SHADE OF PALE ... *Procul Harum* (Deram)	4
20 Jul	BLACK VELVET BAND ... *Johnny Kelly* (Pye)	2
03 Aug	ALL YOU NEED IS LOVE ... *The Beatles* (Parlophone)	1
	BLACK VELVET BAND ... *Johnny Kelly* (Pye)	1
10 Aug	ALL YOU NEED IS LOVE ... *The Beatles* (Parlophone)	1
17 Aug	BLACK VELVET BAND ... *Johnny Kelly* (Pye)	4
14 Sep	SAN FRANCISCO (BE SURE TO WEAR SOME FLOWERS IN YOUR HAIR) ... *Scott McKenzie* (CBS)	1
21 Sep	THE LAST WALTZ ... *Engelbert Humperdinck* (Decca)	5
26 Oct	WHISKEY ON A SUNDAY ... *Danny Doyle* (Tribune)	7
14 Dec	TREAT ME DAUGHTER KINDLY ... *Pat Lynch and Airchords* (Pye)	4

1968

11 Jan	DAYDREAM BELIEVER ... *The Monkees* (RCA)	2
25 Jan	AM I THAT EASY TO FORGET ... *Engelbert Humperdinck* (Decca)	3
15 Feb	MIGHTY QUINN ... *Manfred Mann* (Fontana)	1
22 Feb	MARY FROM DUNGLOE ... *Emmett Spiceland* (Inset)	1
29 Feb	MIGHTY QUINN ... *Manfred Mann* (Fontana)	2
14 Mar	NORA ... *Johnny McEvoy* (Target)	1
21 Mar	LEGEND OF XANADU ... *Dave Dee, Dozy, Beaky, Mick & Tich* (Fontana)	1
28 Mar	DELILAH ... *Tom Jones* (Decca)	3
18 Apr	CHANCE OF A LIFETIME ... *Pat McGeegan* (Emerald)	1
25 Apr	CONGRATULATIONS ... *Cliff Richard* (Columbia)	2

Date disc hit the #1 spot		Number of weeks at No. 1
09 May	SIMON SAYS ... *Dickie Rock and the Miami* (Pye)	1
16 May	A MAN WITHOUT LOVE ... *Engelbert Humperdinck* (Decca)	2
30 May	YOUNG GIRL ... *Union Gap featuring Gary Puckett* (CBS)	2
13 Jun	HONEY ... *Bobby Goldsboro* (United Artists)	4
11 Jul	BLUE EYES ... *Don Partridge* (Columbia)	3
01 Aug	I PRETEND ... *Des O'Connor* (Columbia)	2
15 Aug	HELP YOURSELF ... *Tom Jones* (Decca)	3
05 Sep	LITTLE ARROWS ... *The Dixies* (Pye)	1
12 Sep	HEY JUDE ... *The Beatles* (Parlophone)	1
19 Sep	I'VE GOTTA GET A MESSAGE TO YOU ... *The Bee Gees* (Polydor)	1
26 Sep	HEY JUDE ... *The Beatles* (Parlophone)	2
10 Oct	THOSE WERE THE DAYS ... *Mary Hopkin* (Apple)	5
14 Nov	MY LITTLE LADY ... *The Tremeloes* (CBS)	1
21 Nov	THE GOOD THE BAD AND THE UGLY ... *Hugo Montenegro* (RCA)	4
19 Dec	LILY THE PINK ... *The Scaffold* (Parlophone)	3

1969

09 Jan	QUICK JOEY SMALL ... *Real McCoy* (Target)	2
23 Jan	OB-LA-DI OB-LA-DA ... *The Marmalade* (CBS)	1
30 Jan	LONELY WOODS OF UPTON ... *Sean Dunphy and the Hoedowners* (Dolphin)	8
27 Mar	WAGES OF LOVE ... *Muriel Day* (Dolphin)	1
03 Apr	WHERE DO YOU GO TO (MY LOVELY) ... *Peter Sarstedt* (United Artists)	2
17 Apr	BOOM BANG A BANG ... *Lulu* (Columbia)	2
01 May	GOODBYE ... *Mary Hopkin* (Apple)	1
08 May	GET BACK ... *The Beatles with Billy Preston* (Apple)	6
19 Jun	BALLAD OF JOHN AND YOKO ... *The Beatles* (Apple)	4
17 Jul	IN THE GHETTO ... *Elvis Presley* (RCA)	4
14 Aug	HONKY TONK WOMEN ... *Rolling Stones* (Decca)	1
21 Aug	SAVED BY THE BELL ... *Robin Gibb* (Polydor)	1
28 Aug	WHEN THE FIELDS ARE WHITE WITH DAISIES ... *Sean Dunphy and The Hoedowners* (Dolphin)	1
04 Sep	SAVED BY THE BELL ... *Robin Gibb* (Polydor)	2
18 Sep	IN THE YEAR 2525 ... *Zager and Evans* (RCA)	2
02 Oct	DON'T FORGET TO REMEMBER ... *Bee Gees* (Polydor)	1
09 Oct	BAD MOON RISING ... *Creedence Clearwater Revival* (Liberty)	1

Date disc hit the #1 spot		Number of weeks at No. 1
16 Oct	DON'T FORGET TO REMEMBER ... *Bee Gees* (Polydor)	1
23 Oct	I'LL NEVER FALL IN LOVE AGAIN ... *Bobbie Gentry* (Capitol)	2
06 Nov	TERESA ... *Joe Dolan* (Pye)	1
13 Nov	SUGAR SUGAR ... *The Archies* (RCA)	6
25 Dec	TWO LITTLE BOYS ... *Rolf Harris* (Columbia)	7

1970

12 Feb	LOVE GROWS (WHERE MY ROSEMARY GOES) ... *Edison Lighthouse* (Bell)	4
12 Mar	WANDERING STAR ... *Lee Marvin* (Paramount)	2
26 Mar	ALL KINDS OF EVERYTHING ... *Dana* (Rex)	9
28 May	SPIRIT IN THE SKY ... *Norman Greenbaum* (Pye)	1
04 Jun	QUESTION ... *Moody Blues* (Threshold)	1
11 Jun	YELLOW RIVER ... *Christie* (CBS)	2
25 Jun	TWENTY ONE YEARS ... *Dermot Hegarty* (Release)	2
09 Jul	IN THE SUMMERTIME ... *Mungo Jerry* (Dawn)	1
16 Jul	GOODBYE SAM HELLO SAMANTHA ... *Cliff Richard* (Columbia)	1
23 Jul	IN THE SUMMERTIME ... *Mungo Jerry* (Dawn)	2
06 Aug	THE WONDER OF YOU ... *Elvis Presley* (RCA)	1
13 Aug	LOLA ... *The Kinks* (Pye)	1
20 Aug	THE WONDER OF YOU ... *Elvis Presley* (RCA)	3
10 Sep	TWENTY ONE YEARS ... *Dermot Hegarty* (Release)	3
01 Oct	WHICH WAY YOU GOING BILLY ... *Poppy Family* Decca)	1
08 Oct	BAND OF GOLD ... *Freda Payne* (Columbia)	6
19 Nov	NEW WORLD IN THE MORNING ... *Roger Whittaker* (Columbia)	2
03 Dec	I'LL FORGIVE AND I'LL TRY TO FORGET ... *Margo* (Ruby)	1
10 Dec	NEW WORLD IN THE MORNING ... Ro*ger Whittaker* (Columbia)	1
17 Dec	IF THOSE LIPS COULD ONLY SPEAK ... *Dermot Henry and the Virginians* (Ruby)	2
31 Dec	I HEAR YOU KNOCKING ... *Dave Edmunds* (Mam)	1

1971

07 Jan	IF THOSE LIPS COULD ONLY SPEAK ... *Dermot Henry and the Virginians* (Ruby)	4
04 Feb	MY SWEET LORD ... *George Harrison* (Apple)	7
25 Mar	ANOTHER DAY ... *Paul McCartney* (Apple)	1

Date disc hit the #1 spot		Number of weeks at No. 1
01 Apr	ROSE GARDEN ... *Lynn Anderson* (CBS)	1
08 Apr	HOT LOVE ... *T Rex* (Fly)	2
22 Apr	ROSE GARDEN ... *Lynn Anderson* (CBS)	1
29 Apr	WHEN WE WERE YOUNG ... *Pat Lynch and The Airchords* (Ruby)	1
06 May	HOT LOVE ... *T REX* (Fly)	1
13 May	WHEN WE WERE YOUNG ... *Pat Lynch and The Airchords* (Ruby)	4
10 Jun	I AM I SAID ... *Neil Diamond* (UNI)	2
24 Jun	O'BRIEN HAS NO WHERE TO GO ... *Brendan Shine* (Play)	3
15 Jul	CHIRPY CHIRPY CHEEP CHEEP ... *Middle Of The Road* (RCA)	3
05 Aug	SOMETIMES ... *Red Hurley* (Play)	2
19 Aug	GET IT ON ... *T REX* (Fly)	2
02 Sep	NEVER ENDING SONG OF LOVE ... *New Seekers* (Philips)	3
23 Sep	I'M STILL WAITING ... *Diana Ross* (Tamla Motown)	1
30 Sep	WHAT ARE YOU DOING SUNDAY ... *Dawn* (Columbia)	1
07 Oct	HEY GIRL DON'T BOTHER ME ... *Tams* (Probe)	1
14 Oct	DID YOU EVER? ... *Nancy and Lee* (Reprise)	6
25 Nov	KISS ME GOODBYE ... *Red Hurley* (Play)	1
02 Dec	COZ I LUV YOU ... *Slade* (Polydor)	1
09 Dec	KISS ME GOODBYE ... *Red Hurley* (Play)	1
16 Dec	I DON'T KNOW HOW TO LOVE HIM ... *Real McCoy featuring Tina* (Ruby)	1
23 Dec	O HOLY NIGHT ... *Tommy Drennan* (Columbia)	2

1972

06 Jan	SLANEY VALLEY ... *Larry Cunningham* (Release)	1
13 Jan	I'D LIKE TO TEACH THE WORLD TO SING *New Seekers* (Philips)	2
27 Jan	THE MEN BEHIND THE WIRE ... *Barleycorn* (CRC)	3
17 Feb	TELEGRAM SAM ... *T REX* (T Rex)	1
24 Feb	THE MEN BEHIND THE WIRE ... *Barleycorn* (CRC)	2
09 Mar	GIVE IRELAND BACK TO THE IRISH ... *Wings* (Apple)	1
16 Mar	WITHOUT YOU ... *Nilsson* (RCA)	1
23 Mar	CEOL AN GHRA ... *Sandie Jones and the Dixies* (Play)	1
30 Mar	WITHOUT YOU ... *Nilsson* (RCA)	1
06 Apr	THREE LEAFED SHAMROCK ... *John Kerr* (Pye)	1
13 Apr	BROKEN MARRIAGE VOWS ... *Big Tom & The Mainliners* (Denver)	2
27 Apr	AMAZING GRACE ... *Royal Scots Dragoon Guards* (RCA)	1

Date disc hit the #1 spot		Number of weeks at No. 1
04 May	SUNDAY BLOODY SUNDAY ... *Paddywagon* (Columbia)	1
11 May	WHAT DO I DO ... *Sandie, Joe and The Dixies* (Play)	1
18 May	A THING CALLED LOVE ... *Johnny Cash* (CBS)	4
15 Jun	METAL GURU ... *T Rex* (T Rex)	1
22 Jun	VINCENT ... *Don McLean* (United Artists)	2
06 Jul	OOH WAKKA DO WAKKA DAY ... *Gilbert O'Sullivan* (Mam)	2
20 Jul	SYLVIAS MOTHER ... *Dr Hook and the Medicine* Show (CBS)	7
07 Sep	THE GYPSY ... *Dermot Henry* (Columbia)	2
21 Sep	MAMA WEER ALL CRAZEE NOW ... *Slade* (Polydor)	2
05 Oct	CHILDREN OF THE REVOLUTION ... *T Rex* (T Rex)	2
19 Oct	HOW CAN I BE SURE ... *David Cassidy* (Bell)	1
26 Oct	CLAIR ... *Gilbert O'Sullivan* (Mam)	1
02 Nov	MOULDY OLD DOUGH ... *Lieutenant Pigeon* (Decca)	1
09 Nov	CLAIR ... *Gilbert O'Sullivan* (Mam)	4
07 Dec	MY DING A LING ... *Chuck Berry* (Chess)	2
21 Dec	WHISKEY IN THE JAR ... *Thin Lizzy* (Decca)	2

1973

04 Jan	HAPPY XMAS WAR IS OVER ... *John and Yoko* (Parlophone)	1
11 Jan	WHISKEY IN THE JAR ... *Thin Lizzy* (Decca)	1
18 Jan	LONG HAIRED LOVER FROM LIVERPOOL ... *Little Jimmy Osmond* (MGM)	4
15 Feb	BLOCKBUSTER ... *Sweet* (RCA)	2
01 Mar	I LOVE YOU STILL ... *Big Tom and the Mainliners* (Denver)	2
15 Mar	CUM ON FEEL THE NOIZE ... *Slade* (Polydor)	2
29 Mar	GET DOWN ... *Gilbert O'Sullivan* (Mam)	3
19 Apr	TIE A YELLOW RIBBON ROUND THE OLD OAK TREE ... *Dawn featuring Tony Orlando* (Bell)	6
31 May	SEE MY BABY JIVE ... *Wizzard* (Harvest)	1
07 Jun	DAISY A DAY ... *Danny Doyle* (Release)	3
28 Jun	RUBBER BULLETS ... *10 cc* (UK)	2
12 Jul	SKWEEZE ME PLEEZE ME ... *Slade* (Polydor)	1
19 Jul	WELCOME HOME ... *Peters and Lee* (Philips)	5
23 Aug	WHERE THE THREE COUNTIES MEET ... *Brendan Shine* (Play)	2
06 Sep	YOUNG LOVE ... *Donny Osmond* (MGM)	2
20 Sep	THE DEAN AND I ... *10 cc* (UK)	1

Date disc hit the #1 spot		Number of weeks at No. 1
27 Sep	BALLROOM BLITZ ... *Sweet* (RCA)	3
18 Oct	MY FRIEND STAN ... *Slade* (Polydor)	3
08 Nov	FOR THE GOOD TIMES ... *Perry Como* (RCA)	2
22 Nov	THE HELICOPTER SONG ... *Wolfe Tones* (Dolphin)	4
20 Dec	MERRY XMAS EVERYBODY ... *Slade* (Polydor)	3

1974

10 Jan	I'M GONNA MAKE IT ... *Joe Cuddy* (Rex)	2
24 Jan	YOU WON'T FIND ANOTHER FOOL LIKE ME ... *The New Seekers* (Polydor)	1
31 Jan	TIGER FEET ... *Mud* (Rak)	2
14 Feb	TEENAGE RAMPAGE ... *Sweet* (RCA)	2
28 Feb	DEVIL GATE DRIVE ... *Suzi Quatro* (Rak)	1
07 Mar	JEALOUS MIND ... *Alvin Stardust* (Magnet)	2
21 Mar	CROSS YOUR HEART ... *Tina* (Polydor)	2
04 Apr	BILLY DON'T BE A HERO ... *Paper Lace* (Bus Stop)	1
11 Apr	CROSS YOUR HEART ... *Tina* (Polydor)	1
18 Apr	SEASONS IN THE SUN ... *Terry Jacks* (Bell)	1
25 Apr	WATERLOO ... *Abba* (Epic)	2
09 May	ANY DREAM WILL DO ... *Joe Cuddy* (Rex)	3
30 May	I SEE A STAR ... *Mouth and MacNeal* (Decca)	1
06 Jun	ANY DREAM WILL DO ... *Joe Cuddy* (Rex)	2
20 Jun	I SEE A STAR ... *Mouth and MacNeal* (Decca)	1
27 Jun	ALWAYS YOURS ... *Gary Glitter* (Bell)	2
11 Jul	OLD LOVE LETTERS ... *Big Tom and the Mainliners* (Denver)	1
18 Jul	SHE ... *Charles Aznavour* (Barclay)	1
25 Jul	IF MA COULD SEE ME NOW ... *The Times* (EMI)	4
22 Aug	ABBEYSHRULE ... *Brendan Shine* (Play)	3
12 Sep	NINETEEN MEN ... *Dermot Hegarty* (Release)	3
03 Oct	KUNG FU FIGHTING ... *Carl Douglas* (Pye)	2
17 Oct	ANNIES SONG ... *John Denver* (RCA)	2
31 Oct	EVERYTHING I OWN ... *Ken Boothe* (Trojan)	3
21 Nov	GONNA MAKE YOU A STAR ... *David Essex* (CBS)	4
19 Dec	OH YES YOU'RE BEAUTIFUL ... *Gary Glitter* (Bell)	2

Date disc hit the #1 spot		Number of weeks at No. 1

1975

02 Jan	LONELY THIS CHRISTMAS ... *Mud* (Rak)	2
16 Jan	STREETS OF LONDON ... *Ralph McTell* (Reprise)	2
30 Jan	Ms GRACE ... *The Tymes* (RCA)	1
06 Feb	JANUARY ... *Pilot* (EMI)	4
06 Mar	MAKE ME SMILE (Come Up And See Me) ... *Steve Harley and Cockney Rebel* (EMI)	2
20 Mar	IF ... *Telly Savalas* (MCA)	1
27 Mar	BYE BYE BABY ... *Bay City Rollers* (Bell)	4
24 Apr	LOVE IS ALL ... *Red Hurley* (Release)	2
08 May	OH BOY ... *Mud* (Rak)	3
29 May	STAND BY YOUR MAN ... *Tammy Wynette* (Epic)	3
19 Jun	THREE STEPS TO HEAVEN ... *Showaddywaddy* (Bell)	1
26 Jun	PROUD ONE ... *The Osmonds* (MGM)	1
03 Jul	I'M NOT IN LOVE ... *10cc* (Mercury)	3
24 Jul	TEARS ON MY PILLOW ... *Johnny Nash* (CBS)	1
31 Jul	GIVE A LITTLE LOVE ... *Bay City Rollers* (Bell)	2
14 Aug	BARBADOS ... *Typically Tropical* (Gull)	2
28 Aug	I CAN'T GIVE YOU ANYTHING BUT MY LOVE ... *The Stylistics* (Avco)	3
18 Sep	SAILING ... *Rod Stewart* (Warner Bros)	1
25 Sep	MOONLIGHTING ... *Leo Sayer* (Chrysalis)	2
09 Oct	HOLD ME CLOSE ... *David Essex* (CBS)	2
23 Oct	RHINESTONE COWBOY ... *Glen Campbell* (Capitol)	6
04 Dec	THE COMBINE HARVESTER ... *Brendan Grace* (Solo)	1
11 Dec	IMAGINE ... *John Lennon* (Apple)	1
18 Dec	BOHEMIAN RHAPSODY ... *Queen* (EMI)	6

1976

29 Jan	MAMA MIA ... *Abba* (Epic)	3
19 Feb	TURN OUT THE LIGHTS ... *Brendan Shine* (Play)	3
11 Mar	DREAMING MY DREAMS ... *Marianne Faithfull* (Nems)	5
15 Apr	SAVE YOUR KISSES FOR ME ... *Brotherhood Of Man* (Pye)	1
22 Apr	FERNANDO ... *Abba* (Epic)	7
10 Jun	SISTER MARY ... *Joe Dolan* (Release)	4
08 Jul	SILLY LOVE SONGS ... *Wings* (Parlophone)	2

Date disc hit the #1 spot		Number of weeks at No. 1
22 Jul	BOYS ARE BACK IN TOWN ... *Thin Lizzy* (Vertigo)	1
29 Jul	DON'T GO BREAKING MY HEART ... *Elton John and Kiki Dee* (Rocket)	1
05 Aug	BOYS ARE BACK IN TOWN ... *Thin Lizzy* (Vertigo)	1
12 Aug	DON'T GO BREAKING MY HEART ... *Elton John and Kiki Dee* (Rocket)	4
09 Sep	DANCING QUEEN ... *Abba* (Epic)	6
21 Oct	MISSISSIPPI ... *Pussy Cat* (EMI)	4
18 Nov	IF YOU LEAVE ME NOW ... *Chicago* (CBS)	6
30 Dec	WHEN A CHILD IS BORN ... *Johnny Mathis* (CBS)	3

1977

20 Jan	DON'T GIVE UP ON US ... *David Soul* (Private Stock)	2
03 Feb	AND THE BAND PLAYED WALTZING MATILDA ... *Makem and Clancy* (Blackbird)	3
24 Feb	WHEN I NEED YOU ... *Leo Sayer* (Chrysalis)	3
17 Mar	CHANSON D'AMOUR ... *Manhattan Transfer* (Atlantic)	3
07 Apr	KNOWING ME KNOWING YOU ... *Abba* (Epic)	5
12 May	IT'S NICE TO BE IN LOVE AGAIN ... *Swarbriggss + 2* (EMI)	2
26 May	HAVE I THE RIGHT ... *Dead End Kids* (CBS)	2
09 Jun	BIG TOM IS STILL THE KING ... *Susan McCann* (Top Spin)	2
23 Jun	BACK HOME AGAIN ... *Dickie Rock* (Solo)	4
21 Jul	SAM ... *Olivia Newton John* (EMI)	2
04 Aug	WHEN BENGY WRAPPED HIS TRACTOR ROUND THE OLD OAK TREE ... *Brendan Grace* (Solo)	2
18 Aug	DADDYS LITTLE GIRL ... *Brendan Quinn* (Emerald)	1
25 Aug	ANGELO ... *Brotherhood Of Man* (Pye)	1
01 Sep	I NEED YOU ... *Joe Dolan* (Release)	1
08 Sep	WAY DOWN ... *Elvis Presley* (RCA)	1
15 Sep	I NEED YOU ... *Joe Dolan* (Release)	1
22 Sep	NOBODY DOES IT BETTER ... *Carly Simon* (Elektra)	1
29 Sep	WAY DOWN ... *Elvis Presley* (RCA)	1
06 Oct	SILVER LADY ... *David Soul* (Private Stock)	4
03 Nov	YES SIR I CAN BOOGIE ... *Baccara* (RCA)	1
10 Nov	CALLING OCCUPANTS OF INTERPLANETARY CRAFT ... *The Carpenters* (A&M)	2
24 Nov	BELFAST ... *Boney M* (Atlantic)	1
01 Dec	ROCKIN' ALL OVER THE WORLD ... *Status Quo* (Vertigo)	1
08 Dec	MULL OF KINTYRE ... *Wings* (Parlophone)	10

Date disc hit the #1 spot		Number of weeks at No. 1

1978

16 Feb	FIGARO ... *Brotherhood Of Man* (Pye)	1
23 Feb	TAKE A CHANCE ON ME ... *Abba* (Epic)	1
02 Mar	RARE OLD TIMES ... *Danny Doyle* (Galaxy)	2
16 Mar	WUTHERING HEIGHTS ... *Kate Bush* (EMI)	3
06 Apr	MATCHSTALK MEN AND MATCHSTALK CATS AND DOGS ... *Brian and Michael* (Pye)	3
27 Apr	NIGHT FEVER ... *Bee Gees* (RSO)	3
18 May	RIVERS OF BABYLON ... *Boney M* (Atlantic)	4
15 Jun	ANNIES SONG ... *James Galway* (RCA)	1
22 Jun	YOU'RE THE ONE THAT I WANT ... *John Travolta and Olivia Newton John* (RSO)	8
17 Aug	SUBSTITUTE ... *Clout* (EMI)	1
24 Aug	YOU'RE THE ONE THAT I WANT ... *John Travolta and Olivia Newton John* (RSO)	1
31 Aug	THREE TIMES A LADY ... *Commodores* (Motown)	3
21 Sep	SUMMER NIGHT CITY ... *Abba* (Epic)	1
28 Sep	ONE DAY AT A TIME ... *Gloria* (Release)	1
05 Oct	SUMMER NIGHTS ... *John Travolta and Olivia Newton John* (RSO)	3
26 Oct	SANDY ... *John Travolta* (Polydor)	2
09 Nov	ONE DAY AT A TIME ... *Gloria* (Release)	1
16 Nov	HOPELESSLY DEVOTED TO YOU ... *Olivia Newton John* (RSO)	1
23 Nov	MARY'S BOY CHILD / OH MY LORD ... *Boney M* (Atlantic)	7

1979

11 Jan	YMCA ... *Village People* (Mercury)	4
08 Feb	CHIQUITA ... *Abba* (Epic)	3
01 Mar	TRAGEDY ... *Bee Gees* (RSO)	2
15 Mar	I WILL SURVIVE ... *Gloria Gaynor* (Polydor)	4
12 Apr	BRIGHT EYES ... *Art Garfunkel* (CBS)	3
03 May	HALLELUJAH ... *Milk and Honey featuring Gail Atari* (Polydor)	1
10 May	BRIGHT EYES ... *Art Garfunkel* (CBS)	2
24 May	SUNDAY GIRL ... *Blondie* (Chrysalis)	4
21 Jun	DANCE AWAY ... *Roxy Music* (Polydor)	1
28 Jun	DO YOU WANT YOUR LOBBY WASHED DOWN ... *Brendan Shine* (Play)	4
26 Jul	GREEN FIELDS OF FRANCE ... *Furey Brothers and Davy Arthur* (Banshee)	1
02 Aug	I DON'T LIKE MONDAYS ... *Boomtown Rats* (Mulligan)	4

Date disc hit the #1 spot		Number of weeks at No. 1
30 Aug	WE DON'T TALK ANYMORE ... *Cliff Richard* (EMI)	4
27 Sep	VIVA IL PAPA ... *Caitriona Walsh* (Release)	1
04 Oct	WELCOME JOHN PAUL ... *Jim Tobin* (CMR)	2
18 Oct	MESSAGE IN A BOTTLE ... *Police* (A&M)	1
25 Oct	VIDEO KILLED THE RADIO STAR ... *Buggles* (Island)	2
08 Nov	GIMME GIMME GIMME ... *Abba* (Epic)	2
22 Nov	WHEN YOU'RE IN LOVE WITH A BEAUTIFUL WOMAN ... *Dr Hook* (Capitol)	3
14 Dec	WALKING ON THE MOON ... *Police* (A&M)	1
21 Dec	ANOTHER BRICK IN THE WALL ... *Pink Floyd* (Harvest)	2

THE TOP TEN RECORDS OF THE YEARS 1959 – 1979

This listing is not intended as a guide to the best selling records of 1959-1979, as it obviously does not reflect sales figures. But it does show the most consistently popular discs year by year.

The yearly top tens below are therefore an indication of consistency rather than sales. Based on the Top Ten Irish Hits, ten points are awarded for a number one position, 9 points for a number two, and so on – down to one point for a number 10 placing.

1959

Title	Artist	Points
1. IT DOESN'T MATTER ANYMORE	BUDDY HOLLY	143
2. PETITE FLEUR	CHRIS BARBER	122
3. SIDE SADDLE	RUSS CONWAY	121
4. LIVING DOLL	CLIFF RICHARD	113
5. A PUB WITH NO BEER	SLIM DUSTY	99
5. ROULETTE	RUSS CONWAY	99
7. A FOOL SUCH AS I	ELVIS PRESLEY	96
8. LIPSTICK ON YOUR COLLAR	CONNIE FRANCIS	85
9. ONE NIGHT / I GOT STUNG	ELVIS PRESLEY	78
10. BATTLE OF NEW ORLEANS	LONNIE DONEGAN	74

1960

Title	Artist	Points
1. HE'LL HAVE TO GO	JIM REEVES	168
2. PLEASE DON'T TEASE	CLIFF RICHARD	115
3. CATHY'S CLOWN	EVERLY BROTHERS	112
4. THREE STEPS TO HEAVEN	EDDIE COCHRAN	102
5. A MESS OF BLUES	ELVIS PRESLEY	93
6. ONLY THE LONELY	ROY ORBISON	92
7. IT'S NOW OR NEVER	ELVIS PRESLEY	90
8. MY OLD MAN'S A DUSTMAN	LONNIE DONEGAN	83
9. APACHE	SHADOWS	76
10. WHY	ANTHONY NEWLEY	68

1961

1. SURRENDER	ELVIS PRESLEY	118
2. BUT I DO	CLARENCE 'FROGMAN' HENRY	107
3. RUNAWAY	DEL SHANNON	86
4. HELLO MARY LOU	RICKY NELSON	77
5. JOHNNY REMEMBER ME	JOHN LEYTON	70
6. HIS LATEST FLAME	ELVIS PRESLEY	65
7. WALK RIGHT BACK	EVERLY BROTHERS	64
8. MICHAEL	HIGHWAYMEN	63
9. YOU DON'T KNOW	HELEN SHAPIRO	61
9. YOU'LL ANSWER TO ME	CLEO LAINE	61

1962

1. GOOD LUCK CHARM	ELVIS PRESLEY	123
2. ROCK A HULA BABY	ELVIS PRESLEY	91
3. THE YOUNG ONES	CLIFF RICHARD	90
3. DEVIL WOMAN	MARTY ROBBINS	90
5. SHE'S NOT YOU	ELVIS PRESLEY	84
6. TELSTAR	TORNADOS	83
7. WONDERFUL LAND	SHADOWS	81
8. I'M LOOKING OUT THE WINDOW	CLIFF RICHARD	75
9. LET'S TWIST AGAIN	CHUBBY CHECKER	72
10. LOVESICK BLUES	FRANK IFIELD	70

1963

1. SHE LOVES YOU	BEATLES	114
2. FROM A JACK TO A KING	NED MILLER	113
3. KISS ME QUICK	BRENDAN BOWYER	96
4. IN DREAMS	ROY ORBISON	86
5. I LIKE IT	GERRY and THE PACEMAKERS	84
5. YOU'LL NEVER WALK ALONE	GERRY and THE PACEMAKERS..	84
7. WELCOME TO MY WORLD	JIM REEVES	81
8. BACHELOR BOY/THE NEXT TIME	CLIFF RICHARD	76
9. SUMMER HOLIDAY	CLIFF RICHARD	68
9. TAKE THESE CHAINS FROM MY HEART	RAY CHARLES	68

1964

1. I WON'T FORGET YOU	JIM REEVES	144
2. I LOVE YOU BECAUSE	JIM REEVES	95
3. FROM THE CANDY STORE	DICKIE ROCK	81
4. I WOULDN'T TRADE YOU FOR THE WORLD	BACHELORS	74
5. BLESS YOU	BRENDAY BOWYER	73
6. OH PRETTY WOMAN	ROY ORBISON	72
6. I BELIEVE	BACHELORS	72
8. A HARD DAY'S NIGHT	BEATLES	70
9. IT'S OVER	ROY ORBISON	69
10. NEEDLES AND PINS	SEARCHERS	68

1965

1. HUCKLEBUCK./.I RAN ALL THE WAY HOME	BRENDAN BOWYER	86
2. MY OWN PECULIAR WAY	JOE DOLAN	78
2. EVERY STEP OF THE WAY	DICKIE ROCK	78
4. HELP	BEATLES	72
5. (I CAN'T GET NO) SATISFACTION	ROLLING STONES	71
6. TEARS	KEN DODD	70
7. DON'T LOSE YOUR HUCKLEBUCK SHOES	BRENDAN BOWYER	67
8. IF I DIDN'T HAVE A DIME	TOM DUNPHY	64
9. A WORLD OF OUR OWN	SEEKERS	63
10. CRYING IN THE CHAPEL	ELVIS PRESLEY	59
10. WALKING THE STREETS IN THE RAIN	BUTCH MOORE	59

1966

1. THE MERRY PLOUGHBOY	DERMOT O'BRIEN	86
2. THE SEA AROUND US	LUDLOWS	82
3. PRETTY BROWN EYES	JOE DOLAN	75
4. BLACK AND TAN GUN	PAT SMYTH	73
5. COME BACK TO STAY	DICKIE ROCK	72
6. MURSHEEN DURKIN	JOHNNY McEVOY	71
7. LOVELY LEITRIM	LARRY CUNNINGHAM	69
8. STRANGERS IN THE NIGHT	FRANK SINATRA	62
9. PRETTY FLAMINGO	MANFRED MANN	58
10. SLOOP JOHN B	BEACH BOYS	56

1967

1. BLACK VELVET BAND	JOHNNY KELLY	163
2. WHISKEY ON A SUNDAY	DANNY DOYLE	105
3. THE BOSTON BURGLAR	JOHNNY McEVOY	98
3. FIVE LITTLE FINGERS	FRANKIE McBRIDE	98
5. THE LAST WALTZ	ENGELBERT HUMPERDINCK.	96
6. SAN FRANCISCO	SCOTT McKENZIE	79
7. SEVEN DRUNKEN NIGHTS	DUBLINERS	72
7. RELEASE ME	ENGELBERT HUMPERDINCK	72
7. I'M A BELIEVER	MONKEES	72
10. THIS IS MY SONG	PETULA CLARK	67

1968

1. HEY JUDE	BEATLES	90
2. HELP YOURSELF	TOM JONES	88
3. THOSE WERE THE DAYS	MARY HOPKIN	85
4. LITTLE ARROWS	THE DIXIES	84
5. YOUNG GIRL	UNION GAP	83
6. DELILAH	TOM JONES	81
7. HONEY	BOBBY GOLDSBORO	76
8. THE GOOD, THE BAD AND THE UGLY	HUGO MONTENEGRO	74
9. A MAN WITHOUT LOVE	ENGELBERT HUMPERDINCK	73
10. SIMON SAYS	DICKIE ROCK	70

1969

1. MAKE ME AN ISLAND	JOE DOLAN	137
2. LONELY WOODS OF UPTON	SEAN DUNPHY	122
3. SUGAR SUGAR	ARCHIES	85
4. GET BACK	BEATLES	79
5. DON'T FORGET TO REMEMBER	BEE GEES	78
6. QUICK JOEY SMALL	REAL McCOY	69
6. WHEN THE FIELDS ARE WHITE WITH DAISIES	SEAN DUNPHY	69
8. BALLAD OF JOHN AND YOKO	BEATLES	64
8. OB-LA-DI, OB-LA-DA	MARMALADE	64
8. IN THE GHETTO	ELVIS PRESLEY	64
8. TERESA	JOE DOLAN	64

1970

Title	Artist	Points
1. TWENTY ONE YEARS	DERMOT HEGARTY	217
2. ALL KINDS OF EVERYTHING	DANA	101
3. TWO LITTLE BOYS	ROLF HARRIS	90
4. I'LL FORGIVE AND I'LL TRY TO FORGET	MARGO	87
5. THE WONDER OF YOU	ELVIS PRESLEY	85
6. BAND OF GOLD	FREDA PAYNE	83
7. BRIDGE OVER TROUBLED WATER	SIMON and GARFUNKEL	77
8. IN THE SUMMERTIME	MUNGO JERRY	76
9. LOVE GROWS	EDISON LIGHTHOUSE	68
10. WANDERING STAR	LEE MARVIN	64

1971

Title	Artist	Points
1. O'BRIEN HAS NOWHERE TO GO	BRENDAN SHINE	114
2. WHEN WE WERE YOUNG	PAT LYNCH	98
3. SOMETIMES	RED HURLEY	96
4. MY SWEET LORD	GEORGE HARRISON	92
5. DID YOU EVER	NANCY and LEE	78
6. ROSE GARDEN	LYNN ANDERSON	76
7. HOT LOVE	T REX	75
8. CHIRPY CHIRPY CHEEP CHEEP	MIDDLE OF THE ROAD	73
8. IF THOSE LIPS COULD ONLY SPEAK	DERMOT HENRY	73
10. MAGGIE MAY	ROD STEWART	72

1972

Title	Artist	Points
1. MEN BEHIND THE WIRE	BARLEYCORN	221
2. SYLVIA'S MOTHER	DR. HOOK	84
3. THE GYPSY	DERMOT HENRY	80
4. A THING CALLED LOVE	JOHNNY CASH	79
5. CLAIR	GILBERT O'SULLIVAN	75
6. BROKEN MARRIAGE VOWS	BIG TOM	74
7. PUPPY LOVE	DONNY OSMOND	72
8. CIRCLES	NEW SEEKERS	68
8. I'D LIKE TO TEACH THE WORLD TO SING	NEW SEEKERS	68
10. MOULDY OLD DOUGH	LIEUTENANT PIGEON	55

1973

	Title	Artist	Points
1.	WHERE THE THREE COUNTIES MEET	BRENDAN SHINE	129
2.	TIE A YELLOW RIBBON	DAWN	95
3.	FOR THE GOOD TIMES	PERRY COMO	89
4.	WELCOME HOME	PETERS and LEE	87
5.	DAISY A DAY	DANNY DOYLE	86
6.	LONG HAIRED LOVER FROM LIVERPOOL	LITTLE JIMMY OSMOND	82
7.	I LOVE YOU STILL	BIG TOM	81
8.	AND I LOVE YOU SO	PERRY COMO	80
9.	WHISKEY IN THE JAR	THIN LIZZY	70
10.	GET DOWN	GILBERT O'SULLIVAN	67

1974

	Title	Artist	Points
1.	ANY DREAM WILL DO	JOE CUDDY	124
2.	OLD LOVE LETTERS	BIG TOM	90
3.	ABBEYSHRULE	BRENDAN SHINE	78
4.	NINETEEN MEN	DERMOT HEGARTY	74
5.	GONNA MAKE YOU A STAR	DAVID ESSEX	72
6.	IF MA COULD SEE ME NOW	THE TIMES	68
7.	I SEE A STAR	MOUTH and MacNEAL	65
8.	EVERYTHING I OWN	JOHN HOLT	57
9.	SEASONS IN THE SUN	TERRY JACKS	51
10.	KUNG FU FIGHTING	KARL DOUGLAS	50

1975

	Title	Artist	Points
1.	RHINESTONE COWBOY	GLEN CAMPBELL	89
2.	BYE BYE BABY	BAY CITY ROLLERS	83
3.	WHERE MY EILEEN IS WAITING	JOHNNY McEVOY	67
4.	LAST FAREWELL	ROGER WHITTAKER	61
5.	CAN'T GIVE YOU ANYTHING (BUT MY LOVE)	THE STYLISTICS	56
6.	I'M NOT IN LOVE	10cc	55
6.	SAILING	ROD STEWART	55
8.	THREE STEPS TO HEAVEN	SHOWADDYWADDY	54
9.	LOVE IS ALL	RED HURLEY	53
10.	GIVE A LITTLE LOVE	BAY CITY ROLLERS	52

1976

Song	Artist	
1. MISSISSIPPI	PUSSY CAT	108
2. DANCING QUEEN	ABBA	94
3. DON'T GO BREAKIN' MY HEART	ELTON JOHN and KIKI DEE	93
4. DREAMING MY DREAMS	MARIANNE FAITHFULL	92
5. SISTER MARY	JOE DOLAN	91
6. FERNANDO	ABBA	81
6. DON'T LET LIFE GET YOU DOWN	JOE CUDDY	81
8. SAVE YOUR KISSES FOR ME	BROTHERHOOD OF MAN	79
9. IF YOU LEAVE ME NOW	CHICAGO	78
10. TURN OUT THE LIGHTS	BRENDAN SHINE	71

1977

Song	Artist	
1. IT'S NICE TO BE IN LOVE AGAIN	SWARBRIGGS plus TWO	80
2. AND THE BAND PLAYED WALTZING MATILDA	MAKEM and CLANCY	75
3. BACK HOME AGAIN	DICKIE ROCK	74
4. KNOWING ME KNOWING YOU	ABBA	67
5. I NEED YOU	JOE DOLAN	61
6. WHEN I NEED YOU	LEO SAYER	60
7. SILVER LADY	DAVID SOUL	59
8. BIG TOM IS STILL THE KING	SUSAN McCANN	57
9. HAVE I THE RIGHT	DEAD END KIDS	49
9. DON'T CRY FOR ME ARGENTINA	JULIE COVINGTON	49

1978

Song	Artist	
1. RIVERS OF BABYLON	BONEY M	145
2. ONE DAY AT A TIME	GLORIA	130
3. YOU'RE THE ONE THAT I WANT	JOHN TRAVOLTA and OLIVIA NEWTON JOHN	128
4. SUMMER NIGHTS	JOHN TRAVOLTA and OLIVIA NEWTON JOHN	81
5. MULL OF KINTYRE	WINGS	72
6. MATCHSTALK MEN	BRIAN and MICHAEL	66
7. RARE OLD TIMES	DANNY DOYLE	65
8. TAKE A CHANCE ON ME	ABBA	64
9. MARY'S BOY CHILD	BONEY M	60
10. SUBSTITUTE	CLOUT	52

1979

1. GREEN FIELDS OF FRANCE .... FUREY BROTHERS and DAVEY ARTHUR ... 170
2. DO YOU WANT YOUR LOBBY WASHED DOWN ... BRENDAN SHINE 119
3. WHEN YOU'RE IN LOVE WITH A BEAUTIFUL WOMAN ... DR. HOOK 80
4. BRIGHT EYES .... ART GARFUNKEL 78
5. I WILL SURVIVE .... GLORIA GAYNOR 68
6. HEART OF GLASS .... BLONDIE 60
7. TRAGEDY .... BEE GEES 59
7. I DON'T LIKE MONDAYS .... BOOMTOWN RATS 59
9. YMCA .... VILLAGE PEOPLE 58
10. SUNDAY GIRL .... BLONDIE 54

ROLL OF HONOUR:
IN MEMORY OF

A listing of artists who have departed this life including date of death and where known, the cause of death and age at death.

JANUARY

02 **Tex Ritter** 1974 – heart attack – aged 68
David Lynch (Platters) 1981- cancer – aged 51
04 **Phil Lynott** 1986 – heart and liver failure – aged 36
05 **Billie Anthony** – 1991 series of strokes – aged 58
Sonny Bono 1998 – ski-ing accident – aged 62
07 **Larry Williams** 1980 – self inflicted gunshot wound – aged 44
08 **Ron Goodwin** 2003 – complications due to asthma – aged 77
09 **Dave Dee** (DDBM&T) 2009 – prostate cancer – aged 67
10 **Rod Allen** (The Fortunes) 2008 – liver cancer – aged 63
11 **James Griffin** (Bread) 2005 – cancer – aged 61
12 **Maurice Gibb** (Bee Gees) 2003 – cardiac arrest – aged 53
Randy VanWarmer 2004 – leukemia – aged 48
15 **Nilsson** 1994 – heart attack – aged 52
Marion Ryan 1999 – heart failure – aged 67
Wally Stott 2009 – aged 84
Leroy Smith (Sweet Sensation) 2009 – bronchopneumonia – aged 56
16 **David Whitfield** 1980 – brain haemorrage – aged 53
Will Dub Jones (The Coasters) 2000 – diabetes – aged 71
19 **Carl Perkins** 1998 – throat cancer – aged 65
Wilson Pickett 2006 – heart attack – aged 64
Denny Doherty (Mamas and the Papas) 2007 – kidney failure – aged 66
John Stewart (Kingston Trio) 2008 – stroke – aged 68
21 **Peggy Lee** 2002 – heart attack – aged 81
22 **Telly Savalas** 1994 – bladder cancer – aged 70
Wally Whyton (Vipers Skiffle Group) 1997 – lung cancer – aged 67
23 **Terry Kath** (Chicago) 1978 – accidental gunshot wound to head – aged 31
Vic Ames (Ames Brothers) 1978 – road accident – aged 52

24 **Gordon MacRae** 1986 – cancer – aged 64

25 **Ray Peterson** 2005 – cancer – aged 69

26 **Tommy Dee** 2007 – aged 71

27 **Gene McFadden** (McFadden and Whitehead) 2006 – cancer – aged 57

28 **Jim Capaldi** 2005 – stomach cancer – aged 60

29 **Billy Fury** 1983 – heart failure – aged 42

30 **Luke Kelly** (The Dubliners) 1984 – brain tumour – aged 43

FEBRUARY

02 **Sid Vicious** (Sex Pistols) 1979 – heroin overdose – aged 21

03 **Big Bopper** (J P Richardson) 1959 – plane crash – aged 28

Buddy Holly 1959 – plane crash – aged 22

Ritchie Valens 1959 – plane crash – aged 19

04 **Karen Carpenter** 1983 – complications from anorexia – aged 32

Doris Kenner (Shirelles) 2000 – breast cancer – aged 58

06 **Hugo Montenegro** 1981 – emphysema – aged 55

Carl Wilson (Beach Boys) 1998 – lung cancer – aged 51

Frankie Laine 2007 – cardiovascular disease – aged 93

07 **Matt Monro** 1985 – liver cancer – aged 54

08 **Del Shannon** 1990 – self inflicted gunshot wound – aged 55

09 **Bill Haley** 1981 – heart attack – aged 55

Brian Connolly (The Sweet) 1997 – liver failure – aged 51

10 **Freddie Bell** 2008 – lung cancer – aged 76

12 **Sal Mineo** 1976 – stabbed to death – aged 37

Oliver 2000 – cancer – aged 54

13 **Waylon Jennings** 2002 – diabetic complications – aged 64

14 **Vincent Crane** (Atomic Rooster) 1989 – suicide– aged 45

Mick Tucker (The Sweet) 2002 – leukemia – aged 54

15 **Nat King Cole** 1965 – lung cancer – aged 47

17 **Bob Merrill** 1998 – suicide – aged 76

20 **Ronnie Hilton** 2001 – aged 75

21 **Les Gray** (Mud) 2004 – heart attack – aged 57

22 **Florence Ballard** (Supremes) 1976 – heart attack – aged 32

Brendan O'Dowda 2002 – cancer – aged 76

23 **Stan Laurel** 1965 – heart attack – aged 74

Don Cornell 2004 – emphysema – aged 84

25 **Cyril Stapleton** 1974 – heart attack – aged 59
Donie Collins 1987 – cancer – aged
Johnnie Ray 1990 – liver failure – aged 63
Edward Patten (Gladys Knight and the Pips) 2005 – stroke – aged 65
26 **Cornell Gunter** (The Coasters) 1990 – murdered shot – aged 53
Wendy Richard 2009 – breast cancer – aged 65
27 **Frankie Lymon** 1968 – heroin overdose – aged 25
28 **Doretta Morrow** 1968 – cancer – aged 40
Winifred Atwell 1983 – heart attack – aged 68
Helmut Zacharias 2002 – lung infection – aged 82
Chris Curtis (Searchers) 2005 – long illness – aged 63
Mike Smith (Dave Clark Five) 2008 – pneumonia – aged 64

MARCH

02 **Serge Gainsburg** 1991 – heart attack – aged 62
Dusty Springfield 1999 – breast cancer – aged 59
03 **Danny Kaye** 1987 – heart failure – aged 74
Hurricane Smith 2008 – cancer – aged 85
05 **Richard Kiley** 1999 – bone marrow cancer – aged 76
08 **Billy Eckstine** 1993 – stroke – aged 78
Adam Faith 2003 – heart attack – aged 62
Hank Locklin 2009 – aged 91
09 **Brad Delph** (Boston) 2007 – carbon monoxide poisoning – aged 55
10 **Andy Gibb** 1988 – heart virus – aged 30
15 **Edmund Hockridge** 2009 – aged 89
16 **Johnny Cymbal** 1993 – heart attack – aged 48
Joseph Pope (Tams) 1996 – heart failure – aged 62
18 **John Phillips** (Mamas and the Papas) 2001 – heart failure – aged 65
19 **Paul Kossoff** (Free) 1976 – drug induced heart attack – aged 25
20 **Shay O'Hara** 2009 – leukemia – aged 73
21 **Speedy Keen** (Thunderclap Newman) 2002 – heart failure – aged 56
22 **Dave Guard** (Kingston Trio) 1991 – lymphatic cancer – aged 56
25 **Buck Owens** 2006 – heart attack – aged 74
27 **Ian Dury** 2000 – liver cancer – aged 57
28 **Waldo de Los Rios** 1977 – self inflicted gunshot wound – aged 42

29 **Mantovani** 1980 – aged 74
The Singing Nun 1985 – suicide – aged 51
31 **Phil Cordell** (Springwater) 2007 – aged 59

APRIL

01 **Marvin Gaye** 1984 – gunshot wound – aged 44
02 **Edwin Starr** 2003 – heart attack – aged 61
03 **Gerry Cronin** (Gerry and the Ohio) 1988 – heart attack
Sarah Vaughan 1990 – lung cancer – aged 76
Butch Moore 2001 heart attack – aged 61
Brendan O'Brien 2008 – heart attack – aged 66
05 **Bob Hite** (Canned Heat) 1981 – heart attack – aged 36
Danny Rapp (Danny and the Juniors) 1983 – self inflicted gunshot wound – aged 41
Cozy Powell 1998 – car crash – aged 50
Gene Pitney 2006 – heart attack – aged 66
06 **Tammy Wynnette** 1998 – blood clot on lung – aged 55
Nikki Sullivan (Crickets) 2004 – heart attack – aged 66
07 **Lee Brilleaux** (Dr Feelgood) 1994 – throat cancer – aged 41
Heinz 2000 – motor neurone disease – aged 57
08 **Patrick O'Hagan** 1993 – aged 69
09 **Duke D'Mond** (Barron Knights) 2009 – heart attack – aged 66
10 **Little Eva** 2003 – cervical cancer – aged 59
11 **Harry Secombe** 2002 – prostate cancer – aged 79
14 **Michael Flanders** 1975 – aneurism – aged 53
Burl Ives 1995 – cancer – aged 85
Dorothy Squires 1998 – cancer – aged 83
15 **Anthony Newley** 1999 – cancer – aged 67
Dave King 2002 – aged 72
John Fred 2005 – kidney failure – aged 63
16 **Morris Stoloff** 1980 – aged 81
17 **Eddie Cochran** 1960 – car accident – aged 21
19 **Michael O'Duffy** 2003 – aged 74
20 **John Banks** (Merseybeats) 1988 – aged 44
Steve Marriott 1991 – house fire – aged 44
Benny Hill 1992 – heart attack – aged 68

21 **Lynne Taylor** (Rooftop Singers) 1979 – aged 43
George Lanius (Crescendos) 1996
Nina Simone 2003 – natural causes – aged 70
23 **Pete Ham** (Badfinger) 1975 – suicide (by hanging) – aged 27
25 **John Kerr** 2006 – aged 80
Bobby 'Boris' Pickett 2007 – leukemia – aged 69
Humphrey Lyttleton 2008 – aortic aneurysm – aged 86
30 **Zola Taylor** (Platters) 2007 – pneumonia – aged 73

MAY

01 **Doc Carroll** (Royal Blues) 2005 – cancer – aged 64
Johnny Paris (Johnny and the Hurricanes) 2006 – pneumonia – aged 65
04 **Joe 'Mr Piano' Henderson** 1980 – heart attack – aged 60
06 **Dickie Valentine** 1971 – car accident – aged 41
Gerry Shepherd (Glitter Band) 2003 – cancer – aged 52
08 **Eddy Arnold** 2008 –aged 89
10 **Ciaran Bourke** (Dubliners) 1988 – aged 53
Clive Scott (Jigsaw) 2009
11 **Noel Redding** (Jimi Hendrix Experience) 2003
John Whitehead (McFadden and Whitehead) 2004 – gunshot wound – aged 45
12 **Perry Como** 2001 – natural causes – aged 88
13 **Joan Weber** 1981 – pneumonia – aged 45
Johnnie Wilder (Heatwave) 2006 – aged 56
14 **Keith Relf** (Yardbirds) 1976 – electrocuted – aged 33
Frank Sinatra 1998 – heart failure – aged 82
15 **Frederik** (Nina and Frederik) 1994 – gunshot wound – aged 62
18 **Leroy Anderson** 1975 – aged 66
19 **Odia Coates** 1991 – cancer – aged 49
Freddie Garrity (Freddie of the Dreamers)2006 – blood circulation problem – aged 69
21 **Vaughn Monroe** 1973 – following stomach surgery – aged 61
22 **Willie Devey** (Cadets) 2004 – heart attack
Dermot O'Brien 2007 – lung cancer – aged 74
24 **Gene Clark** (Byrds) 1991 – heart attack – aged 49
25 **Sid Phillips** 1973 – heart attack – aged 65
Desmond Dekker 2006 – heart attack – aged 64
28 **Tony Ashton** (Ashton, Gardner and Dyke) 2001 – cancer – aged 55

JUNE

02 **Bo Diddley** 2008 – heart failure – aged 79

03 **Johnny Grande** (Comets) 2006 – cancer – aged 76

05 **Conway Twitty** 1993 – abdominal aneurysm – aged 59
Mel Torme 1999 – effects of a stroke – aged 73

06 **Billy Brown** 1999 – long illness – aged 55
Billy Preston 2006 – kidney failure – aged 59

09 **Frank Chacksfield** 1995 – Parkinsons disease – aged 81

10 **Alan Blakely** (Tremeloes) 1996 – cancer – aged 54
Johnnie Johnston (Johnston Brothers) 1998 – aged 78
Ray Charles 2004 – complications from acute liver disease – aged 73

12 **Lou Monte** 1989 – emphysema – aged 72
Finbar O'Leary (Dixies) 2002

14 **Rory Gallagher** 1995 – liver failure – aged
Eamonn McGirr (Go Lucky Four) 2004 – complications of paralyis – aged 63
Bob Bogle (The Ventures) 2009 –non Hodgkins Lymphoma – aged 75.

15 **Gary Miller** 1968 – heart attack – aged 44
Ella Fitzgerald 1996 – diabetes – aged 79

16 **Paul Furey** (Furey Brothers) 2002 – cancer – aged 54

19 **Tony Brent** 1993 – heart attack – aged 66
Bobby Helms 1997 – emphysema – aged 60
Lawrence Payton (Four Tops) 1997 – cancer – aged 59

21 **Bert Kaempfert** 1980 – stroke – aged 56
Michael Jackson 2009 – cardiac arrest – aged 50

27 **Pat McGeegan** 1987 – cancer – aged 52
John Entwistle (The Who) 2002 – heart attack – aged 57
Gale Storm 2009 – natural causes – aged 87
Fayette Pinkney (Three Degrees) 2009 – aged 61

28 **Maisie McDaniel** 2008 – suddenly – aged 69

29 **Horst Jankowski** 1998 – lung cancer – aged 62
Rosemary Clooney 2002 – lung cancer – aged 74

30 **Chet Atkins** 2001 – colon cancer – aged 77

JULY

01 **Guy Mitchell** 1999 – surgical complications – aged 72

02 **Renaldo 'Obie' Benson** (Four Tops) 2005 – lung cancer – aged 69

03 **Brian Jones** (Rolling Stones) 1969 – drowning – aged 27
Jim Morrison (Doors) 1971 - aged 27
04 **Barry White** 2003 – kidney failure – aged 58
05 **Ernie K-Doe** 2001 – liver failure – aged 65
Gerry Reynolds (Hi-Lows) 2002 – cancer – aged 49
Gary Street (Fairways) 2003 – aged 55
06 **Louis Armstrong** 1971 – heart attack – aged 71
Denis D'ell (Honeycombs) 2005 – cancer – aged 61
07 **Syd Barrett** (Pink Floyd) 2006 – complications from diabetes – aged 60
08 **Geoff Love** (Manuel and the Music of the Mountains) 1991 – aged 73
09 **Milan Williams** (Commodores) 2006 – cancer – aged 58
10 **Chris O'Mahoney** (Dixies) 1990 – heart attack
12 **Minnie Ripperton** 1979 – breast cancer – aged 31
13 **Les Crane** 2008 – natural causes – aged 72
15 **Bill Justis** 1982 – cancer – aged 55
Johnny Duncan 2000 – bowel cancer – aged 67
16 **Jo Stafford** 2008 – congestive heart failure – aged 90
17 **Chas Chandler** (Animals) 1996 – aortic aneurysm – aged 57
Paul Young (Sad Cafe) 2000 – heart attack – aged 53
Gordon Waller (Peter and Gordon) 2009 – cardiac arrest – aged 64
20 **Roy Hamilton** 1969 – stroke – aged 39
21 **Long John Baldry** 2005 – chest infection – aged 64
22 **Eugene Record** (Chi-Lites) 2005 – cancer – aged 64
Herb Kalin (Kalin Twins) 2006 – heart attack – aged 71
Theo Cahill (Dixies) 1988 – heart attack
24 **Peter Sellers** 1980 – heart attack – aged 54
Charlie Rich 1995 – blood clot in lung – aged 62
26 **Mary Wells** 1992 – throat cancer – aged 48
28 **George Williams** (The Tymes) 2004 – cancer – aged 68
29 **Mama Cass Elliott** 1974 – heart attack – aged 32
Tom Dunphy 1975 – car accident – aged 39
31 **Jim Reeves** 1964 – plane crash – aged 40
Fran O'Toole 1975 – murdered by terrorists – aged 29
Anne Shelton 1994 – died in sleep – aged 65
Les Braid (Swinging Blue Jeans) 2005 – cancer – aged 69

AUGUST

01 **Tommy Makem** 2007 – lung cancer – aged 74
Paul Robi (Platters) 1989– pancreatic cancer – aged 57
02 **Don Estelle** 2003 – long illness – aged 70
Erik Darling (Tarriers) 2008 – Burkitt's lymphoma – aged 74
03 **Dominic Behan** 1989 – cancer – aged 60
Louis Teicher (Ferrante and Teicher) 2008 – heart attack – aged 83
04 **Lee Hazlewood** 2007 – cancer – aged 78
07 **Oliver Hardy** 1957 – celebral thrombosis – aged 65
Esther Phillips 1984 – liver and kidney failure – aged 48
Tony Williams (Platters) 1992 – emphysema – aged 63
08 **Eddie Calvert** 1978 – heart attack – aged 56
09 **Donald Peers** 1973 – bronchial pneumonia – aged 65
13 **Joe Tex** 1982 – heart attack – aged 49
Eve Boswell 1998 – heart attack – aged 74
Les Paul 2009 – pnuemonia – aged 94
14 **Johnny Burnette** 1964 – boat accident drowning – aged 30
Lita Roza 2008 – aged 82
16 **Elvis Presley** 1977 – cardiac arrhythmia – aged 42
Alan Caddy (Tornados) 2000 – aged 60
Ronnie Drew (Dubliners) 2008 – cancer – aged 73
20 **Tony Jackson** (Searchers) 2003 – cirrhosis of liver – aged 63
Carol Young (Kaye Sisters) 2006 – cancer – aged 76
Larry Knetchel (Bread) 2009 – cancer – aged 69
21 **Colm Gilmore** (Colm and the Sundowners) 1997 – cancer
23 **Brendan Murray** (The Seasons) 2002
Hal Kalin (Kalin Twins) 2005 – car crash – aged 71
24 **Warren Covington** (Tommy Dorsey Orchestra) 1999 – aged 78
27 **Big Dee Irwin** 1995 – heart attack – aged 56
29 **Lee Marvin** 1987 – heart attack – aged 63
31 **Carl Wayne** (Move) 2004 – cancer of esophagus – aged 61

SEPTEMBER

02 **Fritz Fryer** (Four Pennies) 2007 – pancreatic cancer – aged 63
03 **Al Wilson** (Canned Heat) 1970 – suicide – aged 27
05 **Les Braid** (Swinging Blue Jeans) 2005 – cancer – aged 67
06 **Tom Fogerty** (Creedence Clearwater revival) 1990 – heart attack – aged 48

07 **Keith Moon** (The Who) 1978 – accidental overdose of prescription drugs – aged 32
James Gilreath 2003 – tractor accident on farm – aged 67
09 **Norrie Paramor** 1979 – cancer – aged 65
12 **Johnny Cash** 2003 – complications from diabetes – aged 71
14 **Grace Kelly** 1982 – car crash – aged 52
Perez Prez Prado 1989 – stroke – aged 72
15 **Richard Wright** (Pink Floyd) 2008 – cancer – aged 65
Cyril McKevitt (The Mainliners) 2009 – heart attack – aged 69
16 **John McCormack** 1945 – pnuemonia – aged 61
Marc Bolan 1977 – car crash – aged 29
Mary Travers (Peter Paul and Mary) 2009 – leukemia – aged 72
Sheb Wooley 2003 – leukemia – aged 82
17 **Frankie Vaughan** 1999 – heart ailment – aged 71
18 **Jimi Hendrix** 1970 – drug overdose – aged 27
19 **Lou Busch** 1979 – car accident – aged 69
Slim Dusty 2003 – cancer – aged 76
Skeeter Davis 2004 – breast cancer – aged 72
Chuck Rio aka Danny Flores (Champs) 2006 – pneumonia – aged 77
Arthur Ferrante (Ferrante and Teicher) 2009 – aged 88
20 **Glen Curtin** 2009 – aged 66
22 **Robert Wilson** 1964 – result of a car accident in 1963 – aged 56
23 **Robbie McIntosh** (Average White Band) 1974
25 **Canon Sydney MacEwan** 1991 – aged 83
26 **Billy Vaughn** 1991 – cancer – aged 72
27 **Gracie Fields** 1979 – pneumonia – aged 81
Jimmy McCulloch 1979 – drug related heart failure – aged 26

OCTOBER

01 **Nick Reynolds** (Kingston Trio) 2008 – acute respiratory disease – aged 75
04 **Mike Gibbins** (Badfinger) 2005 – natural causes – aged 56
07 **Mario Lanza** 1959 – heart attack – aged 38
Johnny Kidd 1966 – car crash – aged 26
10 **Lennie Peters** (Peters and Lee) 1992 – bone cancer – aged 53
11 **Russ Hamilton** 2008 –aged 76
Edith Piaf 1963 – liver cancer – aged 47
12 **Gene Bricker** (Marcels) 1983
John Denver 1997 – plane crash – aged 53

14 **Bing Crosby** 1977 – heart attack – aged 74
15 **Terry Gilkyson** 1999 – natural causes – aged 83
17 **Tennessee Ernie Ford** 1991 – liver failure – aged 72
Teresa Brewer 2007 – neuromuscular disease – aged 76
Levi Stubbs (Four Tops) 2008 – cancer – aged 72
18 **Bryan Johnson** 1995 – cancer – aged 69
20 **Henry Vestine** (Canned Heat) 1997 – respiratory failure – aged 52
22 **Bill Reed** (Diamonds) 2004 – cancer – aged 67
24 **Kim Gardner** (Ashton, Gardner and Dyke) 2001 – cancer – aged 53
25 **Johnny Kelly** 1987 – aged 45
Roger Miller 1992 – lung cancer – aged 56
Richard Harris 2002 – cancer hodgkins disease – aged 72
26 **Alma Cogan** 1966 – ovarian cancer – aged 34
29 **Michael Holliday** 1963 – suicide drugs overdose – aged 38
31 **Larry Hogan** 1998 – heart failure – aged 59

NOVEMBER

04 **Lonnie Donegan** 2007 – heart failure – aged 71
05 **Eamonn Andrews** 1987 – heart failure – aged 64
Billy Guy (The Coasters) 2002 – heart attack – aged 56
Bobby Hatfield (Righteous Brothers) 2003 – heart attack – aged 63
12 **Mitch Mitchell** (Jimi Hendrix Experience) 2008 – natural causes – aged 61
16 **Russ Conway** 2000 – cancer – aged 75
17 **Alan Hull** (Lindisfarne) 1995 – heart attack – aged 50
Don Gibson 2003 – natural causes – aged 75
18 **Ted Heath** 1969 – aged 69
19 **Tom Evans** (Badfinger) 1983 – suicide (by hanging) – aged 36
21 **Will Glahe** 1989 – aged 87
22 **Paul Williams** (Greenbeats) 1967 – car accident
Janet Ertel (Chordettes) 1988 – cancer – aged 74
23 **O. C. Smith** 2001 heart attack – aged 69
24 **Freddie Mercury** 1991 – A.I.D.S. – aged 45
26 **Tommy Dorsey** 1956 – asphyxiation choked to death – aged 51
28 **Guy Marks** 1987 – aged 64
Tony Meehan 2005 – following a fall at his home – aged 62
29 **George Harrison** 2001 – cancer – aged 58

DECEMBER

02 **Mariska Veres** (Shocking Blue) 2006 – cancer – aged 57
Dave Mount (Mud) 2006 – suicide – aged 59
04 **Bernie Dwyer** (Dreamers) 2002 – cancer – aged 62
06 **Roy Orbison** 1988 – heart attack – aged 52
Danny Williams 2005 – lung cancer – aged 63
08 **John Lennon** 1980 – gunshot wound murdered – aged 40
Marty Robbins 1982 – respiratory failure – aged 57
09 **Georgia Gibbs** 2006 – leukemia – aged 87
Michael Botts (Bread) 2005 – colon cancer – aged 61
Freddie Marsden (Pacemakers) 2006 – lung cancer – aged 66
10 **Faron Young** 1996 – suicide self inflicted gunshot wound – aged 64
11 **Sam Cooke** 1964 – gunshot wound – aged 33
12 **Des Wilson** (Cotton Mill Boys) 1990 cancer – aged
13 **Zal Yanovsky** (Lovin' Spoonful) 2002 – congestive heart failure – aged 57
17 **Ruby Murray** 1996 – chronic alcoholism – aged 61
Dennis Peyton (Dave Clark Five) 2006 – cancer – aged 63
19 **Michael Clarke** (Byrds) 1993 – liver failure – aged 47
20 **Bobby Darin** 1973 – heart failure after open heart surgery – aged 47
Michael Conn (Millionaires) 2008 – after long illness
21 **Karl Denver** 1998 – brain tumour – aged 67
22 **Joe Ames** (Ames Brothers) 2007
23 **Jimmy Shand** 2000 – after long illness – aged 92
24 **Rossano Brazzi** 1994 – neural virus – aged 78
Nick Massi (Four Seasons) 2000 – cancer – aged 78
Charlie Drake 2006 – aged 81
25 **Charles Chaplin** 1977 – natural causes – aged 78
Dean Martin 1995 – respiratory failure due to emphysema – aged 78
James Brown 2006 – pneumonia – aged 73
Eartha Kitt 2008 – colon cancer – aged 81
26 **Joe Dolan** 2007 – brain haemorrhage – aged 64
27 **Bob Luman** 1978 – pneumonia – aged 61
28 **Denis Wilson** (Beach Boys) 1983 – drowning – aged 39
Meri Wilson 2002 – car crash – aged 53
30 **Johnny Moore** (Drifters) 1998 – heart attack – aged 64
31 **Ricky Nelson** 1985 – plane crash – aged 45
Floyd Cramer 1997 – lung cancer – aged 64

Title – *Act* (Position) Year of Chart Entry

ALMOST THERE
1954 – 1958

For the purpose of this book, and in order to give a more accurate picture of the most popular records in Ireland for the period September 1954 to December 1958 , we have also checked with newspaper advertisements of the period.

Many record stores, such as Piggotts, McHugh Himself, Tara Record Store and the Gramophone Store, published their own list of best sellers, in their newspapers advertisements of the period, this has assisted us in producing a comprehensive listing of the best selling discs in Ireland from September 1954 to December 1958.

The following is a listing of records that while they did not make the record companies official Best Sellers List, did appear on the best sellers listings of record stores such as Piggotts, McHugh etc.

THE ABC'S OF LOVE – *Frankie Lymon and The Teenagers* (-)....1957
ARE YOU SINCERE – *The Platters* (-)....1958
ARMEN'S THEME• – *Ted Heath and his Music* (-)....1957
AT THE HOP – *Danny and the Juniors* (-)....1958
AT THE HOP – *Nick Todd* (-)....1958

BABY DOLL – *Andy Williams* (-)....1957
THE BALLAD OF DAVY CROCKETT – *Tennessee Ernie Ford* (-)....1956
BANANA BOAT SONG – *Stan Freberg* (-)....1957
THE BEST THINGS IN LIFE ARE FREE• - *Sid Phillips and his Band* (-)....1957
BIG MAN – *Four Preps* (-)....1958
BIRD DOG – *Everly Brothers* (-)....1958
THE BIRDS AND THE BEES – *Dave King* (-)....1956
BLUE MOON – *Elvis Presley* (-)....1956
THE BLUEBELL POLKA• – *Jimmy Shand Band* (-)....1955
THE BOOK OF LOVE – *The Monotones* (-)....1958
BREATHLESS – *Jerry Lee Lewis* (-)....1958
BYE BYE LOVE – *Everly Brothers* (-)....1957

Title – *Act* (Position) Year of Chart Entry

A CERTAIN SMILE – *Johnny Mathis* (-)....1958
CIU CIU BELLA – *Danny Kaye* (-)....1957
C'MON LET'S GO – *Tommy Steele* (-)....1958
COME NEXT SPRING – *Tony Bennet* (-)....1956

DAVY CROCKETT IS HELPING SANTA CLAUS – *Joe Lynch* (-)....1956
THE DONKEY CART• – *Frank Chacksfield and his Orchestra*(-)....1956
DON'T BE CRUEL – *Elvis Presley* (-)....1956
DON'T KNOCK THE ROCK – *Bill Haley and the Comets* (-)....1957
DON'T RINGA THE BELL – *Alma Cogan* (-)....1956

EARTHBOUND – *Mario Lanza* (-)....1956
EL RANCHO ROCK• - *The Champs* (-)....1958
ELEVENTH HOUR MELODY• - *Lou Busch and his Orchestra* (-)....1956

FABULOUS – *Charlie Gracie* (-)....1957
A FALLEN STAR – *The Hilltoppers* (-)....1957
FIRST PUFF TO BALLYJAMESDUFF – *Joe Lynch* (-)....1956
FRAULEIN – *Bobby Helms* (-)....1957
FRIENDLY PERSUASION (Thee I Love) – *Pat Boone* (-)....1957

THE GIRL WITH THE GOLDEN BRAIDS – *Perry Como* (-)....1957
GREAT BALLS OF FIRE – *Jerry Lee Lewis* (-)....1957

HEART – *Max Bygraves* (-)....1957
HOOTS MON• – *Lord Rockingham's X1* (-)....1958
HOUND DOG – *Elvis Presley* (-)....1956
A HOUSE WITH LOVE IN IT – *Vera Lynn* (-)....1956

I MAY NEVER PASS THIS WAY AGAIN – *Perry Como* (-)....1958
I MAY NEVER PASS THIS WAY AGAIN – *Dennis Lotis* (-)....1958
IF WE ONLY HAD OLD IRELAND OVER HERE – *Sean Mooney* (-)....1954
I'M WALKIN' – *Fats Domino* (-)....1957
THE IMMORTAL PERCY FRENCH L.P. – *Brendan O'Dowda* (-)....1958
IN A LITTLE SPANISH TOWN – *Bing Crosby* (-)....1956
IN THE MIDDLE OF A DARK DARK NIGHT – *Guy Mitchell* (-)....1957
IT'S ALL IN THE GAME – *Tommy Edwards* (-)....1958

Title – *Act* (Position) Year of Chart Entry

IT'S ONLY MAKE BELIEVE – *Conway T witty* (-) 1958
IVORY TOWER – *Cathy Carr* (-) 1956

JAILHOUSE ROCK – *Elvis Presley* (-) 1958
JAMAICA FAREWELL – *Edmundo Ros and his Orchestra*(-) 1957
JENNY JENNY – *Little Richard* (-) 1957
JUST SAY I LOVE YOU – *Tony Dalli* (-) 1958

KEWPIE DOLL – *Frankie Vaughan* (-) 1958
KING CREOLE – *Elvis Presley* (-) 1958
KISSES SWEETER THAN WINE – *Jimmie Rodgers* (-) 1958

LAZY MARY – *Lou Monte* (-) 1958
LEFT BANK• – *Winifred Atwell* (-) 1956
(LET ME BE YOUR) TEDDY BEAR – *Elvis Presley* (-) 1957
LET'S ROCK 'N' ROLL• - *Winifred Atwell* (-) 1957
A LETTER TO A SOLDIER – *Terry Burton* (-) 1957
LITTLE CHILD (DADDY DEAR) – *Danny Kaye and Dena Kaye* (-) 1954
LOLLIPOP – *Gary Miller* (-) 1958
LONELY MAN – *Frankie Laine* (-) 1957
LOVE AND MARRIAGE – *Frank Sinatra* (-) 1956
LOVE ME TENDER – *Elvis Presley* (-) 1956

MADAGASCAR• - *Ted Heath and his Music* (-) 1957
MAGIC MOMENTS – *Perry Como* (-) 1958
MAN ON FIRE – *Bing Crosby* (-) 1957
MANDOLIN SERENADE• – *Charles Chaplin* (-) 1957
MARY'S BOY CHILD – *Harry Belafonte* (-) 1957
MAYBE BABY – *The Crickets* (-) 1958
MELODIE D'AMOUR – *The Ames Brothers* (-) 1957
MORE THAN EVER – *Edmund Hockridge* (-) 1958
MOUNTAIN GREENERY – *Mel Torme* (-) 1956
MY DUBLIN BAY – *Rose Brennan* (-) 1956
MY SEPTEMBER LOVE – *Robert Earl* (-) 1956
MY SPECIAL ANGEL – *Malcolm Vaughan* (-) 1957

NORA MALONE – *Teresa Brewer* (-) 1956

Title – *Act* (Position) Year of Chart Entry

OH BOY – *The Crickets* (-)....1958
OH JULIE – *The Crescendos* (-)....1958

PARTY – *Elvis Presley* (-)....1957
PEGGY SUE – *Buddy Holly* (-)....1958

REAL LOVE – *Ruby Murray* (-)....1958
THE RISING OF THE MOON – *Michael O'Duffy* (-)....1957
ROCK WITH THE CAVEMAN – *Tommy Steele* (-)....1956
ROCK-A-BEATIN' BOOGIE – *Bill Haley and the Comets* (-)....1956
ROCK-A-BYE YOUR BABY WITH A DIXIE MELODY – *Jerry Lewis* (-)....1957
ROUND AND ROUND – *Perry Como* (-)....1957

SAIL ALONG SILVERY MOON – *Anne Shelton* (-)....1958
SANTA CLAUS ROLLED AND HIS REINDEER ROCKED – *The Mountaineers* (-)....1956
SCHOOL DAY – *Chuck Berry* (-)....1957
SEE YOU LATER ALLIGATOR – *Bill Haley and the Comets* (-)....1956
6-5 JIVE – *The King Brothers* (-)....1958
SIXTEEN TONS – *Tennessee Ernie Ford* (-)....1956
THE SON OF MARY – *Harry Belafonte* (-)....1958
SORRY SORRY SORRY – *Alma Cogan* (-)....1958
STUPID CUPID – *Connie Francis* (-)....1958
SUGARTIME – *McGuire Sisters* (-)....1958

TAMMY – *Debbie Reynolds* (-)....1957
TEA FOR TWO CHA CHA• - *Tommy Dorsey Orchestra* (-)....1958
A TEAR FELL – *Teresa Brewer* (-)....1956

TEQUILA• - *The Champs* (-)....1958
THAT'LL BE THE DAY – *The Crickets* (-)....1957
THIS SAME HEART – *Edmund Hockridge* (-)....1956
THREE BROTHERS – *Alma Cogan* (-)....1957
TILL• - *Roger Williams* (-)....1958
TOM DOOLEY – *Lonnie Donegan and his Skiffle Group* (-)....1958
TOM DOOLEY – *The Kingston Trio* (-)....1958
TOM HARK• - *Elias and his Zig Zag Jive Flutes* (-)....1958
TORERO – *The Southlanders* (-)....1958

Title – *Act* (Position)	Year of Chart Entry
TULIPS FROM AMSTERDAM – *Max Bygraves* (-)	1958
VALLEY OF TEARS – *Fats Domino* (-)	1957
A VERY PRECIOUS LOVE – *Doris Day* (-)	1958
VOLARE – *Dean Martin* (-)	1958
THE WAYWARD WIND – *Gogi Grant* (-)	1956
WHEN – *Kalin Twins* (-)	1958
WHOLE LOTTA WOMAN – *Marvin Rainwater* (-)	1958
WHY DO FOOLS FALL IN LOVE – *Alma Cogan* (-)	1956
THE WISDOM OF A FOOL – *Norman Wisdom* (-)	1957
WONDERFUL WONDERFUL – *Johnny Mathis* (-)	1957

Title – *Act* (Position) Year of Chart Entry

UNOFFICIAL:
1962 – 1967

During the 1960's several publications namely – Evening Herald (October 1962–1967), Evening Mail (1960–1962), Evening Press (1964), Spotlight Magazine (1965 – 1966) and Top Ten Weekly (1967) – published weekly charts of the Top Ten Best Selling records in Ireland. In the interest of chart history we have listed below the recordings which achieved a Top Ten position on those charts, (together with the highest position and name of publication) but didn't succeed in making the 'official' Irelands Top Ten chart as broadcast by Radio Eireann between October 1962 – December 1966.

ALL DAY AND ALL OF THE NIGHT – *The Kinks* (7) EH........ 1964
AM I LOSING YOU – *Jim Reeves* (8) EM........1961
AMONG THE WICKLOW HILLS – *Gerry and the Ohio* (8) EH........1966
AN OLD CHRISTMAS CARD - *Gerry and the Ohio* (10) EH........1966
ANYWAY THAT YOU WANT ME – The Troggs (10) EH........1967
ARE YOU SINCERE – *The Airchords featuring Pat Lynch* (9) EH........1965
ARE YOU TEASING ME – *The Cadets* (4) EP........1965
AS LONG AS HE NEEDS ME - *Shirley Bassey* (8) EM........1960

BABY I DON'T CARE – *Buddy Holly* (4) EH........1961
BABY TAKE A BOW – *Adam Faith* (6) EH........1962
BE MY BABY – *The Ronettes* (6) EH........1963
BEATLES FOR SALE L.P. – *The Beatles* (5) EP........ 1964
BEYOND THE SHADOW – *Declan Ryan and The Arrivals* (10) EH........1966
BLUE MOON – *The Marcels* (3) EM........1961
BO DIDDLEY – *Buddy Holly* (6) EH........1963
BOSSA NOVA BABY – *Elvis Presley* (7) EH........1963
A BOY WITHOUT A GIRL –*Anthony Newley* (7) EM........1960

THE CADETS L.P. – *The Cadets* (7) EP........ 1964
CAN THIS BE LOVE – *Matt Monro* (10) EM........1961
CHRISTMAS CANDLES – *Maisie McDaniel* (9) EH........1962
THE CLAPPING SONG – *Shirley Ellis* (10) EH........1965
COME AND STAY WITH ME – *Marianne Faithfull* (6) EP........1965

Title – *Act* (Position) Year of Chart Entry

COME ON HOME – *The Springfields* (8) EH 1963
CORRINE CORRINA – *Ray Peterson* (2) EM 1961

DON'T BLAME ME – *Frank Ifield* (8) EH 1964
DON'T LET THE SUN CATCH YOU CRYING – *Gerry and The Pacemakers* (9) EH 1964
DON'T YOU THINK IT'S TIME – *Mike Berry with the Outlaws* (3) EH 1963

EASY GOING ME – *Adam Faith* (5) EM 1961
THE END OF THE WORLD – *Skeeter Davis* (3) EH 1963
EVERYBODY LOVES SOMEBODY – *Dean Martin* (10) EH.................... 1964

FIRST TASTE OF LOVE – Ben E King (9) EM 1961
THE FIRST TIME – Adam Faith with the Roulettes (2) EH....................1963
FORTY SHADES OF GREEN – Johnny Cash (7) EM 1961
FROM A WINDOW – Billy J Kramer with the Dakotas (8) EH.................... 1964

GERONIMO• – The Shadows (4) EH 1963
GIRL DON'T COME – Sandie Shaw (4) EH....................1965
GLOBETROTTER• – *The Tornados* (7) EH 1963
GOOD GOLLY MISS MOLLY – Swinging Blue Jeans (9) EH.................... 1964
GOODNIGHT – Roy Orbison (8)EH....................1965

HE'LL ONLY HURT YOU – Kings Showband featuring Prince Vince (8) EH....................1965
HEY MAMA – *Frankie Vaughan* (9) EH....................1963
HI-LILI HI-LO – *Alan Price Set* (9) NS 1966
HIT THE ROAD JACK – *Ray Charles* (9) EM....................1961

I DON'T CARE – *Los Bravos* (8) EH 1966
I KNOW WHAT IT'S LIKE (TO HAVE LOVED) – *Tom Dunphy of the Royal Showband* (8) NS..........1966
I UNDERSTAND – *Freddie and the Dreamers* (10) EH....................1965
I WON'T COME IN WHILE HE'S THERE – *Jim Reeves* (10) EH 1967
I'LL KEEP YOU SATISFIED – *Billy J Kramer with the Dakotas* (8) EH....................1963
I'M GONNA BE WARM THIS WINTER – *Connie Francis* (6) EH 1963
I'M GONNA GET ME A GUN – *Cat Stevens* (9) TT 1967
INSIDE LOOKING OUT – *The Animals* (8) EH 1966
IRELAND SWINGS – *Brian Coll and the Plattermen* (6) NS 1966
THE IRISH PATROL – *Patrick O'Hagan* (4) EM 1961

Title – *Act* (Position) Year of Chart Entry

IT MIGHT AS WELL RAIN UNTIL SEPTEMBER – *Carole King* (7) EH....1962
IT'S GOOD NEWS WEEK – *Hedgehoppers Anonymous* (9) EH....1965
IT'S MY PARTY – Lesley Gore (9) EH....1963

KID GALAHAD E.P – *Elvis Presley* (4) EH....1962
KISS ME QUICK – *Elvis Presley* (9) EH....1964
KON TIKI• – *The Shadows* (4) EM....1961

THE LEAVING OF LIVERPOOL –*Clancy Brothers & Tommy Makem* (10) EH....1964
LET'S GO STEADY AGAIN – *Neil Sedaka* (10) EH....1963
LIKE STRANGERS – *Everly Brothers* (9) EM....1961
LITTLE BOY SAD – *Johnny Burnette* (5) EM....1961
LITTLE DONKEY – *Nina and Frederick* (4) EM....1960
LITTLE MAN – *Sonny and Cher* (10) EH....1966
LITTLE SISTER – *Elvis Presley* (1) EH....1961
LOSING YOU – Brenda Lee (7) EH....1963
LOVERS OF THE WORLD UNITE – *David and Jonathan* (10) NS....1966
LOVE'S GONNA LIVE HERE – *Royal Blues Showband featuring Shay O'Hara* (10) EP....1965

MAKE THE WORLD GO AWAY – *Eddy Arnold* (6) NS....1966
MAN OF MYSTERY• – *The Shadows* (5) EM....1960
MARIE – *The Bachelors* (7) EH....1965
MELLOW YELLOW – *Donovan* (10) TT....1967
MILORD – *Edith Piaf* (9) EM....1960
MISTY – *Johnny Mathis* (7) EH....1960
MR CUSTER – Charlie Drake (10) EM....1960
A MUST TO AVOID – *Herman's Hermits* (9) EH....1966
MY FRIEND THE SEA – *Petula Clark* (7) EM....1961
MY GIRL JOSEPHINE – Fats Domino (8) EM....1962
MY HEARTACHES GOT HEARTACHES – *Jack Ruane Band* (9) NS....1966
MY LOVE FOR YOU – *Johnny Mathis* (8) EM....1960
MY SHIP IS COMING IN – *Walker Brothers* (7) EH....1966
MY WAY – *Eddie Cochran* (4) EH....1963
MYSTERY GIRL – *Jess Conrad* (6) EM....1961

NATURE'S TIME FOR LOVE – *Joe Brown and the Bruvvers* (7) EH....1963
NO ONE CAN MAKE MY SUNSHINE SMILE – *Everly Brothers* (8) EH....1962

Title – *Act* (Position) Year of Chart Entry

ON MY WORD – *Cliff Richard* (10) EP 1965
OVER UNDER SIDEWAYS DOWN – *The Yardbirds* (10) EH 1966

PROMISES – *Ken Dodd* (10) EH 1966

REMINISCING – *Buddy Holly* (9) EH 1962
THE RISE AND FALL OF FLINGEL BUNT• – *The Shadows* (10) EH 1964
ROYAL SHOWBAND, WATERFORD E.P. – *The Royal Showband* (8) EP 1964
RUBY ANN – *Marty Robbins* (7) EH 1963

SAY I WON'T BE THERE – *The Springfields* (9) EH 1963
SHAPES OF THINGS – *The Yardbirds* (10) EH 1966
SO SAD (TO WATCH GOOD LOVE GO BAD) – *The Greenbeats* (9) EH 1965
SPANISH FLEA• – *Herb Alpert and the Tijuana Brass* (7) NS 1966
STANDING IN THE SHADOWS OF LOVE – *The Four Tops* (10) EH 1967
SUBTERRANEAN HOMESICK BLUES – *Bob Dylan* (10) EP 1965
SUGAR TOWN – *Nancy Sinatra* (9) EH 1967
SUMMER IN THE CITY – *The Lovin' Spoonful* (8) NS 1966
SUNNY – *Bobby Hebb* (9) NS 1966

TELL ME WHEN – *The Applejacks* (5) EH 1964
TERRY – *Twinkle* (8) EH 1965
THAT GIRL BELONGS TO YESTERDAY – *Gene Pitney* (6) EH 1964
THEY'RE COMING TO TAKE ME AWAY HA! HA! – *Napolean XIV* (7) EH 1966
THIS SPORTING LIFE – *Ian Whitcomb* (9) EH 1965
TILL THE END OF THE DAY – *The Kinks* (10) EH 1966
TOBACCO ROAD – *The Nashville Teens* (5) EH 1964
TRAINS AND BOATS AND PLANES –*Billy J Kramer with the Dakotas* (8) EH 1965
TRAVELLIN' MAN – *Ricky Nelson* (3) EM 1961
TRIBUTE TO JIM REEVES – *The Dixielanders* (3) EH 1964
TURN OUT THE LIGHT – *The Creatures* (8) EH 1966
TWELFTH OF NEVER –*Cliff Richard* (8) EH 1964
THE TWIST – *Chubby Checker* (4) EM 1962

WALK RIGHT IN – *The Rooftop Singers* (9) EH 1963
WE ARE IN LOVE – *Adam Faith with the Roulettes* (6) EH 1964
WHAT HAVE THEY DONE TO THE RAIN –*The Searchers* (5) EP 1965

Title – *Act* (Position) — Year of Chart Entry

WHAT IN THE WORLD'S COME OVER YOU – *Alan Dee and the Chessmen*(7) EH..........1965
WHAT'S THE USE – *Sean Fagan and the Pacific Showband* (7) EP..........1965
WHISPERING - *The Bachelors* (9) EH..........1963
WISHING – *Buddy Holly* (5) EH..........1963
WONDERFUL WORLD – *Herman's Hermits* (9) EH..........1965

YOU CAN NEVER STOP ME LOVING YOU – Kenny Lynch (3) EH..........1963
YOU'RE NO GOOD – *Swinging Blue Jeans* (10) EH..........1964
YOU'VE LOST THAT LOVIN' FEELIN' – *Cilla Black* (5) EH..........1965
YOUR CHEATING HEART – *Ray Charles* (7) EH..........1962

ONE TO WATCH:
1962 – 1966

Throughout the period October 1962 to December 1966 the compilers of Irelands Top Ten included a new release each week in their "One To Watch" slot. The majority of the tracks featured in the 'One To Watch' slot made the Top Ten. Rather than list every record in the 'One to Watch' category, I have just listed the records (together with date track was listed) that did not make the Top Ten breakthrough.

1962

08 Oct **MARTA** – Tom Dunphy *HMV POP(I) 1070*

15 Oct **DON'T YOU BELIEVE IT** – Andy Williams *CBS EAAG 116*

05 Nov **LITTLE BLACK BOOK** – Jimmy Dean *CBS EAAG 122*

26 Nov **ESO BESO** – Paul Anka *RCA RCA 1316*

24 Dec **PALABRA D'AMOR** – Roy Donnelly *Gael-linn AN 4*

1963

14 Jan **RUBY ANN** – Marty Robbins *CBS EAAG 128*

25 Feb **WALK RIGHT IN** – Rooftop Singers *Fontana 271 700 ETF*

01 Apr **YOU'RE THE REASON I'M LIVING** – Bobby Darin *Capitol CL(I) 15286*

15 Apr **MR. BASS MAN** – Johnny Cymbal *London HL-R 9682*

27 May **SHY GIRL** – Mark Wynter *Pye 7N 15525*

10 Jun **THERE GOES MY HEART AGAIN** – Fats Domino *HMV POP(I) 1164*

08 Jul **SOME DO SOME DON'T** – Lorne Gibson Trio *Decca F 11684*

05 Aug **SUKIYAKI** – Kyu Sakamoto *HMV POP(I) 1171*

09 Sep **WHISPERING** – Bachelors *Decca F 11712*

16 Sep **THEME FROM THE ONE NIGHTERS** – Royal Showband *HMV IP 1294*

23 Sep **ACE IN THE HOLE** – Leon McAuliff *Decca F 11676*

14 Oct **THE FIRST TIME** – Adam Faith *Parlophone R(I) 5061*

28 Oct **BOSSA NOVA BABY** – Elvis Presley *RCA RCA 1374*

04 Nov **SWEET IMPOSSIBLE YOU** – Brenda Lee *Brunswick 05896*

09 Dec **WOODEN SOLDIER** – Hank Locklin *RCA RCA 1370*

23 Dec **TALK BACK TREMBLING LIPS** – Johnny Tillotson *MGM MGM 1214*

1964

06 Jan **DO YOU REALLY LOVE ME TOO** – Billy Fury *Decca F 11792*

27 Jan **DON'T BLAME ME** – Frank Ifield *Columbia DB(I) 7184*

17 Feb **5-4-3-2-1** Manfred Mann *HMV POP(I) 1252*

02 Mar **OVER YOU** – Freddie and The Dreamers *Columbia DB(I) 7214*

09 Mar **STAY AWHILE** – Dusty Springfield *Philips EBF 1313*

16 Mar **HEIGH-HO** – Big Dee Irwin *Colpix PX 11040*

30 Mar **THEME FOR YOUNG LOVERS** – The Shadows *Columbia DB(I) 7231*

13 Apr **FIONA** – The Hootenannys *Pye 7N 15638*

20 Apr **DON'T LET THE SUN CATCH YOU CRYING** – Gerry and The Pacemakers *Columbia DB(I) 7268*

15 Jun **A LITTLE LOVING** – Fourmost *Parlophone R(I) 5128*

06 Jul **SOMEDAY WE'RE GONNA LOVE AGAIN** – The Searchers *Pye 7N 15670*

07 Sep **EVERYBODY LOVES SOMEBODY** – Dean Martin *Reprise R 20281*

05 Oct **ROOM FULL OF ROSES** – Maisie McDaniel *Fontana ETF 492*

02 Nov **TWELFTH OF NEVER** – Cliff Richard *Columbia DB(I) 7372*

09 Nov **IF THIS WORLD WERE MINE** – The Greenbeats *Pye 7N 15718*

07 Dec **CHRISTMAS CANDLES** – Bing Crosby *Reprise R 20424*

14 Dec **WHAT HAVE THEY DONE TO THE RAIN** – The Searchers *Pye 7N 15739*

1965

18 Jan **I'M LOST WITHOUT YOU** – Billy Fury *Decca F 12048*

08 Feb **ARE YOU TEASING ME** – The Cadets *Pye 7N 15769*

08 Mar **ALL OF A SUDDEN MY HEART SINGS** – Pat McGeegan and The Victors *Decca F 12078*

15 Mar **BRING YOUR LOVE TO ME** – Righteous Brothers *Pye Int. 7N 25297*

22 Mar **WHAT'S THE USE** – Sean Fagan and the Pacific Showband *Pye 7N 15822*

12 Apr **I'M GONNA GET THERE SOMEHOW** – Val Doonican *Decca F 12118*

03 May **SO SAD** – The Greenbeats *Pye 7N 15843*

24 May **WHO KNOWS** – Johnny Flynn Band featuring Roy Donn *Decca F 12141*

07 Jun **RING OF FIRE** – Gerry and The Ohio *Pye 7N 15851*

14 Jun **ON MY WORD** – Cliff Richard *Columbia DB(I) 7996*

21 Jun **THE CLAPPING SONG** – Shirley Ellis *London HLR 9961*

28 Jun **SHE'S ABOUT A MOVER** – Sir Douglas Quintet *London HLU 9964*

30 Aug **WHAT'S NEW PUSSYCAT** – Tom Jones *Decca F 12203*

20 Sep **SOME OF YOUR LOVING** – Dusty Springfield *Philips EBF 1430*

04 Oct **A MILLION MILES AWAY** – Val Doonican *Decca F 12242*

18 Oct **ARE YOU SINCERE** – The Airchords featuring Pat Lynch *Columbia IDB 746*

25 Oct **IN THE CHAPEL IN THE MOONLIGHT** – The Bachelors *Decca F 12256*

29 Nov **HOW CAN YOU TELL** – Sandie Shaw *Pye 7N 15987*

1966

03 Jan **MY SHIP IS COMING IN** – The Walker Brothers *Philips EBF 1454*

10 Jan **HELLO DOLLY** – The Bachelors *Decca F 12309*

17 Jan **BREAKIN' UP IS BREAKIN' MY HEART** – Roy Orbison *London HLU 10015*

07 Feb **SPANISH FLEA** – Herb Alpert and the Tijuana Brass *Pye 7N 25335*

12 Dec **ONE WAY STREET** – Brendan Bowyer and Royal Showband *HMV IP 1306*